1 MONTH OF
FREE
READING

at

www.ForgottenBooks.com

By purchasing this book you are eligible for one month membership to ForgottenBooks.com, giving you unlimited access to our entire collection of over 1,000,000 titles via our web site and mobile apps.

To claim your free month visit:
www.forgottenbooks.com/free116652

ISBN 978-1-5282-7776-1
PIBN 10116652

This book is a reproduction of an important historical work. Forgotten Books uses state-of-the-art technology to digitally reconstruct the work, preserving the original format whilst repairing imperfections present in the aged copy. In rare cases, an imperfection in the original, such as a blemish or missing page, may be replicated in our edition. We do, however, repair the vast majority of imperfections successfully; any imperfections that remain are intentionally left to preserve the state of such historical works.

DEPARTMENT OF THE INTERIOR
BUREAU OF EDUCATION

BULLETIN, 1919, No. 75

MONTHLY RECORD
OF CURRENT EDUCATIONAL
PUBLICATIONS

NOVEMBER, 1919

WASHINGTON
GOVERNMENT PRINTING OFFICE
1919

L11
A4
1919:75-87
(Educ. dept.)

ADDITIONAL COPIES

OF THIS PUBLICATION MAY BE PROCURED FROM
THE SUPERINTENDENT OF DOCUMENTS
GOVERNMENT PRINTING OFFICE
WASHINGTON, D. C.
AT

5 CENTS PER COPY
EDUCATION DEPT.

MONTHLY RECORD OF CURRENT EDUCATIONAL PUBLICATIONS.

Compiled by the Library Division, Bureau of Education.

NOTE.

The record comprises a general survey in bibliographic form of current educational literature, domestic and foreign, received during the monthly period preceding the date of publication of each issue.

This office can not supply the publications listed in this bulletin, other than those expressly designated as publications of the Bureau of Education. Books, pamphlets, and periodicals here mentioned may ordinarily be obtained from their respective publishers, either directly or through a dealer, or, in the case of an association publication, from the secretary of the issuing organization. Many of them are available for consultation in various public and institutional libraries.

Publications intended for inclusion in this record should be sent to the library of the Bureau of Education, Washington, D. C.

PROCEEDINGS OF ASSOCIATIONS.

1730. **Conference of educational associations.** Report of the seventh annual conference . . . held at the University college, London, January 1919. London, 1919. 230 p. 8°.

Contains: 1. H. A. L. Fisher: The art of keeping alive, p. 1–10. 2. Percy Griffith: Drawing and the utility-motive in education, p. 12–18. 3. Lord Gorell: Education of men on military service, p. 24–29. 4. National and international ideals in the teaching of history, [by] F. J. C. Hearnshaw, p. 29–35; [by] Miss A. E. Levett, p. 35–43. 5. Frank Warner: Art in industry, p 54–63. 6. E. W. Maples: The education, welfare, and recreation of the young worker, p. 78–84. 7. Winifred Mercier: The training college, p. 85–92. 8 The utility motive in education, [by] John Adams, p. 96–103; [by] P. B. Ballard, p. 103–108. 9. J. A. Thomson: The eugenic ideal in education, p. 114–23. 10. E. W. MacBride: The principles of sex-instruction, p. 123–37. 11. Miss M. G. Bondfield: The place of the school in society, p. 158–73 12 J. Shelley: What do we mean by freedom for the child? The root problem of educational reconstruction, p. 175–83. 13. Prof. Fleure. Human geography, p. 193–98. 14. James Shelley: Realistic education. Joy as a criterion of educational values, p 199–203. 15. Homer Lane: Factors in children's conduct, p 207–12. 16. Ernest Gray: Continuation schools, p. 217–24.

144508°—19 .   542813   •   3

1731. Education association of western Pennsylvania. Proceedings [Pittsburgh, Pa., November 29–30, 1918] Pittsburgh, University of Pittsburgh, 1919. 114 p. 8°. (University of Pittsburgh bulletin, vol. 15, no. 3, March 1, 1919)

Contains: 1. S. A. Courtis: Educational efficiency revealed by standard tests, p. 6–9. 2. L. L. Thurston: Mental tests for college entrance, p. 16–17. ' 3. E. C. Noyes: Report of a committee of the Allegheny county principals' round table on essentials in English, p. 27–42. 4. W. S. Small: State and national legislation for physical education, p. 55–57. 5. F. T. Jones: Standardizing tests in physics and chemistry, p. 82–85. 6. Orton Lowe: What economic occupations of educational value can be devised for children under fourteen years of age in mining towns—how relate the occupations to school work? p. 86–93. 7. A. C. Callen: The problem of educating the adult in mining towns in subjects pertaining to mining, p. 93–103. 8. Josiah Keely: The educated versus the uneducated miner as an asset to coal company, p. 103–9. 9. J. G. Becht: How obtain more general financial support for schools in mining towns, p. 112–14.

EDUCATIONAL HISTORY AND BIOGRAPHY.

1732. Boyer, Charles C. History of education. New York [etc.] C. Scribner's sons [1919] viii, 461 p. plates. 12°.

The thematic purpose of this volume is to show that historically education has been a progressive adjustment of claims in the exercise of human freedom.

1733. Wells, Benjamin W. Alcuin the teacher. Constructive quarterly, 7 : 531–52, September 1919.

CURRENT EDUCATIONAL CONDITIONS.

GENERAL AND UNITED STATES.

1734. Cestre, Charles. Coup d'œil sur la civilisation américaine. Revue internationale de l'enseignement, 39 : 247–65, July–August 1919.

Opening lecture of the course in American literature and civilization at the Sorbonne in Paris, December 3, 1918.

Emphasizes the community of ideals of France and America.

1735. Claxton, Philander Priestley. Education for the establishment of democracy in the world. Washington, Government printing office, 1919. 22 p. 8°.

Address before the National education association at Milwaukee, Wis., July 2, 1919.

1736. Gerwig, George W. Report of secretary of the Board of public education, Pittsburgh, 1918–1919. Pittsburgh, Pa., 1919. 2 pamphlets. 8°.

These reports contain sections on Character as a national asset, and on Education and reconstruction.

1737. Marquardt, W. W. Aims of our public schools. Philippine education, 16 : 97–100, August 1919.

An address by the former Director of education of the Philippines before the Rotary club of Manila on the work of the Bureau of education of the Philippines and the results that are being attained.

1738. North Carolina. University. School of education. A study of the public schools in Orange county, North Carolina. Chapel Hill, N. C., The University, 1919. 32 p. illus. 8°. (University of North Carolina record, no. 166, June 1919. Extension series no. 32)

1739. Price, Theodore H. The school and the workaday beyond. Outlook, 123 : 178–80, October 1, 1919.

An address delivered at a conference of masters in church schools, held at St. Paul's school, Concord, N. H., September 18, 1919.

Presents differences between boys educated in the public schools and those educated in preparatory schools. Says that public school graduates are more efficient in the business world than preparatory school graduates.

1740. **Boz, Firmin.** La culture française aux États-Unis. Minerve française, 1 : 87–98, June 1, 1919.

1741. **Way, J. E.** The earmarks of autocracy in American schools. Educational monthly, 68 : 360–64, September 1919.

1742. **Wood, Will C.** New occasions and new duties. Sierra educational news, 15 : 403–11, September 1919.
> Reconstruction in education. Speaks particularly of conditions in California.

FOREIGN COUNTRIES.

1743. **Blakesley, John H.** Education: its aims and means. Nineteenth century, 86 : 535–46, September 1919.
> Criticises state interference in education. Conditions in England described.

1744. **Cohn, Adolphe.** Reopening of the École normale supérieure. Educational review, 58 : 181–200, October 1919.
> The reopening exercises of the school took place on March 23, 1919, at Paris, and were attended by the highest educational authorities of France. Gives speeches of Ernest Lavisse, President Poincaré, etc.

1745. **Delvolvé.** L'école et les universités. Revue pédagogique, 75 : 79–94. August 1919.
> Deals with the relations between the university and the public school in France. The author discusses the same subject from the university point of view in an article in the Revue de métaphysique et de morale, March–April 1919.

1746. **Fries, Wilhelm.** Zur schulreform in Deutschland und Österreich. Lehrproben und lehrgänge aus der praxis der höheren lehranstalten (Halle a. d. S.) heft 140 : 1–20, July 1919.
> Reviews various recent works on the new era in education in Germany and Austria.

1747. **Inman, Samuel Guy.** Educational leaders of Mexico. Educational foundations, 31 : 104–108, October 1919.

1748. **Litt, Theodor.** Die höhere schule und das problem der einheitsschule. Monatschrift für höhere schulen (Berlin) 18 : 280–93, July–August 1919.
> Based on a program brochure by Karl Reinhardt entitled Die neugestaltung des deutschen schulwesens, Leipzig, 1919.

1749. **Strong, John,** *ed.* The education (Scotland) act, 1918, with annotations. With list of new educational authorities. Edinburgh, Oliver and Boyd, 1919. xi, 125 p. 8°.

1750. **Thompson, J. M.** Reflections of a temporary schoolmaster. Contemporary review, 116 : 327–31, September 1919.
> Discusses public school life in England. Student morals and religion.

1751. **Torres, Arturo.** The educational system of the republic of Cuba. Bulletin of the Pan American union, 49 : 352–57, September 1919.
> Prepared from data furnished by Dr. Ramiro Guerra, professor of education in the Normal school of Habana, and information contained in the Columbus Memorial library of the Pan American union.

EDUCATIONAL THEORY AND PRACTICE.

1752. **Palmer, Frank H.** Repression, impression, expression in the process of education. Education, 40 : 98–107, October 1919.
> Presents among other topics the socialized recitation and student self-government.

1753. **Ward, C. H.** Educational bolshevism. Outlook, 123 : 130–33. September 24, 1919.
> Criticises the methods of modern pedagogists in building up mountains of data and then making "practical applications of their inductions without any knowledge of the practice of teaching."

1754. Winship, A. E. Danger signals for teachers. Chicago, Forbes & company, 1919. 204 p. 12°.
  Some hints designed to help teachers in their work.

EDUCATIONAL PSYCHOLOGY; CHILD STUDY.

1755. Moritz, Robert E. The new comedy of errors. Educational review, 58: 219–38, October 1919.
  Defends the doctrine of formal discipline in education. Criticises the "modernists" for their views.

1756. Wrightson, Hilda A. Sense training for children's development in the form of simplified games and exercises. New York, The McCann company [1919] 221 p. plates. 12°.

EDUCATIONAL TESTS AND MEASUREMENTS.

1757. Bachman, Frank P. Subject-matter standards. School and society, 10: 411–16, October 11, 1919.
  A formulation of the standards that should control in judging instruction on the side of subject-matter and teaching methods.
  A second article by the same author on this subject is contained in School and society, 10 : 454–57, October 18, 1919, under the title "Teaching standards."

1758. Chase, H. W. and Carpenter, C. C. The response of a composite group to the Stanford revision of the Binet-Simon tests. Journal of educational psychology, 10: 179–88, April 1919.
  Study based on a test of 103 children in the elementary school of Chapel Hill, N. C., by the Stanford revision of the Binet tests.

1759. Courtis, Stuart A. The Gary public schools. Measurement of classroom products. New York city, General education board, 1919. xxii, 532 p. 12°.
  The eighth part of the report of a survey of the schools of Gary, Ind., made by the General education board on invitation of the board of education and the superintendent of schools of that city.

1760. Jordan, R. H. The use of tests and scales as supervisory instruments. Journal of education, 90: 255–56, September 18, 1919.
  Mentions a number of ways in which mental tests and scales may assist the supervisor.

1761. Madsen, I. N. and Sylvester, R. H. High school students' intelligence ratings according to the Army Alpha test. School and society, 10: 407–10, October 4, 1919.
  Results of the Alpha test given to the high-school students of Rockford, Ill., Madison, Wis., and Sioux City, Iowa.

1762. Mead, Cyrus D. The effect of exempting pupils proficient in handwriting. Journal of educational psychology, 10: 179–88, April 1919.
  A controlled test in handwriting carried out over the greater part of the school year of 1917–18 with three fifth and two sixth grades, in all, 203 pupils.

1763. Rogers, Agnes L. The scope and significance of measurement in early elementary education. Kindergarten-primary magazine, 32: 40–44, October 1919.
  An address given before the International kindergarten union, at Baltimore, Md.
  Also in Kindergarten and first grade, 4 : 299–304, October 1919.

1764. Scott, Colin A. An eighth grade demonstration class and the three R's. Journal of educational psychology, 10: 189–218, April 1919.
  Tests of arithmetic and silent reading in school of South Hadley, Mass.

1765. Van Wagenen, M. J. Educational tests and scales: their origin. School education, 39: 44, 46–47, October 1919.
  To be continued.

SPECIAL METHODS OF INSTRUCTION.

1766. **Branom, Mendel E.** The project method in education. Boston, R. G. Badger [1919] 282 p. 8°.

Deals with the general principles of project teaching, and with the use of projects in the manual arts and in history and geography.

1767. **Follett, Wilson.** Schooling without the school. Harper's magazine, 139 : 700–08, October 1919.

The story of the home training of the author's little daughter, who learned to use a typewriter at the age of three years before she could read. Mr. Follett describes his method of teaching, which he thinks will call out of any normal child the eager powers and abilities hidden away within him.

1768. **Levin, Samuel M.** The use of the problem method in history teaching. Education, 40 : 111–20, October 1919.

Emphasizes the importance of history teaching, and advocates the problem method as " an instrumentality of inestimable worth."

1769. **Lull, H. G.** What are problems and projects. Chicago schools journal, 2 : 19–25, September 1919.

Procedures in project-problem instruction.

SPECIAL SUBJECTS OF CURRICULUM.

SPELLING.

1770. **Randall, John.** Phonetic spelling as an engineering problem. Educational review, 58 : 239–52, October 1919.

An effort to show what might be developed " by treating English spelling from the viewpoint of the efficiency engineer rather than that of the specialist."

ENGLISH AND COMPOSITION.

1771. **Carr, W. L.** The English vocabulary of the high school freshman. Classical journal, 15 : 29–29, October 1919.

Discusses the value of Latin as an aid in improving a pupil's English.

1772. **Froehlich, Hugo B.** A new basis for the study of English. Industrial-arts magazine, 8 : 436–38, November 1919.

Vitalizing the teaching of English through the manual arts.

1773. **Leonard, Sterling L.** Composition targets. English journal, 8 : 401–11. September 1919.

Suggests among other things cooperative attempts to rate oral and written themes by all teachers.

1774. **Magee,** *Mrs.* **Helen B.** On the value of journal and letter writing as an introduction to a freshman course in exposition writing. English journal, 8 : 429–32, September 1919.

1775. **Tressler, J. C.** Salvaging from the English scrap-heap. English journal, 8 : 412–18, September 1919.

Describes a method of testing the efficiency of dictation in teaching written composition.

FOREIGN LANGUAGES.

1776. The study of languages. Pennsylvania gazette, 18 : 12–13, October 3, 1919.

ANCIENT LANGUAGES.

1777. **Grant, W. L.** The study of the classics in translation: an Ontario attempt. Bookman, 50 : 230–35, October 1919.

Describes an experiment made in Upper Canada college by holding a definite class for the study of classical literature in translation. Favors this method for many students.

1778. Hoffman, Horace Addison. Everyday Greek; Greek words in English, including scientific terms. Chicago, Ill., The University of Chicago press [1919] ix, 107 p. 12°.

> This book is adapted for use in schools and colleges, and for private study and reference. It is particularly serviceable for students of medicine.

1779. MacVey, Anna P. The classical club as an educational agency. Classical journal, 15 : 30–36, October 1919.

> Discusses the encouragement of classical studies through the medium of classical clubs.

1780. Robinson, Mary C. An experiment in teaching Latin for the sake of English. Classical journal, 15 : 42–49, October 1919.

> An experiment tried in the high school of Bangor, Maine.

1781. Shorey, Paul. What to do for Greek. Classical journal, 15 : 8–19, October 1919.

> A plea for the classics in the high schools, especially Greek.

HISTORY.

1782. Suggestions for teachers of history. Historical outlook, 10 : 377–87, October 1919.

> A symposium : (1) Yorktown day, October 19, by T. W. Gosling, p. 377 ; (2) Current events revised, by W. H. Ellison, p. 881 ; (3) A college museum, by M. P. Clarke, p. 383 ; (4) American history in fiction, by G. Buck, p. 384.

GEOGRAPHY.

1783. Brown, Robert M. Geography in recent books on education. Journal of geography, 18 : 268–74, October 1919.

1784 ——— Geography in recent school surveys. Educational review, 58 : 207–18, October 1919.

> Study based on the following school surveys : Cleveland, 1916 ; Grand Rapids, Mich., 1916 ; St. Louis, 1918 ; Elyria, Ohio, 1918 ; San Francisco, 1917 ; Gary, 1918.

SCIENCE.

1785. Davis, Bradley M. Introductory courses in botany. School science and mathematics, 19 : 629–32, October 1919.

> To be continued.

1786. Libby, Walter. A function of the history of science. Educational review, 58 : 201–6, October 1919.

> Advocates the study of the history of science in colleges as a bond of reconcilement between divergent educational ideals.

MATHEMATICS.

1787. Barnes, H. O. Geometry by analysis. School review, 27 : 612–18, October 1919.

> Says that pupils become more efficient in demonstration of originals, and show more initiative.

MISCELLANEOUS.

1788. Pollock, Horatio M. Mental hygiene in the school. American education, 23 : 60–63, October 1919.

> The ground to be covered in teaching mental hygiene includes the following : mental habits, mental food, exercise, rest, environment, and pathological conditions.

1789. Reynolds, Harriet C., ed. Thoughts on humane education. Suggestions on kindness to animals and notes on their habits and usefulness. Washington, D. C., Humane publishing company, 1919. 200 p. plates. 16°.

> The introduction is written by Dr. P. P. Claxton.

1790. Whitney, Albert W. Safety in education in the public schools. Teacher's journal, 19 : 130–34, October 1919.

> Tells what has been done in safety work in the St. Louis public schools.

KINDERGARTEN AND PRIMARY SCHOOL.

1791. Claxton, P. P. The economics of the kindergarten. Outlook, 123 : 136-37, September 24, 1919.

RURAL EDUCATION.

1792. Root, Rosamond. The specific equipment of teachers to meet the new course of study. Rural school messenger, 9 : 29-33, September 1919.

This is one of a series of contributions given in a symposium on " The new demands in rural life and education " at the meeting of the National education association in Milwaukee, July 1919.

1793. Wilson, G. M. The reorganized course of study for modern rural life. School and home education, 39 : 26-28, October 1919.

Read at the meeting of the National education association, Milwaukee, July 1, 1919.

SECONDARY EDUCATION.

1794. Breslich, E. R. A committee on results. School review, 27 : 600-11, October 1919.

Describes the work of a committee in the University high school of the University of Chicago known as a committee on results, and "charged with the responsibility of stimulating testing throughout the school and of coordinating such work done by the various departments."

1795. Briggs, Thomas H. What is a junior high school? Educational administration and supervision, 5 : 283-301, September 1919.

Results of a questionnaire sent to representative men, who have shown the most interest in the junior high school movement, in order to find out what is considered essential and what non-essential for a junior high school.

1796. Cook, J. H. Principles underlying the organization of public high school curricula. High school journal, 3 : 167-71, October 1919.

Applied especially to North Carolina high schools.

TEACHERS: TRAINING AND PROFESSIONAL STATUS.

1797. California. State normal school, San Diego. The curriculum of the model and training school. Sacramento, California state printing office, 1919. 178 p. illus. 8°. (State normal school, San Diego, Cal. Bulletin, vol. 7, no. 3, August 1919)

1798. Crabbe, John G. How to secure an adequate student constituency for state normal schools and colleges. American school, 5 : 237, 253, August 1919.

Read before the Department of normal schools, National education association, Milwaukee, July 3, 1919.

Offers some suggestions for a plan of advertising to increase the attendance of students at normal schools.

1799. Gay, Edwin F. Does a university career offer "no future"? Journal of education, 90 : 367-68, October 16, 1919.

From the New York Times, September 14, 1919.

The exodus of college professors and the necessity of paying the college teacher a decent salary.

1800. Hall, Newton M. The laborer and her hire. Outlook, 123 : 133-36, September 24, 1919.

A discussion of teachers' salaries.

1801. Mead, A. R. An example of cooperation in teacher training in a small city. School and society, 10 : 393-97, October 4, 1919.

Cooperation in teacher training in Delaware, Ohio.

1802. Northend, Charles. Professional improvement. Pennsylvania school journal, 68 : 73-76, August 1919.

Improvement of teachers in service by professional reading, visits to schools, teachers' meetings, etc.

1803. **Strong, E. A.** Academic degrees in normal schools. American schoolmaster, 12:294–99, September 1919.

Part of an address to the degree classes of the State normal college, Ypsilanti, Mich., June 1919.

Calls attention to a very radical change, with respect to degrees and diplomas, which has come over the educational world during these twenty or twenty-five years.

HIGHER EDUCATION.

1804. **Brodrib, C. W.** Thoughts on Oxford. Contemporary review, 116:316–20. September 1919.

1805. **Collard, F.** Deux universités belges en Hollande: Amersfoort et Utrecht. Revue internationale de l'enseignement, 39:266–77, July-August 1919.

The story of two institutions of higher education established among the interned Belgian soldiers and refugees in Holland during the world war.

1806. **Lowell, A. Lawrence.** Universities from within. World's work, 38:620–25, October 1919.

Discusses academic instruction and moral training. Salaries for instructors.

1807. **Pierce, Frederick E.** American scholarship. Yale review, 9:119–30, October 1919.

Criticises "the appalling inadequacy" of German scholarship in the humanities, and the evil effects of such scholarship on American higher education.

1808. **Princeton university.** Endowment committee. Princeton. Princeton. N. J., Endowment committee of Princeton university, 1919. 95 p. 12°.

CONTENTS.—Preface, President J. G. Hibben.—1. Why Princeton needs endowment.—2. Summary of specific needs.—3. Schedule of endowments.—4. Geographical distribution of students.—5. Princeton's national tradition.—6. Princeton's educational policy.

1809. **Wertenbaker, Thomas Jefferson.** The preceptorial method. Princeton alumni weekly, 20:10–12, October 1, 1919.

The preceptorial system at Princeton university.

SCHOOL ADMINISTRATION.

1810. **Flanders, J. K.** Some effects of federal aid upon secondary education. Educational administration and supervision, 5:325–34, September 1919.

1811. **Staples, C. L.** A critique of the U. S. Bureau of education. Education, 40:78–97, October 1919.

Discusses the educational appropriations made to the Federal bureau of education. Criticises the meagerness of the appropriations, and urges the creation of a Department of education, with a secretary of education.

1812. **Swift, Fletcher Harper.** Common school finance in Alabama. Educational administration and supervision, 5:303–24, September 1919.

This study was begun before the recent federal survey of education in Alabama was announced. "The striking agreement of the conclusions in the present study with those of the [Federal] Commission, most of which were arrived at entirely independently, lends interest and strength to the criticisms and recommendations of both."

SCHOOL MANAGEMENT.

1813. **Brown, J. Stanley.** Supervision of study in the grades. Chicago schools journal, 1:10–13, June 1919.

1814. **Cast, G. C.** Free text-books in the high school. Nebraska teacher, 22:62–65, October 1919.

The writer is convinced that the free text-book, at least in the high school, is a positive evil from the viewpoint of sound pedagogy. Presents the more obvious reasons for considering the free text-book harmful.

1815. **Kendall, Calvin N.** Plain talk about schools. Journal of education, 90:311–12, October 2, 1919.

A few suggestions for making schools better and happier.

1816. **Leonard, Sterling Andrus.** The social recitation. Chicago schools journal, 1:2–9, June 1919.

SCHOOL ARCHITECTURE.

1817. Koos, Leonard V. Space provisions in the floor plans of modern high school buildings. School review, 27 : 573–99, October 1919.

Study based on a tabulation of the kinds of space-provision made in the floor-plans of 156 high school buildings erected during the decade 1908–17.

SCHOOL HYGIENE AND SANITATION.

1818. Bardeen, C. R. Medical supervision of students at Wisconsin. Modern medicine, 1 : 468–77, October 1919. Illus.

In conclusion, the writer says that the aims of medical supervision at the University of Wisconsin embrace the study and care of the health of the community as a whole, including the hygiene of the environment, and the study and care of the health of students as individuals both immediate and in relation to their future.

1819. Friedel, V. H. The interallied congress of hygiene in Paris. American journal of school hygiene, 3 : 61–65, September 1919.

Translated by Lawrence A. Averill. Reprinted from School hygiene (London), 10 : no. 2, June 1919.

The principal resolutions regarding school hygiene adopted by the congress.

1820. Howe, William A. Oral hygiene, a state health educational function. 10 p. 8°.

Reprinted from the Journal of the National dental association, vol. 6, no. 8, August 1919.

Read before the National dental association at its twenty-second annual session, Chicago, Ill., August 5–9, 1918.

1821. Howes, Willard B. Medical supervision of Framingham (Mass.) schools. Boston medical and surgical journal, 181 : 427–31, October 2, 1919.

Gives table showing the prevalence of certain physical defects in different age groups.

1822. Marcus, Leopold. Open-air classes. Journal of the American medical association, 73 : 1057–59, October 4, 1919.

Work of the Bureau of child hygiene, New York city. Paper read before the section of preventive medicine and public health at the Seventieth annual session of the American medical association, June, 1919.

1823. Thaler, William H. The evolution of hygiene as a factor in education. School and society, 10 : 450–54, October 18, 1919.

1824. Withers, John W. The dental clinic and the public schools. *In* Report of Missouri state dental association. Annual meeting, St. Louis, April 14–16, 1919. Dental cosmos, 61 : 1016–21, October 1919.

PHYSICAL TRAINING.

1825. Doeblin, Maud I. "Come, let us play with our children." Froebel. Current education, 23 : 246–50, October 1919.

The importance of play in the education of the child.

1826. Pearl, N. H. *and* **Brown, H. E.** Health by stunts. New York, The Macmillan company, 1919. x, 216 p. illus. 16°.

An effort on the part of two physical directors, who have had unusual opportunity for observation and experimental work with boys in the upper elementary grades and in the high school grades, to give in convenient form plans to develop an interest by our boys in various wholesome athletic exercises.

SOCIAL ASPECTS OF EDUCATION.

1827. Fell, E. E. The aims and advantages of the parent-teachers' association. Moderator-topics, 40 : 36–37, 47, September 25, 1919.

1828. Piggott, H. E. The cooperation of home and school. Journal of education and school world (London) 51 : 593–95, September 1919.

1829. **Snedden, David.** Educational sociology: its province and possibilities. American journal of sociology, 25: 129–49, September 1919.

Discusses the value of sociology to government, religion, domestic life, and education. Says that the two sciences most fundamental to education are sociology and psychology. Presents possible objectives of research in educational sociology.

1830. **Webb, J. C.** Socialization as an educational objective. Journal of education, 90: 339–40, October 9, 1919.

CHILD WELFARE.

1831. **American child hygiene association.** Transactions of the ninth annual meeting, Chicago, December 5–7, 1918. Baltimore, Press of Franklin printing company, 1919. 354 p. 8°. (Miss Gertrude B. Knipp, secretary, 1211 Cathedral Street, Baltimore, Md.)

Formerly the American association for study and prevention of infant mortality.

Contains: 1. Mrs. W. L. Putnam: President's address [Child welfare] p. 17–31. 2. Mrs. W. P. Lucas: The work of the children's bureau of the American Red cross in France, p. 33–40. 3. Anna E. Rude: The progress of children's year, p. 59–64. 4. Mrs. I. C. Wood: Report of the Elizabeth McCormick memorial fund on the program of the children's year in Illinois, p. 69–73. 5. Anna E. Rude: What the Children's bureau is doing and planning to do, p. 75–80. 6. Taliaferro Clark: The plans of the United States public health service, p. 85–92. 7. S. Josephine Baker: Lessons from the draft, p. 181–88. 8. Pansy V. Besom: How to conduct a survey in the interest of child welfare work, p. 198–205. 9. Report of the Committee on teaching courses, p. 252–53; Discussion, p. 253–58.

1832. **U. S. Children's bureau.** Standards of child welfare. A report of the Children's bureau conferences May and June, 1919. Washington, 1919. 459 p. 8°. (Conference series no. 1. Bureau publication no. 60)

CONTENTS.—Section I. The economic and social basis for child welfare, p. 21–77.—Section II. Child labor, p. 79–141.—Section III. The health of children and mothers, p. 143–304.—Section IV. Children in need of special care, p. 305–407.—Section V. Standardization of child welfare laws, p. 409–27.—Section VI. Standards, p. 429–44.

RELIGIOUS EDUCATION.

1833. **Erb, Frank Otis.** Organizing the young people's department of the Sunday school. Religious education, 14: 305–11, October 1919.

1834. **Hartshorne, Hugh.** Childhood and character; an introduction to the study of the religious life of children. Boston, Chicago, The Pilgrim press [1919] viii, 282 p. 12°.

1835. **Johns, Ralph Leslie.** The problem of Old Testament instruction. Biblical world, 53: 481–92, September 1919.

1836. **Johnson, George.** The curriculum of the Catholic elementary school. A discussion of its psychological and social foundations. Washington. D. C., 1919. 121 p. 8°.

A dissertation submitted to the faculty of philosophy of the Catholic University of America in partial fulfillment of the requirements for the degree of doctor of philosophy.

1837. **Lampe, M. W.** The religion of university students, as seen in the University of Pennsylvania. Alumni register (University of Pennsylvania) 22: 14–21, October 1919.

1838. **Rhinelander, Philip Mercer.** Theology and education. Churchman, 120: 15–17, September 6, 1919.

MANUAL AND VOCATIONAL TRAINING.

1839. **National society for vocational education.** Addresses delivered at the twelfth annual convention, St. Louis, Mo., February 20–22, 1919. New York city, National society for vocational education, 1919. 4 v. 8°. (Bulletin, no. 28, 29, 30, 31)

> Contains: Bulletin no. 28, Lessons of the war, The states and the Smith-Hughes act, Women in industry, 96 p.; Bulletin no. 29, Federal aid to commercial education, Recent developments in commercial education, Retail selling education, 79 p.; Bulletin no. 30, Industrial education, Trade tests, Unit trade schools, General industrial schools, Shopwork on productive basis, Teacher training—State supervision, Training and upgrading of women workers, 72 p.; Bulletin no. 31, Agricultural education, Supervision, Two current problems, Relations to agricultural extension, 29 p.

1840. **Bennett, Charles A.** Industrial art education—America's opportunity. School and society, 10: 373–77, September 27, 1919.

> Emphasizes the value of art education from the economic standpoint.

1841. **Binnion, R. B.** Academic education as related to vocational education. Texas school journal, 36: 12, 14, 21, 29, May 1919.

1842. **Boone, Richard G.** Teaching printing in the schools of California. Sierra educational news, 15: 436–39, September 1919.

1843. **Dooley, William H.** Principles and methods of industrial education, for use in teacher training classes; with an introduction by C. A. Prosser. Boston, New York [etc.] Houghton Mifflin company [1919] xi, 257 p. 12°.

> According to the introduction, the value of this book lies in its compact summing up of facts and principles; its "sampling" of methods and devices in organizing material for purposes of instruction, all of which can be a constant stimulus to vocational teachers in training classes to reflect and reason independently.

1844. **Ladd, Robert M.** Class work in industrial chemistry. School science and mathematics, 19: 633–42, October 1919.

1845. **McKinney, James.** Some essentials in teacher training as they apply to trades and industries. Manual training magazine, 21: 41–45, October 1919.

1846. **Thomas, Earl Baldwin.** Theodore Roosevelt and industrial education. Manual training magazine, 21: 39–40, October 1919.

1847. **Vaughn, S. J.** First aid to the inexperienced—III. Class management, or, How to handle the boys. Industrial-arts magazine, 8: 427–32, November 1919.

> The third article in a series on starting a grade class in woodworking.

VOCATIONAL GUIDANCE.

1848. **Whitney, Frank P.** Choosing a vocation in junior high school. Education, 40: 120–25, October 1919.

> Material gathered from pupils of the Collinwood junior high school, Cleveland, Ohio, regarding their prospective vocations, etc.

VOCATIONAL TESTS; ARMY PERSONNEL.

1849. **U. S. War Department.** Adjutant general's department. Classification division. The personnel system of the United States army. Vols. 1–2. Washington, D. C., 1919. 2 v. 8°.

> Vol. I. History of the personnel system.—Vol. II. The personnel manual.
> Volume I traces the development of the personnel work of the army as it steadily solved the problems arising and finally ripened into an organized system. Volume II gives detailed instructions for the actual operation of the personnel system as finally evolved and in use during the latter part of 1918.

AGRICULTURAL EDUCATION; HOME ECONOMICS.

1850. **Cooley, Anna M.** Teaching home economics; by Anna M. Cooley, Cora M. Winchell, Wilhelmina H. Spohr, Josephine A. Marshall, of Teachers college, Columbia university, New York. New York, The Macmillan company, 1919. xii, 555 p. 12°.

> Part I of this book deals with the history and place of home economics as an organized study in the school program. In Part II the organization of courses of study in home economics is presented—in the elementary school, high school, rural schools, and in agencies other than schools. Part III tells how to plan lessons in home economics. The subject of Part IV is Personnel, materials, and opportunities in the teaching of home economics. A comprehensive bibliography of the literature of the entire subject concludes this part of the book. Part V, Addenda, contains numerous typical courses of study selected from various institutions.

1851. **Hunt, Thomas Forsyth.** The future of agricultural education. School and society, 10 : 381–88, October 4, 1919.

> Some observations on agricultural education during the past as bearing upon its possible future.

PROFESSIONAL EDUCATION.

1852. **Hayford, John F.** Reflections of an S. T. E. E. president. Bulletin of the Society for the promotion of engineering education, 10 : 1–14, September 1919.

> Presidential address at the 27th annual meeting of the society, June 25–28, 1919. Deals with various phases of engineering education in this country.

1853. **U. S. War Department.** Committee on education and special training. The engineer school at Camp Humphreys. A report on methods of teaching engineering. Washington [1919] 76 p. 8°.

1854. **Wood, Helen.** Value of the clinical method of teaching in nursing schools. American journal of nursing, 20 : 8–12, October 1919.

CIVIC EDUCATION.

1855. **Leighton, Etta V.** Our little citizens. Primary education, 27 : 483–85, October 1919. illus.

> Civic instruction and the "Tiny Town" movement in Springfield, Mo.

1856. **Ray, P. Orman.** The ignorant "educated" and the universities. School and society, 10 : 388–93, October 4, 1919.

> Deplores the lack of instruction in American government in our universities. Says "Not only do thousands enter the colleges and universities each year deplorably ignorant of such matters, but it is possible for most of them to leave the university at the end of four years hardly less ignorant."

1857. **Rosenstein, David.** Government, training and welfare. School and society, 10 : 441–50, October 18, 1919.

> "A comment on a collection of papers written by leading specialists, under the title, 'Experts in city government,' edited by Major E. A. Fitzpatrick, of Wisconsin, and bespeaking interest in the growing movement for college and university training for public service."

1858. **Snedden, David.** Some new problems in education for citizenship. International journal of ethics, 30 : 1–15, October 1919.

> An address given before the Columbia institute of arts and sciences, January 28, 1919.
> Writer says that means must be devised of convincing our youth that their chief responsibilities as active or dynamic citizens must be met, not through their abilities to solve complex social and political problems for themselves, but through their abilities to employ specialists to solve these problems for them

1859. **Tildsley, John L.** What Government does for the citizen. Outlook, 123 : 126–29, September 24, 1919.

> First of a series of articles on community civics—a practical educational course in citizenship.

AMERICANIZATION OF IMMIGRANTS.

1860. Arnold, Earl C. The elimination of illiteracy. Education, 40: 65–71, October 1919.

Advocates immediate steps to Americanize the 13,000,000 foreigners in this country, many of whom can neither read nor write our language.

1861. Avery, Lewis B. A new heaven. School and society, 10: 416–22, October 11, 1919.

The Americanization movement and the efforts of the public schools in the movement.

1862. Somers, Arthur S. The gospel of Americanism. Brooklyn, N. Y., Brooklyn training school for teachers, 1919. 11 p. 8°. (Brooklyn training school for teachers. Bulletin no. 4.)

Commencement address before the class of 1919 of the Brooklyn training school for teachers.

The teacher's function in Americanizing our alien population.

EDUCATION OF SOLDIERS.

1863. Erskine, John. Universal training for national service. American review of reviews, 60: 416–20, October 1919.

Discusses the advantages of converting the army training cantonments into permanent training schools where much of the equipment used for war purposes could be constantly used for purposes of peace.

1864. Houston, Harry. Teaching illiterates in France. Journal of education, 90: 319–20, October 2, 1919.

Teaching American soldiers in France.

REEDUCATION OF WAR INVALIDS.

1865. Conférence interalliée pour l'étude de la rééducation professionnelle et des questions qui intéressent les invalides de la guerre, Paris, May 8–12, 1917. Compte rendu. Tome I–II. Paris, Imprimerie Chaix, 1919. 2v. 4°.

EDUCATION OF WOMEN.

1866. Allix, André. A technical course in economic geography. Journal of geography, 18: 252–59, October 1919.

The French text of this article is appearing in L'École du travail, Paris. Describes the work of the Higher technical school for girls, Lyons, France. Gives program of studies, and bibliography.

1867. Gerould, Katharine Fullerton. Cap-and-gown philosophers. Delineator, 95: 7, 59–60, October 1919.

Reviewed in Literary digest, October 11, 1919, p. 57–58, 62, 66.

Tabulates and digests the answers received from 600 woman's college seniors, mostly in the East, to the following questions: 1. Do you plan to live at home next year? 2. Are your plans for the future in harmony with those of your parents for you? 3. If you could do exactly as you wanted, what occupation would you follow: Stage, business, writing, editing, law, medicine, etc.? 4. How much money, approximately, did it cost you to dress, per year, in college? 5. At how much money per year, do you estimate the value of your services as a wife and housekeeper, provided you sacrifice a "career" to home life? 6. Which of the monthly magazines do you enjoy the most? 7. How much money do you think a man and girl need to marry on? 8. How many children do you want? 9. If you follow a professional or business career, would you attempt marriage and motherhood in addition, if you met the right man? 10. Provided you could not have both marriage and a business or professional career, which would you sacrifice? 11. What do you think of women smoking?

NEGRO EDUCATION.

1868. A declaration of principles by representative Negroes of North Carolina,
Raleigh, September 26, 1919. Raleigh, N. C., Office of superintendent
of public instruction, 1919. 12 p. 8°.

> The declaration given in this pamphlet was adopted by a conference of
> leading Negroes called by Dr. E. C. Brooks, State superintendent of public
> instruction, with a view to inaugurating a broad educational policy for both
> races in North Carolina and promoting confidence and harmony.

1869. Williams, W. T. B. Hampton graduates as teachers. Southern workman, 48 : 503–7, October 1919.

EDUCATION OF DEAF.

1870. Society of progressive oral advocates. Proceedings of the second annual
convention, St. Louis, June 23–25, 1919. Volta review, 21 : 229–60,
October 1919.

> Contains : 1. M. A. Goldstein : The lessons from the war, p. 631–34. 2. J.
> W. Davis : Phonics in the schools, p. 635–38. 3. E. A. Gruver : The subnormal
> deaf, p. 641–44. 4. Mrs. E. C. Evans : What the parent can accomplish through
> organized effort, p. 647–50. 5. Enfield Joiner : Work of the section of defects
> of hearing and speech at U. S. Army general hospital no. 11, p. 651–55. 6.
> Frederick Martin : Stammering, p. 655–59.

1871. De Land, Fred. Some notes about the American association to promote
the teaching of speech to the deaf. Volta review, 21 : 663–69, 701–702,
October, November 1919.

> Third and fourth papers of series.

1872. Monro, Sarah J. Phonetics and word study. A plan for pronunciation
and speech drill, fifth year's work. Volta review, 21 : 669–72, October
1919.

EDUCATIONAL EXTENSION.

1873. Bulletin of the Metropolitan museum of art, vol. 14, no. 9, September 1919.

> Contains : 1. Gustave Straubenmüller : The place of the art museum in edu-
> cation, p. 191–93. 2. Walter Sargent : The place of the art museum in
> elementary education, p. 193–94. 3. Royal B. Farnum : The place of the art
> museum in secondary education, p. 194–96. 4. F. L. Ackerman : College and
> museum, p. 196–98.

1874. Drummond, Alec M. Plays for the time. English journal, 8 : 419–28,
September 1919.

> Gives a list of plays suitable for the educational theatre, based on appro-
> priateness to the time.

LIBRARIES AND READING.

1875. Richardson, Mary C. The importance of the library in the school system. Public libraries, 24 : 334–35, October 1919.

BUREAU OF EDUCATION: RECENT PUBLICATIONS.

1876. Financial and building needs of the schools of Lexington, Kentucky.
Washington, 1919. 50 p. (Bulletin, 1919, no. 68)

1877. Home gardening for city children of the fifth, sixth, and seventh grades;
by Ethel Gowans. Washington, 1919. 72 p. (U. S. School garden
army)

1878. The junior college; by F. M. McDowell. Washington, 1919. 139 p. (Bulletin, 1919, no. 35)

1879. Lessons in school-supervised gardening for the southeastern states. Vegetables. Washington, 1919. 53 p. (U. S. School garden army)

1880. A manual of school-supervised gardening for the northeastern states.
Pt. I—Vegetables. Washington, 1919. 74 p. (U. S. School garden
army)

DEPARTMENT OF THE INTERIOR
BUREAU OF EDUCATION

BULLETIN, 1919, No. 76

COMMUNITY AMERICANIZATION

A HANDBOOK FOR WORKERS

By

FRED CLAYTON BUTLER
DIRECTOR OF AMERICANIZATION, BUREAU OF EDUCATION

WASHINGTON
GOVERNMENT PRINTING OFFICE
1920

CONTENTS.

LETTER OF TRANSMITTAL.

DEPARTMENT OF THE INTERIOR,
BUREAU OF EDUCATION,
Washington, September 30, 1919.

SIR: Except for a quarter million North American Indians, descendants of the natives whom the white settlers found here, the people of the United States are all foreign born or the descendants of foreign-born ancestors. All are immigrants or the offspring of immigrants. The oldest American families are so new in this country that they have hardly forgotten the traditions and the home ties of the countries from which they came. Though we are now more than a hundred millions of people between our double oceans, we have yet to celebrate the three hundredth anniversary of the founding of the second of the colonies out of which the Nation has grown; 150 years ago there were less than three millions of us.

From all the world we have come, mostly sons of the poor, all striving to better our conditions in some way, all looking for a larger measure of freedom than was possible for us in the countries from which we came. Here, free from the domination of autocratic government and from the poisoning influences of decadent aristocracies, forgetting our fears and servile habits, we have elevated the best from all countries into a common possession, transfused and transformed it by our highest and best ideals, and called it Americanism. A new thing is this in the world, and withal the most precious possession the world has. Though incomplete, and still in the formative stage, growing richer and grander as the years go by, constantly clearing and purifying itself, its form and spirit are quite well determined.

To enter into this common heritage of the best of all, to be inspired with these ideals, to learn to understand the institutions which guarantee our freedom and rights and enable us to work together for the common good, to resolve to forget all purely selfish means for the work of the highest welfare of our country and of the world, is to become Americanized. To give to the foreign-born population in the United States, and all others, the fullest and freest opportunity for this, is what we in the Bureau of Education mean by Americanization. Every part of our program is directed to this end.

5

Americanization is a process of education, of winning the mind and heart through instruction and enlightenment. From the very nature of the thing it can make little or no use of force. It must depend, rather, on the attractive power and the sweet reasonableness of the thing itself. Were it to resort to force, by that very act it would destroy its spirit and cease to be American. It would also cease to be American if it should become narrow and fixed and exclusive, losing its faith in humanity and rejecting vital and enriching elements from any source whatever.

Our program of education does not compel but invites and allures. It may, therefore, probably must, in the beginning be slow; but in the end it will be swift and sure.

Americanization is not something which the Government or a group of individuals may do for the foreign born or others. It is what these persons do for themselves when the opportunity is offered and they are shown the way; what they do for the country and the thing called democracy. The function of the Government and all other agencies interested in Americanization is to offer the opportunity, make the appeal, and inspire the desire. They can and should attempt nothing more than to reveal in all their fullness the profit and the joy of working together for the common good and the attainment of our high ideals, to create the desire to have a part in the inspiring task, to show the way by which each may do his part best, and to help him set his feet firmly on the way.

Therefore, the real work of Americanization must be a community affair. Federal and State Governments can only help the several communities to discover their problems, inspire them to the task of its solution, direct their efforts, and coordinate their work. To assist in doing this is the purpose of the manuscript transmitted herewith for publication as a bulletin of the Bureau of Education. Its spirit and the methods it advocates are, I believe, in harmony with the soundest and best policies of Americanization.

Respectfully submitted.

P. P. CLAXTON,
Commissioner.

The SECRETARY OF THE INTERIOR.

FOREWORD.

Americanization is in the end a task for the individual citizen and not for the Government. The individual can be successful in so human a problem only by having a sympathetic knowledge of his task and of those with whom he must deal.

To supply at least the foundations of this knowledge is the purpose of this book. The contents are taken largely from the lives and experiences of successful workers in Americanization as revealed at the conference of May, 1919. Those who desire a fuller knowledge of the work are referred to the complete proceedings of that conference. That volume may be secured from the Government Printing Office at a cost of 35 cents.

It is evident that such a book as this must be written for the lay-. man. The expert will find little or nothing herein that is new. The technical phases of the problem are being covered by other writers in books which will be issued in the near future as bulletins of the Bureau of Education. These will include " The Training of Teachers for Americanization," " The Teaching of English to the Foreign Born," and " The Teaching of Native Illiterates."

THE AUTHOR.

7

COMMUNITY AMERICANIZATION.

Chapter I.

GENERAL PRINCIPLES.

Americanization can never be a cold, calculating process of the brain. It must spring from hearts filled with love for men. "There is no way by which we can make anyone feel that it is a blessed and splendid thing to be an American, unless we ourselves are aglow with the sacred fire—unless we interpret Americanism by our kindness, our courage, our generosity, our fairness."[1]

There are, however, ways and methods of Americanization which will be successful and those which will merely harm the cause. Americanization is in some respect an art, requiring great skill of its workers. It is a difficult and a delicate art, for we are dealing with human hearts, with primal passions, with inherited prejudices, with minds which are supersensitive and which are prone to read into our purposes motives which we do not possess.

DEFINITION.

We have given too much time in the past to seeking a technical definition for Americanization. It is well to know whither we are headed, but nothing is to be gained by trying to set forth in so many words such a technical definition. Anyone who is American at heart knows that we have in purpose nothing of Prussianization. We seek nothing through force or fear. Indeed we might seek long and find no better definition of Americanization than is contained in the golden rule: "As ye would that men should do to you, do ye also to them likewise."

Oversensitive workers have feared that even the "Americanization" might give offense and have sought, without much success, to find a new term for our purpose. The word Americanization is a good word. It can offend only those who read into its meaning that which has never been intended. Technically it means "the making of America" or "the process of making Americans." Surely there

---

[1] Franklin K. Lane.

is nothing in either of these definitions that could offend. Instead, then, of spending time seeking new combinations of words to take its place, let us bend our efforts to giving Americanization its proper meaning.

America is a brotherhood. Men of many races have chosen to become members. We who are already initiated through the accident of birth or choice by immigration are now to extend the hand of fellowship to the later comers. Upon the tact, skill, and diligence with which we do our part will depend in no small measure the future of America.

But though it is difficult for us as yet to picture definitely what we wish to produce, to visualize the composite American of the future, it is necessary that we formulate some idea, set before ourselves some fairly tangible objective, so that our efforts may be effective. Can we not then take as this objective— the creation of a homogeneous people?[1]

KNOWLEDGE NEEDED.

We must first of all, if we are to do our task properly, possess the American spirit ourselves. We should have some knowledge of those whom we are seeking to initiate into our brotherhood. We must know the difficulties under which they are laboring in this new land. We must come to have a real respect for them as men and for their possibilities as members.

We can succeed only if we approach our task with hearts beating in sympathy with the needs of our fellow men, with visions unclouded by the hates or passions of war, "with charity for all and malice toward none." Unless we are ourselves convinced that these people from other lands are desirable potential Americans, that we need them here, that they come not with empty hands but with arts, crafts, sciences, music, ideals, which will add to the wealth of our common heritage—unless we feel that to us is given not so much a duty as a great opportunity, we shall fail.[2]

I believe that there is one and only one way by which you can make a good American, and that is by sympathy, by understanding. If we are to deal wisely in this larger day, we must get within the man and look out with his eyes not only upon this strange world in which he has landed but upon the land from which he came; for has not America become as a foster mother to these strugglers? We want an avenue of communication opened to reach that man's soul. And as he surveys this land and knows its people he will come to understand the country and to love the people.

The whole of this continent is to him now the cramped apartment, the dirty street, and the sweatshop or the factory. To the sweep of the great land and its many beckonings, his eyes are closed. And in his isolation and ignorance and disappointment there is a fruitful nesting place for all the hurtful microbes that attack society.[3]

---

[1] John Ihlder, in Conference Proceedings.
[2] F. C. Butler, in Conference Proceedings.
[3] Franklin K. Lane.

OUR OWN ATTITUDE.

Just as the teacher must have in her heart a deep love for little children if she is to succeed in her work, so must the Americanization worker possess a spirit of respect, tolerance, and sympathy. Nor can we pretend to such a feeling if we have it not. The foreign-born people among whom we must work, with their senses sharpened by our neglect, and exclusiveness of the past, will be quick to detect the slightest feeling of patronage or superiority. Indeed they can discern it even when we ourselves may think we do not have it. Unless we can meet our new Americans as man to man, seeking to learn from them as well as to teach, we will never be able to make the cordial and sympathetic contact which is so essential.

One of the reasons the alien shuts the door in your face to-day is because she has too often fallen a victim to disinterestedness that was really self-interest, and to assistance that was self-advertising; and to undisciplined, spasmodic efforts that drew her into the whirlpool of uplift, but left her worse off than before. Somehow unless you can learn to meet her with directness and simplicity and sincerity as a friendly understanding human being, measuring the day's success more by loss than by gain, by purpose rather than by fulfillment, you will fail at the task of Americanization.

If Americanization service appeals to you primarily as a chance to educate yourself, lay it aside. Such education will certainly be a big by-product, but you have not the right to ask the foreigner to pay for your education nor America to liquidate your mistakes.

If you have racial prejudice and inhospitality in your heart and a sense of Anglo-Saxon superiority in your mind and go with your hands bearing gifts, you will ultimately set America back rather than forward at this critical time.[1]

MUST KNOW OUR PEOPLE.

There is only one way in which we can learn a proper respect for the people among whom we are to work, and that is by knowing them. Invariably, workers among the foreign born come to have a love for them. Their simple, homely traits of frankness, sincerity, and a sort of childlike simplicity endear them to those who learn to look beyond the superficial externals.

We have been too prone to judge whole groups by the acts of individuals. The newspapers have unconsciously and unintentionally helped to give us distorted pictures of a whole race by closing their stories of crime with such statements as "the murderer is a Hungarian" or "the criminal is a Greek." If they cared to do so, they could not infrequently close with a statement that "the scoundrel is a native-born American," but this they do not do. Such statements have had a tendency to connect in our minds criminality with our foreign-born people. Obviously, this is a deep injustice. Having for

[1] Frances A. Kellor.

the most part only a dense ignorance of the virtues of our new Americans, many have unwittingly ascribed to them only vices.

And, because of this ignorance of ours, we tend to group these people in large masses and to ascribe to each member of a group those characteristics which we have been pleased to ascribe to the group as a whole. With such a grouping established, we are constantly ready to believe ill of those concerning whom we know so little. The fault of an individual becomes the fault of "his people." The unreliability of some Poles causes us to believe all Poles unreliable; the Italian acceptance of overcrowded dwellings causes us to accept statements that all Italians prefer to live in overflowing tenements. Then, when a crisis comes, a time of emotional strain, resentment blazes out against a whole group, innocent with guilty. And in response comes resentment for injustice. That the injustice was unintentional, based merely on lack of understanding, does not lessen the emotion on one side or the other.[1]

To the native born we must say: Know the people with whom you are working. Do not fall into the error of feeling that there is a magical process which can be applied to all national groups to accomplish your end. Standpoint, method of application, and form of procedure must be based upon the psychology of the folk, upon their customs and beliefs, upon their perceptive bases. You can not gain the cooperation of those whom you do not know. The method followed with the Pole will not always gain results when applied without change to the Italian or the Jew or the Croatian.

One can not gain the confidence of those he detests or of those he does not appreciate and whose ideals and dreams he can not sympathize with. I come into frequent contact with an excellent woman who is perfectly enthusiastic about the theory of community organization, yet she can not succeed in her work among the Russian-Jewish people, whom she is hoping to organize, because it is instinctively felt by them, despite all her efforts, that she despises them.[2]

Not only must we eliminate the obnoxious and insulting nicknames which we thoughtlessly bestowed upon our new Americans in the past, such as "Dago," "Wop," and "Hunky," but we should cease to speak of them even as foreigners. That man can never be thoroughly assimilated who hears himself constantly referred to as a "foreigner." It will be noted that the Bureau of Education uses the term "foreigner."

KNOW THEIR DIFFICULTIES.

Yes; more sympathy and interest and real brotherhood on the part of native Americans toward the foreign born is needed if this Americanization movement is to be a success. And this sympathy and interest can be awakened only by a greater knowledge concerning these various races immigrating to this country, by a knowledge of their characteristics, their history, and their past and present conditions in their native lands, for Americans must remember that these "foreigners," too, have had their glorious history, their patriotic struggles, and their great men of literature, art, science, and every line of human endeavor.[3]

Such a knowledge on our part of these peoples would show us that many of the conditions under which they are living in this country,

[1] John Ihlder, in Conference Proceedings.
[2] Nathan Peyser, in Conference Proceedings.
[3] Albert Mamaty, in Conference Proceedings.

and which we so greatly deplore, are not of their choosing. Indeed, in most cases their environment is far below that of their former lives. They have been driven into it in the past through many reasons, not the least of which have been the selfishness and exclusiveness of the native born.

We have decried the failure on the part of the new Americans to adopt the ways and standards of our land, quite forgetting that through our own aloofness they were not coming into contact with those customs. Mary Antin in her own life story points out that the Americanization of her family began as soon as they moved into an American neighborhood. Yet, just as her mother was gladly learning American ways from these neighbors, the native born moved away because, as they said, " they did not want to live next to a Russian Jew."

Physically, the port of entry seems to be the gateway to America, but mentally, socially, and culturally it is not more than the outer office, the reception hall of the new country. The real entrance to American life comes very often much later, through long and sometimes saddening experiences in industry or commerce or in pleasanter pathways leading through night school, social center, fraternal or other organization, conducted by sympathetic Americans or by kinsmen who have preceded by some years the later comers.[1]

WRONG METHODS.

Some there are who would Americanize by law, who would force the knowledge and use of the English language and of naturalization and citizenship. A few talk of deportation and imprisonment, as though the lip service gained in such fashion could serve America. Such only harm the cause. Too often the foreign born, hearing them, forget that they are but the unthinking few who serve only to accentuate the good sense and judgment of the majority.

You can not make Americans that way. You have got to make them by calling upon the fine things that are within them, and by dealing with them in sympathy, by appreciating what they have to offer us, and by revealing to them what we have to offer them. And that brings to mind the thought that this work must be a human work—must be something done out of the human heart and speaking to the human heart and must largely turn upon instrumentalities that are in no way formal, and that have no dogma and have no creed and which can not be put into writing and can not be set upon the press.[2]

Americanization is a mutual process. We shall fail if we do not receive as well as give. That Americanization would be futile which incorporated these foreign-born peoples into our lives and lost to America all that they have to give. America is the child of many races, but is herself stronger and nobler than any of her progenitors. This is so because each people has brought with it a wealth of art,

---

[1] Harry A. Linsky, in Conference Proceedings.
[2] Franklin K. Lane.

of song, of custom, of ideals, all of which together form a wondrous
heritage.

The native-born worker must not face the problem with the feeling
that his task is entirely that of putting something across to the
foreign group. It consists just as surely of carrying something back
from the group with which he is working. Americanization is a twofold process. It is a process of reciprocal adjustment. The newcomer is having his standards modified, his point of view changed,
his experiences enlarged, his equipment of languages added to, his
grasp of our political structure and ideals strengthened, and his
standards of living altered; but he is just as surely modifying our
point of view, enlarging our experiences, modifying our industrial
organization, and causing changes in our economic values and our
political organization. He is bringing with him the values and experiences and spiritual riches of his racial and national life, and he is
contributing these to us.[1]

MUST HAVE TOLERANCE.

Many are too prone to think that we must cast out all that is new
or unusual in order to Americanize. They are apt to feel that the
newcomers in order to be good Americans should resemble themselves in all their ways as nearly as possible! They would cast out
with the same naïve abandon as the child does the weeds in her
mother's posy bed.

Those who go out to "Americanize" in the spirit of saving the country
from disaster, or of reforming the heathen by abolishing all that looks un-
familiar, are less likely to Americanize the foreign born than to provincialize
America. There is surely nothing dangerously un-American in spaghetti or
marionettes, or even funerals with six barouches of flowers and 100 coaches![2]

Let us then give over all thought of trying to make the American
from other lands just exactly the same sort of an American that
we are ourselves. It is conceivable that men may be good Americans at heart and still not understand a word of the English language. Men may wear wooden shoes and still stand ready to die
for America or to serve her devotedly. Let us seek, therefore, to
tell the true from the false, the meat from the husks, the essential
from the superficial.

You can not work against nature. You can never completely transform a
man or woman that was not born and raised in this country, or at least that
did not come here as a child so as to go through the American public schools,
into just such an American as you are. It is impossible. But it is also unnecessary.

---

[1] Nathan Peyser, in Conference Proceedings.
[2] Esther Everett Lape, in Ladies Home Jour.

A man is not "foreign" because he was born in a foreign land or because he does not speak good English, but because he clings to or is actuated by un-American or anti-American ideas.[1]

We can never crush out of men's hearts the love they hold for their childhood homes. Nor would we do so if we could. The heart which could so easily and quickly forget the land of its birth could never love with a deep devotion the land of its adoption.

None of us would wish that the immigrant or the descendant of immigrants—which includes all of us—should fail in pride of ancestry. With that would go loss of self-respect. Whatever the people or the peoples from which our fathers came, they have something to contribute to the greater, richer American life of the future. And that contribution we want, whether it be the German Christmas tree and the sentiment that surrounds it or the Italian love of gayety and color."[2]

OUR FOREIGN COLONIES.

Austria was never a nation. It was merely a federation of many diverse peoples. Some there are who plead for the continuance of the foreign colonies in America. They even argue that these people came to America for freedom to live as they choose; that if they desire to keep their Polish or Italian or other national solidarity and life and customs, they should be permitted to do so. Such pleaders mistake sentimentality for sense. Such a course could result only in America becoming a second Austria and subject to its fate.

The various peoples in Austria were conquered by superior strength and incorporated into the whole without their consent. All peoples in America have come to this land of their own choice. They come presumably ready and willing to abide by its laws and ways. There is no place here for a branch of any other nation. To these new peoples we offer the great institutions of this land which our fathers fought and died to secure and maintain. They are given freely with only the stipulation that these peoples shall cast their lot with us and be one of us. Such as do not care to accept this simple requirement are free to go whence they came. Of those that remain we ask that they shall learn our language, that they shall leave their feuds and hatreds at the gate, that they shall renounce allegiance to their old and prepare to live or die for the glory of the new—America.

For the growth of foreign colonies in America, the native born are equally at fault. We have resented the purchase of property on our streets by anyone even having a foreign name. Through our own clannishness we have forced these new Americans to live among themselves if they would find aught in life to enjoy. Yet we should not

---

[1] Alberty Mamatey, in Conference Proceedings.
[2] John Ihlder, in Conference Proceedings.

forget that this gathering into groups is but a natural thing. We have our American colonies in London, and Paris, and Mexico.

The segregation and clannishness of the immigrant groups is erroneously called a characteristic peculiar to them. All of us choose our homes among those people with whom we feel comfortable, with the result that all of us really live segregated in districts. Those who come from the same country naturally feel unity. We have, then, in segregation merely a manifestation of a common human characteristic.[1]

BREAKING UP GROUPS.

We can dissolve these colonies only as we offer a fuller life to those who live in them. When the inhabitants of our foreign districts find full fellowship in our communities and equality of treatment and of opportunity, they will find in the new relation a happiness greater than in the old and disintegration will come about naturally.

Could we start with a clean slate in this work of Americanization, the task would be simple. We must, however, reckon with the bitterness and the heartburning, the misunderstanding and resentment, caused by our long years of neglect and injustice. We Americans take a great deal of injustice toward ourselves, all as a part of the game. We know that some time when we get around to it we will take a day off and clean up that injustice that bothers us; in the meantime we suffer from it with a grin. Our foreign-born friends, however, are prone to nourish the feeling of a slight or wrong.

When an immigrant sees unfair practices he is likely to be affected much more than is the American, because of his faith that such things are not found in democracy. He must be led to see that all, including himself, owe a duty to help prevent such things. He must see that the power in a democracy is in the people and that there is not some outside power to which to appeal and which to blame. We can get no great distance in civic improvement until all persons recognize a personal responsibility for evil conditions and count it a moral and religious duty to stop them. We can not depend upon the Government as something apart from ourselves to right wrongs. We must right the wrongs ourselves, for we are the Government. An immigrant ought to be given the desire to become a citizen so that he can do his share; as a foreigner he is quite helpless, but as a citizen he can help in realizing fair play.[2]

FIGHTING BOLSHEVISM.

There is a negative school of Americanization abroad in the land. It would Americanize America by "fighting Bolshevism" by word and laws, by more police power, more restrictions, more espionage. It is right that our Nation should stand on guard for the principles on which it was founded. But no campaign was ever won merely by the zealous punishing of a minority. The America of the future will be built not by our fear for it, but by the belief of one hundred million citizens in it.[3]

---

[1] H. A. Miller, in Conference Proceedings.
[2] A Program for Citizenship. National Catholic War Council.
[3] Esther Everett Lape.

Americanization workers may be tempted to fight Bolshevism and the other " isms " that attack society from time to time. They should consider whether they are not merely helping in this way to attract attention to these various " causes " and thus assist in advertising them. Bolshevism is an effect, not a cause, and it is always wasted effort to attack effects, leaving the causes untouched. Bolshevism is the natural fruit of ignorance and injustice. Let us therefore bend our efforts to the eradication of these causes, and the effects will disappear of themselves.

Our responsibility is not to be met, however, with cries and shouts and pieces of paper, like Chinese exorcising evil spirits. It is not to be met with the chantings of the charms of democracy nor with boasting of great things done. It can be met only by doing the things that remain to be done to make America the better land it ought to be.[1]

So my interest in this movement is as much an interest in ourselves as in those whom we are trying to Americanize, because if we are genuine Americans they can not avoid the infection; whereas, if we are not genuine Americans, there will be nothing to infect them with and no amount of teaching, no amount of exposition of the Constitution, no amount of dwelling upon the idea of liberty and of justice will accomplish the object we have in view, unless we ourselves illustrate the idea of justice and of liberty.[2]

---

[1] Franklin K. Lane.
[2] Woodrow Wilson.

Chapter II.

. A COMMUNITY SURVEY.

Before there can be an intelligent solution found for the problem of a community, there must be a study made of its needs. In planning such a survey there is a tendency to go into too much detail. Not only is it difficult to assimilate properly such a vast amount of detail as many surveys provide, but the task of doing so disheartens the workers. Most such detailed surveys are carefully tied up in bundles and left to gather dust on closet shelves.

It is doubtful if a house-to-house survey is justified. The questions asked are apt to be personal, if not impertinent. Agitators of trouble are quick to impute ulterior motives to such a survey. The foreign-born people, not yet acquainted with the reasons for the survey, are very apt to misunderstand the purpose. They associate it with the visits of the police in their former lands. Instead of helping, a house-to-house survey is almost sure to hinder. Nor is it necessary.

There are sources of information available in every community that will give the workers all the information necessary, at least in the beginning of the work. In every community of size there are large numbers of people ready at hand to receive instruction and assistance. Only when the helping hand has been extended to all of these will a community find it necessary to search the homes for persons to help.

Surveys of any sort or the tasks of gathering statistics of any kind are without value unless use is made of those facts when secured. Practically all of the information needed by committees can be secured from a few sources. For information relative to individuals, the industries are ready at hand with contacts with probably nine-tenths of the foreign born in a community.

A suggestive survey is given below. Needless to say this must be fitted to each particular community, rejecting such parts as do not well apply. The questionnaires supplementing the survey plan have been designed in order that only pertinent points be presented to the several types of agencies involved. The duplication in some of the questionnaires caused by the existence of several possible sources of information on a given subject may be used for purposes of checking up or averaging estimates; or, on the other hand, the duplication may be obviated by utilizing the most important questionnaires first and striking out those portions in all subsequent ones upon which data have already been secured.

18

TENTATIVE PLAN FOR COMMUNITY SURVEY.

I. IMMIGRANT POPULATION—COMPOSITION AND CHARACTERISTICS.

A. Summary of data from United States Census (by wards in larger cities):

1. Population (total) _____
2. Color and nativity (native and foreign born—white; Negro) _
3. Foreign nationalities in larger cities _____
4. Males of voting age _____
   a. Citizenship of foreign-born white _____

5. Illiteracy _____
6. Inability to speak English _____
7. School age and attendance _____
8. Map of community, showing location of chief immigrant settlements _____

Remarks:

B. Summary of data for community secured through questionnaires, etc.

1. Estimated number of foreign born and of foreign parentage by foreign-language groups:

Foreign-language groups (in order of predominance).	Approximate number foreign born and foreign parentage.	Approximate number foreign born.	Approximate number foreign parentage.

Total population of foreign birth or parentage, _____
Remaining population, _____
   Remarks:

2. Males of military age—native and foreign born:
Number registered—native, _____; naturalized, _____; declarants, _____; aliens, _____.
(Information can be secured from 1917–18 records of draft boards.)
   Remarks:

3. Estimated number of immigrants in the community's industrial plants:

Names and address of factories.	Total number employees.	Approximate number immigrant employees.	Number of classes for immigrants.

Remarks and suggestions:

II. STATUS OF EDUCATIONAL FACILITIES AVAILABLE TO IMMIGRANTS.

A. Public day schools with any considerable number of immigrant children (foreign born or of foreign parentage) attending:

Names and addresses of schools.	Total number of children attending.	Number of children of immigrants attending.

Remarks and recommendations:

19

B. Public-school classes, evening and day, for immigrants above regular school age.

Names and addresses of schools.	Number of immigrant classes.	Average total number attending per year.	Number hours instruction per year.

Remarks.—Amount of money appropriated for these classes—legislation governing them. Are these schools covering the situation adequately? Is the subject matter taught adapted to the needs and interests of the immigrants? Do these classes hold their pupils? List of sources for further information, etc.

C. Private day schools with any considerable number of immigrant children attending.

Names and addresses of schools.	Total number children attending.	Number of children of immigrants attending.

Remarks and recommendations:

D. Private-school classes, evening and day, for immigrants above regular school age:

Names and addresses of schools.	Number of immigrant classes.	Average total number attending per year.	Number hours instruction per year.

Remarks and recommendations:

E. Factory classes:

Name and address of factory.	Approximate number immigrant employees.	Number of immigrant classes.	Average total number attending.	Number hours instruction per year.

Remarks: Basis of cooperation between factory and school board, etc.
Recommendations:

F. Libraries:

Addresses of libraries patronized by immigrants.	Maintained by.	Days and hours open.	Estimated number immigrant patrons.	Total number books— foreign, English.	Estimated circulation of books per year among immigrants, foreign, English.

Note.—List also county and State traveling libraries if these reach immigrants in your community to any extent.

Remarks: Is the number of foreign-language books in keeping with the foreign-language speaking population? ———
Recommendations:

G. Reading rooms:

Addresses of reading rooms patronized by immigrants.	Maintained by.	Estimated number immigrant patrons.	Number foreign language papers.	Number English papers.

Remarks and recommendations:

III. OTHER FACILITIES AVAILABLE TO IMMIGRANTS.

Note.—List county and State institutions in addition to community facilities wherever the former affect immigrants to any extent.

A. Racial churches:

Names and addresses of racial churches.	Approximate membership.

Remarks:

B. Racial organizations:

Names and addresses.	Approximate membership.	Affiliations.

Remarks and recommendations:

C. Foreign-language newspapers circulating to any extent in your community:

Names and addresses.	Approximate circulation.

Remarks: Utility for publicity for various lines of cooperation, etc. (The Ayer Newspaper Annual will be found helpful in securing addresses.)
Recommendations:

D. Community centers reaching immigrants:

Names and location.	Approximate total number reached.	Approximate number of immigrants reached per year (give by foreign language groups, if possible).

Remarks: State what funds are available for this work; legislation upon which it depends. What basis of cooperation is there between the schools and community centers, etc.?

E. Legal aid societies:

Names and location.	Total number reached per year.	Approximate number of immigrants reached per year.

Remarks: Are there any special information and translation facilities furnished for immigrants? etc.

F. Information bureaus reaching immigrants:

Names and addresses.	Approximate number aided per year.	Number immigrants reached per year.

Remarks: The nature and scope of the bureaus; the use of interpreters; foreign language literature, etc.

G. Housing committees, bureaus, etc.

Names and addresses.

Remarks: Findings of conditions among immigrants, etc.

H. Charity organizations:

Names and addresses.	Total number assisted per year.	Number immigrants assisted per year.

Remarks: Plan of charity organization in the community. Conditions among immigrants, etc.

I. Recreational facilities:

  1. Playgrounds:

Names and locations.	Approximate total number reached per year.	Approximate number immigrant children reached per year (give by foreign language groups if possible).	Gymnasium (yes or no).

    Remarks: Legislation upon which the work rests, appropriations, cooperation with schools, etc., scope of the work. Relation to immigrants.

  2. Gymnastic organizations:

Names and addresses.	Native or racial.	Approximate average membership per year.	Approximate average membership of immigrants per year.

    Remarks:

J. Health agencies:

  1. Visiting nurse organizations:

Names and addresses.	Total number visited per year.	Approximate number immigrants reached per year.

    Remarks and recommendations: Especially as to immigrants.

  2. Free dispensaries and hospitals:

Names and addresses.	Nature of work; general, dental, etc.	Total number reached per year.	Approximate number immigrants reached per year.

    Remarks and recommendations: Especially as to immigrants.

  3. Child welfare organizations:

Names and addresses.	Approximate number immigrants reached per year.

    Remarks: Nature and scope of work actually carried on in the community. Work with immigrants.
    Recommendations:

  4. Health inspection bureaus:

Names and addresses.	Number cases per year.	Number cases among immigrants per year.

    Remarks and recommendations:

K. Penal institutions:

Names and addresses.	Approximate average number immigrant prisoners per year.

    Remarks and suggestions:

QUESTIONNAIRE TO SCHOOL SUPERINTENDENTS.

Number and Characteristics of Immigrant Nationalities:

1. Present estimated immigrant population of your city or town (foreign born or foreign parentage). Give estimate according to following classification.

Foreign language groups.	Approximate number foreign born and foreign parentage.	Approximate number foreign born.	Approximate number foreign parentage.

(Totals.)

2. Total population of your city, _____.
3. Chief occupations of the given nationalities, _____
4. Any segregated foreign section? Give location, _____
5. Give, if possible, some of the characteristics of the chief nationalities represented; their social and political status, etc., _____
   _____

Educational Facilities Available to Immigrants:

6. Day schools with any considerable number of children of immigrants attending.

Name and location of school.	Total number of children attending.	Approximate number of children of immigrants attending.

Remarks and recommendations: Give a general description of the work for immigrants' children carried on in the various schools.

7. Classes, evening and day, for immigrants above regular school age;

Names and location of schools.	Number of immigrant classes.	Average total number attending per year.	Number hours instruction per year.

Remarks: Amount of money appropriated for these classes; legislation governing them. Are these schools covering the situation adequately? Is the subject matter taught adapted to the needs and interests of the immigrants? Do these classes hold their pupils? List of sources for further information, etc.

8. Factory classes attended largely by immigrants and in any way connected with the school system:

Names and addresses of schools.	Number of immigrant classes.	Average total number attending.	Number hours instruction per year.

Remarks: Basis of cooperation between factory and school board, etc.

Recommendations:

9. Libraries in any way connected with the school system:

Addresses of libraries patronized by immigrants.	Maintained by.	Days and hours opened.	Estimated number immigrant patrons.	Estimated circulation among immigrants per year. Adult. Juvenile.	Total number books. Foreign. English.	Estimated circulation per year among immigrants. Foreign. English.

Remarks and recommendations:

10. Reading rooms:

Addresses of reading rooms patronized by immigrants.	Maintained by.	Days and hours open.	Estimated number immigrant patrons.	Number foreign language papers.	Number English papers.

Remarks: Give basis of cooperation between schools and libraries, also reading rooms, etc. Number of bilingual books, texts for teaching English, etc.

Recommendations:

11. Playgrounds affiliated with the school system and reaching immigrants:

Names and locations.	Approximate total number reached per year.	Approximate number immigrant children reached per year (give by foreign language groups, if possible).	Gymnasium (yes or no).

Remarks: Legislation upon which the work rests, appropriations, cooperation with schools, etc., scope of the work.

12. Community centers affiliated with the school system and reaching immigrants:

Names and locations.	Approximate total number reached per year.	Approximate number immigrants reached per year (give by foreign language groups, if possible).

Remarks: State what funds are available for this work; legislation upon which it depends. What basis of cooperation is there between the schools and community centers, etc.?

13. Health and other welfare work carried on in public schools:
Give summary of the health work that is being carried on in the schools; names and addresses of the schools affected and of the organizations which are cooperating. To what approximate extent does this work reach the immigrant?

QUESTIONNAIRE FOR RACIAL LEADERS.

1. What is the estimated number of people speaking the _____ language in _____?
2. Of the above, approximately what is the number of foreign born _____? Approximately what is the number of foreign parentage _____? Can you give estimate of number unable to speak English (not counting children) _____?
3. How many segregated districts of your people in _____? Outline if possible on map. Describe each district as to number speaking the _____ tongue; number and names of churches; number and names of parochial schools; number and names of public schools; number and kind of business establishments, etc.

Remarks and recommendations:

4. Public schools with any considerable number of children of your people attending:

Names and addresses of schools.	Approximate number of children of your people attending.

Remarks and recommendations:

5. Public school classes, evening and day, for immigrants above regular school age, attended to any extent by your people?

Names and addresses of schools.	Number of classes for immigrants.	Number of your people attending.

Remarks and suggestions:

Have you any criticism or suggestions to offer regarding these schools? Are they teaching your people the things most needed by them and in which they are most interested? Are the methods of teaching in these schools really adapted to the needs, interests, and understanding of your people? Would teachers who could speak both English and _____ be preferable, in your opinion, to the majority of those studying English? Do these classes hold their pupils; if not, why not? Give approximate statement of extent to which your people are attending classes other than English.

6. Private day schools (parochial, etc.) with any considerable number of children of your people attending:

Names and addresses of schools.	Approximate number of children of your people attending.

Remarks and suggestions:

7. Private-school classes (parochial, etc.), evening and day, for immigrants above school age attended to any extent by your people:

Names and addresses of schools.	Number of immigrant classes per school.	Number of your people attending.

Remarks and suggestions:

List also names and addresses of men giving private lessons to individuals or groups. Give approximate statement of extent to which your people attend classes other than English.

8. Libraries patronized to any extent by your people:

Names and addresses.	Maintained by.	Days and hours open.	Est. number of your people who are patrons	Number books. For- eign.	Eng- lish.	Est. circu. among im mig. per year. For- eign.	Eng- lish.

Remarks and suggestions:

Are the foreign-language books owned by your people's organizations circulated anywhere near the extent to which they reasonably might be expected to circulate?

9. Reading rooms patronized to any extent by your people:

Names and addresses of reading rooms.	Maintained by.	Estimated number your people who are patrons.	Number foreign-language papers in each.	Number English papers.

Remarks and suggestions:

10. Foreign-language newspapers circulated to any extent among your people:

Names and addresses.	General nature.	Approximate circulation.

Remarks and suggestions:

Give also *native* American newspapers circulated to any extent among your people. (NOTE.—Complete lists of foreign-language newspapers and addresses can be secured from the "Ayer Newspaper Annual.") Have your newspapers been used to any extent for purposes of publicity among foreign born?

11. Churches attended to any extent by your people:

Names and addresses.	Approximate membership or at least number of churchgoers of your people.

Remarks:

12. Organizations of your people:

Names and addresses.	Approximate membership.	Affiliations.

Remarks and suggestions: If possible, give general nature of the more important organizations.

13. Organizations other than your own reaching your people to any extent: (Names and addresses and approximate number of your people reached by each.)

   (a) Fraternal, social, and gymnastic organizations (Elks, Odd Fellows, Knights of Columbus, Y. M. C. A., Y. W. C. A., etc.); also political clubs.
   (b) Community centers.
   (c) Legal-aid societies.
   (d) Information bureaus.
   (e) Housing committees.
   (f) Charity organizations.
   (g) Health agencies (visiting-nurse organizations, free dispensaries, child-welfare organizations, health-inspection bureaus, etc.).
   Remarks and recommendations:

QUESTIONNAIRE TO CLERGYMEN.

1. Name and address of your church ---------------------------------------
2. Approximately, how many people of foreign birth or of foreign parentage have you in your parish? ---------------- Give a rough estimate of the number (1) foreign born ---------------- (2) of foreign parentage ------------------.
3. What foreign-language groups are represented in your parish? Approximate number of each --
4. What is the estimated number of people speaking the --------------------- language in ---------------------? Of these, what is the approximate number foreign born? --------------------. Approximate number of foreign parentage? ------------------.
5. What are their chief occupations? --
6. What are some of their chief characteristics? ----------------------------
7. How many segregated districts of --------------------- speaking people in ---------------------? Outline, if possible, on map. Describe each district as to number speaking the --------------------- tongue, number and names of churches, number and names of parochial schools, number and kinds of business establishments, etc.

   Other remarks and suggestions.
8. Have you a parochial day school connected with your church? ----------- How many children of --------------------- parents attend? ----------- ---------------- If any others, give racial group and number. How many teachers? ---------------------.

   Other remarks and suggestions.

   Give names and addresses of other parochial schools attended to any extent by children of --------------------- parents. If possible, give the approximate number of these children attending each, mentioning also the approximate total number of pupils attending each of these schools.
9. Have you an evening school for immigrants? ------------------. How many --------------------- speaking immigrants attend? Number of classes? ----------------. Days and hours per week? ----------------. Hours per year? ------------------.
10. Libraries patronized to any extent by --------------------- speaking people?

Names and addresses.	Maintained by.	Days and hours open.	Estimated number of .... speaking people patrons.	Total number of books. For- eign.	Eng- lish.	Estimated circulation per year. For- eign.	Eng- lish.

   Remarks and suggestions: Are the foreign-language books in the various libraries of --------------------- (or of your district) circulated anywhere near the extent to which they reasonably might be expected to circulate? ---------------------.
11. Reading rooms patronized to any extent by --------------------- speaking people?

Names and addresses.	Maintained by.	Days and hours open.	Estimated number .... speaking who are patrons.	Number foreign language papers.	Number English papers.

   Remarks and recommendations:

12. Have you a playground in connection with your church or parochial school? _____. Approximate number of _____ speaking children patronizing it _____. Total number patronizing it _____.

   Remarks and suggestions: Is there a gymnasium connected with the playground? _____

13. Organizations reaching your people to any extent with which you maintain cooperation:

   (a) Community centers.
   (b) Legal-aid societies.
   (c) Information bureaus.
   (d) Housing committees, etc.
   (e) Charity organizations.
   (f) Recreational and gymnasium organizations.

QUESTIONNAIRE TO LIBRARIES.

1. Name and address of the library or libraries with which you are connected:
_____

2. Maintained by? (City or organization.)_____

3. Give the days and hours on which it is open_____

4. Give an estimate of the number of immigrant patrons of your library:
_____

5. What is the total number of books?_____ Foreign_____ _____ English_____

6. Give an estimate of the number of books circulated among immigrants: Foreign_____ English_____.

7. How many librarians and assistants?_____

8. Is the number of foreign language books in your library in keeping with the foreign language speaking population of your community?_____

_____

9. Are there any branches or stations connected with your library? If so, give names and addresses_____

_____

   NOTE.—Fill out separate questionnaire for each branch and station.

10. Have you any special provisions for assisting immigrants—open-shelf book sections containing literature adapted to the needs and interests of immigrants, foreign language or bi-lingual explanations, attendants understanding the special needs of immigrants and knowing the languages chiefly spoken in your community?_____

11. Do you conduct any extension activities which include the participation of immigrants—story hours, lectures, etc?_____

12. Have you any special facilities for Americanization workers—up-to-date bibliographies, reference works on immigration and Americanization, files of latest newspapers, clippings, etc., arranged on special open-shelf section _____

13. If your library does not come under the city library system, state whether you maintain any cooperation; and, if so, what, with the city, county, or State library authorities_____

   Further remarks and suggestions.

Reading Rooms.

1. Address of reading room (or reading rooms) with which you are connected_____
2. Maintained by? (City or organization)_____
3. Give the days and hours on which it is open_____
4. Give an estimate of the number of immigrant patrons of your reading room _____
5. What is the total number of newspapers and periodicals_____
   Foreign_____ English_____
   NOTE.—If possible give list of papers (with addresses) both English and foreign which are read to any extent in your community.
6. What are the newspapers and periodicals (list) which appear to be most in demand by your patrons: Foreign_____
   English_____
7. How many attendants_____
8. Is the number of foreign language newspapers and periodicals in your reading room adequate for the foreign-language speaking population of your community?_____
9. Have you any special provisions for aiding immigrants—foreign language or bi-lingual explanations, attendants understanding the languages chiefly spoken in your community, etc.?_____
10. Have you any special facilities for Americanization workers—up-to-date bibliographies, files of latest clippings, etc.?_____
    Further remarks and suggestions.

Chapter III.

EDUCATIONAL PHASES OF THE PROBLEM.

Americanization is as broad as life itself. It is weaving into the warp and woof of the life of the community those who come to make it their home. In such assimilation education in English is, of course, the first step.

While, theoretically, it may be conceded that a foreigner may become a good American in spirit without knowing our language, it is quite generally granted that, if there is to be a community of interest, there must be a common language for conveying thought.[1]

LEARNING THE LANGUAGE.

There is no one thing so supremely essential in a Government such as ours, where decisions of such importance must be made by public opinion, as that every man and woman and child shall know one tongue—that each may speak to every other and that all shall be informed.

There can be national unity neither in ideals nor in purpose unless there is some common method of communication through which may be conveyed the thought of the Nation. All Americans must be taught to read and write and *think* in one language; that is a primary condition to that growth which all nations expect in a government of us, and which we demand of ourselves.[2]

The public schools must teach English, and the work of the schools must be done in English. In this country we have established and we maintain public schools in all of the States in order, first, that children may be prepared for life by an education which will enable them to make a living, and for intelligent living, and for the duties and responsibilities of citizenship, and, secondly, that the State and Nation may be well served by them.

We compel parents and guardians to send their children to school in order that the State may not be cheated out of that which it is preparing to get. In doing this we must require that the schools to which children are permitted to go in lieu of attendance at the public schools shall teach the things which the public schools are teaching. In other words, that they shall all teach English; that the work of the school shall be conducted in English, so that the children growing to manhood and womanhood may have a familiar knowledge of this language.[3]

The Constitution of the United States specifically reserves to the States all rights which are not definitely given to the Federal Government. Education, not being specifically intrusted to the Government at Washington, is therefore left to the States. All laws regulating education must consequently emanate from the State legislatures and not from the Congress.

---

[1] H. H. Goldberger, in Conference Proceedings.
[2] Franklin K. Lane.
[3] P. P. Claxton, in Conference Proceedings.

Community workers should therefore place before the legislatures of their States any need for new legislation regarding the conduct of the schools. The Federal Government can only suggest. The position taken by the United States Bureau of Education, as outlined above by Commissioner Claxton, is that English must be the primary language of all schools public and private; that the administration of the schools shall be in English; that such foreign languages as are taught shall be taught merely as parts of the course of study and confined to their regular class periods. Says Dr. Claxton further:

This does not mean that people are to forget their own language. The Bureau of Education has no sympathy with any policy that would limit knowledge in any direction. It does mean, however, that all shall know the English language, shall be able to understand it, to speak it, to write it, to express themselves easily in it.

What foreign languages shall be taught must necessarily be decided by each community and State for itself. Workers everywhere can render no better service than to see that the educational authorities of their city, county, and State enact regulations which will conform to the position taken by the Federal Bureau of Education.

FORMING CLASSES.

Both policy and justice require that there be no compulsory education of adults in America. It is our task rather to create in the hearts and minds of our new citizens an earnest desire to equip themselves with the language of their new land. Through all of the agencies at hand we must work skillfully to demonstrate to the non-English speaking the great advantages of reading and writing and speaking the language of America. Then we must make so easily available to everyone the facilities for learning English that it will be within the power of every person to secure such an education if he desire it.

The first essential in teaching English is a teacher. The rapid disintegration of classes of the foreign born in the past can be traced in nearly every case to the teacher who did not understand her problem. It has been the natural thing to do to place in charge of classes of the foreign born regular teachers of the public school. It has unfortunately not been generally recognized that the teaching of a child has little relation to the teaching of a grown man and woman, and that the methods and materials used for children will drive away rather than hold the interest of adults.

It is useless to form a class of foreign-born people until there is first available a teacher who has made a study of the task of teaching the non-English speaking. Such a teacher should by all means take a course in this science in some of the normal schools or colleges which are now offering such instruction. Failing in this, he or she should at least make a personal study of the subject. The books prepared for the Bureau of Education by Messrs. Goldberger and Mahoney should be carefully studied, together with some of the number of good textbooks which are now available.

THE PUBLIC SCHOOLS.

Education is a public responsibility and a public function. The educational authorities in relatively but a few of the many communities of the country have as yet met their responsibility and provided classes at such times and places that foreign-born adults may attend them. Community workers should, therefore, bend their energies to arousing a public sentiment that will enable their authorities to meet this problem. This requires that funds shall be provided. This in turn necessitates that the people shall be taught that the education of those adults who are either illiterate or unable to use the English language is a public duty equally with that of educating the children. This task constitutes a program in itself. Campaign for night schools, for schools in industries, or wherever men can be brought together. Arouse your community to its duty. Have adequate funds provided. Get behind your superintendent of schools and support him in his desire to educate the illiterate adults of your community.

The responsibility for this task should be placed definitely upon the shoulders of the public-school system. If they can not be aroused or enabled to undertake the work, provide the classes under other auspices, but do not cease your efforts until the educational authorities finally meet their responsibility.

Classes may be formed in industries, during or after working hours, in the public schools, either in daytime or night, in halls, lodges, stores, homes, churches, or wherever a group can be brought together of such a minimum number as may be decided upon. The classes being formed and some one made responsible for maintaining the attendance and caring for the physical equipment, the public-school authorities should furnish the necessary teacher. Thus the school system becomes the hub around which all of the agencies of the community may work. This, it is generally acknowledged, is the ideal method of meeting the problem. But until the public-school system can be empowered or awakened the need must be met in such ways as can be provided.

Somewhere in every community can surely be found some person who is willing to volunteer for this patriotic service. It may be some woman of human understanding who taught school before she was married and who can spare a few hours a week now. Wherever

AMERICANIZATION IN THE CONCRETE.

An American of Armenian birth who, after several years in America, has met his mother and his brother at the wharf. This group pictures in striking fashion just what Americanization means. Here in this "Land of Equal Chance," with the friendly help of the native-born Americans, that hopeless, hunted look of fear and care will gradually give way, and in its place will come that confident look of self-reliance, of optimism, of determination, of prosperity, of equality, which radiates from the other. Here is truly Americanization in the concrete.

MAKING AMERICANS.

View of the school of the Ford Motor Co., at which the employees of this company are taught to speak, read, and write the language of America. This company, which numbers among its employees men born in nearly every country of earth, was one of the first to undertake the work of Americanization upon a definite and practical basis.

AN INDUSTRIAL STUDY HOUR.

Splendid interest in their work has been one of the many results of the English and civic classes conducted by the Seng Co., of Chicago. Note the well-lighted room and convenient blackboards, seats, and benches.

possible, funds should be raised to recompense such persons for their work. Teachers who work upon purely a volunteer and unpaid basis must possess exceptional interest and determination not to lag sooner or later in their efforts.

Even though there are no funds available, it is a shortsighted and unprogressive school board which will not at least permit the use of the school buildings. Any community that cares can do the rest. "Are future Americans not to be taught English and not to be prepared for citizenship because the school tax does not provide for paying the janitor for night work or for turning on the electric light?"[1]

RECRUITING THE CLASSES.

It is human nature to be interested in those things in which we have a part. None of us becomes wildly enthusiastic over those things which come to us ready-made and complete. Classes of the foreign born will be more popular and more permanent if the foreign born themselves have an important part in planning them.

Make it a community matter. Let the foreign born recruit the classes through their Liberty Loan groups, or lodges, or benefit associations. Let them have a voice in determining what shall be taught (the waiters and shopkeepers and peddlers want more arithmetic, perhaps, than the man who is intent only on preparing for his second papers); and when the classes are organized, turn them into clubs and keep them in touch with the town.[1]

Without the support of the leading spirits of the foreign group, progress will be slow. This support can be realized only by the display of a sympathetic, appreciative attitude, by the paying of full credit to the worth of the people, and by the presentment of reasonable aims and ideals which the foreign born can observe actually applied among the native born of his community. Gain the confidence and active support of the editors of newspapers, the heads of unions and fraternal organizations, and the problem of reaching the masses is largely solved.

We condemn the immigrant for not learning to speak English, yet there are more towns and cities that give no opportunities to learn English than there are municipalities that do. There are more towns that have not established classes for foreign men and women than there are boards of education that have. In the principal city of one of the eastern States I have heard prominent citizens declaiming against the large Italian and Polish population for not learning the English tongue. It did not seem to occur to these estimable Americans that the fault was their own. A survey of the school buildings of this city showed that only one was provided with lighting facilities, and in none of them had evening classes ever been provided to enable the Poles and Italians to learn the American tongue.[2]

---

[1] Esther Everett Lape.
[2] Dr. Nathan Peyser, in Conference Proceedings.

146580°—20——3

CAMPAIGNING FOR PUPILS.

Some communities have started their work among the foreign born with great community " drives " similar to a Liberty Loan campaign. The wisdom of such methods has been questioned.

I am convinced that in this matter the vigorous community drive, with its great publicity and with its inevitable reflection, by implication, upon the patriotism of the alien residents, is not the best way to begin. A better way is to have one or more industries begin quietly and quite as a matter between the management and the employees. The management may, of course, make it understood that they want the employees to acquire the knowledge, but that the privilege of learning English during the day at the plant is offered on the ground that existing facilities in the community are not sufficient or are not convenient. Nothing succeeds like success, and when such a class is found to be in progress in an important industry it is not long until the others, particularly industries in competing lines, either competing for labor or for the local market, or both, fall into line.

One forceful personality, or a small working committee engaged in selling this proposition to one establishment after another or to groups of industries organized for trade purposes, is to be preferred to a regiment of copy writers and speakers.[1]

Whether the work be instituted class by class or by a great community drive, it is essential that the purposes be laid plainly before those whom it is hoped to reach. It is essential also that they shall be convinced of the value to themselves of attendance upon the classes.

The utilization of this positive point of view is exhibited in a learn-English campaign recently conducted in New York City under the joint auspices of the board of education and the Educational Alliance.

The aim was not to coerce or compel, but to persuade and convince. The basis of the drive was publicity, to bring home to the non-English speaking group on the lower East Side of New York City the need for learning English and the personal and family advantages to be derived, and to enlighten them on the values and the opportunities offered. It was explained that English was to be a tongue additional to their Yiddish, their Italian, their Greek, their Hungarian, or their Ladino. It was essential that they learn English in order that they might come closer to their children, retain their confidence and respect, and thus avert the frequent domestic tragedy of the foreign home. It was conveyed to them that without English they were dependent upon their children for guidance and interpretation whenever they left their homes.[2]

Those workers who are concerned with the formation of classes of the foreign born should read the papers submitted at the Americanization Conference by Messrs. Goldberger, Streyckmans, and Peyser.

MAINTAINING ATTENDANCE.

While a falling off in attendance must be expected in any class of volunteer students, whether foreign or native born, this fact should not keep those in charge of the classes from seeking other

[1] W. M. Roberts, in Conference Proceedings.
[2] Nathan Peyser, in Conference Reports.

causes and removing them. Incompetent teachers, wrong methods, lack of proper material, unsuitable environment or equipment, lack of tact—these are among the usual causes of disintegration.

The paper of H. H. Goldberger in the Conference Proceedings will be found especially helpful in meeting the problem of maintaining attendance. "Make the night school your club" is one of the methods he advocates of maintaining the interest of the students. "Teach democracy by practicing it" is another.

In a school of about 25 classes of adult foreigners the problem was to create this social spirit. Each of the 25 classes was organized as a unit, as a club, electing its own staff of officers, the officers meeting as delegates with the executive officer of the school. This body of delegates and school officials, called "the general organization," assumed the duty of considering ways and means to make the school fit the needs of the pupils and to make itself a neighborhood force.

Almost at the beginning the general organization felt the need of formulating a constitution and electing general officers. The assembly at which candidates were nominated for office by the foreign born had their peculiar fitness pointed out by their fellow pupils. The subsequent election by the foreign born and the canvass of the result were worth a wilderness of textbook instruction in the method by which a democracy elects its officers. The pupils sought the honor of holding office almost as spiritedly as men do in political life, and once elected they sought in accomplishment an excuse for reelection.[1]

GRADING THE CLASSES.

While the technical methods of class instruction are fully covered in the bureau publications by Messrs. Goldberger and Mahoney previously referred to, it may not be amiss to point out here to those who are forming classes the necessity of grading them carefully. Failure to do this is another fertile cause of disintegration.

Grading the men is a very important process and comes next in the program. Too much importance can not be attached to this grading, for there is a very wide variance in the different minds and aptitudes of these foreign-born people who are seemingly on the same basis so far as knowledge of the English language is concerned. For instance, the men and women who are illiterate in their own language, never having gone to school or learned to read or write in their native land, present one problem. An entirely different one is presented by the men and women who have received considerable schooling in their native land but have not yet learned to speak and read or write the English language.

For practical purposes four grades seem necessary:

Grade 1. Those who are illiterate in their own language and who speak little and read or write little or no English.

Grade 2. Literate in their own language, speak and read a little English.

Grade 3. Those who speak and read English fairly well and write a little.

Grade 4. Those who speak, read, and write fairly well but need a better understanding of English and are ready for the citizenship course.[2]

[1] H. H. Goldberger, in Conference Proceedings.
[2] Winthrop G. Hall and Gren O. Pierrel.

CLASSES IN THE HOME.

We have at last learned that we must take the school to the man in the factory and to the woman in the home. Immigrant women especially can rarely be interested in " going to school," but they are interested in their children, in the cost of living, in sewing, and in cooking. Let them meet anywhere, in a home, a " model apartment," a neighborhood center, or a school, on any basis they will, to knit, to make the lace of the old country, with a few American women, to be instructed, to cook, perhaps using the school's domestic-science equipment, to form a mother's club, or to continue their Red Cross auxiliary on another basis.[1]

The importance of carrying education to the woman in the home of the foreign born can not be overemphasized. The children in the schools and the father in the factory are bound to come into touch with Americanizing influences even though such influences be not intelligently planned and directed. They are sure to take on some American ways and manners of life. The wife and mother, however, is left isolated in the home. She sees her husband and children gradually becoming as of another race; she hears them speaking oftentimes in a language she can not understand; she feels herself ignored and avoided by her American neighbors; finally perchance she finds herself an outcast in her own home, belittled or ridiculed by her own children. This tragedy of injustice reflects itself in the criminal records of the courts where the offenders born of foreign parents number two and one-half times greater than those born of native parents.

The women of the races from southeastern Europe are usually shy and timid. They have often been discourteously treated by their American neighbors and are left either in a mood fearful of further discourtesy or resentful of past treatment. Then, too, the women of these races are not permitted by custom to have the freedom granted to our American women. They are often forbidden by their husbands to leave their homes or to attend social or public functions. All of these factors combine to make the problem of reaching the foreign-born woman a most difficult one. But it can be done.

California is one State which provides teachers from the public schools for work in the homes. The domestic science workers of the department of agriculture carry Americanism into the homes and classes which they attend. The visiting nurses, the school-teachers, the settlement workers—all are in strategic positions to reach the foreign-born woman.

A FIELD FOR WOMEN.

Volunteer workers can do much in this problem. It is one which comes peculiarly within the province of the women's clubs and

---

[1] Esther Everett Lape.

patriotic societies. But it is one which requires careful tact, sympathy, and sincere, friendliness if the worker is not to do more harm than good. The approach is of the utmost importance.

A worker who often passed a certain building noticed a large group of foreign women sitting on the benches sunning their babies and visiting together, and observed that it was practically the same group day after day. So the worker visited with them about the babies and the weather and other topics of mutual interest until she won their confidence, and they came to realize that she was not only friendly, but that she had many things of value to tell them. At this point the worker suggested having a club meeting on the days which she could be with them and talk over the problems which interested them. Thus camouflaged, she held a class in city civics for several months, and when the weather no longer made the sidewalk club practical, a series of home meetings were inaugurated and have continued through two winters, with a summer session in between.[1]

If the worker have the ingenuity and the tact to approach the foreign-born women more in the rôle of one seeking help than of one giving it, her chances of success will be materially increased. Few of us like to be openly aided, while we all take pride in extending a helping hand. Most friendly relations have been established with immigrant women by getting them to teach the native women their dances, their arts, their cookery. If the native women will bring their foreign-born sisters to them in this spirit they will both receive and give.

When proper contacts have been made and friendly relations established, the next step can be taken. The foreign-born woman whose acquaintance has been made can easily bring to her home or to a park or to some of the little shops a group of her neighbors for helpful talks by native-born women upon the problems of life in the new country. The second step to actual instruction in English is a short one.

In almost every immigrant colony one may find an intelligent immigrant woman, either a mother of a family who has been long in this country or has even been born and reared here, or an elder daughter who has received a public-school education, speaks English satisfactorily, and who, at the same time, speaks the immigrant's language and knows the families in the colony more or less thoroughly. Such a woman should be approached first, should be induced to accept training, and then become an organizer or teacher of the adult immigrant women in the colony. She will be able to effect an organization which may be called the "Women's Club" or "Mothers' Club." Instead of creating an entirely new body, such organizations as exist could and should be utilized; there may be clubs, some cooperative association or a benefit society, or, of course, there may be no organization at all and every detail may have to be initiated. In that case the woman chosen as organizer will cause to be appointed as leaders of the new organization the more developed immigrant women.[2]

[1] Mrs. Harriet P. Dow, in Conference Proceedings.
[2] Peter A. Speak, in Conference Proceedings.

Advantage should be taken of every gathering of women of the foreign born to present something of America and American life. Wherever they have clubs of their own for any purpose, speakers and teachers may be provided.

Right near the school was an Ukrainian Church in which there were gathered a club of servant girls once a week, their night off, on Thursday nights. We found out about that club and sent a representative to ask permission to give those people a half hour of English instruction. Permission was granted, and one night the teacher asked this group of Ukrainian servant girls to come to the school, about two blocks away, and take part in the social activities of that evening. They came, and as a result they asked that we organize them as a permanent class in the school building.[1]

We can probably never hope to bring the foreign-born women in any large numbers to our schools for either day or night classes. We must reach all we can in this way, but to the greater number the school must be taken wherever we may find them together in groups. Mrs. Dow tells of a school that began in one corner of a New York playground, where the women had gathered to keep watch of their children at play.

The summer classes of a backyard playground were so successful that a near-by flat was rented and the classes became all-year-round groups. Classes in the little foreign store and kitchen classes have been successful. Why should classes be held in these homely places, when more attractive and comfortable places might be secured? Because they are the familiar spots, because the foreign mother is often less shy in these known surroundings, and, most important of all, because they are accessible and save time and effort for the mother. Few of us realize how much work many of these women have to do.[2]

CLASSES IN INDUSTRY.

Employers have a place of peculiar power in the problem of transforming immigrants into good citizens. Making contact with new Americans in industry has been likened to " collecting revenue at its source." Here we are able to touch almost 100 per cent of the non-English speaking people. Here we find them ready at hand for our instruction. We must therefore look to industry more and more to assist us by forming these people into classes that we may teach them the English language and something of America.

The more forward-looking employers have already tried to meet this problem. In fact many of them have not only undertaken class work but have trained and employed their own teachers. Here is a task for the community workers: To convince the employers of their city of the wisdom and profit of helping the community to provide their adult employees with a primary education, if they do not already possess it. We must urge employers where it is at all possi-

[1] H. H. Goldberger, in Conference Proceedings.
[2] Mrs. Harriet P. Dow, in Conference Proceedings.

ble to permit the men to be taught on company time. There can be no doubt that if these men are not "docked" for the time spent in classes the number we can reach will be much greater.

Manufacturers may well aid in the work, if they wish, by increasing the wages at least slightly of those employees who learn to speak English. That they will be justified in this there can be no doubt. Employers everywhere testify that their men are more efficient, loyal, and valuable after they secure a knowledge of the English language.

Wage discrimination is one of the best ways to stimulate the alien's desire for Americanization. The non-English-speaking alien is a less valuable employee and should be made to understand it. He is also the great accident hazard, and it is needless to say that the workman who understands deaf and dumb signs only is the less efficient employee. For this reason the alien who becomes Americanized should receive a higher wage than the one who is not. And the wage scale should be graduated to cover each step in the proceess of citizenship.[1]

The classes in industry should teach the men the vocabulary of their trade and the means of protecting themselves from the particular hazards of that occupation. This will be the employer's direct return for his investment.

The safety department of an industry should also become a factor in Americanization. While we are apt to interpret safety work in terms of the industry, it is of just as much value to the individual. To be careless is to be a poor citizen. To be made to feel that industry has no interest in its employees beyond their work and wages tends to develop a spirit of laissez faire, which is thoroughly un-American. Lessons on safety precautions are just as essential in a class for new Americans as are lessons in the history of our Government.[2]

PLANT DIRECTOR.

Wherever possible the employer should designate some member of his staff as plant director of Americanization, who will be the point of contact of the school authorities with his men.

The success of any Americanization program in industry depends, of course, upon the hearty cooperation of the management. A wise manager, in order to secure success in such a venture will have some man appointed as a supervisor of Americanization in the plant, who is definitely responsible for the promotion of the program and who is released from other duties, so that he will have sufficient time to carry it out. It is unnecessary to say that this supervisor must be a person who appreciates the value of education, who recognizes the need for Americanization work in the plant, and who has a sympathy with these foreign-born men and their problems and a real appreciation of their backgrounds.[3]

Workers interested in the formation of classes in industry should read the papers persented upon this subject at the Americanization

---

[1] William Lamkie, in Conference Proceedings.
[2] Charles H. Paull, in Conference Proceedings.
[3] Winthrop G. Hall and Gren O. Pierrel.

Conference by Messrs. Roberts, Weber, Speek, and Rindge. Upon the subject of a plant director the first named has this to say:

All of the teaching under any plan for carrying on classes in the industrial plants should be under the direction of the public schools. Only in this way can all parties concerned—the employer, the employee, and the public—be certain that the work is wholly disinterested.

There must be some one delegated by the factory management to see that all obligations assumed by the plant are fully carried out, and this person must always be on the job. It will not do merely for him to say " there is the room and the men are at liberty to come at the agreed time." The most satisfactory arrangement is to have the general responsibility vested in a member of the employment department, or welfare department, under whose direction an employee, such as a foreman, timekeeper, or one of the men of the group taking instruction, is responsible for seeing that the room is always in order; that reports wanted by the management are made; that at the close of the lesson the door is locked, books and materials put away safely, and all is ready for factory use next day. Such attendants are usually paid a small amount in overtime for this service. Their help is at times exceedingly valuable. They relieve the teacher of responsibility when complaints are made that the room was not left in proper condition for use for other purposes between class periods.[1]

In some cities several plants have joined hands to employ a director of Americanization. This may be a most suitable way out, particularly with smaller plants.

Three years ago, through the chamber of commerce at Farrell, a director of Americanization was hired through the efforts of 10 of the leading industries in this section. The school board finally consented to the use of two school buildings for the evening classes. At the end of the first school year the register showed a total of 400 students, with an average attendance of 175. The second year found the school more prosperous than ever before. The third year, after the industries had proven that every class for foreign-born pupils could be made a success, the school board took over this activity and operates it now under a special budget.[2]

THE FOREMEN.

Unless the sympathetic cooperation of the foremen of a plant can be secured, the work will be difficult.

Before any attempt is made to organize a program the foremen should be called together, not once but many times, and have presented to them the needs of their foreign-born men and how they may be met, and the extremely important part which the foremen have in making this program successful.[3]

The foremen are not only in position to know the problems of the foreign born in industry, but they can help as can no other in solving them. Their cooperation is necessary if the men are to be relieved from their tasks to attend the classes. They can protect the students

---

[1] W. M. Roberts, in Conference Proceedings.
[2] A. H. Wyman.
[3] Winthrop G. Hall and Gren O. Pierrel.

from overtime work that will interfere with their studies. An encouraging word now and then from the foremen will assist wonderfully in maintaining attendance. If the employees come to feel that their foremen and employers are anxious to have them better themselves, a spirit will enter into their work that can be secured in no other way.

The foremen can—

approach the leaders of the various racial groups in the shop and explain to them clearly just what is proposed in the plant and the reasons for its being done, thereby enlisting their intelligent interest and cooperation. Then the foremen together with these racial group leaders will take the census of the plant, discovering all men and women who speak little or no English, who can not read or write, and also discover men who are not American citizens. Having the census taken, it is very helpful to have meetings of the various racial groups and to have a speaker of their own group present the opportunities which the management is offering to them and the reasons why they should avail themselves of this chance to better understand American ideals and traditions [1].

No matter what may be the exigencies of his position, a wide-awake foreman will attempt to get into personal contact with the men who are under him, and if he himself has an appreciation of American ideals, he can not fail to impart some of that appreciation to the men with whom he comes in contact. Too much emphasis can not be placed upon the necessity for the foreman maintaining a proper attitude toward the men working under him. He is the industry's personal representative in the workroom, and with him rests more than with anyone else the daily interpretation of the industry's attitude toward American ideals as they are related to employment. In a number of industries, at the present time, definite work is being carried on in the education of foremen to an appreciation of the opportunities which they have for cooperating with Americanization work, and for becoming active agents in carrying it on.[2]

THE EMPLOYER'S INFLUENCE.

No other task before the workers in Americanization of a community compares in importance with that of securing the cordial sympathy and cooperation of the manufacturers and other employers.

It is not that the employer is either legally or morally responsible for a nation-wide task. He is simply in a strategic position. He has a determining influence in Americanization. If inside the plant he has one set of rulings for the natives and another set for the foreign born; if he has company houses for the native born and tar-paper bunks for the foreign born; if he has a scientific employment system for the native born and gets the foreign born by the bulk from the padrone; if he has hearings on discharge for skilled workmen and nothing at all for the non-English-speaking foreign born but the word (often an oath) or the temper of the foreman; if he has different standards of justice and operation for native and foreign born, he is not carrying his end in building up an American citizenship in that town. The workman

---

[1] Winthrop G. Hall and Gren O. Pierrel.
[2] Charles H. Paull, in Conference Proceedings.

spends most of his waking hours in the factory. His judgment of that town and his judgment of America are going to be largely based upon what he finds in the job.[1]

Americanization workers, however, should guard against leaving the entire problem to industry. The conditions of the job vitally influence the viewpoint of the immigrant as has been stated, but the social and community conditions have an equal bearing upon whether or not that immigrant is to become a loyal citizen of America.

Outside the plant, too, the employer and the town must work together. It is not the employer's business to teach his men English; and yet the public school can hardly do it without his cooperation in giving the school authorities a list of all foreign-born employees, in furnishing facilities for factory classes, in following up school records, and in other ways constantly backing up the public policy of the town.

It would be far too sweeping to say that the Americanization of an industrial town depends upon the employer. Employers justly resent that position, and so do the foreign born. The latter want Americanization through American fellowship and American institutions, supplied as the public policy of a nation and a community, not by the " welfare " projects of one man or of one corporation. And yet unless the industry is solidly behind the community, working with it at every turn, it will take a long time to put America into your town.[1]

---

[1] Esther Everett Lape.

Chapter IV.

SOCIAL PHASES OF THE PROBLEM.

In communities where the American public has come to know the immigrant for what he is—and there are such communities—the problem of Americanization has been stripped of much of its difficulty. The school authorities should foster in every possible way the interest of the American public in the people who attend the evening schools. Because—let it be said again and again—the task of Americanization is one, not for the American school alone, but for the American people, operating through every instrumentality of an organized social life. The teacher can do comparatively little working alone.[1]

Neither education nor naturalization will make true Americans. Many an American whose heart beats true to the ideals of America can speak English but brokenly. On the other hand, many an enemy of all that America stands for speaks our language fluently, and may, in fact, have been born in the shadow of our flag. Our task, therefore, is much broader than mere education and naturalization, important as they are. Our duty to our new Americans will not be done until we have Americanized the schools their children will attend, Americanized the water their families drink, Americanized the air they breathe, and the houses they live in; Americanized their play, their work, their surroundings.

We want to interpret America in terms of fair play; in terms of the square deal. We want in the end to interpret America in healthier babies that have enough milk to drink. We want to interpret America in boys and girls and men and women that can read and write. We want to interpret America in better housing conditions and decent wages, in hours that will allow a father to know his own family. That is Americanization in the concrete—reduced to practical terms. That is the spirit of the Declaration of Independence put into terms that are social and economic.[2]

As has already been stated, a number of factors have combined to cause the foreign born in many instances to dwell together in colonies. Our cities have failed in most cases to extend to these colonies the same watchful care regarding health and safety that has been given to the better portions of our communities. The result has been to make these colonies synonymous with housing evils, overcrowding, and filth. It may be stated as a fact that the conditions of life in which immigrants have been thrust in our American cities are far below the standards in health and decency to which the majority of them have been accustomed in their own countries.

---

[1] John J. Mahoney and Charles M. Herlihy, in "First Steps in Americanization."
[2] Franklin K. Lane.

IMPROVING ENVIRONMENT.

Were we able to trace to their source the many "isms" and the social unrest which now afflict us, we would doubtless be startled to find how great a factor in such discontent is the present housing situation in America. Statistics show that, as conditions are at present, 60 per cent of our laboring people can never expect to own their own homes or afford to do so. The matter of providing homes for our people, therefore, becomes a matter for community and national concern. It can no longer be left to profit-seeking individuals.

It will be a sorry day for America when a large portion of its people lose hope for the future, and that man can not entertain any large hope who can never expect even to own the house in which he lives.

You can not shut a man up in a reeking tenement and give him no more than will buy macaroni for himself and his wife and his babies, and give him no opportunity to breathe the fresh air, and no opportunity to know this great country, and then say that man is to blame if his mind holds false ideas regarding our country.[1]

Thousands of the immigrants of the white races will be so completely Americanized in the second generation that they can not be told from native Americans. Their children in the next generation will be among our leading artists, statesmen, and business and professional men. Yet a provincial arrogance and a feeling of race superiority often lead the native-born Americans to resent the efforts of the foreign born to improve their conditions and get out of the foreign environment in which they have found themselves. Before we can solve our problems of Americanization, we must not only improve this environment of the foreign born, but we must assist them in getting into the environment of the native born.

To us there is no force in the argument that certain people prefer to live in tenement houses; that they are lonesome if not huddled in stifling rooms; that they feel bereft when the garbage is removed; that they are uncomfortable and unhappy when clean.[2]

The conditions commonly imposed upon workmen from foreign countries, such as being herded together in shacks, I maintain are un-American and will result in un-American practices. The wives of foreign workmen are no happier under such conditions than could your wives or mine be. It is just as impossible for them to rear American children in the American way under such conditions as it would be for your wives to rear your children in the American way under such un-American conditions.[3]

Houses! Houses that a man can really own or rent. That is the first answer to many a town's Americanization problem. In hundreds of towns, now, cham-

---

[1] Franklin K. Lane.
[2] John Ihlder, in Conference Proceedings.
[3] E. E. Bach, in Conference Proceedings.

bers of commerce, real estate men, bankers, and mortgage holders have a real opportunity to develop housing projects that will give the town permanent industrial stability and make it wholly American. Every architect, town planner, civil or sanitary engineer in a town where a very few "company houses" and a great many grimy, squat little cottages or unpainted shacks chronically out of repair are the rule, is challenged by that town's Americanization task. It is useless to preach "American standards of living" to foreign-born people whom the town permits to live like that.[1]

The change can be brought about in two ways: First, by the enforcement of law requiring not only the proper design and construction of all dwellings but their proper maintenance. This method is essential, for by no other means can every dwelling be reached and the minimum American standards applied to all. This method means, however, a new Americanism on the part of the native born. It means efficient government; it means sewer and water main extension into parts of our cities and towns now neglected, and the enforcement of house connection with sewers and mains; it means regular and frequent collection of garbage and rubbish. If many of the un-Americanized among us live as they do, it is because those most sure of their Americanism fail in their duties as citizens.[2]

I remember one beautiful little town with the railroad track running through it like a dead line. On one side they had, and enforced, admirable health ordinances. The paved streets stopped short of the foreign district; so did the drainage, so did the city water system, so did the fire hose and the fire plugs. The condition in that town is the rule, not the exception.

The trouble is that, though the sewers do not cross the railroad track, the germs do. Malaria, whooping cough, yellow fever, and Spanish influenza, once given a foothold, will have the right of way in that town as long as the dead line exists and as long as American health standards apply to only one-half or two-thirds of the population.

But if you expect the foreign born to cross the track to your night schools, first carry America over the track to them, in houses, in sewers, in water pipes, in sidewalks. You can not make them part of *our* Nation if they are not part of *your* town.

The American future does not consist merely in teaching the foreign-born English or in holding meetings to decry bolshevism and sign up the 100 per cent Americans. It is a matter of boards and concrete and timber and housing laws and inspectors to enforce them. The spiritual process of Americanization works only in souls that look out of windows that open on American streets. It is hard to feel patriotic devotion for a country when your part of it is a muddy maze of alleys full of stagnant pools, privies, refuse, dogs, cats, chickens, ducks, geese, and children—even if some of them are yours.

The changing of the housing conditions in the immigrant sections of an old city, where real estate values are high and a building project must be profitable, indeed, in order to pay the man who undertakes it, is not a matter about which we can lightly make suggestions. But, by some combination of American government in such of our cities there must be made new conditions of housing that hold alike for foreign born and native, if we are longer to cherish the illusion that there is such a thing as an American standard of living.

---

[1] Esther Everett Lape.
[2] John Ihlder, in Conference Proceedings.

Individual citizens can be useful, not by urging impossible reforms upon people who have neither the power nor the money to carry them out, but by helping carefully and scrupulously to get a real recognition of the facts in every quarter; and by throwing the weight of their influence toward every project to build decent homes for rental or purchase at fair prices. Nobody has a keener sense than the immigrant of the wisdom of investing in his own home. Many of the "migratory workmen" among them are migratory simply because they never find any city or community that offers the many inducement to settle down.[1]

Until government recognizes that the housing of the people is a matter for the attention of the State, each community must solve its own problems as best it can. Public-spirited citizens, industries, and the municipality must cooperate to improve the housing situation of the community.

Americanization workers should take the initiative in such improvement in the homes of the foreign born and endeavor in every possible way to rally the forces to the community that those homes may be brought to a fair American standard.

RECREATION.

Many communities have decried certain habits and customs of their foreign-born people in the matter of amusement and recreation. Few communities, however, have definitely undertaken to provide worth-while programs in lieu of that which they condemn. Active, restless humans are like the rich, black soil of a garden; something must grow, either plants or weeds. It is heartbreaking work as well as backbreaking to try to keep rid of weeds by pulling them up. The better way is to plant something good to take their place and gradually to run them out.

No portion of our people stands more in need of intelligently planned and directed play than our foreign born. Here is a task for the Americanization workers of a community.

Recreation may well begin with the night schools, for, as has been pointed out, these classes must be vivified with the social element if they are to be successful. Through the class organization social nights may be set aside when the wives, families, and friends of the foreign-born men may meet together. This will greatly stimulate interest in the class and help the families to appreciate what the men are doing in these Americanization classes. Such social events help as nothing else will to fuse the various races represented, to cause them to forget their inborn racial prejudices, and to discover that their fellows are men " for a' that."

An interesting incident of this sort is described by Mr. Golderberger:`

The party took the form of a school dance; pupils and teachers brought their friends, and we invited a number of students from Columbia. The pupils

---

[1] Esther Everett Lape.

made all arrangements for music, for the sale of tickets, for refreshments, and for the reception and comfort of visitors. But the dance promised to be a failure. The clans and cliques, the nationalities and language groups refused to mix. It seemed for a time as if the device of a dance would be but another abortive attempt to make one out of many. Evidently old habits and prejudices were not to be startled out of their complacency so easily

The music played, but the nations merely congested the floor and gave little room to the dozen or two couples dancing, Jew with Jew, Greek with Greek. * * * Then some one proposed a "Paul Jones."

After several figures of the "Paul Jones" the music for the next dance struck up, and Greek was no longer Greek and Jew no longer Jew, for there in that immense hall were several hundred whirling couples mixed up delightfully, even with undoubted good Americans who would probably have resented the insinuation that they needed a baptism of Americanism.[1]

One of the great by-products of recreation is that it brings not only the various foreign races together, but it does or should bring the native American into the melting pot. Nothing will cause the latter to lose his deplorable exclusiveness and unfriendliness so quickly as to mix with the foreign-born people, learn to know them, see them in their beautiful dances and interesting games, and come to understand that they have many things which he has not.

Special occasions may be set aside when the races may successively take charge of the program with a Polish Day or an Italian Night and show the dances, games, and songs of that race. The general management of such affairs should be in the hands of committees which represent various nations. It is not at all difficult to turn out a great crowd of Poles, for instance, to witness a Polish program, but if care is not used to keep the management cosmopolitan, there is danger that such events may merely increase the racial solidarity instead of lessening it. Properly organized, these field days, games, dances, pageants, and the like can become powerful factors in assimilation. Let the foreign born—yes, urge them—to bring out the costumes of the old countries and revive the joyous memories of the home land.

While pageantry that leads thoughts back to the lands of their fathers is good so far as we of native birth are concerned, because it makes us realize that those people have something of value to contribute, and while it is of value as showing one group among them what another has to contribute that is of value, is there not danger that we shall be too easily satisfied and take the easier way, the way that meets with the least resistance from the alien groups? Is there not danger that we shall content ourselves with pageantry that does not Americanize those who take part and who compose the greater part of the audience, and because of this content fail to do the hard things necessary to make the aliens visualize clearly what they expect America to be to them—not the land of their fathers, but the land of their children, is what we want them to think most about.[2]

---

[1] H. H. Goldberger, in Conference Proceedings.
[2] John Ihlder, in Conference Proceedings.

The foreign born in some cities have shown a very tactful consideration in one interesting way—the carrying exclusively of the American flag. In some great parades in Chicago with dozens of races taking part with their characteristic floats, only the American flag has been carried. The foreign costumes and environment were all there, but of foreign flags there were none. This is as it should be. The flag is an emblem of allegiance, of sovereignty, and only the American flag in America should receive this homage. Native-born Americans may fly the flags of foreign lands on certain days, out of courtesy to those nations, but it is a delicate tribute that the foreign born have so often paid of carrying only the flag of America and not that of their former land. Such an action, however, should come from the free initiative of the foreign born and not through prohibition by the native born.

Recreation and pageantry and music are so full of possibilities for Americanization, that this whole book might be devoted to them alone. Any earnest committee can find a hundred ways of bringing joy and health and Americanism into the lives of their foreign born through these avenues. Imagine, for instance, with what joy these music-loving people would greet a male quartette, a chorus, or even a phonograph and a bunch of good records if they should appear in their streets at the close of a hot summer day. Motion pictures can now be produced effectively from little portable machines. Why not try the experiment of carrying some good music and some interesting films into the too-vacant lives of your foreign born?

In one of the dirtiest and most unlovely of our American industrial towns I went one stifling Sunday afternoon in August into a ramshackle moving-picture house. It was the only amusement place there and had just been opened by an Italian of the district. The place was full of men, women, and children, all starched and bedecked, tired mothers surrounded by active families with floating ribbons. For several hours they sat there watching with tensest interest one of the dullest plays ever reeled off, a tiresome story of the rivalry of two chemists. Here and there, it is true, graceful and beautiful ladies appeared on the scene, quite irrelevantly, for the film had been so cut that the plot, if the play had ever had one, was lost. The uncritical absorption of the audience stimulated me to closer attention, and I soon discovered the charm. It was the scenes, recurring at intervals, of beautiful American countrysides, magnificent country roads, bordered with cool hedgerows, down which glided the inevitable magnificent automobiles, carrying the inevitable beautiful girl in filmy summer clothing. There was joy and the grace of life. Marooned in the ugliest town of America they were all, on that stifling day in that stifling little hall, taking cool and expansive joy rides along American highways which they had never seen.

I have seen night-school classes of men who have literally forgotten how to laugh. For them I would trust more to an hour's rollicking fun as an Americanization agency than to all the civics that could be put into a month's lessons. Bring groups of your various races, men and women together, in a party often with plenty of Americans, and if you can not get a joyous party out of it, it will not be the fault of the foreign born.

Bring them into the "community sings," side by side with you, and make them warmly welcome until they feel that the community things belong to them, too. Bring them in on your music, your orchestras, bands, art exhibits. You will find many a man and woman holding humble positions in American industry, in whom lives the old-world suceptibility to line and color and note.

I saw a group of foreign-born women, old, stout, apathetic, brought together after many years in America in their very first party of any kind here. Somebody skillfully lured them into a dance they had known in the old country. Could you have seen the stiff, toil-thickened bodies break into old motions, the breaking of old joys over faces grown immobile, you would have seen a new meaning in the thing you call "Americanization." [1]

COMMUNITY CENTERS.

A public recreation hall in a community is a prime necessity. Public meetings, lectures, amateur theatricals, dancing, public celebrations, sporting activities, etc., may be held and centered there. It is the neutral place, where all community members, natives, and immigrants of various races, religions, and tongues meet each other, learn to know each other, and influence each other, where the much-needed social visiting among the natives and immigrants may take its inception.[2]

I am not urging the absurdity that men can be transformed into Americans by a course in school. This is but a beginning. Knowledge of our language is but a tool. * * * Our strange and successful experiment in the art of making a new people is the result of contact, not of caste, of living together, working together for a living, each one interpreting for himself and for his neighbors his conception of what kind of social being man should be, what his sympathies, standards, and ambitions should be.

Now, this can not be taught out of a book. It is a matter of touch, of feeling, like the growth of friendship. Each man is approachable in a different way, appealed to by very contradictory things. One man reaches America through a baseball game, another through a church, a saloon, a political meeting, a woman, a labor union, a picture gallery, or something new to eat. The difficulty is in finding the meeting place where there is no fear, no favor, no ulterior motives, and above all, no soul-insulting patronage of poor by rich, of black by white, of younger by elder, or foreign born by native born, of the unco' bad by the unco' good. To meet this need the schoolhouse has been turned into a community center. It is a common property, or should be. All feel entitled to its use.[3]

What an opportunity for the school of the community, the school conducted by native-born citizens of native and of foreign parentage. The school has a vital hold upon the most influential member of the family—the child; it reaches into practically every home in the community; it represents an institution upon which the foreigner looks with the greatest respect. The most suitable point of contact, the vital approach, is at hand—the children of the family. Through its opportunities for the organization of mothers' clubs and parents' associations, through the activity of home visitor and home teacher, through its close relationship with boards of health and all other public

---

[1] Esther Everett Lape.
[2] Peter A. Speek, in Conference Proceedings.
[3] Franklin K. Lane.

agencies, through its contact with the most influential citizens in the neighborhood, the school possesses the power to form a powerful functioning community organization. With the school as a center, with the public school, the day school, the school of the children as a starting point, a social organization can be built up. an organization embracing foreign and native-born citizens, English speaking and non-English speaking, educated and illiterate. The schools of the community can unite in such a movement, federate their parents' and teachers' organizations, affiliate with other social agencies in the district, and thus gather about them the entire community. The school building will become the meeting place, the public forum, the social center, the evening school, the recreation house, the civic center; it can become the neighborhood house, where contacts are made, where newcomers are welcomed, where troubles are told, and where organized action is taken for neighborhood improvement. Here formal and informal education can take place. Here the one group can gain from the other groups and in turn can contribute the best which it possesses.[1]

A number of books have been prepared dealing with the schoolhouse as a community center, and committees are urged to make a special study of the possibilities of this phase of the work. Bureau of Education Bulletin No. 11 of 1918, "A Community Center, What it is and How to Organize it," by Dr. Henry E. Jackson, will be very helpful. "Community Center Activities," written by Clarence Arthur Perry and published by the department of recreation of the Russell Sage Foundation, is also valuable.

IMPOSITION.

The protection of our immigrants from imposition and exploitation has been placed by law under the jurisdiction of the Bureau of Immigration, Department of Labor, and in this work local committees may receive much assistance from the Commissioner of Immigration and his deputies.

The foreign born are peculiarly at the mercy of the unscrupulous of all races. The many schemes that have been devised to take his money away from the immigrant could scarcely be enumerated. Grafters in the guise of Government officials have met him at the very gate of the steamship wharf and assessed him with fictitious fees. The hack driver has driven him around a block or two to his destination a few doors from where he started and charged him five prices. Employment agents, land swindlers, rooming-house bureaus—the immigrant has been the prey of the unprincipled of them all.

After a few experiences with these "apaches" of America, it is small wonder that many of the immigrants have become bitter toward the whole land. An embittered immigrant is not good tim--ber for citizenship. Community committees, therefore, may well

---

[1] Nathan Peyser, in Conference Proceedings.

give a large portion of their time and energy to protecting the newcomer from imposition and to helping him to recover from those who have defrauded him. The best way of doing this is through a legal-aid society.

The foreign born does not know what his rights are, nor how to get them. In every city there should be a place, well advertised in foreign sections and in industries, where complaints may be lodged and where persons unable to pay anything can get free advice, and those who can pay can be referred to capable lawyers making reasonable charges. The principle of the legal-aid bureaus in a few cities is capable of great extension.[1]

Bring some of your public-spirited judges and lawyers together and get them to see the need of lending these newcomers a helping hand. Gather a few cases of local injustice—unfortunately, they are to be found everywhere—and lay them before the members of the bar. If possible, employ some young man who is a graduate from a high-grade law school, and who has the soul and enthusiasm, to act as attorney for the organization. The legal-aid society must have the cordial support of the bar behind it, as the society is purely the representative of the bar in extending legal assistance.

Where a legal-aid society can not be formed, a group of citizens can still do effective work in eliminating imposition.

The foreign born, in a new environment, is the victim of all sinister forces that try to exploit him. A body of men who sympathize with him should sit down with the foreign born, talk over his difficulties, give him advice, and guide him in the course he should pursue. This would result in two things—the foreign born would become more confident because he has a friend to whom he can turn, and the exploiters would soon go to hiding.[2]

Every city needs a well-organized and really official information service where non-English speaking men and women can find out about jobs, licenses for peddling and for news stands, factory and fire laws, naturalization, the location of the county clerk's office, clinics, doctors, legal aid, compulsory school laws, child-labor laws, and workmen's compensation.[1]

Such a bureau can perform Americanization service of the greatest importance. The immigrant, ignorant of our customs, is sadly handicapped in his efforts to secure justice. The very interpreters through whom he must make his plea are often in league against him.

Most of the protections needed for immigrants are vouchsafed by existing laws to be found in our case and statute books. But law in books is one thing and law in action, unfortunately, is quite another. This is only saying what we all know, that laws are not self-enforcing. A law affords real protection only when it is given life through enforcement.

Therefore, the prevention through law of exploitation requires as its third and most essential element an administration of justice, accessible to all, workable by all, equipped with proper administrative machinery for the prompt and full enforcement of the laws.

---

[1] Esther Everett Lape.
[2] Peter Roberts, in Conference Proceedings.

To-day, under existing conditions, delay, inability to pay costs, and inability to engage counsel are causing gross denial of justice to immigrants in all parts of the country. This means for them bitter disillusionment. It brings them to the conviction that there is no law for them; that America has only laws that punish and never laws that help. From this it is only a short step to open opposition to all law. Wherever we deny justice to an immigrant, we prepare a fertile field in which the seeds of anarchy, sedition, and disorder quickly take root.

The immigrant judges American institutions more by the courts than by anything else. When he is brought into the criminal court for selling without a license, or when he comes into the civil court to collect the wages due him, our American institutions themselves are on trial. According to the treatment he receives so will he judge us and our institutions.

Education, social service, community work are all splendid. They can carry the immigrant a long distance, but not the final distance. The last part of the road can be covered only by experience. You can labor unceasingly to teach the immigrant respect for our institutions, but your entire effort will amount to nothing if the immigrant, when he comes into personal contact with our institutions, finds that they do not deserve respect.

When we can secure in every city a modern municipal court, with its domestic relations session, its small claims and conciliation session, possessed of that indispensable administrative arm called the probation staff, working harmoniously in definite alliance with immigration commission, industrial commission, public defender, and legal aid organization, we shall have established a complete ring of protection.

Then, and not until then, can we end exploitation.[1]

The courts ought to be, and often are, a potent force in Americanization. But often, sometimes without the judge's even suspecting it, the foreign born leaves court with a burning sense of injustice that long defers Americanization. Take a single example: The workman who can not collect his wages and must lose a day's work each time he goes to court, only to have the clever lawyer for the contractor get the case adjourned. Are they equal? The conciliation courts, first tried in Cleveland, for the informal settlement of claims for not over $30 are a simple and practicable way of ending delays in these small wage cases that mean everything to a workman who needs each week's wages to pay for the next week's food and rent, and for milk and medicine for the baby.

The need is that some group of Americans in your village shall be interested in seeing to it that American law is quite as majestic and quite as equitable a thing in the open stretches as it is in the lofty city courts; that good and fair interpreters are provided; that the alien knows his rights under the law; that all the usual guarantees are provided, and that the offender sees the penalty inflicted as the just result of the operation of American law and not as a personal conspiracy between perhaps a clerk of the company, an offended saloonkeeper (from whom perhaps he did not buy the wine for the christening), and an officer of the law whose ear the interpreter and the complainant can get while the alien can not.

In the village, even more than in the town and city, your foreign born need the community's aid in their struggle toward American citizenship. If the right American in the village does not show interest, the wrong one often does.[2]

---

[1] Reginald Heber Smith, in Conference Proceedings.
[2] Esther Everett Lape.

Half the judges are compelled to designate shysters around the Tombs to represent people who have no attorney, because there is no one else to designate. It seems to me that is one of the prolific sources of abuse. These shysters get a hold upon the court and upon the people coming into the courts, because the judges have to recognize them. It seems to me this great body can go back to their respective communities and provide some one who is decent, straightforward, on the level, to be assigned to this work, and the judges will meet us more than halfway.[1]

The foreign born are to-day the prey as never before of the medical "quacks" of the country. As the American newspapers and magazines have been casting out these frauds more and more, they have devoted their efforts to the foreign born.

In one year, recently, the County Medical Association of New York prosecuted complaints against 196 "specialists" or "institutes" offering treatment for all ills under the sun, from "frost-bitten lungs" to cancer, including, of course, venereal diseases. The social results of such mistreatment stagger the imagination. It would be interesting to know how many "dependent and delinquent aliens" have become public charges by depending for the saving of their health upon this kind of "American" institution. Ninety-eight per cent of the victims were then reported to be, and always are, foreign born.

One of the "specialists" prosecuted in New York employed no fewer than five persons of different nationalities to distribute foreign-language circulars among their countrymen in that city. Some of the advertising men are employed upon a commission basis. Most of the concerns keep within the law by hiring some worn-out and discredited M. D. actually to take the money from the patient.

Part of this problem is obviously for the district attorney and the county medical association. Where does the layman come in? In getting the facts and reporting them, and in giving public support when prosecutions are made.[2]

A word of warning against the quality of paternalism creeping into this as well as all other Americanization work, is given by Mr. Smith:

To employ the law and the administration of justice for the elimination of exploitation is the only sure way, and, further, it is the only democratic method. It is the American way.

Other plans which have been attempted or suggested run too far in the direction of paternalism. They attempt to put the immigrant under tutelage, and they endanger the whole program of Americanization, for they are un-American in conception and execution. We can not supervise the immigrant in his every act; we can not have a policeman at his elbow every minute, we can not make his decisions for him, in order to prevent a possible misstep; we can not deprive him of liberty of motion, of thought, of speech, and of action. In a word, we must not attempt to play the rôle of the benevolent despot.[3]

THRIFT.

Closely connected with the removal of imposition and exploitation is the matter of the encouragement of thrift. The foreign born

---

[1] B. G. Lewis, in Conference Proceedings.
[2] Esther Everett Lape.
[3] Reginald Heber Smith, in Conference Proceedings.

in America must in some way "get ahead" if they are to find the fullest measure of happiness and satisfaction in their new home. If they can be protected from the sharper, a great step forward will be made. They must, however, also be taught the ways in which best to invest their savings.

In every foreign district in America men both of foreign and native birth, but especially the former, have rented stores and painted the word "bank" on the window. They have then invited the people, particularly those of their own race, to deposit their money with them. The claim has been made that many of these "banks" conduct definite campaigns to create distrust of American banks in the minds of the new Americans. They offer to forward savings to the banks in the old country, and there is no doubt that many millions of dollars are taken out of circulation in America for deposit in foreign banks. The postal savings department of this Government has reduced this outflow to a considerable extent, but there are many regulations in the conduct of the postal savings banks which prevent the foreign born from using them as they should be used.

Many of the private "banks" undoubtedly do an honest business, and not a few perform service of great value to the foreign born in advising them and lending them assistance in their financial affairs. Communities, however, should take steps to see that these "banks" come under the supervision of the banking authorities. They should by no means be legislated out of existence, at least until other agencies of equal value are provided to render the same service.

The immigrant patronizes the racial or immigrant bank mainly because his language need is not met by the American banks. In normal times enormous sums, running into the hundreds of millions, are annually sent to foreign countries for saving and investment as well as for the support of dependents. The large contributions which the foreign born have made in the different campaigns for the Liberty loan are conclusive proof that if approached by their own racial leaders, or by Americans in the proper fraternal spirit, they will invest their savings in America rather than in their native country.[1]

How many of the distinguished banks in your city carry the foreign born's savings and investments, or have interpreting facilities to make it possible to do so, or are open at hours when workmen can go to them?

Without encouragement from American banks, the foreign born have usually done one of three things with their money: They have sent it abroad through their fellow-countryman, the notary or the padrone or steamship agent (who does not always transmit it) ; or they have put it with the "private banker," who has not always been under State banking laws; or they carry it around from job to job.[2]

---

[1] An. Rept. Bu. of Immigration, Mass.
[2] Esther Everett Lape.

In the very nature of the relations existing between the immigrant and his former home, there will always be large amounts of money transferred to the old country. Much of it will go to maintain parents whom the immigrant can not bring to America. Some will always go to be invested in the native land. Whether this is entirely an evil is a question for economists to solve. It may be well for community workers to consider another side of this matter before taking any radical steps to curb the forwarding of funds.

In this case, however, there is also the firm, economic justification for our readily accepting the practice of foreigners in sending their money abroad. This money can only go over in one of two ways—either it goes over in the form of gold or goes in the form of credits, which are ultimately paid by export of goods from this country. Our feeling about the undesirability of the foreigners sending their savings abroad is nothing but a relic of the old mercantile notion that it was a desirable thing for the United States to pile up gold within its own borders, which is, of course, thoroughly discredited by modern economic thinkers.

When the foreigner sends his money abroad he either tends to reduce the supply of gold in this country, which in itself is sometimes an advantage, inasmuch as it tends to keep the price level from rising, or else he establishes credits in foreign countries, which results in the increase of. exports of goods from our own country, and either one of these things is an advantage.[1]

The really vast amounts contributed to the financing of the war by the foreign born through the Liberty Loans and the War Savings Stamps gives some indication of the possibilities of saving among them. Community workers can perform few tasks of more value than that of providing for their foreign born some method of systematically investing their savings in ways equally as safe and convenient as the Liberty Loan plans. Great numbers of the foreign born have been given the habit of coming regularly to our banks with their Liberty Loan payments. This habit must be maintained, if possible.

The foreign born are naturally thrifty. Actual ways of saving need to be taught here less than among our careless native born. Too often among the foreign born—

Saving money becomes at once the job and the recreation. The women and children sell wood or do something else to help it along. The family lives on incredibly small sums in order that the hoard may grow faster. This is what Theodore Roosevelt had in mind when he said that one of the big tasks of Americanization was showing the foreign-born family that in America they *must not* live on $2.50 a month, because in America that is not living at all.

I always hear with some apprehension, therefore, the propaganda about "thrift campaigns" among the foreign born. Many foreign born, like many Americans, doubtless need it. But sometimes they need, rather, to learn good American spending. There are Polish women in the stockyards who can not be persuaded to take enough from their savings to buy the children's shoes. There are mothers who, obsessed with saving, put their children into day nurseries too soon in order that they may join their husbands in the factory; or

---

[1] H. P. Fairchild, in Conference Proceedings.

who evade the compulsory-school laws and put the children to work too early. A combination of *only* earning and saving conjures up a very dreary picture of family Americanization.[1]

In this unwise saving the native born have too often encouraged their foreign-born brothers in order that something might be sold them at a profit. We have urged them to buy properties beyond their means, thus forcing them to live on a scale un-American in its meanness. A public sentiment can be created in a community which will greatly lessen such imposition.

At first the landlords of these newcomers are, of course, native Americans. Their interest is usually purely financial. They differentiate among the various alien nationalities chiefly on the ground of promptness in meeting payments. There are middle-western capitalists who speak with enthusiasm of the Poles as borrowers; there are New England bankers who grow eloquent on the marvelous ability of the Italians to buy a three-decker on a shoe string and pay off the mortgage in an incredibly small number of years. They never think how these admirable debtors are living. They never inquire whether the Pole's children go to school or go to work just as soon as the law allows. They never ask how many families from his native village the thrifty Italian has crowded into his wooden three-decker. Those are their debtor's affairs and of no interest to them so long as payments are made on the nail.[2]

EMPLOYMENT.

His unfamiliarity with the language naturally places the foreign born at a disadvantage in securing and retaining employment. Some industries are making rules against the employment and even the retention of workers who can not understand the English language. At first glance this rule might seem to make for Americanization. As a matter of fact, however, it makes for injustice, for society has as yet provided no general facilities whereby the foreign born can study the language. To discharge them from their positions for failing to learn that which we ourselves have not given them the opportunity to learn is futile and unjust. If all industries were to issue an announcement that after a certain date—say 6 or 8 years from now—they would employ only English-speaking people, undoubtedly a great impetus would be given to the study of English. But even such action ought not to be taken until the States and the Nation have first made easily available to every person the facilities for the study of the language.

In the meantime and until we ourselves have performed what is so plainly our manifest duty, the foreign born must be given employment. They must not only be given an equal chance, but it is a question whether justice does not demand that their weakness be met

---

[1] Esther Everett Lape
[2] John Ihlder, in Conference Proceedings.

by exceptionally favorable treatment, as one would favor an employee who lacked an arm or a leg.

Get in your own heart, if you please, in the first place, some sympathy with that man who is in a foreign land. Let the best of your nature come out, the tolerant part, the kindly part. If you are an employer give him opportunity that you would not give to others. Deal with him not as one whose labor you buy, but as a human soul, and we can transform that man before a generation has passed.

There is only one way to translate yourself to him and that is by your conduct to the foreigner who is here—by translating America into square dealing, into justice, into kindliness.[1]

If community workers will create such an advisory bureau as has heretofore been described, great assistance can undoubtedly be rendered to the foreign born in the matter of employment. Such a bureau can act as "the next friend" of the foreign born before the Federal, State, and municipal employment bureaus. Such a bureau can make something of a study, if it will, of the abilities of each applicant. Hands capable of producing the most exquisite embroidery have been found scrubbing floors in office buildings because there was no way provided through which they might be placed at their proper work. The foreign born, driven by immediate necessity, drift into the first occupation which offers itself, regardless of the abilities they possess for valuable creative work in some special activity.

One night, in New York City, at a local draft board last year, I watched a long line of Sicilians. Every one of them had migrated from the same small village, Sciacca. They all now lived on Elizabeth Street, and they were all fish peddlers. One of them had been directed to that occupation, and the rest had followed him. In this case it was natural enough, since Sciacca is a sea village. But in another American community 17 men out of one small racial group became scissors grinders, though no one of them had had in the old country a job even faintly resembling scissors grinding. A little information about jobs would change many careers.[2]

Particularly in the matter of placing the immigrant upon the land can the community committee be helpful. Whether this be a place where he may satisfy his craving for cultivation by raising his own vegetables or whether it be upon a place large enough to earn his whole living matters not. A large portion of our new Americans were raised upon the land and know no other trade.

Nothing ties a foreign-born workman to a town or a job so much as a house to live in and a truck patch to work. It is a wholly American illusion that the foreign born love shacks and barracks and boarders. Many of them buy lots at the first opportunity, but they have not the money to build houses except on really easy terms.

We have kept the old country peasant in the coast State factory, although he wants to farm and although America needs his peasant faculty upon our

---

[1] Franklin K. Lane.
[2] Esther Everett Lape.

western lands awaiting development, upon our "abandoned farms" in New England and elsewhere, and even in the desert places. Millions of our foreign-born "industrials" in mill and foundry are country born and bred. They understand farming. They go at it with the sturdy patience and submission born of generations that do not expect to get their living in any other way. They know the careful, close methods of agriculture that could be grafted to admirable advantage upon the lavish, careless, wasteful American methods of cultivation.

The "conquest" of the waste places of America will never be altogether a matter of huge irrigation projects or solar motors or whatever the successful device may be. It must be also a matter of that human labor and patience which, in high degree, so many foreign born bring. When we have really learned to distribute the foreign born to the land, the food problem of the world will be nearer solution than it now is.[1]

NATURALIZATION.

There is a great field of usefulness for community committees in creating among the foreign born a desire for naturalization. They can assist the judges and examiners in many ways. They can lessen the burden of the process by having the rules adapted to local conditions. They can add greatly to the honor and dignity of the ceremony by holding receptions or public programs, at which the new citizen is presented with his papers or with some insignia of his new status. These ceremonies should include not only the wives of the new citizens, who automatically become citizens through the naturalization of the husband, but they may well include those young men and women, native or foreign born, who by reason of having become of age have acquired citizenship.

Such a ceremony may well be held twice each year, or at least annually. Many communities have adopted the permanent plan of holding a public reception, with suitable ceremonies, to all new citizens on the Fourth of July. Heretofore the foreign born have taken out their citizenship papers with the same lack of ceremony that accompanies the issue of a dog license, while our own native boys and girls have drifted unnoticed into the great honor of citizenship.

Campaigns for "100 per cent naturalization" and similar drives should be discountenanced. It should be perfectly obvious that forced or overstimulated naturalization can result, as a rule, only in mere lip service and in men who are citizens in name only.

Do we wish him to obtain citizenship and to make the best of it? Then show him the best side of citizenship—its privileges, its opportunities, and its possibilities for good. Make the act of naturalization a holy act and the day one to be remembered. Make his concept of citizenship a practical one. Base it upon neighborhood improvement, home development, child protection, communal organization.[2]

---

[1] Esther Everett Lape.
[2] Nathan Peyser, in Conference Proceedings.

The matter of naturalization is under the jurisdiction of the Bureau of Naturalization, Department of Labor, and community committees are urged to cooperate with the Commissioner of Naturalization and his examiners in all matters pertaining to this important factor in the process of Americanization.

COST OF LIVING.

As a rule the better and more dependable stores are not convenient to the foreign born. Thus they are left to the mercies of hucksters and those keepers of small stores whose prices must necessarily be high because of the limited amount of their business. Community committees may, therefore, with great profit study ways and means of bringing the consumers among the foreign born closer to the producers. Cooperative buying plans, curb markets, and the like may be instituted which will reduce materially the extreme cost of living among the foreign born and permit them with the same expenditure materially to raise their standard of living.

Domestic science teachers and those women with such training or experience can, through classes of foreign-born women, render most valuable assistance. The field is not one for "reformers" or "uplifters." It is a field for a woman filled with love for her sister women, anxious to help and with the tact to offer assistance without offending. It can not be urged too strongly that ways must be studied out to make the necessary contact with the women of the foreign born by giving them opportunities to teach as well as to learn. .

A young domestic science teacher who was working with a group of foreign-born mothers taught them how to make gingerbread, a very good thing in itself. The trouble was that the teacher was very young and was having her first experience, and she felt that she had taken these mothers several generations ahead in their knowledge of the art of cooking. The mothers, in an innocent act of friendliness, taught her differently. A few days after the gingerbread lesson they sent her a large plate of that delicious "stroudel," that wonderful pastry that we can never learn to make with the skill that these foreign women inherited as part of their birthright. The young teacher was wise, even in her youthful inexperience, and she invited the group to teach her how to make the "stroudel." Her greatest return for this spirit of exchange came during the days which followed, and it was part of her work to teach the conservation of wheat, sugar, and other ingredients dear to the hearts of all good housekeepers. These women not only were willing for the sake of the teacher to learn to use the food substitutes but became missionaries and taught other foreign women.[1]

Those communities which provide material assistance in securing, plowing, and harrowing garden plats can thereby perform Americanization service which will at once create thrift, provide recrea-

---

[1] Mrs. Harriet P. Dow, in Conference Proceedings.

tion, reduce the cost of living, and encourage fellowship! Surely no more valuable work in citizenship can be undertaken. In many communities whole blocks of unkept vacant lots have been turned into beautiful gardens by the foreign born through the stimulus of assistance in securing and preparing the lots, regular inspection, and a system of prizes. Such lots may be prepared for planting at a small cost of money and labor when done by wholesale, where the effort required to prepare a single lot is often prohibitive.

EDUCATING THE COMMUNITY.

Some one has proposed the following definition of Americanization as presenting the most pressing phase of the problem: "The preparation of the hearts of the native born to receive into full fellowship those born in other lands." There can be no doubt that the failure of the foreign born to find their place in America can often be traced to the neglect and lack of understanding of those born of immigrants of other generations.

Community committees should encourage in every possible way the meeting together as neighbors and citizens of a common community of those of all races, including the American. Americanization waits upon mutual respect, which in turn waits upon acquaintance. Community forums, pageantry, recreation, community sings, and other methods have been described. The moving-picture theaters, the churches, the lodges, the labor unions, the women's clubs offer other facilities for the welding together of our peoples which will be taken advantage of by committees with vision and purpose.

The American and foreign-language press will be glad to cooperate with community committees by printing live news and contributed articles which will point the way to this fuller understanding which is so necessary. They will without doubt be glad to eliminate from their own columns any matter which committees will point out to them as being harmful to this better understanding.

Speakers' bureaus have been formed in some communities to carry to the foreign born correct information in regard to America's purpose and ideals. Heretofore this opportunity has been left to those with an " ism " to urge, to the ignorant and unscrupulous. In New York City a " flying squadron " has been formed under what is almost a military discipline to carry on such a propaganda of patriotism. Wherever they find the enemies of this Government at work upon the " soap box," there representatives of the flying squadron are ordered with soap boxes of their own. The distorted and insidious arguments of the agitator are met by a calm and intelligent presentation of the facts. Such a squadron can perform valiant service in any community, not only in combating dangerous propaganda but in presenting, wherever men may gather, the community's duty in the creation of a homogeneous citizenship.

From the handbook of the flying squadron of the National Security League of New York are taken the following excellent suggestions to speakers:

Speakers should choose a definite subject and develop it. Do not talk at random. Use simple English. Avoid vulgar and profane language. Do not be patronizing. Be earnest always. Never lose your self-control. Assume that your audience is patriotic. Announce that you will answer pertinent questions at the close of your speech. Do not tolerate hostile interruptions.

Begin with a positive, concrete, striking statement. Tell your audience something at the start that will immediately grip their attention. Use short sentences. Try to make one word do the work of two. Avoid fine phrases. You aren't there to give them an earfull, but a mindfull. Talk to the back row of your audience; you'll hit everything closer in. Talk to the simplest intelligence in your audience; you'll touch everything higher up. Be natural and direct. Sincerity wears no frills. Speak slowly. A jumbled sentence is a wasted sentence. Finish strong and short.

In California this plan has been used in carrying messages by speakers in foreign languages to those who understand only those languages:

These certified foreign speakers should go wherever foreign groups are found—to their own gathering places. They should stress particularly—

(a) The obligation that democracy places upon the citizen.

(b) The fact that national unity can not be secured while race prejudice exists.

(c) The advantages of democracy to the foreign born and his children.

(d) The impossibility of securing national unity unless each citizen becomes an effective unit.

(e) The contribution of the foreign born to America and the world.

(f) The necessity for all to learn English—the language of America.[1]

---

[1] From the program of State Commission of Immigration and Housing of California.

Chapter V.

ORGANIZING THE COMMUNITY.

A community about to interest itself in Americanization should, first of all, take stock of its resources. This can be done through a survey or similar study in which both the existing facilities and the possible facilities for work are determined as accurately as possible. Such a study will show what activities can be entered upon without adding to the equipment at hand. When a community takes stock of its resources, it should look not only for physical equipment but also for existing organizations and individuals capable of rendering effective service. The next step is to bring these resources together, under a single purpose, with a willingness to pool their interests for the common good. Such a scheme as this does not rob any agency of its individuality. It simply directs individuality into the most effective channels.[1]

Americanization, in the last analysis, must be a community problem. The foreign born come in contact but little if at all with the Federal Government. Unless the people of the communities make the foreign born a part of the life of that community, they can never be a part of the life of the Nation. Just as the Nation raised its enormous funds for war by asking each community to produce its quota, so this task of bringing our boreign-born people into full citizenship must depend upon the communities.

The field for work as described in the previous pages is a great one. Here is a task in which every power for good in every community can find a part. Here is a task that no one agency alone can ever solve. All the forces of the community must be mobilized and coordinated. It should not be necessary to create new agencies. Every community has agencies which, properly enthused and directed, can carry out the work.

It is not possible definitely to lay out a program for each agency for the reason that the number and strength of these agencies vary so materially in different communities. Suggestions can only be made as to some of the ways in which the various agencies can serve. Without coordination and cordial teamwork, but little can be accomplished. The ambitions and jealousies of organizations must be controlled and eliminated for the sake of a better America. Just as that man is not a good member of an organization who is not willing to submerge himself for the sake of the organization, so that organization is not a good member which is not willing to submerge itself

---

[1] Charles H. Paull, in Conference Proceedings.

COMMUNITY COMMITTEES

Coordinating the

EXISTING AGENCIES

THE CHURCHES.
THE CHAMBER OF COMMERCE.
THE SCHOOLS.
THE CITY AND COUNTY OFFICIALS.
THE LODGES AND SOCIETIES.
THE WOMEN'S ORGANIZATIONS.
THE PHILANTHROPIC INSTITUTIONS.
THE CHARITABLE SOCIETIES.
THE GRANGES.
THE MOVING-PICTURE THEATERS.
THE VISITING NURSES.

THE COUNCILS OF DEFENSE.
THE ROTARY AND OTHER CLUBS.
THE LABOR UNIONS.
THE BOY AND GIRL SCOUTS.
THE PATRIOTIC ORGANIZATIONS.
THE RACIAL ORGANIZATIONS.
THE MANUFACTURERS.
THE TEACHERS.
THE COUNTY FARM BUREAU.
THE PLAYGROUNDS.
THE DOCTORS.

THE PROGRAM

COMMUNITY CENTERS.—The formation of community centers in the sc ols and elsewhere and their use as means of education, recreation, entertainment, fellowship, and the inculcation of the fundamentals of the Americanization program.

EDUCATION.—The organization of ight schools for adults for the teaching of English, civics, and other educational and vocational subjects.

LEAGUES OF FOREIGN-BORN.—Organization of Americanization leagues of the foreign born in order that they may have an important part in working out tlar own problems.

INDUSTRIAL.—Formation of classes within the industries for the teaching of English and the fundamentals of the trade.

EDUCATIONAL CLASSES.—Encouragement of sses in physical culture, first aid, domestic arts, English, etc., by various philanthropic and social organizations.

PERSONAL CONTACT.—Encouragement of personal contact in a proper spirit through visiting nurse associations, school nurses, parent-teacher associations, fod demonstrations, etc.

NATIVE BORN.—Education of the native born for a ore sympathetic and tolerant treatment and understanding of the foreign born and their problems, for greater rtesy in dealing with them, nd for the elimination of nicknames.

RECREATION.—Provision of healthful and interesting recreation and occupation to take the place of undesirable customs or activities. Extension of playgrounds and parks. Provisions for ayts ard parades and of community singing for the stimulation of patriotism and nationalization.

H   SIG.—Elimination of (fee and unsuitable housing conditions; bette sanitation; adequate building and sanitary codes; increased work for public health and faty; child welfare.

PROTECTION.—Elimination of grafting upon foreign born by translators; interpreters; steamship, foreign-exchange, and employment-agents. Legal aid and advice.

EMPLOYMENT.—Cooperation with the State and Federal ncles in peculiar problems of) mployment of the foreign born.

THRIFT.—Encouragement of thrift through postal savings, thrift stamps, and tber Government securities.

COST OF LIVING.—Protection from imposition in) ate cost of living through provision of public markets, introduction of new sources of food supply, fatg, etc.

for the sake of a cause. There must be a great deal of give and take, particularly where the work in a community is already in progress.

It is a community job; it is hopeless to leave it all to a school superintendent without money or power and with too much to do already. In a number of such towns private organizations together or singly have set the ball rolling. They have made arrangements for the opening of the school at night for the men, and in the afternoon for the mothers. Through the foreign lodges and by personal visits, with committees of the foreign born, they have enrolled the classes, held shop meetings, interested employers in factory classes, worked out a co-operative arrangement with the naturalization courts and the judges, arranged community nights and entertainments regularly where foreign born and native townsmen danced and sang together, celebrated "graduations" as town events, held citizenship receptions for the newly naturalized, and in general made the foreign-born classes feel the continuing interest of the community.[1]

THE CENTRAL COMMITTEE.

Some person or body within each community must be made definitely responsible for the carrying out of the necessary work. The ideal plan would be for the National Government to employ the Federal director and a number of regional directors in charge of the work with groups of States, the State government to employ a State director, and for the community to employ a community director. The problem being fundamentally one of education, all of these directors might well be a part of their respective educational systems. In the larger communities, especially those with large numbers of foreign-born people, a more or less extensive organization would be necessary. In the smaller places, some teacher might give part of this time to the necessary executive work connected with the problem.

In the communities there should be a committee representative of the different agencies at work in Americanization or those which should be at work. Of this committee the director should be the executive officer. Under the plan outlined above, the State directors would take the initiative in appointing the community committees. They may, however, be appointed in other ways, such as by joint action of the leading agencies themselves, by the superintendent of schools, by chamber of commerce, or otherwise. Care should be taken, however, to see that these committees are thoroughly representative. The foreign born themselves should have adequate representation, as should the industries, labor, the schools, the women, the various organizations, etc.

For the financing of the work, budgets may be provided through the board of education or through the municipal government, through the chamber of commerce, or through a special fund contributed for the purpose by the citizens. Later it is hoped that both

---

[1] Esther Everett Lape.

the State and Nation will be enabled to join with the communities in providing teachers specially trained for the work. Our communities should not wait for this action, however, but should proceed at once with such facilities as are at hand or that can be provided.

THE VARIOUS AGENCIES.

The industries.—As has heretofore been pointed out, the industries are in a position to be of the greatest possible influence and assistance in Americanization. Unless we can reach the foreign born at their work, we can never expect to reach them all.

If the employers representing the dominant industries in any industrial city remain indifferent as to whether or not the men know the language, it would require extraordinary effort on the part of other agencies in the community to get them started to learning English.[1]

Through the interesting of the foremen, of the racial leaders in the plants, and of the men themselves, industries can create interest in the classes. Through kindly encouragement, through protection from interfering overtime, through bonuses or increased wages for graduates of the classes, industries may exert great influence upon continued attendance.

Through proper cooperation between the industries and the local school authorities the men can become better workmen by being taught those things which have a direct bearing upon their work.

In a majority of instances nonindustrial agencies have taken the attitude that education for new Americans must be largely general, and have failed to appreciate how much they were losing when they ignored the vocational interests of the individual. The result has too often been that the school or other organization has looked upon local industries as being wholly unappreciative of educational values, while industries, on the other hand, have · considered Americanization schemes as being more or less impractical.[2]

Every department of the industry can be brought into play in the work of Americanization: Employment, safety, welfare, recreational, and legal.

Another point of definite contact with employees is through the legal department. Industries are beginning to appreciate the value of offering legal assistance to their non-American employees in order to protect them from unscrupulous lawyers, frequently of their own nationality. This legal department extends its work in such a way that it saves a great many days of labor to the company during the year. Aside from dealing with strictly legal problems, it undertakes such tasks as paying taxes for the men, so that they will not be required to lose a portion of a day from their work.[2]

---

[1] W. M. Roberts, in Conference Proceedings.
[2] Charles H. Paull, Industrial Report, Solvay Process Co.

In fact the very atmosphere of the plant has a direct bearing upon the quality of the citizenship its employees will possess.

Satisfactory working conditions are among the most potent factors in the building of Americans. Pure air, good light, pure drinking water, ample washing facilities, sanitary conditions, toilet arrangements, safety, first aid, hospital facilities, workmen's relief funds, cooperative activities of whatever sort, all are common factors of contentment, which are in the lap of the employer to be used or discarded as he regards his duty to those whose toil and labor add to his material prosperity.[1]

The schools.—The part the schools may play has already been discussed at length in previous chapters. The schools should be the wheel upon which all the other activities may turn. This means that they will have to realize that education does not consist merely of " book learning." Unless the schools step to the front and take charge of the whole educational problem, other agencies will come in and do so, thus weakening the educational system still further. Where the schools or any other agency in a community are not functioning as they should in this problem, the efforts of the committee in charge should be directed largely to arousing such agencies to proper activity rather than to creating new agencies to undertake their work.

The task of Americanization as it has been outlined in previous chapters is much broader than mere education. School boards may not now feel that they can undertake such work as improvement of housing conditions or the elimination of imposition notwithstanding the direct bearing such work may have upon the receptivity of the minds of the foreign born in their classes. More than a century elapsed in the conduct of our public schools before the school authorities recognized that the health of the pupils and their home conditions were a part of their educational problem.

There is no reason why the community director, even though he be employed by the school board, may not direct the work of various committees or agencies in all phases of Americanization, even though they seem to be only slightly connected with education. Such matters as housing may be turned over to a chamber of commerce or a civic club, but the central committee should always maintain an interest in it, to see that the foreign born receive proper attention. The task of the central committee after all is not to perform the various necessary tasks, but rather to see that they are performed by the proper agencies.

The use of the school buildings must constitute an important part in any community program of Americanization. We must remember that the school gymnasiums and swimming pools may become quite as important factors in Americanization as the classroom. In fact,

---

[1] E. E. Bach, in Conference Proceedings.

we must stand ready to assist the foreign born in any direction their talents or desires may take them. In New York—

A group of sewing machine operators, tailors, and workers in sedentary trades desire gymnasium classes. Within a short time, men who spent their leisure hours in playing pinochle and stuss, and who regarded baseball as a time-killing device of roughnecks and loafers, were playing the American game with Talmudic punctiliousness for its rules and with a degree of enthusiasm sufficient to make up for their past neglect.

Other foreigners who desired an opportunity to discuss current topics formed a debating society; still others wanted to express themselves dramatically, and they were encouraged to do so in the presentation of a play. [1]

The school auditoriums may be made to function as real melting pots in which the valuable components of each race may be fused and the dross removed. For until we mingle with our foreign-born people, visit with them, not as sociologists but as neighbors, we shall never get to know them, nor they us. Until then they will continue to be merely Italians or Hungarians or Poles.

The use of the school buildings for public debates, for pageantry, for celebrations, songfests, and all sorts of social activities, even dances, must become general.

I believe that more and more thought will be given to our school system as the most serviceable instrumentality we possess for the development of a better America. It has been, we must confess, a very much taken-for-granted institution. * * * It is the beginning of things for the boys and girls, but to the man and the woman it is almost a thing outside of life. This should no be so, for it may be the very center of the social, the intellectual, and in the smaller places of the economic life.[2]

The racial organizations.—These bodies of our foreign-born people who have banded together because of mutual interests and memories have not been brought into the work of Americanization in the past as they should have been. Americanization leagues composed of three members chosen by each organization of foreign-born (including three native Americans) have been most successful in many cities. Such a body meeting frequently will build up a fine spirit among the representatives of the various races, and they will carry back a mutual understanding to the bodies they represent. Each group of representatives will become the missionaries among the people of their race to win their full support to the Americanization program. They will become the recruiting officers for the educational classes.

I find the best agency of all for spreading this work among the immigrants is the non-English-speaking person. If you want to get the Greeks into your class, get a few leading Greeks to work among their own people. I have a Greek fruit dealer now telling his people in the Greek language the story of

---

[1] H. H. Goldberger, in Conference Proceedings.
[2] Franklin K. Lane.

what the school department of the city is willing to do for the Greek people, saying that the school department will furnish teachers, books, supplies, equipment of all kinds, if 12 or more Greeks will meet in any place convenient to them. We are not attempting to pull them into the school buildings; we will go to them. Our motto is, if the immigrants will not come to the school, we will take the school to them.[1]

When we remember how spiritedly the foreign-born people through their organizations entered into our Liberty Loan campaigns during the war, we can estimate the power that can be exerted for Americanization by their cooperation. Dealing with the groups of foreign born, especially those of different races, naturally calls both for tact and a knowledge of their racial peculiarities. Mrs. Dow gives two instances showing the use of tact and the lack of it.

An enthusiastic committee in an eastern city arranged a loyalty week parade last year. On one block they placed the Greeks of the community. What happened? Two national factions were represented, the people's party and the royalists. The group that had the larger representation stayed, the others with their beautiful flag of white and blue, with their gaily costumed men, women, and children and their band went home. The other faction would have done the same had they been the outnumbered ones. A small group of Americans or an American band between the two groups would have avoided the issue.

In one industrial town where there is almost an equal number of Hungarians and Slovaks a community Fourth of July celebration was planned. The question of precedence in the order of march presented a problem. A social worker who knew and understood the situation solved the difficulty. She visited the lodges and societies of both racial groups and explained the meaning of the holiday and purpose of the parade. She then asked the lodges to send representatives to a meeting of the parade committee, and have them draw lots to see who should lead the foreign groups in the parade, with the understanding that the alternate groups should lead the next year. The plan has continued with success even through the stress of war times when factional feelings have been most sensitive.[2]

Properly brought into the full direction of the work in a community, the foreign born will enter whole-heartedly into carrying out the program, but—

You must feel welcome before you can give it. Manner goes further than words. Unless you think rightly of the newcomer, and recognize in him a man and brother, with inalienable human rights and needs and a soul, you will not be able to do him any good, and might better leave him alone. If you look upon him as an inferior, he will know it and regard you with resentment. If you think of him as an interloper, he will think of you as intolerant. If you meet him as a man, he will respond with amazing gratitude.[3]

What should particularly be appreciated by the native born is that the point of view that the foreign element in the United States is a menace, as is so often expressed to-day, is most injurious in its effects upon possible cooperation.

[1] Laurence J. O'Leary, in Conference Proceedings.
[2] Mrs. Harriet P. Dow, in Conference Proceedings.
[3] Howard B. Grose, D. D.

We can not hope to have the love and support and loyalty of an individual upon whom we are continually casting animadversion and whose inner worth and decency we are ever impugning. The immigrant group is a asset, a bulwark, and a promise for the future. The newcomer to our shores is not to be looked upon with suspicion and distrust as a possible anarchist or criminal, but rather as our guest. He remains our guest during good behavior until he becomes a citizen. and then he becomes one of us. As both guest and citizen he is a member of the community and should be protected against unjust attacks.[1]

The newspapers.—Messrs. Mahoney and Herlihy, in their book, The First Steps in Americanization, point out the following ways in which the newspapers may aid in creating interest in the English classes:

The daily and weekly newspapers in a city or town are always willing to give free publicity to the notices about the opening of evening schools. This form of publicity is strictly limited, however, in its scope. The immigrant who can read in his own language most frequently relies on his own newspapers for the news which is of interest to him. The leaders in each nationality, however, do read the English papers and can be counted on to transmit the information about the opening of evening schools to many of their fellow countrymen. The notices should be telling in form, and the information presented in a style which will attract attention.

The immigrants' newspaper is a good medium for publicity, but one which is ordinarily not sufficiently used by the school authorities. The people who conduct these papers are invariably disposed to cooperate with public-school officials. It means only the effort of locating the offices of these little sheets and presenting the "stuff." And the "stuff" must be appealingly presented, as a rule, if it is to secure any results. It should be remembered that the average immigrant has had no particular reason in the past to think very highly of what the evening school had to offer. Those who attended, either perforce or voluntarily, at any time prior to the period covered by the last half dozen years, as a general rule got little. They remember that fact. They shrug a careless shoulder when the season for reopening school rolls around. This well-founded prejudice must be wiped away. Almost everywhere during the past few years one finds evening school organization and instruction improved. And the next few years will see the improvement in a much more marked degree. Through skillful and striking and persistent publicity this idea must be made to permeate our foreign quarters. Notices of the opening of evening schools should be published at least two weeks before the opening night and reprinted several times after the first week. Then, too, the editors should be reached personally. They are, ordinarily, men of unusual, sometimes of extraordinary, intelligence. If properly approached they are not at all unwilling to conduct an editorial campaign for Americanization purposes. Group leaders also prove of service here. Every little foreign settlement has these leaders. They shape and mold opinion. Sometimes it is a young lawyer, sometimes the politician, sometimes the fruit dealer or the undertaker. It is highly important that such people be enlisted actively in the cause of the schools. The schoolman, notoriously a poor advertiser, has overlooked these people heretofore. They should not be overlooked. They should be induced to indorse in print the school's program. They should be induced to contribute in their publications occasional signed articles, setting forth their belief in the Americanization movement and urging attendance at the evening schools. Once their interest is aroused, their influence will be manifested in various ways.

---

[1] Dr. Nathan Peyser, in Conference Proceedings.

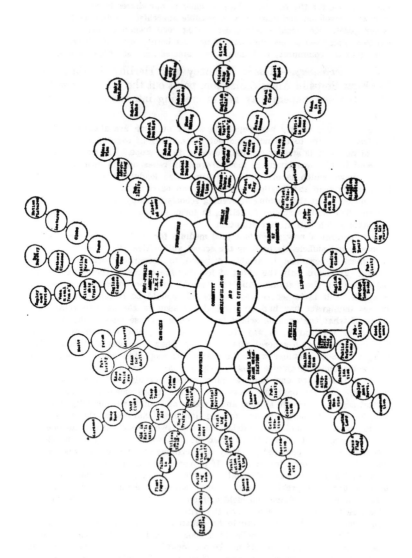

In every task the committee undertakes to further the cause of Americanization the newspapers, both those in English and those in foreign tongues, can render powerful assistance. Publicity is the greatest antidote for imposition and injustice. It is the lever that must be used to pry the community out of its rut and start it upon its way as a force in Americanization.

The churches.—The churches may aid in Americanization not only by bringing the foreign born together in classes where they may be taught by teachers (preferably furnished by the public schools), but by definite work through their men's, women's, and children's classes and organizations. This work must not be allowed to assume the slightest form of proselyting or the workers will forfeit the confidence of those they seek to help, and will bring discredit upon the whole task of Americanization.

This department is saying very frankly to church people who inquire of us as to methods of Americanization that they will not only fail in their purpose, but they will make the work very hard for us if they attempt through the work of Americanization to win converts for their own religious creed. We can succeed in Americanization only if we enter the work in a spirit of purest unselfishness. If we approach these foreign-born people with the hope of winning them to our particular religious or political faith, we will create only a resentment and a mistrust of our whole movement. Church organizations will find ample field for their efforts among people of their own faith.

The interest of America in this problem is too vital and pressing to permit the work to be used as an entering wedge for propaganda, religious or political.[1]

Chambers of commerce.—Where these organizations are truly representative of the entire community and not merely of the business element, they offer particularly influential auspices for Americanization work. They possess funds, executives, and committees which are or should be representative of all interests of the community. Where they have committees at work upon phases of the problem, they should be careful to see that such elements as labor, the foreign born, the women, and the schools are represented in the membership of the committee and not merely business men alone. In a number of cities the work of Americanization has been initiated by the chamber of commerce, which has then gradually turned the problem over to the various organizations able to serve leaving a central federated committee in charge.

Labor unions.—These bodies, reaching as they do large numbers of foreign born through their membership and work, can be of great assistance in encouraging the foreign born to take advantage of the English classes. Sometimes classes may be formed to meet in the union halls where they could not be reached elsewhere. The American Federation of Labor has adopted a platform calling for the broadest dissemination of education and the local unions in carrying

---

[1] Fred C. Butler, in Conference Proceedings.

out this program can help greatly with the educational work of their community. The labor leaders and newspapers should be interested in the community work at an early stage and given an active part in planning and carrying out the program.

Libraries.—Adequate supplies of books written in simple English, particularly those regarding America, its customs, institutions, and history, should be provided for the intermediate and advanced students of English among the foreign born. While there remain great numbers of people in America who read only foreign languages, libraries should see that books in those languages of the proper content are provided for the instruction and entertainment of this class. Some libraries have questioned the wisdom of supplying books printed in foreign languages. To do this, however, as a temporary expedient would seem to be both wise and helpful. Until we have' given all our foreign-born people an opportunity to learn English, we must see that their proper wants are cared for in such languages as they can read.

Librarians can serve the greatest need by taking the library to the foreign-born people through branches easily accessible to them and by properly advertising to them through their press and racial leaders the fact that books are available for their special needs. Teachers of classes of the foreign born may be invited to bring their pupils to the library, where the librarian may explain the book supply and methods used.

I know of a city that had an excellent public library well up in the native section of the city, and a very extensive Polish population at the *other* end of the city. And of course there was about as much connection between them as there is between Greenland's icy mountains and India's coral strand. Finally, a group of women, in the impetus of " children's year," established a health center in the Polish neighborhood. That meant that an American woman spent her days if not her nights there; and that meant that pretty soon she found out that one of the things those people wanted most was something to read. Many of them were literate in their own language. They could not read English, and this happened to be one of the cities where public funds for night schools had never been supplied. The library authorities decided to open a branch there in an unused room in the health center. A small collection of Polish books was secured; ideas and interest began to circulate; and it is a very dull American indeed who does not see that the interest aroused among the Poles in that neighborhood by that library of Polish books could be used to very rich advantage to introduce them to American books.[1]

Parent-teacher associations.—Because these organizations bring together people with a common interest—the child—they form excellent agencies for real race assimilation. Here the messages of the doctor and dentist and lawyer, the health official and policemen and firemen may be conveyed to the mothers. Here the foreign-born woman can come into full fellowship in a mutual problem with the

---

[1] Esther Everett Lape.

native born. These associations can be most helpful in eliminating race prejudice both on the part of the parents and of the children. The parent-teacher association can become a real neighborhood power, and through it a real neighborhood spirit can be built.

Domestic science workers.—Teachers of home economics possess an excellent approach to the foreign-born woman. In fact such a worker is a teacher and preacher of Americanism in every home she enters. Home economics workers are urged to make a study of the problem of Americanization and of the racial characteristics of the people in their districts, in order that this movement may have the benefit of their great influence. They should read the chapter on The home Teacher in Mr. Mahoney's book on Training the Teacher for Americanization.

Women's organizations.—The field for service for the American women is obviously the woman in the foreign-born home. Women's organizations, whether civic or patriotic, can render a great service in supporting the home teachers of the communities where such are provided by the public schools. Where such teachers are not provided the organized women should work to secure them and in the meantime carry on the work in the best way possible through volunteer workers who have prepared themselves by study for this work.

Reciprocity is the great thing. Make Americanization an exchange of points of view as well as of seeds and plants and recipes. By all means show the foreign-born woman the importance of swatting the fly, or teach her the germ theory of disease; but let her teach you how to cook spaghetti or how to make lace; give her a pattern for the baby's nightgown, but let her give you a pattern for your embroidery. In Springfield classes of American women are studying what immigrants from the various countries have contributed to their town; it would be a healthful study for any American. But give them a chance to contribute even more than they do—in music, art, craft, or simply in the understanding of the grace of life which even the simplest peasants often possess. The Cleveland's Woman's Club which voted a group of Polish women straight into their membership had at last hit upon the real secret; and a certain other woman's club that did "Americanization work" by pinning roses on all the men in the war that became citizens had not.[1]

In smaller towns the same methods employed by the settlements in cities should take place—mutual visiting, social intercourse, and beyond all else the development of common tasks. Foreign-born citizens should be placed on all civic and educational committees. Nobody likes to be done good to. Everyone likes to help. Social reform agencies have been remiss in this. Neighborhood men and women should be placed on all committees relating to neighborhood problems, for the foreign born will become Americanized only as they participate in community life.[2]

In every city, the field for cooperation with physicians and boards of health is wide. In New York City a group of women have established a series of maternity centers for the instruction of expectant mothers by physicians in co-

[1] Esther Everett Lape.
[2] Mrs. V. G. Simkhovitch, in Conference Proceedings.

operation with the board of health. In Chicago the Women's Club has cooperated with the board of health in employing a woman physician after school hours. And in Chicago, again, a part of the baby-welfare campaign has been run in the parks in immigrant sections, with outdoor movies. Good foreign-speaking workers or nurses are valuable in any part of the health work.[1]

In Philadelphia the Octavia Hill Association buys old houses in neglected sections of the city, puts the dwellings in good condition and manages them. This association has not only proven that good management pays, but that it can be used as a direct and powerful factor in Americanization.

The Octavia Hill Association's rent collectors are much more than rent collectors. They are friendly visitors. They take as much interest in the upkeep of the house as does the best tenant. They not only respond to a tenant's desires for improvements, they tactfully stimulate such desires. They take an interest in family problems and help to solve them. The covers of the association's rent books contain the names and addresses of neighboring agencies that may be of assistance—the nearest social settlement, public bath-house, library, free clinics, playground. If trouble comes, the friendly rent collector is a friend to whom the tenant turns for information and advice. And all the time, as occasion offers, this unusual rent collector gives hints as to American standards of living, of opportunities for rising in the New World.[2]

Patriotic societies.—Such organizations may well be given the task of holding the community celebrations welcoming into citizenship those who have become citizens during the year either through reaching their majority or through naturalization. They may take charge of the patriotic programs at the community centers and schools.

Semipublic institutions.—The Young Men's Christian Association and the Young Women's Christian Association have been active for a number of years in Americanization work, and the war has encouraged a number of other organizations of similar character to undertake the work. These organizations are usually provided with buildings which are available to the people of all races and creeds. Many of them have organized classes, trained and employed teachers, and have graduated large numbers of the foreign born with a good working knowledge of English. Community committees may well support and extend the work of such organizations. In some cities such organizations do not themselves conduct the classses, but merely form them and secure a teacher from the public schools. As the schools take up this work more and more and are able to secure an adequate supply of properly trained teachers, the responsibility should be placed upon the board of education. In the meantime we should welcome the assistance of such teachers as we are able to secure.

---

[1] Esther Everett Lape.
[2] John Ihlder, in Conference Proceedings.

Lodges and clubs.—These organizations, like the chambers of commerce and labor unions, can render valuable service in a community program, and they should be utilized to the fullest possible measure.

Visiting nurses.—The nurse that goes into the home of the foreign born can, like the domestic science worker and the home teacher, render yeoman service. The nurse possesses the confidence of the foreign-born woman to an unusual degree and is in a position to be of great assistance to community committees. Read address of Mrs. Bessie A. Harris, in Conference Proceedings.

A visiting nurse may sometimes more quickly than anything else give America a start in the village. The experiment was tried once in a small and very desolate foreign-born community quite without American institutions, on the island to which the garbage of New York City is carried by barges and reduced.

The infant mortality of the island was great. The ignorance of the foreign-born mothers, the poor drainage, badly built houses on filled-in creeks, condensed milk, etc., easily explained it. With the cooperation of the Health Department of the City of New York a nurse was put upon the island. Gradually the mothers began coming to the nurse's office and became interested in the infant scales and bathtubs and the ways of using them. The office became also an emergency dispensary—there was no regular doctor on the island—a gathering place for the children, a social center.

The signs of an American community began to appear; organizations came into being;. a "little mothers' league" of the older girls whom the nurse instructed to help their mothers with the babies; a Boy Scout group; a society of Camp Fire Girls; an Altar Society which, by dint of regular sweeping and dusting and evergreen decoration, made a different place of the musty old church. It is better if the nurse is authorized by the local or State health authorities; but it is a good deal better to have a nurse on private funds and private authority than not to have one at all.[1]

The doctors and lawyers.—The medical and legal profession can be of great assistance in Americanization in eliminating quackery, imposition, and exploitation. They can assist in the education of the foreign born through talks before the parent-teacher associations, in the community centers, and in the schools. They can serve upon committees on legal and medical aid and in many ways become a potent force for the raising of the standards of life in a community.

The banks.—The banks individually or as a clearing house association should take steps to meet the needs of the foreign born, if we are to encourage among them proper methods of saving their money. If the banks do not remain open at times that meet the needs of these people, a joint office of all the banks might be arranged which could be so opened. Such an office can also be placed in that portion of the city where it is most accessible to those of foreign birth. Some such plans must be worked out if we are to eliminate the " quack " banker who thrives upon the credulity of the foreign born.

[1] Esther Everett Lape.

The city officials.—Practically every city and county officer comes into contact with the foreign born and affects his opinion of the justice and fairness of American institutions. Such officials have an unusual opportunity to create favorable impressions of this country. Too often the man who speaks English brokenly or who is dressed poorly gets scant attention and less courtesy from public officials, policemen, firemen, street-car conductors, and others in places of authority. Through the heads of these various departments, community committees can bring about an improvement in such situations which will be far-reaching.

The boys and girls.—Here is an opportunity for Americanization at its source. Through the children in the schools, through the boys' and girls' organizations, the elimination of insulting nicknames and of racial prejudice, may be carried out. The boys and girls should invite the immigrant children to their parties and exercises exactly as they invite other children. They should help them with their struggle with the new language and not laugh at their mistakes. The children of the foreign born should be encouraged to tell the native born boys and girls about their former country, about its greatness and its heroes.

Other organizations.—It is impossible to name all the organizations which stand ready to assist in this great work. It is impossible to suggest ways in which all may serve. It is impossible to designate any work which may be undertaken exclusively by any one organization. Team work must prevail. We must all put aside our pride of organization when America asks us to serve.

Finally.—It is our duty to show friendship without paternalism; encourage education without compulsion; extend hospitality unstintingly; provide information on matters which pertain to his (the foreign born's material welfare; protect him from common abuses—shyster lawyers, un-American propagandists, and social leeches; cultivate and maintain proper contact with his organization leaders; make him feel that he is a desirable and invaluable asset to the commonwealth, rather than a liability; afford him opportunities for self-improvement, for an understanding of American history, and a working of the civic machinery.[1]

And the test of our democracy is in our ability to absorb that man and incorporate him into the body of our life as an American. He will learn to play the game, to stand to the challenge that makes Americans; the unfostered self-sufficiency of the man who knows his way and has learned it by fighting for it will yet be his.[2]

---

[1] E. E. Bach, in Conference Proceedings.
[2] Franklin K. Lane.

Chapter VI.

BIBLIOGRAPHY.

For the guidance of those who desire to prepare themselves more fully for the work of Americanization a brief list of available books covering the various phases of the work is given herewith.

Americanism.

BRYCE, JAMES. The American Commonwealth. Vol. 2, Chapters, cl, cli, cxiv. New York [etc.], Macmillan Co.

DE TOCQUEVILLE. Democracy in America. 2 vols. Colonial Press, 1862.

FOERSTER, NORMAN, and PIERSON, W. W., editors. American ideals. Boston [etc.], Houghton Mifflin Co. $1.25.

HILL, DAVID J. Americanism: what is it. New York, D, Appelton & Co., 1916. $1.25.

KELLOR, FRANCES A. Straight America. New York [etc.], Macmillan Co., 1916. 50 cents.

LANE, FRANKLIN K. The American spirit. (Addresses in war time.) New York, Frederick A. Stokes Co., 1918. 75 cents.

ROOSEVELT, THEODORE. American ideals and other essays. New York, G. P. Putnam's Sons, 1901. $1.50.

————. The great adventure. New York, Charles Scribner's Sons, 1918. $1.

VAN DYKE, HENRY. The spirit of America. New York [etc.], Macmillan Co., 1910. $1.50.

Background of the races.

BAGOT, R. Italians of to-day. Chicago, F. G. Browne, 1913. $1.25.

BALCH, E. G. Our Slavic fellow citizens. New York, Charities Publication Committee, 1910. $2.50.

BARNES, MARY C., and BARNES, LEMUEL C. The new America—a study in immigration. New York [etc.], Fleming H. Revell & Co., 1913. 50 cents.

BOGARDUS, EMORY S. Essentials of Americanization. Parts 2 and 3. Los Angeles, Calif., University of Southern California Press, 1919.

CLARK, FRANCIS F. Old homes of new Americans (races of former Austro-Hungarian empire). Boston [etc.] Houghton Mifflin Co., 1913. $1.50.

COMMONS, JOHN R. Races and immigrants in America. New York [etc.], Macmillan Co., 1915. $1.50.

GRAHAM, STEPHEN. With the poor immigrants to America. (Slavs.) New York [etc.], Macmillan Co., 1914. $2.25.

KNOX, GEORGE WILLIAM. The spirit of the Orient. New York, Thomas Y. Crowell & Co., 1906. $1.50.

STEINER, EDWARD A. On the trail of the immigrant. New York [etc.], Fleming
H. Revell & Co., 1906. $1.50.

RUPPIN, ARTHUR. The Jews of to-day. New York, Henry Holt & Co., 1913.
$1.75.

VAN NORMAN, L. E. Poland, knight among nations. New York [etc.], Fleming
H. Revell & Co., 1907. $1.50.

The following articles published in the Literary Digest will be found to be
especially valuable. They have the advantage of being concise and to the point.

Americans of Austrian birth (Sept.
28, 1918).

Columbus Day (Oct. 12, 1918).

Greeks in America (Dec. 7, 1918).

Armenians in the United States
(Jan. 4, 1919).

Czecho-Slovak Republic (Jan. 11,
1919).

Swedes in the United States (Jan. 25,
1919).

Jugo-Slavia (Feb. 1, 1919).

Norwegians in the United States
(Feb. 8, 1919).

Poland (Feb. 15, 1919).

Danes in the United States (Feb. 22,
1919).

Lithuania (Mar. 1, 1919).

Poles in the United States (Mar. 8,
1919).

Greece (Mar. 15, 1919).

Spaniards in the United States (Mar.
22, 1919).

Armenia (Mar. 29, 1919).

Bohemians in the United States
(Apr. 5, 1919).

Roumania at the peace table (Apr.
12, 1919).

Lithuanians in the United States
(Apr. 19, 1919).

Syrians in the United States (May 3,
1919).

Ukraine (May 10, 1919).

Finns in the United States (May 24,
1919).

Lettonia (May 31, 1919).

Jugo-Slavs in the United States
(June 7, 1919).

Esthonia (June 14, 1919).

Letts in the United States (June 21,
1919).

Finland (June 28, 1919).

Community centers.

CLARK, IDA C. Little democracy. New York, D. Appleton & Co., 1918. $1.50.

JACKSON, HENRY E. A community center—what it is and how to organize it.
Washington, Government Printing Office, 1918. (U. S. Bureau of Education. Bulletin, 1918, No. 11.) 10 cents.

——— A community center. New York, [etc.], Macmillan Co., 1918. $1.
Contains reproduction of United States Bureau of Education bulletin, 1918, no. 11,
together with additional material.

KING, IRVING. Social aspects of education. New York, Macmillan Co. $1.60.

MACIVER, ROBERT M. Community. New York [etc.] Macmillan Co., 1917. $3.75.

QUICK, HERBERT. The brown mouse. Indianapolis, Ind., Bobbs-Merrill Co.,
1915. $1.25.

TERRY, CLARENCE A. Community center activities. Cleveland (Ohio) Foundation Survey. Educational Extension. 25 cents.
Contains references on various phases of the work.

——— First step in community center development. New York, Russell Sage
Foundation, Publication Dept., 130 East 22d St.

WARD, EDWARD J. The social center. New York, D. Appleton & Co., 1913. $1.50.

Education of the foreign born.

ENGLISH TEXTS.

AUSTIN, RUTH. Lessons in English for foreign women. New York [etc.], American Book Co., 1913.

BESHGETURIAN, AZNIV. Foreigners' guide to English. Yonkers, N. Y., World Book Co., 313 Park Hill Ave., 1917.

CHANCELLOR, WILLIAM E. Reading and language lessons for evening schools. New York [etc.], American Book Co., 1912.

COLE, R. E. Everyday English for every coming American. Cleveland, Ohio, Y. M. C. A., Educational Dept., 1914.

FIELD and COVENEY. English for new Americans. New York [etc.], Silver, Burdett & Co., 1911.

GOLDBERGER, HENRY H. English for coming citizens. New York [etc.], Charles Scribner's Sons, 1918.

HOUGHTON, FREDERICK. First lessons in English for foreigners. New York [etc.], American Book Co., 1911.

MARKOWITZ and STARR. Everyday language lessons. New York [etc.], American Book Co., 1914.

PRICE, ISAAC. Direct method of teaching English to foreigners. New York, Frank Beattys & Co., 1913.

ROBERTS, PETER. English for coming Americans. New York, Association Press, 347 Madison Ave.

A series of books, pamphlets, charts, and cards. Descriptive price list can be secured on request from the publisher.

CIVICS TEXTS.

CARR, JOHN FOSTER. Guide to the United States for the immigrant. New York, Immigrant Educational Society, 241 Fifth Ave.

Issued in several languages.

DUNN, ARTHUR W. Community and the citizen. (Boston [etc.], D. C. Heath & Co., 1907.

For advanced classes.

HILL and DAVIS. Civics for new Americans. Boston [etc.], Houghton Mifflin Co., 1915.

PLASS, ANNA A. Civics for Americans in the making. Boston [etc.], D. C. Heath & Co., 1912. 50 cents.

RICHMAN and WALLACH. Good Citizenship. New York [etc.], American Book Co., 1908. 45 cents.

ROBERTS, PETER. Civics for coming Americans. New York, Association Press, 347 Madison Ave., 1917. 50 cents.

SHARPE, MARY F. Plain facts for future citizens. New York [etc.], American Book Co., 1914. 48 cents.

WEBSTER, HANSON HART. Americanization and citizenship. Boston [etc.], Houghton Mifflin Co. 40 cents.

ZMRHAL, J. J. Primer of civics—for the guidance of immigrants. Chicago, Illinois Society of the Colonial Dames of America, 1362 Astor Street, 1912.

Bi-lingual texts in Italian, Polish, Bohemian, Lithuanian, and other languages.

TRAINING FOR TEACHING.

BAHLSEN, LEOPOLD. Teaching of modern languages. Boston [etc.], Ginn & Co., 1905. 50 cents.

BERLITZ, M. D. The Berlitz method for teaching a language. (English part. Book 1.) New York, Berlitz & Co., 28–30 West 34th Street, 1915. $1.

COLVIN *and* BAGLEY. Human behavior—a first book in psychology for teachers. New York [etc.], Macmillan Co., 1913. $1.

GOLDBERGER, HENRY H. How to teach English to foreigners. New York, A. G. Seller, 1224 Amsterdam Ave., 1918. 75 cents.

GOUIN, FRANCOIS. The art of teaching and studying languages. New York [etc.], Charles Scribner's Sons, 1892.

JESPERSEN, O. How to teach a foreign language. New York [etc.], Macmillan Co., 1904. 90 cents.

MAHONEY *and* HERLIHY. First steps in Americanization. Boston [etc.], Houghton Mifflin Co., 1918.

ROBERTS, PETER. Teacher's manual—English for coming Americans. New York, Association Press, 347 Madison Ave., 1909.

SWEET, H. The practical study of languages. New York, Henry Holt & Co. $1.50.

UNITED STATES. DEPARTMENT OF THE INTERIOR. Bureau of Education. Civic education in elementary schools as illustrated in Indianapolis, Ind. Washington, Government Printing Office, 1915. (Bulletin, 1915, no. 17.) 5 cents.

———— ———— ———— Lessons in community and national life. Washington, Government Printing Office, 1919. 45 cents.

———— ———— ———— The teaching of community civics. Washington, Government Printing Office, 1915. (Bulletin, 1915, no. 23.) 10 cents.

ELIMINATION OF EXPLOITATION.

BOSTON LEGAL AID SOCIETY, 39 Court Street, Boston, Mass. Annual reports.

IMMIGRANTS PROTECTIVE LEAGUE, 920 South Michigan Ave., Chicago, Ill. Sixth annual report, 1915.

LEGAL AID SOCIETY OF CHICAGO, 230 Northwestern University Building, Chicago, Ill. Annual reports.

LEGAL AID SOCIETY OF NEW YORK, 239 Broadway, New York City. Annual reports.

NATIONAL ALLIANCE OF LEGAL AID SOCIETIES. Third biennial convention, October 11–12, 1916. Proceedings. Cincinnati, Ohio, Legal Aid Society, 103 Lincoln Inn Court.

SMITH, REGINALD HEBER. Justice and the poor. New York, Charles Scribner's Sons. $1.50.

HOUSING IMPROVEMENT.

Housing awakening. *In* Survey, 1910–11.

A series of articles running through thirteen numbers of the Survey; published by Survey Associates, 105 East Twenty-second Street, New York City. $2.65.

Howe, Frederick C. The modern city and its problems. Chapters 19 and 20. New York [etc.], Charles Scribner's Sons, 1915. $1.50.

Hutton, J. E. Welfare and housing. New York, Longmans, Green & Co., 1918. $1.50.

National Housing Association, 105 East Twenty-second street, New York City. Housing problems in America. Proceedings, 1919. Vol. 7. $2.

——— Tenement-house problem. (de Forest and Veiller, L., *editors*.) 1903. Postpaid, $3.40.

Veiller, L. Housing reform. New York, Survey Associates, 105 East Twenty-second Street, 1910. $1.25.

——— Model housing law. New York, Survey Associates. $2.

THE IMMIGRANT'S MIND.

Antin, Mary. The promised land. Boston [etc.], Houghton Mifflin Co., 1912. $2.

Bridges, Horace J. On becoming an American. Boston, Marshall Jones Co., 212 Sumner Street, 1918. $1.75.

Cohen, Rose. Out of the shadow. New York, George H. Doran Co., 1918. $2.

Ravage, M. E. An American in the making. New York, Harper & Brothers, 1917. $1.40.

Riis, Jacob. The making of an American. New York [etc.], Macmillan Co., 1901. $3.

Steiner, Edward A. From alien to citizen. New York, Fleming H. Revell & Co., 1914. $2.

Stern, E. G. My mother and I. New York [etc.], Macmillan Co., 1917. $1.

RECREATION.

Addams, Jane. The spirit of youth and the city streets. New York [etc.], Macmillan Co. $1.25.

Bancroft, Jessie H. Games for the playground, home, school, and gymnasium. New York [etc.], Macmillan Co. $1.50.

Bancroft and Pulvermacher. Handbook of athletic games. New York [etc.], Macmillan Co. $1.50.

Beegle and Crawford. Community drama and pageantry. Yale University Press. $1.50.

Bryant, Sarah Cone. Stories to tell children. Boston [etc.], Houghton Mifflin Co. $1.

Curtis, Henry S. Practical conduct of the play. New York [etc.], Macmillan Co. $1.50.

——— The play movement and its significance. New York [etc.], Macmillan Co. $1.50.

——— Play and recreation for the open country. Boston [etc.], Ginn & Co. $1.25.

Elsom and Trilling. Social games and group dances. Philadelphia, Lippincott & Co. $1.75.

146580°—20——6

FERRIS, HELEN. Girls' clubs. New York, E. P. Dutton & Co. $2.

JOHNSON, GEORGE E. Education by plays and games. Boston [etc.], Ginn & Co. 90 cents.

LEE, JOSEPH. Play in education. New York [etc.], Macmillan Co. $1.50.

MACKAY, CONSTANCE D'ARCY. Patriotic drama in your town. New York, Henry Holt & Co. $1.25.

Y. M. C. A. Community recreation. National War Work Council, Y. M. C. A., 347 Madison Avenue, New York City 20 cents.

O

DEPARTMENT OF THE INTERIOR
BUREAU OF EDUCATION

BULLETIN, 1919, No. 77

STATE AMERICANIZATION

THE PART OF THE STATE IN THE EDUCATION AND ASSIMILATION OF THE IMMIGRANT

By

FRED CLAYTON BUTLER
DIRECTOR OF AMERICANIZATION, BUREAU OF EDUCATION

WASHINGTON
GOVERNMENT PRINTING OFFICE
1920

CONTENTS.

LETTER OF TRANSMITTAL.

DEPARTMENT OF THE INTERIOR,
BUREAU OF EDUCATION,
Washington, September 30, 1919.

SIR: In the United States all public education is primarily the function of the several States and not of the Federal Government. Whatever help, financial or otherwise, the Federal Government may finally give to that very important phase of education which we call Americanization—education of adult foreign-born persons in our language, American life and ideals, government, and industrial and social opportunities—the States must continue to perform the important tasks of organizing the work in their several municipalities and of giving them the necessary immediate oversight and direction. To assist State school officials in these important tasks Dr. Fred Clayton Butler, Director of Americanization of the Bureau of Education, has prepared the manuscript which I am transmitting herewith for publication as a bulletin of the Bureau of Education.

Respectfully submitted.

P. P. CLAXTON,
Commissioner.

The SECRETARY OF THE INTERIOR.

5

FOREWORD.

There are many thousands of people who are in a position to exert great influence in the work of Americanization, through their leadership or membership in State legislatures, State bureaus and departments, and State organizations, official and voluntary.

The primary purpose of this book is to lay before that body of men and women some concrete suggestions of ways by which the States may serve effectively in the education and the assimilation into full fellowship and citizenship of our foreign-born people.

The States are rapidly coming to see the importance of this problem, and many are taking official action. The conception of the task varies greatly, and some of the methods advocated in some States seem unwise to those who have long studied the question. It seems wise, in order to bring about a common understanding of the problem, that this present work should be issued immediately.

Those interested in the opportunity to render service in this task through the States are urged to read the book "Community Americanization" in order to secure a fuller understanding of the principles underlying the problem. They are also referred, for the expert phases of Americanization, to three other bulletins which will be printed by the Bureau of Education coincidently with the present one: "Teaching English to the Foreign Born," "Teaching Native Illiterates," and "Training Teachers for Americanization."

THE AUTHOR.

STATE AMERICANIZATION.

Chapter I.

GENERAL PRINCIPLES.

During the heat and passion of war, some of the American people lost for a time that sense of justice and fair play which has always characterized this Nation. We permitted our righteous hatred of Germany's barbarism to overflow upon even those who left Germany because of her methods. Even those who bore German names, though of native parentage and intensely patriotic to America, were keenly conscious in many cases of an underground current of suspicion and resentment.

Chauvinists in some instances sought to translate this unhealthy mental attitude into law, and some of the States passed acts which we now see were not entirely fair and just. The good sense and judgment of the American people can be trusted to reassert themselves and eliminate from the statutes those regulations which were inspired by war passions rather than by wise deliberation.

There has always been in America a group, happily a very small one, which has advocated "America for Americans only," meaning by "Americans" themselves and those others who were accidentally born in this country. If America is to be a place merely for the select, it must be obvious that the matter of birth is too uncertain to be used as a qualifying factor. The fathers wisely decreed that the gates of America shall be open to all who meet certain reasonable requirements. It is therefore a condition which confronts us and not a theory

ILLITERATES IN THE DRAFT.

We have in this country to-day, according to a census now 10 years old, eight and one-half millions of people who are either entirely illiterate or can not read and write the language of America. Although this number is of itself greater than the number of all the people of the Dominion of Canada, our draft statistics show us that it is probably far under the correct number. Of 1,552,000 men who were examined in the draft Army, 386,000, or 24.9 per cent, were unable to read an American newspaper or write a letter. If this may be taken as a typical cross-section of the American people (and these were all men between

7

21 and 31 years old—the group which presumably was most recently out of our schools), then there are probably more nearly 18,000,000 people in this country who can not read our laws or who must receive their patriotic impulses from newspapers published in foreign languages.

Now, despite the efforts of those who would close our gates to all immigration, these people are here. They can not be returned to the land of their birth. In fact it is probable that more than half of them were born in America. Their presence here and their needs constitute a problem. This is the problem of Americanization.

All must admit that if America is to be really a nation and not a group of races, there must at least be a common tongue. Although this country was discovered by an Italian and settled largely by the French and Spanish, fate has decreed that English is to be the language of America. It is not unfair therefore to ask that all who come to America to make this their home shall equip themselves with the English language. This does not mean that they must give up the language of their native land, but merely that they shall also learn the language of America, that we may understand them and that they may understand us.

SUASION BETTER THAN FORCE.

There are those who would insist that the immigrant be forced to learn the English language, and there are those also who would insist that he be forced to give up the use of his mother tongue. Calm thought will of itself demonstrate the unwisdom of the latter course. We have been too prone to blame the foreign born for not learning English, when only a very few of our communities have made any provision whereby they might learn it. Only a few cities have provided schools for adults conducted at such hours that an adult may attend.

It would seem to be wiser and fairer, before trying force, to provide facilities and then attempt to create a desire to learn upon the part of the foreign born. Such a policy is not only in keeping with the traditional liberty of America, but it is a sound economical and political procedure.

The minor child, however, is a ward of the State, and here compulsion may be used without any infringement of constitutional or moral rights. Let us therefore see that no boy or girl reaches the age of 21 without the ability to read and write and think in English. Let us also make the facilities for adults to secure an education in English so general that they will be available to all. Proper organized effort and the cooperation of all agencies concerned can then be depended upon to bring, of their own free will, the non-English-speaking into the classes.

In all of our dealings with the foreign born we should remember that until they are naturalized they are guests of our nation and protected by solemn treaties entered into by this Government with the countries from which they came. We can, as a rule, apply no restrictions to aliens in America which will not thereby automatically permit other nations to apply similar restrictions to Americans abroad, and it should not be forgotten that many thousands of our people are resident in other countries, engaged in business, in the arts, and in the sciences. They are hostages for the fair treatment of other peoples here.

CITIZENSHIP LAWS TOO LOOSE.

It is no intrusion upon the immigrant's liberty to insist that he should be able to read and write English as a requisite to his becoming a citizen. We have without a doubt been too free with the priceless privilege of citizenship. Aliens in large numbers have applied for their citizenship papers because they could then secure a hunting license at a cheaper fee or because they could then keep a dog, which privilege local laws forbade an alien. This is of course a travesty upon the honor and pride of the nation. A number of States still grant citizenship, or rather the right to vote, upon the mere statement of intention to become a citizen. Such statements are in thousands of cases never fulfilled. Here then is a first task for the States—to bring their laws concerning the right to vote up to a standard with those of other States, to the end that there shall be a voting citizenship based upon uniform requirements.

Laws have been introduced in State legislatures tending to prohibit racial organizations and to abolish the foreign-language press. It is hoped that here also the good judgment of the American people will assert itself. To prohibit association based upon a common mother tongue or upon racial kinship would be another invasion of liberty which could not be justified before the law. Our own people form in groups around all sorts of common desires and objects. Our fraternal organizations are exclusive in their membership to those who believe in the particular ideals advocated in their respective rituals. We have our Chicago societies in New York and our New York societies in Chicago. We have our California societies and our Illinois and other societies wherever men from those States live in large numbers away from the homeland they love so well. This is a most human tendency and of itself can work no harm. The harm is caused when those gathered together cherish and advocate theories contrary to the welfare of this Nation. And such may gather together as well in the form of a college fraternity as in that of a racial organization.

The racial organizations of this country, numbering as they do millions of our foreign born among their membership, can be a great and most invaluable factor in the task of assimilating and educating our immigrants. Many of these organizations as a matter of fact make full citizenship in America within a certain period of years one of their essentials for membership. All of them when properly approached, we may be sure, will join whole-heartedly with us in any wise and necessary program for Americanization.

THE FOREIGN-LANGUAGE PRESS.

The foreign-language press similarly constitutes a great and powerful force that will offer itself for the education of its readers. There are undoubtedly millions of people in this country who can read satisfactorily only their native foreign tongue. To destroy, even if we could do so, our only means of bringing our story to their minds would be folly. A little reflection would show how difficult it would be to prohibit the publication of newspapers or magazines or books in foreign tongues. We would then have to prohibit the importation of anything printed other than in English. Some of the great master-pieces of the world would be ruled out of our land. Our scientists and artists would be provincialized. But it is idle even to discuss such an action in America. Here again wisdom advises that we direct our efforts at the cause rather than at the effect. When all of our people have been furnished with the proper educational facilities for learning English, the need for papers published here in foreign tongues will disappear. In fact, already the more forward-looking publishers of foreign-language newspapers are printing a part of their paper in English in order that they may hold that portion of their clientele which is gradually acquiring the English language. Other publishers may be depended upon to see that such a plan is both patriotic and good business.

Some people assume that whatever is printed or said in a language which they themselves can not understand must necessarily be pernicious. As a matter of fact a careful translation of large numbers of foreign publications in America reveals nothing so dangerous as much that appears openly in the English language. This is not intended as a plea for the foreign-language press in America. It is a plea for level-headedness in dealing with a problem so intimately connected with a proper solution of our task. We hope and believe that the day will soon come when the foreign-language press will gradually be transformed into publications in English, not through compulsion, but through the removal of the special need which they now serve.

ENGLISH LANGUAGE FIRST NEED.

As has already been pointed out, the first essential in the proper assimilation of our foreign-born people is the provision of facilities for learning the English language. The Constitution, not having specifically placed education in the control of the Federal Government, thereby reserves it to the States. The first task, therefore, for State workers is to bring about a public sentiment that will demand the provision of facilities for the education of adults in English, civics, and American history. It is hoped that the Federal Government will soon decide to join the States in a cooperative movement toward such an end. In the meantime the States should act independently.

State legislators should recognize that the proper education of our foreign born goes much further than mere "book learning." Laws enacted to provide such education should be so elastic that facilities may be provided wherever the foreign born may be brought together in groups. Only a comparatively small portion of these people can ever be brought into our night schools. We must reach the greater number with classes in industrial plants, in their lodges and labor unions, and even in their churches. The public-school authorities should be authorized to send properly trained teachers wherever the necessary minimum number of such people can be formed into a class and at such hours of the day or night as will be most convenient to their needs.

Just as the teeth and general health and even the home conditions of the child are recognized as a proper field for the supervision of the school authorities, so legislators should recognize that the environment of the foreign born and their community and social conditions are a part of the problem as well as the mere teaching of English. The public-school authorities should be permitted a broad discretion in the field of work and not limited too strictly to pure education. As will be described later, the public-school system should be the hub around which all the forces of the State and community may work in this problem.

In his book on Community Americanization,[1] the writer has set forth the following essential requirements for those who would serve the Nation in this task:

We must first of all, if we are to do our work properly, possess the American spirit ourselves. We should have some knowledge of those whom we are seeking to initiate into our brotherhood. We must know the difficulties under which they are laboring in this new land. We must come to have a real respect for them as men and for their possibilities as members.

These requirements apply with equal or greater force to those who plan to work along State lines, and all such are urged to read Community Americanization both for the broader treatment it gives of these requirements and for a proper knowledge of the program they are urged to bring about within the communities of the State.

---

[1] Bureau of Education, Bulletin, 1919, No. 76.

Chapter II.

STATE LEGISLATION.

Purely as a suggestion to the authorities of other States, the laws of the State of New York which affect the education of adolescents are included herein. Suggestions are also added which will enable the school authorities of a State to make cooperative arrangements with the National Government when it shall adopt the necessary legislation.

Every minor between 16 and 21 years of age who does not possess such ability to speak, read, and write the English language as is required for the completion of the fifth grade of the public or private schools of the city or school district in which he resides shall attend some day or evening school or some school maintained by an employer, as hereinafter provided, in the city or district in which he resides throughout the entire time such school is in session; provided that no such minor be required to attend, if the commissioner of health of the city, town, village, or district where such minor resides, or an officer, deem such minor physically or mentally unfit to attend.

Any minor subject to the provisions of this section who willfully violates any provisions of this section shall be punished by a fine not exceeding $5.

Every person having in his control any minor subject to the provisions of this section shall cause such minor to attend a school as hereby required; and if such person fails for six sessions within a period of one month to cause such minor to so attend school, unless the commissioner of health or the executive officer of the board or department of health of the city, town, village, or district where such minor resides, or an officer thereof designated by such board, department, or commissioner shall certify that such minor's physical or mental condition is such as to render his attendance at school harmful or impracticable, such person shall, upon complaint by a truant officer and conviction thereof, be punished by a fine of not more than $20.

Whoever induces or attempts to induce such minor to absent himself unlawfully from school or employs such minor, except as is provided by law, or harbors such who, while school is in session, is absent unlawfully therefrom, shall be punished by a fine of not more than $50.

The employer of any minor subject to the provisions of this section shall procure from such minor and display in the place where such minor is employed the weekly record of regular attendance upon a school, and it shall be unlawful for any person to employ any minor subject to the provisions of this section until and unless he procures and displays said weekly record as herein provided. It shall be the duty of the teacher or principal of the school upon which he (such minor) attends to provide each week such minor with a true record of attendance.

Any employer may meet the requirements of this act by conducting a class or classes for teaching English and civics to foreign-born in shop, store, plant, or factory, under the supervision of the local school authorities, and any minor subject to the provisions of this act may satisfy the requirement by attendance upon such classes.

12

Night schools wherein the common branches and such additional subjects as may be adapted to students applying for instruction are taught on three nights each week, for two hours each night, shall be maintained by the board of education—

(1) In each city of the first class throughout the duration of the day-school term.

(2) In each city of the second class on at least 100 nights.

(3) In each city of the third class on at least 80 nights.

(4) In each city not subject to the foregoing provisions and in each school district where 20 or more minors between the ages of 16 and 21 years are required to attend school, or where 20 or more persons over the age of 16 years make application for instruction in a night school, for at least 75 nights.

All night schools shall be free to all persons residing in the districts or city.

The commissioner of education is hereby authorized to divide the State into zones and to appoint directors thereof, teachers, and such other employees as may be necessary to promote and extend educational facilities for the education of illiterates and of non-English-speaking persons.

The board of estimate and apportionment of a city, the council of a city, or the common council of a city, the board of supervisors of a county, the board of trustees of an incorporated village, the town board of a town may make appropriations to aid and promote the extension of education among the illiterates and non-English-speaking persons within the jurisdiction of these respective bodies.

No person, after January 1, 1922, shall become entitled to vote by attaining majority, by naturalization, or otherwise, unless such person is also able, except for physical disability, to read and write English.

The State law should provide that such minors as are unable to read and write English with the specified facility should attend school for a minimum of 200 hours each year, even though it be necessary for them to attend the regular day public school.

The law should also designate the commissioner, or superintendent of education, the State superintendent of public instruction, or other chief educational officer, as the official representative of the State authorized to complete any necessary cooperative arrangements with the Federal Government.

The State treasurer should be designated specifically as the officer authorized to receive Federal funds.

The chief educational officer of the State should be authorized to negotiate and arrange with the Federal Government for the expenditure of any joint funds at any time available.

When the Federal Government makes a specific appropriation of funds for expenditure in each State, further action by the State legislatures will be necessary to make appropriations meeting the requirements of such Federal acts, unless blanket appropriations may be provided in anticipation of such action by the National Congress.

A map of the State of New York, showing the proposed zoning, is printed herewith. It is proposed to divide the State into 15 zones. These zones have been worked out on the following basis: (1) Purposes of local administration; (2) number of illiterates and non-English speaking in each district (8,000 to 12,000); (3) natural geographical divisions. The divisions should be upon county lines.

It is proposed to organize in New York under a director or supervisor a representative group of local Americanization committees, similar to the plan explained in the book "Community Americanization." These committees will represent all the activities and

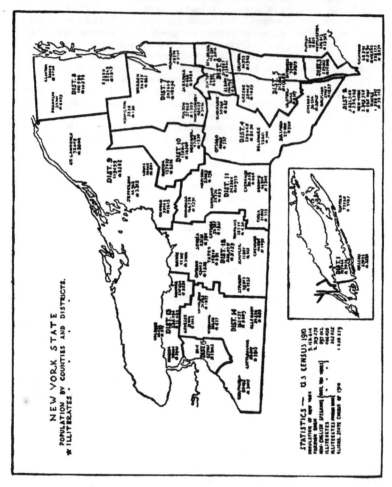

forces functioning in Americanization service; for example, public schools, civic bodies, chambers of commerce, rotary clubs, women's organizations, industries, foreign societies and leaders, social and civic forces, including Young Men's Christian Association, Knights of Columbus, Young Men's Hebrew Association, etc.

The function of this director will be to administer the State's activities through the local forces, to coordinate the local activities behind the public school extension program, to arouse and focus public attention and enlist volunteer activity upon constructive Americanization, to supervise the teachers trained for this work, through local cooperation of public school authorities, and to arrange local training centers when and where needed.

Other State legislation will be necessary in order to protect the foreign born from imposition, exploitation, adverse housing conditions, etc. These needs will be brought out from time to time as the work progresses. Such progressive and modern measures as small-claims courts, public defenders, etc., should be studied and provided whenever found advisable.

Chapter III.

THE STATE AND THE COMMUNITY.

It is obvious that the national problem of Americanization is too large and too widespread to be solved from the City of Washington. To care for it properly there must be decentralization similar to that followed in the plans of the Federal Reserve Banking System, for instance. Under such a plan, there would be regional directors directly representing the National Government in groups of States. These regional directors would establish cooperative working relations with the State directors and would place at the disposal of the latter all the facilities of the National Government available for the work.

The plan already adopted by New York for the work in that State follows similar lines, with regional directors for the several groups of counties. The uniform adoption of such a plan throughout the Nation would give a simple, effective, and business-like working organization with direct lines from the Federal director, through the regional directors, the State directors, the district directors to the community directors. The adoption of this plan is urged upon those in authority in the States.

The work of Americanization vitally concerns several different State departments, such as health, labor, etc., but fundamentally the task is one of education. It seems far better therefore to have this work made a part of the educational machinery of the State unless it can be made a separate department of the State's work. The education of our foreign-born people is a task for our educational scientists, and not for the layman who knows nothing of the process of transforming men's minds.

THE COMMISSION PLAN.

Some States, notably California, have already organized for this work along lines quite different from the New York plan. In California the task of improving the environment and protecting the interests of the foreign born was a number of years ago placed in the hands of a special commission, that of immigration and housing. Excellent work has resulted. Here a body of men and women, giving a part of their time, have directed the work through an execu-

16

tive secretary and assistants, while under the New York plan the responsibility is placed upon a State director reporting to the State commissioner of education. The New York plan may be adopted and the advantages of the California plan incorporated by appointing an advisory State committee which will represent all the State interests involved in Americanization.

This committee should include representatives of the various State bureaus affected, the principal racial organizations of the State, the industries, the federation of labor, the women's organizations, patriotic societies, etc. Such a committee would coordinate all the activities of the principal State organizations, eliminate duplication of effort, bring harmony of purpose, and be a powerful factor in advising and aiding the State director in carrying on the work.

A State department or commission (or committee) should be democratic, and made up of citizens who have had actual experience with immigrants and who represent various viewpoints in connection with the problem. The commissioners should preferably be leaders in their fields who could not give full time, but who would determine general policies and employ a staff of experts for the work of administration. Obviously, the smaller communities or private agencies can not afford to retain the services of experts in all the various lines of Americanization work, but the State can do so, and it can make them available for surveys and advisory work in each community. The State department, working in cooperation with the National department, thus has a concentrated power to inform each community as to its problems and as to the newest and most successful methods for attacking these problems. Few, if any, States can afford to maintain a department sufficiently large to do all the direct field work; and, indeed, it is questionable if the State should perform such functions. However, the State organization should be flexible and so developed that, on short notice, it can send experts in any line to the aid of the community.

THE STATE'S RESPONSIBILITY.

But it is not to be assumed that the State should await the call of the community. The initiative must be assumed by the State; it should keep in close contact with the National department, and also with the work being done in other States, and should assume responsibility for inaugurating work and programs, the value of which has been proved, not only in communities which have already recognized their Americanization problems but also in the backward communities which have failed to realize that they have any such problem. The California commission has boldly faced this question and has sent staffs of investigators into the most backward communities to make surveys, and has then confronted the community government and social agencies with a frank and full report of the conditions, pointing out the work that the local community agencies must undertake to meet the situation. When persuasion has failed, the commission has resorted to public exposure of existing conditions, and publicity has usually achieved the desired end.

In this connection it might be pointed out that the most progressive communities should always cooperate with the State department in compelling backward communities to undertake this work, because in many ways the Americanization problem can not be isolated, nor can it be solved by isolated action; it is what we might term a "migratory problem." For example, especially in our Western States, the greater percentage of foreign-born people are migratory workers, therefore in the fields of housing and sanitation the community does not fully protect itself by establishing proper and high standards, because the flow of migratory workers from one community to another has the effect of constantly reducing or endangering these standards. The same example holds good in the fields of education. These are clear instances of a low-standard community affecting a high-standard community, whereas the reverse is, unhappily, not true unless there is a centralized State agency to serve as a clearing-house for the establishment of uniform standards in all communities.

DEFINITE POLICY NECESSARY.

Simultaneously with the development of an organization for energizing communities and for rendering expert assistance and guidance, the State department must develop, as it goes along, a definite Americanization policy. It must not fall into the error of adopting some printed program or of hastily writing out a program in the seclusion of an executive session. It must establish direct contact with the foreign born, preferably by means of the establishment of complaint offices for handling cases of exploitation, in order that it may find out from the immigrants themselves what problems and difficulties have confronted them in the particular State. The State policy must be framed to meet such facts, not to test theories. In addition, the department must survey every field that has a possible bearing upon the broader work of Americanization, for it is bound to find fields where the State must do the direct work, because legal technicalities and the inherent nature of the work itself will make it impossible for communities to undertake it.

The State, in developing a policy, must realize that the community or the local private agency is apt to see only some one small angle of the Americanization problem, and the scope of its work may become too rigidly set in a narrow field. It is the duty of the State to maintain a clear and broad vision of the problem as a whole, and to keep the communities and local agencies out of the ruts and up on the open road leading to a set goal of accomplishment. Furthermore, the private agencies or charities have too long borne the burdens in this field. They have done noble pioneer work, but this is a public problem, the responsibility of the State, and we should no longer impose upon such generosity. The State can bring pressure to bear upon local units of government to make them undertake this work in their communities. Furthermore, the State, since it represents the people, can make an Americanization program truly democratic, and there will be none of the suspicion of self-aggrandizement or religious proselyting that unfortunately often attaches to the program of private agencies.

OPPORTUNITY UNLIMITED.

The opportunities for the States and the Nation are unlimited. They can centralize or focus public attention upon inadequate standards that are discovered and practically compel immediate improvements that could be achieved by the communities single-handed only in several decades.

Under our forms of government the responsibility in educational matters is largely that of the States. Therefore the State Americanization department should study and point out the defects in our public-school system which retard the school end of Americanization, and it should boldly lead the communities in a fight to make of our educational system in fact what we boast of it in fancy. The States, with the backing of the Nation, must aid and, where necessary, force the community in raising the standards of education in making of teaching a real profession, made up of trained teachers paid a decent wage, sufficient at least to maintain the American standard of living. If the community does not secure this backing and guidance of the State, its work in the schooling field of Americanization is a weak, almost futile, compromise with the shortcomings of our educational system.[1]

---

[1] Mr. George L. Bell, formerly attorney and executive officer of the California Immigration and Housing Commission, in an address before the National Conference on Methods of Americanization.

Chapter IV.

STATE SURVEY.

One of the first tasks for a newly organized State department of Americanization is to make a study of the problem, of the agencies already at work, and of the agencies available for the work. Every effort should be made to limit the information gathered to that which is essential, in order that the resulting data may not be so voluminous as to be confusing. There is incorporated herewith a suggestive survey.

TENTATIVE PLAN FOR STATE AMERICANIZATION SURVEY.

I. IMMIGRANT POPULATION—COMPOSITION AND CHARACTERISTICS.

A. Summary of Data from Census of 1910 for State and Chief Cities.

1. Population.
2. Color and nativity.
3. Foreign nationalities.
4. Males of voting age.
   a. Citizenship of foreign-born white.
5. Illiteracy.
6. Inability to speak English.
7. School age and attendance.
8. Map showing per cent of foreign white by counties, in total population, etc.

Remarks:

B. Summary of Data for Cities and Towns, secured through questionnaires, etc. (See attached questionnaires.)

1. Immigrant and Total Population Compared, 1910 and present.

Cities and towns.	Population, 1910 census.	Number foreign-born and foreign parentage in 1910.	Present population.	Estimate of present number foreign-born and foreign parentage.

Remarks:

2. Males of Military Age—Native and Foreign-born.
   a. Number Registered.

1. Native ....
2. Naturalized ....
3. Declarants ....
4. Aliens ....
   (Information can be secured from 1917-18 records of draft boards.)

Remarks:

3. Immigrants in Industry.

Cities and towns.	Approximate total number employees.	Approximate number immigrant employees.	Number classes for immigrants.

Remarks and suggestions:

II. STATUS OF EDUCATIONAL FACILITIES.

A. Public Day Schools for Children.

Cities and towns	Number of public schools attended largely by children of immigrants.	Total number of children attending.	Number of children of immigrants attending.

Remarks and recommendations:

19

B. Public School Classes, Evening and Day, for Immigrants above Regular School Age.

Cities and towns.	Total number of adult immigrants.	Number of immigrant classes.	Average total number attending.	Number hours instruction per year.	Money appropriated last year.

Remarks: Legislation governing these classes. Are they covering the situation adequately? Is the subject matter taught adapted to the needs and interests of the immigrants? Do the classes as a whole hold their pupils? etc.
Recommendations:

C. Private Day Schools.

Cities and towns.	Number of private schools attended largely by children of immigrants.	Total number of children attending.	Total number of children of immigrants attending.

Remarks and recommendations:

D. Private School Classes, Evening and Day, for Immigrants above Regular School Age.

Cities and towns.	Number of classes.	Average total number attending.	Hours per year.

Remarks:

E. Factory Classes.

Cities and towns.	Approximate number immigrant employees.	Number of classes.	Average total number of immigrants attending.	Number of hours per year.

Remarks: Showing especially the cooperation furnished by the school authorities.
Recommendations:

F. Libraries.

Cities and towns.	Number libraries patronized by immigrants.	Estimated number immigrant patrons.	Number books— Foreign. English.	Estimated circulation among immigrants per year. Foreign. English.

Remarks: Is the number of foreign-language books in keeping with the foreign-language speaking population?
Recommendations:

G. Reading Rooms.

Cities and towns.	Number reading rooms patronized by immigrants.	Estimated number immigrant patrons.	Number papers. Foreign. English.

Remarks and suggestions:

III. OTHER FACILITIES AVAILABLE FOR IMMIGRANTS.

A. Racial Churches.

Cities and towns.	Number of racial churches.	Approximate membership.

Remarks and suggestions:

B. Racial Organizations.

Cities and towns.	Number of racial societies.	Approximate membership.

> *Remarks:* Possibilities of cooperation Accomplishments of foreign language societies, etc. Mention, if possible, enrollment of immigrants in English-speaking organizations such as Elks, Odd Fellows, Woodmen of the World, etc.
>
> *Recommendations:*

C. Foreign language newspapers published in ....

Cities and towns.	Number foreign-language papers.		Total circulation.
	Daily.	Other.	

> *Remarks:* Mention newspapers from other States which circulate to any extent in ...., etc.
>
> *Suggestions:*

D. Community Centers.

Cities and towns.	Number.	Approximate number of immigrants reached.

> *Remarks:* What funds are available in general for this work, and the legislation upon which it depends? What basis of cooperation is there between schools and community centers?
>
> *Suggestions:*

E. Legal Aid Societies.

Cities and towns.	Number of offices.	Approximate number of immigrants reached per year.

> *Remarks and suggestions:*

F. Information Bureaus Reaching Immigrants.

Cities and towns.	Number of offices.	Number of immigrants reached per year.

> *Remarks:* Describe the general nature and scope of the work, use of interpreters, foreign language translations, etc.
>
> *Suggestions:*

G. Housing Committee, Bureaus, etc.

Cities and towns.	Number.

> *Remarks:* Summary of reported housing conditions among immigrants.
>
> *Suggestions:*

H. Charity Organizations.

Cities and towns.	Number of agencies.	Total number assisted per year.	Number immigrants assisted per year.

> *Remarks:* Description of general plan of organization in the State, etc.
>
> *Suggestions:*

I. Recreational and Gymnastic Facilities

Cities and towns.	Number play-grounds.	Approximate number immigrants reached per year.	Number other recreational and gymnastic agencies.

Remarks and suggestions:

J. Health Agencies.

Cities and towns	Visiting nurse organ.	Approximate number immigrants reached per year.	Free dispensary.	Approximate number immigrants reached per year.	Child-welfare organ.	Approximate number immigrants reached per year.

Health inspection bureaus.	Approximate number immigrant cases per year.

Remarks: Institutions maintained by State and county governments and extent to which they reach immigrants.

Suggestions:

K. Penal Institutions.

Cities and towns.	Number.	Number of immigrants.

Remarks: Extent to which they are maintained by county and State government.

Suggestions:

Chapter V.

COORDINATION OF FORCES.

A State committee or commission having been formed or a State director appointed, there are certain definite steps that may be taken to inaugurate a State-wide program. If the legislature of the State has not yet recognized its duty and responsibility in the matter of Americanization, and the committee is an unofficial one, its first efforts should be directed toward securing the necessary legislation and appropriations properly to undertake the work.

Assuming that an unofficial committee has been appointed, representing the various State agencies and interests involved in Americanization, the first step should be to appoint an executive director and provide funds for operation. A temporary director may be secured from the State educational department or from the State university in its extension department. Either of these organizations may be induced to provide temporarily the services of such a man in order that the movement may be inaugurated and the educational system of the State made the auspices for its continuance.

At least a nominal fund may be secured by calling for contributions upon each of the State agencies working in the field of Americanization. The plans of the committee may be put in concrete form and a fund raised by public subscription from the industries, chambers of commerce, public-spirited citizens and other sources.

SECURING LEGISLATION.

The director and funds provided for a short period at least, a State-wide campaign should be undertaken to show the need for adequate legislation, to arouse the communities to action and to create a public sentiment which will enable the legislature at its first meeting to provide the necessary funds. When the legislature takes action, the unofficial committee may be disbanded or may offer its services in an advisory and coordinating way to the official charged with the responsibility for the work. It would seem wise for each State director to name some sort of a State committee to act as an advisory cabinet. Such a committee should preferably be representative of influential State forces or organizations rather than of sections of the State. If each of the great State agencies can thus be coordinated, even though unofficially, mutual understanding, harmony of action, and elimination of duplication will be greatly promoted.

23

One of the first tasks in Americanization is the provision of a body of properly trained teachers. The normal schools and State university may be induced to institute courses for the special training required and the committee can aid in securing recruits for the classes. Teachers' institutes may be held in various parts of the State. The Bureau of Education bulletin "Training Teachers for Americanization" will be found most helpful in planning the work of such classes or institutes.

State laws should be provided, if necessary, making English the primary language of the schools of the State, both public and private. All of the subjects of the school should be taught in English, and the school itself should be conducted in English in order that the future citizens of America may learn not only to talk but to think in the language of this land. Each State and community must decide for itself what foreign languages may be taught in the schools, but such languages should be taught in classroom periods exactly as all other subjects are taught and should not dominate the school.

It is hoped that the Federal department may be enabled to take an active part in bringing about the organization of the States and in forming expert agencies of service at Washington to assist the States and through them the communities in solving the problems relating to Americanization. The State department or committee must, however, undertake the task of correlating all of the agencies of the States—educational, industrial, racial, and social—in order that they may serve with methods, materials, and expert service the needs of the communities. The State department must also take the initiative in organizing or federating the forces of the community exactly as has been recommended for those of the State.

FINAL TASK THE COMMUNITY'S.

The great task of educating, protecting, and assimilating our foreign-born people must be performed by the communities where these people live and work. These communities must be organized and set at work. It should be unnecessary to create any new machinery within a community, for every community has already of its own initiative formed organizations and societies which are ready for the work. The task is to bring them together in one united force.

Practically all local agencies are branches of a State organization of similar character. It is those State organizations which possess such local agencies which must first be coordinated. Once the State organization is brought fully into the work, the way will be made easy for all of the community committees to make cooperative contact with the local agencies.

The State chamber of commerce, wherever it exists, should be a powerful factor in bringing back of the State program the influential and representative bodies which compose its membership. The State association of commercial secretaries whose members are the executive officers of the local chambers can wield a most helpful influence.

The State federation of labor, with its hundreds of local unions, is a necessary factor, for through the unions direct influence may be brought to bear upon the non-English-speaking workmen to enter the classes wherever they may be formed. Organized labor has recently taken a strong stand for the education of the illiterate and non-English-speaking people.

The State association of manufacturers represents a group which is indispensable in the work of Americanization. The active support and complete sympathy of the manufacturers must be secured by each community, and this can be greatly advanced by first securing the cooperation of the State association.

The State departments of education, of health, of industrial relations, and those other bureaus which are concerned in the broader aspects of Americanization should of course be brought into the plans. The State university, through its educational extension work, can be of very great assistance not only in the educational phases of the work but in the social aspects as well. Through its traveling libraries, film service, community center, and other work, the extension division can directly assist the communities in practical Americanization.

The State federation of women's clubs and the women's patriotic organizations can start a great force at work in every community in the State, and they should be brought completely into the plans of the State committee.

The special educational branches, such as home economics, kindergarten, and school nursing, can through their State leaders be of material assistance. The State organizations of the doctors, visiting nurses, lawyers, bankers, dentists, architects, and others can not only render direct assistance, but they can in turn spur their individual members to proffer their help to the local committees.

The State library association, the State Young Men's Christian Association, Young Women's Christian Association, Knights of Columbus, Young Men's Hebrew Association, and other semi-public institutions, the Boy and Girl Scouts, the social workers, the churches and the church organizations—all of these should be interested in the work.

Of an importance which is very great are the racial organizations. Many of the local racial societies are formed into State groups, and if the interest, sympathy, and support of the latter are once secured, that of the former will follow naturally.

In bringing all of these active agencies into a common program, great tact on the part of the State committee or director will be required.   Many of these agencies are already at work in the field.   It will not be an easy task to incorporate them into a common program, but it can be done.   The interests of the State and Nation are involved, and each organization must be impressed with the necessity for teamwork if the proper results are to be secured.

With vision, sympathy, tolerance, and a sincere friendliness toward the foreign born by those in authority within the States, with adequate funds for the provision of educational facilities for their needs, and with earnest and cordial cooperation on the part of all the powerful forces of the Nation, State, and community, America can within a decade weld all of its various peoples into one great, harmonious, homogeneous whole and the words of its national motto be at last achieved—"One out of many."

O

DEPARTMENT OF THE INTERIOR
BUREAU OF EDUCATION

BULLETIN, 1919, No. 78

SCHOOLS AND CLASSES FOR THE BLIND, 1917-18

PREPARED BY THE STATISTICAL DIVISION OF THE BUREAU OF EDUCATION

Under the supervision of
H. R. BONNER
Collector and Compiler of Statistics

[Advance Sheets from the Biennial Survey of Education
in the United States, 1916–1918]

WASHINGTON
GOVERNMENT PRINTING OFFICE
1920

SCHOOLS AND CLASSES FOR THE BLIND, 1917-18.

CONTENTS.—Number of schools reporting—Dual schools—Control—Instructors—Number of pupils—Graduates—Enrollment by grades—Enrollment by courses of study—Value of property—Volumes in libraries—How the States provide for the education of their blind—Receipts—Total expenditures—Statistical tables.

TABLE 1.—*Review of statistics of schools for the blind, 1900 to 1918.*

	1900	1901	1902	1903	1904	1905	1906	1907	1908
Number of schools reporting.	37	39	39	38	39	40	39	41	40
Instructors:									
Men	144	173	163	155	171	175	162	176	183
Women	293	299	324	313	321	330	317	342	339
Total	437	472	487	468	492	505	479	518	522
Pupils:									
Boys	2,104	2,222	2,363	2,374	2,304	2,401	2,264	2,318	2,304
Girls	1,917	1,977	1,952	1,989	1,932	2,040	1,941	2,041	2,036
Total	4,021	4,199	4,315	4,363	4,236	4,441	4,205	4,359	4,340
Graduates:									
Boys								75	70
Girls								71	54
Total	171	160	141	165	135	170	118	146	124
Pupils in industrial courses	2,235	2,649	2,948	2,667	2,684	3,201	2,871	2,924	2,832
Instrumental music	1,883	1,998	2,242	2,233	2,338	2,354	2,266	1,990	2,066
Vocal culture	1,815	2,237	2,076	2,216	2,016	2,211	2,095	1,707	1,895
Volumes in the library:									
In raised type								88,493	95,325
In ink								40,026	41,126
Total	94,689	103,626	105,804	106,655	121,062	125,581	105,785	128,519	136,451

	1909	1910	1911	1912	1913	1914	1915	1916	1918
Number of schools reporting.	41	48	53	60	64	62	62	61	62
Instructors:									
Men	187	178	195	202	205	202	211	198	201
Women	347	353	406	450	460	463	491	489	527
Total	534	531	601	652	665	665	702	687	728
Pupils:									
Boys	2,271	2,263	2,453	2,639	2,615	2,601	2,731	2,724	2,867
Girls	2,142	2,060	2,217	2,353	2,358	2,370	2,522	2,431	2,519
Total	4,413	4,323	4,670	4,992	4,973	4,971	5,253	5,155	5,386
Graduates:									
Boys	47	39	56	59	55	63	57	50	85
Girls	55	50	38	52	64	45	55	58	78
Total	102	89	94	111	119	108	112	108	163
Pupils in industrial courses	2,960	2,855	3,041	3,268	3,523	3,754	3,702	3,577	8,164
Instrumental music	2,013	1,752	1,936	2,207	2,354	2,467	2,417	2,450	2,437
Vocal culture	1,855	1,317	1,853	2,057	2,073	2,556	2,228	2,306	2,370
Volumes in the library:									
In raised type	104,864	80,774	87,400	135,339	109,112	115,096	127,247	137,284	149,621
In ink	51,687	34,754	40,354	53,482	53,830	49,468	54,788	60,622	52,402
Total	156,551	115,528	127,754	188,821	162,942	164,564	182,035	197,906	202,023

NUMBER OF SCHOOLS REPORTING.

This report, for 1917–18, includes the statistics of 62 schools for the blind. In addition to these, 9 other such schools, known to be in existence, did not submit a report. The list of institutions not reporting this year follows. By including these schools this chapter serves as a complete directory of schools for the blind.

Arkansas School for the Blind, Little Rock, Ark.
Florida School for the Deaf and Blind (both white and colored), St. Augustine, Fla.
Georgia Academy for the Blind (colored only), Macon, Ga.
Louisiana State School for the Blind, Baton Rouge, La.
Tennessee School for the Blind (colored only), Nashville, Tenn.
Virginia State School for Colored Deaf and Blind Children, Newport News, Va.
Racine Day School for the Blind, Racine, Wis.
Catholic Institute for the Blind, One hundred and seventy-fifth Street and University Avenue, New York City.

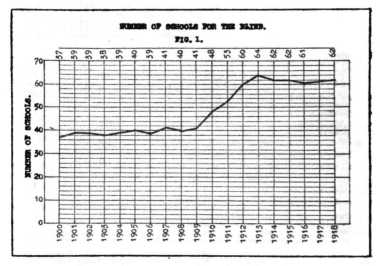

NUMBER OF SCHOOLS FOR THE BLIND.
FIG. 1.

The Institution for the Deaf, Blind, and Orphans (colored only) at Taft, Okla., has had thus far no blind pupils to report.

The Austine Institution for the Deaf and Blind, Brattleboro, Vt., no longer admits blind pupils and is not properly included in this chapter.

The highest number of schools reporting in any year was in 1913, when 64 schools were represented. The increase from 41 schools in 1909 to 64 schools in 1913 is very pronounced. The decrease since the latter date is due to the failure of certain institutions to report and not to an actual decrease in the number of such schools, as will be noted from the list of delinquent schools given above.

DUAL SCHOOLS.

Thirteen of the 62 schools reporting in 1918 are dual schools, i. e., they are schools for both deaf and blind. These schools, therefore, will appear again in the chapter on "Schools for the deaf," wherein the statistics relating to all schools for the deaf will be found. Altogether, 14 States provide for such dual schools, viz, Alabama (colored only), California, Colorado, Florida (both white and colored), Idaho, Maryland (colored only), Montana, Oklahoma (colored only), North Carolina (colored only), South Carolina (both white and colored), Texas (colored only), Utah, Virginia (both white and colored), and West Virginia. As explained in a preceding paragraph, the dual schools in Florida and Oklahoma (colored only) are not represented in the statistics of this report.

In addition to the 13 dual schools represented herein, there are 2 other schools of this character which did not report in 1918. They are listed in the first paragraph of this chapter. So far as the reports indicate, all dual schools are State institutions.

CONTROL.

Ten of the schools for the blind included in this report are maintained as a part of the city public school system and are located as follows: Chicago, Ill.; Detroit, Mich.; Jersey City, N. J.; Newark, N. J; New York City; Cincinnati, Cleveland, Mansfield, and Toledo, Ohio; and Milwaukee, Wis. Four schools are under private control or management: St. Joseph's Asylum for Blind Girls, Prince Bay, N. Y.; the International Sunshine Society, Summit, N. J., and Brooklyn, N. Y.; New York Institute for the Education of the Blind (412 Ninth Avenue), New York City; and Brooklyn Home for Blind, Crippled, and Defective Children, Port Jefferson, N. Y. The Perkins Institution and Massachusetts School for the Blind, Watertown, Mass., is under private control but receives State aid. All other schools listed in this chapter in the detailed statistical tables are State institutions.

INSTRUCTORS.

The number of instructors in schools and classes for the blind has increased almost steadily since 1900, from 437 at that time to 728 in 1918, or an increase of over 66 per cent within this period. The curve representing the total number of instructors is governed very largely by the curve in figure 1, which represents the number of schools reporting. Despite the fact that fewer schools have reported since 1913, the number of instructors has continued to increase. The largest number reported in any year was 728, in 1918.

The majority of the teachers in schools for the blind are women. In 1900 the men numbered about half as many as the women. In 1918 over 72 per cent of all teachers in these schools were women.

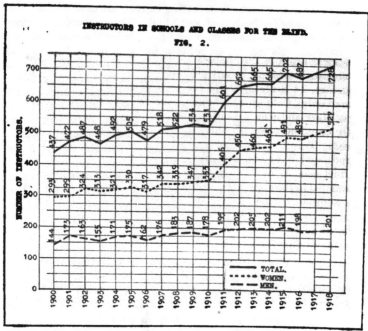

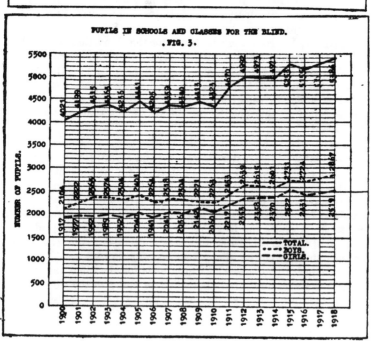

NUMBER OF PUPILS.

The number of pupils in schools and classes for the blind in 1918 was 5,386. In 18 years, as shown in figure 3, the number of pupils has increased from 4,021 to 5,386, or over 31 per cent. The "total" curve in this figure follows in general the same course as that shown in figure 1, representing the number of schools.

In a preceding paragraph it was shown that the number of teachers increased 66 per cent within this same period of 18 years. These percentages imply that teachers are not obliged to instruct so many pupils at present as they did several years ago. The average number of pupils per teacher in 1900 was 9, as against 7 in 1918.

The number of boys slightly exceeds the number of girls in schools for the blind. This difference has been practically the same since 1900, as shown in figure 3, indicating that the data within this period have been remarkably consistent.

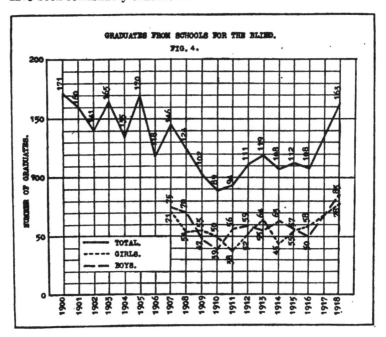

GRADUATES FROM SCHOOLS FOR THE BLIND.

FIG. 4.

GRADUATES.

The data on the number of graduates prior to 1910 are not very reliable, since the blank used in collecting this information did not specify that only graduates from the secondary school should be reported. This indefiniteness in the question accounts for the zigzag nature of the curve in figure 4 prior to that date. In general, since

1910 the number of graduates has increased. The relatively high numbers, 111 and 119, respectively, reported in 1912 and 1913, are due largely to the high points in the curve in figure 1 representing these years, when an unusual number of schools reported. The number of graduates has been about equally divided between boys and girls. The interweaving of the curves representing boys and girls in figure 4 is probably due to the small number of graduates reported annually.

ENROLLMENT BY GRADES.

The distribution of pupils by grade groups is shown in Table 3. In the kindergarten, 498 pupils were enrolled; in grades,1 to 4, 2,138 pupils; in grades 5 to 8, 1,614 pupils; and in classes corresponding to the high-school grades, 1,005 pupils. Only 2 of the 62 schools reporting did not make this distribution by grade groups. Of the 5,245 pupils represented in this distribution, 9 per cent were in kindergartens, 41 per cent in grades 1 to 4, 31 per cent in grades 5 to 8, and 19 per cent in high school. About one-fifth of those in high schools graduated. One-half the pupils are below the fifth grade and the other half are in the fifth grade or above.

ENROLLMENT BY COURSES OF STUDY.

The number of pupils enrolled in the different courses of study in schools and classes for the blind are represented graphically in figure 5. The number reported in 1918 was 3,164. Of this number, 1,686 pupils were boys and 1,478 girls. Since 1900 the curve for the number of pupils in industrial or trade training courses has stood above the curves for the enrollment in music courses. The trend of this curve follows that in figure 1, showing that the enrollment in trade courses is proportional to the number of schools reporting. The highest number of pupils in these courses was reported in 1914, when the greatest number of schools reported. The decided drop in 1918 is probably due to war conditions. Presumably most of the trade courses are taught by men, and the draft would necessarily deplete the male teaching force. Further, there was a special demand for men who could teach trade-training courses. In corresponding courses in the other chapters of this Biennial Survey a decrease is shown for 1918.

The number enrolled in music courses is also shown in figure 5. In general the number in instrumental music exceeds the number in vocal culture. A decided drop in the number in vocal culture is noted in 1910 and a decided increase in 1914, which are both probably due to erroneous reports. In general these two curves do not rise so rapidly as the upper curve for enrollment in trade courses. This tendency indicates that increased emphasis is placed on industrial work.

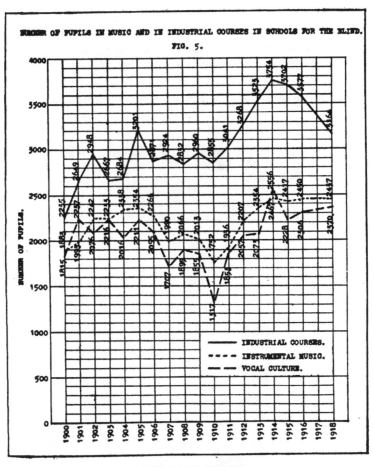

NUMBER OF PUPILS IN MUSIC AND IN INDUSTRIAL COURSES IN SCHOOLS FOR THE BLIND.

FIG. 5.

VALUE OF PROPERTY.

Altogether, 54 schools reported the value of property as follows: Buildings and grounds, $11,586,064; apparatus, furniture, library, etc., $1,378,231; permanent endowment or productive funds, $3,306,964. In 1915-16, 48 schools reported for these items $10,152,802, $916,426, and $3,590,278, respectively. A slight decrease in productive funds is shown. The 6 additional schools reporting the value of property in 1918 may account largely for the increased value of buildings and grounds and for apparatus, etc. Assuming that the 8 schools not reporting the value of property in 1918 had the average value of $214,557 for buildings and grounds, and $25,523 for apparatus, etc., the total value of the former item for the 62 schools reporting would be $13,302,520 and for the latter item,

$1,582,415. These amounts are probably high, since city schools for the blind usually do not report the value of property, inasmuch as separate buildings for blind pupils are seldom provided.

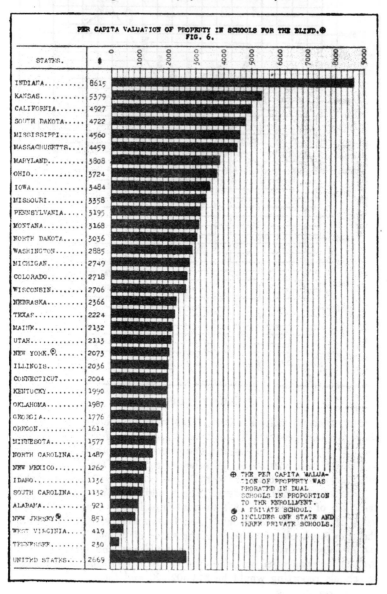

PER CAPITA VALUATION OF PROPERTY IN SCHOOLS FOR THE BLIND.⊕
FIG. 6.

STATES.	$
INDIANA	8615
KANSAS	5379
CALIFORNIA	4927
SOUTH DAKOTA	4722
MISSISSIPPI	4560
MASSACHUSETTS	4459
MARYLAND	3808
OHIO	3724
IOWA	3484
MISSOURI	3358
PENNSYLVANIA	3195
MONTANA	3168
NORTH DAKOTA	3036
WASHINGTON	2885
MICHIGAN	2749
COLORADO	2718
WISCONSIN	2706
NEBRASKA	2366
TEXAS	2224
MAINE	2132
UTAH	2113
NEW YORK.⊙	2073
ILLINOIS	2036
CONNECTICUT	2004
KENTUCKY	1990
OKLAHOMA	1987
GEORGIA	1776
OREGON	1614
MINNESOTA	1577
NORTH CAROLINA	1487
NEW MEXICO	1262
IDAHO	1156
SOUTH CAROLINA	1132
ALABAMA	921
NEW JERSEY.✿	851
WEST VIRGINIA	419
TENNESSEE	230
UNITED STATES	2669

⊕ THE PER CAPITA VALUA-
TION OF PROPERTY WAS
PRORATED IN DUAL
SCHOOLS IN PROPORTION
TO THE ENROLLMENT.
✿ A PRIVATE SCHOOL.
⊙ INCLUDES ONE STATE AND
THREE PRIVATE SCHOOLS.

VOLUMES IN LIBRARIES.

In schools for the blind two kinds of libraries are usually found, one with books in raised type and the other with books printed in ink. The statistics on the number of volumes in libraries are not very reliable, since dual schools sometimes reported the number of volumes printed in ink with the library used by the department for the deaf, and since often a school reported the total number of volumes interchangeably, under one nomenclature or the other. As shown in Table 1 the data on the number of volumes in ink vary considerably from year to year, being the lowest in 1910, when 34,754 volumes were reported, and highest in 1916, when 60,622 volumes were reported. The number of volumes in raised type shows a more stable tendency, rising almost steadily from 88,493 volumes in 1907 to 149,621 volumes in 1918. The data on libraries previous to 1907 do not distinguish between these two types. The totals for each year more nearly represent the general tendency to increase the number of volumes. In Table 5 it will be noted that in several instances the library statistics in dual schools have been included in the chapter on schools for the deaf, thereby decreasing correspondingly the number of volumes reported in this chapter. The average total number of volumes in the libraries of the 48 schools reporting is 4,270.

HOW THE STATES PROVIDE FOR THE EDUCATION OF THEIR BLIND.

An index as to the interest manifested by a State in educating its blind is the per capita investment for each blind person in its institutions. In figure 6 it is seen that Indiana has property valued at $8,615 for each person in its school for the blind. Kansas ranks second, with a per capita valuation of $5,379. The corresponding average per capita for the United States is $2,669. In the construction of this figure, only those schools were used that reported both the valuation of property and the total enrollment for the year. . A State having large schools necessarily has a lower per capita valuation than a State with a small school, where the per capita cost of housing, etc., is necessarily high. This fact must be considered in judging a State near the bottom of the list. The data on which figure 6 is based are shown in Table 2. In the case of dual schools the valuation of property has been prorated between deaf and blind in proportion to the enrollment in each as shown in the detailed tables of this chapter.

It should be remembered that the schools included in the construction of this figure are not all State institutions. The school representing New Jersey is a private school. Only one of the four schools for New York is a State institution. In all other instances the State is represented by State institutions.

12 BIENNIAL SURVEY OF EDUCATION, 1916–1918.

RECEIPTS.

In all, 49 schools for the blind reported their receipts aggregating $2,385,049, or an average of $48,674 per school. Of this total, $2,304,278 was itemized as follows: $1,724,969, or about 75 per cent, came from public funds; $89,101, or over 4 per cent, from private benefactions; $267,336, or over 11 per cent, from endowment funds; and $222,872, or almost 10 per cent, from other sources. The significant implication of these data is that about three-fourths of the income of all schools for the blind comes from public sources, usually from the State.

Thirteen schools represented in this report did not give a statement of their income. If these schools each received the average indicated above, the total receipts of all 62 schools reporting would be $3,017,811. This total is only a gross estimate and should be used with caution. The schools not submitting any report whatever for 1917–18 have not been considered in estimating this total.

EXPENDITURES.

Altogether, 52 schools for the blind reported their expenditures, amounting to $2,459,252, or an average of $47,293 per school. Of this amount $2,404,169 was itemized by function as follows: For buildings and other lasting improvements, $393,032, or over 16 per cent; for teachers' salaries, books, etc., $547,663, or almost 23 per cent; and for other salaries and all other current expenses, $1,463,474, or about 61 per cent. If the average for the 10 schools not reporting expenditures was the same as that for those reporting, the total expenditures for the 62 schools represented in this report would be $2,932,182. This amount is almost equal to the estimated total receipts for the same schools given above, viz, $3,017,811. This comparatively slight difference signifies that these totals are essentially correct. The validity of these estimates is further supported by the fact that receipts usually exceed expenditures.

Figure 7 shows the amount of money spent in 1918 on each person in schools for the blind in the different States represented. The States are arranged in the order of the per capita cost for current expenses. Montana spent $1,178 for each person for current expenses and $556 additional for buildings, sites, or other permanent improvements. Maine ranks second with a per capita of $865, and Massachusetts third with a per capita cost of $845. The corresponding per capita amount going for current expenses for the United States is $428 and for outlays $82. This graph is a good index as to the importance which a State attaches to the education of its blind. In the case of dual schools the expenditures have been prorated between deaf and blind in proportion to the enrollment in each type of school as shown in Table 6.

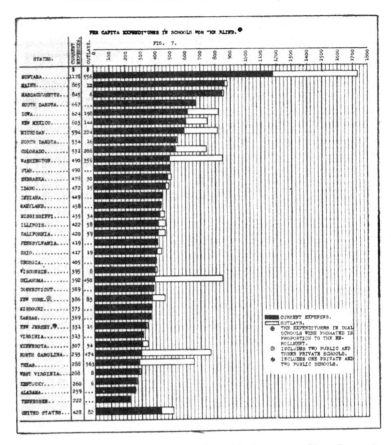

It should be kept in mind in reading this figure that New Jersey is represented by a private school and two city schools for the blind; New York by one State, one city, and three private schools; and Ohio by one State and two city schools. It is altogether proper, however, to include these municipal and private schools in ranking the States, since it is evident that these city and private schools are patronized by State pupils, and, therefore, reduce the responsibility of the State in providing for these blind pupils in a State institution. All the private schools represented in this report receive public funds and usually pupils are admitted at the request of some State officer. They serve, therefore, in several ways as State schools and are properly included in the graph.

TABLE 2.—*Per capita expenditures and per capita value of property in schools for the blind, 1917-18.*

States.	Per capita expenditures.						Per capita value of property.			
	Schools reporting.	Enrollment in these schools.	Total current expenses.	Outlays.	Current expenses per capita.	Outlays per capita.	Schools reporting.	Enrollment in these schools.	Value of property in these schools.	Value per capita.
United Stat	52	4,805	$2,054,743	$392,942	$428	$82	48	4,854	$12,955,780	$2,669
Alabama	2	115	29,737		259		1	115	105,935	921
California	1	99	41,580	5,807	420	59	1	99	487,760	4,927
Colorado	1	46	24,426	9,476	531	206	1	46	125,028	2,718
Connecticut	2	54	20,999		389		2	54	108,223	2,004
Georgia	1	76	30,750		405		1	76	135,000	1,776
Idaho	1	22	10,380	1,000	472	15	1	22	25,000	1,136
Illinois	1	206	88,000	12,000	422	58	1	206	419,400	2,036
Indiana	1	119	53,858		449		1	119	1,025,229	8,615
Iowa	1	101	63,000	20,000	624	198	1	101	351,900	3,484
Kansas	1	103	38,000		369		1	103	554,000	5,379
Kentucky	2	148	38,451	855	260	6	2	148	295,632	1,990
Maine	1	27	23,365	321	865	12	1	27	57,565	2,132
Maryland	2	135	47,622		438		2	133	506,500	3,808
Massachusetts	1	312	263,758	1,794	845	6	1	312	1,391,058	4,459
Michigan	2	195	115,981	43,676	594	224	2	195	534,907	2,740
Minnesota	1	157	48,123	5,320	307	34	1	157	247,630	1,577
Mississippi	1	58	25,251	2,000	435	34	1	58	264,500	4,567
Missouri	1	125	46,618		373		1	125	419,724	3,358
Montana	1	24	28,272	13,344	1,178	556	1	24	76,039	3,168
Nebraska	1	67	31,000	2,000	478	30	1	67	158,500	2,366
New Jersey	3	76	25,189	1,168	331	15	1	47	40,000	811
New Mexico	1	52	31,376	7,500	603	144	1	52	65,600	1,262
New York	5	723	278,744	59,649	386	83	4	594	1,232,597	2,075
North Carolina	2	224	65,544	106,300	293	474	2	224	333,196	1,487
North Dakota	1	28	14,950	450	534	16	1	28	85,000	3,036
Ohio	3	257	107,084	5,000	417	19	1	200	744,801	3,724
Oklahoma	1	111	43,500	50,000	392	450	1	111	220,600	1,987
Oregon							1	35	56,500	1,614
Pennsylvania	2	408	171,119		419		2	408	1,303,480	3,195
South Carolina							1	61	69,077	1,132
South Dakota	1	18	12,000		667		1	18	85,000	4,722
Tennessee	1	207	45,853		222		1	207	47,600	230
Texas	1	73	21,024	22,119	288	363	2	304	676,072	2,224
Utah	1	39	19,110		490		1	39	82,417	2,113
Virginia	1	64	20,000		313		1	64	44,470	697
Washington	1	59	28,920	21,000	490	356	1	59	169,212	2,881
West Virginia	1	76	21,888	608	288	8	1	76	31,800	411
Wisconsin	2	201	79,271	1,555	395	8	1	140	378,829	2,703

TABLE 3.—*Summary of statistics of schools for the blind, 1917: 18.*

States	Number of schools reporting	Instructors — Men	Instructors — Women	Instructors — Total	Pupils enrolled — Boys	Pupils enrolled — Girls	Pupils enrolled — Total	Pupils in the kindergarten — Boys	Pupils in the kindergarten — Girls	Pupils in the kindergarten — Total	In classes corresponding to grades 1 to 4 — Boys	In classes corresponding to grades 1 to 4 — Girls	In classes corresponding to grades 1 to 4 — Total	In classes corresponding to grades 5 to 8 — Boys	In classes corresponding to grades 5 to 8 — Girls	In classes corresponding to grades 5 to 8 — Total	In classes corresponding to high school grades — Boys	In classes corresponding to high school grades — Girls	In classes corresponding to high school grades — Total	Graduates in 1918 — Boys	Graduates in 1918 — Girls	Graduates in 1918 — Total	Pupils in Industrial department — Vocal culture	Pupils in Industrial department — Instrumental music	Pupils in Industrial department — Boys	Pupils in Industrial department — Girls	Pupils in Industrial department — Total
	2	**3**	**4**	**5**	**6**	**7**	**8**	**9**	**10**	**11**	**12**	**13**	**14**	**15**	**16**	**17**	**18**	**19**	**20**	**21**	**22**	**23**	**24**	**25**	**26**	**27**	**28**
United States	62	201	527	728	2,867	2,519	5,386	261	237	499	1,161	967	2,128	828	786	1,614	512	492	1,005	85	78	163	2,370	2,437	1,686	1,478	3,164
Alabama	2	7	8	15	57	58	115				30	18	48	13	22	35	3	7	10	3	3	6	20	70	37	27	64
Arkansas	1			4	15	14	29				4	4	8	4	7	11	3	3	6	1	1	3	27	18	13	12	25
California	1	14	14	19	50	40	90				18	14	32	15	4	19	11	11	14	1	1	0	76	76	20	19	39
Colorado	2	7	12	11	27	19	46				17	12	27	8	6	9	4	3	8	0	0	0	41	28	20	19	34
Connecticut	2	4	8	9	29	29	54				12	12	24	6	9	16	3	5	8	1	0	1	41	15	15	19	34
Georgia	1	2	9	11	40	36	76	1	1		23	17	40	11	10	21	6	9	15				74	68	9		9
Idaho	1	2	3	5	16	6	22	1			4	3	9	4	4	10	6	6					30	19	22	50	22
Illinois	1	10	22	32	138	119	257	8	10	18	41	39	80	44	42	88	38	38	61	2	4	7	88	78	97	56	97
Indiana	2	4	13	17	63	56	119	8	8	16	29	20	49	23	23	37	9	8	14	7	3	3	98	94	68	55	119
Iowa	1	5	14	14	51	50	101	4	2	6	17	18	35	15	15	18	14	14	37	1	1	8	88	58	40	35	75
Kansas	1	2	11	15	58	45	103	5	5	10	26	18	44	12	13	25	12	12	7	2	2	9	33	48	52	45	48
Kentucky	2	2	12	15	77	71	148	16	6	20	30	28	58	22	19	41	11	11	43	1	1	1	148	55	41	24	44
Maine	1		10	9	21	9	27				30	4	4	16	21	37	13	13	81	6	6	6	38	88	58	24	33
Maryland	2	4	13	17	61	74	185	6	6	10	49	48	256	4	11	12	17	17	62	1	0	0	27	101	87	82	98
Massachusetts	1	7	13	49	134	160	312	18	13	35	63	40	103	40	25	25	22	22	65	2	3	15	92	58	88	66	98
Michigan	1	2	11	28	105	105	210	10	10	15	11	11	14	6	6	10	10	10	10	0	0	9	27	60	87	90	167
Minnesota	3	7	12	16	90	61	157	13	17	19	41	13	24	13	12	30	3	3	3	1	1	1	92	57	88	50	186
Mississippi	1	4	11	12	30	28	58	8	9	11	15	15	33	12	9	24	2	2	2	3	1	2	58	94	81	25	46
Missouri	2	5	13	18	68	57	135	11	11	17	18	17	17	8	5	7	1	1	10	8	8	6	10	212	180	197	49
Montana	1	2	3	2	15	9	24	3	3		63	6	103	3	5	2	2	2	30	3	3	5	38	58	102	68	19
Nebraska	2	2	6	6	41	26	67	10	10	5	11	11	14	6	6	10	7	7	10	0	0	0	36	35	10	8	18
New Jersey	1	10	10	10	43	83	76	13	13	9	11	18	24	18	12	30	1	1	3	1	1	1	44	12	12	25	28
New Mexico	3	1	6	8	27	25	52	2	2	4	148	15	33	8	2	4	2	2	121	10	10	2	284	28	180	197	52
New York	1	13	21	81	373	359	734	53	55	108	148	108	256	111	133	244	61	61	39	3	3	25	96	38	102	66	377
North Carolina	2	6	9	30	134	90	224	3	3	17	63	40	103	40	25	65	22	22		1	1	3	98				168

TABLE 3.—*Summary of statistics of schools for the blind, 1917-18—Continued.*

States	Number of schools reporting	Instructors			Pupils entered			Pupils in the kindergarten			In classes corresponding to grades 1 to 4			In classes corresponding to grades 5 to 8			In classes corresponding to high school grades			Graduates in 1918			Pupils in—				
		Men	Women	Total	Boys	Girls	Total	Boys	Girls	Total	Boys	Girls	Total	Boys	Girls	Total	Boys	Girls	Total	Boys	Girls	Total	Vocal culture	Instrumental music	Industrial department		
																									Boys	Girls	Total
1	2	3	4	5	6	7	8	9	10	11	12	13	14	15	16	17	18	19	20	21	22	23	24	25	26	27	28
North Dakota	1	1	4	5	13	15	28	0	0	0	4	5	10	6	3	9	3	6	9	0	0	0	26	18	7	0	7
Ohio	1	22	38	60	201	178	379	8	4	12	78	70	148	70	68	146	20	24	44	11	3	11	236	229	130	90	220
Oklahoma	1	5	11	16	67	44	111	20	19	39	15	15	30	28	5	30	9	3	12	0	1	1	100	40	19	35	67
Oregon	1	1	4	5	19	16	35	5	1	6	9	9	15	5	4	10	4	1	4	0	0	0	31	31	19	16	35
Pennsylvania	2	14	37	51	207	201	408	37	24	61	70	69	139	37	45	82	47	40	87	14	7	14	130	140	121	121	212
South Carolina	2	3	8	11	44	43	87	0	0	0	17	20	37	14	13	27	13	10	24	0	0	0	87	70	44	43	87
South Dakota	1	1	3	4	6	12	18	3	3	3	6	3	9	0	3	3	9	2	9	3	3	1	21	10	6	12	18
Tennessee	1	12	12	17	114	93	207	7	7	14	45	35	80	33	32	65	36	26	62	4	4	8	81	100	90	81	171
Texas	2	15	24	39	105	132	304	0	0	0	31	69	150	44	38	82	32	26	58	1	1	0	38	147	82	83	165
Utah	1	3	4	7	17	22	39	0	0	0	6	12	18	11	7	18	3	3	3	0	0	0	38	10			
Virginia	1	3	9	12	24	40	64	0	0	0	16	26	42	5	8	13	3	0	9	2	2	2	45	55	30	30	40
Washington	1	7	7	10	33	23	59	0	0	0	13	12	25	16	2	18	4	2	6	0	0	0	2	35	40	15	55
West Virginia	1	6	6	12	51	25	76	0	0	0	28	13	41	14	6	14	9	6	15	0	0	0	60	35	42	65	117
Wisconsin	2	6	17	23	116	85	201	5	7	12	43	30	73	51	30	81	17	18	35	4	2	4	112	100	83	65	117

TABLE 4.—*Summary of statistics of receipts, expenditures, and property of schools for the blind, 1917-18.*

		Receipts					Expenditures					Property					
													Volumes in library				
States	Number of schools reporting	From State, county or city	From private benefactions for permanent equipment and current expenses	From productive endowment funds	From other sources	Total	Number of schools reporting	For building and lasting improvements	For teachers' salaries, books, etc.	For other salaries and all other current expenses	Total	Number of schools reporting	In raised type	In ink	Value of buildings and grounds	Value of scientific apparatus, instruments, furniture, library, etc.	Permanent endowment or productive funds
1	2	3	4	5	6	7	8	9	10	11	12	13	14	15	16	17	18
United States	49	$1,724,090	390,101	267,336	222,872	$2,385,049	52	$388,082	$547,068	$1,463,474	$2,499,282	54	149,621	52,402	$11,586,064	$1,378,231	$3,306,994
Alabama	2	28,290				28,290	2		7,189	22,555	29,787	2	1,928	575	97,113	8,822	
California	1	47,520				47,620	1	5,807	22,374	19,206	47,387	2	2,000		461,390	26,391	24,055
Colorado	1	35,742				35,742	1	5,476	24,426		33,902	1	1,498		98,272	26,756	
Connecticut	2	11,500	5,973	1,909	375	126,846	2		24,468		120,999	2	551	158	107,096	1,126	40,873
Georgia	1	30,000				30,000	1	1,000	5,480	4,900	130,750	1	1,500	1,200	125,000	10,000	0
Idaho	1	9,794				9,794	1		51,000	37,000	11,380		15,000	5,000	25,000		
Illinois	1	100,000				100,000	1	12,000	25,246	28,612	100,000	1	6,984	3,451	319,400	100,000	0
Indiana	1	53,839			241	54,100	1		10,000	53,000	53,838	1	600	3,000	983,100	42,129	
Iowa	1	70,000			13,200	83,200	1	20,000			53,000	1	600	3,000	326,900	26,000	
Kansas	1	38,000				38,000	1	835	15,089	23,000	38,000	1	1,500	500	500,000	54,000	0
Kentucky	2	38,992			359	39,351	2	321	13,800	24,651	39,306	2	1,200	800	275,000	20,682	46,000
Maine	1	6,975		99	12,465	19,559	1		2,556	20,800	23,686	1			65,397	2,168	14,263
Maryland	1	37,500			71,533	145,438	2	1,794	12,391	46,708	59,099	1	4,450	1,525	496,000	10,500	0
Massachusetts	1		36,017	118,463		263,513	1		31,140	232,018	265,552	3	14,791	9,708	1,215,690	175,422	2,070,425
Michigan	2	134,998	0	0	65,644	1 212,702	2	43,766	5,000	110,981	159,747	3	8,080	1,632	418,784	116,123	0
Minnesota	1	53,443	0			53,443	1	5,320		48,123	53,443	1	4,500	1,500	235,900	16,830	0
Mississippi	1		0	600	0	600	1	2,000	10,000	15,261	27,251	1	800	600	260,000	14,500	1,500
Missouri	1	46,619				46,619	1	13,344	10,732	35,886	46,618	1	3,548	102	379,352	40,372	0
Montana	0	(2)				(2)			14,495	13,776	41,616	1			66,388	9,651	

1 Includes totals not itemized.　　2 No report on receipts.

TABLE 4.—*Summary of statistics of receipts, expenditures, and property of schools for the blind, 1917-18*—Continued.

States.	Number of schools reporting.	Receipts.					Number of schools reporting.	Expenditures.				Number of schools reporting.	Volumes in library.		Property.		
		From State, county, or city.	From private benefactions for permanent equipment and current expenses.	From productive endowment funds.	From other sources.	Total.		For building and lasting improvements.	For teachers' salaries, books, etc.	For other salaries and all other current expenses.	Total.		In raised type.	In ink.	Value of buildings and grounds.	Value of scientific apparatus, instruments, furniture, library, etc.	Permanent endowment or productive funds.
1	2	3	4	5	6	7	8	9	10	11	12	13	14	15	16	17	18
Nebraska	1	$30,000			$3,000	$33,000	1	$2,000	$12,500	$18,500	$33,000	1	1,000	1,000	$125,000	$33,500	0
New Jersey	3	22,218			4,451	26,679	3	1,168	2,387	19,468	26,357	1	53	92	30,000	10,415	
New Mexico	1	32,468	$25,366	$6,902	296	39,625	1	7,500		31,376	38,876	1	774		60,000	5,000	0
New York	4	185,351		69,684	35,108	315,512	5	59,649	65,977	212,787	338,388	6	8,670	5,335	1,065,014	170,083	
North Carolina	2	157,732		0	0	157,732	2	105,300	23,748	41,706	171,844	2	2,600	1,478	818,992	14,204	806,018
North Dakota	1	0		13,573	627	14,200	1	450	5,480	9,470	15,400	1	800	900	75,000	10,000	0
Ohio	3	113,404				113,404	3	5,000	36,080	71,004	112,084	1	2,450	900	670,800	74,200	
Oklahoma	1	98,500				93,500	1	50,000	17,000	26,500	93,500	1	900	2,200	190,000	30,600	
Oregon	2	102,381	21,762	40,000	13,011	177,174	2		45,858	125,261	177,119	2	23,969	4,846	50,000	6,500	900,018
Pennsylvania															1,245,661	57,819	
South Carolina	1	(¹)		1,500		(²)	1	0	3,000	9,000	(²)	1	600	600	67,077	$2,300	0
South Dakota	1	39,982				39,982	1	22,119	12,553	33,300	45,583	1	1,300	1,200	70,000	15,000	
Tennessee	1	44,019		3,030		44,143	1		4,086	16,995	43,143	1	6,000	2,150	25,000	22,600	0
Texas	1	15,620				18,660	1		6,370	12,740	19,110	1	21,800	260	553,512	122,560	
Utah												2	2,000		75,685	6,782	
Virginia	1	20,000				20,000	1	21,000	4,000	16,000	20,000	1	800	200	41,705	2,675	99,840
Washington	0	(²)				(⁴)	0		16,485	12,485	49,920	1	700		186,135	11,077	
West Virginia	1	23,560			1,216	24,776	1	608	9,728	12,160	22,496	1	300	75	30,400	1,400	
Wisconsin	2	86,532			1,376	87,908	2	1,855	21,696	57,685	80,286	2	1,908	2,025	269,334	80,405	0

¹ Includes totals not itemized.   ² No report on receipts.   ³ No report on expenditures.   ⁴ Includes $300, the value of the library in another school.

TABLE 5.—Statistics of schools for the blind, 1917-18.

Location	Institution	Instructors		Pupils enrolled		Pupils in the kindergarten		In classes corresponding to grades 1 to 4.		In classes corresponding to grades 5 to 8.		In classes corresponding to high-school grades.		Graduates in 1918.		Pupils in				Volumes in library.		Property		
																Vocal culture.	Instrumental music.	Industrial departments.				Value of buildings and grounds.	Value of scientific apparatus, instruments, furniture, library, etc.	Permanent endowment or productive fund.
1	2	Men 3	Women 4	Boys 5	Girls 6	Boys 7	Girls 8	Boys 9	Girls 10	Boys 11	Girls 12	Boys 13	Girls 14	Boys 15	Girls 16	17	18	Boys 19	Girls 20	In raised type. 21	In ink. 22	23	24	25
Talladega, Ala.	Alabama School for the Blind	4	8	47	47	0	0	30	18	13	22	3	3	3	3	30	63	33	27	1,926	575	$85,000	$8,000	
Do.	Alabama School for the Negro Deaf and Blind	3	6	10	11	(¹)	0	4	4	4	7				1	4	7	4	12			*12,113	*$822	
Little Rock, Ark.	Arkansas School for the Blind	1	3	15	14	0	4	18	4	4	7	3	3	7	3	27	18	13	12	2,000	(²)	461,369	26,391	$27,055
Berkeley, Calif.	California School for Deaf and Blind (Negro).	5	14	30	49	4	0	17	14	15	18	11	13	2	1	79	76	20	19	² 1,498	(?)	*68,272	*³,756	
Colorado Springs, Colo.	Colorado School for the Deaf and the Blind.			27	19	0	0	17	10	6	4	4	5	0	0	41	26	20	19			13,000	⁴ 125	
Farmington, Conn.	Nursery for Blind	1		4	4															51	58	94,098	⁴ 1,000	
Hartford, Conn.	Connecticut Institute for the Blind (school department).	2	2	25	21	1	2	4	2	9	6	6	9	2	0	5	25	15	19	500	100			
Macon, Ga.	Georgia Academy for the Blind	2	3	40	36	1	0	23	17	11	10	6	9		2	74	58	9	9	1,500	1,200	125,000	10,000	40,873
Gooding, Idaho	Idaho State School for the Deaf and the Blind.	4		16	6			5	3	4	1	6	2	1	2	20	19	16				*25,000		
Chicago, Ill.	Chicago Public Schools for the Blind.	1	3	33	18	8	1	11	5	8	6	6	7	1	1	30	25	2	0					0
Jacksonville, Ill.	Illinois School for the Blind.	9	19	105	101	10	10	30	34	34	31	19	21	2	2	30	97	45	50	15,000	5,000	319,400	100,000	0
Indianapolis, Ind.	Indiana School for the Blind.	8	13	63	56	0	0	29	26	26	14	8	15	2	4	84	63	56	3,451	³ 6,984	983,100	42,128	
Vinton, Iowa	Iowa College for the Blind.	5	11	51	50	0	0	18	20	20	13	13	15	4	2	8	53	40	35	600	3,000	326,900	25,000	
Kansas City, Kans.	Kansas State School for the Blind.	4	11	58	45	2	0	18	26	12	13	12	5	33	52	48	33	1,500	500	500,500	54,000	
Louisville, Ky.	Kentucky School for the Blind.	2	9	65	63	8	12	29	24	15	9	9	10	1	128	36	46	45	1,200	800	250,000	19,394	40,000
Do.	Kentucky School for the Blind (Negro department).	1	3	12	8		0		3	3	1	1	20	9	9		25,000	1,238	6,000
Portland, Me.	Maine Institution for the Blind.	3	2	22	5														55,397	2,168	18,253

* Prorated. † School not graded. ¹ Included in chapter on schools for the deaf. ² Data for 1915-16. ³ Data for 1916-17. ⁴ Value of library. ⁵ Approximate.

TABLE 5.—*Statistics of schools for the blind, 1917–18—Continued.*

Location	Institution	Instructors Men	Instructors Women	Pupils enrolled Boys	Pupils enrolled Girls	Pupils in the kindergarten Boys	Pupils in the kindergarten Girls	In classes corresponding to grades 1 to 4 Boys	Girls	In classes corresponding to grades 5 to 8 Boys	Girls	In classes corresponding to high school grades Boys	Girls	Graduates in 1918 Boys	Girls	Vocal culture	Instrumental music	Industrial departments Boys	Girls	Volumes in library In raised type	In ink	Value of buildings and grounds	Value of scientific apparatus, instruments, furniture, library, etc.	Permanent endowment or productive fund
1	2	3	4	5	6	7	8	9	10	11	12	13	14	15	16	17	18	19	20	21	22	23	24	25
Overlea, Md.	Maryland School for the Blind.	3	10	50	62	7	8	23	26	13	17	7	12	2	7	35	30	44	46	4,000	1,200	$450,000	$10,500	
Do.	Maryland School for the Colored Blind and Deaf.	3	3	11	12	1	3	7	4	8	4	0	1	0	0	23	21	8	10	450	325	$46,000		
Watertown, Mass.	Perkins Institution and Massachusetts School for the Blind.	8	41	152	160	19	16	53	54	37	44	43	46	6	9	88	86	78	80	14,791	9,708	1,215,636	175,422	3,070,425
Detroit, Mich.	Detroit Public Day School for the Blind.	0	2	2		0	0	2	4	3	4	1	1	0	0	0	0	0	0	250	1.80			0
Lansing, Mich.	Michigan School for the Blind.	4	15	63	79	5	11	30	27	25	28	13	13	1	1	11	55	53	64	3,900	1,452	314,784	66,097	0
Saginaw, Mich.	Michigan Employment Institution for the Blind.	4	4	36	17			27	10	25	5	3	3	0	0	16	34	21	16	3,880	100	104,000	50,028	
Faribault, Minn.	Minnesota School for the Blind.	4	12	96	61	16	11	54	44	17	26	7	7	0	1	92	57	68	50	4,000	1,000	285,900	11,720	0
Jackson, Miss.	Mississippi Institute for the Blind.	11	11	30	28	0	0	16	11	8	5	11	3	2	2	58	45	21	25	800	600	250,000	14,500	1,500
St. Louis, Mo.	Missouri School for the Blind.	5	13	68	57	9	9	20	18	26	6	7	7	2	3	8	69	16	50	3,568	102	379,352	40,372	0
Boulder, Mont.	Montana Schools for Deaf, Blind, and Backward Children.	2	6	15	9	0	0	8	1	6	5	1	1	0	0	10	14	12	0			$66,388	$9,651	0
Nebraska City, Nebr.	Nebraska School for the Blind.	2	6	41	26	10	9	9	6	5	4	7	3	0	0	35	35	10	7	1,000	1,000	125,000	33,500	0
Jersey City, N. J.	Public School Classes for the Blind.	0	3	7	8	0	0	3	3	4	0	1	2	0	0	38	0	8	8	53	92		415	
Newark, N. J.	...do.	0	6	24	28	3	3	9	9	5	8	7	2	0	0	0	12	12	0					
Summit, N. J.	International Sunshine Society, Department for the Blind (Arthur Home).		3			10	5									20						30,000	10,000	
Alamogordo, N. Mex.	New Mexico Institute for the Blind.	1	6	27	25		17	18	15	4	3	2	5	0	0	44	35	27	25	774		60,000	5,600	
Batavia, N. Y.	New York State School for the Blind.	5	13	105	83	22		30	21	27	20	26	26	4	2	130	77	42	28	5,280	3,500	478,000	61,884	
Brooklyn, N. Y.	International Sunshine Society, Department for the Blind.	1	5	14	14	5	4	7	4	6	8					16	22			100	200	28,435	3,795	
New York (412 Ninth Avenue), N. Y.	New York Institute for the Education of the Blind.	5	15	73	33	0	0	32	12	28	11	18	10				56	73	33	2,500	600	411,079	53,009	

Location	Name																					
New York, N. Y.	New York Public School Classes for the Blind.																					*2,500
Fort Jefferson, N. Y.	Brooklyn Home for Blind, Crippled, and Defective Children.																					51,683
Prince Bay, Staten Island, N. Y.	St. Joseph's Asylum for Blind Girls.																					0
Raleigh, N. C.	State School for the Blind and the Deaf.																					
Do.	State School for the Blind and the Deaf (colored department).																					200,000
Bathgate, N. Dak.	North Dakota School for the Blind.																					
Cincinnati, Ohio.	Cincinnati School for the Blind.																					
Cleveland, Ohio.	Cleveland School for the Blind.																					
Columbus, Ohio.	Ohio State School for the Blind.																					
Mansfield, Ohio.	Public School Classes for the Blind.																					
Toledo, Ohio.	do.																					
Muskogee, Okla.	Oklahoma School for the Blind.																					
Salem, Oreg.	Oregon State School for the Blind.																					786,018
Philadelphia (Sixty-fourth and Malvern, West), Pa.	Pennsylvania Institution for the Instruction of the Blind.																					
Pittsburgh, Pa.	Western Pennsylvania Institution for the Blind.																					20,000
Cedar Spring, S. C.	South Carolina School for the Deaf and Blind.																					
Do.	South Carolina School for the Deaf and Blind (Negro).																					
Gary, S. Dak.	South Dakota School for the Blind.																					0
Nashville, Tenn.	Tennessee School for the Blind.																					
Austin, Tex.	Texas School for the Blind.																					0
Do.	Deaf, Dumb and Blind Institute for Colored Youths.																					
Ogden, Utah.	Utah School for the Deaf and the Blind.																					0
Staunton, Va.	Virginia School for the Deaf and the Blind.																					
Vancouver, Wash.	Washington State School for the Blind.																					
Romney, W. Va.	West Virginia Schools for the Deaf and the Blind.																					99,840
Janesville, Wis.	Wisconsin School for the Blind.																					
Milwaukee, Wis.	Milwaukee Public Day School for the Blind.																					0

*Promoted.
1 Data for 1915-16.
2 Included in column 9.
3 Included in column 10.
4 Value of library.
5 Includes statistics of schools for colored deaf.
6 Included in chapter on schools for the deaf.

TABLE 6.—*Statistics of receipts and expenditures of schools for the blind, 1917–18.*

Location	Institution	Receipts					Expenditures			
		From State, county, or city.	From private benefactions for permanent equipment and current expenses.	From productive endowment funds.	From other sources.	Total.	For building and lasting improvements.	For teachers' salaries, books, etc.	For other salaries and all other current expenses.	Total.
1	2	3	4	5	6	7	8	9	10	11
Talladega, Ala.	Alabama School for the Blind	$23,460				$23,460		$5,980	$18,782	$24,762
Do.	Alabama School for the Negro Deaf and Blind	*4,580				*4,580		*1,202	*3,773	*4,975
Berkeley, Calif.	California School for the Deaf and Blind	*47,520				*47,520	*$5,807	*22,374	*19,206	*47,387
Colorado Springs, Colo.	Colorado School for the Deaf and the Blind	*35,742				*35,742	*9,476	*24,425		*33,902
Farmington, Conn.	Nursery for Blind		*5,973	$1,909	$375	7,089				7,089
Hartford, Conn.	Connecticut Institute for the Blind		0			19,757				13,910
Macon, Ga.	Georgia Academy for the Blind	11,500				1 30,000	1,000	5,480	4,900	1 30,750
Gooding, Idaho	Idaho State School for the Deaf and the Blind	*9,794				*9,794				11,380
Jacksonville, Ill.	Illinois School for the Blind	100,000				100,000	12,000	51,000	37,000	100,000
Indianapolis, Ind.	Indiana School for the Blind	53,859			241	54,100		25,248	28,612	53,858
Vinton, Iowa	Iowa College for the Blind	70,000			13,200	88,200	20,000	15,000	53,000	83,000
Kansas City, Kans.	Kansas State School for the Blind	38,000				38,000		12,000	23,000	38,000
Louisville, Ky.	Kentucky School for the Blind	33,743			359	34,102			21,352	34,057
Do.	Kentucky School for the Blind (negro department)	5,249				5,249	765	1,800	3,399	5,249
Portland, Me.	Maine Institution for the Blind			96	12,485	19,559	150	2,556	20,809	23,686
Overlea, Md.	Maryland School for the Blind	6,975				37,376	321	9,888	37,784	47,622
Do.	Maryland School for the Colored Blind and Deaf					*8,062		2,553	*8,924	*11,477
Watertown, Mass.	The Perkins Institution and Massachusetts School for the Blind	37,500	36,017	118,463	71,533	263,513	1,794	31,140	232,618	265,553
Lansing, Mich.	Michigan School for the Blind	98,748	0	0	940	1 111,787	43,616	(a)	67,556	111,071
Saginaw, Mich.	Michigan Employment Institution for the Blind	36,250	0		64,666	100,945	250	6,000	43,426	48,676
Faribault, Minn.	Minnesota School for the Blind	53,443	0		0	53,443	5,880		48,122	53,443
Jackson, Miss.	Mississippi Institute for the Blind	0	0	600	0	600	2,000	10,000	15,351	27,251
St. Louis, Mo.	Missouri School for the Blind	46,619				46,619	0	10,732	35,586	46,618
Boulder, Mont.	Montana Schools for Deaf, Blind, and Backward Children						1 13,844	14,496	*13,776	*41,618
Nebraska City, Nebr.	Nebraska School for the Blind	30,000			3,000	33,000	2,000	12,500	18,500	33,000
Jersey City, N.J.	Public School Classes for the Blind	900				900		1,356		1,838
Newark, N.J.	International Sunshine Society, Department for the Blind (Arthur Home).	3,334				3,334				3,334
Summit, N.J.	...do...	18,094			4,461	22,545	1,168	1,031	19,668	21,067

Location	Institution							
Alamogordo, N. Mex.	New Mexico Institute for the Blind	32,488		6,902	234	30,636	7,500	12,728	31,376	38,876
Batavia, N.Y.	New York State School for the Blind	82,347		1,661	1,900	84,236	8,116		64,835	85,030
Brooklyn, N.Y.	International Sunshine Society, Department for the Blind	10,837	2,617		1,424	16,529	463	470	14,170	15,103
New York (412 Ninth Avenue), N.Y.	New York Institute for the Education of the Blind	39,904		68,023	31,776	139,792	41,887	18,946	67,815	128,645
New York, N.Y.	New York Public School Classes for the Blind							29,458	798	30,256
Port Jefferson, N.Y.	Brooklyn Home for Blind, Crippled and Defective Children	52,183	22,752			74,935	9,183	4,305	65,149	78,597
Raleigh, N.C.	State School for the Blind and the Deaf	*157,732	0	0	0	*157,732	*105,300	*23,748	*41,796	*171,844
Do.	State School for the Blind and the Deaf (colored department)	0	0	13,573	627	14,200	460	6,450	9,470	16,400
Bathgate, N. Dak.	North Dakota School for the Blind	12,562				12,852		8,691	664	9,345
Cincinnati, Ohio	Cincinnati School for the Blind	100,000				100,000	5,000	25,000	70,000	100,000
Columbus, Ohio	Ohio State School for Blind	842				842		2,389	310	2,699
Mansfield, Ohio	Public School Classes for the Blind	93,500				93,500	50,000	17,000	26,500	93,500
Muskogee, Okla.	Oklahoma School for the Blind	51,081				122,751		34,528	80,853	115,675
Philadelphia (64th and Malvern Ave.), Pa.	Pennsylvania Institution for the Instruction of the Blind	51,300	21,742	38,506	11,472	54,428	0	11,036	44,408	55,444
Pittsburgh, Pa.	Western Pennsylvania Institution for the Blind	15,500		1,584	1,539	16,500		3,000	9,000	12,000
Gary, S. Dak.	South Dakota School for the Blind	39,982		1,500		39,982		12,553	33,300	45,853
Nashville, Tenn.	Tennessee School for the Blind	44,019				44,019	*22,119	4,088	*16,586	*43,143
Austin, Tex.	Deaf, Dumb, and Blind Institute for Colored Youths	15,620		*3,030		18,650		*6,370	*12,740	*19,110
Ogden, Utah	Utah School for the Deaf and the Blind	*20,000				*20,000		*4,000	*16,000	*20,000
Staunton, Va.	Virginia School for the Deaf and the Blind						21,000	16,485	12,435	49,920
Vancouver, Wash.	Washington State School for the Blind	*22,560			*1,216	*24,776	*608	*9,728	*12,160	*22,496
Romney, W. Va.	West Virginia Schools for the Deaf and the Blind	76,734			1,375	78,110	1,555	12,920	56,554	71,080
Janesville, Wis.	Wisconsin School for the Blind	9,798				9,798		8,666	1,131	9,798
Milwaukee, Wis.	Milwaukee Public Day School for the Blind									

*Prorated.   1 For white and colored departments.   2 Includes totals not itemized.   3 Included in following column.

DEPARTMENT OF THE INTERIOR
BUREAU OF EDUCATION

BULLETIN, 1919, No. 79

SCHOOLS FOR THE DEAF
1917-18

PREPARED BY THE STATISTICAL DIVISION OF
THE BUREAU OF EDUCATION

UNDER THE SUPERVISION OF H. R. BONNER
COLLECTOR AND COMPILER OF STATISTICS

[Advance sheets from the Biennial Survey of Education, 1916–1918]

WASHINGTON
GOVERNMENT PRINTING OFFICE
1920

SCHOOLS FOR THE DEAF, 1917-18.

TYPES OF SCHOOLS INCLUDED.

From an administrative viewpoint three types of schools for the deaf are included in this chapter: First, those controlled and supported by the State; second, those controlled and financed by private organizations; and, third, those operated as a part of the city public school systems. This latter type is referred to herein as city day schools, since children attend them during school hours generally and are not housed in dormitories as is usually the case in State and private institutions. These three types of schools are kept separate and distinct throughout the chapter. All States, except Delaware, Nevada, New Hampshire, New Jersey, and Wyoming have State schools for the deaf. Some of the schools in Massachusetts, New York, and Pennsylvania included with the State schools are only semipublic, i. e., they are partly controlled by private organizations but serve as State institutions, receiving pupils at public expense. Some of these schools admit pupils at public expense from other States than the one in which the school is located.

DUAL SCHOOLS.

Altogether, 13 dual State schools are included in this report. The Florida State School for the Deaf and Blind (both white and colored departments), St. Augustine, and the Virginia State School for Colored Deaf and Blind, Newport News, did not report. Altogether, there are 15 dual schools in 14 different States. South Carolina and Virginia each provide two dual schools, one for white and the other for colored youth. In Florida, white and colored pupils are taught in different departments of the same school. Dual schools are limited to State institutions. For a more detailed discussion of this type of school, see the chapter on schools for the blind.

3

SCHOOLS NOT REPORTING.

In addition to the two dual schools mentioned above, five other schools for the deaf did not report in 1918. They are given here so that this publication may form a complete directory of such schools throughout the United States:

St. Joseph's Deaf-Mute Institute, St. Louis, Mo.
The Davidson School of Individual Instruction, Tamworth, N. H.
New Mexico Asylum for the Deaf and Dumb, Santa Fe, N. Mex.
Reno Margulies School for the Deaf, New York, N. Y.
Racine Day School for the Deaf, Racine, Wis.

TABLE 1.—*Review of statistics of all schools for the deaf, 1900 to 1918.*

	1900	1901	1902	1903	1904	1905	1906	1907	1908
Number of schools reporting:									
State	56	57	57	56	57	56	59	58	55
City day	41	46	49	54	64	64	60	52	51
Private	17	15	15	17	16	16	16	17	16
Total	114	119	121	127	137	136	135	127	122
Instructors:									
State—									
Men	344	386	379	384	386	416	436	373	349
Women	668	709	739	746	780	786	806	828	741
Total	1,012	1,095	1,118	1,130	1,166	1,202	1,242	1,201	1,090
City day—									
Men	5	7	9	5	5	5	6	5	6
Women	94	100	113	116	130	135	137	136	146
Total	99	107	122	121	135	140	143	141	152
Private—									
Men	17	20	16	19	17	12	10	10	13
Women	56	59	59	70	68	71	70	67	70
Total	73	79	75	89	85	83	80	77	83
Pupils:									
State—									
Male	5,389	5,560	5,862	5,800	5,909	5,662	5,848	5,818	5,508
Female	4,398	4,509	4,762	4,728	4,869	4,659	4,786	4,759	4,534
Total	9,787	10,069	10,624	10,528	10,778	10,321	10,634	10,577	10,042
City day—									
Male	409	433	457	469	522	578	574	602	628
Female	340	347	378	412	460	515	537	522	566
Total	749	780	835	881	982	1,093	1,111	1,124	1,194
Private—									
Male	211	213	202	233	227	256	222	232	245
Female	267	281	277	290	280	282	303	301	298
Total	478	494	479	523	507	538	525	533	543
Graduates:									
State	393	299	283	226	232	193	238	232	269
City day	3	6	14	3	15	6	2	15	18
Private	9	17	22	26	24	23	13	23	26
	405	322	319	255	271	222	256	270	313

TABLE 1.—*Review of Statistics of all schools for the deaf, 1900 to 1918.*—Continued.

	1909	1910	1911	1912	1913	1914	1915	1916	1918
Number of schools reporting:									
State	57	57	57	64	68	68	68	69	68
City day	53	53	55	58	62	65	64	71	69
Private	17	20	20	19	17	18	18	19	18
Total	127	130	132	141	147	151	150	159	155
Instructors:									
State—									
Men	385	378	371	410	366	375	468	442	372
Women	835	830	874	930	941	969	991	1,076	1,003
Total	1,220	1,208	1,245	1,340	1,307	1,344	1,459	1,518	1,375
City day—									
Men	5	5	8	10	9	8	18	17	18
Women	168	184	210	224	228	249	270	290	305
Total	173	189	218	234	237	257	288	307	323
Private—									
Men	11	16	14	15	12	14	17	19	20
Women	85	85	77	69	73	74	84	97	103
Total	96	101	91	84	85	88	101	116	123
Pupils:									
State—									
Male	5,915	5,681	5,887	6,057	5,976	6,106	6,222	6,415	6,070
Female	4,971	4,718	4,853	5,187	5,094	5,240	5,237	5,369	5,246
Total	10,886	10,399	10,740	11,244	11,070	11,346	11,459	11,784	11,316
City day—									
Male	697	780	811	949	1,049	1,130	1,151	1,312	1,309
Female	622	728	796	979	883	894	958	1,050	1,182
Total	1,319	1,508	1,607	1,928	1,932	2,024	2,109	2,362	2,482
Private—									
Male	245	282	274	217	216	232	218	239	326
Female	321	357	419	301	300	257	294	348	318
Total	566	639	691	518	516	489	512	587	644
Graduates:									
State	178	156	72	130	180	150	211	203	206
City day			1	2	1	1	1		5
Private	13	7	2	1	1			3	3
	191	163	75	133	182	151	212	206	214

NUMBER OF SCHOOLS.

As will be observed in figure 1, the total number of schools reporting in 1918 was 155. Of this number, 68 are State or semi-State
institutions, 69 are city day schools, and 18 are private schools. The
highest number of schools reporting in any year was in 1916, when
159 reports were received. The decrease this year is due to the
failure of a few schools to report and not to an actual decrease in the
total number of schools throughout the United States. The number
of State and private schools for the deaf since 1900 has remained
practically the same. The increase in the number of such schools
has been due very largely to the formation of city day-school classes
for the deaf. The number has increased from 41 in 1900 to 71 in 1916
and to 69 in 1918. The number of private schools was about the

same in 1918 as it was in 1900. At no time within this period did the number exceed 20. The number of State schools increases slowly but steadily. It is evident that the drop in the total curve in figure 1 from 1907 to 1911 is due to the failure of a number of city day schools to report, since a corresponding synchronous fluctuation is observed in the "long-dash" curve representing these schools and classes as is shown in the "total" curve. The number of schools reporting has a marked influence on the summarized data. For example, note the corresponding drops in 1908 in figure 1, repre-

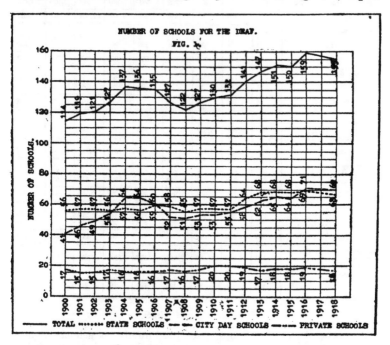

senting the number of schools; in figure 2, representing the number of instructors; and in figure 3, representing the number of pupils. The deviation from the line of tendency in any year is due more generally to incompleteness of reports than to any other single factor. A truer condition would be presented if lines should be drawn connecting only the highest points in the figures.

INSTRUCTORS.

Since 1900 the number of instructors in schools for the deaf has increased from 1,184 to 1,821, or 54 per cent, as shown in figure 2. The number of men instructors has remained practically constant, the corresponding increase being from 366 to 410 within this period of 18 years. The greater proportion of the increase has been in the number of women teachers. In 1900 there were 818 and in 1918 1,411 women teachers in schools for the deaf. The increase within this period has been over 72 per cent.

The teaching "load" in these schools has lessened within the period under consideration. In 1900 the average number of pupils per teacher was 9.3. In 1918 the corresponding average was only 7.9. These figures indicate that the teaching "load" has been

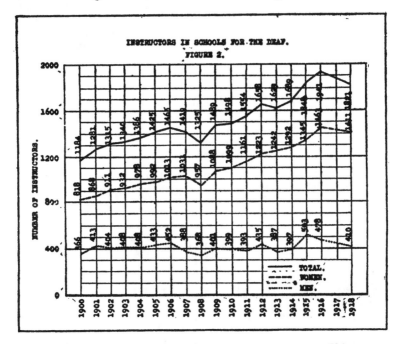

decreased about 15 per cent within a period of 18 years. This means that teachers have greater opportunity for giving individual instruction. It is an index of increasing efficiency.

The number of pupils per teacher is largest in city day-school classes and smallest in private schools. The average number of pupils per teacher in the former in 1918 was 7.7 and in the latter 5.2. The corresponding average in State schools is 8.2. It is evident, therefore, that larger numbers of pupils are taught by a teacher in State schools for the deaf than in city or private institutions. More individual attention is evidently given to pupils in private than in either State or city schools.

PUPILS.

A rather unexpected situation is revealed by figure 3. A very
large proportion of the pupils in schools for the deaf is found in
State institutions; of the 14,442 pupils reported in 1918, 11,316, or 78
per cent, were enrolled in State institutions; in 1900 the corresponding
ratio was 89 per cent. While the actual *number* of pupils in State
institutions has steadily increased, these schools are enrolling a smaller
and smaller *proportion* of all such pupils. The reason is found in the
increasing importance of city day school classes for the deaf. The
enrollment in these classes has increased from 749 in 1900 to 2,482 in
1918. It has increased 231 per cent within this period. The number of pupils enrolled in private schools, not serving as State institutions, has not materially increased within this period. The very
rapid rise in the upper curve in figure 3 does not indicate that the number of deaf persons in the population has increased so rapidly, but
that a greater interest is manifested by States and cities in the education of the deaf and consequently that a greater proportion of deaf
persons are enrolled in school.

ENROLLMENT BY GRADES.

By assembling the data on enrollment by grade-groups found in
the summary tables the following distribution is obtained:

Enrollment by grades.

Grades.	Enroll-ment in State schools.	Per cent.	Enroll-ment in private schools.	Per cent.	Enroll-ment in city schools.	Per cent.	Total enroll-ment.	Per cent.
Kindergartens........	1,312	12.2	99	15.4	213	8.6	1,624	11.7
Grades 1 to 4.........	5,890	54.8	317	49.3	1,513	61.2	7,720	55.6
Grades 5 to 8.........	3,007	27.9	205	31.9	719	29.0	3,931	28.3
High school..........	548	5.1	22	3.4	30	1.2	600	4.4
Total..........	10,757	100.0	643	100.0	2,475	100.0	13,875	100.0

This summary does not include the total enrollment in all schools
for the deaf, since several schools did not make a complete distribution of their total enrollment. The percentages in the last column
show very accurately, however, the relative proportion of pupils in
the different grade-groups. Over one-half of the enrollment is found
in grades 1 to 4, inclusive. Less than one-twentieth of it is found in
high-school grades, about one-ninth in kindergartens, and over one-
fourth in grades 5 to 8, inclusive. City schools have relatively small
percentages of deaf pupils in kindergartens and in high schools. Private schools have relatively a high percentage of pupils in kindergartens, but below the average percentage in high schools.

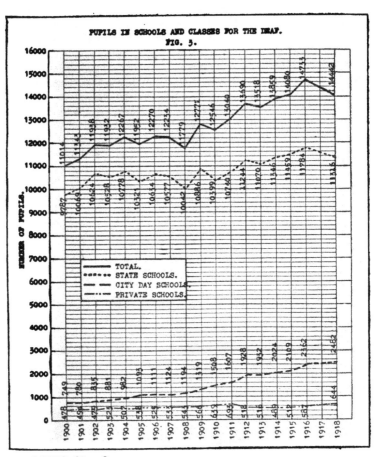

PUPILS IN SCHOOLS AND CLASSES FOR THE DEAF.

FIG. 3.

GRADUATES.

Prior to 1911 the blank on which the statistics were collected did not specify that only graduates from secondary schools should be reported. Consequently, many schools reported the number completing the elementary as well as the secondary course as shown in Table 1. Since 1911 a more stable increase in the number graduating from secondary schools is shown, as will be noted in figure 4. Practically all graduates are found in State institutions, indicating that city boards of education have not generally provided secondary schools for deaf children. In fact only five cities reported pupils in high-school grades. The reports show that 28 State institutions have 548 pupils enrolled in high-school classes. Altogether, there are enrolled in high-school classes of five city schools for the deaf only 30 pupils, and in four private schools only 22 pupils. Of these numbers, 206, 5, and 3 pupils graduated from State, city, and private schools, respectively. The number of graduates from city and private secondary schools for the deaf has been almost negligible, as shown in figure 4.

PUPILS TAUGHT SPEECH.

The following table shows the number of pupils in each type of school who were taught speech during the year.

Pupils taught speech.

Items.	State schools.	Private schools.	City day schools.	Total.
Pupils taught speech...........................	7,814	537	2,406	10,757
Pupils taught by the oral method.................	6,992	499	2,208	9,699
Pupils taught by the auricular method............	282	38	115	435

Of the 14,442 pupils enrolled in schools for the deaf, 10,757, or 74 per cent, were taught speech during the year. In all three types of schools combined, 9,699 pupils were taught by the oral method, i. e., they were taught to speak and to understand the speech of others by lip reading or speech reading. Only 435 pupils were taught by the auricular method, which consists in attempting to improve the hearing of those not absolutely deaf.

VOLUMES IN LIBRARIES.

As shown in Tables 5, 8, and 11, the total number of volumes in the libraries of schools for the deaf is 144,281 volumes in State institutions, 2,225 volumes in private schools, and 7,153 volumes in city day schools. In the case of three dual State schools the number of volumes given in the detailed tables includes the number of volumes (printed in ink) in schools for the blind. On the other hand, the

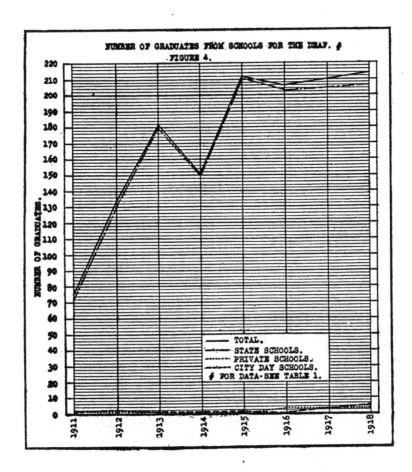

NUMBER OF GRADUATES FROM SCHOOLS FOR THE DEAF. #
FIGURE 4.

library in another school of this type has been reported with schools for the blind. The total number of volumes reported in all schools for the deaf is 153,659, or an average of 1,652 volumes per school reporting this information. This average in State institutions is 2,531 volumes; in private schools, only 318 volumes; and in city day schools, 247 volumes. It should be remembered, however, that other libraries are also accessible to children enrolled in city schools for the deaf. The library facilities in private schools are not nearly so adequate as those in State institutions.

VALUATION OF PROPERTY.

The following summary shows the number of schools reporting and the valuation of the property reported for each type of school represented:

Property.

Kind of property.	State schools.		Private schools.		City day schools.		Total.	
	Number reporting.	Value.	Number reporting.	Value.	Number reporting.	Value.	Number reporting.	Value.
Buildings and grounds.......	63	$18,266,754	9	$425,913	7	$458,600	79	$19,151,267
Scientific apparatus, furniture, instruments, etc......	53	1,581,471	8	24,759	21	49,015	82	1,655,245
Endowment or productive funds....................	10	1,838,347	2	87,419	1	8,400	13	1,934,166
Total.................	....	21,686,572	....	538,091	....	516,015	....	22,740,678

Only 5 State schools did not report the value of buildings and grounds, and 15 did not give the value of apparatus, etc. Assuming that each State school not reporting had the same average value of property as those reporting, viz, $289,948 for buildings and grounds and $29,839 for apparatus, etc., the total value of the former for the 68 institutions represented in this report would be $19,716,494 and of the latter $2,029,056. In the case of dual State schools, the valuation of property has been prorated between schools for the blind and deaf in proportion to the enrollment in each. The total valuation of property in private schools and in city day schools can not be estimated with any degree of accuracy, since so few schools of each type reported this information. In the case of city schools for the deaf, a part of the regular public school buildings is often used as classrooms for the deaf. Consequently few of these schools could supply the data desired.

Altogether, 13 schools reported a total endowment of $1,934,166. The greater part of this belongs to State or semi-State schools.

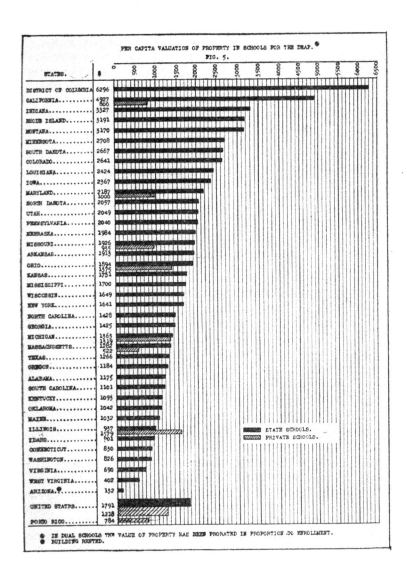

PER CAPITA VALUATION OF PROPERTY IN SCHOOLS FOR THE DEAF.
FIG. 5.

A good index as to how well a State provides for its deaf is found in the valuation of property for each one enrolled in its schools for the deaf. A great variation obtains in this respect, as will be noted from figure 5. The District of Columbia, ranking highest, has an average per capita of $6,296; while West Virginia, ranking lowest, has an average per capita value of only $402. Arizona, with a per capita of $132, rents the buildings used by its school for the deaf. The average per capita for the United States is $1,791 for State or semi-State institutions and $1,218 for private schools. California and the District of Columbia seem to form a separate class in the investments which they have made for deaf pupils. The next highest State, Indiana, has only about three-fifths the per capita value shown for California and only about one-half that shown for the District of Columbia. Little information would be derived from attempting to show the per capita value of property in city schools for the deaf, since so few cities report the valuation of property.

RECEIPTS.

The receipts of city day schools for the deaf are inseparably bound up with the total receipts of city public schools. So few city schools for the deaf reported receipts that it was not thought advisable to tabulate the returns.

Amounts received from the various sources for State and private schools.

Source of revenue.	Amount for State schools (59 schools reporting).		Amount for private schools (8 schools reporting).	
	Amount reported.	Per cent of total.	Amount reported.	Per cent of total.
From State, city, or county............................	$3,420,387	89.6	$6,828	7.8
From private benefactions.............................	19,800	.5	41,851	47.6
From productive endowment fund.....................	171,121	4.5	4,340	4.9
From other sources....................................	206,625	5.4	34,867	39.7
Total amount distributed..............................	3,817,933	100.0	87,886	100.0
Total amount...	[1] 4,494,484	....	87,886	....

[1] Part of this amount was not itemized as to source.

In State schools almost 90 per cent of the revenue comes from public sources, and in private schools over half the revenue comes from private benefactions and productive funds. In private schools almost 40 per cent comes from other sources, most of it presumably from tuition fees. In State or semi-State schools only 5 per cent of the revenue comes from private benefactions or productive endowment.

Only 59 State schools reported receipts, the total being $4,494,484, or an average of $76,177 per school. If each of the 9 State schools not reporting receipts received the same average amount, the total receipts for State schools would be $5,180,077. This estimate for State schools does not take into account the 3 State schools which submitted no report whatever. Not even a gross estimate is possible in case of private schools, since only 8 out of 18 reported their receipts.

EXPENDITURES.

Altogether 61 State schools for the deaf reported expenditures, the aggregate amount reported being $4,292,789, or an average of $70,378 per school. If the other 8 State schools not reporting incurred the same average expenses, the total amount spent by the 68 State schools reporting in 1918 would be $4,855,822, which is almost as much as the estimated total receipts for the same schools, viz, $5,180,077. The total amount spent by the 8 private schools reporting was $102,990, or an average of $12,874 per school. The unusual amount of $42,682 spent for buildings by one private institution has materially increased this average. Omitting this one relatively large school from consideration, the average expenditure in the other 7 schools is only $5,525.

Distribution of expenditures in State and private schools.

Expenditures.	Amount spent by State schools.	Per cent of total.	Amount spent by private schools.	Per cent of total.
For buildings and lasting improvements....................	$438,091	10.6	$50,089	48.6
For teachers' salaries, books, etc......................	1,267,945	30.6	20,173	19.6
For other salaries and other current expenses..............	2,430,530	58.8	32,728	31.8
Total amount distributed............................	4,136,566	100.0	102,990	100.0

In State schools about one-tenth of the total expenditures are made for outlays. In private schools the expenditures for the same purpose were unusual in 1918. In State schools about three-tenths of the expense is incurred for instruction. In both types of schools the expenditures made for "other salaries and other current expenses" are about double the amount spent for teachers' salaries, books, etc., i. e. for instruction. Presumably, the greater portion of this large group of expenditures is incurred because pupils are housed and boarded in the school dormitories.

Only 49 city day schools for the deaf reported their expenditures. Usually, financial accounts for such schools are not kept by the teacher or principal, but by the superintendent or the board of education. Table 17 shows the amount spent by each of the 49 cities reporting. The total amount spent for all purposes was $294,952, or an average cost of $195 per pupil enrolled. Assuming that this average applies to all pupils enrolled in such schools, viz, 2,482 pupils, the total cost of maintaining all city day schools for the deaf would be $483,990. The total amount spent for instruction, usually for teachers' salaries, was $215,330, or an average of $1,080 per teacher. This average represents rather accurately the average salaries of teachers in city day schools for the deaf. It may be slightly too high, since it includes both the salary of the teacher and other expenses of instruction, such as books, pencils, paper, etc. In many instances the round numbers given in Table 17 indicate that only the teachers' salaries were reported under this item of expenditure (column 4).

The per capita expenditures in schools for the deaf is shown graphically by States in figure 6. Montana ranks highest both in the total expense incurred, $1,734, and in the amount spent for current expenses, $1,178. The District of Columbia ranks second, with a per capita current expense of $713. Texas had the smallest per capita for current expenses, $139. The average per capita for current expenses for the United States is $358, and for outlays, $41. The corresponding averages for the United States for private schools are $238 and $225, respectively.

The "open" portion of the bars represent per capita expenditures for buildings and other lasting improvements. This item will vary considerably from year to year for the various States, and consequently is not considered in ranking the States. It is shown additionally to indicate the total per capita expense incurred by any State for the year considered. Where the open bar is long, the State represented evidently incurred an unusual expense for permanent improvements. In the case of dual schools the expenditures have been prorated between deaf and blind schools in proportion to the number of pupils in each type of school.

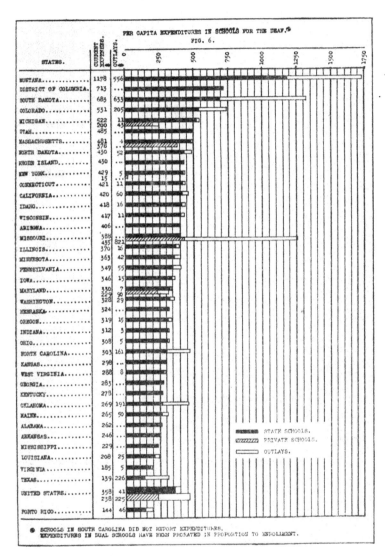

PER CAPITA EXPENDITURES IN SCHOOLS FOR THE DEAF.

FIG. 6.

STATES.	CURRENT EXPENSES.	OUTLAYS.
MONTANA	1178	556
DISTRICT OF COLUMBIA.	713	...
SOUTH DAKOTA	683	633
COLORADO	531	205
MICHIGAN	522	11
	200	43
UTAH	485	...
MASSACHUSETTS	481	4
	378	..
NORTH DAKOTA	430	52
RHODE ISLAND	430	...
NEW YORK	429	5
	15	..8
CONNECTICUT	421	11
CALIFORNIA	420	60
IDAHO	418	16
WISCONSIN	417	11
ARIZONA	406	...
MISSOURI	388	...
	455	821
ILLINOIS	370	16
MINNESOTA	363	42
PENNSYLVANIA	349	55
IOWA	346	15
MARYLAND	330	7
	229	90
WASHINGTON	328	29
NEBRASKA	324	...
OREGON	319	15
INDIANA	312	3
OHIO	308	5
NORTH CAROLINA	303	161
KANSAS	298	...
WEST VIRGINIA	288	8
GEORGIA	283	...
KENTUCKY	278	...
OKLAHOMA	269	191
MAINE	265	50
ALABAMA	262	...
ARKANSAS	246	...
MISSISSIPPI	229	...
LOUISIANA	208	25
VIRGINIA	185	5
TEXAS	139	226
UNITED STATES	358	41
	238	225
PORTO RICO	144	46

STATE SCHOOLS.
PRIVATE SCHOOLS.
OUTLAYS.

● SCHOOLS IN SOUTH CAROLINA DID NOT REPORT EXPENDITURES.
EXPENDITURES IN DUAL SCHOOLS HAVE BEEN PRORATED IN PROPORTION TO ENROLLMENT.

TABLE 2.—*Per capita value of property in schools for the deaf, 1917–18.*

States.	State institutions.				Private institutions.			
	Number of schools reporting.	Enrollment.	Value of property.	Value per capita.	Number of schools reporting.	Enrollment.	Value of property.	Value per capita.
United States......	64	10,970	$29,648,126	$1,791	9	362	$460,672	[1] $3,180
Alabama............	2	218	256,065	1,175				
Arizona............	1	38	5,000	132				
Arkansas...........	2	366	700,000	1,913				
California..........	1	195	960,765	4,927	1	40	32,000	800
Colorado...........	1	144	380,304	2,641				
Connecticut........	2	266	220,810	830				
District of Columbia....	2	162	1,020,000	6,296				
Georgia............	2	212	302,600	1,425				
Idaho..............	1	61	55,000	901				
Illinois............	1	377	353,257	937	1	131	206,886	1,579
Indiana............	1	298	961,597	3,327				
Iowa..............	1	191	452,354	2,367				
Kansas............	1	223	385,950	1,731				
Kentucky..........	2	316	345,300	1,093				
Louisiana..........	1	145	351,500	2,424				
Maine.............	1	113	116,720	1,032				
Maryland..........	2	150	328,009	2,187	2	48	46,009	1,090
Massachusetts......	2	191	244,960	1,282	1	18	9,400	522
Michigan..........	1	291	396,660	1,363	1	34	45,843	1,319
Minnesota.........	1	242	655,371	2,708				
Mississippi.........	2	176	299,134	1,700				
Missouri...........	2	282	543,000	1,926	1	50	46,943	985
Montana...........	1	78	247,260	3,170				
Nebraska..........	1	185	367,000	1,994				
New York..........	8	1,881	3,086,576	1,641				
North Carolina.....	2	362	516,804	1,428				
North Dakota......	1	100	205,664	2,057				
Ohio..............	1	489	926,390	1,894	1	24	[2] 33,000	1,375
Oklahoma.........	2	316	329,255	1,042				
Oregon............	1	103	122,000	1,184				
Pennsylvania.......	5	1,135	2,315,282	2,040				
Porto Rico.........					1	39	30,600	784
Rhode Island......	1	94	300,080	3,191				
South Carolina.....	1	123	135,423	1,101				
South Dakota......	1	60	160,080	2,667				
Texas.............	2	556	703,928	1,266				
Utah..............	1	115	235,583	2,049				
Virginia...........	1	211	145,500	690				
Washington........	1	143	118,113	826				
West Virginia......	1	174	69,990	402				
Wisconsin.........	1	188	310,000	1,649				

[1] Per capita value, excluding Porto Rico, is $1,218.   [2] Data for 1915–16.

TABLE 3.—*Per capita expenditures in State and private schools for the deaf, 1917-18.*

States.	State institutions.						Private institutions.					
	Number reporting	Enrollment.	Current expenses.	Outlays.	Current expenses per capita.	Outlays per capita.	Number reporting	Enrollment.	Current expenses.	Outlays.	Current expenses per capita.	Outlays per capita.
United States	62	10,779	$3,854,508	$438,291	$358	$41	8	223	$52,901	$50,089	$238	$225
Alabama	2	218	57,154	....	262	....						
Arizona	1	38	15,445	0	406	0						
Arkansas	2	366	89,939	0	246	0						
California	1	195	81,909	11,700	420	60						
Colorado	1	144	76,490	29,592	531	205						
Connecticut	1	198	83,385	2,109	*421	11						
District of Columbia	2	162	115,539	....	713	....						
Georgia	2	212	60,000	....	283	....						
Idaho	1	61	25,520	1,000	418	16						
Illinois	1	377	139,600	6,000	370	16						
Indiana	1	298	92,808	945	312	3						
Iowa	1	191	66,139	3,000	346	15						
Kansas	1	223	66,672	0	298	0						
Kentucky	2	316	87,709	....	278	....						
Louisiana	1	145	30,249	3,638	208	25						
Maine	1	113	29,971	5,526	265	50						
Maryland	2	150	49,561	1,058	330	7	2	46	10,538	4,136	229	90
Massachusetts	2	191	91,810	692	481	4	1	18	6,805	....	378	....
Michigan	1	291	151,903	3,132	522	11	1	34	6,808	1,473	200	43
Minnesota	1	242	87,961	10,500	363	42						
Mississippi	2	176	40,224	0	229	0						
Missouri	2	282	109,500	....	388	....	2	52	22,634	42,682	435	821
Montana	1	78	91,856	43,364	1,178	556						
Nebraska	1	185	60,000	....	324	....						
New York	8	1,881	807,222	9,690	429	5	1	34	500	....	15	....
North Carolina	2	362	109,770	58,349	303	161						
North Dakota	1	100	42,999	5,231	430	52						
Ohio	1	489	150,775	2,500	308	5						
Oklahoma	2	316	85,075	60,462	269	191						
Oregon	1	103	32,858	1,510	319	15						
Pennsylvania	5	1,135	395,817	6,200	349	55						
Porto Rico							1	39	5,616	1,798	144	46
Rhode Island	1	94	40,493	....	430	....						
South Dakota	1	60	41,000	38,000	683	633						
Texas	2	556	77,549	125,481	139	226						
Utah	1	115	55,890	....	485	....						
Virginia	1	211	39,000	1,000	185	5						
Washington	1	143	46,904	4,144	328	29						
West Virginia	1	174	50,112	1,392	288	8						
Wisconsin	1	188	77,700	2,076	417	11						

TABLE 4.—*Summary of statistics of instructors and pupils in State schools for the deaf, 1917–18.*

States.	Number of schools reporting.	Instructors.			Pupils enrolled.			Pupils in the kindergarten.			In classes corresponding to grades 1 to 4.			In classes corresponding to grades 5 to 8.			In classes corresponding to high-school grades.		
		Men.	Women.	Total.	Boys.	Girls.	Total.	Boys.	Girls.	Total.	Boys.	Girls.	Total.	Boys.	Girls.	Total.	Boys.	Girls.	Total.
1	2	3	4	5	6	7	8	9	10	11	12	13	14	15	16	17	18	19	20
United States	68	372	1,003	1,375	6,070	5,246	11,316	723	589	1,312	3,196	2,604	5,980	1,531	476	3,007	263	285	548
Alabama	2	7	16	23	116	102	218	6	4	10	61	58	119	18	16	34	14	10	24
Arizona	1	3	6	9	25	13	38				21	8	30	9	16	8			
Arkansas	2	12	20	32	189	177	366	16	22	38	95	28	160	73	129	204	4	10	14
California	1	15	15	30	118	77	195	16	6	13	36	36	54	47	36	83	4	7	15
Colored o.	1	8	17	25	75	69	144	7	0	0	51	43	94	23	24	47	1	2	3
Connecticut	2	8	36	44	140	126	36	39	36	76	53	37	90	42	38	80	5	14	19
District of Columbia	2	13	22	25	84	44	62	3	1	4	7	21	21	49	7	35	4	3	7
Georgia	2	2	19	21	117	95	43	33	17	50	66	65	131	16	13	29	4	0	4
I abd.	1	1	8	9	34	27	61	8	4	12	16	15	31	6	14	21	0	0	0
Illinois	1	12	34	46	193	184	77	0	0	0	164	154	318	29	30	59	0	0	0
Indiana	1	7	18	25	149	100	91	28	28	56	107	90	197	10	22	32	4	9	13
Iowa	1	10	18	28	91	100	81	0	0	0	68	65	133	10	23	33	7	18	22
Kansas	2	15	23	38	130	93	23	27	20	47	80	38	88	69	44	73	11	11	24
Kentucky	1	4	10	14	154	168	45	9	9	18	85	87	172	32	41	73	12	12	3
Louisiana					76						34	23	57	27	27	54	2	1	
Maine	1	3	11	14	59	54	13	7	3	10	30	31	61	22	20	42	0	0	0
Maryland	2	7	17	24	81	89	20	20	17	37	29	32	61	16	26	32	16	13	29
Massachusetts	1	10	24	34	101	90	81	3	8	23	36	38	74	63	50	113	16	12	31
Michigan	1	11	24	35	160	131	291	35	23	58	76	82	134	62	45	78	16	15	0
Minnesota	1	4	24	38	140	102	242	0	0	0	134	124	57	63	43	54	16	16	
Mississippi	2	3	12	15	83	83	76	2	3	5	42	43	85	45	33	78	4	4	8
Missouri	2	17	15	32	158	124	282	0	0	0	104	88	192	49	34	83	0	0	0
Montana	1	3	7	10	39	39	78	8	3	11	20	21	41	7	11	18	4	4	8
Nebraska	1	4	17	21	98	87	85	11	9	20	58	46	104	23	26	48	6	7	13
New York	8	53	190	243	1,063	848	1,81	204	156	360	641	430	971	214	216	490	22	19	41
North Carolina	2	13	36	50	217	146	82	0	0	0	44	90	244	71	38	109	4	4	81
North Dakota	1	4	9	13	16	35	100	36	24	90	10	24	35	10	30	05	0	0	0
Ohio	1	10	80	91	285	223	49	8	8	144	142	311	35	41	95	4	8	8
Oklahoma	2	12	9	21	154	163	30	6	6	20	81	18	164	38	26	43	7	13	25
Oregon	1	2	10	12	60	43	03	8	6	14	22	12	40	28	19	12	1	1	43

Pennsylvania	5	28	111	139	622	513	1,135	168	141	309	240	186	426	141	137	278	31	23	54
Rhode Island	1	1	14	15	49	45	94	6	5	11	16	13	29	27	27	54	0	0	0
South Carolina	2	5	15	20	75	81	156	0	0	0	30	37	67	27	29	56	18	15	33
South Dakota	1	2	11	13	27	33	60	4	9	13	18	12	30	5	11	16	......	1	1
Tennessee	2	9	11	20	141	129	270	......	......	......	98	90	188	43	39	82	......	......	......
Texas	2	20	52	72	278	278	556	0	0	0	191	205	396	63	61	124	18	15	33
Utah	1	3	16	19	62	53	115	0	0	0	38	34	72	14	13	27	7	9	16
Vermont	1	0	5	5	24	19	43	......	......	......	16	13	29	8	6	14	0	0	0
Virginia	1	7	20	27	108	103	211	5	5	10	63	55	118	29	25	54	1	4	5
Washington	1	7	10	17	80	63	143	13	9	22	39	30	69	27	23	50	1	1	2
West Virginia	1	6	15	21	94	80	174	12	8	20	66	54	120	16	18	34	0	0	0
Wisconsin	1	9	18	27	112	76	188	0	5	5	63	35	98	39	26	65	10	10	20

TABLE 5.—Summary of graduates and miscellaneous items in State schools for the deaf, 1917–18.

States	Graduates in 1918 Boys	Girls	Total	Pupils in teacher training classes Boys	Girls	Total	Pupils taught speech during the year Boys	Girls	Total	Pupils taught by oral method Boys	Girls	Total	Pupils taught by auricular method Boys	Girls	Total	Pupils in the industrial department Boys	Girls	Total	Volumes in library	Value of buildings and grounds	Value of scientific apparatus, furniture, instruments, library, etc.	Amount of permanent endowment or productive fund
1	2	3	4	5	6	7	8	9	10	11	12	13	14	15	16	17	18	19	20	21	22	23
United States	102	104	216	3	43	46	4,278	3,536	7,814	3,741	3,251	6,992	161	121	282	3,096	2,751	5,847	144,281	$18,266,754	$1,581,471	$1,838,347
Alabama	0	0	0				62	59	121	60	58	118	2	1	3	7	7	14	950	242,887	13,178	0
Arizona							25	13	38	25	13	38				14	10	24				
Arkansas	0	0	0		2	2	87	80	167	76	79	155	11	1	12	167	144	311	450	500,000	5,000	
California	7	7	14				78	65	143	78	65	143	78	65	143	111	71	182	6,000	906,885	200,000	71,245
Colorado	1	2	3				49	48	97	49	48	97				75	69	144	3,650	307,728	61,870	
Connecticut	0	3	3		2	2	196	33	229	140	125	265	4	2	6	159	25	184	3,060	212,810	72,576	0
District of Columbia	3	0	3	2	6	8	65	24	89	14	17	31				24	25	49	6,000	1,000,000	8,000	0
Georgia	0	0	0				88	81	169	76	68	144	2	2	4	25	27	52	1,200	300,000	20,000	
Idaho	0	0	0				26	25	51	24	23	47				34	27	61		55,000	2,000	
Illinois							113	99	212	54	65	119	2	2	4	71	65	136	12,225	353,287	162,907	
Indiana	4	9	13				57	68	125	57	68	125				63	93	156	3,000	818,600	66,354	
Iowa	4	5	9				66	49	115	66	49	115				38	78	116	6,325	383,900	26,650	
Kansas	5	3	8				92	112	204	92	112	204				83	134	215	3,449	389,300	16,300	16,000
Kentucky	10	10	20				60		60	60						83	104	187	2,300	329,000	1,500	7,000
Louisiana												54	6		6	40		40	2,200	350,000		
Maine	0	0	0				57	52	109	57	52	109	11	5	16	47	41	88	800	101,100	16,720	
Maryland	2	3	5				74	66	140	58	57	115	1		1	46	34	80	3,100	316,000	12,000	
Massachusetts	4	2	6		10	10	102	89	191	102	89	191				69	56	125	4,100	226,500	18,400	
Michigan	6	4	10				98	80	178	98	80	178				60	85	145	5,000	398,660		3,340
Minnesota																				563,863	91,508	299,758
Mississippi	0	0	0				77	71	148	11	4	15	10	15	25	0	10	10	3,400	270,091	29,043	0
Missouri	12	11	23				86	64	150	69	61	130				125	96	220	2,500	543,000	31,434	0
Montana	2	3	5				29	24	53							28	39	67	2,000	215,826	12,000	
Nebraska							60	61	120							66	61	127	1,650	355,000		
New York	12	5	17		5	5	908	741	1,649	789	647	1,436	26	10	36	484	461	945	30,773	2,854,048	232,528	1,082,404

North Carolina																								
North Dakota																								
Ohio																								
Oklahoma																								
Oregon																								
Pennsylvania																								
Rhode Island																								
South Carolina																								
South Dakota																								
Tennessee																								
Texas																								
Utah																								
Vermont																								
Virginia																								
Washington																								
West Virginia																								
Wisconsin																								

TABLE 6.—Summary of receipts and expenditures of State schools for the deaf, 1917-18.

States	Number of schools reporting	Receipts (only 59 schools reporting).					Expenditures.			
		From State, county, or city.	From private benefactions for permanent equipment and current expenses.	From productive endowment fund.	From other sources.	Total.	For building and lasting improvements.	For teachers' salaries, books, etc.	For other salaries and all other current expenses.	Total.
1	2	3	4	5	6	7	8	9	10	11
United States	61	$3,420,387	$19,800	$171,121	$206,625	$4,494,484	$438,291	$1,267,945	$2,430,530	$4,292,798
Alabama	2	53,025			445	53,026		18,739	38,415	57,164
Arizona	1	15,000	0	0	445	15,445		6,740	8,705	15,445
Arkansas	2	78,615			4,100	80,715	11,700	11,817	78,122	89,939
California	1	93,476		0		93,476	29,592	43,966	37,973	93,609
Colorado	1	111,879				111,879		76,490		106,082
Connecticut	1	62,173	1,786	21,999		85,958	2,109	45,091	38,294	86,494
District of Columbia	2	60,000	0	0	0	116,580		22,000	38,000	115,539
Georgia	2	60,000	0	0	0	60,000	1,000	22,000	38,000	60,000
Idaho	1	27,206	0	0	0	27,206	6,000	11,580	13,560	26,520
Illinois	1	159,100		0		159,100	6,000	11,580	139,560	145,600
Indiana	1	103,448	0	0	6,161	103,448	945	25,701	67,107	93,783
Iowa	1	66,370			2,832	72,831	3,000	14,000	52,139	69,139
Kansas	2	66,500			4,318	66,382	3,000	19,810	46,962	66,672
Kentucky	1	82,948		350		87,536		24,390	63,318	87,708
Louisiana	1	29,800		1,570	900	33,270	3,636	15,411	14,838	33,887
Maine	1	35,362		135	1,664	38,497	5,526	12,500	17,471	38,497
Maryland	2	37,500			13,789	48,657	1,068	17,337	32,224	50,612
Massachusetts	2	57,437	4,201	11,963		87,390	692	41,884	49,926	92,594
Michigan	1	121,000	0	0	38,799	159,799	3,132	29,287	122,616	155,020
Minnesota	1	106,300	0	0	7,263	113,563	10,500	31,421	56,540	98,406
Mississippi	2	47,700			60	50,340		7,094	32,530	40,221
Missouri	2	109,500				109,500	0	35,000	74,500	109,630
Montana	1	60,000				60,000	43,364	47,066	44,790	135,260
Nebraska	1	60,000				60,000		26,000	34,000	60,000
New York	8	392,389	5,688	97,672	67,	1,061,214	9,690	227,701	579,521	816,921

North Carolina	1	197,268			168,338	8,048	58,349	40,816	66,954	164,119
North Dakota	1				62,780		5,231	16,589	28,440	46,230
Ohio	1	149,595	72		149,657		2,000	34,872	96,903	185,276
Oklahoma	2	127,356	0		127,356		60,462	33,265	51,780	145,887
Oregon	1	28,778	0	900	29,678	900	1,510	9,020	23,838	34,368
Pennsylvania	5	330,355	23,390	8,125	387,545	25,675	6,200	185,419	210,398	402,017
Rhode Island	1	96,500	0	0	104,183	7,683				60,463
South Dakota	1	69,000	5,000		74,000		38,000	48,003	41,000	79,000
Texas	2	225,451			225,451	0	125,481	18,630	29,546	203,030
Utah	1	47,350	8,970	0	56,330		0		37,290	53,890
Virginia	1	40,000			40,000		1,000	22,000	17,000	40,000
Washington	1	50,331			51,048	727	4,144	5,214	41,660	51,048
West Virginia	1	83,940			56,724	2,784	1,392	22,272	27,840	51,594
Wisconsin	1	76,895	0	0	76,895	0	2,076		77,700	79,776

1 Includes $9,463 not itemized.   2 Includes $487,718 not itemized.

TABLE 7.—*Summary of statistics of instructors and pupils in private schools for the deaf, 1917–18.*

States.	Number of schools reporting.	Instructors.			Pupils enrolled.			Pupils in the kindergarten.			In classes corresponding to grades 1 to 4.			In classes corresponding to grades 5 to 8.			In classes corresponding to high school grades.		
		Men.	Women.	Total.	Boys.	Girls.	Total.	Boys.	Girls.	Total.	Boys.	Girls.	Total.	Boys.	Girls.	Total.	Boys.	Girls.	Total.
1	2	3	4	5	6	7	8	9	10	11	12	13	14	15	16	17	18	19	20
Total...........	18	20	103	123	326	318	644	52	47	99	165	152	317	92	113	205	15	7	22
California.........	1	1	6	7	40	....	40	....	....	....	20	....	20	16	....	16	2	....	2
Georgia...........	1	....	4	4	2	12	14	1	4	5	1	6	7	....	2	2	....	....	....
Illinois..........	1	....	17	17	69	62	131	5	8	13	42	30	72	23	24	47	0	0	0
Louisiana.........	1	1	8	9	25	32	57	0	0	0	20	19	39	5	13	18	0	0	0
Maryland..........	2	....	12	12	3	43	46	....	4	4	2	29	31	....	11	11	0	0	0
Massachusetts......	1	....	1	1	8	10	18	8	10	18	0	0	0	0	0	0	0	0	0
Michigan..........	1	3	2	5	22	12	34	0	0	0	18	10	28	4	2	6	0	0	0
Missouri..........	2	3	13	16	25	27	52	14	12	26	9	9	18	2	6	8	....	....	....
New York..........	2	5	12	17	39	23	62	7	1	8	10	6	16	10	9	19	12	7	19
Ohio..............	1	2	3	5	13	11	24	3	1	4	5	3	8	5	7	12	....	....	....
Pennsylvania......	2	....	9	9	24	26	50	7	3	10	11	14	25	5	9	14	1	0	1
Porto Rico........	1	0	5	5	17	22	39	0	0	0	6	5	11	11	17	28	....	....	....
South Dakota......	1	....	1	1	....	1	1	....	....	....	....	1	1	....	....	....	....	....	....
Wisconsin.........	1	5	10	15	39	37	76	7	4	11	21	20	41	11	13	24	0	0	0

TABLE 8.—*Summary of statistics of graduates and miscellaneous items in private schools for the deaf, 1917–18.*

Location.	Graduates in 1918.			Pupils taught speech during the year.			Pupils taught by oral method.			Pupils taught by auricular method.			Pupils in the industrial department.			Volumes in library.	Property (9 schools reporting).		
																	Value of buildings and grounds.	Value of scientific apparatus, furniture, instruments, library, etc.	Amount of permanent endowment or productive fund.
	Boys.	Girls.	Total.	Boys.	Girls.	Total.	Boys.	Girls.	Total.	Boys.	Girls.	Total.	Boys.	Girls.	Total.				
1	2	3	4	5	6	7	8	9	10	11	12	13	14	15	16	17	18	19	20
Total...........	3	0	3	305	232	537	282	217	499	23	15	38	121	196	317	2,225	$425,913	$24,759	$87,419
California.........	2	....	2	35	....	35	25	....	25	10	....	10	20	....	20	500	32,000	....	....
Georgia...........	....	....	....	2	15	17	2	12	14	....	3	3	....	....	....	....	....	....	....
Illinois..........	0	0	0	90	....	90	90	....	90	0	0	0	68	68	400	200,000	6,886	....
Louisiana.........	0	0	0	27	47	16	25	41	4	2	6	12	22	34	....	....	....	....
Maryland..........	0	0	0	3	45	48	3	43	46	0	2	2	0	0	0	500	42,500	3,500	100
Massachusetts......	0	0	0	8	10	18	8	10	18	0	0	0	0	0	0	....	8,400	1,000	87,319
Michigan..........	0	0	0	21	12	33	21	12	33	0	0	0	2	8	10	225	43,570	2,273	0
Missouri..........	....	....	....	21	24	45	19	20	39	2	4	6	16	18	34	....	41,843	5,100	....
New York..........	....	....	....	21	7	28	21	7	28	0	0	0	7	6	13	300	....	....	....
Ohio..............	....	....	....	13	11	24	13	11	24	....	....	....	10	10	20	....	30,000	3,000	....
Pennsylvania......	1	....	1	24	26	50	21	25	46	3	1	4	18	24	42	200	....	....	....
Porto Rico........	....	....	....	17	22	39	17	22	39	....	....	....	9	15	24	100	27,600	3,000	0
South Dakota......	....	....	....	1	1	....	1	1	....	....	....	....	....	....	....	....	....	....	....
Wisconsin.........	0	0	0	30	32	62	26	29	55	4	3	7	27	25	52	....	....	....	....

TABLE 9.—*Summary of receipts and expenditures of private schools for the deaf, 1917–18.*

States.	Number of schools reporting.	Receipts.					Expenditures.			
		From State, county, or city.	From private benefactions for permanent equipment and current expenses.	From productive endowment fund.	From other sources.	Total.	For building and lasting improvements.	For teachers' salaries, books, etc.	For other salaries and all other current expenses.	Total.
1	2	3	4	5	6	7	8	9	10	11
United States...	8	$6,828	$41,851	$4,340	$34,867	$87,886	$50,089	$20,173	$32,728	$102,990
Maryland	2	2,250	1,933	0	9,674	13,857	4,136	2,791	7,747	14,674
Massachusetts	1	2,429	1,409	4,340	41	8,219	......	2,390	4,415	6,805
Michigan	1	0	5,918	0	3,507	9,425	1,473	3,765	3,043	8,281
Missouri	2	......	27,444	......	21,016	48,460	42,682	10,360	12,274	65,316
New York	1	0	500	0	0	500	0	500	0	500
Porto Rico	1	2,149	4,647	0	629	7,425	1,798	367	5,249	7,414

TABLE 10.—*Summary of statistics of instructors and pupils in city day-school classes for the deaf, 1917–18.*

States.	Number of schools reporting.	Instructors.			Pupils enrolled.			Pupils in the kindergarten.			In classes corresponding to grades 1 to 4.			In classes corresponding to grades 5 to 8.			In classes corresponding to high school grades.		
		Men.	Women.	Total.	Boys.	Girls.	Total.	Boys.	Girls.	Total.	Boys.	Girls.	Total.	Boys.	Girls.	Total.	Boys.	Girls.	Total.
1	2	3	4	5	6	7	8	9	10	11	12	13	14	15	16	17	18	19	20
United States	69	18	305	323	1,300	1,182	2,482	103	110	213	792	721	1,513	384	335	719	17	13	30
California	6	0	20	20	69	85	154	5	7	12	41	54	95	20	21	41	....	1	1
Georgia	1	....	1	1	3	4		1	....	1	....	3	3	....					
Illinois	3	3	37	40	163	153	316	9	13	22	120	102	222	34	38	72	....	....	....
Iowa	1	....	1	1	4	4	8	0	1	1	4	3	7	....					
Louisiana	1	....	2	2	5	9	14	1	2	3	4	7	11	....					
Massachusetts	2	2	38	40	162	157	319	10	7	17	87	93	180	66	46	112	....	....	..
Michigan	13	3	31	34	145	119	264	16	7	23	84	76	160	45	29	74	2	5	7
Minnesota	2	0	6	6	23	30	53	2	6	8	13	11	24	8	13	21	....		
Missouri	2	1	10	11	64	43	107	5	2	7	57	37	94	2	4	6	....		
New Jersey	2	....	14	14	55	50	105	7	6	13	12	15	27	36	29	65	....		
New York	1	3	37	40	185	189	374	7	19	26	118	119	237	67	51	111	....		
Ohio	6	1	28	29	106	98	204	7	8	15	74	66	140	25	24	49	....		
Oregon	1	....	2	2	13	12	25	2	4	6	5	4	9	6	4	10	....		
Texas	1	....	2	2	10	4	14	0	0	0	8	4	12	2	0	2	....		
Washington	4	2	10	12	43	45	88	4	7	11	23	22	45	16	16	32	....		
Wisconsin	23	3	66	69	252	181	433	27	21	48	142	105	247	64	40	104	15	8	23

TABLE 11.—*Summary of statistics of graduates and miscellaneous items in city day school classes for the deaf, 1917–18.*

States	Graduates in 1918			Pupils in teacher training classes			Pupils taught speech during the year			Pupils taught by oral method			Pupils taught by auricular method			Pupils in the industrial department			Property			
	Boys	Girls	Total	Boys	Girls	Total	Boys	Girls	Total	Boys	Girls	Total	Boys	Girls	Total	Boys	Girls	Total	Volumes in library	Value of buildings and grounds	Value of scientific apparatus, furniture, instruments, library, etc.	Amount of permanent endowment or productive fund
1	2	3	4	5	6	7	8	9	10	11	12	13	14	15	16	17	18	19	20	21	22	23
United States	3	2	5	0	15	15	1,261	1,145	2,406	1,143	1,065	2,206	60	55	115	398	374	772	7,153	$458,600	$49,015	$8,400
California	1	0	1				61	77	138	66	81	147	12	14	26	9	13	22	185			
Georgia							1	2	3	1	2	3										
Illinois					2	2	148	138	286	163	153	316				2	2	4			50	
Iowa							4	4	8	4	4	8							200	2,500	100	
Louisiana		1	1				5	9	14	5	9	14										
Massachusetts	1	0	1		1	1	162	157	319	162	157	319	10	14	24	40	48	88	2,257	235,500	38,300	8,400
Michigan					2	2	145	119	264	55	44	99	16	13	29	16	16	32	168		100	
Minnesota							23	30	53	23	30	53	0	0	0	12	30	42	30		500	
Missouri							57	35	92	22	18	40								15,000		
New Jersey							54	50	104	54	50	104				7	2	9	1,192			
New York							185	189	374	185	189	374	1	1	2	88	90	178	306	142,600	4,300	
Ohio							106	98	204	105	97	202				67	69	136				
Oregon							13	12	25	13	12	25				7	8	15				
Texas							10	4	14	10	4	14										
Washington	1	1	2				43	45	88	43	45	88	2	2	4	9	7	16			50	
Wisconsin					10	10	244	176	420	232	170	402	19	11	30	141	89	230	2,490	63,000	6,615	

TABLE 12.—*Statistics of State schools for the deaf, 1917–18.*

Location	Institution	Instructors		Pupils enrolled		Pupils in the kindergarten		In classes corresponding to grades 1 to 4		In classes corresponding to grades 5 to 8		In classes corresponding to high school grades		Graduates in 1918		Pupils in teacher-training classes		Pupils taught speech during year		Pupils taught by oral method		Pupils taught by auricular method		Pupils in industrial department		Property		
		Men	Women	Boys	Girls	Boys	Girls	Boys	Girls	Boys	Girls	Boys	Girls	Boys	Girls	Boys	Girls	Boys	Girls	Boys	Girls	Boys	Girls	Boys	Girls	Volumes in library	Value of buildings and grounds	Value of scientific apparatus, furniture, etc.	Amount of permanent endowment, or productive funds
1	2	3	4	5	6	7	8	9	10	11	12	13	14	15	16	17	18	19	20	21	22	23	24	25	26	27	28	29	30
Talladega, Ala.	Alabama School for the Deaf	5	15	99	88	6	4	56	56	18	16	10	10	0	0	0	0	0	0	58	58	1	1		7	7	875	$225,000	$12,000	
Do.	Alabama School for the Negro Deaf and Blind.	2	1	17	14	(¹)														13	13			75		450	$17,887	*1,178	
Tucson, Ariz.	Arizona State School for the Deaf.	3	5	25	13	11		21	21	4	4	14	10					6	13	25	25	11			14	10	450		5,000	0
Little Rock, Ark.	Arkansas Deaf Mute Institute	10	17	173	154	11	14	85	73	73	73	4	4	0	0	0	0	87	80	79	76	11	0	158	130				
Do.	Arkansas Deaf Mute Institute, Colored Department.	3	2	16	16	2		28	9	56	16	6	0	0	0			9	9	9	9	0	0	9	14				
Berkeley, Calif.	California School for Deaf and Blind.	15	17	118	77	7	7	51	47	23	36	8	7	7	7	2		78	78	78	65	78	65	111	71	26,000	500,000	200,000	
Colorado Springs, Colo.	Colorado School for Deaf and Blind.	8	23	106	92	7	0	33	33	36	24	4	2	1	2	0	0	49	48	65	49	0	0	75	60	3,650	908,895	51,870	847,190
Hartford, Conn.	American School, at Hartford, for the Deaf.	6	13	34	31	32	28	51	21	23	33	10	4	0	0	0	0	106	48	92	92	0	0	143	69	2,000	307,728	72,576	
Mystic, Conn.	The Mystic Oral School for the Deaf.	2	13	34	31	7	8	20	20	6		4		0	0	0	0	33	33	33	33	4	2	16	25	1,050	178,950	8,000	0
Washington, D. C.	Columbia Institution for the Deaf: Gallaudet College.	10	5	60	33			7	14	10	17			3	3		1	3	3	0	0	0	0	(⁶)	25	6,000	1,000,000	20,000	0
	Kendall School.	3	17	24	25	3	1	45	14	16	16	3	0	0	0	1	1	24	23	17	17	0	0	24	25				
Cave Spring, Ga.	Georgia School for the Deaf.	1	7	96	78	33	17	21	17	13	13	0	0	0	0	0	0	76	76	76	76	0	0	17	20	200	300,000	2,000	
Do.	Georgia School for the Deaf (Negro).	1	2	21	17	0	0	21	17			0	0	0	0	0	0	12	13	0	0	0	0	8	7				
Gooding, Idaho	Idaho School for the Deaf and the Blind.	1	8	34	27	8	4	16	16	6	5	3	3	0	0	0	0	26	25	23	24	2	2	34	27	1,200	55,000		0

¹ Prorated.
² School is not graded.
³ Printed in ink.
⁴ Includes also statistics of school for the blind.
⁵ Male and female.
⁶ Data for 1915–16.
⁶ Pupils in senior year required to take some occupational course.

TABLE 12.—*Statistics of State schools for the deaf, 1917–18*—Continued.

Location	Institution	Instructors Men	Women	Pupils enrolled Boys	Girls	Pupils in the kindergarten Boys	Girls	In classes corresponding to grades 1 to 4 Boys	Girls	In classes corresponding to grades 5 to 8 Boys	Girls	In classes corresponding to high school grades Boys	Girls	Graduates in 1918 Boys	Girls	Pupils in teacher-training classes Boys	Girls	Pupils taught speech during year Boys	Girls	Pupils taught by oral method Boys	Girls	Pupils taught by auricular method Boys	Girls	Pupils in industrial department Boys	Girls	Volumes in library	Value of buildings and grounds	Value of scientific apparatus, furniture, etc.	Amount of permanent endowment or productive funds
Jacksonville, Ill.	Illinois School for the Deaf	12	34	193	184	0	0	164	154	30	30	0	0	0	0	0	0	99	113	70	65	0	0	71	66	12,225	$353,257	$162,907	
Indianapolis, Ind.	Indiana State School for the Deaf	(1)	(1)	149	146	28	28	107	90	10	15	4	9	0	4	0	0	90	90	0	0	0	0	63	98	3,000	818,600		$16,000
Council Bluffs, Iowa	Iowa School for the Deaf	7	18	91	100	0	0	68	65	16	22	7	13	4	0	0	0	68	57	57	68	0	0	86	78	6,236	383,900	66,354	
Olathe, Kans.	Kansas State School for the Deaf	10	18	130	93	0	0	50	38	66	44	11	11	5	0	0	0	49	49	65	66	0	0	81	134	3,449	336,300	96,000	7,000
Danville, Ky.	Kentucky School for the Deaf	13	21	138	149	27	20	72	75	30	39	12	12	0	0	0	0	92	92	92	92	0	0	79	89	2,300	309,000	15,000	
Do.	Kentucky School for the Deaf (Negro)	2	2	18	13	0	0	13	13	2	0	2	1	0	0	0	0	0	0	0	0	0	0	4	15		20,000	1,300	
Baton Rouge, La.	Louisiana State School for the Deaf	4	10	69	54	9	9	34	23	27	27	1	0	0	0	0	0	60	54	54	54	0	0	40	—	200	350,000	1,500	
Portland, Me.	Maine School for the Deaf	3	11	59	54	3	3	30	20	20	20	0	0	0	0	0	0	57	57	56	57	0	2	47	41	800	101,100	16,620	3,340
Frederick, Md.	Maryland State School for the Deaf	5	13	64	59	14	14	19	16	16	12	0	0	2	2	0	0	64	64	56	80	8	3	32	25	3,100	262,000	12,000	
Overlea, Md.	Maryland School for the Colored Blind and Deaf	2	4	17	17	3	3	10	10	4	4	0	0	0	0	0	0	10	10	2	2	0	0	14	12		*34,000	2,400	56,958
Beverly, Mass.	New England Industrial School for Deaf-Mutes	1	6	15	15	8	8	10	7	2	0	0	0	2	0	0	0	18	18	16	16	1	0	14	12	800	10,000	16,000	212,790
Northampton, Mass.	Clarke School for the Deaf	10	21	86	75	23	23	25	25	60	60	13	15	4	4	0	0	86	86	86	75	0	0	55	44	3,300	216,500	91,508	0
Flint, Mich.	Michigan School for the Deaf	11	24	140	131	0	0	58	58	53	53	0	0	6	6	0	0	98	98	98	80	0	0	60	85	5,086	390,000	5,000	0
Faribault, Minn.	Minnesota School for the Deaf	11	24	75	102	0	0	39	39	35	25	0	0	0	0	0	0	75	75	80	80	0	0	—	—	5,000	563,985		
Jackson, Miss.	Institute for the Deaf and Dumb	2	10	18	18	0	0	4	4	10	10	0	0	0	0	0	0	68	68	35	37	0	0	35	30	3,400	270,091	29,043	
Do.	Institute for the Deaf and Dumb (Negro)	1	2	2	2	0	0	0	0	2	2	0	0	0	0	0	0	3	2	3	3	0	0	2	—				
Fulton, Mo.	Missouri School for the Deaf	16	15	150	118	0	0	95	88	45	28	0	0	11	11	0	0	85	65	75	80	0	0	116	90	2,500	$543,000		
Do.	Missouri School for the Deaf (Negro)	1	0	8	6	0	0	6	6	2	2	0	0	0	0	0	0	0	0	0	0	0	0	9	5				

Location	Institution																														
Boulder, Mont.	Montana School for Deaf and Blind	3	7	39	39	8	3	20	21	7	11	4	4	2	3		20	21	11	4	10	15	28	3	2,000	* 215,826	* 31,434		
Omaha, Nebr.	Nebraska School for the Deaf	1	17	98	87	11	9	58	46	23	25	6	7				60	61	60	61			66	61	1,650	355,000	12,000	
Albany, N. Y.	The Albany Home School for the Oral Instruction of the Deaf	5	0	26	22	5	5	14	12	7	5						24	21	25	21	1	1	10	8		² 40,000	¹ 3,000	
Buffalo, N. Y.	Le Couteulx St. Mary's Institution for the Improved Instruction of Deaf Mutes	4	27	100	82	17	6	68	45	14	26	1	5	1	1	3	89	79	76	86	3		64	60	3,000	257,500	35,400	
Malone, N. Y.	Northern New York Institution for Deaf Mutes	1	12	57	53	21	22	11	14	19	14	3	3	2	2	0	57	53	57	53			14	53	1,200	184,925	27,249	
New York (904 Lexington Ave.), N. Y.	Association for the Improved Instruction of Deaf Mutes. In-	6	31	148	128	31	21	75	66	41	41	1	0	0	0	2	148	128	148	128	0	0			1,983	279,383	42,000	
New York (Station M) N. Y.		18	33	275	175	89	66	128	68	50	41	8	2	5	1	0	253	161	248	158	5	3	186	109	11,490	700,000	26,000	1,082,404
Rochester, N. Y.	Western New York Institution for Deaf Mutes	5	21	94	86	5	4	65	59	16	14	8	9	3	1	0	94	86	0	0			53	50	10,100	200,000	73,259	0
Rome, N. Y.	Central New York Institution for Deaf Mutes	2	13	61	33	9	6						0	0	0	0	61	33	61	33			45	33		130,000		
Westchester, N. Y.	St. Joseph's Institute for the Improved Instruction of Deaf Mutes	11	53	272	269	24	26	180	168	67	75	1	0	1	0	0	182	180	174	168	8	12	150	150	3,000	1,062,240	25,620	
Morganton, N. C.	North Carolina School for the Deaf	9	26	166	104	0	0	108	68	55	29	2	7	0	0	4	144	95	144	95	0	0	52	76	3,100	550,000	30,000	0
Raleigh, N. C.	North Carolina School for the Blind and the Deaf (Negro)	4	9	51	41			36	32	15	9						31	27	31	27			20	32		* 131,008	* 5,796	
Devils Lake, N. Dak.	North Dakota School for the Deaf	4	9	48	52			31	24	16	20	1	5	0	3		32	37	32	37			31	29	1,850	205,664		1,800
Columbus, Ohio	State School for the Deaf	16	36	266	223	35	24	169	142	35	30	15	10	9	5	2	177	157	175	155	0		117	84	6,500	925,500	800	0
Sulphur, Okla.	Oklahoma School for the Deaf	9	20	140	148			75	76	49	46	16	26		1		83	98	83	98					735	210,000	26,255	
Taft, Okla.	Institute for Deaf, Blind and Orphans (Negro)	2	0	14	14	6	8	6	6				1				14	14	14	14			4	6	102	90,000	3,000	
Salem, Oreg.	Oregon State School for the Deaf	2	10	60	43	8	6	22	18	23	19		10	1	1		47	36	47	36			42	40	1,200	117,000	5,000	0
Swissvale (Edgewood Park), Pa.	Western Pennsylvania Institution for the Instruction of the Deaf and Dumb	10	22	149	135	46	44	68	60	22	23	13	8				139	129	139	129			67	80	4,930	628,092	35,386	86,800
Philadelphia (2201 Belmont Ave.), Pa.	Home for the Training in Speech of Deaf Children before They Are of School Age	1	8	39	26												39	26	39	26					1,000	87,405		
Philadelphia (Mount Airy), Pa.	Pennsylvania Institution for the Deaf and Dumb	13	57	323	271	95	85	125	91	85	80	18	15	12	8	4	323	271	323	271			238	198	4,000	1,000,000	250,000	300,000
Pittsburgh (Black Hills), Pa.	De Paul Institute for Deaf Mutes	3	12	47	47	6	9	28	19	13	19						47	47	46	47	1		18	27	300	113,849	² 3,000	
Scranton, Pa.	Pennsylvania State Oral School for the Deaf	1	12	64	34	21	3	22	16	21	15	0	0	0	0		64	34	64	34	0		43	19	300	189,000	8,500	0
Providence, R. I.	Rhode Island Institute for the Deaf	1	14	49	45	6	5	16	13	27	27	0	0	0	0	0			49	45			33	32		300,000		0
Cedar Springs, S. C.	South Carolina School for the Deaf and the Blind	4	13	60	63	0	0	24	29	21	23	15	11	0	0	0	30	33	28	31	2	2	60	63	1,200	* 135,423		
Do.	South Carolina School for the Deaf and the Blind (Negro)	1	2	15	18	0	0	6	8	6	6	3	4	0	0	0	0	0	0	0	0	0	15	18	100			
Sioux Falls, S. Dak.	South Dakota School for the Deaf	2	11	27	33	4	9	18	12	5	11		1	1	0	0	15	25	15	25	3		9	14		150,000	10,000	
Knoxville, Tenn.	Tennessee School for the Deaf and the Dumb	8	11	121	124			84	86	37	38		2	5			55	54										

* Prorated.   ¹ Work is done by correspondence.   ² Data for 1915-16.

Table 12.—Statistics of State schools for the deaf. 1917–18—Continued.

Location	Institution	Instructors Men	Instructors Women	Pupils enrolled Boys	Pupils enrolled Girls	Pupils in the kindergarten Boys	Pupils in the kindergarten Girls	In classes corresponding to grades 1 to 4 Boys	In classes corresponding to grades 1 to 4 Girls	In classes corresponding to grades 5 to 8 Boys	In classes corresponding to grades 5 to 8 Girls	In classes corresponding to high-school grades Boys	In classes corresponding to high-school grades Girls	Graduates in 1918 Boys	Graduates in 1918 Girls	Pupils in teacher training classes Boys	Pupils in teacher training classes Girls	Pupils taught speech during year Boys	Pupils taught speech during year Girls	Pupils taught by oral method Boys	Pupils taught by oral method Girls	Pupils taught by auricular method Boys	Pupils taught by auricular method Girls	Pupils in industrial department Boys	Pupils in industrial department Girls	Volumes in library	Value of buildings and grounds	Value of scientific apparatus, furniture, etc.	Amount of permanent endowment or productive funds
1	2	3	4	5	6	7	8	9	10	11	12	13	14	15	16	17	18	19	20	21	22	23	24	25	26	27	28	29	30
Knoxville, Tenn.	Tennessee School for the Deaf and the Dumb (Negro).	1		20	5		0	11	4	6	1	13	13	3	6	0	0	135	159	48	41	0	0	8	83	4,000	$687,000	$52,500	0
Austin, Tex.	Texas School for the Deaf.	16	44	235	237	0	0	163	169	59	55	13	9	3	0	0	0	12	18	8	14	4	4	98	30	150	*61,488	*2,940	0
Do.	Texas Deaf, Dumb and Blind Institute for Colored Youth.	3	16	43	41	0	0	38	34	5	6	7	0	0	0	0	0	62	53	56	49	0	0	4	31	3,500	*224,365	*11,218	0
Ogden, Utah.	Utah School for the Deaf and the Blind.	0	5	62	19	5	5	16	13	14	13	0	4	0	0	0	0	24	19	24	19	0	0	26	16		*138,205	*7,385	
Brattleboro, Vt.	Austine Institution for the Deaf and the Blind.	7	20	24	103	13	5	39	55	8	25	1	1	1	4	0	0	79	81	79	81	1	1	14	43	1,700	89,660	28,423	
Staunton, Va.	Virginia School for the Deaf and the Blind.	7	10	106	63	12	5	39	30	29	23	1	1	0	1	0	0	62	55	49	44	1	2	62	37	1,275	*69,600	*300	
Vancouver, Wash.	Washington State School for the Deaf.	6	15	90	80	0	9	66	54	27	18	0	0	0	0	0	0	74	65	68	63	0	0	42	5	450	300,000	10,000	
Romney W. Va.	West Virginia Schools for Deaf and Blind.	9	18	94	76	0	0	63	35	16	26	10	10	1	3	0	0	82	51	82	51	6	0	75	25	500			
Delavan, Wis.	Wisconsin School for the Deaf.	9	18	112	76	0	0	63	35	39	26	0	0	1	3	0	0	82	51	82	51	6	0	35	25			10,000	0

* Printed.

Table 13.—*Statistics of receipts and expenditures of State schools for the deaf, 1917-18.*

Location.	Institution.	Receipts.					Expenditures.			
		From State, county, or city.	From private benefactions for permanent equipment and current expenses.	From productive endowment fund.	From other sources.	Total.	For building and lasting improvements.	For teachers' salaries, books, etc.	For other salaries and all other current expenses.	Total.
1	2	3	4	5	6	7	8	9	10	11
Talledega, Ala.	Alabama School for the Deaf	$45,895				$45,895		$16,941	$32,804	$49,745
Do.	Alabama School for the Negro Deaf and Blind	*7,130				*7,130		*1,798	*5,611	*7,409
Tucson, Ariz.	Arizona State School for Deaf	15,000			$445	15,445		6,740	8,705	15,445
Little Rock, Ark.	Arkansas Deaf Mute Institute	76,615			4,100	80,715	0	11,817	78,122	89,939
Do.	Arkansas Deaf Mute Institute, colored department									
Berkeley, Calif.	California School for Deaf and Blind	*93,476				*93,476	*11,700	*43,936	*37,973	*93,609
Colorado Springs, Colo	Colorado School for Deaf and Blind	*111,879				*111,879	*29,592	*78,490	(1)	*106,082
Hartford, Conn	American School, at Hartford, for the Deaf	62,173	$1,786	$21,999		85,958	2,109	45,091	38,294	85,494
Washington, D. C.	Columbia Institution for the Deaf					116,580				115,539
Cave Spring, Ga.	Georgia School for the Deaf	60,000			0	60,000		22,000	38,000	60,000
Do.	Georgia School for the Deaf (Negro)									
Gooding, Idaho	Idaho School for the Deaf and the Blind	*27,206			0	*27,206	1,000	11,830	13,680	28,520
Jacksonville, Ill.	Illinois School for the Deaf	159,100			0	159,100	6,000		139,600	145,600
Indianapolis, Ind.	Indiana State School for the Deaf	103,448			0	103,448	945	25,701	67,107	93,753
Council Bluffs, Iowa	Iowa School for the Deaf	66,370			6,161	72,531	3,000	14,000	52,139	69,139
Olathe, Kans	Kansas State School for the Deaf	66,500			2,832	69,332		19,810	46,862	66,672
Danville, Ky	Kentucky School for the Deaf	76,190			4,239	80,779		23,057	57,774	80,831
Do.	Kentucky School for the Deaf (Negro)	6,678		30	79	6,757		1,333	5,544	6,877
Baton Rouge, La	Louisiana State School for the Deaf	29,800		1,50	900	32,270	3,638	15,411	14,838	33,587
Portland, Me	Maine School for the Deaf	35,382		25		35,497	5,526	12,500	17,471	35,497
Frederick, Md.	Maryland State School for the Deaf	37,500			1,694	39,194	1,058	14,347	22,771	38,176
Do.	Maryland School for the Colored Blind and Deaf					*9,453	692	*2,990	*9,453	*9,453
Beverly, Mass.	New England Industrial School for Deaf Mutes	5,200	4,201	2,45	523	12,360		6,374	5,301	12,367
Northampton, Mass.	Clarke School for the Deaf	52,237		9,38	13,266	75,021	0	35,510	44,625	80,135
Flint, Mich.	Michigan School for the Deaf	121,000	0	0	38,799	159,799	3,132	29,287	122,616	155,035
Faribault, Minn.	Minnesota School for the Deaf	106,300	0	0	7,263	113,563	10,500	31,431	56,540	98,461

1 Included in preceding column.

* Prorated.

Location	Institution	Receipts					Expenditures			
		From State, county, or city.	From private benefactions for permanent equipment and current expenses.	From productive endowment fund.	From other sources.	Total.	For building and lasting improvements.	For teachers' salaries, books, etc.	For other salaries and all other current expenses.	Total.
1	2	3	4	5	6	7	8	9	10	11
Jackson, Miss.	Institute for the Deaf and Dumb	$47,700		0	$2,640	$50,340	0	$7,694	$32,530	$40,224
Do.	Institute for the Deaf and Dumb (Negro)									
Fulton, Mo.	Missouri School for the Deaf	109,500				109,500		35,000	74,500	109,500
Do.	Missouri School for the Deaf (Negro)									
Boulder, Mont.	Montana School for the Deaf and Blind						*$43,364	47,086	44,700	*135,220
Omaha, Nebr.	Nebraska School for the Deaf	60,000				60,000		28,000	34,000	60,000
Albany, N.Y.	Albany Home School for the Oral Instruction of the Deaf	17,740				17,740		4,200	14,260	18,460
Buffalo, N.Y.	Le Couteulx St. Mary's Institution for the Improved Instruction of Deaf Mutes	65,312	$2,391			67,703		20,427	47,145	67,572
Malone, N.Y.	Northern New York Institution for Deaf Mutes	49,873			717	50,890		5,068	33,843	39,511
New York (904 Lexington Ave.), N.Y.	Association for the Improved Instruction of Deaf Mutes					321,383		46,105	60,652	106,757
New York (Station M.), N.Y.	New York Institution for the Instruction of the Deaf and Dumb	147,550	1,886	$97,672	735	247,543	9,690	63,727	169,684	242,001
Rochester, N.Y.	Western New York Institution for Deaf Mutes	64,227	0	0	11,026	75,252	0	20,827	40,748	61,575
Rome, N.Y.	Central New York Institution for Deaf Mutes	47,587	0	0	230	47,817	0	16,728	31,086	47,816
Westchester, N.Y.	St. Joseph's Institute for the Improved Instruction of Deaf Mutes	0	1,711	0	65,140	233,186		51,019	182,211	233,220
Morganton, N.C.	North Carolina School for the Deaf	85,500	0	0	8,068	98,568	14,649	31,004	51,750	97,463
Raleigh, N.C.	North Carolina School for the Blind and the Deaf (Negro)	*64,768				*94,768	*43,700	*9,782	*17,204	*70,666
Devils Lake, N. Dak.	North Dakota School for the Deaf					62,700	5,231	16,559	26,463	43,220
Columbus, Ohio	State School for the Deaf	149,567		72		149,567	2,402	54,872	96,403	153,275
Sulphur, Okla.	Oklahoma School for the Deaf	101,700				101,656	10,000	23,286	36,124	69,881
Tuft, Okla.	Institute for Deaf, Blind, and Orphans (Negro)	25,655	0	0	0	25,676	50,000	10,000	15,538	75,656
Salem, Oreg.	Oregon State School for the Deaf	26,776			900			9,000	23,638	34,366
Swissvale, Pa.	Western Pennsylvania Institution for the Instruction of the Deaf and Dumb	84,139	0	5,152	1,575	90,866	1,510	36,819	60,675	97,384
Philadelphia (2201 Belmont Ave.), Pa.	Home for the Training in Speech of Deaf Children before They Are of School Age	23,400	2,125	238	100	26,893		13,094	16,730	29,824

Location	Institution									
Philadelphia (Mount Airy), Pa.	Pennsylvania Institution for the Deaf and Dumb	170,000	6,000	18,000	24,000	218,000	......	120,000	98,000	218,000
Pittsburgh (South Hills), Pa.	De Paul Institute for Deaf Mutes	......	......	......	......	......	......	16,767	35,098	15,767
Scranton, Pa.	Pennsylvania State Oral School for the Deaf	52,816	0	0	......	62,816	0,300	9,789	......	51,082
Providence, R.I.	Rhode Island Institute for the Deaf	96,500	0	0	7,683	104,183	0	......	......	40,448
Sioux Falls, S. Dak.	South Dakota School for the Deaf	69,000	......	5,000	......	74,009	38,000	......	41,000	79,000
Austin, Tex.	Texas School for the Deaf	174,800	0	......	0	174,800	100,000	48,350	10,000	158,350
Do., Tex.	Texas Deaf, Dumb, and Blind Institute for Colored Youths	*50,561	0	*8,970	0	*50,561	*25,481	*4,988	*19,540	*49,060
Ogden, Utah	Utah School for the Deaf and the Blind	*47,380	......	......	......	*56,380	0	*18,630	*87,260	*55,980
Staunton, Va.	Virginia School for the Deaf and the Blind	*40,000	......	......	......	*40,000	*1,000	*22,000	*17,000	*40,000
Vancouver, Wash.	Washington State School for the Deaf	50,321	......	......	727	51,048	*4,144	6,214	41,660	51,048
Romney, W. Va.	West Virginia Schools for Deaf and Blind	*53,940	......	......	*2,784	*56,724	*1,898	*22,272	*27,840	51,504
Delavan, Wis.	Wisconsin School for the Deaf	76,886	0	0	0	76,886	2,076	......	77,700	79,776

* Promised.   1 Includes totals not itemized.   2 Data for 1915-16.

TABLE 14.—Statistics of private institutions for the deaf, 1917-18.

Location	Institution	Instructors		Pupils enrolled.		Pupils in the kindergarten.		In classes corresponding to grades 1 to 4.		In classes corresponding to grades 5 to 8.		In classes corresponding to high school grades.		Graduates in 1918.		Pupils taught speech during the year.		Pupils taught by oral method.		Pupils taught by auricular method.		Pupils in the industrial department.		Volumes in library.	Value of buildings and grounds.	Value of scientific apparatus, furniture, instruments, library, etc.	Amount of permanent endowment or productive fund.
		Men.	Women.	Boys.	Girls.	Boys.	Girls.	Boys.	Girls.	Boys.	Girls.	Boys.	Girls.	Boys.	Girls.	Boys.	Girls.	Boys.	Girls.	Boys.	Girls.	Boys.	Girls.				
1	**2**	**3**	**4**	**5**	**6**	**7**	**8**	**9**	**10**	**11**	**12**	**13**	**14**	**15**	**16**	**17**	**18**	**19**	**20**	**21**	**22**	**23**	**24**	**25**	**26**	**27**	**28**
Oakland, Calif.	St. Joseph's Home for Deaf Mutes.	1	6	40	12	1	4	20	6	16	2			2		35	15	25	12	10	3	20	20	500	$32,000		$28
Macon, Ga.	Miss Arbaugh's School for Deaf Children.		4	2		1		1	30		24					2		2	25								
Chicago, Ill.	Ephpheta School for the Deaf.	1	17	69	62	5	8	41	19	23	13					90	27	90	32		3	68		400	200,000	$4,886	
Chinchuba, La.	Chinchuba Deaf-Mute Institute.		8	25	32	0	0	20	23	5	9					20	32	16		4		22					
Baltimore, Md.	St. Francis Xavier's School for the Deaf.	1	7	3	32				6		2					3	12	3	11	2		0	0	500	$40,000	$3,200	$100
Kensington, Md.	Home School for Little Deaf Children.		5	8	11		4	2	0	0	2					8	10	8	10	0		0	0		2,500	300	87,319
West Medford, Mass.	The Sarah Fuller Home for Little Deaf Children.		1		10	8	10	0	0		0						12		12	0		2	8		8,400	1,000	
North Detroit, Mich.	Evangelical Lutheran Deaf-Mute Institute.	3	2	22	12	0	0	18	10	4	2	7	6			21		21	1	0		16	18		43,570	2,273	0
Joplin, Mo.	Joplin Day School for the Deaf.	0	1	1	1					1	1	5	1			1	1	1	19			7	6			5,100	
St. Louis, Mo.	Central Institute for the Deaf.	3	12	24	26	14	12	18	10	1	5	5				20	23	18		2	4	10	10	225	41,843		0
New York, N.Y.	Society for the Welfare of the Jewish Deaf.	1	2	18	16	7		9	9	5	5						7		7	0		7					
New York (1 Mt. Morris Park W.), N.Y.	Wright Oral School.	4	10	21	7	7	1	6	5	5	5	7				21	11	21	11					300		0	
Cincinnati (R.F.D. 11, box 15, Lockland), Ohio.	St. Rita School for the Deaf.	2	8	13	11	8	1	5	8	5	7	5				13		13				10	10		$30,000	$3,000	0

Location	Institution																					
Lansdowne, Pa.	The Sanitarium School																					0
Philadelphia (1805 Vine St.), Pa.	Archbishop Ryan Memorial Institute for the Deaf																					
Santurce, P. R.	St. Gabriel's School for the Deaf	5	17	22	0	0	6	5	11	17		17		22	17	22	1		9	13	100	27,600	3,000
Lead, S. Dak.	Black Hills School for the Deaf	1		1				1						1		1							
St. Francis, Wis.	St. John's Institute for Deaf Mutes	10	39	37	7	4	21	20	11	13	30	32	26	20	4	3	27	25				

¹ Includes both sexes.   ² Data for 1915-16.

TABLE 15.—*Receipts and expenditures of private schools for the deaf, 1917-18.*

Location	Institution	Receipts.					Expenditures.			
		From State, county, or city.	From private benefactions for permanent equipment and current expenses.	From productive endowment fund.	From other sources.	Total.	For building and lasting improvements.	For teachers' salaries, books, etc.	For other salaries and all other current expenses.	Total.
1	2	3	4	5	6	7	8	9	10	11
Baltimore, Md.	St. Francis Xavier's School for the Deaf	$2,250	$1,833		$2,774	$6,857	$136	$1,103	$4,627	$5,996
Kensington, Md.	Home School for Little Deaf Children	0	100	0	6,900	7,000	$4,000	1,688	3,120	8,808
West Medford, Mass.	The Sarah Fuller Home for Little Deaf Children	2,429	1,409	$4,340	41	8,219		2,380	4,415	6,805
North Detroit, Mich.	Evangelical Lutheran Deaf-Mute Institute	0	5,918		3,507	9,425	1,473	3,765	3,043	8,281
Joplin, Mo.	Joplin Day School for Deaf							1,000		1,000
St. Louis, Mo.	Central Institute for the Deaf		27,444	0	21,016	48,460	42,682	9,360	12,274	64,316
New York (40 West 115th St.), N. Y.	Society for the Welfare of the Jewish Deaf		500			500	0	500	0	500
Santurce, P. R.	St. Gabriel's School for the Deaf	2,149	4,647	0	629	7,425	1,708	367	5,249	7,414

¹ Data for 1915-16.

TABLE 16.—*Statistics of city day classes for the deaf, 1917–18.*

Location.	Institution.	Instructors. Men.	Instructors. Women.	Pupils enrolled. Boys.	Pupils enrolled. Girls.	Pupils in the kindergarten. Boys.	Pupils in the kindergarten. Girls.	In classes corresponding to grades 1 to 4. Boys.	In classes corresponding to grades 1 to 4. Girls.	In classes corresponding to grades 5 to 8. Boys.	In classes corresponding to grades 5 to 8. Girls.	In classes corresponding to high-school grades. Boys.	In classes corresponding to high-school grades. Girls.	Graduates in 1918. Boys.	Graduates in 1918. Girls.	Pupils in teacher-training classes. Boys.	Pupils in teacher-training classes. Girls.	Pupils taught speech during the year. Boys.	Pupils taught speech during the year. Girls.	Pupils taught by oral method. Boys.	Pupils taught by oral method. Girls.	Pupils taught by particular method. Boys.	Pupils taught by particular method. Girls.	Pupils in industrial department. Boys.	Pupils in industrial department. Girls.	Volumes in library.	Value of buildings and grounds.	Value of scientific apparatus, furniture, instruments, library, etc.	Amount of permanent endowment or productive fund.
1	2	3	4	5	6	7	8	9	10	11	12	13	14	15	16	17	18	19	20	21	22	23	24	25	26	27	28	29	30
Eureka, Calif.	Eureka Deaf School.																												
Los Angeles, Calif.	Oral Day School for Deaf Children.																												
Oakland, Calif.	Oakland School for the Deaf (Santa Fe School).																									85			
Sacramento, Calif.	Sacramento Day School for the Deaf.																									100			
San Diego, Calif.	Public School for the Deaf.																												
San Francisco, Calif.	San Francisco Oral Day School for the Deaf.																												
Atlanta, Ga.	Atlanta Day School for the Deaf.																									200	$2,500	$550	
Aurora, Ill.	Aurora School for the Deaf.																											100	
Chicago, Ill.	Chicago Public Day Schools for the Deaf.																												
Rochelle, Ill.	Rochelle Public Day School for the Deaf.																									510	$95,000	$3,300	$3,400
New Orleans, La.	New Orleans Day Class for the Deaf.																									1,747	137,500	35,000	
Boston, Mass.	Horace Mann School for the Deaf.																												
Randolph, Mass.	The Boston School for the Deaf.																												
Bay City, Mich.	Bay City Day School for the Deaf.																												
Calumet, Mich.	Calumet Day School for the Deaf.																												
Detroit, Mich.	Detroit Day School for Deaf.																									0		100	0
Grand Rapids, Mich.	Oral School for the Deaf and Hard of Hearing.																												
Houghton, Mich.	Houghton Day School for Deaf.																												
Iron Mountain, Mich.	Iron Mountain Oral Day School for Deaf.																												
Ivanwood, Mich.	Day School.																												
Jackson, Mich.	School for the Deaf.																												
Lansing, Mich.	Lansing School for the Deaf.																												
Manistee, Mich.	Manistee Day School for the Deaf.																									100			
Saginaw, Mich.	Oral School for the Deaf.																									46			0

Sault Ste. Marie, Mich.	Oral Day School for the Deaf.
Traverse City, Mich.	Traverse City Day School for the Deaf.
Minneapolis, Minn.	Special Classes for Deaf Children.
St. Paul, Minn.	Special Day School for the Deaf.
Kansas City, Mo.	Day School for the Deaf.
St. Louis, Mo.	Gallaudet School for the Deaf.
Jersey City, N. J.	Classes for the Deaf.
Newark, N. Y.	School for the Deaf.
New York (225 East 23d St.), N. Y.	Public School 47.
Ashtabula, Ohio.	Ashtabula Day School for the Deaf.
Canton, Ohio.	Canton Day School for the Deaf.
Cincinnati, Ohio.	Oral School.
Cleveland, Ohio.	Cleveland Public Day School for the Deaf.
Dayton, Ohio.	Dayton School for the Deaf.
Toledo, Ohio.	Toledo Public School for the Deaf.
Portland, Oreg.	Portland Day School for the Deaf.
Houston, Tex.	Houston Public Schools for the Deaf.
Everett, Wash.	Everett School for the Deaf.
Seattle, Wash.	Seattle Day School for the Deaf.
Spokane, Wash.	Spokane Day School for the Deaf.
Tacoma, Wash.	Tacoma Day School for the Deaf.
Antigo, Wis.	School for Deaf.
Appleton, Wis.	Appleton Day School for the Deaf.
Ashland, Wis.	Ashland Day School for the Deaf.
Black River Falls, Wis.	Day School for the Deaf.
Bloomington, Wis.	Bloomington Day School for the Deaf.
Eau Claire, Wis.	Eau Claire Oral Day School for the Deaf.
Fond du Lac, Wis.	Fond du Lac Deaf School.
Green Bay, Wis.	Green Bay Oral Day School for the Deaf.
Janesville, Wis.	Janesville Public School for the Deaf.
Kenosha, Wis.	School for the Deaf.
La Crosse, Wis.	La Crosse Oral Day School for the Deaf.
Madison, Wis.	Madison Day School for the Deaf.
Marinette, Wis.	Marinette Day School for the Deaf.
Marshfield, Wis.	Marshfield Oral Day School for the Deaf.
Milwaukee, Wis.	Milwaukee School for the Deaf.
New London, Wis.	New London Day School for Deaf and School for Defective Speech.
Oshkosh, Wis.	Day School for the Deaf and Defective Speech.
Rice Lake, Wis.	Rice Lake Day Oral School.
Richland Center, Wis.	Oral Day School for the Deaf.
Sheboygan, Wis.	Sheboygan Day School for the Deaf.
Stevens Point, Wis.	Oral Day School.
Superior, Wis.	Superior Day School for the Deaf.
Wausau, Wis.	Wausau Day School for the Deaf.

Table 17.—*Expenditures in 49 city day schools for the deaf, 1917–18.*

Location of school.	Number of teachers.	Number of pupils.	For teachers' salaries, books, and other expenses, of Instruction.	For all other purposes.
1	2	3	4	5
Sacramento, Calif.	2	16	$2,904	$193
San Diego, Calif.	1	6	1,080	....
Aurora, Ill.	1	13	950	361
Chicago, Ill.	38	296	52,953	....
Rochelle, Ill.	1	11	1,000	110
Dubuque, Iowa.	1	8	1,100	50
Boston, Mass.	18	136	29,868	13,531
Randolph, Mass.	22	163	9,900	[1] 29,450
Calumet, Mich.	1	12	1,380	....
Grand Rapids, Mich.	6	20	4,738	1,374
Iron Mountain, Mich.	1	5	600	....
Jackson, Mich.	1	14	1,200	....
Saginaw, Mich.	1	6	1,200	....
Sault St. Marie, Mich.	1	9	1,050	....
Traverse City, Mich.	1	13	1,215	....
Minneapolis, Minn.	4	36	4,175	....
St. Paul, Minn.	2	17	1,950	35
Jersey City, N. J.	2	21	1,497	100
Canton, Ohio.	1	12	1,300	....
Cincinnati, Ohio.	8	33	7,200	....
Cleveland, Ohio.	16	124	18,894	5,979
Dayton, Ohio.	1	9	1,600	....
Toledo, Ohio.	2	20	2,711	274
Portland, Oreg.	2	25	2,200	....
Spokane, Wash.	1	11	1,125	....
Tacoma, Wash.	5	26	2,000	200
Antigo, Wis.	1	10	1,051	886
Appleton, Wis.	2	7	2,126	65
Ashland, Wis.	1	8	1,498	....
Black River Falls, Wis.	1	7	(2)	1,913
Bloomington, Wis.	1	2	585	89
Eau Claire, Wis.	7	39	4,676	3,764
Fon du Lac, Wis.	2	19	2,627	....
Green Bay, Wis.	9	35	(2)	10,478
Janesville, Wis.	1	3	1,000	....
Kenasha, Wis.	2	15	1,918	....
La Crosse, Wis.	2	14	1,310	....
Madison, Wis.	2	13	1,700	706
Marinette, Wis.	1	7	823	632
Marshfield, Wis.	1	7	930	473
Milwaukee, Wis.	22	158	27,305	6,913
New London, Wis.	4	11	1,225	482
Oshkosh, Wis.	2	19	1,593	....
Rice Lake, Wis.	1	8	1,546	....
Richland Center, Wis.	1	7	899	....
Sheboygan, Wis.	2	12	1,693	....
Stevens Point, Wis.	1	8	1,479	....
Superior, Wis.	1	6	1,214	297
Wausau, Wis.	2	16	2,342	1,287
Total.	209	1,513	215,330	79,622

[1] Includes board and lodging. [2] Included in column 5.

DEPARTMENT OF THE INTERIOR
BUREAU OF EDUCATION

BULLETIN, 1919, No. 80

TEACHING ENGLISH TO THE FOREIGN BORN

A TEACHER'S HANDBOOK

By

HENRY H. GOLDBERGER

INSTRUCTOR IN METHODS OF TEACHING ENGLISH TO FOREIGNERS
TEACHERS COLLEGE, COLUMBIA UNIVERSITY

WASHINGTON
GOVERNMENT PRINTING OFFICE
1920

TABLE 17.—*Expenditures in 49 city day schools for the deaf, 1917–1*

Location of school.	Number of teachers.	Number of pupils.	Expenditures.	
			For teachers' salaries, books, and other expenses of instruction.	For all other purposes.
1	2	3	4	5
Sacramento, Calif.	3		$2,904	$298
San Diego, Calif.	1		1,080	
Aurora, Ill.	1	13	950	361
Chicago, Ill.	26		52,953	
Rochelle, Ill.	1	11	1,000	110
Dubuque, Iowa.	1		1,100	39
Boston, Mass.	19		29,868	12,521
Randolph, Mass.	22	163	9,900	[1] 29,450
Calumet, Mich.	1	12	1,380	
Grand Rapids, Mich.	6	20	4,738	1,374
Iron Mountain, Mich.	1	3	600	
Jackson, Mich.	1	14	1,200	
Saginaw, Mich.	1	6	1,200	
Sault St. Marie, Mich.	1	9	2,050	
Traverse City, Mich.	1	13	1,215	
Minneapolis, Minn.	4	36	4,175	
St. Paul, Minn.	2	17	1,950	35
Jersey City, N. J.	2	21	1,497	109
Canton, Ohio.	1	12	1,300	
Cincinnati, Ohio.	8	33	7,200	
Cleveland, Ohio.	16	124	18,894	5,979
Dayton, Ohio.	1	9	1,600	
Toledo, Ohio.	2	20	2,711	394
Portland, Oreg.	2	25	2,200	
Spokane, Wash.	1	11	1,125	
Tacoma, Wash.	5	26	2,000	290
Antigo, Wis.	1	10	1,051	385
Appleton, Wis.	2	7	2,126	65
Ashland, Wis.	1	8	1,498	
Black River Falls, Wis.	1	7	[2]	1,913
Bloomington, Wis.	1	2	585	99
Eau Claire, Wis.	7	39	4,676	3,704
Fon du Lac, Wis.	2	19	2,627	
Green Bay, Wis.	9	35	[2]	10,478
Janesville, Wis.	1	3	1,000	
Kenasha, Wis.	2	15	1,918	
La Crosse, Wis.	2	14	1,310	
Madison, Wis.	2	13	1,700	705
Marinette, Wis.	1	7	823	632
Marshfield, Wis.	1	7	930	693
Milwaukee, Wis.	22	158	27,305	6,912
New London, Wis.	4	11	1,225	462
Oshkosh, Wis.	2	19	1,593	
Rice Lake, Wis.	1	8	1,546	
Richland Center, Wis.	1	7	899	
Sheboygan, Wis.	2	12	1,693	
Stevens Point, Wis.	1	8	1,479	
Superior, Wis.	1	6	1,214	367
Wausau, Wis.	2	16	2,342	1,287
Total.	209	1,513	215,330	79,622

[1] Includes board and lodging.   [2] Included in column 5.

DEPARTMENT OF THE INTERIOR
BUREAU OF EDUCATION

BULLETIN, 1919, No. 80

TEACHING ENGLISH TO THE FOREIGN BORN

A TEACHER'S HANDBOOK

By

HENRY H. GOLDBERGER

INSTRUCTOR IN METHODS OF TEACHING ENGLISH TO FOREIGNERS
TEACHERS COLLEGE, COLUMBIA UNIVERSITY

WASHINGTON
GOVERNMENT PRINTING OFFICE
1920

CONTENTS.

LETTER OF TRANSMITTAL.

DEPARTMENT OF THE INTERIOR,
BUREAU OF EDUCATION,
Washington, D. C., October 8, 1919.

SIR: There is, I believe, nothing in the Constitution or the laws of the United States or of any of the States compelling the use of the English language, or prohibiting the free use of any other tongue. Any person has a right in this country to express himself and to get his information, inspiration, guidance, and hope through any language within his power. But English is the common language of the country, understood and spoken by more than 95 per cent of the people. It is the language of the Constitution and of the statute laws of the United States and of all the States, the language of our courts of law and of all assemblies designed for other than special classes of the population. Practically all the books which reveal American ideals and interpret American life are printed in English, as are all our more important magazines and newspapers intended for general circulation, and all the reports and bulletins of the administrative departments of Federal and State Governments published for the instruction and guidance of the people. It is the language of commerce, business, and general social intercourse, the common means of communication. Any man or woman in America who does not know English is doomed to live only in the small world of some one racial group and remain a stranger in the larger world of the whole people, and must suffer a constant handicap in business and social converse. Through lack of understanding rather than through ill will, any individual or group ignorant of the English language may at any time endanger the public peace. It is therefore of great importance both to the welfare of the country and to the happiness and prosperity of those among us who have recently come from countries of other speech than ours that these be given every possible opportunity to learn English, that they be induced to make use of these opportunities, and that the methods of teaching be adapted to their needs, so that the task of learning a new language after they have passed the age when languages are most easily learned may be made as easy and attractive as possible. To offer the opportunity and formulate the method is a large part of the task of Americanization in which this

5

bureau is engaged. The manuscript herewith transmitted for publication as a bulletin of the Bureau of Education has been prepared at the request of this bureau by Dr. Henry H. Goldberger, who has had much experience in teaching English to foreigners and in preparing teachers for this work. The methods set forth are based on sound principles, and the bulletin should be very helpful as a guide both to teachers of the foreign born and to those who are engaged in preparing such teachers.

Respectfully submitted.

P. P. CLAXTON,
Commissioner.

The SECRETARY OF THE INTERIOR.

PREFACE.

The process of transforming the mind of a man who speaks and thinks in one language, so that an entirely different language can be used easily and naturally, is a difficult one. Only within the past few years has this process been given the general study it deserves. Recently a number of colleges and universities have been making investigations of the subject, and it is now commencing to take definite form as a science.

At the National Conference on Methods of Americanization, held under the auspices of the Department of the Interior in May, 1919, three sessions were devoted to the methods of teaching English to the foreign born. At the close of the conference a committee of leading teachers of immigrants was appointed and asked to submit to this division a report which would embody the underlying principles of this problem. The report of this committee is presented as a supplement hereto. The thanks of the department are due to the men who served upon this committee.

Based upon the report of this committee as well as upon the best thought of the country as it was brought out at the 1919 conference, this division asked Dr. Henry H. Goldberger, of New York, to prepare a simple and concise handbook for teachers upon the subject of teaching English to the foreign born. Dr. Goldberger is very generally recognized as one of the leading educators of the country in this science. That this new work of his will prove of inestimable value to those who will be called to teach our foreign-born people, I feel most confident.

This book is not intended as a text but rather as a suggestive outline upon which the teacher can build to suit the needs of the particular peoples whom she is to teach, and their various degrees of literacy. There are many good textbooks upon the market with which the teacher can supplement this present work. A short bibliography of such texts is printed herewith.

If the teacher has not herself taken a course of training in this new science of teaching the foreign born, she is urged to read carefully Mr. Mahoney's book, "Training Teachers for Americanization," also published as a bulletin by the Bureau of Education.

FRED C. BUTLER,
Director of Americanization,
Bureau of Education.

TEACHING ENGLISH TO THE FOREIGN BORN.

CHAPTER I.

GENERAL PRINCIPLES.

Learning a language is an exceedingly difficult process if the learner already has one language which serves his purpose. Many of us know very little of our own language even though we were born to it and have spent a great many years in perfecting our knowledge. With the exception of people actuated by a thirst for knowledge or for culture, few of us take the trouble to learn a second language unless we are compelled to do so by our inability to communicate with people with whom for social or economic reasons we wish to communicate. The foreign born who live in America, like Americans who live in foreign lands, prefer to live among their own kind, to speak their own languages at home, to patronize shops where their own languages are spoken and to read books and newspapers printed in the mother tongue. They learn so much of the language of America as they need in getting along with English-speaking people. If all their needs are satisfied in Polish or Italian, the Poles and Italians do not find it necessary to learn English.

The method of coercion advocated by some is hardly the method by which independent, liberty-loving, self-determining Americans are to be fashioned. But aside from its effect on the American spirit, compulsion in learning the language of a country has heretofore failed to justify itself in the European countries where it has had a long and troublesome trial and is hardly likely to succeed in our country.

As long as Americans consciously isolate one of foreign birth by social ostracism, by characterizing him with an opprobrious epithet, by leaving him to his own devices in distinct foreign sections, so long will we have the problem of finding adequate incentives for his learning English as a step toward his Americanization. With a wider understanding of our responsibility and a broader-minded attitude on the part of Americans, this condition will no doubt ultimately disappear.

152285°—20——2

The schoolroom, whether in a factory, church, home neighborhood house, or school building, can approximate ideal conditions and provide adequate incentives by ridding itself of the traditional schoolroom atmosphere and attitude in dealing with adults, some of whom have never áttended school and others who have attended have learned to associate unpleasant restrictions with their school days.

SOCIALIZING THE TEACHING.

Comparatively few of the immigrants to America ever go to school in this country, and yet the great majority speak enough English to make themselves understood and to understand us. These have picked up their knowledge of English in social and business intercourse without formal lessons. Many others, those who were thrown in with English-speaking people, did not find it necessary to speak English in their limited environment. By approximating life conditions the school can overcome some of the psychological objections to "going to school," can select what the pupils can use in their activities, and, above all, can furnish an adequate motive for application in learning what the pupils realize is vital to them. The foreign born are inclined to associate school with children. Hence in many schools instead of forming "classes" for the teaching of English, teachers have attempted other adult forms of organization; for example, groups of women have been formed in sewing circles, canning and preserving clubs, dressmaking clubs, cooking, millinery, health and dancing clubs. Men have been organized into clubs for—

Lunch.	Cooperative buying.	Dancing.
Savings.	Singing.	Health.
Sanitation.	Better housing.	Industrial training.
Benefit.	Athletics.	Citizenship.
Social purposes.	Recreation.	Debating.

The effect of such organization is—

1. The relationship of teacher-pupil gives way to another relationship that obtains in the world outside of the schoolroom.

2. Free communication is fostered.

3. The necessity for expressing himself in English becomes real to the learner.

4. It is a means of approach to people when the classroom would not attract.

5. For the teacher, it serves the purpose of supplying him with a knowledge of what English the pupils require to know. Thus, in a dancing class, the pupils asked to be taught: (1) How to introduce a friend; (2) how to refuse to dance; (3) how to ask a lady to dance; (4) how to ask a friend to the dance; (5) how to ask a friend to take refreshments; and (6) how to invite a friend to visit you.

THE LEARNER'S POINT OF VIEW.

A guiding principle for the selection both of content and of method in teaching English to the foreign born may be found in the principle of use, i. e., teach to-day such English as the pupil can use at once in his contact with English-speaking people. For beginners, understanding the language of the people with whom they come in contact is more important than understanding the language of Lowell and of Emerson; to be able to address an English-speaking person is more vital than to be able to recite a bookful of English useful only in the classroom; to read the common signs, warnings, and directions printed in English is more necessary than to read an English story; to write a simple letter more desirable than to write an essay on "How I spent my birthday." Always the foreign born desires to be taught such English as he can use at once in the world outside of the classroom. And this English he desires to use in making himself understood to people who do not speak his own language. If it is a question of choice between using his native language and using English, he will always use his native tongue. Hence the school must select out of the vast body of English such content as will serve the purpose of the foreign born in making himself understood to English-speaking people. He does not desire to be taught a vocabulary or a sentence structure useful in talking to his brother or to his mother. He wants to talk and will willingly undergo hardships to learn to speak to his English-speaking neighbor, to his foreman, to the policeman, to the salesman. When the teacher does not consciously select usable English, the pupil doubts his own ability to master so difficult a language, becomes discouraged at his inability to use what he has learned, and discontinues his efforts to learn.

What is most important for a person who is learning English as a new language? It will readily be seen that this matter of "importance" is largely determined by personal considerations, for what is important to one person may not be important to another. On the following topics, however, the great mass of non-English-speaking people will, if they are to talk to those who speak English, be required to have some English knowledge:

1. Statements of the pupil's relationship with those with whom he comes in contact: Name, address, occupation, greetings, salutations, farewells, inquiries, showing gratitude. Statements about himself and those in whom he is most interested: Age, weight, illness, good health, pain, hunger, and thirst.

2. Schoolroom activities, objects, and descriptive words and phrases: Standing, walking, reading, writing, speaking, opening, closing, coming, and going.

3. Daily extra school needs: Buying, selling, repairing, cooking, eating, looking for work, working, riding, walking, together with counting, weighing, measuring and the units used by the pupils, visiting, enjoyments, spending leisure time and holidays, and recreations.   .

4. Vocational expression: Occupations and technical expressions.

5. The house and family: Renting, furnishing, cleaning, and beautifying the home; the members of the family and their relationships.

6. The community: The pupil's relationship to the school, the church, the lodge, trade or labor organizations, the newspaper, theater, the post office, and local agencies for the promotion of his well being and security, such as police, sanitation, licenses, and local ordinances.

7. Local and national holidays: National ideals as exemplified in the lives of great Americans.

8. Formal civics: The relation of the city, State, and Nation.

CHAPTER II.

ORGANIZATION AND ADMINISTRATION.

The best work can be done only when teachers are working with groups that are fairly homogeneous. If only enough pupils enter to form one class, a teacher may have to do individual or group teaching, especially if the members of the class are not all beginners.

Effective group teaching is accomplished by dividing the class into two or three sections on the basis of some ability, such as is used in the formation of whole classes. Each group is then taught as if it were a class by itself, while the other groups are given written work or reading to do by themselves.

The pupil's knowledge of English is the best basis for the organization of whole classes of foreign born or of groups within a single class. The following is a suggested organization for three groups or classes:

1. Beginners—to be subdivided into two groups:
    (a) Those who speak no English, but who can read and write their own languages.
    (b) Those who speak no English, but are illiterate in their own languages.
2. Intermediate:
    Those who have completed the work for the beginners' classes; or—
    Those who have never gone to school before but who can make themselves understood in English, and can read the beginning lessons in an English to foreign text.
3. Advanced:
    Those who have completed the intermediate class; or—
    Those who can carry on a conversation in English and can read and understand a simple newspaper article.

Beginners' classes may be further subdivided on the basis of nationality, their previous education, age, and sex. These subdivisions are, however, valuable only in the beginning, and should not be retained for long, because they tend to stratify groups of foreign born and to emphasize the formation of national cliques, thus counteracting Americanization forces.

13

METHODS OF TEACHING.

THE DIRECT METHOD.

The first question in teaching English to immigrants is "Should the teacher use the native language of the pupil in teaching him English?" For most teachers there is no difficulty in deciding the question because they know no foreign languages. However, even for teachers who know several languages, it is best that they use a direct method only, i. e., that they teach English by using English as the means of instruction. Such is the best practice throughout the country to-day and it is founded on good reason. Language is acquired by use, by associating verbal expressions with objects, ideas or experiences. Translation methods force the pupil to associate one language form (English) with another language form (Italian) and a pupil so taught must always think of the equivalent native word before he can think of the English expresison. Translation methods do not enable the pupil to think of an object, or to have an idea and to think of the English words to express the idea. Direct methods enable the pupil to say and think something in English. Since the problem with most foreign-born people in America is to train them to speak rather than to read or to write, the Direct Method is advocated.

This must not be understood to mean that the teacher should not know the foreign language of his pupil. On the contrary such knowledge is decidedly helpful in understanding the pupil's difficulties and his point of view. But it does mean that the teacher must refrain from *using* the foreign language in teaching. Every time the teacher resorts to translation in making clear a word or a sentence, she is making it easier for herself at the expense of the pupil's progress. The more English the pupil hears and uses the sooner will he be able to speak.

THE SYNTHETIC METHOD.

For a long time it was thought that a knowledge of a language could be "built up" as we build a house or put up a piece of machinery by adding one part to another. Language, however, is not a machine but an organism; it grows large and strong by use just as the muscles of a body do. This has been understood and applied for several centuries in the teaching of language. Every few years, however, some old things are "rediscovered" and so it happens that there are rediscovered the method of teaching English by "building" with the elements. Thus the alphabet method purposes to build words by means of the letters. Happily, this is no longer done anywhere. A word method would use single isolated words to build phrases and sentences. In order to teach single words teachers resort to the device of pointing out objects and saying, "This is a hat,"

"This is a book." Used occasionally to point out the meaning of a new word, "This is a latch," the device is valuable, but of course no one ever learned to speak in this way. One might know the meanings of all the words in the dictionary and be unable to put five of them together in a sentence. But besides the impossibility of learning to speak by it the method is exceedingly wasteful psychologically. Each individual word is taught separately. There is no connection between hat, coat, chair, desk, ceiling, floor, that makes one remember the other words if you think of one of them. Hence these single words must be drilled over and over mechanically to make them stick deep since they have no support from each other. Such teaching is tiring, grinding, mechanical drill.

The process of building sentences by declining pronouns or by conjugating verbs is equally futile in teaching a person to speak English.

After a pupil has learned "I walk, thou walkest, he walks, we walk, you walk, they walk," he can not ask his way while out walking, nor can he be quieted and kept on the drill by the promise that some day he will be able if he sticks long enough. The answer is he does not, and the school must adjust its teaching to his needs.

ANALYTIC-SYNTHETIC METHODS.

Quite generally synthetic processes of teaching language have been replaced by analytic processes especially where the emphasis has been on spoken rather than on written language. In analytic methods the pupil begins not with an element—a letter or a word—but with a larger unit which is useful or interesting for its own sake. Thus the pupil may begin with a whole sentence or even with a larger unit, a series of sentences about some topic or theme. This is the basis of François Gouin's procedure in developing the theme. On the theme to "open the door" the teacher may construct a series of sentences to describe the act; thus:

```
I walk to the door_____ I walk.
I stop at the door_____ I stop.
I stretch out my hand_____ I stretch.
I turn the knob_____ I turn.
I push the door_____ I push.
The door moves_____ moves.
I let go the knob_____ I let go.
```

The procedure in constructing themes is as follows:

1. The teacher selects an "end" worth while to his pupil, e. g., "To go to work," "to look for a job," "to visit the doctor."

2. The teacher then constructs a series of sentences each describing a certain act tending toward the accomplishment of the end sought in the theme.

3. The sentences must be short and so worded that the meaning of each and every part of each sentence may be made clear to the foreign born by means of actions, dramatizations, and by the use of objects or pictures.

4. The sentences must be related to each other, either in time sequence or by cause and effect.

5. Not more than 10 sentences can profitably be used in any one theme, because of the difficulty of memorizing more than that number.

The advantages to be derived from using the theme method are as follows:

1. It can be used with beginners without the intermediation of a foreign language. To make it usable in this way, however, it is necessary that the teacher bear in mind that each sentence must be such as to be made clear by objects, actions, and dramatizations. When, however, the pupil has acquired sufficient knowledge of English to dispense with objectifying, the method should no longer be used, but rather the simple English which the pupil knows should then be employed to give him further command of the language.

2. The method emphasizes the teaching of sentences rather than of isolated meaningless words and phrases. The fact that the sentences are coherent and related to each other, makes it easier for the pupils to understand, to learn and to recall them.

3. In the process of developing a theme, sufficient variety of drill is provided to make possible the easy retention of sentence form.

The theme method, nevertheless, has a number of limitations; it is not a panacea for teaching English. Moreover, it must be understood that merely cutting up a paragraph into a number of short lines and placing a word to the right will not facilitate the problem of teaching English. As soon as a foreigner understands a little English, the theme becomes a very artificial process and a distinctly schoolroom device. It is a bridge or a crutch for as long as the pupil needs an interpreter. The theme procedure is therefore supplemented by other methods in order to work out a coherent lesson unit.

In addition to the themes developed in the lesson units, the following theme subjects may be used when necessary:

To go to work.	To write a letter.
To bathe.	To visit (the museum).
To go to a restaurant.	To clean the house.
To look for work.	To go to the library.
To take the train.	To send money home.
To look for rooms.	To introduce a friend.
To pay rent.	To telephone.
To buy groceries.	To cook dinner.
To go to the doctor.	To deposit money.
To spend a holiday.	To draw out money.
To go to school.	

Conversation between teachers and pupils is the most natural way of teaching English and is the most valuable exercise for practical reasons. The earliest exercises are designed to furnish the teacher with necessary information about the pupils, their needs and their interests. Thus the teacher asks such questions as the following:

With whom do you board?
Where were you born?
Who is your employer?
How many hours a day do you work?
How many children have you?

A later development in the process of securing free conversation is that of questioning on the subject of the theme and of the reading matter. Thus the pupils know the theme " Going to school:"

I put on my hat and coat. I say Goodbye.
I walk to school. I enter the building.
I come into the room.

The teacher now asks the following questions:

Mr. ——, do you walk to school?
Does Mr. —— walk to school?
Walk around the room, Mr. ——.
Walk to the front of the room, Mr. ——.
Please put your hat on, etc.

For teaching idiomatic expressions, the method of dramatization is most successfully used. To illustrate: Two pupils are instructed to take the parts of salesman and of customer. As the dialogue proceeds, the teacher asks other pupils to express the same thoughts in better English, at the same time writing the correct expressions on the board. After other pupils have gone through the same exercise, the class is instructed to copy those expressions which they like best. The following topics suggest conversations of a practical nature from which a teacher may select those which are most needed by his pupils:

Buying an article, e. g., a hat, shoes, cigars, suit, clothing, furniture.
Repairing shoes, clothing, machinery, furniture.
Renting a flat, a room at a boarding house or hotel.
Ordering a meal, an expressman.
Checking a trunk.
Asking one's way in street, in car, in department store, at a railroad terminal.
Telling time.
Applying for position, raise in salary, day off.
Getting a license to peddle, to sell liquors, to marry.
Sending money home.
Ordering insurance policy, fire, life, accident.
Opening bank account.
Introducing a friend.
Seeing a friend off.
Inviting someone to call, to dinner, theater, to visit.
Complaining to policeman, foreman.

Going to a doctor, a dentist.
Taking a child to school, to be vaccinated.
Conversation on the weather.
In the witness chair.

HOW TO USE A TEXTBOOK.

1. A language is learned primarily through the ear, and only secondarily through the eye. Children and illiterate adults are able to speak English even though the eye has not aided them in the acquisition. Reading a text may be made a most valuable aid in teaching spoken English as well as in teaching reading, provided the text material is properly constructed, and provided further, that the teacher make some use of the text to insure that the learner has understood its meaning.

2. Ordinarily, the tendency is very strong to ask foreign-born pupils "to read" without making sure that the reading means anything. The process of reading then consists of a series of mispronunciations punctuated by the corrections of the teacher. Each mispronunciation helps to impress itself on the pupil's mind, and the right pronunciation is acquired by accident, if it is acquired at all.

3. It must be borne in mind that a foreign-born pupil, merely because he is foreign born, is not, therefore, childish and that he resents being treated as a child. "I am a little buttercup" is not proper reading material for an able-bodied foreign-born laborer. The teacher must select such books as appeal to the personal interest of the pupils and stimulate the further desire to read. Books which usually begin with a vocabulary developed by the "This is a hat," "This is a chair," procedure do not make good reading material. Vocabularies are to be explained by teachers in oral lessons, as provided for in these lesson units. Above all, the teacher must remember that the function of reading is to get thought from the printed page, and that in order to get this thought, the meaning of the language and the recognition of the symbols which express that language to us, must be well understood before the pupil is asked to read. Hence the following procedure should in all cases be followed in a reading lesson:

A. An introduction.
   The function of the introduction is—
   (a) To interest the class in the subject matter of a lesson by reference to a picture, a previous conversation, or experience.
   (b) To overcome the mechanical difficulties of understanding and of recognizing new words by means of drills on the board, introducing new words in conversation, by illustrating, objectifying, but never at this early stage, by requiring definitions or by looking them up in the dictionary.

B. Oral reading by the teacher as a model of pronunciation, enunciation, and expression.

• C. Silent reading by the pupils to enable them to conquer one difficulty at a time and to get the thought. While the pupils read silently, the teacher walks about the room helping those who need her help.

D. Testing the pupils' understanding of the reading matter by questions—by having them obey directions; by dramatizations; by summaries; by discussions.

E. Oral reading by the pupils.

4. As a test of understanding of the reading matter, the teacher must have some other means than oral reading. Modern textbooks are beginning to supply such tests in a series of questions based on the reading matter to insure that the pupil understands, to give him a reason for rereading, and to supply a natural method of drill. For example, in a recent textbook, the following lesson appears:

WASHING MY HANDS.

My hands are dirty. I turn up my sleeves. I take soap from a dish. I dip the soap into the water. I rub the soap on my hands. I wash my hands in the water. I dry my hands on a towel. My hands are clean.

Exercises.

Are your hands clean or dirty?
My hands are _____.
What do you turn up?
I _____ my sleeves.
Where is the soap?
The soap is in the _____.
What do you do with the soap?
I _____ the soap into the water.
What do you rub on your hands?
I rub the _____ on my _____.
With what do you dry your hands?
I dry my hands with a _____.

At the beginning the questions are simple and the answers suggested. Later on the question becomes more difficult, and the pupil finds the answer in the text. Still later, the questions are such as to call for the reconstruction of the pupil's thought together with an answer in the pupil's own words, thus making for progress in acquiring a vocabulary and in using it for conversational purposes.

NOTE BOOKS FOR PUPILS.

Each pupil should have a notebook in which to keep the written work assigned and such personal jottings as the pupil desires to make.

TEACHER'S PREPARATION.

The teacher's work will proceed with greater profit to the pupils and increased pleasure to herself if in addition to following the directions in the lesson units, she will prepare the work carefully for each lesson. Such preparation had better be written out and should include:

1. What you expect to teach.
2. How you expect to take it up.
3. Special pupils whom you expect to call on.
4. Information about pupils, about their lives, needs, vocations, etc., that will affect the teaching.
5. The results of interviews with employers, employment managers, foremen, etc., concerning the special English requirements of their employees.

REGISTRATION OF PUPILS.

Teachers should be furnished as soon as possible with a form of registration card, on which the following data should be recorded: Name, address, age, married or single, country of birth, occupation, employer, employer's address, and such other information as local conditions may require. When necessary the aid of interpreters should be secured to obtain the required information.

REGULARITY OF ATTENDANCE.

A pupil who stays away from one lesson finds it easy to stay away from a second. Such pupils unless followed up speedily drop out. The teacher must therefore take such interest in the pupil as to be solicitous about him. The best way to show personal interest is to call on him personally when his absence is unexplained. If that be impossible, appoint a committee of his classmates to call. The least effective means to secure the return of an absent pupil is to write letters and postal cards.

PROMPTNESS.

When pupils enter the classroom in a body, e. g., in a factory, no difficulty is experienced with late entrants. When, however, the pupils come from home, the ever-present danger is that they will defer their time of going to school, especially if the teacher waits for all to arrive before beginning the lesson. When the first pupil comes in at the door, the successful teacher is on her feet welcoming him and engaging him in conversation, correcting his written work, hearing him read, explaining a difficulty, or giving him an opportunity to copy something from the board or from a book.

CHAPTER III.

DETAILED LESSON UNITS.

In the lesson plans that follow, a variety of exercises, methods, and devices are used. No attempt has been made to follow any one method exclusively. Throughout the lessons, however, one main purpose governs the selection of subject matter and of method, i. e., the availability of the lesson content for use by the pupil. These lessons are intended moreover for beginning pupils only and especially are intended to precede the more advanced lessons to be found in the better grade of recent textbooks.

The lessons are arranged in units of six or seven kinds of exercises, each dovetailing with, supporting, and supplementing the other. There are 10 such lesson units. The main substance of each lesson unit consists of a short theme. Out of the theme are developed all other drills and formal exercises. Each unit is complete in itself, and should be mastered by the pupil before he is permitted to continue to the next. Pupils, however, differ so greatly in their ability to learn that no one can foretell the number of lessons or the number of hours of instruction required by any given class to complete the work of a single unit. It is necessary, however, that the teacher devote sufficient time to each exercise, and especially that the teacher do not overemphasize the importance of any one exercise by devoting too much time to it. The following table suggests the maximum time limit for each exercise:

Exercise.	Two-hour session.	One and one-half hour session.	One-hour session.
	Minutes.	Minutes.	Minutes.
Conversation	20	15	10
Theme	35	30	20
Word drill	10	5	[1] 5
Sentence drill	10	5	[1] 5
Writing	30	25	20
Incidental reading	10	5	[1] 5
Physical training	5	5	5
	120	90	60

[1] Alternate lessons.

LESSON UNIT I.

1. CONVERSATION:

Establish friendly relations with the members of the class; a hearty handshake, a captivating smile and an optimistic outlook are essential to the stock-in-trade of a teacher of adults. Take pains to become interested in the individual under instruction rather than in the subject matter which you teach. One of the best ways of approach with people who speak no English is to introduce yourself and to ask that they introduce themselves in turn to you. Thus the teacher says: "My name is ———." "What is your name?"

Have each person say, "My name is ———."

To vary the procedure ask, "What is his (or her) name?"

Let the pupils say, "His (her) name is ———."

Use such expressions as "Good," "That's good," "You understand," to encourage the pupils. If a pupil does not understand, pass on to another and come back to him. Above all, show no signs of impatience, and keep smiling.

Teach "Good evening," "Good morning," "Good afternoon," or "Good night," as suits the time of day when the class meets and when you dismiss it. Let the pupils answer in the same way.

2. DEVELOP THE THEME:

Getting up in the morning.

I open my eyes. (Dramatize.)

I look at the clock. (Show on a clock or on a diagram on the blackboard.)

It is six o'clock. (Show the time on a clock face.)

I get out of bed. (A picture will do.)

The water runs into the sink. (A model or a picture.)

I wash myself. (Dramatize.)

I dress myself. (Dramatize.)

I comb my hair. (Dramatize.)

I brush my teeth. (Dramatize.)

It is half past six. (Show clock face.)

3. PROCEDURE:

1. Stand in front of the class and command attention. Shut your eyes and say, "I shut my eyes."

Open your eyes slowly and say, "I open my eyes."

2. Let the class perform the act of opening the eyes and saying "I open my eyes." Let individual pupils do this and say the words.

3. Open your eyes once more, say, "I open my eyes" and write "I open my eyes" on the board.

4. Let pupils perform the act, say the words, and read the words from the board.

NOTE: Don't worry about their knowing the letters or the sounds of the letters. They "read" when they are able to say "I open my eyes" and to realize that the marks on the board mean "I open my eyes," even though they may for the time being be unable to recognize a single word or a single letter.

5. In the same way teach as many of the other sentences in the theme as you can in about 30 minutes. Make sure that every member of the class understands each sentence by performing the act and saying the words describing it or by indicating the meaning. Thus the sentence "It is half past six" may be illustrated on a clock face or on a diagram.

6. Let the pupils copy as many of the sentences as you have taught.

7. While the class is trying to copy select the illiterates and group them by themselves. Whenever possible illiterates should be taught in a class by themselves, as their progress will be much slower. When the number under instruction does not warrant forming a special class of illiterates, it is best to group them and to furnish them with special exercises while the rest of the class is being taught. Thus, while the class is copying from the board, the illiterates may be practicing the writing of their names from the individual copies furnished by the teacher.

8. Test the pupils' understanding of the sentences taught by directing them to perform the act while you speak the sentence; thus, say "Mr. ———, wash yourself." Mr. ——— performs the act of washing and says, "I wash myself."

4. READING:

Review the theme or so much of it as you have taught by having the pupils perform the act and speak the sentence. Now let them read each sentence as a whole. Make sure they do not chop off each word separately, "I-open-my-eyes." If they are inclined to do this, let them once more *say* the sentence fluently.

5. WORD DRILL:

So far the pupil has been taught to recognize an entire sentence. He must be taught to recognize individual words as well in order that he may be able to read new sentences. For this purpose the following exercises are intended:

1. Point to "open," "eyes," "my," "I." Have pupils recognize them and say them as rapidly as possible. If they fail, point to the entire sentence and let pupils repeat the sentence until they come to the word you want them to read.

2. Write the words in column in irregular order, e. g.,

    my
    I
    open
    eyes

Have pupils read the words.

3. Call the words of a sentence in any order and let pupils find them on the board.

4. Write or print each word on a stiff card about 6 inches square. Let the pupils read the word as you present the card.

5. Teach the recognition of as many of the words of a theme as the pupils can master in a 10-minute lesson. If all exercises under this head can not be used in one lesson, reserve some of them for future lessons in word drill.

6. Rearrange the words taught and have pupils read them; thus—

    "Look at my eyes."
    "My eyes look."
    "Open the clock."
    "Look at the bed."
    "I wash my eyes."
    "Open the bed."

6. PHONIC DRILL:

Adults who read their own language will find little difficulty in recognizing the sounds of most English consonants. They will find difficulty in recognizing some phonograms like ight, ought, alm, aw, eau, eigh. For them, exercises in phonic recognition serve the purpose of extending their reading vocabularies.

Illiterates must be taught to associate the correct sound with each consonant as it occurs in a word whose meaning they know and which they can pronounce as a whole. The purpose of these exercises in phonics is to furnish the pupil with a key to the recognition of new words. Separate "look" into l-ook;

sound "ook;" pupils sound l and "ook." Similarly, sound b-ed, r-un, g-et, dr-ess, p-ast.

Now combine as many of the sounds as form real words, making sure the pupils understand the words thus formed, e. g., from l-ook, b-ed, r-un, p-ast, g-et, h-alf, the pupils form b-ook, l-ed- r-ed, l-ast, g-un, p-et, h-at, h-ook, bl-ock, br-ook, b-un, b-et.

LESSON UNIT II.

1. CONVERSATION:

Teach pupils to give their addresses and to write them; thus you say, " I live at 145 State Street." "Where do you live, Mr. Brown?"

If Mr. Brown does not understand repeat the question and pass on to someone else who does, and then go back to Mr. Brown. Have pupils write their names and addresses. Furnish a copy to each illiterate and let him practice writing his name first, and then his address. While the others are writing help the illiterates.

2. DEVELOP THE THEME:

Making the fire.

> It is cold.
> I take some paper.
> I put the paper into the stove.
> I put some wood on the paper.
> I strike a match.
> I light the paper.
> The paper burns.
> The wood burns.
> I put some coal on the fire.
> It is warm.

NOTE: If possible have a stove and all the necessary materials for making a fire. If this is not possible have all other material and go through the process of making a fire without, of course, lighting the paper.

3. WORD DRILL:

Drill on rapid recognition of words like cold, take, some, paper, wood, fire, etc. Follow procedure in Unit I.

4. SENTENCE DRILL:

Sentence reading after sentences have been developed by the procedure in Theme I. Form new sentences on the board; make sure the pupils understand the meaning by having them perform the act and then let them read—

> " Put wood on the paper."
> "Take some cold water."
> "I put the warm water on my eyes."
> "Put the cold water on the stove."
> "I wash myself with warm water."

5. PHONIC DRILL:

Review the rapid recognition of b, r, g, p, l, cl, d, dr, b, br, ed, et, ess, un, ast, ook.

Teach the sounds of—

> *t* from take.
> *s* from some.
> *m* from match.
> *w* from warm (w is formed by pursing the lips as for whistling oo).
> *f* from fire.

Form new words—

take	some	match	look
bake	come	latch	cook
lake		catch	
wake			
run	get	fire	last
gun	wet	wire	mast
sun		hire	fast
fun		tire	

6. PHYSICAL EXERCISES:

The object of these exercises is twofold:

1. To furnish relaxation when the class tires. Hence these exercises should be given at the middle of the period devoted to English instruction.

2. To teach the vocabulary of the parts of the body in a natural way. Perform each act to indicate its meaning. Let the class follow you.

Class stand.

Face the windows.

Breathe in.

Breathe out. (Do this eight time, the teacher counting out loud " one, two, three, four, five, six, seven, eight." Say " Through your nose. Shut your mouth." Interpret the meaning by performing the acts.)

Face front.

Arms upward, stretch. Down. (Count four.)

LESSON UNIT III.

1. CONVERSATION:

Review "My name is ———." "I live at ———."

Teach "How do you do?" "I am well, thank you."

Teach them to write "I am a ——— (occupation)." I work for ——— (name of employer)."

NOTE: In the case of women unemployed, teach instead "My husband (brother, father, etc.) is a ———." "He works for ———."

2. REVIEW OF THEMES:

Write one of the two themes so far learned on the board, omitting an important word in each sentence. Let the pupils copy the theme from the board, filling in the omitted word from memory. Fill in the blank spaces and let the pupils compare their work with the work on the board. Thus,—

I ——— my eyes.

I look at the ———.

It ——— six o'clock.

I ——— out of bed.

The water runs into the ———.

3. INCIDENTAL READING:

Prepare a set of cards about six inches square on which are neatly printed such signs as the pupils are likely to see in their daily walks or in their places of employment. Exhibit one of these hereafter at every lesson and spend about five minutes in letting the pupils respond by action to them. Thus place EXIT, or ENTRANCE over the doors or over roped-off sections of a room and see that pupils enter and go out by the proper doors.

Similarly, show one sign during each succeeding lesson, paying especial attention to the signs in factories and in the neighborhood. Suggest that pupils copy signs which they see and do not understand and bring them into the classroom for explanation. It is necessary that pupils know what these signs mean.

It is not necessary that they know how to spell the words: NO SMOKING, NO ADMITTANCE, DANGER, CURRENT ON, PAY WINDOW, MEN WANTED, FIRE ESCAPE.

4. PHYSICAL TRAINING:
Same as before.
Introduce "Turn head to the right". "Front". Four times.

5. DEVELOP THE THEME:

Eating breakfast.

It is seven o'clock.
I am hungry.
The table is set.
I walk to the table.
I sit down.
I eat my breakfast.
I drink a glass of milk (tea—coffee—cocoa).
I eat a piece of bread and butter.
I drink a glass of water.
I get up from the table.

6. WORD DRILL:

it	look	get	clock	bread
sit	book	let	block	head
old	some	walk	down	
cold	come	talk	town	
ear	table	drink	eat	
dear	fable	ink	meat	
	gable	sink	beat	
			heat	

7. SENTENCE DRILL:

Let the pupils read these sentences silently, carry out the directions, and then read aloud:

Set the table.
Wash the glass.
Take a piece of bread.
Warm the milk.
Put some butter on the bread.
Sit at the table.
Put some cold water into the glass.

LESSON UNIT IV.

1. CONVERSATION:
Review greetings:

"How do you do?"
"My name is ————."
"I live at ————"
"I am a ————."
"I work for ————."

Teach: "I am ———— years old." "I am married (single)."
Writing: Have pupils fill in blank spaces in the above after they have had practice in doing so orally.

2. DEVELOP THE THEME:

Going to work.

It is half past seven.
It is very cold on the street.
I put on my hat and coat.
I say " Good-by."
I do not walk.
I ride to the shop.
I enter the shop.
I take my hat and coat off quickly.
I put on my working clothes.
The whistle blows.
I begin to work.

3. WORD DRILL:

Rapid recognition of quickly, clothes, good-by, whistle, walk, very.

street	coat	take	shop
meet	boat	bake	stop
hat	past	cake	shop
cat	last	very	shut
blow	quickly	vinegar	shake
show	quietly		show

4. SENTENCE DRILL:

Put your hat on quickly (slowly).
Walk until the whistle blows.
Run quickly to bed.
What time is it?
Blow your whistle.
Take your hat off.
Do not take your coat off.

5. REVIEW OF THEMES:

Have pupils fill in blank spaces in sentences taken from the themes. See Theme III.

6. PHYSICAL TRAINING:

Same as before.
Teach " Bend your knees. Up." Four times.

7. INCIDENTAL READING:

One sign.

LESSON UNIT V.

1. CONVERSATION:

Review previous conversational expressions.

Teach—Hours of work, e. g., " I work from 8 o'clock in the morning until 6 o'clock at night."

By this time the pupils have heard counting several times; teach them to count to 100.

To test them, ask such questions as " How many hands have you? " (Show hands.)

" How many fingers have you? "
" How many children have you? "
" How many rooms have you? "
" How many hours do you work? "
" How much do you earn? "
" How many days in the week? " (Say Monday, Tuesday, Wednesday, etc., to make them understand.)

2. DEVELOP THE THEME:

The noon hour.

I am hungry (thirsty).
The whistle blows just at 12 o'clock.
I stop work.
I wash my hands and face.
I dry my hands and face with a towel.
I go to the lunch room.
I sit at the table.
I buy a cup of coffee.
I put some sugar into the coffee.
I eat my lunch.
I rest from 12 to 1.
The whistle blows again.
I begin to work again.

3. WORD DRILL:

lunch	rest	hand	face
bunch	rest aurant	land	place
		band	race
		and	
dry	stop	lun*ch*	wa*sh*
why	drop	*ch*urch	*sh*ave
my			shop
just	whistle (hoo-isl)	sugar	
jump	why (hoo-ai)	sure	
	where		
	when		
	who		
	whose		
	whom		

4. SENTENCE DRILL:

After teaching the theme as it stands, let one pupil go through the actions once more and you describe his actions in the third person, thus:

" He (she) is hungry."
" He stops work."
" He washes his hands and face."
" He dries his hands and face with a towel."
" He goes to the lunch room," etc.

Drill the pupils on describing another's acts in the third person. Point out the *s* which is usually added when speaking of another, i. e., I walk. He-she-walk*s*.

5. INCIDENTAL READING:

Teach one sign.

Teach the meaning of two or three words used in the industry of the pupil.

Where all the pupils are employed in the same industry, the teacher may obtain some of the tools or materials used and build a theme around them after the manner in which the general themes in these lessons are built. When pupils are not in the same industry the pupils may be encouraged to bring the materials and small tools to school. The teacher then labels each object by attaching a card to the object. Thus the teacher labels a pick, a spade, a shovel and pronounces the word. Where the objects themselves can not be brought to the classroom use pictures, drawings, diagrams, models, etc. Not more than two or three objects should be taught in one lesson in this way.

For women not in industry, teach in this lesson and in every succeeding lesson the names of two or three objects which they buy or about which they will likely want to talk to English-speaking people, e. g., baby, milk, bath, scrub, oatmeal, articles of clothing, food, furniture, etc.

6. PHYSICAL TRAINING:

Review all previous exercises.
Teach "Arms on hips, place. Down." Four times.

LESSON UNIT VI.

1. CONVERSATION:

Review giving names, addresses, occupations, counting objects.

Teach asking the price of a number of articles such as hat, coat, shoes, gloves, rent of a room, a day's work, etc. Thus:

Question.—How much does this hat cost? or, How much do you want for this hat?

Answer.—This hat costs three dollars. (Write three dollars on the board.)

Each pupil should be called upon to ask and to answer the question.

By writing the cost of various articles on the board, the pupils will learn to read American money. Thus, $1.75; 16 cents or 16¢; 2 for a quarter, etc.

2. DEVELOP THE THEME:

Stopping work.

I work hard.
I am tired.
The whistle blows again at six o'clock.
I stop work.
I take off my working clothes.
I wash myself.
I put on my hat and overcoat.
I walk into the street.
I open the door.
I enter the house.
" Good evening. How do you do? "

3. WORD DRILL:

Again, tired, working, evening, overcoat.

hard	blow	street	enter
card	blows	meet	entrance
lard	flow	feet	
	flows		
	show		
	shows		

working	evening	getting
stopping	making	morning
going	washing	

4. SENTENCE DRILL:

Have pupils dramatize the sentences and let each change them using " he " or " she " instead of " I."

5. WRITING:

Have pupils fill in blank spaces for the verbs in the theme using the third person, thus:

He ——— hard.
He ——— work.
He ——— off his working clothes.

6. INCIDENTAL READING:

Teach one sign.

Teach the meanings of two or three words used in the pupils' industry or homes.

7. PHYSICAL TRAINING:

Review all previous exercises.

Teach "Rise on toes. Down." Four times. "Get your heels off the floor." Indicate meaning.

LESSON UNIT VII.

1. CONVERSATION:

Review asking questions about the cost of articles.

Review "I am married (single)."

Teach the names of relatives, e. g., father, mother, brother, sister, child, son, daughter, cousin, uncle.

Begin with some pupil who you know is married. Say, "Are you married?"

> He answers: "I am married."
> "What is your wife's name?"
> "Have you a child?" (If he does not understand, mention the name of his child.)
> "You are his father (or mother)."

Do the same with all the pupils in the class, developing in this way the meanings of the other words showing relationships by recalling their known relationships.

2. DEVELOP THE THEME:

Eating supper.

The table is set.

I have a knife, a fork, and a spoon near my plate.

My wife puts the supper on the table. (Waitress, waiter, Mrs. X.)

My boy John sits down (or Mr. ——).

My girl Mary sits down (or Miss ——).

My wife sits down (or Mrs. ——).

I sit down next to my wife.

We eat our supper.

After supper I smoke my pipe.

NOTE: Change the words in the theme as needed to meet different conditions.

3. WORD DRILL:

Set	wife	it	table	pipe
get	life	its	able	ripe
let	knife	sit		wipe
met		sits		
		knit		
		knits		
boy	our	supper	plate	smoke
joy	sour	upper	late	joke
toy			slate	poke
				stoke
				coke

4. SENTENCE DRILL:

I eat my breakfast at 7 o'clock.

You eat your lunch at 12 o'clock.

We eat our supper at 6 o'clock in the evening.

My wife sets the table.

She puts some bread on the table.

Next to my plate is a knife.

I cut bread with the knife.

I put sugar into my coffee with the spoon.

I hold meat with the fork.

. **5. WRITING:**

Have pupils fill blank spaces in the theme. Thus,

I eat my breakfast at ——— o'clock.

You eat your lunch at ——— o'clock.

We eat our supper at ——— o'clock.

6. INCIDENTAL READING:

Teach one sign.

Teach the names of two or three objects in industry or home. It is advisable to associate some action with the object rather than have it merely pointed out. Thus, "I drive the nail with the hammer", helps to associate "drive" with "nail" and "hammer." This makes it easier to teach and easier to remember than by teaching "This is a nail." "This is a hammer."

7. PHYSICAL TRAINING:

Review all previous exercises.

Teach " Bend bodies to the right. To the left." Four times.

LESSON UNIT VIII.

1. CONVERSATION:

Review the names of the members of the pupils' families by asking about them; thus, "Mr. X, how is your wife?"

Teach him to answer "She is well, thank you."

After you have reviewed the various members of the family, let the pupils question each other.

Teach the names of the countries from which the pupils came; thus, begin with a pupil whose birthplace you know, and say, " Mr. Frank, were you born in Russia?"

Teach him to say "I was born in Russia."

Ask the other pupils "Where were you born?"

As they are given, write the names of the countries on the board. Then write "I was born in ———," and let the pupils fill in the country of birth.

2. DEVELOP THE FOLLOWING CONVERSATION:

Dramatize the lesson by taking part yourself; after the thought has been developed, write the sentences on the board and let the pupils dramatize.

The bell rings.

" Come in."

" Good evening."

" Good evening, Mr. ———. Please take a seat."

" Thank you. How do you feel, Mrs. X?"

" I am very well, thank you. How is Mrs. ———?"

" She is very tired."

" Did she wash clothes to-day?"

" Yes, and she ironed them, too."

" How are the children?"

" My boy is well but the girl is sick."

" What is the matter with her?"

" The doctor says she needs a rest."

" I hope she feels better."

" Thank you. You are very kind."

3. WORD DRILL:

iron, thank, children, doctor, kind, too.

child	ring	ringing	well	need
wild	rings	bringing	fell	needs
mild	bring	evening	tell	feed
	brings		sell	feeds
knife	thank		kind	feel
knee	thin			heel
know				steel
				kneel

4. SENTENCE DRILL:

Review Theme I by changing the sentences to the second person; thus: you open your eyes. You look at the clock.

In later lessons other previous themes may be changed to the first person plural: "We open our eyes."

Or to the third person plural: "They open their eyes."

Not more than one variation, however, should be attempted in one lesson.

5. WRITING:

Dictate three or four sentences from Theme I. Have pupils write and then compare their work with a correct copy on the board.

6. INCIDENTAL READING:

Teach one sign.

Teach the meaning of two or three words used in the pupils' industries or homes.

7. PHYSICAL TRAINING:

Review previous exercises.

Teach "Point in front of you." "Point back of you."

LESSON UNIT IX.

1. CONVERSATION:

Review telling the time by indicating it on a clock face or on a diagram
Teach "What time is it?"

"Ten minutes past two."
"A quarter past three."
"Half past eight." etc.

Test by asking such questions as—

"What time do you get up in the morning?"
"What time do you go to lunch?"
"When do you go to sleep?"
"What time do you go to bed on Saturday—on Sunday, etc.?"

2. DEVELOP THE THEME:

Putting the children to bed.

It is 9 o'clock.
My children are tired.
John is sleepy.
Mary yawns and nods.
"Go to bed, children."
"It is late."
"Good night, papa and mamma."
They kiss me.
They go to bed.
The house is quiet.
I read the newspaper.

3. WORD DRILL:

bed	go	house	night
red	so	mouse	fright
fed	no		might
good	kiss	nod	bright
wood	miss	God	light
	hiss		

4. SENTENCE DRILL:

At 9 o'clock my children go to bed.
They are very tired and sleepy.
They go to bed early.
John is healthy and strong.
Mary is sickly and weak.

5. WRITING:

Teach pupils to address an envelope to themselves.

> Mr. John Brown,
> 43 State Street,
> Oriole, Ill.

and then an envelope to some one to whom they are likely to write, e. g., the teacher, the foreman, the employer, the landlord, some relative, etc.

6. INCIDENTAL READING:

Teach one sign.
Teach the meanings of two or three words used in the pupils' industries or homes.

7. PHYSICAL TRAINING:

Review previous exercises.
Teach "Forward march." "Halt."

LESSON UNIT X.

1. CONVERSATION:

Review the days of the week.
Ask such questions as—
  "What day is this?"
  "What day was yesterday?"
  "What day will to-morrow be?"
  "On what day do you rest?"
  "On what day do you go to church?"
  "On what day were you married?"

From now on write the date on the board during each lesson and have the pupils copy it into their notebooks; thus, Tuesday, November 18, 1919.

2. DEVELOP THE THEME:

Going to bed.

It is late.
I feel sleepy.
I go to my bedroom.
I undress myself.
I put on my night clothes.
I turn out the gas. (Blow out the lamp.)
The house is dark.
I get into bed.
I cover myself with a blanket.
I fall asleep.

3. WORD DRILL:

late	undress	turn	fall
ate	unhappy	burn	all
hate	unwilling		tall
gate	unable		ball
			call

dark	remark
bark	shark
mark	park

4. SENTENCE DRILL:

Change the sentences in the theme to the past tense by prefixing " Yesterday " to each sentence, thus, Yesterday it was late. I felt sleepy, etc.

5. WRITING:

Review addressing an envelope.

Teach proper heading and salutation and close to a business letter:

---

                        25 Pershing Avenue,
                            Downey, Ohio.

Mr. Thomas Smith,
  15 Broad Street,
    Oriole, Pa.

Dear Sir:

                  Yours truly,

---

6. INCIDENTAL READING:

Teach one sign; one motto.

Construct sentences with words taught by phonic drills. Have pupils read them silently, then aloud.

7. PHYSICAL TRAINING:

Review previous exercises.

Teach " Close fists. Open fists. Stretch your fingers." Eight times.

SUBSEQUENT LESSON UNITS.

Probably the most effective work in teaching English to foreigners can be done when classes are organized in industries, with the co-operation of the employers. Experience has shown that adults find it irksome to return to school in the evening after a hard day's work in factory or shop. The familiar environment of the " shop," the customary business attitude of the workers, help to provide an atmosphere of seriousness and continuity which is lacking when pupils leave their work for home to return later to a school. The break between work and school must not be so abrupt as to require extraordinary energy from the pupil in putting himself into an entirely new frame of mind. Psychologically, there is a great gain when the worker, without any undue strain, is at the same time the pupil—when the work attitude is carried over into the pupil attitude.

The gain is not only psychological. The selection of lesson material and of method of instruction is controlled by the needs, interests and desires of the pupil. The more nearly alike these needs, interests and desires in learning English are, the more likely is the teacher to satisfy the pupils and to adjust his teaching to meet their ever present needs. This condition is best obtained where the pupils of any given class work at the same processes, in the same industry, requiring the same English sentences to express their ideas. Every industry has its own technical expressions, its own procedure, its own customs. The successful teacher of English to men and women in industry must make himself thoroughly familiar with all these, and must base his lessons on the English useful to the pupils in the specific work at which they are engaged. Instead of teaching a pupil how to apply for an imaginary job, the teacher must connect his present job with the unique procedure in getting it. Rather than teach a carpenter the English that goes with laying bricks, the teacher must plan the lesson to be of value to the carpenter. It is better for the pupil to understand the signs posted in his factory than the signs in any other factory.

To the teacher the time expended in familiarizing himself with local industrial conditions, will be time well spent. Not only will he secure a body of subject matter for his English instruction which will be far superior to any ready-made lessons, but by relating his lessons to the pupils' vocations he will secure the interest of his pupils and the active cooperation of their employers. The teacher must bear in mind that his success depends largely on the backing of employers and industrial managers. The latter must be made to feel that, aside from patriotic consideration, teaching English to their non-English-speaking workers is a necessity; that it pays in better understanding, in better workmanship, in improved spirit.

Obviously, it is not possible to draw up a series of lessons to be effective in the great variety of industries found in our country. Merely by way of suggestion, the following lessons are presented with the further statement that the teacher must adapt the lesson to the situation as he finds it and must add other lessons usable in the industry of the pupil:

Looking for work.

John is a molder (rammer, presser, fireman, etc.).
He has no job.
He wants to work.
He walks around the streets. He is looking for work.
He sees a sign " Molders wanted."

He walks into the factory.

The foreman (employment manager, superintendent) comes in.

"Do you want molders?"

"Yes. Have you any experience?"

"I have three years' experience."

"For whom did you work?"

"I worked for Johnson & Company."

"How much do you want?"

"I want ——— dollars a day."

"We pay by the week. We pay ——— a week."

"We pay by the piece. We pay ——— a piece."

"All right, I'll take the job."

"When can you begin to work?"

"I can begin to-morrow morning."

"All right. Here is a ticket with your number. I shall expect you."

Beginning work.

John came to the factory at 7 o'clock.

He walked in.

The foreman said, "Good morning, John. Come with me."

He showed John how to punch the clock.

Then John put his hat and coat into a locker.

He put on a pair of overalls.

The foreman said, "Come with me to the foundry" (drying room, machine shop, etc.).

Everybody was working.

The foreman called Mike.

"Mike, this is John. He will work with you."

The two men shook hands.

John walked away with Mike and began to work.

Pay day.

To-day is pay day.

The cashier (pay clerk, paymaster, foreman, etc.) comes into the factory.

He carries a leather bag.

In the bag are envelopes.

Each envelope holds the pay of a workman.

The men stand in line.

The cashier (pay clerk, paymaster, foreman, etc.) says, "What is your name?"

"My name is John Brown."

"What is your number?"

"My number is 465."

"Here is your envelope."

"Thank you."

John opens the envelope.

He counts the money.

It is right.

AN ACCIDENT.

A man was hurt in our factory.

He did not obey the danger sign.

The sign read, "Danger. Do not touch."

He could read English, but he was careless.
He touched a piece of hot metal.
The hot metal burned his hand.
He fell down and fainted.
We took him to the emergency room.
The doctor treated his hand.
Then he put a bandage on the man's hand and sent him home.
The man will not be able to work for a week.

PLANING A BOARD.

I am a carpenter.
I take a board.
It is rough.
I put it into the vise.
I go to the tool rack.
I take a jack plane.
I plane one side of the board.
I open the vise.
I take out the board.
I turn the board around.
I plane the other side.
The board is smooth on two sides.

SUPPLEMENT A.

(*Report of the Committee on Methods of Teaching English to the Foreign Born.*)

Mr. Fred C. Butler, *Director of Americanization, Washington, D. C.*

Dear Sir: The committee upon Methods of Teaching English to the Foreign Born, appointed at the National Conference on Methods of Americanization, held in Washington in May, 1919, submits its report as follows:

Introduction.—Teaching English to non-English-speaking people is merely one phase of the general problem of foreign-language instruction. Because of this the principles underlying a comprehensive method of teaching English to the foreign born are the same as those that underlie the teaching of a foreign language to American men and women of equal education and intelligence.

It is the understanding of this committee that the suggestions regarding method were intended to apply to teaching English to beginners, since this phase of the work differs more widely from the customary methods employed in teaching English to the intermediate and advanced groups.

Types of method.—Methods of teaching foreign languages may be classified in many ways. When we think of the language that is used as a means of communication between teacher and pupil we may class the method as either direct or indirect—indirect when the teacher is able to speak the language of the pupils and uses it in the teaching; direct when the teaching is carried on entirely in the new language.

Again the methods may be classed as synthetic or analytic according to the unit of advance used in the teaching. The method may be said to be synthetic when the attempt is made to build a vocabulary by the mastery of isolated words and then out of this material it is attempted to construct sentences. A method may be said to be analytic when the sentence is taken as the unit and is later analyzed into its separate parts.

It is the opinion of this committee that the results achieved by the intelligent use of the direct method, which is not synthetic in plan but which does depend upon the sentence as the unit of language, are the most satisfactory. The direct method to be satisfactory, however, must be completely and carefully organized and the material for the early lessons must be selected with great care.

Source of lesson material.—The committee feels that grave mistakes have been made in the past in the choice of lesson material for classes of the foreign born because too much emphasis has been placed upon the literary features of the English language and too little placed upon the actual every-day English that the pupil needs for his home, industrial, and community life. Instead of selecting material for its literary value, it is better to select the subject matter of the lessons from the field of common, every-day experiences of the individual, to the end that he may learn to express himself in English on subjects about which he is likely to have the opportunity of talking to English-speaking people.

38

Classification of pupils.—It is a well-known fact that individuals differ in intellectual power and educational attainments. Classes, after all, are only groups of individuals, and it has been found possible to adjust the groupings of these individuals in such fashion that each class can make the greatest amount of progress in the shortest time. The following principles of classification will be found valuable in this respect:

(1) *Grouping according to race.*—When dealing with real beginners, those who can speak and understand no English, it is adviseable to recognize the principle of classification by race. In this way racial antipathies are avoided and groups that are homogeneous both as to racial backgrounds and intellectual achievements can be brought together. Later on, after the preliminary lessons have been given, it will be advisable to break down the barriers of race by organizing the classes upon some other basis.

(2) *Classification by sex.*—Where numbers warrant, it is often advisable to classify men and women separately. If such a course is impossible on account of lack of numbers, divide the class into two groups, placing the women in one group and the men in another.

(3) *Classification on the basis of knowledge of English.*—The third principle of classification is found in the amount of English that is already the property of the pupils. Three main groups are possible on this basis: Beginners, intermediates, and advanced. In the first class should be placed those who do not speak, understand, read or write any English, or very little English. In the second group may be placed those who are able to speak much English rather poorly or a little English quite well, who are able to read simple English sentences with understanding, and who are able to write short sentences from dictation. In the third group may be placed those who are able to talk on subjects of general interest, who are able to read simple news items in the daily paper, and who are able to write a short business letter with some degree of correctness.

Detailed classification of beginners.—Experience has shown that it is advantageous to make subdivisions of those who are classed as beginners. In general, it is more advantageous to group in one beginning class the illiterates—those who are unable to read or write their own language. These may be again subdivided into a group that does not speak or understand any English and another group that speaks and understands little English. Likewise it is advantageous to group together those who are educated in their own language, and these may be again subdivided into those who speak and understand no English and those who speak and understand some English. The following outline will explain this plan of grouping:

(1) Beginners:
    (*a*) Illiterate.
        (Speak and understand no English.)
        (Speak and understand some English.)
    (*b*) Educated in own language.
        (Speak and understand no English.)
        (Speak and understand some English.)

(2) Intermediate beginners:
    (*a*) Speak much English rather poorly or a little English quite well.
    (*b*) Read simple English sentences with understanding.
    (*c*) Write short sentences from dictation.

(3) Advanced beginners:
    (*a*) Talk about matters of general interest.
    (*b*) Read simple news items in daily paper.
    (*c*) Write short business letter.

As indicated in the introduction, the essential work of this committee was to deal with methods for beginners. It seems wise, however, to suggest that when pupils have reached the stage of advanced beginners they are able to apply their English to gaining instruction about our history, our institutions, our civics, and such other general topics as may be of particular value to individual classes, e. g., study of the post office and its departments, of the weather bureau and its value to the citizen, buying real estate, building a home, borrowing money, and so forth.

Principles governing the organization of material.—Following the idea mentioned above, the subject matter of each lesson should be selected from the common, every-day experience of pupils. Each lesson should be organized around one central idea which constitutes the general end. In the early lessons this central idea or theme should be developed in not more than 15 sentences. It should be noted that the sentence rather than single words is taken as the unit of language. The sentences should follow one another according to logical sequence in time, since this is a great aid to the memory of the pupil. It is advisable to arrange the sentences in groups so that natural resting places will occur in the theme. Ordinarily, 15 sentences should be arranged in three groups of five each. However, in suggesting 15 sentences as the maximum number for the early lessons, it is not intended to set this as a standard. A theme may consist of three or four sentences, or it might be possible to have more than 15. The short theme that follows will indicate the application of the principles so far mentioned:

Making the fire.

1. I close the dampers.
2. I shake the grate.
3. I take out the ashes.
4. I put the ashes in an iron pail.
5. I take off the lids. (Covers.)
6. I place paper in the fire-box.
7. I place wood in the fire-box.
8. I put on a shovelful of coal.
9. I strike a match.
10. I light the paper.
11. I open the dampers.
12. I put on the lids. (Covers.)
13. I brush off the stove.
14. The fire burns.
15. I put on more coal.
16. I close the stove-pipe dampers.

In cases if illiterates and pupils of low mentality, the sentences in a given lesson should be short and very simple, closely connected and few in number. It will be found that some classes learn more rapidly than others. Consequently, teachers may find that all the sentences in the theme can not be developed in one lesson. If such is the case, they should develop only as many as the class can assimilate and leave the others to be taken up at a later time.

It will be noted that the connecting idea between the sentences in the theme is that of succession in time expressed by the words "and then" understood. The language used in the theme should be objective, i. e., such that is easily dramatized or made intelligible to the pupil through the use of objective material.

Principal governing the teaching process.—We have already recognized the importance of teaching the foreign-born to speak and understand English as well as to read and write it. To develop the ability to speak and understand the language, attention must be given to ear training, since it is through the ear that we master language. We have already noted that the sentence is the unit of language. Our method then should deal from the beginning with sentences rather than with vocabulary lists. In each sentence the most important word is the verb. This should receive special drill and attention because it is in the use of verbs that a large proportion of the mistakes of language occur.

In transmitting the idea to the mind of the pupil one or all of the following devices may be employed:

(1) Dramatization: (a) Action; (b) gesture; (c) play of features and inflection of the voice.

(2) Objects.

(3) Pictures. The use of figurative language should be postponed until the pupils have developed sufficient vocabulary so that explanations of abstractions may be made. In teaching the theme, however, which is composed of objective language, the teacher should also use such expression as " That is good." " I like that." " Please try again," etc. These constitute expressions of commendation, judgment, or admonition, and may be classed under the heading of subjective language. It will be found unnecessary to explain the meaning of these phrases since the expression of the features and the inflection of the voice convey the idea. Out of the objective language found in the theme and the subjective language contributed by the teacher, conversation will be naturally developed, and conversations furnish excellent drill in the use of language.

Many of the textbooks for the teaching of English to the foreign-born, emphasize the objective features of the direct method and many of the earlier pages are devoted to exercises revolving about selected lists of words arranged in such fashion as " This is a hat." " Is this a coat?" " What is this?" "This is a book," etc. While this arrangement of material does not appear in the theme plan as outlined above, the teacher may use question and answer exercises to good advantage in reviewing what has already been taught by the theme plan. The great importance of variety in review work can not be too strongly emphasized. Other devices for accomplishing this result are as follows:

(a) Question the pupils, requiring answers that use words taught in the sentences of the various themes.

(b) Let the pupils question each other about the lessons as soon as they have gained sufficient vocabulary.

(c) Give commands either orally or in writing on the blackboard using vocabulary previously taught and requiring a pupil to execute a command and then tell what he did.

(d) Dramatize universal activities, e. g., buying a hat, applying for work, making a deposit in a savings bank, etc.

Teaching English grammar through use.—The formal rules and definitions of grammar should have little place in this method, but a great amount of drill in the use of grammatical forms and expressions can be obtained by the use of variants which can be introduced into the original theme. On general principles it will probably be found advantageous through a series of lessons to substitute for the personal pronoun " I " that occurs as the subject of each sentence in the early themes, the other personal pronouns. It will also be found possible by the use of the key words " to-day," " yesterday," and " to-morrow " to get splendid drill in the tenses by teaching the pupils to say, " To-day I walk to the door." " Yesterday I walked to the door." " To-morrow I shall walk to the door," etc.

Teaching the English sounds.—Experience has shown that sound drills are valuable in classes of foreign-speaking people to aid in the correction of foreign accent, enunciation, and pronunciation, and sometimes to furnish a key for the recognition of new words. Care should be taken to avoid a waste of time in this field, however, and the phonic period should be kept separate in order that the reading exercise may not lose its continuity. Sound drills should be centered around words that appear in the themes, but no pupils should be asked to practice the sounds until the teacher has carefully shown how the sounds are developed.

Teaching procedure.—A common mistake, especially in the teaching of English to men and women who do not speak or understand any English, has been to rely upon the printed page as the instrument by which to teach the language. Experience has shown, however, that spoken language is best mastered through the ear. As a consequence, the teaching procedure should place its first emphasis upon oral instruction and practice in speaking. Drill in the reading of the language should be thought of as a second step in the teaching process for beginners. The pupil should first be taught the meaning of the theme through the devices of action, gesture, play of features, inflection of the voice, together with the use of objects and pictures. After the ears of the pupils have become accustomed to the sounds of the sentences as voiced by the teacher and after they have grasped the meaning, they should then learn through imitation and repetition to say the English sentences. The process of oral instruction and the practice in speaking should continue until the completed theme has been mastered.

As soon as the pupils are able to repeat the sentences of the lesson understandingly, the teacher should write the lesson on the blackboard, sentence by sentence, having the class read each sentence several times after it has been so written. When the complete lesson is on the blackboard it should be read in concert by the class as a whole and then, if possible, in whole or in part by each member of the class. This lesson should then be copied into a notebook provided for this purpose. In the above procedure, use is first made of the ear in listening, then of the mouth in repeating, then of the eye in reading from the blackboard, and then of both the eye and the hand in copying into the notebook. Teaching according to this plan intensifies the language impressions made and increases the student's chances of retaining the lessons taught.

Limitations on the features of dramatization, use of objects, etc.—The committee desires to lay particular stress upon the importance of modifying the application of a method according to the particular needs of the class. It is for that reason that so much attention is given to the principle of classification in the earlier part of this report. In classes of beginners who do not speak or understand any English, it will be found necessary to make use of the suggested devices for dramatization, use of objects, etc,. in order that understanding may be aroused in the minds of the pupils. Care should be taken, however, that the use of these devices should be gradually discontinued as the class improves in its knowledge of English. Likewise, there may be classes of beginners who have picked up some knowledge of English through their association with English-speaking people. The teacher who makes the mistake of resorting to detailed dramatization and object teaching with these classes will immediately forfeit the respect of the pupils and will discover a great loss of interest in the lessons.

While it is possible to use similar lesson material with intermediate beginners, namely, those who can already speak and understand some English, the teacher should begin the work of reading from the blackboard, leaflet, or book at once using objects and action-work only when necessary.

How long should the theme form of lesson organization be used?—The committee recognizes that a difference of opinion exists as to the number of lessons that should be introduced in the theme form. We feel that the matter of passing from the theme plan to the paragraph plan depends upon the ability and previous preparation of the student rather than upon any stated number of lessons. As a rule, with real beginners, 25 or 30 themes of about 15 sentences each may be used to advantage before lessons are organized in regular paragraph form.

Respectfully submitted.

W. M. ROBERTS, *Chairman.*
Asst. Superintendent of Schools, Chicago, Ill.
CHAS. E. FINCH,
Director of Immigrant Education, Rochester, N. Y.
H. H. GOLDBERGER,
Principal Public School 18, New York City,
Instructor, Methods of Teaching English to Foreigners,
Columbia University.
PETER ROBERTS,
Secretary Industrial Department,
Internaltional Committee, Y. M. C. A.
T. E. SPENCER,
Supervisor of Educational Extension, St. Louis, Mo.
CHAS. F. TOWNE,
Director of Immigrant Education, Massachusetts.

SUPPLEMENT B.

BIBLIOGRAPHY.

ENGLISH TEXTS.

Austin, Ruth. Lessons in English for foreign women. New York [etc.], American Book Co., 100 Washington Square east, 1913. 35 cents.

Beshgeturian, Azniv. Foreigners' guide to English. Yonkers, N. Y., World Book Co., 313 Park Hill Avenue, 1914. 60 cents.

Chancellor, William E. Reading and language lessons for evening schools. New York, American Book Co., 1912. 30 cents.

Cole, R. E. Everyday English for every coming American. Cleveland, Ohio, Y. M. C. A., Educational Department, 1914.

Field and Coveney. English for new Americans. New York [etc.], Silver, Burdett & Co., 1911. 60 cents.

Goldberger, Henry H. English for coming citizens. New York [etc.], Charles Scribner's Sons, 1918. 80 cents.

Houghton, Frederick. First lessons in English for foreigners. New York, American Book Co., 1911. 40 cents.

Markowitz and Starr. Everyday language lessons. New York, American Book Co., 1914. 40 cents.

Price, Isaac. Direct method of teaching English to foreigners. New York, Frank Beattys & Co., 1913. 45 cents.

Roberts, Peter. English for coming Americans. New York, Association Press, 347 Madison Avenue.

> Series of books, pamphlets, charts and cards. Descriptive price list can be secured on request.

CIVICS TEXTS.

Carr, John Foster. Guide to the United States for the immigrant. New York, Immigrant Educational Society, 241 Fifth Avenue.

Dunn, Arthur W. Community and the citizen. (For advanced classes.) Boston [etc.], D. C. Heath & Co., 1907.

Hill and Davis. Civics for new Americans. Boston [etc.], Houghton Mifflin Co., 1915. 80 cents.

Plass, Anna A. Civics for Americans in the making. New York [etc.], D. C. Heath & Co., 1912. 50 cents.

Richman and Wallach. Good citizenship. New York [etc.], American Book Co., 1908. 45 cents.

Roberts, Peter. Civics for coming Americans. New York, Association Press, 347 Madison Avenue, 1917. 50 cents.

Sharpe, Mary F. Plain facts for future citizens. New York [etc.], American Book Co., 1914. 48 cents.

United States. Department of the Interior. Bureau of Education. Civic education in elementary schools as illustrated in Indianapolis. Washington, Government Printing Office, 1915. (Bulletin, 1915, No. 17.) 5 cents.

———— ———— ————. Lessons in community and national life. Washington, Government Printing Office, 1918. (Series A, B, and C.) 45 cents.

———— ———— ————. The teaching of community civics. Washington, Government Printing Office, 1915. (Bulletin, 1915, No. 23.) 10 cents.

44

Webster, Hanson Hart. Americanization and citizenship. Boston [etc.], Houghton Mifflin Co. 40 cents.
Issued in several languages.

Zmrhal, J. J. Primer of civics. Chicago, The Illinois Society of the Colonial Dames of America, 1362 Astor Street, 1912.
Bilingual texts in Italian, Polish Bohemian, Lithuanian, and other languages.

TRAINING FOR TEACHING.

Bahlsen, Leopold. Teaching of modern languages. Boston [etc.], Ginn & Co., 15 Ashburton Place, 1905. 50 cents.

Berlitz, M. D. The Berlitz method for teaching a language. English Part—Book 1. New York, Berlitz & Co., 28-30 West Thirty-fourth Street, 1915. $1.00.

Colvin and Bagley. Human behavior—a first book in psychology for teachers. New York, The Macmillan Co., 64 Fifth Avenue, 1913. $1.00.

Goldberger, Henry H. How to teach English to foreigners. New York, A. G. Seiler, 1224 Amsterdam Avenue, 1918. 75 cents.

Gouin, François. The art of teaching and studying languages. New York [etc.], Charles Scribner's Sons, 597 Fifth Avenue, 1892.

Jespersen, O. How to teach a foreign language. New York [etc.], The Macmillan Co., 64 Fifth Avenue, 1904. 90 cents.

Mahoney and Herlihy. First steps in Americanization. Boston [etc.], Houghton Mifflin Co., 1918.

Roberts, Peter. Teacher's manual—English for coming Americans. New York, Association Press, 347 Madison Avenue, 1909.

Sweet, H. The practical study of languages. New York, Henry Holt & Co., 19 West Forty-fourth Street. $1.50.

AMERICANISM.

Bryce, James. The American commonwealth. Vol. 2. Chapters CI, CII, CXIV. New York [etc.], The Macmillan Co., 64 Fifth Avenue.

deTocqueville. Democracy in America. 2 vols. Colonial Press.

Foerster, Norman, and Pierson, W. W., editors. American ideals. Boston, [etc.], Houghton Mifflin Co. $1.25.

Hill, David J. Americanism: What it is. New York, D. Appleton & Co., 29-35 West Thirty-second Street, 1916. $1.25.

Kellor, Frances A. Straight America. New York, The Macmillan Co., 1916. 50 cents.

Lane, Franklin K. The American spirit. Addresses in war time. New York, Frederick A. Stokes Co., 443 Fourth Avenue, 1918. 75 cents.

Roosevelt, Theodore. American ideals and other essays. New York, G. P. Putnam's Sons, 2 West Forty-fifth Street, 1901. $1.50.

—— The great adventure. New York [etc.], Charles Scribner's Sons, 597 Fifth Avenue, 1918. $1.00.

Van Dyke, H. The spirit of America. New York, The Macmillan Co., 1910. $1.50.

THE IMMIGRANT'S MIND.

Antin, Mary. The promised land. Boston [etc.], Houghton Mifflin Co., 1912. $2.00.

Bridges, Horace J. On becoming an American. Boston, Marshall Jones Co., 212 Sumner Street, 1918. $1.75.

Cohen, Rose. Out of the shadow. New York, George H. Doran Co., 244 Madison Avenue, 1918. $2.00.

Ravage, M. E.   An American in the making.   New York, Harper & Bros., 325 Pearl Street, 1917. $1.40.
Riis, Jacob.   The making of an American.   New York [etc.], The Macmillan Co., 64 Fifth Avenue, 1901. $3.00.
Steiner, Edward A.   From alien to citizen.   New York [etc.], Fleming H. Revell & Co., 158 Fifth Avenue, 1914. $2.00.
Stern, E. G.   My mother and I.   New York, The Macmillan Co., 1917. $1.00.

BACKGROUND OF THE RACES.

Bagot, R.   Italians of today.   Chicago, Ill., F. G. Browne, 1913. $1.25.
Balch, E. G.   Our Slavic fellow citizens.   New York, Charities Publication Committee, 105 East Twenty-second Street, 1910. $2.50.
Barnes, Mary C., and Barnes, Lemuel C.   The new America—a study in immigration.   New York [etc.], Fleming H. Revell Co., 158 Fifth Avenue, 1913.   50 cents.
Bogardus, Emory S.   Essentials of Americanization.   Parts 2 and 3.   Los Angeles, Cal., University of Southern California Press, 1919. $1.50.
Commons, John R.   Races and immigrants in America.   New York [etc.], The Macmillan Co., 64 Fifth Avenue, 1915. $1.50.
Graham, Stephen.   With the poor immigrants to America (Slavs).   New York, The Macmillan Co., 1914. $2.25.
Knox, George William.   The spirit of the orient.   New York, Thomas Y. Crowell & Co., 426 West Broadway, 1906. $1.50.
Steiner, Edward A.   On the trail of the immigrant.   New York [etc.], Fleming H. Revell & Co., 158 Fifth Avenue, 1906. $1.50.
Ruppin, Arthur.   The Jews of today.   New York, Henry Holt & Co., 19 West Forty-fourth Street, 1913. $1.75.
Van Norman, L. E.   Poland, knight among nations.   New York, Fleming H. Revell & Co., 1907. $1.50.

DEPARTMENT OF THE INTERIOR
BUREAU OF EDUCATION

BULLETIN, 1919, No. 81

STATISTICS
OF NORMAL SCHOOLS
1917-18

LB 2846 -

By

L. E. BLAUCH and H. R. BONNER

[Advance sheets from Biennial Survey of Education
in the United States, 1916-1918]

WASHINGTON
GOVERNMENT PRINTING OFFICE
1920

TYPES OF SCHOOLS REPRESENTED.

This report includes data on public and private normal schools. It does not include data on the State teachers' colleges of Colorado, Iowa, and New York. These institutions are included under statistics of universities, colleges, and professional schools in another chapter of the Biennial Survey.

The normal schools have been classified chiefly on the basis of control. Those under State control are State normal schools. The State normal schools of Pennsylvania were, prior to 1911, only partly under State control. They were owned by corporations. Of the 18 trustees for each institution, 6 were appointed by the superintendent of public instruction. The code of 1911 provided for the purchase of the institutions by the State.[1] Six of them have become the property of the State under this act.

A city normal school is one under the control of the city board of education.

The definition of a county normal school varies somewhat in the different States.[2] Wisconsin has the only true county normal schools. They are separate from the regular public schools in control, school plant, and all other respects. In Michigan the county training classes have their own boards. In Ohio the county normal schools are operated in connection with first-grade high schools. They are under the supervision of the county superintendent, and he nominates the director of the school. The county normal schools of Wisconsin and Ohio are included here, as are also several from Michigan. Eighteen other States make provision for the training of teachers in a number of secondary schools.

Private schools are under private control. On this basis several schools formerly included under public normal schools have been included with the private schools for the purposes of this study.

---

[1] School Code of Pennsylvania and Other Laws. Act of May 18, 1911, Harrisburg, 1911, p. 101.
[2] See "Rural Teacher Preparation in County Training Schools and High Schools," by H. W. Foght. Bu. of Educ., Bul., 1917, No. 31.

3

TABLE 1.—*Review of statistics of all normal schools, 1900-1918.*

1	1899-1900	1901-2	1903-4	1905-6	1907-8	1909-10	1911-12	1913-14	1915-16	1917-18
	2	3	4	5	6	7	8	9	10	11
Number of schools reporting	¹ 305	282	269	264	250	264	277	281	279	·308
Number of instructors:										
a. Total in all courses—										
Men	1,856	1,783	1,859	2,057	2,031	2,195	2,294	2,505	2,700	3,166
Women	2,511	2,636	3,067	3,345	2,982	3,719	3,982	4,243	4,606	5,386
Total	4,367	4,419	4,926	5,402	5,013	5,914	6,276	6,748	7,306	8,552
b. In normal courses—										
Men	1,466	1,469	1,491	1,525	1,273	1,360	1,631	1,772		¹1,796
Women	1,617	1,808	2,023	2,131	1,965	2,400	2,834	3,127		¹3,153
Total	3,083	3,277	3,514	3,656	3,258	3,760	4,465	4,899		¹4,949
Number of students enrolled:										
a. Total in all courses—										
Men	47,851	45,946	40,330	46,316	32,599	37,823	28,745	26,526	30,591	21,287
Women	68,696	74,913	72,746	86,876	76,714	94,615	80,541	88,190	101,586	116,887
Total	² 116,549	² 120,859	² 113,076	² 133,192	² 109,313	² 132,438	109,286	115,016	132,177	138,174
b. In normal courses—										
Men	24,157	19,683	16,749	16,382	16,146	19,746	19,880	19,247	22,940	13,281
Women	45,894	45,375	46,898	52,555	55,721	68,815	70,124	76,089	88,732	96,822
Total	69,551	65,058	63,627	68,937	71,887	88,561	89,994	96,236	111,672	110,053
Graduates from normal courses:										
Men	2,989	2,209	2,053	1,670	1,984	2,161	2,325	2,430	3,085	2,170
Women	8,370	7,796	8,795	9,326	11,045	13,279	15,083	18,228	21,449	22,351
Total	11,359	10,005	10,848	10,996	13,079	15,430	18,278	20,658	24,534	24,601
Enrollment in model schools	35,397	43,256	55,007	51,739	51,060	66,180	42,338	63,001	57,580	83,608

Receipts for the year:									
a. From State, city, and county for improvements	$718,507	$906,301	$916,443	$1,549,906	$3,421,190	$2,635,836	$1,720,442	$3,688,891	$4,016,760	$4,221,006
b. From State, city, and county for current expenses	$2,782,123	$3,289,642	$3,927,209	$4,648,156	$4,648,700	$6,678,152	$7,056,965	$8,973,677	$10,134,158	$11,630,637
c. Total receipts from State, city, and county	$3,500,630	$4,146,143	$4,842,652	$6,198,062	$8,067,980	$9,310,990	$9,287,407	$12,637,268	$14,150,918	$15,751,983
d. Total receipts, all sources	$5,231,856	$5,761,291	$6,898,700	$8,296,830	$11,981,346	$14,688,220	$13,328,101	$17,495,763	$20,140,199	$22,728,205
Number of volumes in libraries	807,963	908,032	1,068,769	1,159,128	1,289,062	1,521,528	1,585,142	1,799,486	1,849,034	2,172,637

1 The institution at Geneva, Ohio, is omitted from all these data (1899–1900).
2 Engaged half time or more in instructing resident students in normal courses.
3 A number of pupils in model schools are included in these data.

TABLE 2.—*Review of statistics of State normal schools, 1900-1918.*

1	1899-1900	1901-2	1903-4	1905-6	1907-8	1909-10	1911-12	1913-14	1915-16	1917-18
	2	3	4	5	6	7	8	9	10	11
Number of schools reporting	127	135	137	137	142	151	161	172	174	172
Number of instructors:										
a. Total in all courses—										
Men	899	996	1,101	1,166	1,284	1,503	1,696	1,902	2,099	2,563
Women	1,300	1,447	1,777	1,852	1,766	2,337	2,651	3,072	3,357	4,073
Total	2,199	2,443	2,878	3,018	3,050	3,840	4,347	4,974	5,426	6,636
b. In normal courses—										
Men	823	901	1,025	1,092	890	1,000	1,373	1,515		1,587
Women	952	1,118	1,355	1,488	1,358	1,598	2,116	2,386		2,571
Total	1,775	2,019	2,380	2,580	2,248	2,598	3,489	3,901		4,158
Number of students enrolled:										
a. Total in all courses—										
Men	19,834	21,428	21,428	24,374	19,911	25,690	21,758	21,717	25,524	18,183
Women	40,475	44,326	47,427	56,055	53,100	68,453	64,245	74,232	86,044	102,074
Total	60,309	65,754	68,855	80,429	73,011	94,143	86,003	96,949	111,568	120,257
b. In normal courses—										
Men	11,801	11,662	10,768	12,119	12,478	16,628	16,965	17,165	20,140	12,408
Women	29,854	32,100	33,498	38,587	43,663	54,819	57,788	64,907	74,826	84,211
Total	41,655	43,762	44,266	50,706	56,141	71,447	74,753	82,072	94,966	96,619
Graduates from normal courses:										
Men	1,800	1,556	1,250	1,127	1,459	1,692	2,073	2,194	2,818	1,896
Women	5,545	5,285	5,750	6,297	7,965	9,497	12,085	14,516	17,081	17,716
Total	7,345	6,841	7,000	7,424	9,424	11,189	14,158	16,710	19,899	19,612
Enrollment in model schools	20,921	24,680	32,482	28,211	26,082	37,887	32,252	36,722	39,411	54,320

Receipts for the year:									
a. From State, city, and county for improvements	$968,432	$908,801	$915,343	$1,519,606	$3,040,476	$2,008,088	$1,634,395	$3,371,948	$3,757,187	$4,182,716
b. From State, city, and county for current expenses	$2,285,061	$2,798,725	$3,395,431	$4,131,352	$4,110,477	$5,854,729	$7,119,376	$8,399,518	$9,548,074	$11,263,150
c. Total receipts from State, city, and county	$2,953,493	$3,702,526	$4,310,774	$5,650,958	$7,150,953	$7,947,817	$8,753,770	$11,771,466	$13,305,261	$15,435,866
d. Total receipts, all sources	$3,717,188	$4,221,762	$5,152,158	$6,496,650	$8,840,140	$10,436,061	$11,427,842	$15,283,037	$17,463,141	$20,512,706
Number of volumes in libraries	574,184	673,677	903,157	878,461	1,036,701	1,207,106	1,389,299	1,455,326	1,540,282	1,865,044

1 Engaged half time or more in instructing resident students in normal courses.
2 A number of pupils in model schools are included in these data.
3 Of this number 18,500 were in public or in partly public schools.

TABLE 3.— *Review of statistics of city and county normal schools, 1900–1918.*

1	1890–1900	1901–2	1903–4	1905–6	1907–8	1909–10	1911–12	1913–14	1915–16	1917–18
	2	3	4	5	6	7	8	9	10	11
Number of schools reporting:										
City	27	26	27	34	34	32	34	36	37	34
County	3	1	2	3	4	8	22	25	21	45
Total	30	27	29	37	38	40	56	61	58	79
Number of instructors:										
a. Total in all courses—										
Men	94	79	81	104	110	127	149	152	162	236
Women	456	561	564	763	620	718	750	678	750	742
Total	550	640	645	867	730	845	899	830	912	978
b. In normal courses—										
Men	71	61	61	90	101	101	111	121		¹ 104
Women	254	275	318	337	374	472	455	518		¹ 425
Total	325	336	379	427	475	573	566	639		¹ 529
Number of students enrolled:										
a. Total in all courses—										
Men	1,378	3,961	180	4,807	3,032	3,512	299	404	434	277
Women	6,187	10,807	6,100	14,047	12,095	13,428	7,601	7,210	8,349	8,071
Total	² 7,565	² 14,758	² 6,280	² 18,854	² 15,127	² 16,940	7,900	7,614	8,783	8,348
b. In normal courses—										
Men	148	99	58	152	469	341	299	309	404	264
Women	4,444	4,489	6,049	7,737	6,438	7,432	7,601	7,049	8,339	7,983
Total	4,592	4,588	6,107	7,889	6,907	7,773	7,900	7,388	8,743	8,287
Graduates from normal courses:										
Men	19	62	30	43	59	91	105	77	111	132
Women	1,646	1,648	1,913	2,096	2,168	2,445	3,060	2,925	3,365	3,276
Total	1,665	1,710	1,943	2,139	2,227	2,536	3,165	3,002	3,476	3,408
Enrollment in model schools	10,637	14,855	17,193	20,060	19,869	22,772	7,145	13,683	14,021	26,306

Receipts for the year:									
a. From State, city and county for improvements.	$50,000	$2,500	$100	$30,300	$379,714	$642,760	$905,590	$179,543	$256,673	$88,350
b. From State, city, and county for current expenses.	$451,182	$386,300	$485,715	$457,180	$504,763	$771,559	$422,010	$519,359	$567,645	$269,526
c. Total receipts from State, city, and county.	$501,182	$388,800	$485,815	$517,480	$884,467	$1,314,319	$489,906	$698,902	$827,218	$297,876
d. Total receipts, all sources.	$504,616	$392,190	$500,297	$531,961	$902,385	$1,319,906	$496,521	$705,080	$844,162	$313,481
Number of volumes in libraries.	39,229	50,022	45,485	59,388	76,713	96,920	89,933	129,391	145,270	163,111

1 Engaged half time or more in instructing resident students in normal courses.
2 A number of pupils in model schools are included in these data.
3 The reported expenditures were as follows: (1) For outlays, $64,881; (2) for current expenditures, $1,354,104; (3) total expenditures, $1,418,985.

TABLE 4.—*Review of statistics of private normal schools, 1900–1918.*

1	1899–1900	1901–2	1903–4	1905–6	1907–8	1909–10	1911–12	1913–14	1915–16	1917–18
	2	3	4	5	6	7	8	9	10	11
Number of schools reporting	148	119	108	90	70	73	60	48	47	67
Number of instructors:										
a. Total in all courses—										
Men	863	708	687	787	637	565	449	451	469	367
Women	755	628	726	730	596	664	581	493	499	571
Total	1,618	1,336	1,413	1,517	1,233	1,229	1,030	944	968	948
b. In normal courses—										
Men	572	507	406	343	282	259	147	136	....	¹105
Women	411	415	350	306	253	330	263	223	....	¹157
Total	983	922	755	649	535	589	410	359	....	¹262
Number of students enrolled:										
a. Total in all courses—										
Men	26,639	20,567	18,722	17,135	9,656	8,621	6,688	4,706	4,033	2,827
Women	22,036	19,780	19,219	16,774	11,519	12,734	8,695	6,748	7,193	6,742
Total	²48,675	²40,347	²37,941	²33,909	²21,175	²21,355	15,383	11,453	11,826	9,569
b. In normal courses—										
Men	12,208	7,932	5,923	4,111	3,199	2,777	2,596	1,773	2,396	533
Women	11,096	8,786	7,331	6,231	5,620	6,564	4,735	4,083	5,567	4,463
Total	23,304	16,718	13,254	10,342	8,819	9,341	7,331	5,856	7,963	4,996
Graduates from normal courses:										
Men	1,170	591	773	500	466	368	147	159	156	142
Women	1,179	863	1,132	933	962	1,337	808	787	1,003	1,339
Total	2,349	1,454	1,905	1,433	1,428	1,705	955	946	1,159	1,481
Enrollment in model schools	3,889	3,521	5,332	3,468	5,079	5,521	2,941	2,726	3,248	2,978

Receipts for the year:										
a. From State, city, and county for improvements.	$875	......	......	......	$1,000	......	$19,151	$2,080	......	$17,963
b. From State, city, and county for current expenses.	$45,880	$54,817	$46,083	$29,624	$31,550	$48,854	$24,580	$54,900	$18,439	$17,963
c. Total receipts from State, city, and county....	$45,955	$54,817	$46,083	$29,624	$32,550	$48,854	$43,731	$36,980	$18,439	$17,962
d. Total receipts, all sources....	$1,010,152	$1,147,339	$1,246,245	$1,270,219	$2,238,521	$2,932,261	$1,404,738	$1,507,646	$1,802,806	$1,947,622
Number of volumes in libraries....	194,550	191,429	260,127	220,284	185,638	217,493	155,920	144,770	103,482	153,872

1 Engaged half time or more in instructing resident students in normal courses.   2 A number of pupils in model schools are included in these data.

TABLE 5.— *Review of the number of normal schools reporting, 1900–1918.*

United States.

Alabama.
Arizona.
Arkansas.
California.
Colorado.

Connecticut.
Delaware.
District of Columbia.
Florida.
Georgia.

Idaho.
Illinois.
Indiana.
Iowa.
Kansas.

Kentucky.
Louisiana.
Maine.
Maryland.
Massachusetts.

Michigan.
Minnesota.
Mississippi.
Missouri.
Montana.

Nebraska.
Nevada.
New Hampshire.
New Jersey.
New Mexico.

New York
North Carolina
North Dakota
Ohio
Oklahoma

Oregon
Pennsylvania
Rhode Island
South Carolina
South Dakota

Tennessee
Texas
Utah
Vermont
Virginia

Washington
West Virginia
Wisconsin
Wyoming

[1] Four others did not report.

NUMBER OF SCHOOLS REPORTING.

The number of normal schools reporting since 1900 is shown in Tables 1–5 and in figure 1. One fact to be noted is the steady

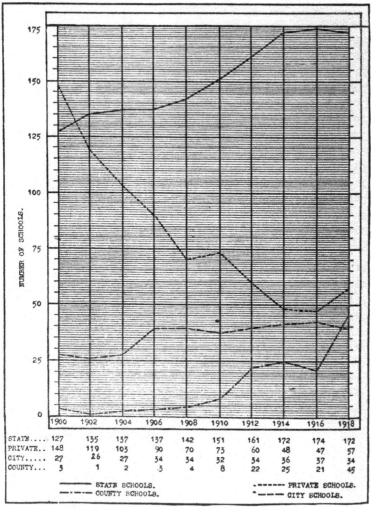

	1900	1902	1904	1906	1908	1910	1912	1914	1916	1918
STATE....	127	135	137	137	142	151	161	172	174	172
PRIVATE..	148	119	103	90	70	73	60	48	47	57
CITY.....	27	26	27	34	34	32	34	36	37	34
COUNTY...	5	1	2	.3	4	8	22	25	21	45

——————— STATE SCHOOLS.　　　.------- PRIVATE SCHOOLS.
—.——.— COUNTY SCHOOLS.　　　*——— CITY SCHOOLS.

Fig. 1.—Number of normal schools reporting, 1900–1918.

increase in the number of State normal schools. This is the case despite the fact that several States have abandoned their State normal schools as separate institutions and that a number of State normal schools have become State teachers' colleges, and consequently are now reported under "Universities, Colleges, and Professional Schools." The institutions located at the following places were transferred to the latter list at the respective dates: Cedar Falls, Iowa, 1911; Greeley, Colo., 1912; Albany, N. Y., 1913.

In several States normal schools are organized as part of a State college or university. The statistics of such State normal schools are included in the data of these higher institutions since they have become so organized. The following States, with the respective numbers of institutions, are cases in point: Florida 1, Nevada 1, Ohio 2, Utah 1, Wyoming 1. The two universities in Ohio which do this work were included in the data cited herein for the years 1908, 1910, and 1912.

The State Normal and Industrial College for Colored Persons at Tallahassee, Fla., was included in the reports on normal schools until 1911 and at the same time under the "Agricultural and Mechanical Colleges." A similar statement applies to the Georgia State Industrial College for Colored Persons, Savannah, Ga., until 1907.

There has also been an increase in the number of city normal schools. In 1918 there were 26 per cent more reports than in 1900. The corresponding increase in the number of State normal schools is 35 per cent.

Nearly all of the county normal schools have been established since 1900. Those in Wisconsin were established under a law enacted in 1899. Twenty-five reported from Wisconsin in 1918. Those of Ohio are of more recent date and reported for the first time in 1918. Twenty-one of the latter are included in the data of Tables 1–5 and in figure 1.

Another observation to be made is the decrease in the number of private normal schools. Table 5 shows this decrease to have occurred in most of the States having such schools. The increase in 1918 is partly due to including 25 kindergarten training schools in 1918, while in 1916 only 14 reported. The decrease in private normal schools is probably largely accounted for by two causes, first, increased cost of conducting schools; and, second, the increased public provision for higher education and for this type of training.

The 57 private normal schools reporting in 1918 are classified as follows:

Kindergarten training schools...................................... 25
General normal schools and colleges................................ 19
Normal schools of physical education.............................. 8
Industrial and technical normal schools........................... 5

The data for 1918 include 24 normal schools for colored persons distributed as follows (see Tables 32-39):

State normal schools... 15
City normal schools....................,........................... 2
Private normal schools... 7

From Table 5 one may gain a fair knowledge of the change in the number of the various kinds of normal schools in the different States. Of course a number of schools fail to make reports at times, but, in general, the data given indicate the increase or the decrease.

LENGTH OF SESSIONS.

TABLE 6.—*Distribution of normal schools according to the number of weeks of school in the year, 1917–18.*[1]

Number of weeks in school year.	Number of schools.				Number of weeks in school year.	Number of schools.			
	State.	City.	County.	Private.		State.	City.	County.	Private.
30				2	42	44		2	6
32				5	43	4			1
33				1	44	16	1	1	
34			.	7	45	6	2		
35				3	46	22		2	1
36	11	6	19	17	47	3			
37	1	1			48	21			2
38	14	6	2	2	50	1			
39	6			3					
40	19	18	19	6	Total number of reports	171	34	45	57
41	3			1					

[1] Including summer session of 1917.

The length of time which the normal schools were in session during the year 1917-18 is shown in Table 6. For State normal schools the most common number of weeks is 42. This usually includes a summer session of 6 weeks. The most common length of session for city normal schools is 40 weeks, for county normal schools 40 weeks, and for private normal schools 36 weeks.

NUMBER OF INSTRUCTORS.

The number of instructors in normal schools since 1900 has steadily increased, as is shown in Table 1. This increase, as is quite evident from figure 2, has been in public normal schools. In 1918 there were more than twice as many instructors reported in State normal schools as in 1900. In the same time the number in city and county normal schools increased approximately 78 per cent, while the number in private normal schools decreased approximately 41 per cent.

From figure 3 it is observed that the average size of faculty in State normal schools has increased regularly and rapidly. This indicates that those institutions are becoming larger and are doing more

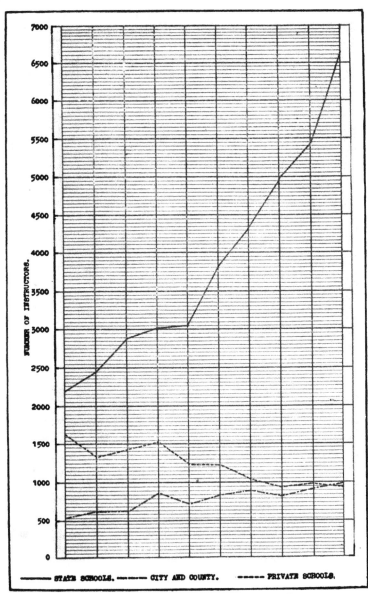

FIG. 2.—Number of instructors in normal schools, 1900-1918.

work. The data seem to indicate that the faculties of city and county normal schools are becoming smaller. This is due largely to the increase in the number of county normal schools, most of which have small faculties, as will be noted later.

The average size of faculty in private normal schools is increasing. Since it was noted above (see fig. 1 and Table 5) that the number of

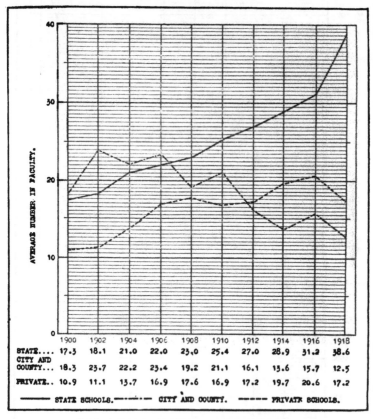

	1900	1902	1904	1906	1908	1910	1912	1914	1916	1918
STATE....	17.3	18.1	21.0	22.0	23.0	25.4	27.0	28.9	31.2	38.6
CITY AND COUNTY...	18.3	23.7	22.2	23.4	19.2	21.1	16.1	13.6	15.7	12.5
PRIVATE..	10.9	11.1	13.7	16.9	17.6	16.9	17.2	19.7	20.6	17.2

————— STATE SCHOOLS.—·—·—· CITY AND COUNTY. ————— PRIVATE SCHOOLS.

FIG. 3.—Average size of faculties in normal schools 1900–1918.

these institutions is decreasing, it is obvious that the smaller schools are going out of existence, while the larger ones are surviving. The decrease in the size of faculty in 1918 is partly due to including more kindergarten training schools, which generally have small faculties. With those eliminated in 1918 which were not included in 1916 (13 schools, with a total of 96 instructors) the average size of faculty in private normal schools was 20.3 in 1918.

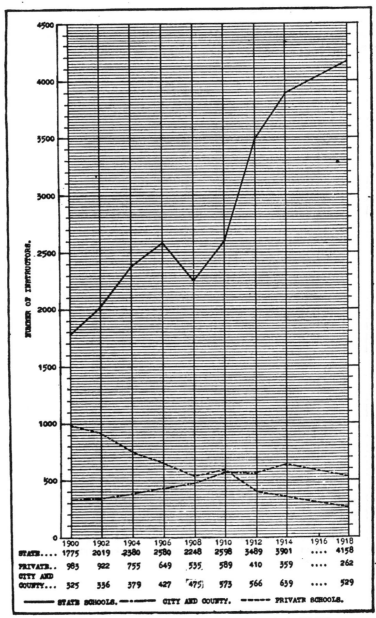

FIG. 4.—Number of instructors in normal courses in normal schools, 1900-1918.

The number of instructors in normal courses in State normal schools shows an increase since 1900 (see fig. 4). So does also the number in city and county normal schools, except from 1916 to 1918. The number in private normal schools shows a general rapid decrease.

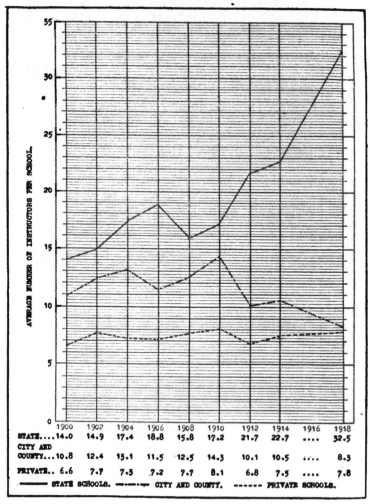

	1900	1902	1904	1906	1908	1910	1912	1914	1916	1918
STATE....	14.0	14.9	17.4	18.8	15.8	17.2	21.7	22.7	....	32.5
CITY AND COUNTY...	10.8	12.4	13.1	11.5	12.5	14.3	10.1	10.5	....	8.3
PRIVATE..	6.6	7.7	7.3	.7.2	7.7	8.1	6.8	7.5	....	7.8

——— STATE SCHOOLS. —·—··— CITY AND COUNTY. —————— PRIVATE SCHOOLS.

FIG. 5.—Average number of instructors per school in normal courses, 1900-1918.

Figure 5 is of interest as showing the relative average number of instructors per school in normal courses in the different kinds of institutions. The average is highest in the State schools and lowest in private schools. With the 13 kindergarten training schools, as above mentioned, eliminated in 1918, the average number in private schools for that year is 9.8. The decrease in the city and county schools since 1910 is probably due to the increase in the number of county normal schools, which have small faculties.

The total number of instructors and the number in normal courses are compared in figure 6.[1] There is not much regular change in the

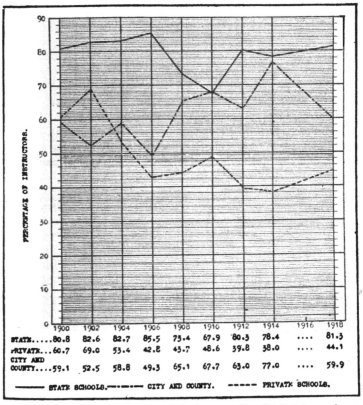

	1900	1902	1904	1906	1908	1910	1912	1914	1916	1918
STATE.....80.8		82.6	82.7	85.5	73.4	67.9	80.3	78.4	....	81.3
PRIVATE...60.7		69.0	53.4	42.8	43.7	48.6	39.8	38.0	....	44.1
CITY AND COUNTY....59.1		52.5	58.8	49.3	65.1	67.7	63.0	77.0	....	59.9

————— STATE SCHOOLS. —··—··— CITY AND COUNTY.   ————— PRIVATE SCHOOLS.

Fig. 6.—Percentage of instructors in normal schools who were teachers of students in normal courses, 1900–1918.

percentage of State normal school faculties which are giving normal courses. In city and county normal schools the percentage increased from 1900 to 1914. In private normal schools the percentage decreased, thus indicating that those which survived tend to devote more energy to instruction in other than normal courses.

[1] In these ratios for 1918 only those schools are used which reported both sets of data.

TABLE 7.—*Distribution of normal schools according to the total number of instructors, including the presidents and principals, 1917-18.*

Number of instructors.	Number of schools.				Number of instructors.	Number of schools.			
	State.	City.	County.	Private.		State.	City.	County.	Private.
1		1	1	1	46– 50	8			
2		1	5	1	51– 55	6	1		1
3		1	15		56– 60	11			
4		3	12	4	61– 65	5			
5		1	5		66– 70	3			
					71– 75	1			
1– 5		7	38	6	76– 80	3			
6–10	3	5	6	16	81– 85	2			
11–15	13	3		9	86– 90	1	1		
16–20	13	6		8	91– 95	2			
21–25	20	1		8	96–100	2			
26–30	24	5		3	More than 100	2	1		1
31–35	14	1		1					
36–40	22	1		2	Total number of reports	172	34	44	55
41–45	16	2							

The size of faculty in the various normal schools in 1918 may be noted from Table 7. The county schools generally have the smallest faculties, and the State schools the largest. The typical size of the State normal school faculty is from 21 to 40.

TABLE 8.—*Distribution of normal schools according to the number of instructors engaged half time or more in instructing resident students in normal courses, 1917-18.*

Number of instructors.	Number of schools.				Number of instructors.	Number of schools.			
	State.	City.	County.	Private.		State.	City.	County.	Private.
1	1	1	16	4	26–30	14	2		
2	1	3	4	4	31–35	10			
3		1	10	4	36–40	13	1		
4	2	2	4	6	41–45	11	2		
5	1	2	1	1	46–50	7			
					51–55	4	1		
1– 5	5	9	35	19	56–60	5			
6–10	12	2	2	9	More than 60	1 8			
11–15	13	3		5					
16–20	12	5		2	Total number of reports	133	27	37	37
21–25	19	2		2					

1 64, 66, 70, 74, 87, 90, 94, and 108.

Table 8 is similar to Table 7 in its make-up. The summer school faculty is included in the total for the year, which tends to increase the size of the faculty represented in this table over the average number in the faculty during the regular year (for the size of summer school faculty see Table 30).

NUMBER OF STUDENTS ENROLLED.

Since 1912 there has been an increase in the total enrollment (see Table 1, item 3 *a*). Figure 7 shows that the increase was largely in State normal schools. The total enrollment in private normal schools shows a decided falling off.

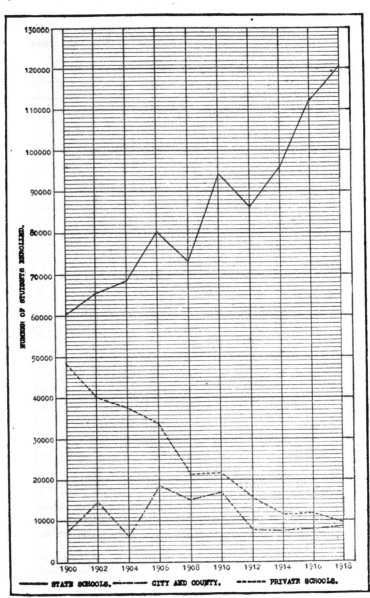

FIG. 7.—Number of students enrolled in normal schools, 1900–1918.

A more reliable set of data than the total enrollment for the period 1900–1918 is the enrollment in normal courses (see fig. 8). The curves of figure 8 are fairly regular. Again, it may be observed that the number in State normal schools increased rapidly, the number in

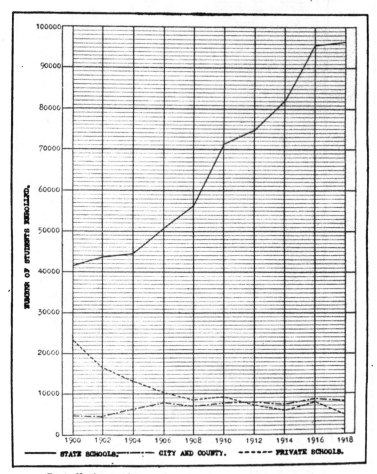

FIG. 8.—Number of students enrolled in normal courses in normal schools, 1900–1918.

city and county normal schools almost as rapidly, while those in private normal schools decreased. From this figure the relative numbers in each type of school may be easily noted. The State normal schools are by far the most important in the training of teachers, and their relative importance has been rapidly increasing.

TABLE 9.—*Comparisons on enrollment in normal schools, 1900-1918.* (*For data see Tables 2-4.*)

	1900	1902	1904	1906	1908	1910	1912	1914	1916	11918
1	2	3	4	5	6	7	8	9	10	11
Average number of students enrolled per school:										
State	475	487	502	587	514	623	534	553	646	699
City and county	250	547	217	510	397	424	141	125	137	106
Private	332	339	368	377	311	293	257	239	253	177
Average number of students per school enrolled in normal courses:										
State	328	324	326	370	395	473	464	477	551	582
City and county	153	170	211	213	182	194	141	121	151	104
Private	158	140	129	115	126	128	122	122	169	93
Average number of students per instructor:										
State	27.5	26.9	23.7	26.7	23.9	24.5	19.8	19.3	20.7	18.9
City and county	13.7	23.1	9.7	21.7	20.7	20.0	8.8	9.2	8.7	8.5
Private	30.1	30.2	26.8	22.4	17.1	17.3	14.9	12.1	12.2	10.1
Average number of students in normal courses per instructor in normal courses:										
State	23.5	21.7	18.6	19.7	25.0	27.5	21.4	21.0	......	17.4
City and county	14.1	13.8	16.1	18.5	14.5	13.6	14.0	11.5	......	14.7
Private	23.7	18.1	17.1	15.9	16.5	15.8	17.9	16.3	......	15.8
Percentage of all students who were in normal courses:										
State	69.2	66.6	64.4	63.1	76.9	76.0	86.9	85.4	85.1	83.0
City and county	60.7	31.1	97.3	41.8	45.6	45.8	100.0	96.6	99.5	99.0
Private	47.8	41.4	34.9	30.5	41.6	43.8	47.6	51.1	67.3	56.4

1 In computing the data for this year only those schools were used which reported both sets of data which were being compared.

A number of comparisons are made in Table 9 between the number of schools, the number of instructors, and the number of students enrolled. Marked changes occur with regularity in only a few cases. Item 5 of this table seems to indicate that from 1906 to 1916 private normal schools devoted an increasing amount of attention to training teachers. This tendency seems different from that noted above in figures 3, 5, and 6.

TABLE 10.—*Distribution of normal schools according to the total enrollment of resident students, 1917-18.*

Number enrolled.	Number of schools.				Number enrolled.	Number of schools.			
	State.	City.	County.	Private.		State.	City.	County.	Private.
1- 25	......	7	21	11	901-1,000	10	......	......	......
26- 50	......	3	8	7	1,001-1,100	4	......	......	1
51- 75	3	3	9	5	1,101-1,200	4	......	......	......
76-100	3	5	6	6	1,201-1,300	3	......	......	1
					1,301-1,400	5	1	......	......
1-100	6	18	44	29	1,401-1,500	1	......	......	......
101-200	16	6	1	13	1,501-1,600	2	......	......	......
201-300	19	5	......	4	1,601-1,700	1	......	......	......
301-400	17	1	......	2	1,701-1,800	1	......	......	......
401-500	21	......	......	2	More than 1,800	1 9	......	......	......
501-600	15	1	......	......					
601-700	14	1	......	......	Total number of reports	172	34	45	54
701-800	6	......	......	1					
801-900	16	1	......	1					

1 1,803 2,050, 2,094, 2,144, 2,480, 2,526, 2,700, 2,840, and 2,846.

The status of enrollment in 1918 is shown in Tables 10, 11, 12, 32, 36, and 38. The total enrollment for the year includes the enrollment in the summer session of 1917. This means that some schools, especially those with large summer schools, are likely to have a much larger total enrollment than they would have had if the data only for the regular year, not including the summer, had been used. Similar remarks apply to the data of Tables 11 and 12.

TABLE 11.—*Distribution of normal schools according to the number of resident students enrolled in normal courses, 1917–18.*

Number of students.	Number of schools.				Number of students.	Number of schools.			
	State.	City.	County.	Private.		State.	City.	County.	Private.
1– 25	1	6	22	22	701– 800	5			
26– 50	4	3	6	8	801– 900	13	1		
51– 75	6	3	10	5	901–1,000	7			
76–100	4	5	5	2	1,001–1,100	4			
					1,101–1,200	3			
1–100	15	17	43	37	1,201–1,300	1			
101–200	18	6	1	11	1,301–1,400	4	1		
201–300	27	5		2	1,401–1,500	3			
301–400	15	1		1	More than 1,500	[1] 9			
401–500	21			3					
501–600	11	1			Total number of reports	166	33	44	54
601–700	10	1							

[1] 1,563, 1,566, 1,777, 2,017, 2,050, 2,280, 2,526, 2,700, 2,846

TABLE 12.—*Distribution of normal schools according to the number of resident students enrolled in other than normal courses, 1917–18.*

Number of students.	Number of schools.		Number of students.	Number of schools.	
	State.	Private.		State.	Private.
1–100	25	10	601–700	1	
101–200	22	2	701–800	3	
201–300	14	1	More than 800	[1] 2	[1] 2
301–400	7	2			
401–500	4		Total number of reports	81	17
501–600	3				

[1] 1,036 and 1,755.   [2] 1,041 and 1,042.

TABLE 13.—*Distribution of normal schools according to the number of attendance or enrollment weeks, in resident normal courses, 1917–18.*[1]

Number of weeks.	Number of schools.				Number of weeks.	Number of schools.			
	State	City.	County.	Private.		State.	City.	County.	Private.
0– 499		1	8	12	20,000–22,499	3			
500– 999	1	4	9	9	22,500–24,999	6			
1,000– 1,499	3	3	3	3	25,000–27,999	5			
1,500– 1,999	4		5	1	27,500–29,999	1			
2,000– 2,499	3	3	3	4	30,000–32,499	1			
					32,500–34,999	2			
0– 2,499	11	11	28	29	35,000–37,499	3			
2,500– 4,999	19	9	3	9	37,500–39,999	2			
5,000– 7,499	22	2		7	More than 40,000	2			
7,500– 9,999	16	1		2					
10,000–12,499	21	1			Total number of reports	150	27	31	47
12,500–14,999	10	1			Number reporting attendance weeks	78	7	18	20
15,000–16,499	13								
17,500–19,999	13	2							

[1] In a number of cases where attendance weeks were not reported the enrollment weeks were computed by multiplying the number of weeks per term or semester by the number of students enrolled during the term or semester.

A better means of comparing the amount of service which the schools render is the number of attendance weeks. Table 13 gives these for resident students in normal courses. For a number of schools not reporting this item the enrollment weeks were computed and the results included in Table 13. The number thus computed is somewhat higher than the actual number of enrollment weeks, the difference being greater in the cases of the longer terms. This number is also higher than the number of attendance weeks, but it is nevertheless a rough approximate means of comparison and is more nearly correct than the enrollment.

TABLE 14.—*Distribution of normal schools according to the number of nonresident students enrolled in extension and correspondence courses, 1917–18.*

Number of students.	Number of schools.			Number of students.	Number of schools.		
	State.	City.	Private.		State.	City.	Private.
1- 50	21	......	3	251–300	2	......	......
51–100	13	......	1	301–350	3	......	......
101–150	9	1	1	More than 350	[1] 6	[1] 1	......
151–200	2	1	1				
201–250	1	......	......	Total number of reports..	57	3	6

[1] 401, 460, 611, 635, 647, and 652.   [1] 735.

Extension and correspondence courses were important phases of activity in a number of schools in 1918. Some knowledge of the situation may be obtained from Tables 14, 32, 36, and 38. The number of State normal schools reporting on these courses is as follows:

Correspondence courses only.. 25
Extension courses only... 17
Correspondence and extension courses.............................. 15
Total number reporting.. 53

Three city normal schools reported extension courses, as did also five private normal schools. One private normal school gave correspondence courses.

GRADUATES FROM NORMAL COURSES.

Table 1 shows that the number of graduates from normal courses in normal schools increased with fair regularity from 1902 to 1916. Figure 9 indicates that this increase has been in public normal schools and chiefly in the State institutions. It also shows the relative importance of the three types of institutions in the training of teachers as measured by the number of graduates from normal courses.

Whether the number of graduates is keeping pace with the demand can not be ascertained since the number of new teachers entering the profession annually is not known.

To determine the relative numbers of men and women who graduated from normal courses in normal schools, index numbers were computed (see fig. 10). The index numbers of the number of men graduates were found by dividing the number for each year considered (see Table 1) by the average number for the years 1900–1918.

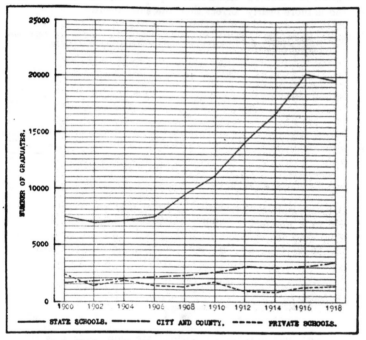

Fig. 9.—Number of graduates from normal courses in normal schools, 1900–1918.

In the same way the index numbers were computed for the number of women graduates.

The relative increase or decrease in the number of graduates is shown by the steepness of the slope of the curves between the dates considered. Thus, for example, from 1906 to 1908 both curves have practically the same slope, thus indicating that the increase in the number of men graduates and in the number of women graduates was relatively about the same. From 1908 to 1910 the number of women graduates increased relatively much more than did the number of men graduates. In general the number of women increased more rapidly relatively than did the number of men. The number of men decreased rapidly from 1900 to 1906, then increased until 1916. The falling off from 1916 to 1918 was likely due to the war.

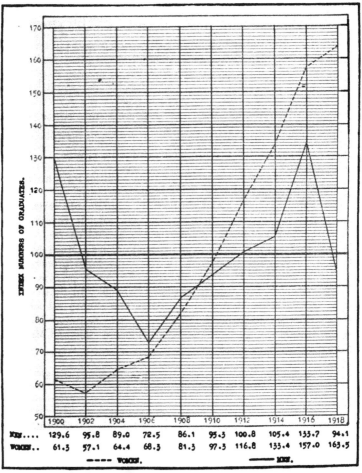

| KEY.... | 129.6 | 95.8 | 89.0 | 72.5 | 86.1 | 95.3 | 100.8 | 105.4 | 133.7 | 94.1 |
| WOMEN.. | 61.3 | 57.1 | 64.4 | 68.3 | 81.3 | 97.3 | 116.8 | 133.4 | 157.0 | 163.5 |

- - - - WOMEN.　　───── MEN.

FIG. 10.—Index numbers of the number of men and women graduates in all normal schools, 1900–1918.

The number of women shows a fairly regular increase from 1902 to 1916. The variation in the curve from 1916 to 1918 was also probably due to the war.

TABLE 15.—*Distribution of normal schools according to the number of hours of practice teaching which each student receives in the normal courses, 1917–18.*

Number of hours.	Number of schools.					Number of hours.	Number of schools.				
	State.[1]	City.	County.	Private.	Total.		State.[1]	City.	County.	Private.	Total.
1- 49	10	1	17	3	31	550–599	1	3	......	......	4
50- 99	23	4	23	10	60	600–649	6	1	......	1	8
100–149	34	2	3	10	49	650–699	1	......	......	1	2
150–199	39	1	......	2	42	700–749	2	1	......	1	4
200–249	13	2	......	2	17	750–799	......	......	......	1	1
250–299	6	......	......	1	7	800 or over	......	2	......	5	7
300–349	5	2	......	1	8	Median hours	180	462	54	180	......
350–399	6	1	......	4	11						
400–449	5	2	......	2	9	Total number of reports	159	32	43	48	282
450–499	5	3	......	1	9						
500–549	3	7	......	3	13						

[1] The five most common numbers are the following: 180 hours, 24 schools; 120, 16; 200, 8; 600, 6; 60, 6.

PRACTICE TEACHING AND FACILITIES FOR IT.

The amount of practice teaching and the facilities for it are important items in normal schools.

From Table 15 it is clear that there is considerable variation in the importance attached to it. Thirty-one schools require fewer than 50 hours per student completing the normal course, while in 7 schools each student received at least 800 hours. Much emphasis is placed on practice teaching in a relatively large proportion of city normal schools. The large numbers of hours in private schools generally occur in kindergarten training schools. In State normal schools the variation is not so marked. The county schools give less attention to it than do the others. It is to be noted, however, that the normal courses in the county schools of Ohio and Michigan are only one year in length.

TABLE 16.—*Distribution of normal schools according to the number of pupils enrolled in model and practice schools, 1917–18.*

Number of pupils enrolled.	Number of schools.				Number of pupils enrolled.	Number of schools.			
	State.	City.	County.	Private.		State.	City.	County.	Private.
1- 50	7	1	11	18	551–600	3	1	......	......
51–100	8	......	1	3	601–650	1	1	......	......
101–150	27	......	2	5	651–700	2	1	......	......
151–200	21	......	......	1	701–750	1	......	......	......
201–250	18	......	1	2	751–800	1	3	......	......
251–300	22	1	2	......	801–850	2	6	......	......
301–350	11	1	......	......	More than 850	11	7	......	......
351–400	7	2	......	1					
401–450	5	2	......	......	Total number of reports	158	30	17	31
451–500	9	1	......	1					
501–550	2	3	......	......					

The practice teaching facilities are measured largely by the enrollments in model and practice schools. Here again there is much variation, as is shown in Table 16. As is to be expected the city normal schools have large model and practice school enrollments, due to the fact that the whole city system is available for it. County normal schools generally have small model and practice schools.

LIBRARIES.

The number of volumes in libraries of normal schools rapidly increased from 1900 to 1918 (see Table 1). In Tables 2–4 this increase is seen to have occurred chiefly in the State normal schools. The number in city and county schools also increased, but the number in private schools decreased.

The average size of libraries in the State schools was more than doubled from 1900 to 1918 (see fig. 11). That of private schools also increased.

TABLE 17.—*Distribution of normal schools according to the number of bound volumes in libraries, 1917–18.*

Number of volumes.	Number of schools.				Number of volumes.	Number of schools.			
	State.	City.	Coun- ty.	Pri- vate.		State.	City.	Coun- ty.	Pri- vate.
1-500	6	5	18	14	12,001-13,000	4			
501-1,000	5	2	12	8	13,001-14,000	2			
					14,001-15,000	10			
1-1,000	11	7	30	22	15,001-16,000	4			
1,001-2,000	9	7	10	7					
2,000-3,000	12	1	1	4	More than 16,000	32	2		2
3,001-4,000	12	4		3					
4,000-5,000	11	1			(a) 16,001-20,000	10			
5,001-6,000	7		1	1	(b) 20,001-24,000	8	2		
6,001-7,000	15	2		3	(c) 24,001-28,000	7			1
7,001-8,000	9	1		2	(d) More than 28,000	¹ 6			² 1
8,001-9,000	11	2		1					
9,001-10,000	5	1			Total number of reports	166	28	42	45
10,001-11,000	7								
11,001-12,000	5								

¹ 30,000; 43,831; 45,300; 57,412; 76,623; and 90,000. ² 40,187.

The data on the number of volumes in the libraries of normal schools for 1918 are exhibited in Table 17. This makes clear the great variation in the size of libraries. A number of the State institutions are very well provided, 32 having more than 16,000 volumes each. A number of them, however, are inadequately provided. The libraries of county normal schools are generally small.

VALUE OF PROPERTY.

The total property valuation of normal schools may be noted in Tables 33, 36, and 39. The variation in this item is shown in Table 18. From this it appears that a number of the institutions are well-to-do in this respect. The valuation of more than half of the schools falls between $200,000 and $550,000.

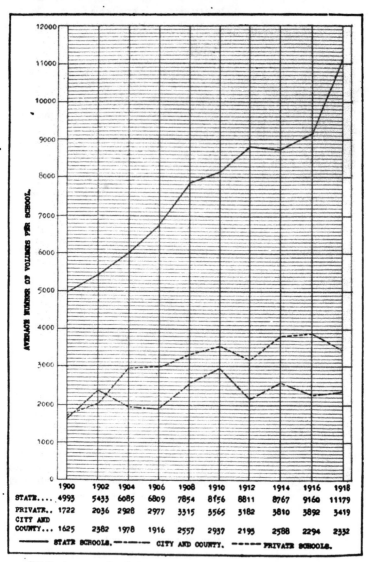

	1900	1902	1904	1906	1908	1910	1912	1914	1916	1918
STATE....	4993	5433	6085	6809	7854	8156	8811	8767	9160	11179
PRIVATE..	1722	2036	2928	2977	3315	3565	3182	3810	3892	3419
CITY AND COUNTY...	1625	2382	1978	1916	2557	2937	2195	2588	2294	2332

———— STATE SCHOOLS. —·——·— CITY AND COUNTY. ————— PRIVATE SCHOOLS.

FIG. 11.—Average number of volumes per school in the libraries of normal schools, 1900–1918.

Table 18.—*Distribution of normal schools according to the total value of property, including endowment, 1917-18.*

Value of property.	Number of schools.				Value of property.	Number of schools.			
	State.	City.	County.	Private.		State.	City.	County.	Private.
$0- $9,999	1	7	24	9	$450,000-$499,999	10	......	......	1
10,000- 19,999	......	......	1	6	500,000- 549,999	9	......	......	......
20,000- 29,999	1	......	2	1	550,000- 599,999	11	1	......	......
30,000- 39,999	3	......	4	......	600,000- 649,999	4	......	......	......
40,000- 49,999	2	2	3	1	650,000- 699,999	2	......	......	......
					700,000- 749,999	2	......	......	......
0- 49,999	7	9	34	17	750,000- 799,999	6	......	......	......
50,000- 99,999	7	4	......	5	800,000- 849,999	7	......	......	......
100,000-149,999	10	1	......	8	850,000- 899,999	1	......	......	......
150,000-199,999	9	1	.	2	900,000- 949,999	4	......	......	......
200,000-249,999	22	4	......	3	950,000- 999,999	0	1	......	......
250,000-299,999	10	2	......	2	More than 1,000,000	1 6	2 1	......	3 2
300,000-349,999	16	......	......	......					
350,000-399,999	12	1	......	......					
400,000-449,999	13	......	......	......	Total number of reports	168	25	34	40

1 1,013,440; 1,064,043; 1,087,531; 1,143,857; 1,150,000; 1,315,000. 2 1,292,085. 3 3,765,022; 3,812,203.

INCOME OF NORMAL SCHOOLS.

The receipts of normal schools have increased very rapidly since 1900. (See Tables 1-4 and fig. 12.) The data show that this increase has occurred very largely in the State schools.

From figure 13 it is evident that the State normal schools in more recent years are securing a smaller percentage of their income from public appropriations than was the case from 1900 to 1908. This means that more is being received from such sources as fees, gifts, productive funds, etc.

TABLE 19.—*Average receipts of normal schools per school, 1900-1918.*

Sources.	1900	1902	1904	1906	1908	1910	1912	1914	1916	1918
State	$30,721	$33,506	$40,568	$47,421	$65,001	$70,041	$71,424	$88,854	$102,004	$118,545
City and county	29,677	39,219	41,691	33,248	60,159	62,853	17,086	19,056	19,731	1 18,670
Private	9,807	14,165	17,553	18,146	43,898	49,699	31,926	47,114	56,340	46,372

1 Expenditures.

The average income of normal schools shows a rapid increase in the State and in the private schools. (See fig. 14.) The drop in the curve for private schools in 1912 was due partly to the fact that several large schools were included in 1910 but not in 1912. The decrease shown in the city and county schools occurred largely because fewer large schools and more small schools reported their income in later years.

The derivation of the income of State normal schools in 1917-18 is set forth in figure 15. These percentages were obtained by comparing the total receipts, less the income from public funds for

150407°—20——3

increase of plant, with the amount received from public funds for current expenses. In Wisconsin the income from fees, etc., is turned over to the State. The State appropriations, therefore, in Wisconsin cover all receipts for State normal schools. In computing these percentages the State plan was not followed. The

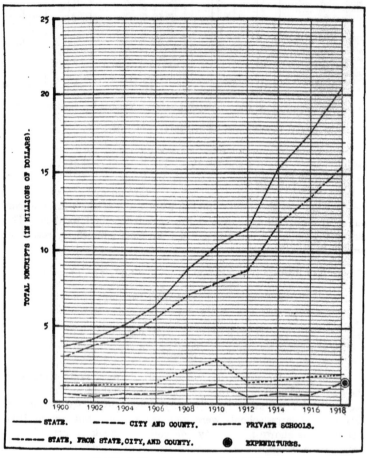

FIG. 12.—Total receipts of normal schools, 1900–1918.

receipts from the various sources were considered as in other States for the reason that the State in reality appropriated so much less from public funds, since such receipts really contribute to the State appropriations. A similar remark may be made in the case of several other States. (See Table 34 and footnotes.) It is obvious from figure 15 that there is much variation in the policies of the different States in the support of their State normal schools. In California almost all of the income for current expenses was received from public funds, while in Pennsylvania only 20 per cent was so obtained. In the latter State a number of the schools are yet semi-private.

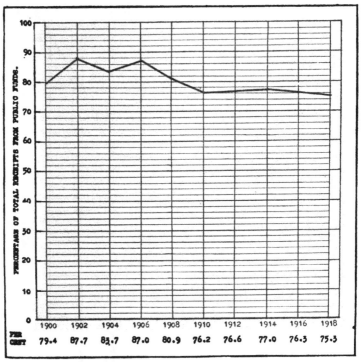

FIG. 13.—Percentage of total receipts for State normal schools which was appropriated from public funds, 1900–1918.

EXPENDITURES.

The variation in total expenditures of normal schools in 1917–18 is set forth in Table 20. One State school spent less than $7,500, while 54 spent more than $100,000. The county schools are the smallest as measured by expenditures. Only two private schools expended more than $60,000.

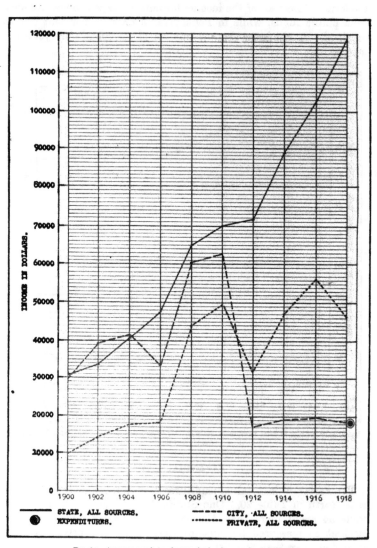

FIG. 14.—Average receipts of normal schools per school, 1900–1918.

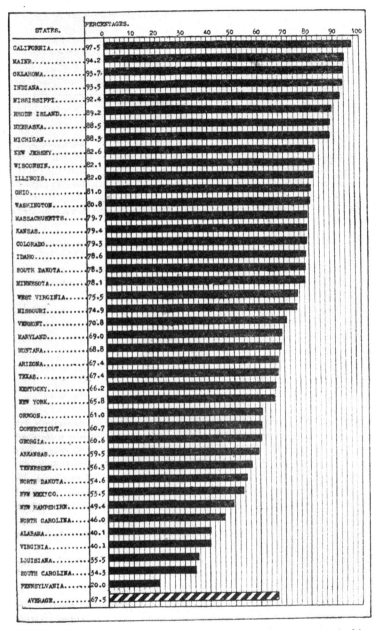

STATES.	PERCENTAGES.
CALIFORNIA	97.5
MAINE	94.2
OKLAHOMA	93.7
INDIANA	93.5
MISSISSIPPI	92.4
RHODE ISLAND	89.2
NEBRASKA	88.5
MICHIGAN	88.3
NEW JERSEY	82.6
WISCONSIN	82.1
ILLINOIS	82.0
OHIO	81.0
WASHINGTON	80.8
MASSACHUSETTS	79.7
KANSAS	79.4
COLORADO	79.3
IDAHO	78.6
SOUTH DAKOTA	78.3
MINNESOTA	78.1
WEST VIRGINIA	75.5
MISSOURI	74.9
VERMONT	70.8
MARYLAND	69.0
MONTANA	68.8
ARIZONA	67.4
TEXAS	67.4
KENTUCKY	66.2
NEW YORK	65.8
OREGON	61.0
CONNECTICUT	60.7
GEORGIA	60.6
ARKANSAS	59.5
TENNESSEE	56.3
NORTH DAKOTA	54.6
NEW MEXICO	53.5
NEW HAMPSHIRE	49.4
NORTH CAROLINA	46.0
ALABAMA	40.1
VIRGINIA	40.1
LOUISIANA	35.5
SOUTH CAROLINA	34.3
PENNSYLVANIA	20.0
AVERAGE	67.5

FIG. 15.—Percentages of total current expenses of State normal schools which were appropriated from public funds, 1900–1918.

TABLE 20.—*Distribution of normal schools according to the total current expenditures, 1917–18.*

Expenditures.	Number of schools.				Expenditures.	Number of schools.			
	State.	City.	County.	Private.		State.	City.	County.	Private.
$0– $2,499		4	21	4	$80,000–$89,999	12			
2,500– 4,999		1	9	6	90,000– 99,999	13			
5,000– 7,499	1	3	9	5	100,000–109,999	8	1		
7,500– 9,999				2	110,000–119,999	14	1		
					120,000–129,999	5	1		
0– 9,999	1	8	45	17	130,000–139,999	8			
10,000– 19,999	10	5	2	12	140,000–149,999	2	1		
20,000– 29,999	9	5		8	150,000–159,999	3	1		
30,000– 39,999	4	3		2	More than $160,000	[1] 14			[2] 2
40,000– 49,999	21	1		1					
50,000– 59,999	15	1		3	Total number of reports	168	24	47	45
60,000– 69,999	14								
70,000– 79,999	15	1							

[1] 161,440; 165,645; 174,644; 179,746; 191,780; 198,202; 199,212; 207,075; 226,407; 240,391; 252,600; 253,564; 272,759; 313,167.
[2] 315,908; 397,360.

TABLE 21.—*Distribution of normal schools according to the annual salaries of the presidents and principals, 1917–18.*

Annual salaries.	Number of schools.				Annual salaries.	Number of schools.			
	State.	City.	County.	Private.		State.	City.	County.	Private.
$1– $499		1	8		$4,500–$4,999	6	2		
500– 999		1	8	2	5,000– 5,499	21	4		1
1,000–1,499	4	2	12	8	5,500– 5,999	4	1		
1,500–1,999	4	4	8	13	6,000– 6,499	3	1		
2,000–2,499	15	6	10	4	6,500– 6,999	0			
2,500–2,999	10	6	3	2	7,000– 7,499	1			
3,000–3,499	33	2		1					
3,500–3,999	34	1		2	Total number of reports	166	30	41	33
4,000–4,499	31								

Table 21 shows the distribution of the salaries of principals and presidents of normal schools. Here, too, considerable differences obtain. No county normal school principal received $3,000. Most of the county normal school directors in Ohio received $950 and $1,000. Of the State normal school principals and presidents, 133 received $5,000 or more. Eleven city normal school principals received $3,000 or more. The corresponding figure for private normal school presidents and principals was four.

Classification of expenditures.—In the tables which follow the items are made up as follows:

(1) Business administration includes salaries of boards, their traveling expenses, and similar items.

(2) The salary of the principal needs no explanation.

(3) Other expenses of educational administration include the salary of office assistants (clerical) and other office expenses. (Items 1, 2, and 3 constitute the cost of administration.)

(4) Salaries of deans and teachers need no explanation.

(5) Textbooks, supplies, etc., include such supplies as are used in instruction. (Items 4 and 5 constitute the cost of instruction.)

(6) Operation of school plant includes wages of janitors, engineers, etc., and wages paid persons connected with demonstration farms and with dormitories; cost of fuel, water, and light; janitors' supplies; and similar expenses of operation.

(7) Maintenance of school plant includes repair of buildings and upkeep of grounds, repair and replacement of equipment, and similar items.

(8) Auxiliary agencies include salaries of librarians (sometimes reported under salaries of instructors), books and library supplies, athletics and promotion of health, lunches, lecture courses, printing, etc.

(9) Fixed charges include rent, insurance, contributions, and contingencies. (Items 8 and 9 constitute the expenses for miscellaneous items.)

Detailed expenditures of 58 State normal schools.—For a detail study of expenditures of State normal schools, 58 schools were selected. Those chosen reported the total number of attendance weeks and distribution of their expenditures. Several other schools reported these data, but due to the nature of the method used only a limited number could be included. The list is thought to be a fair sample. It contains schools from 27 of the 42 States which have State normal schools. From Table 22 it appears that they fairly represent the situation with regard to the number of attendance weeks, since the schools included therein have from 1,558, in the smallest, to 39,116 in the largest school. The greatest possible variation on this score, as indicated in Table 13, is limited to a little over 40,000 attendance weeks in the largest school. The schools selected are also representative with regard to the total current expenses, since the total current expenses vary from $12,576, in the school having the lowest amount, to $199,212 in the school having the largest amount, as shown in Table 26. The highest corresponding expenditure incurred by any State normal school is $313,167, as shown in Table 20. The general tendencies in the distribution of expenditures can be noted from a study of the practice in these schools. Any other school can easily be compared with these data if the number of attendance weeks and the distribution of expenditures are known.

TABLE 22.—*Fifty-eight State normal schools arranged in order of magnitude according to the number of attendance weeks, 1917-18.*

	Location of institution.	Number of attendance weeks	Nonresident students.[1]		Location of institution.	Number of attendance weeks.	Nonresident students.[1]
1	2	3	4	1	2	3	4
1	Los Angeles, Calif.	39,116	611	30	Providence, R. I.	11,090	183
2	Normal, Ill.	33,421	310	31	Lock Haven, Pa.	10,994	......
3	Warrensburg, Mo.	32,196	460	32	Edinboro, Pa.	10,670	......
4	Prairie View, Tex.²	28,344	......	33	Fredericksburg, Va.	10,222	......
5	Kent, Ohio	26,944	88	34	Ellensburg, Wash.	10,088	112
6	Carbondale, Ill.	26,647	......	35	Platteville, Wis.	9,896	11
7	Springfield, Mo.	26,250	......	36	Richmond, Ky.	9,618	......
8	Pittsburg, Kans.	26,192	112	37	Bowling Green, Ohio	8,766	635
9	Aberdeen, S. Dak.	25,963	401	38	Fayetteville, N. C.²	8,478	......
10	San Marcos, Tex.	24,253	......	39	Oswego, N. Y.	8,463	......
11	Farmville, Va.	22,489	......	40	Minot, N. Dak.	8,164	49
12	Cape Girardeau, Mo.	20,267	91	41	Lowell, Mass.	7,914	......
13	Kearney, Nebr.	18,905	......	42	Ellendale, N. Dak.	7,570	......
14	St. Cloud, Minn.	18,888	......	43	Chadron, Nebr.	7,481	20
15	Stevens Point, Wis.	18,741	37	44	Springfield, S. Dak.	7,286	......
16	Cheney, Wash.	18,274	332	45	Albion, Idaho.	7,253	31
17	Shippensburg, Pa.	17,854	5	46	Fresno, Calif.	7,200	......
18	La Crosse, Wis.	17,760	......	47	Duluth, Minn.	6,960	......
19	Oneonta, N. Y.	17,664	......	48	Cullowhee, N. C.	6,805	......
20	Buffalo, N. Y.	17,577	......	49	Worcester, Mass.	6,560	......
21	Durant, Okla.	16,814	......	50	Shepherdstown, W. Va.	6,560	......
22	Kutztown, Pa.	15,909	......	51	Lewiston, Idaho.	6,389	10
23	Slippery Rock, Pa.	15,243	......	52	Keene, N. H.	6,370	......
24	Pine Bluff, Ark.²	14,456	......	53	Commerce, Tex.	6,249	......
25	Whitewater, Wis.	14,116	......	54	Westfield, Mass.	6,091	......
26	Millersville, Pa.	13,621	......	55	Willimantic, Conn.	4,021	......
27	Livingston, Ala.	12,000	......	56	North Adams, Mass.	4,010	114
28	Fitchburg, Mass.	11,854	......	57	Presque Isle, Me.	2,309	......
29	Menomonie, Wis.	11,594	......	58	Johnson, Vt.	1,558	27

[1] These students were enrolled in extension and in correspondence courses. They are not considered in any ratios which are used in this discussion of expenditures.
² For colored persons.

In this study of expenditures of 58 State normal schools each institution is assigned a significant number. Table 22 shows the scheme of numbering used. The schools are here arranged in serial order according to the number of attendance weeks, the one with the largest number of attendance weeks being number 1, etc. The number of a school, therefore, denotes the relative size of the institution which it represents. Thus school number 29 is about the average size, school number 4 is large, school number 57 is small, etc. This scheme is to be kept in mind as the reader follows the discussion and reads the accompanying figures.

In this study no account is taken of the nonresident students in extension and in correspondence courses. The number so enrolled is given in Table 22. These, of course, add to the amount of current expenditures, but there is no convenient means of including them in the ratios which are used. Possibly the exclusion of nonresident students may explain why certain schools have relatively very high expenditures per attendance week.

The data of Table 24 were derived from the corresponding data of Table 23 by dividing each item for each school by the number of attendance weeks reported for the school, that is, by dividing for each school the data in columns 3 to 16, inclusive, of Table 23 by the data in column 2 of the same table. Table 23 also shows the median cost and the upper and the lower limits of the middle half of the costs for the various purposes.

To obtain the median here used the various costs per attendance week for the same purpose in the different schools were arranged in serial order, the largest being first. The middle cost was then taken as the median. When there was an even number of costs in the series so arranged, the higher one of the two middle costs was taken as the median. In a similar manner the upper and the lower limits of the middle half of the costs were obtained, the series being divided into four nearly equal parts, instead of into two parts as in the case of the median. The middle half is frequently called the "zone of safety."

Table 24 is to be read as follows: School No. 58 spends per attendance week $18.25 for all current expenses, $1.35 for the salary of the principal, $0.34 for other expenses of educational administration, $9.82 for salaries of deans and teachers, $0.68 for textbooks and supplies for instruction, etc.

In order to facilitate comparison, the data of Table 25 were computed. These were obtained from Table 24 by dividing each item in it by the median for the corresponding item. Table 25 is thus a table of ratios as is indicated by its heading. The median ratios and the upper and the lower limits of the middle half of the ratios are given. These aid in interpreting the data of the table.

Table 25 is to be read as follows: School No. 58 spends per attendance week 2.84 times the median amount (see Table 24 for median amount) for all current expenses, 4.66 times the median amount for the salary of the principal, 2.12 times the median amount for other expenses of educational administration, etc.

TABLE 23.—*Expenditures for various purposes in 58 State normal schools, 1917-18.*

Name of school	Number of school (see Table 22)	Number of attendance weeks	Total current expenses	Administration — Business	Educational — Salary of principal	Educational — Other expenses	Instruction — Deans and teachers	Instruction — Text-books, supplies, etc.	Operation of school plant	Maintenance	Miscellaneous — Auxiliary agencies and sundry activities	Miscellaneous — Fixed charges, as rent, insurance, etc.	Miscellaneous — Administration	Total — Instruction	Total — Miscellaneous	Total — Salaries of principals, deans, and teachers
	2	3	4	5	6	7	8	9	10	11	12	13	14	15	16	17
Johnson, Vt.	58	1,558	$25,437		$2,100	$540	$15,300	$1,060	$3,606	$2,102	$3,729	$700	$2,640	$16,360	$3,729	$17,400
Lewiston, Idaho	51	6,389	104,927	$719	3,500	4,385	55,250	2,583	15,887	20,216	5,049		7,385	55,250	5,749	56,750
North Adams, Mass.	56	4,013	61,983	8,396	3,250	3,326	20,853	2,602	28,081	3,891		0	6,675	23,436	2,644	24,103
Willimantic, Conn.	55	4,021	50,126		3,500	700	29,685	2,602	7,602	3,671	2,644		6,919	33,287	2,644	33,185
Menomonie, Wis.	29	11,564	132,317		6,000	0	48,421	5,384	56,044	3,231	4,641	0	14,396	54,005	4,641	54,631
Keene, N.H.	52	6,370	71,568	62	3,500	946	41,583	5,496	18,781	830	400		4,506	47,079	400	45,083
Commerce, Tex.	53	6,249	96,087		3,000	6,711	43,003	8,643	2,900	900	1,200		9,711	51,676	1,200	46,083
Bowling Green, Ohio	37	9,295	90,235	3,522	4,000	6,870	52,071	2,835	19,069	312	6,856		8,963	54,996	6,586	55,371
Fresno, Calif.	46	9,346	73,846		4,500	1,800	53,785	2,296	9,411		6,856		6,300	54,071	6,586	57,288
Ellensburg, Wash.	34	10,080	96,443	8,783	4,500	3,008	42,866	3,976	17,394	2,584	3,500		18,256	62,206	3,500	56,733
Presque Isle, Me.	57	2,300	22,086		2,200	120	11,616	600	6,980	500	50		2,320	12,216	50	13,816
Minot, N. Dak.	40	8,164	74,246	2,900	1,754	1,907	24,676	1,250	23,250	13,669	7,997	43	2,361	25,926	8,040	42,430
Oswego, N.Y.	39	8,463	74,733		1,900		41,558	2,400	16,731	9,937	7,500		5,000	44,661	2,490	45,388
Albion, Idaho	45	7,253	53,240	2,800	1,375	275	29,878	2,694	14,731	5,880	2,213	278	5,967	33,472	2,490	33,283
Lowell, Mass.	41	7,914	64,881	2,017	3,083	1,243	42,645	3,880	11,960	1,161	880	0	4,006	46,575	880	45,788
Slippery Rock, Pa.	28	15,243	122,777	3,790	4,500	720	28,986	1,127	16,485	61,656	4,454	1,099	9,000	30,113	5,553	33,498
Westfield, Mass.	54	6,091	47,764		3,250	2,481	19,008	2,146	15,094	5,415	1,750		5,731	21,654	1,221	22,286
Fitchburg, Mass.	28	11,854	90,551		4,000	8,140	42,450	7,255	24,120	5,170	1,750		7,140	50,190	1,221	46,450
Duluth, Minn.	47	6,990	52,100		5,000	3,650	30,450	650	8,660	3,800	1,700		7,650	31,300	1,750	35,450
Providence, R.I.	30	11,000	83,000		4,000	2,500	47,600	7,000	17,000	3,300	1,700		6,000	31,500	1,700	51,500
Platteville, Wis.	35	9,896	73,217		3,750	1,770	44,226	2,700	12,559	2,575	4,847	780	5,590	46,908	5,927	47,986
Chadron, Nebr.	43	7,181	54,074		3,000	180	35,668	650	9,646	1,000	930		5,182	39,315	930	41,665
Kutztown, Pa.	22	15,909	110,741	2,113	3,000		28,060	3,792	29,743	40,201	2,935	847	5,113	31,882	3,902	31,000
Lock Haven, Pa.	31	10,094	76,519	2,741	2,700	980	18,132	3,583	20,772	22,395	2,935	484	7,621	22,065	3,965	20,982
Worcester, Mass.	49	6,580	45,597	2,297	3,208	1,041	28,503	3,280	11,258	1,723	397		6,546	25,788	397	26,711

School	2	3	4	5	6	7	8	9	10	11	12	13	14	15	16	17
Cape Girardeau, Mo.	12	20,207	139,200	1,257	3,000	10,278	61,983	4,093	26,125	22,728	8,297	781	15,435	65,924	8,988	65,703
Fredericktown, Va.	33	10,222	69,715	1,783	3,000	1,000	28,882	1,171	20,704	7,170	5,030	676	5,783	30,033	5,708	31,882
Shepherdstown, W. Va.	50	9,560	43,033	0	3,250	14,780	17,460	1,016	5,990	500	807		17,260	18,476	807	19,990
Ellendale, N. Dak.	42	7,570	48,650		3,600	1,107	22,069	967	14,636	2,201	2,700	1,560	4,417	23,026	4,350	25,319
Richmond, Ky.	36	9,618	59,541	1,982	3,600	1,724	34,364		16,409	492	900		7,288	34,364	900	37,994
St. Cloud, Minn.	14	18,888	114,837		5,000	7,087	55,817	3,472	19,575	21,220	2,066		12,087	59,299	2,066	60,817
Millersville, Pa.	26	13,631	82,663	1,200	5,000	480	24,436	3,506	39,766	4,728	4,962	2,621	5,680	27,941	7,583	128,435
Normal, Ill.	2	33,421	199,212	2,602	5,000	2,710	123,117	13,669	39,042	4,370	8,517	185	10,312	136,786	8,702	128,117
Springfield, S. Dak.	44	7,288	42,984	2,199	3,350	2,346	17,889	444	16,560	1,202	344		6,645	18,333	344	20,889
Edinboro, Pa.	32	10,670	62,724	1,415	3,350	790	16,978	3,672	16,742	1,284	17,703	789	5,556	20,640	18,492	20,328
Prairie View, Tex.	4	28,344	165,645	3,156	2,000	1,638	37,071	1,927	71,495	44,237	4,121		6,794	38,998	4,121	39,071
Kearney, Nebr.	13	18,905	109,774		3,000	7,160	57,959	5,182	20,909	10,457	5,107		10,160	63,141	6,107	60,989
Cheney, Wash.	16	18,271	103,010		5,000	2,800	54,000		28,800	2,980	9,850	1,068	7,800	64,000	6,850	59,000
Whitewater, Wis.	25	14,116	79,452		4,000	3,572	51,243	2,008	11,206	2,202	4,154		7,572	63,261	5,522	55,243
La Crosse, Wis.	18	17,760	93,555		4,250	2,618	63,402	3,072	10,086	3,145	6,280	702	6,988	66,474	6,962	67,652
Pittsburg, Kans.	8	26,192	137,855	1,200	4,500	6,170	101,828	3,540	13,354	3,900	3,948	1,153	11,670	105,868	3,063	107,328
Stevens Point, Wis.	15	18,741	96,409	3,870	4,000	3,838	59,419	3,989	16,062	11,683	4,468	1,091	7,838	63,408	5,630	63,419
Farmville, Va.	11	22,489	113,489		4,300	3,772	48,348	176	37,530		7,088		6,775	48,521	5,977	52,645
Los Angeles, Calif.	1	39,116	191,780	4,459	6,000		142,683		20,030	8,425	7,000	3,840	13,642	142,683		148,683
San Marcos, Tex.	10	24,253	115,945		3,600	4,053	64,551	7,150	20,780	5,640	6,331		7,653	71,701	10,171	68,151
Carbondale, Ill.	6	26,647	123,236		5,000	3,400	66,405	11,361	21,669	8,200	7,200		8,400	77,787	7,200	71,405
Aberdeen, S. Dak.	9	25,963	117,917		4,000	5,973	63,381	5,280	27,500	9,090	3,259		14,407	63,661	3,259	62,381
Kent, Ohio	5	26,944	119,816		4,500	4,675	63,750	3,700	33,316	4,100	6,775		67,450	67,450	5,775	68,250
Oneonta, N. Y.	19	17,664	74,196	4,459	3,800	1,100	51,750	3,519	9,327	2,124	2,566	855	4,900	55,289	2,566	55,550
Buffalo, N. Y.	20	17,577	68,966		3,600	2,882	46,390	2,400	11,704	1,622	1,150		5,700	48,790	1,150	49,980
Springfield, Mo.	7	26,250	96,266		4,000	1,660	71,086	6,000	12,500			1,200	5,680	77,086	4,668	75,086
Shippensburg, Pa.	17	17,854	64,180		4,000	1,589	17,990	2,754	23,642	10,147	3,265		5,589	20,744	9,992	21,900
Warrensburg, Mo.	27	32,196	102,386	1,500	4,000	780	70,563		6,550		3,992		6,100	79,563	9,700	88,563
Livingston, Ala.	21	12,000	34,459	(¹)	3,100	1,000	19,989	400	6,270	1,000	1,500		5,280	20,339	2,700	25,089
Durant, Okla.		16,814	47,081		3,000	2,832	32,047	1,010	9,443	670	1,059		5,832	33,047	4,069	35,047
Cullowhee, N. C.	48	6,805	15,444		2,000	330	9,298	5,704	3,816	610	650	100	2,330	9,298	1,090	11,298
Pine Bluff, Ark.	24	14,456	26,922	700	2,040	650	12,546	337	3,642	5,276	238	160	3,390	18,250	398	18,588
Fayetteville, N. C.	38	8,478	12,576		1,200	288	8,860		1,206				1,488	4,206		5,069

¹ Included in educational administration.

The data on expenditures which the 58 schools reported are assembled in Table 23. The numbers in column 2 refer to the ranking numbers used in Table 22. The data in column 13 are the sums of the data in columns 4, 5 and 6. In a similar way the data of column 14 combines columns 7 and 8; those of column 15, columns 11 and 12; and those of column 16, columns 5 and 7.

TABLE 24.—Expenditures per attendance week for various purposes in 58 State normal schools, 1917-18.

Name of school	Number of school (see Table 22).	Total current expenses.	Administration			Instruction		Operation of school plant.	Maintenance.	Miscellaneous			Total		
			Business.	Educational		Deans and teachers.	Text-books, supplies, etc.			Auxiliary agencies and sundry activities.	Fixed charges, as rent, insurance, etc.	Administration.	Instruction.	Miscellaneous.	Salaries of principals, deans, and teachers.
				Salary of principal.	Other expenses.										
1	2	3	4	5	6	7	8	9	10	11	12	13	14	15	16
Johnson, Vt.	58	$18.23		$1.35	$0.34	$9.83	$0.68	$2.31	$1.35	$2.40		$1.69	$10.50	$2.40	$11.17
Lewiston, Idaho	51	16.42		.56	.68	8.65		2.43	3.16	.79	$0.11	1.23	8.65	.90	9.20
North Adams, Mass	56	15.45	$0.18	.81	.83	5.20	.64	7.00	.97	.66		1.64	5.84	.66	6.01
Willimantic, Conn	55	12.47	.72	.87	.17	7.38	.65	1.89	.67	.40	.00	1.22	8.03	.40	8.25
Menomonie, Wis	29	11.41		.52	.00	4.19	.47	4.83	.28			1.24	4.66		4.71
Keene, N. H.	52	11.24	.01	.55	.15	6.53	.86	2.95	.13	.06		.71	7.39	.06	7.08
Commerce, Tex.	53	10.58		.48	1.06	6.99	1.38	.40	.10	.19		1.56	8.37	.19	7.37
Bowling Green, Ohio	37	10.30	.40	.49	.16	5.94	.32	2.13	.08	.78		.90	6.26	.78	6.43
Fresno, Calif.	46	10.23		.63	.25	7.33	.18	1.03	.33	.47		.87	7.51	.47	7.95
Ellensburg, Wash.	34	9.57	.87	.45	.50	5.48	.39	1.72	.16			1.82	5.87		5.93
Presque Isle, Me.	57	9.54	.31	.95	.06	5.03	.26	3.01	.22	.02	.01	1.00	5.29	.02	5.98
Minot, N. Dak.	40	9.46	.14	.22	.22	3.02	.15	2.85	1.67	.96		.78	3.17	.96	3.24
Oswego, N. Y.	39	8.84	.28	.45		3.92	.40	1.70	1.17	.08	.04	.39	3.32	.08	5.37
Albion, Idaho	45	8.72		.40	.08	4.12	.36	2.31	.81	.34	.06	.77	4.48	.34	4.68
Lowell, Mass.	41	8.20		.49	.16	5.39	.49	1.61	.15	.11	.00	.55	5.88	.11	5.78
Slippery Rock, Pa.	23	8.06	.25	.29	.06	1.91	.07	1.08	4.04	.29	.07	.29	1.96	.36	2.20
Westfield, Mass	54	7.84		.53	.40	3.13	.42	2.47	.80			.81	3.55		3.66
Fitchburg, Mass.	28	7.58		.34	.27	3.62	.61	2.04	.00	.10		.61	4.23	.10	3.96
Duluth, Minn	47	7.49		.72	.38	4.38	.12	1.23	.55	.11		1.10	4.50	.11	3.10
Providence, R. I.	30	7.48		.36	.23	4.28	.63	1.64	.20	.15		.59	4.91	.15	4.64
Platteville, Wis.	35	7.40		.39	.18	4.47	.27	1.27	.26	.49		.57	4.74	.56	4.95
Chadron, Nebr.	43	7.23		.40	.02	5.17	.09	1.29	.13	.13		.43	5.26	.13	5.57
Kutztown, Pa.	22	6.96	.13	.10		1.77	.24	1.87	2.63	.18	.07	.33	2.01	.23	1.89
Lock Haven, Pa.	31	6.96	.25	.24	.18	1.65	.38	1.80	2.03	.30	.05	.67	2.03	.24	1.89
Worcester, Mass.	40	6.95	.35	.49	.16	3.58	.35	1.72	.25	.04	.04	1.00	3.98	.04	4.07

Cape Girardeau, Mo.
Fredericksburg, Va.
Shepherdstown, W. Va.
Ellendale, N. Dak.
Richmond, Ky.

St. Cloud, Minn.
Millersville, Pa.
Normal, Ill.
Springfield, S. Dak.
Edinboro, Pa.

Prairie View, Tex.
Kearney, Nebr.
Cheney, Wash.
Whitewater, Wis.
La Crosse, Wis.

Pittsburg, Kans.
Stevens Point, Wis.
Farmville, Va.
Los Angeles, Calif.
San Marcos, Tex.

Carbondale, Ill.
Aberdeen, S. Dak.
Kent, Ohio
Oneonta, N. Y.
Buffalo, N. Y.

Springfield, Mo.
Shippensburg, Pa.
Warrensburg, Mo.
Livingston, Ala.
Durant, Okla.

Cullowhee, N. C.
Pine Bluff, Ark.
Fayetteville, N. C.

First quartile[1]
Median
Third quartile[2]

1 Upper limit of the middle half of the expenditures per attendance week.

2 Lower limit of the middle half of the expenditures per attendance week.

TABLE 25.—*Ratios between the amounts spent per attendance week in 58 State normal schools for the various purposes, and the corresponding median amounts spent for those purposes, 1917–18.*

Name of school.	Number of school (see Table 22).	Total current expenses.	Administration			Instruction		Operation of school plant.	Maintenance.	Miscellaneous.		Total.			
			Business.	Salary of principal.	Other expenses.	Deans and teachers.	Text-books, supplies, etc.			Auxiliary agencies and sundry activities.	Fixed charges as rent, insurance, etc.	Administration.	Instruction.	Miscellaneous.	Salaries of principals, deans, and teachers.
	2	3	4	5	6	7	8	9	10	11	12	13	14	15	16
Johnson, Vt.	58	2.84		4.66	2.12	3.20	2.88	1.75	4.66	10.00		3.02	3.15	9.80	3.34
Lewiston, Idaho	51	2.55		1.90	4.25	2.83		1.88	10.90	3.29	2.20	2.30	2.59	3.80	2.76
North Adams, Mass	56	2.40	1.08	2.60	5.19	1.69	2.67	6.30	3.36			2.93	1.75		2.80
Willimantic, Conn	58	2.94	4.13	3.00	1.06	2.40	2.71	1.43	2.31	2.75		2.18	2.40	2.64	2.44
Menomonie, Wis	59	1.77		1.79	.00	1.37	1.96	3.66	.97	1.67		2.22	1.40	1.60	1.41
Keene, N. H.	62	1.75	.06	1.90	.94	2.13	3.58	2.23	.45	.25		1.77	2.21	.24	2.12
Commerce, Tex.	53	1.65		1.65	6.38	2.24	6.76	.35	.34	.70		2.79	2.45	.76	2.21
Bowling Green, Ohio	37	1.60	2.36	1.69	.63	1.94	1.33	1.65	.31	3.25		1.77	1.87	3.12	1.93
Fresno, Calif.	48	1.59		2.14	1.56	2.39	.75	.78	1.14	1.96		1.55	2.25	1.88	2.38
Ellensburg, Wash	34	1.49	6.12	1.66	3.12	1.70	1.62	1.30	.55			3.25	1.76		1.78
Presque Isle, Me.	57	1.48		3.26	.31	1.64	1.06	2.26	5.75	.08		1.79	1.58	.08	1.79
Minot, N. Dak	40	1.37	2.00	.76	1.37	.98	.68	2.16	5.04	4.08	.20	1.39	.95	.99	.97
Oswego, N. Y.	39	1.36	.82	1.55	.19	1.00	1.67	1.75	2.79	1.25	.80	1.05	1.59	.24	.61
Albion, Idaho	45	1.36	1.65	1.59	1.00	1.34	1.50	1.14	.53	.46	.00	1.37	1.33	1.36	1.37
Lowell, Mass	41	1.28		1.34		1.76	2.04					.98	1.76	.44	1.73
Slippery Rock, Pa.	23	1.26	1.47	1.00	.31	.62	.29	.32	13.98	1.21	1.40	1.05	.59	1.44	.66
Westfield, Mass	64	1.22		1.88	2.60	1.09	1.75	1.87	3.07	.43		1.99	1.06	.40	1.10
Fitchburg, Mass	26	1.18		1.17	1.99	1.18	2.54	1.54	2.07	.44		1.97	1.35	.44	1.19
Duluth, Minn	47	1.16		2.48	2.27	1.43	.40	.93	1.90	.63			1.47	.60	1.53
Providence, R. I.	30	1.16		2.24	1.44	1.39	2.62	1.17	1.00			1.06			1.39
Platteville, Wis	36	1.15		1.24	1.12	1.46	1.12	.96	.90	2.04	1.40	1.02	1.42	2.24	1.45
Chadron, Nebr	43	1.12	.77	1.38	.13	1.68	.37	.98	.45	.76	1.00	.57	1.67	.52	1.67
Kutztown, Pa.	22	1.08	1.47	.83	1.12	.54	1.00	1.41	8.72	1.25	.08	1.30	.61	.92	.60
Lock Haven, Pa.	31	1.08	2.06	1.60	1.00	1.17	1.58	1.30	7.90	.17		1.70	1.18	1.36	.55
Worcester, Mass	49	1.08					1.46							.16	1.22

Cape Girardeau, Mo	12	1.07	.35	.66	3.22	.99	.83	.98	3.86	1.71	.80	1.36	.97	1.80	.97
Fredericksburg, Va	33	1.06	1.00	1.00	.63	.92	.46	1.54	2.52	2.04	1.40	1.00	.88	2.24	.93
Shepherdstown, W. Va	50	1.02	......	1.31	14.06	.87	.67	.69	.28	.50	......	4.70	.84	.48	.91
Ellendale, N. Dak	42	1.00	.00	1.48	.94	.95	.54	1.47	1.00	1.54	4.20	1.04	.91	2.32	1.00
Richmond, Ky	36	.96	1.47	1.31	1.12	1.16	......	1.30	.17	.38	......	1.36	1.07	.36	1.18
St. Cloud, Minn	14	.95	......	.90	2.37	.96	.75	.79	3.86	.58	......	1.14	.94	.56	.96
Millersville, Pa	26	.94	.53	1.00	.25	.58	1.08	2.04	1.21	1.50	3.80	.75	.61	2.20	.62
Normal, Ill	2	.93	.47	.52	.50	1.20	1.71	.89	.45	1.04	.20	.55	1.22	1.04	1.15
Springfield, S. Dak	44	.92	1.76	1.41	1.12	.80	.25	1.72	.59	.21	......	1.59	.75	.20	.85
Edinboro, Pa	32	.91	.77	1.10	.44	.52	1.46	1.19	.41	6.92	1.40	.93	.58	6.92	.57
Prairie View, Tex	4	.91	.65	.24	.37	.43	.29	1.91	5.38	.58	......	.43	.41	.56	.41
Kearney, Nebr	13	.90	......	.55	2.37	1.00	1.12	.84	1.90	1.13	......	.96	1.00	1.08	.97
Cheney, Wash	16	.88	......	.93	.94	.96	......	1.20	.48	2.26	......	.75	.89	2.16	.97
Whitewater, Wis	25	.88	......	.97	1.56	1.18	.58	.61	.55	1.21	1.60	.95	1.13	1.48	1.14
La Crosse, Wis	18	.82	......	.83	.94	1.16	.71	.43	.62	1.45	.80	.70	1.12	1.56	1.17
Pittsburg, Kans	8	.82	......	.72	1.50	1.26	.58	.39	.45	.63	......	.80	1.20	.60	1.22
Stevens Point, Wis	5	.82	......	.72	1.25	1.08	.87	.64	1.00	1.00	.40	.73	1.01	1.04	1.01
Farmville, Va	11	.78	......	.66	.37	.70	.04	1.26	1.79	.43	1.00	.54	.65	1.60	.70
Los Angeles, Calif	1	.76	.59	.52	.63	1.19	......	.39	.72	.75	......	.63	1.09	.72	1.14
San Marcos, Tex	10	.74	......	.52	1.06	.87	1.21	.65	.79	1.08	3.20	.57	.88	1.68	.84
Carbondale, Ill	6	.72	......	.66	.81	.81	1.79	.61	1.07	1.13	......	.57	.87	1.08	.80
Aberdeen, S. Dak	9	.71	1.00	.52	1.44	.73	.83	.80	1.21	.54	......	.98	.73	.52	.72
Kent, Ohio	5	.69	......	.59	1.06	.77	.58	.91	.52	1.04	......	.61	.75	1.00	.76
Oneonta, N. Y	19	.65	......	.72	.37	.95	.83	.40	.41	.63	......	.48	.94	.60	.94
Buffalo, N. Y	20	.61	......	.60	.75	.86	.58	.51	3.10	.25	......	.57	.83	.24	.85
Springfield, Mo	7	.56	......	.52	.37	.88	.96	.36	......	......	......	.38	.88	......	.85
Shippensburg, Pa	17	.56	......	.76	.56	.33	.63	1.00	1.96	.75	1.00	.55	.35	.92	.37
Warrensburg, Mo	3	.49	.29	.45	.06	.80	......	.16	......	1.29	......	.34	.74	1.24	.78
Livingston, Ala	27	.45	......	.90	.50	.54	.13	.39	.28	.54	2.00	.61	.51	.92	.58
Durant, Okla	21	.44	......	.62	1.06	.62	.25	.38	.14	1.00	......	.63	.59	.96	.63
Cullowhee, N. C	48	.35	......	1.00	.31	.45	......	.42	......	......	......	.61	.41	......	.50
Pine Bluff, Ark	24	.29	.29	.48	.25	.28	1.67	.19	.14	.17	.60	.41	.38	.28	.30
Fayetteville, N. C	38	.23	......	.48	.19	.15	.17	.11	2.14	.13	.40	.30	.15	.20	.18
First quartile[1]	......	1.28	1.65	1.55	1.56	1.48	1.67	1.54	2.79	1.50	1.60	1.55	1.42	1.68	1.45
Second quartile[2]	......	1.00	1.00	1.00	1.00	1.00	1.00	1.00	1.00	1.00	1.00	1.00	1.00	1.00	1.00
Third quartile[3]	......	.78	.53	.66	.44	.80	.58	.64	.52	.54	.80	.61	.75	.52	.78

[1] Upper limit of the middle half of the ratios. [2] Median. [3] Lower limit of the middle half of the ratios.

Explanation of Fig. 16. How 58 State normal schools spend their money.

To read curves observe:

Schools are numbered according to the total number of attendance weeks in each, No. 1 being the largest and 58 the smallest. (See Table 22.) Each radius represents a school.

Beginning with school No. 58, schools are arranged around the circle in the order of the cost (current expenses) per attendance week; No. 58 having the highest cost; No. 51, the next highest; No. 56, the next highest; etc. The spiral curve shows what part this cost per attendance week is of the median cost. Thus, school No. 58 spends 2.84 times the median cost, which is indicated by circle No. 1. The arrows in the central part of each figure indicate the schools which fall within the "middle half" on the cost per attendance week.

In each part of figure 16, some function of expenditures is shown by means of the "dotted" zigzag curve In each case the median is 1. If a school falls between the two heavy "long-dash" circles, it is within the "middle half" or "safety zone" on the function charted.

For illustration, note the third radius representing school No. 56 in each chart, Parts I–VI. This school spends almost two and a half times as much per attendance week for current expenses as the median cost. This relationship is indicated by the relative distances of the "spiral" and the "median" from the "0" circle on radius 56. The cost in this school is considerably above "middle half."

In Part I this school spends almost three times as much for administration per attendance week as the median cost. On this score the cost is also above the "middle half," since the "dotted" curve meets radius 56 beyond the outer "long-dash" circle.

In Part II this school spends for instruction per attendance week 1.75 times the median cost. On this score, also, the cost is above the "middle half."

In Part III this school spends for the operation of its plant over 5 times as much per attendance week as the median cost. Again, it is considerably above the "middle half."

In Part IV, a similar statement applies for the cost of maintenance.

In Part V no data were submitted on the cost of miscellaneous items.

In Part VI certain items in Parts I and II are combined to show the amount spent per attendance week for the salaries of principals, deans, and teachers. In school No. 56 the amount spent for salaries per attendance week is 1.8 times the median cost. The cost is above the "middle half," since the dotted curve meets this radius beyond the outer "long-dash" circle.

By noting the distances of the points on the curves from the "0" circle, it is possible in figure 16 to compare the expenditures of one school with those of any other school for any function of expense. In Part I, for example, school No. 53 spends over twice as much per attendance week for administration as does school No. 52, since the "dotted" curve meets radius 53 twice as far from the "0" circle as the point of intersection of this curve with radius 52 is distant from the "0" circle.

The data of Table 25 are illustrated in figure 16, Parts I to VI. ᵀn all parts of figure 16 and in Tables 23, 24, and 25, the order of the schools is the same. Attention is again called to the fact that the numbers of the schools indicate the relative sizes of the schools as measured by the number of attendance weeks. This means that the numbers have a significance in the interpretation of figure 16.

The spiral curve indicates the ratios between the amounts spent per attendance week for all current expenses and the median amount for all current expenses (see Table 25, column 2). The spiral curve was used to represent the total current expenses rather than to represent any single function of expense so that comparison might easily be made. The spiral could represent any other item, in which case the spiral would not be the same and the order of schools would be governed by the order of the deviations of the function from the median. Schools falling within the middle half on the total cost of current expenses per attendance week are indicated in the middle of figure 16 ("Middle half—Current expenses").

The limits of the middle half of the ratios on the various other items (administration, instruction, etc.) are indicated by the "long-dash" circles. Thus if the "dotted" curve meets any radius between the two "long-dash" circles, the school represented by that radius spends for the item considered an amount within the middle half as indicated at the bottom of Table 24.

It is to be noted in considering the middle half that it may be creditable to an institution to be located either below or above the middle half on certain items. Thus, for instance, it would seem altogether creditable for a school to be above the middle half on

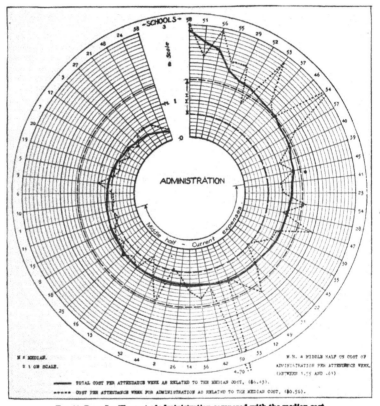

Fig. 16, Part I.—The cost of administration compared with the median cost.

cost of instruction or to be below the middle half on expenses of operation of school plant. A school having a very high total cost per attendance week will not usually fall within the middle zone on any item of expense. Thus the "dotted" curve will seldom enter this zone for the 14 schools having the highest cost per attendance week. Similarly, the "dotted" curve will usually fall below this zone for the 15 schools having the lowest cost per attendance week.

The dotted curve of figure 16, Part I, shows that the cost for administration per attendance week, in general, tends to be high when the cost for current expenses per attendance week is high, and low when the cost per attendance for current expenses is low, which is indicated by the fact that the dotted curve tends to follow the spiral curve. In several cases there are notable exceptions such as schools Nos. 52 and 39, which are low on this item, and schools Nos.

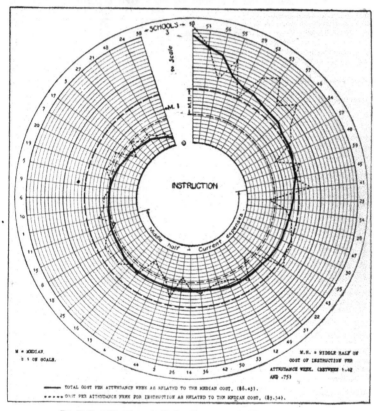

FIG. 16, PART II.—The cost of instruction compared with the median cost.

9, 27, 21, and 48, which are comparatively high on this item. There is perhaps some error in the reports in the cases where the curve for administration falls beyond the scale.

Attention is called to the fact that on the spiral curve practically all of the schools above the middle half (No. 58, through 51, to and including 45) are indicated by large numbers, which means that they are the smaller schools. This likely accounts for the high cost per attendance week for current expenses in these institutions. Most of the schools below the median on the spiral (No. 36, through 14, to and including 38) are indicated by small numbers, thus signifying that they are the larger schools. This seems to point out that the larger schools are the less expensive.

Two types of comparisons are possible in these figures. The first type is that of noting how one particular school stands on any one

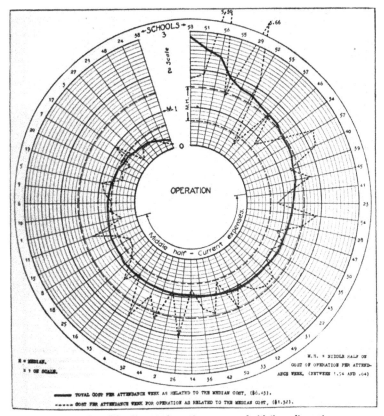

Fig. 16, Part III.—The cost of operation as compared with the median cost.

item, or on all items of expense as related to the central tendency, median of middle half. Thus by noting school No. 52 on all the parts of figure 16 it is evident that this school is high (above the median) on the cost per attendance week for each purpose, though relatively not so high on the operation of school plant (see fig. 16, Part III) as on the other items. It enters the "safety zone" on no function of expense. It is very high on maintenance and on miscellaneous items.

It must be kept in mind that it is a small school, as is indicated by the high number (52), and that its total current expenses per attendance week are high as indicated by the spiral curve. In similar manner it may be noted that school No. 2 is below the middle half on administration, above the median but within the middle half on instruction, below the median but within the middle half on operation, etc.

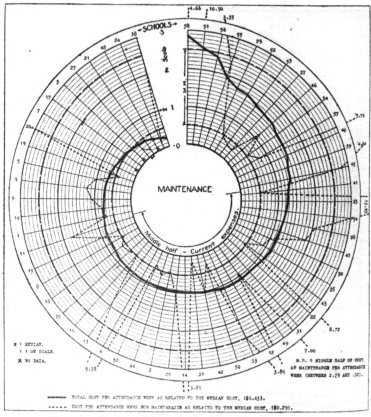

FIG. 16, PART IV.—The cost of maintenance as compared with the median cost.

The second type of comparison is that of showing how the expenditures of one school compare with those of another school for the same purpose. In this the distances of the points from the "0" circle are to be noted and compared. Thus, school No. 53 spends about twice as much per attendance week for administration as does school No. 52, as is explained in the directions for reading the figures.

The observation may be made that some items show much greater general variation from the median than do others, as is indicated by the different widths of the "middle half" on the different parts of figure 16. The "safety zones" are of different widths in the different charts. The least variation from the median is in the cost of instruction (see fig. 16, Part II) and in salaries of principals, deans, and teachers (see fig. 16, Part VI), and the greatest variation is in the cost

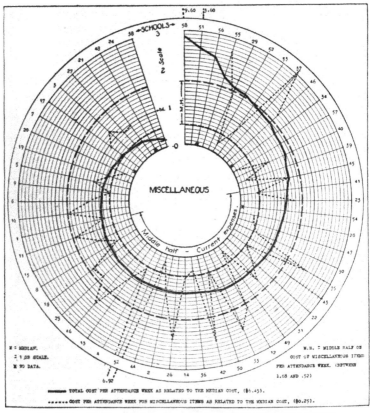

FIG. 16, PART V.—The cost of miscellaneous items as compared with the median cost.

of maintenance. In the latter case some schools may have included outlays in reporting maintenance.

The relative proportion of the total current expenses going for each function of expense can be noted approximately on figure 16, Parts I–VI. If the expenditures for the various purposes in each school were ideally distributed, as indicated by the medians in Table 24, there would be no fluctuation from the spiral curve and the dotted

curve would fall on the spiral curve in each part of figure 16. In
general, it is creditable to an institution to have minor deviations
from the "spiral." When the percentage for any one item is above
the median percentage for that item the "dotted" curve in general
falls outside the spiral, and when the percentage for one item is less
. than the median percentage for that item the "dotted" curve falls
within the spiral. In Part I school No. 53 is an illustration of the

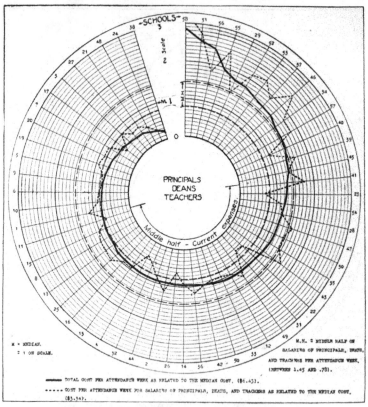

FIG. 16, PART VI.—The salaries of principals, deans, and teachers as compared with the median cost.

former, where the "dotted" curve meets the radius beyond the spiral
point. Judging from the median, this school spends too high a
proportion of its total current expenses for administration. This
same fact is evident in Table 27, which shows that this school spends
14.6 per cent for administration, as compared with 8.7 per cent in
the median school. In Part I school No. 52 is an example of the
latter, where the dotted curve falls inside the spiral curve, and where

the percentage spent for administration is less than the median (Table 27, column 12). This comparison holds in general, though there are slight differences due to the fact that the median is used instead of arithmetical average. The variation is usually restricted to about 10 per cent. In other words, when the proportion going for any function varies less than 10 per cent from the median proportion going for that purpose, the dotted curve is likely to fall on the opposite side of the spiral from that indicated by the table of percentages. Where this variation is greater than 10 per cent the dotted curve falls within or without the spiral curve as indicated by the table of percentage.

THE SALARY OF THE PRINCIPAL.

TABLE 26.—*Total current expenses and salaries of principals of 58 State normal schools, 1917–18.*

Number of school (see Table 22).	Total current expenses. Amount.	Ratio to median.	Salary of principal. Amount.	Ratio to median.	Number of school (see Table 22).	Total current expenses. Amount.	Ratio to median.	Salary of principal. Amount.	Ratio to median.
1	2	3	4	5	6	7	8	9	10
2	$199,212	2.61	$5,000	1.39	39	$74,782	0.96	$3,800	1.06
1	191,780	2.51	6,000	1.67	19	74,186	.96	3,800	1.06
4	165,645	2.16	2,000	.56	46	73,645	.95	4,500	1.25
12	139,200	1.82	3,900	1.08	35	73,217	.94	3,750	1.04
8	137,855	1.80	5,500	1.53	52	71,568	.93	3,500	.97
29	132,317	1.73	6,000	1.67	33	69,715	.91	3,000	.83
6	123,236	1.61	5,000	1.39	20	68,966	.90	3,500	.97
23	122,777	1.61	4,500	1.25	53	66,087	.86	3,000	.83
5	119,816	1.57	4,500	1.25	41	64,881	.85	3,063	.85
9	117,917	1.54	4,000	1.11	17	64,180	.84	4,000	1.11
10	115,945	1.52	3,600	1.00	45	63,240	.83	3,375	.94
14	114,837	1.50	5,000	1.39	32	62,724	.82	3,350	.93
11	113,489	1.48	4,300	1:19	56	61,983	.81	3,250	.90
22	110,741	1.45	3,000	.83	36	59,541	.78	3,600	1.00
13	109,774	1.43	3,000	.83	43	54,074	.71	3,000	.83
51	104,927	1.37	3,500	.97	47	52,100	.68	5,000	1.39
16	103,010	1.35	5,000	1.39	55	50,126	.66	3,500	.97
3	102,385	1.34	4,000	1.11	42	48,650	.64	3,250	.90
15	98,409	1.29	4,000	1.11	54	47,764	.62	3,250	.90
34	96,442	1.26	4,500	1.25	21	47,061	.62	3,000	.83
7	95,256	1.24	4,000	1.11	49	45,597	.60	3,208	.89
18	93,555	1.22	4,250	1.18	50	43,033	.56	2,500	.69
37	90,325	1.18	4,300	1.19	44	42,984	.56	3,000	.83
28	89,851	1.17	4,000	1.11	27	34,459	.45	3,100	.86
30	83,000	1.08	4,000	1.11	58	28,437	.37	2,100	.61
26	82,693	1.08	4,000	1.11	24	26,922	.35	2,040	.57
25	79,452	1.04	4,000	1.11	57	22,036	.29	2,200	.61
40	77,346	1.01	1,754	.49	48	15,444	.20	2,000	.56
31	76,519	1.00	2,700	.75	38	12,576	.16	1,200	.33
(1)	109,774	1.43	4,250	1.18					
(2)	76,346	1.00	3,600	1.00					
(3)	59,541	.78	3,000	.83					

1 Upper limit of the middle half of the amounts or of the ratios.
2 Median.
3 Lower limit of the middle half of the amounts or of the ratios.

Figure 17 (see page 58) shows the salaries of the principals of State normal schools as compared to the number of attendance weeks (indicated by the number of the school) and as compared to the total amount for current expenses (indicated by the spiral curve). This figure is to be read like figure 16, except that the order of the schools is not the same as in figure 16. The data are given in Table 26.

Location of institution.[1]	Rank according to the number of attendance weeks.	Administration			Instruction				Miscellaneous		Total			
		Business.	Educational. Salary of principal.	Other expenses.	Deans and instructors.	Text-books, supplies, etc.	Operation of school plant.	Mainte-nance of school plant.	Auxili-ary agencies and sundry activities.	Fixed charges as rent, insur-ance, etc.	Admin-istra-tion.	Instruc-tion.	Miscella-neous.	Salaries of prin-cipals, deans, and teachers.
	2	3	4	5	6	7	8	9	10	11	12	13	14	15
		Per cent.	*Per cent.*	*Per cent.*	*Per cent.*	*Per cent.*	*Per cent.*	*Per cent.*	*Per cent.*	*Per cent.*	*Per cent.*	*Per cent.*	*Per cent.*	*Per cent.*
Johnson, Vt.	58		7.4	1.9	63.8	3.7	12.7	7.4	13.1		9.3	67.5	13.1	6.12
Lewiston, Idaho	51		8.3	4.2	52.6		16.1	19.3	4.8		7.5	56.2	5.5	5.59
North Adams, Mass.	56	1.4	5.1	5.4	33.6	4.2	45.3	6.3		.7	10.6	37.8		3.88
Willimantic, Conn.	55		7.0	1.4	59.2	5.2	15.2	6.3	5.3		9.8	64.4	5.3	3.62
Menomonie, Wis.	29	6.4	4.5		36.7	4.1	42.3	2.5	3.5	0	10.9	40.8	3.5	4.12
Keene, N. H.	52	.0	4.9	1.3	58.2	7.6	26.4	1.1	.5		6.2	65.8	.5	6.31
Commerce, Tex.	53		4.5	10.1	65.2	13.1	4.4	.9	1.8		14.6	78.8	1.8	6.97
Bowling Green, Ohio	37	3.9	4.8	1.0	57.6	3.1	21.1	.9	7.6		9.7	60.7	7.6	6.24
Fresno, Calif.	46		6.1	2.4	71.7	1.7	10.1	3.2	4.8		8.5	73.4	4.8	7.78
Ellensburg, Wash.	34	9.1	4.7	6.1	57.3	4.1	18.0	1.7			18.9	61.4		6.20
Presque Isle, Me.	57	3.6	10.0	.6	52.7	2.7	31.5	2.3	10.2	.5	10.6	55.4	.2	6.27
Minot, N. Dak.	40	1.6	2.2	2.3	31.8	1.6	30.1	17.6	.7		8.1	33.4	10.8	6.40
Oswego, N. Y.	39		5.1		55.6	4.5	19.2	9.3	3.5	.4	8.7	60.1	.7	6.07
Albion, Idaho	45	3.2	5.3	.4	47.3	4.1	26.5	9.3	1.4	.0	8.9	51.4	3.9	5.26
Lowell, Mass.	41		4.7	1.9	65.6	6.0	18.4	1.8			6.6	71.8	1.4	7.06
Slippery Rock, Pa.	23	3.1	3.7	.5	23.6	.9	13.4	50.2	3.7	.9	7.8	24.5	4.6	2.73
Westfield, Mass.	54		6.8	5.2	39.8	5.3	31.6	11.3			12.0	45.1		4.96
Fitchburg, Mass.	28		4.4	3.5	47.8	8.1	28.8	8.0	1.4		7.9	55.9	1.4	5.22
Duluth, Minn.	47		9.6	5.1	58.5	1.6	16.5	7.3	1.4		14.7	60.1	1.4	6.81
Providence, R. I.	30		4.8	3.0	57.2	8.4	20.5	4.0	2.1		7.8	65.6	2.1	6.20
Platteville, Wis.	35		5.1	2.4	60.4	3.7	17.2	3.5	6.6	1.1	7.6	64.1	7.7	6.55
Chadron, Nebr.	43		5.6	.4	71.5	1.2	17.8	1.8	1.7		6.0	72.7	1.7	7.71
Kutztown, Pa.	22	1.9	2.7		25.3	3.4	26.9	36.3	2.4	.8	4.6	28.7	3.5	2.80
Lock Haven, Pa.	31	3.6	3.5	2.6	23.8	6.1	27.1	29.3	4.4	.6	9.7	28.9	6.0	2.78
Worcester, Mass.	49	5.0	7.0	2.3	51.6	6.0	24.7	3.8	.6		14.3	56.6	.6	5.96

Institution[1]													
Cape Girardeau, Mo.	12	.9	2.8	7.4	44.4	2.9	18.7	16.7	6.9	.6	11.1	47.8	6.5	4.77
Fredericksburg, Va.	13	2.6	4.8	1.4	41.4	1.7	29.7	10.7	7.2	—	8.3	43.1	8.2	4.57
Shepherdstown, W. Va.	50	.0	4.8	34.1	40.8	2.8	13.9	1.2	1.9	1.0	40.1	42.9	8.9	4.64
Ellendale, N. Dak.	50	—	6.7	3.4	40.5	2.0	30.2	4.5	6.7	—	—	47.8	8.9	5.20
Richmond, Ky.	32	3.3	6.1	2.9	57.7	—	27.7	.8	1.5	3.2	12.3	57.7	1.5	5.88
St. Cloud, Minn.	14	—	4.4	6.2	48.6	8.0	17.0	18.5	2.8	—	10.6	51.6	2.3	5.80
Millersville, Pa.	26	1.5	4.8	.6	29.5	4.2	44.5	5.7	6.0	3.2	6.9	38.7	9.2	3.48
Normal, Ill.	2	1.8	2.5	1.8	31.8	4.9	19.6	2.2	4.3	.1	6.1	68.7	4.4	3.48
Springfield, S. Dak.	44	6.1	7.0	3.1	41.6	5.0	38.6	2.8	2.8	—	15.2	42.6	.8	4.86
Edinboro, Pa.	32	2.3	6.8	1.3	27.1	5.8	26.7	2.0	26.2	1.8	8.9	32.9	20.5	3.24
Prairie View, Tex.	4	1.9	1.2	1.0	22.4	1.2	48.1	26.7	2.5	—	4.1	28.6	2.5	2.36
Kearney, Nebr.	13	—	2.8	6.5	62.8	4.7	19.0	9.5	4.7	—	9.3	57.5	4.7	5.56
Cheney, Wash.	16	—	4.9	2.7	82.4	—	82.0	2.8	9.5	—	7.6	82.4	9.5	5.72
Whitewater, Wis.	25	—	5.0	4.5	64.5	2.5	14.1	2.8	6.2	1.4	9.5	67.0	6.6	5.95
La Crosse, Wis.	18	—	4.5	2.8	67.8	3.3	10.8	3.4	6.7	.7	7.3	71.0	7.4	7.22
Pittsburg, Kans.	8	—	4.0	4.7	73.8	2.5	9.7	2.5	2.8	—	8.7	76.8	2.8	7.78
Stevens Point, Wis.	15	—	4.6	3.9	60.4	4.1	15.3	5.6	4.6	1.2	7.9	64.5	5.7	4.44
Farmville, Va.	11	1.1	3.8	1.1	42.4	—	83.1	10.3	7.0	.9	7.0	42.7	7.9	4.64
Los Angeles, Calif.	1	2.0	3.1	2.0	74.4	—	14.1	4.4	3.7	—	7.1	74.4	8.7	7.75
San Marcos, Tex.	10	—	3.1	3.5	67.8	6.1	17.9	4.9	5.5	3.8	6.6	61.8	8.8	5.88
Carbondale, Ill.	6	—	4.1	2.8	63.9	9.2	17.6	6.6	5.8	—	6.9	63.1	5.8	5.80
Aberdeen, S. Dak.	9	8.8	3.4	5.1	49.5	4.4	23.8	7.7	2.8	—	12.3	53.9	2.8	5.29
Kent, Ohio.	5	—	4.8	3.9	53.1	4.7	27.0	3.4	7.7	—	8.7	55.2	5.7	5.09
Oneonta, N. Y.	19	—	5.1	1.5	60.8	4.7	12.6	2.9	8.4	—	6.6	74.5	3.4	7.49
Buffalo, N. Y.	20	—	5.1	3.2	67.3	2.5	17.0	2.3	1.6	—	8.3	70.8	1.6	7.24
Springfield, Mo.	7	—	4.2	1.8	74.6	6.3	13.1	15.8	5.8	1.3	6.0	80.9	6.3	7.88
Shippensburg, Pa.	17	—	6.2	2.6	28.1	4.3	26.8	—	2.8	—	8.7	82.4	9.8	3.48
Warrensburg, Mo.	3	1.6	3.0	.8	77.6	—	6.4	2.9	4.3	3.5	6.2	77.6	9.8	8.15
Livingston, Ala.	27	—	9.0	2.8	58.0	1.2	18.2	1.5	8.6	—	11.9	69.2	7.8	6.70
Durant, Okla.	21	—	6.4	6.0	68.1	2.1	7.3	—	—	—	12.4	70.2	8.6	7.45
Cullowhee, N. C.	48	2.6	12.9	2.1	60.2	—	24.7	2.3	2.3	1.5	15.1	60.2	2.8	7.81
Pine Bluff, Ark.	24	—	7.6	2.4	46.6	21.2	13.5	41.9	1.8	1.3	12.6	67.8	3.1	5.42
Fayetteville, N. C.	38	—	9.6	2.3	30.8	2.7	9.6	—	—	—	—	33.5	—	4.04
Median		2.6	4.8	2.5	53.8	4.1	19.0	4.4	4.3	1.1	8.7	57.7	3.9	

[1] The institutions are named in order of current expense per attendance week, the one with the highest rate being named first, etc. See Table 24, column 2, for the current expense per attendance week. The institutions at Kutztown, Pa., and Lock Haven, Pa., had the same current expense per attendance week.

To show what proportion of their total current expenses the schools spend for the various purposes the data of Table 26 were computed. This table is to be read as follows: The institution at Johnson, Vt., expended 7.4 per cent of its total current expense for the salary of the principal, 1.9 per cent for other expenses of educational administration, 53.8 per cent for deans and teachers, etc.

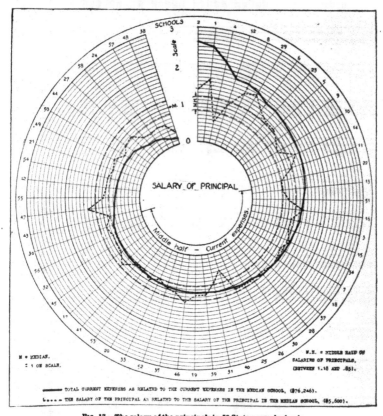

Fig. 17.—The salary of the principals in 58 State normal schools.

Explanation of figure 17. The salary of the principal in 58 State normal schools.

To read curves observe:
  Schools are numbered as in figure 16. (See Table 22.)
  Beginning with school No. 2, schools are arranged around the circle in the decreasing order of their total current expenses. Thus, school No. 2 spends 2.61 times as much as the median, or school No. 31; school No. 1 spends 2.51 times the median, etc.
  The salary of the principal in school No. 2 is 1.39 times the median salary, which is indicated by circle No. 1. The salary of this principal is above the "middle half" since the "dotted" curve meets this radius above the outer "long-dash" circle.
  This school, being No. 2, is second in size as measured by the total number of attendance weeks. Consequently a higher salary than would be indicated by the "middle zone" is to be expected. The total current expenses in this school are higher than those in any other of these 58 schools. The large amount of money expended is another index as to the importance of this principalship and tends to justify a salary above the "middle half."
  The salary of one principal may be compared with that of another by noting the relative distances of the "dotted" curve from the "0" line. Thus, the salary paid the principal in school No. 1 is 3 times as much as the salary of the principal in school No. 4. These two schools are nearly equal in size and incur about the same current expenses. School No. 4 is for colored persons.

TABLE 28.—*Percentages of total current expense of each of 58 State normal schools, which were expended for the different purposes, arranged in order of magnitude.*

[Brace indicates middle half of the percentages.]

	Administration.		Instruction.				Miscellaneous.		Totals.			
		Educational.										
Business.	Salary of principal.	Other expenses.	Deans and teachers.	Textbooks, supplies, etc.	Operation of school plant.	Mainte- nance.	Auxiliary agencies and sundry activities.	Fixed charges as rent and insurance.	Adminis- tration.	Instruc- tion.	Miscel- laneous.	Salaries of principals, deans, and teachers.
1	2	3	4	5	6	7	8	9	10	11	12	13
	13.0		77.6		45.3				40.1	80.9		8.15
	10.0	34.3	74.6		44.5	50.2			18.9	78.3		7.88
	9.6	10.1	74.4		43.1	41.9	28.2		15.2	77.6	29.5	7.78
	9.6	7.4	73.8	21.2	42.3	36.3	13.1		15.1	76.3	13.1	7.78
	9.0	6.5	71.7	13.1	38.6	29.3	10.3		14.7	74.5	10.8	7.75
	7.6	6.2	71.5	9.2	36.8	26.7	9.8		14.6	74.4	9.8	7.71
	7.4	6.0	69.8	8.4	33.1	19.3	9.5		14.3	73.4	9.5	7.49
	7.0	5.4	68.1	8.1	31.6	18.5	8.6		12.6	72.7	9.2	7.45
	7.0	5.2	67.8	7.6	31.5	17.6	7.6		12.4	71.8	8.9	7.31
	7.0	5.1	67.3	6.9	30.2	16.3	7.2		12.3	71.0	8.8	7.24
	6.8	5.1	65.8	6.3	30.1	15.8	7.0		12.3	70.8	8.6	7.23
	6.7	5.1	65.2	6.1	29.7	13.3	6.7		12.0	70.2	8.2	7.05
	6.4	4.7	64.5	6.0	28.0	11.3	6.6		11.9	68.7	7.9	6.97
	6.2	4.5	61.8	5.8	27.7	10.7	6.0		11.9	67.8	7.8	6.95
	6.1	4.2	60.4	5.3	27.1	10.3	5.9		11.1	67.0	7.7	6.81
	6.1	3.9	60.4	5.2	27.0	9.5	5.8		10.9	65.8	7.6	6.79
	5.8	3.9	60.2	5.1	26.9	9.3	5.7		10.6	65.6	7.4	6.62
9.1	5.6	3.5	59.2	5.0	26.8	8.0	5.7		10.6	64.5	6.6	6.55
6.4	5.3	3.5	58.5	4.7	26.7	7.7	5.5	3.5	10.6	64.4	6.5	6.44
5.1	5.3	3.2	58.2	4.7	26.5	7.4	5.3	3.3	9.8	64.1	6.3	6.43
5.0	5.2	3.1	58.0	4.5	26.4	7.3	5.2	3.2	9.7	63.1	5.8	6.38
3.9	5.1	3.0	57.7	4.4	24.7	6.6	5.0	3.2	9.7	61.8	5.7	6.31
3.8	5.1	2.9	57.6	4.3	24.7	6.3	4.8	1.5	9.5	61.4	5.7	6.27
3.6	5.1	2.9	57.3	4.2	23.3	5.7	4.8	1.4	9.3	60.7	5.5	6.24
3.6	5.1	2.8	57.2	4.2	21.1	5.6	4.7	1.3	9.3	60.2	5.3	6.20
3.3	5.0	2.8	55.7	4.1	20.5	5.3	4.5	1.3	9.1	60.1	5.0	6.20
3.2	4.9	2.7	55.6	4.1	19.6	4.9	4.4	1.3	8.9	60.1	4.8	6.12
3.1	4.9	2.6	53.9	4.1	19.2	4.5	4.3	1.2	8.9	59.2	4.7	6.07
[1]2.6	[1]4.8	[1]2.5	[1]53.8	[1]4.1	[1]19.0	[1]4.4	[1]4.3	[1]1.1	[1]8.7	[1]57.7	[1]4.6	[1]5.88
2.6	4.8	2.4	53.1	3.7	18.8	4.0	3.7	1.0	8.7	57.5	4.4	5.96
2.3	4.8	2.4	52.8	3.7	18.4	3.8	3.7	.9	8.5	57.5	3.9	5.80
2.0	4.7	2.4	52.7	3.5	18.2	3.5	3.5	.9	8.3	56.6	3.8	5.73
1.9	4.7	2.4	52.6	3.4	18.0	3.4	3.5	.8	8.3	56.2	3.7	5.69
1.9	4.5	2.3	52.4	3.3	17.9	3.4	3.4	.7	8.1	56.2	3.5	5.59
1.6	4.5	2.3	51.6	3.1	17.8	3.2	2.8	.7	7.9	55.9	3.5	5.56
1.5	4.5	2.3	49.5	3.1	17.6	2.9	2.8	.6	7.9	55.4	3.4	5.42
1.5	4.5	2.1	48.6	3.0	17.2	2.9	2.7	.6	7.8	53.9	3.1	5.30
1.4	4.4	2.0	47.8	2.9	17.0	2.8	2.5	.5	7.7	52.4	2.8	5.29
1.3	4.3	1.9	47.3	2.7	17.0	2.8	2.3	.4	7.6	51.6	2.8	5.26
1.1	4.2	1.9	46.6	2.7	16.5	2.5	2.3	.1	7.5	51.4	2.5	5.22
.9	4.1	1.8	45.3	2.5	16.3	2.5	2.1		7.5	47.3	2.3	5.20
	4.0	1.5	44.4	2.5	15.2	2.5	1.9		7.3	47.3	2.1	4.86
	4.0	1.4	42.6	2.3	15.2	2.3	1.8		7.3	45.1	1.9	4.72
	3.9	1.4	41.6	2.1	14.1	2.3	1.8		7.1	43.1	1.8	4.66
	3.8	1.3	41.4	2.0	13.9	2.3	1.7		6.9	42.9	1.7	4.64
	3.8	1.3	40.6	1.7	13.5	2.2	1.6		6.9	42.7	1.6	4.64
	3.7	1.3	39.8	1.7	13.4	2.0	1.5		6.7	40.8	1.5	4.57
	3.5	1.1	36.7	1.6	13.1	1.8	1.4		6.6	40.8	1.4	4.12
	3.4	1.0	33.6	1.6	12.7	1.8	1.4		6.6	37.8	1.4	4.04
	3.3	1.0	31.8	1.2	12.6	1.7	1.4		6.2	33.7	1.4	3.88
	3.1	.8	30.8	1.2	11.8	1.5	.8		6.2	33.5	.8	3.43
	3.1	.6	29.5	1.2	10.4	1.2	.7		6.0	33.4	.7	3.43
	2.8	.6	28.1	1.0	10.1	1.1	.6		6.0	32.9	.6	3.40
	2.8	.5	27.1	.9	9.7	.9	.5		6.0	32.4	.5	3.24
	2.7	.4	25.3	.1	9.6	.9	.2		6.0	28.9	.2	2.80
	2.5	.4	23.8		7.3	.8			5.1	28.7		2.73
	2.2		23.6		6.4				4.6	24.5		2.73
	1.2		22.4		4.4				4.1	23.6		2.36

[1] Median.

Table 28 shows the percentages of Table 25 arranged in serial order. This gives some idea of the variation among the different percentages expended for the various functions. It also shows the middle half of each group of percentages. With its use the relative expenditures of an institution can easily be compared with the general practice of the 58 schools. Thus, for example, school No. 2 falls below the middle half on the percentage expended for business administration, below the middle half on the salary of the president, below the middle half on other expenses of educational administration, above the middle half on the salaries of deans and teachers, above the middle half on textbooks and supplies of instruction, within the middle half on operation of school plant, below the middle half on maintenance, within the middle half on auxiliary agencies and sundry activities, and below the middle half on fixed charges.

ACCURACY.

Every precaution was taken to secure accuracy in this study of normal schools. There may be, however, some errors in the computed data. There seem to be a few errors in certain reports as has been noted above in the discussion of the wide deviation from the median in the cost of maintenance. There is also a slight error due to using the median instead of the arithmetical mean as the average. The median is a counting average and is not much affected by extremely high or low cost. Thus, in Table 24 the sum of the median amounts in columns 3-11, inclusive, is $5.76, while the median amount in column 2 is $6.43. To be ideal a school would spend $6.43 per attendance week and at the same time to be ideal on the distribution of its expenditures the total cost per attendance week would be only $5.76. The variation here, it will be noted, is restricted to about 10 per cent. A similar error may be noted in Table 28. The sum of the median percentages in columns 1-9, inclusive, is 96.6, instead of 100. This is due to the fact that the median is a counting average and is not mathematically exact, which means that extremely high and low cost do not materially affect it. In the case of the arithmetical mean or common average, extremely high cost or low cost affects the average very materially. In this chapter, in this study of expenditures, it is thought best to use the median rather than the arithmetical average because extremely high costs for any purpose may be due to erroneous reports. By its use the general effect of an erroneous distribution of expenditures in a few schools is minimized. The median, therefore, shows the central tendency better than the arithmetical average in studying expenditures.

SUMMER SESSIONS, 1917.

TABLE 29.—*Distribution of normal schools according to the number of weeks in the summer sessions of 1917.*

Weeks in summer session.	Number of schools.		Weeks in summer session.	Number of schools.	
	State.	Private.		State.	Private.
4	9	4	10	14	
5	2	2	11	4	
6	65	8	12	18	2
7					
8	12		Total number of reports	130	16
9	6				

The summer sessions of normal schools are an important item. There were 130 reported in State normal schools and 16 in private normal schools for the summer of 1917.

From Table 29 it is evident that the most common length of summer session was 6 'weeks, and the next most common was 12 weeks.

TABLE 30.—*Distribution of normal schools according to the number of instructors in the summer sessions of 1917.*

Number of instructors.	Number of schools.		Number of instructors.	Number of schools.	
	State.	Private.		State.	Private.
1-5	4	2	41-45	10	
6-10	13	4	46-50	2	
11-15	16	4	51-55	3	
16-20	18	2	56-60	4	
21-25	17	2	More than 60	[1] 8	
26-30	12	1	Total number of reports	125	16
31-35	9	1			
36-40	9				

[1] 61, 70, 74, 79, 81, 88, 92, and 98.

From Table 30 some knowledge of the size of faculty in the summer sessions may be noted. A total of 3,582 instructors, an average of almost 29 per school, was reported by 125 State schools, while 16 private schools reported a total of 240 instructors, an average of 15 per school.

TABLE 31.—*Distribution of normal schools according to the number of students enrolled in the summer sessions of 1917.*

Students enrolled.	Number of schools.		Students enrolled.	Number of schools.	
	State.	Private.		State.	Private.
1–25.	1	4	501–600.	12	1
26–50.	6	1	601–700.	7	....
51–75.	5	2	701–800.	5	....
76–100.	4	3	801–900.	3	....
			901–1,000.	1	....
1–100.	16	10	1,001–1,100.	4	....
101–200.	25	3	More than 1,100.	¹ 9	....
201–300.	17	....			
301–400.	13	....	Total number of reports....	116	15
401–500.	4	1			

¹ 1,254, 1,333, 1,377, 1,505, 1,606, 1,700, 1,731, 1,960, and 2,255.

The size of the student body is shown in Table 31. A number of summer schools are very large, 13 enrolling more than 1,000 students. A total of 52,810 students was reported enrolled by 116 State schools, an average of about 445 per school, while 15 private normal schools reported for the summer an enrollment of 1,814, an average of about 121 per school.

CHANGES IN THE NORMAL SCHOOL LIST.

I. State normal schools:

Reporting in 1916 but not in 1918—

> Moundville, Ala., State Normal School.
> El Rito, N. Mex., Spanish-American Normal School.
> Memphis, Tenn., West Tennessee State Normal School.
> Murfreesboro, Tenn., Middle Tennessee State Normal School.
> Athens, W. Va., Concord State Normal School.

Reporting in 1918 but not in 1916—

> Commerce, Tex., East Texas Normal College.
> Eau Claire, Wis., State Normal School.

No longer rated as a normal school—

> Pembroke, N. C., Indian Normal College.

Transferred to the list of private normal schools—

> Tuskegee, Ala., Tuskegee Normal and Industrial Institute.
> Hampton, Va., Hampton Normal and Agricultural Institute.

II. City normal schools:

Reporting in 1916 but not in 1918—

> Shenandoah, Iowa, Western Normal College.
> Cohoes, N. Y., Cohoes Training School.

Reporting in 1918 but not in 1916—

> Albert Lea, Minn., Albert Lea High School.
> Pittsburgh, Pa., Pittsburgh Training School for Teachers.

III. County normal schools:
    Reporting in 1918 but not in 1916—

        Ludington, Mich., Mason County Normal School.
        Manistee, Mich., Manistee County Normal School.
        All of the county normal schools of Ohio which reported.

IV. Private normal schools:
    Reporting in 1916 but not in 1918—

        Pea Ridge, Ark., Pea Ridge Masonic College.
        Madison, Fla., Florida Normal Institute.
        Marion, Ind., Marion Normal Institute.
        Muncie, Ind., Muncie National Institute.
        Bloomfield, Iowa, Normal and Scientific Institute.
        Boston, Mass., Boston Normal School of Gymnastics.
        New York, N. Y., Jenny Hunter Kindergarten Training School.
        Philadelphia, Pa., Froebellian School for Women.
        Memphis, Tenn., La Moyne Normal Institute.
        Richmond, Va., Richmond Training School for Kindergartners.

    Reporting in 1918 but not in 1916—

        Chicago, Ill., Normal School of Physical Education.
        Chicago, Ill., Technical Normal School of Chicago.
        Ammendale, Md., Ammendale Normal Institute.
        Cambridge, Mass., Lesley Normal School.
        Santee, Nebr., Santee Normal Training School.
        Newark, N. J., Newark Normal School for Physical Education and
            Hygiene.
        Bridgeport, Conn., Connecticut Froebel Kindergarten and Primary
            Training School.
        Hartford, Conn., Culver-Smith Kindergarten Training School.
        Washington, D. C., Columbia Kindergarten Training School.
        Miami, Fla., Miami Kindergarten Normal School
        Chicago, Ill., Pestalozzi-Froebel Kindergarten Training School.
        Springfield, Mass., Springfield Normal Kindergarten Training School.
        Grand Rapids, Mich., Grand Rapids Kindergarten Training School.
        Cincinnati, Ohio, Cincinnati Kindergarten Training School.
        Oberlin, Ohio, Oberlin Kindergarten Training School.
        Harrisburg, Pa., Froebel Kindergarten Training School.
        Dallas, Tex., Dallas Kindergarten Training School.
        Fort Worth, Tex., Fort Worth Kindergarten and Teachers' Training
            School.

GENERAL SUMMARY.

State normal schools.—Of the types of normal schools herein discussed the State schools are by far the most important in the training of teachers. These institutions have increased in number in the period 1900-1918. They have also increased in size as measured by the average size of faculty, the average enrollment, the average size of library, and the average income.

The distribution tables on the number of instructors, the enrollment, the amount of practice teaching, the model and practice school enrollment, the property valuation, the size of library, and the total expenditures indicate that there is great variation among the different State normal schools in these respects.

Wide differences exist in the policies of the different States regarding their State normal schools. Several States provide many institutions, while a number of States provide only one or two. Only 42 States have State normal schools separately organized; 3 States have State teachers' colleges.

The policies of administration and control are very different in the different States. In Wisconsin, for example, all receipts which the schools received from fees, productive funds, etc., are turned over to the central State authorities. All available receipts for the schools come directly from State appropriations. A somewhat similar policy of centralized control obtains in several other States, as in Massachusetts and Connecticut. In most States, however, administrative control is not so highly centralized, the individual schools having greater freedom in this matter.

A third difference in State policies pertains to the financial support of the State normal schools. Figure 15 shows that the proportion of total income for current expenses which comes from public funds varies in the different States, it being over 97 per cent in one State and about 20 per cent in another.

It is a notable fact that in later years a smaller percentage of the income of State normal schools was appropriated from public funds than was the case in the earlier part of the period 1900–1918 (see fig. 13).

The study of expenditures shows that there is great variation in this item as to the total amounts spent by the different schools, as to the proportionate amounts spent for various purposes.

The summer schools are a very important feature in the work of the State normal schools.

City and county normal schools.—The number of city normal schools remained almost the same throughout the period considered. Several of these are large institutions, as was noted in the discussion of the distribution tables. Others are not so large, the instructors being few in number and the enrollment frequently small. These schools usually have large practice schools and give much attention to this phase of training.

The county normal schools are of more recent development than are the city normal schools. In late years they have increased rapidly in number. They are becoming an important factor in the training of teachers.

Private normal schools.—The number of private normal schools decreased rapidly in the period 1900–1918. In general, the average private normal school of later years is larger than was the average private normal school of earlier years. This means one of two things, either that the larger schools tend to survive or that the schools which continue are becoming larger. Private normal schools tend to become a less important factor in the training of teachers. They are yet, however, important in training teachers, especially teachers for special phases of work, such as physical education and kindergarten teaching.

150407°—20——5

TABLE 32.—*State normal schools—Number and personnel, 1917–18.*

			Instructors.						Students.							Graduates in 1918.		Enrollment in model schools.
States.	Schools reporting.	Summer sessions reporting.	Total for year. Men.	Total for year. Women.	Summer session. Men.	Summer session. Women.	Half-time or more in normal courses. Men.	Half-time or more in normal courses. Women.	Total for year. Men.	Total for year. Women.	Summer session. Men.	Summer session. Women.	Normal courses. Men.	Normal courses. Women.	Extension and correspondence courses.	Men.	Women.	
1	2	3	4	5	6	7	8	9	10	11	12	13	14	15	16	17	18	19
United States	172	127	2,563	4,073	1,698	1,894	1,587	2,571	18,183	101,974	5,971	46,839	12,408	84,211	‡8,088	1,896	17,716	‡64,320
Alabama	7	7	62	77	50	45	29	33	311	2,091	57	422	228	1,367	58	62	280	1,036
Arizona	2	1	30	32	12	13	29	31	216	755	15	214	64	497	30	4	139	587
Arkansas	2	1	25	17	10	10	14	12	226	696	16	284	94	449		12	29	65
California	8	6	75	227	33	67	77	219	202	4,238	51	729	202	4,238	687	53	1,111	3,497
Colorado	1	1	14	23	14	23	14	23	85	462	25	325	25	395	135	1	54	252
Connecticut	4	1	36	107	16	6	12	47	107	963	103	346	107	952	70	4	334	4,045
Georgia	3	1	21	97	4	6	12	36	17	1,902		136	9	1,728	60	1	406	540
Idaho	2	1	18	42	8	14	8	14	85	872	51	272	69	829	41	2	95	568
Illinois	5	5	129	165	121	128	123	165	1,148	6,059	278	3,704	902	5,818	902	81	491	2,164
Indiana	1	1	32	10	32	10			683	1,367	342	1,035	683	1,367		35	109	275
Kansas	3	3	99	133	99	133	27	28	1,148	4,703	511	3,003	624	3,219	254	116	471	1,086
Kentucky	3	3	41	55	41	50	27	22	441	1,756	36	376	395	1,642		21	112	538
Louisiana	1	1	28	31	15	15	7	40	281	1,309	165	771	202	1,088	4	28	231	489
Maine	5	1	14	70	1	6	12	16	26	654	2	62	26	654		11	297	1,265
Maryland	3	2	15	23	12	9			15	619	4	288	15	574		4	136	295
Massachusetts	10	2	86	217	14	13	82	212	186	2,529	53	223	198	2,529	114	32	910	4,756
Michigan	4	4	121	185	100	150	67	93	851	5,214	483	3,282	808	5,066	1,233	144	1,550	1,612
Minnesota	5	5	64	112	51	61	64	141	140	3,573	68	1,921	140	3,573	64	32	608	2,836
Mississippi	1	1	16	11	16	11			92	745			92	745		6	25	17
Missouri	6	5	130	143	136	126	59	71	1,410	5,489	821	3,962	1,057	4,209	868	282	843	1,150
Montana	1	1	12	14	8	12	8	12	22	513	11	228	12	451	138	2	67	500
Nebraska	4	4	63	103	63	73	85	100	489	3,081	145	1,923	277	1,855	0	37	308	592
New Hampshire	5	1	12	57	6	10	10	28		274				274			122	
New Jersey	8		19	106			10	71	88	2,014			88	2,014	250	87	1,078	1,455
New Mexico	2	2			26	32			441	1,385	205	903	231	1,006		10	66	160

	1	2	3	4	5	6	7	8	9	10	11	12	13	14	15	16	17	18
New York	10	3	78	240	12	27	40	128	510	3,943	33	1,098	113	3,357	258	50	1,431	8,465
North Carolina	6	—	53	156	37	53	37	71	472	2,628	33	1,353	190	1,242	—	10	160	796
Ohio	4	4	52	71	43	46	51	63	243	1,628	80	1,853	143	1,477	49	19	284	796
North Dakota	2	1	52	66	28	46	28	48	143	1,881	89	1,416	143	1,981	728	18	259	551
Oklahoma	7	7	165	115	162	110	63	58	1,777	6,706	871	5,087	636	2,082	310	76	405	838
Oregon	1	1	8	20	6	12	8	20	40	850	3	397	40	850	6	—	155	2,674
Pennsylvania	13	5	166	222	29	28	70	111	1,337	5,253	55	396	1,194	5,107	183	282	1,688	2,760
Rhode Island	1	1	11	61	9	12	11	14	10	471	10	190	10	471	42	—	114	446
South Carolina	2	2	59	86	24	33	27	36	330	2,587	54	1,193	190	2,251	501	29	224	649
South Dakota	4	4	57	118	35	42	35	47	471	2,033	65	884	308	1,601	—	15	191	649
Tennessee	2	2	30	41	22	38	24	29	270	944	100	400	155	740	—	23	110	331
Texas	6	6	165	115	141	108	98	78	1,626	5,599	591	2,928	1,638	5,439	27	104	334	821
Vermont	2	2	6	31	5	24	6	29	—	394	—	374	—	394	—	—	46	161
Virginia	5	5	70	172	48	93	42	121	145	4,073	40	2,323	28	2,805	710	1	345	2,700
Washington	3	3	64	97	63	81	63	95	212	2,200	54	595	198	2,112	118	35	729	2,167
West Virginia	6	4	54	55	14	11	18	27	526	1,242	51	305	70	442	188	30	250	2,970
Wisconsin	10	10	238	283	129	98	185	179	1,458	5,950	344	2,522	999	5,311	—	172	1,075	2,494
Colored only.																		
Alabama	2	2	28	26	17	12	10	11	141	406	9	154	89	346	8	11	23	407
Arkansas	1	1	14	7	—	—	3	2	108	283	—	49	8	16	—	3	4	—
Kentucky	1	1	13	12	13	12	11	8	106	307	14	49	60	193	—	8	33	61
Maryland	1	1	4	3	4	—	4	2	6	80	1	44	6	79	—	1	11	33
Missouri	—	—	14	11	—	—	0	0	40	—	—	—	11	26	—	11	26	80
North Carolina	3	3	26	37	12	11	14	14	365	939	73	444	58	351	—	5	4	484
Oklahoma	1	1	15	10	15	10	16	12	144	532	22	278	29	229	—	8	39	30
South Carolina	1	1	40	19	7	8	11	14	284	489	8	153	144	310	—	29	48	45
Tennessee	1	1	17	26	9	23	21	14	130	259	—	—	16	57	—	5	16	106
Texas	1	1	21	11	24	11	3	17	300	932	12	258	300	932	—	47	110	30
Virginia	1	1	23	46	10	22	—	—	118	750	—	—	13	406	—	1	11	—
West Virginia	—	—	16	10	—	—	—	—	101	182	—	—	3	35	—	3	35	233
United States	15	13	233	228	111	110	93	91	1,905	5,301	140	1,431	766	2,980	8	132	360	1,461

[1] 5,375 in extension courses, 2,276 in correspondence courses, 437 in both (not separated) courses.

[2] Of this number 18,599 are in public or in partly public schools.

TABLE 33.—State normal schools—Property, 1917-18.

States	Schools in the State	Bound volumes in the library. Number of reports	Number	Library apparatus, machinery, furniture. Number of reports	Value	Grounds and buildings. Number of reports	Value	Amount of endowment funds. Number of reports	Amount	Total value of property, including endowments.
	2	3	4	5	6	7	8	9	10	11
United States	176	166	1,855,644	162	$8,251,883	167	$8,459,495	68	$2,043,782	$68,755,150
Alabama	8	7	27,250	6	104,165	6	812,300	6	0	916,465
Arizona	2	2	17,680	2	215,665	2	925,825	0	0	1,144,490
Arkansas	2	2	6,567	2	37,043	2	289,597	2	0	326,640
California	8	8	122,682	8	391,533	8	3,120,744	0	0	3,512,097
Colorado	1	1	6,000	1	8,500	1	60,000	0	0	68,500
Connecticut	4	4	53,307	3	45,000	3	545,000	1	0	520,000
Georgia	3	3	21,091	3	132,000	3	1,075,700	1	1,000	1,208,700
Idaho	2	2	9,456	2	73,354	2	356,246	1	7,658	439,258
Illinois	5	4	95,426	5	545,826	5	3,104,751	1	108,225	3,758,803
In land	1	1	76,623	1	315,000	1	1,000,000	1	0	1,315,000
Kansas	3	3	73,831	3	104,500	3	2,181,000	1	255,357	2,540,870
Kentucky	3	2	13,374	1	93,568	1	840,840	2	0	984,408
Louisiana	1	1	9,916	1	158,720	1	361,600	0	0	520,300
Maine	5	5	11,900	5	58,000	5	652,200	4	0	710,202
Maryland	3	3	5,650	2	27,500	3	901,500	0	0	928,500
Massachusetts	10	9	65,901	6	157,450	9	3,361,585	7	1,500	3,520,535
Michigan	4	4	107,400	8	273,698	4	2,114,547	0	0	2,458,245
Minnesota	5	5	144,132	5	207,483	5	2,051,865	1	30,000	2,289,346
Mississippi	1	1	6,060	1	32,208	1	424,948	0	0	457,158
Missouri	6	5	96,251	5	238,484	5	2,085,000	2	1,000	2,379,484
Montana	1	1	10,220	1	18,000	1	269,000	0	0	287,009
Nebraska	4	4	54,571	4	217,000	3	1,264,000	0	0	1,471,000
New Hampshire	2	2	9,000	2	14,000	2	370,000	2	0	384,000
New Jersey	3	3	25,743	3	217,224	3	1,802,030	1	0	2,023,754
New Mexico	2	2	15,000	2	45,730	2	279,619	0	4,500	328,240

New York	10	9	103,767	10	668,498	10	3,349,800	3	250,000	4,287,989
North Carolina	6	6	10,435	5	61,783	6	1,195,550	4	0	1,257,312
North Dakota	4	4	27,892	4	172,589	4	1,127,242	2	373,452	1,673,312
Ohio	2	2	31,000	2	173,647	2	1,316,263	0		1,489,913
Oklahoma	7	7	39,970	7	162,062	7	1,137,817	2		1,299,839
Oregon	1	1	6,220	1	20,000	1	215,000	1	0	226,002
Pennsylvania	13	12	104,241	13	825,767	13	5,998,185	3	0	6,823,050
Rhode Island	1	1	23,600	1	150,000	1	650,000	1	0	800,000
South Carolina	2	2	21,199	2	186,709	2	1,252,822	1	1,008,214	1,419,531
South Dakota	4	4	26,980	4	106,653	4	1,262,300	2		2,370,166
Tennessee	4	2	4,452	2	31,755	2	431,734	0	0	463,489
Texas	6	6	70,333	6	320,050	6	1,750,063	1		2,070,113
Vermont	2	2	10,528	2	22,712	2	44,000	0	0	66,712
Virginia	5	5	23,685	5	184,483	5	1,470,379	3	2,845	1,657,707
Washington	3	3	48,000	3	175,443	3	1,168,260	1	0	1,342,705
West Virginia	7	6	30,932	6	120,388	6	1,457,000	4	0	1,557,388
Wisconsin	10	10	191,299	10	1,010,914	10	4,349,075	5	0	5,369,989
Colored only.										
Alabama	2	2	8,250	2	32,000	2	287,300	2	0	269,300
Arkansas	1	1	2,150	1	1,537	1	88,500	1	0	90,037
Kentucky	1	1	3,701	1	9,372	1	124,000	0		133,372
Maryland	1	1	250	1	2,500	1	32,000	0		34,500
Missouri	1	1	3,914	1	4,636	1	205,000	0		209,636
North Carolina	3	3	2,284	3	10,850	3	146,645	2		157,495
Oklahoma	1	1	300	1	6,000	1	176,000	0		182,000
South Carolina	1	1	550	1	25,000	1	307,000	0		332,000
Tennessee	1	1	1,452	1	16,755	1	146,734	0		163,489
Texas	1	1	500	1	25,000	1	343,950	0		368,950
Virginia	1	1	1,500	1	36,483	1	222,379	1	0	258,862
West Virginia	1	1	1,800	1	6,000	1	290,000	1	0	296,000
United States	15	15	25,651	15	176,133	15	2,309,508	7	0	2,485,641

TABLE 34.—State normal schools—Receipts, 1917-18.

States.	Schools in the State.	From student fees. Tuition, etc. Num-ber of re-ports.	Amount.	Board, room, etc. Num-ber of re-ports.	Amount.	From productive funds. Num-ber of re-ports.	Amount.	From public funds. For increase of plant. Num-ber of re-ports.	Amount.	For current expenses. Num-ber of re-ports.	Amount.	From all other sources. Num-ber of re-ports.	Amount.	Total available for use. Num-ber of re-ports.	Amount.
1	2	3	4	5	6	7	8	9	10	11	12	13	14	15	16
United States	176	142	$1,417,099	107	$2,762,525	50	$147,583	96	$4,182,716	170	$11,253,150	96	$1,022,479	170	$20,512,706
Alabama	8	6	44,211	5	76,174	4	397	3	3,000	7	106,000	6	36,178	7	294,960
Arizona	2	2	6,425	2	79,814	1	2,491	3	152,500	2	193,000	1	4,750	2	438,975
Arkansas	2	2	5,876	2	19,251	1	960	2	61,996	2	59,430	2	13,636	2	161,149
California	8	5	7,476	3	0	3	0	8	1,060,846	8	699,141	6	10,676	8	1,778,139
Colorado	1	1	6,500	0		0		1	19,555	1	65,134	1	11,000	1	102,229
Connecticut	4	4	78,989	2	2,006	0		2	22,951	4	125,226	0		4	229,550
Georgia	3	3	19,178	2	68,992	0		1	82,500	3	155,000	2	12,900	3	338,640
Idaho	2	2	3,025	2	39,927	0		1	75,400	2	179,496	2	6,097	2	303,944
Illinois	5	5	42,153	5	76,942	1	6,494	5	182,146	5	656,518	2	30,483	5	994,726
Indiana	1	1	7,000	1	0	1		1	86,347	1	227,469	1	9,000	1	329,816
Kansas	3	3	70,674	0	43,666	1	12,384	3	199,389	3	384,945	1	11,500	3	657,983
Kentucky	3	3	7,337	3	103,687	0		1	0	3	171,000	3	36,639	3	288,640
Louisiana	1	1	12,610	1	6,000	1	6,273	0	0	1	66,750	1	2,283	1	193,603
Maine	5	2	0	2	33,791	2	0	2	0	5	104,536	3	2,500	5	111,036
Maryland	3	1	857	1		0		0		3	90,000	3	2,506	3	116,184
Massachusetts	10	8	$3,565	8	$161,920	1	0	3	140,000	9	683,080	7	2,813	9	974,280
Michigan	4	4	68,176	0		2	5,636	2	116,522	4	591,533	3	8,902	4	785,569
Minnesota	5	4	21,161	3	72,617	4	5,408	1	34,230	5	409,399	2	15,413	5	545,122
Mississippi	1	1	8,736	0		0		1	6,500	1	48,000	1	229	1	58,465
Missouri	5	5	111,416	1	30,101	1	55	2	18,144	0	480,904	3	19,406	0	659,696
Montana	1	1	3,896	1	30,248	0	0	1	52,500	1	75,000	0		1	161,683
Nebraska	4	3	$9,610	3	$8,328	0		2	19,145	3	282,500	2	18,869	3	334,452
New Hampshire	3	3	33,369	2	$28,014	1	170	1	0	3	66,500	2	6,227	3	106,061
New Jersey	3	0		2	$75,774	1	0	1	3,000	3	362,919	1	20	2	441,883
New Mexico	2	2	11,966	2	$26,018	1	5,415	2	35,512	2	96,942	2	40,043	2	199,380

New York	10	4	¹2,783	0	184,815	0	256	5	113,006	10	560,403	1	280,714	10	940,783
North Carolina	4	6	45,905	0	78,304	2	48,994	3	82,330	0	218,640	5	22,053	0	556,718
North Dakota	4	4	33,115	4	66,561	4	0	2	6,338	4	289,320	2	38,333	4	446,411
Ohio	2	2	7,563	2	13,961	0		2	179,140	2	361,078	1	1,541	2	482,059
Oklahoma	7	3		2		1	0	4	84,098	7	896,401	2	5,133	7	456,181
Oregon	1	1	6,844	0		0		1	25,000	1	85,181	1	16,276	1	82,991
Pennsylvania	13	13	362,205	12	716,885	3	6,887	2	59,320	13	309,356	1	126,575	3	1,001,338
Rhode Island	1	1	9,000	0		0		0		1	74,000	0		1	83,000
South Carolina	2	2	49,222	2	140,330	1	22,072	2	52,914	2	134,076	0		2	444,360
South Dakota	4	4	39,164	3	8,276	3		3	248,535	4	261,352	0	67,818	4	569,069
Tennessee	6	2	7,370	3	40,616	1	2,047	0		2	79,978	1	12,000	2	141,920
Texas	2	6	68,861	3	106,595	3	12,648	0	406,221	6	505,957	4	54,794	6	1,100,180
Vermont	5	1		3	13,610	2	39	0		2	40,100	5	2,189	0	56,631
Virginia	2	5	30,749	3	261,687	1	428	3	12,000	5	290,383	2		5	598,251
Washington	3	2	23,772	3	46,236	1	900	3	51,215	3	340,666	2	61,000	8	475,139
West Virginia	7	5	17,601	3	40,776	1	0	2	10,000	0	221,275	2		0	310,440
Wisconsin	10	10	⁵113,07·	4	⁵58,976	2	⁴7,784	10	538,813	10	1,006,198	3	17,76	10	1,544,999
Colored only.															
Alabama	2	1	2,962	1	840	1	0	0	20,000	2	20,000	2	99,617	2	53,419
Arkansas	1	1	795	1	246	0	990	0	12,000	1	12,000	1	13,636	1	27,637
Kentucky	1	1	288	1	11,456	1		0	21,000	1	21,000	1	14,102	1	46,846
Maryland	1	0		0		0		0		1	10,000	1	440	1	10,440
Missouri	1	0		0		0		1		1	33,682	1	6,983	1	40,966
North Carolina	3	3	2,711	3	16,137	1	256	1	0	3	22,449	3	5,024	3	46,577
Oklahoma	1	0		1	13,961	0		0		1	50,537	1	5,133	1	69,031
South Carolina	1	1	2,432	1	6,000	0		0	44,500	1	20,000	1	67,818	1	140,750
Tennessee	1	1	2,783	1	18,243	0		1		1	26,669	1	12,000	1	60,687
Texas	1	1	8,778	1	108,596	1	12,648	0	68,150	1	74,147	1	12,500	1	284,819
Virginia	1	1	6,676	1	42,637	0		1	2,000	1	30,250	1	17,571	1	99,134
West Virginia	1	1	2,070	1	15,591	1	0	1		1	51,850	1	16,880	1	86,391
United States	15	11	29,495	12	234,709	5	13,894	6	114,650	15	372,574	15	201,704	15	966,996

¹ This does not include the items in the following notes: 2, 3, 5, and 6.
² $1,323 of this is not included in column 16.
³ $24,715 of this is not included in column 16.
⁴ The report of the State Normal School at Chadron is not included in this table as the receipts were not completely reported.
⁵ Not included in column 16.
⁶ $15,549 of this is not included in column 16.

TABLE 35.—State normal schools—Expenditures, 1917-18.

States	Number reporting	Administration — Business	Educational — Salary of principal	Educational — Other expenses	Instruction — Deans and teachers	Instruction — Text-books, supplies, etc.	Operation of school plant.	Maintenance.	Auxiliary agencies and sundry activities.	Fixed charges (rent, insurance, etc.).	Total current expenses.	Outlays (capital acquisition and construction).	Payment of indebtedness.
	2	3	4	5	6	7	8	9	10	11	12	13	14
United States	163	$244,444	$600,066	$414,605	$7,348,370	$564,657	$3,159,937	$1,236,834	$667,485	$88,777	$14,525,175	$2,944,174	$193,974
Alabama	6	24,284	16,100	7,025	95,654	7,253	49,339	24,121	4,912	2,803	231,533	4,811	
Arizona	2	8,208	9,900	5,945	115,536	24,179	43,433	16,644	54,163	2,274	280,202	129,712	4,135
Arkansas	2	1,158	5,040	3,217	46,736	5,704	17,760	18,295	2,011	3,900	103,821	70,459	
California	8	8,751	32,419	20,536	463,430	23,415	76,339	43,214	31,353		699,457	58,488	
Colorado	1	8,964	4,050	2,415	43,655	2,800	6,037	5,500	7,210	400	81,031	1,500	1,016
Connecticut	4	3,604	14,000	2,700	139,204	9,332	22,543	8,679	6,576		205,638	22,951	
Georgia	2	530	6,460	3,060	75,883	1,896	25,846	7,749	4,742	978	125,196	179,522	
Idaho	2	2,017	6,875	4,660	85,128	2,594	32,556	26,096	7,261	835	166,167	35,400	
Illinois	5	2,602	25,000	17,335	409,544	32,372	171,485	28,072	29,755	714	717,000	117,847	
Indiana	1	1,535	7,000	5,300	135,000	3,155	81,691	6,375	12,704		253,564	73,046	
Kansas	3	1,321	15,000	24,233	318,033	16,540	76,691	5,750	22,013		480,080	54,350	
Kentucky	3	5,162	10,200	8,049	105,439	4,000	37,654	16,262	1,850		198,616		
Louisiana	1	1,800	4,000	3,115	56,163	4,419	32,104	36,360	58,640	1,701	198,202	1,545	6,030
Maine	5		11,950	1,735	59,741	1,735	21,740	1,925	475		99,301	250	
Maryland	3	1,562	7,400	2,007	30,784	3,187	23,478	4,902	4,476	7	77,803		
Massachusetts	9	2,297	30,521	21,480	280,413	32,741	307,557	59,382	4,235	5,627	738,606	149,000	
Michigan	4	15,773	18,750	23,995	519,645	24,748	129,200	14,396	32,633		784,778	121,375	
Minnesota	5	4,650		26,098	247,803	17,890	99,871	49,773	14,669		486,060	5,784	
Mississippi	1	2,865	3,500	2,371	29,237	973	6,013	183	3,324		48,465	10,000	
Missouri	6	4,187	20,990	18,638	345,855	14,062	88,941	37,175	34,402	6,451	570,611	8,000	5,088
Montana	1		4,000	4,068	46,529	493	16,055	1,501	2,945	225	75,916	54,000	
Nebraska	4	62	12,000	16,720	218,427	15,132	70,775	24,267	18,047		375,358	230,823	
New Hampshire	2			1,952	56,448	6,931	28,343	2,699	940		104,435		
New Jersey	3	10,079	15,900	7,627	173,734	37,338	82,893	61,896	12,728	1,732	403,925	2,244	
New Mexico	2	387	7,947	6,079	60,526	29,563	8,148	47,646	3,616	156	163,068	19	

New York	10	7,150	37,630	10,200	381,004	34,679	92,278	43,313	11,200	657	618,331	241,825		
North Carolina	6	5,784	12,600	6,351	154,312	15,433	208,668	37,083	41,108	637	432,176	76,506		
North Dakota	4	7,455	14,004	10,629	146,968	8,265	82,681	26,141	17,328		318,301	85,050		
Ohio	2	7,522	8,800	5,545	115,821	6,635	51,875	4,912	12,631		210,141	62,509		
Oklahoma	7	960	17,930	15,981	238,064	3,706	37,973	11,887	18,556	4,842	344,407	47,110	2,100
Oregon	1		3,000	1,400	30,644	44,894	14,292	1,000	3,500		54,488	28,255	
Pennsylvania	13	23,613	47,000	15,369	343,112	7,000	405,191	286,030	123,799	30,177	1,319,794	97,454	166,346
Rhode Island	1		4,000	2,500	47,500	11,645	17,000	3,300	1,700		83,000		
South Carolina	2	21,568	7,000	6,218	107,639	13,043	88,947	38,220	68,318	7,343	326,928	42,322	2,023
South Dakota	4	6,628	13,000	10,104	131,905		89,504	34,823	8,203		328,110	106,042	
Tennessee	1	2,500	2,400	1,900	17,600	900	13,548	4,000	2,306	5,690	45,033	7,096	
Texas	6	12,856	17,800	14,402	381,648	31,086	118,421	88,891	16,962	915	687,755	429,299	
Vermont	2		4,100	765	22,487	1,787	8,385	3,886	4,354	3,281	46,659		8,166
Virginia	5	10,802	15,000	5,917	133,062	8,859	135,771	47,108	71,570	732	431,382	27,945	
Washington	3	11,977	14,300	11,701	181,071	9,468	64,864	13,782	22,980	20	330,875	60,915	
West Virginia	6		15,900	20,040	139,460	5,046	32,702	12,900	10,064		226,522	10,000	
Wisconsin	10	17,496	42,750	35,444	596,338	39,042	171,644	31,368	56,122	6,680	906,882	280,714	
Colored only.													
Alabama	2		3,800	1,705	25,030		12,312	1,524	630	985	45,356	3,161	
Arkansas	1	700	2,040	650	12,546	5,704	3,642	610	950	400	26,922	914	
Kentucky	1	54	2,440	1,500	19,811	1,335	12,465	5,942	420		44,406		
Maryland	1	1,083	1,400		2,082	67	12,830	215			7,068		
Missouri	1				20,551		13,999	2,797			38,450		
North Carolina	3	171	3,400	1,187	14,679	1,180	8,134	10,239	926	311	40,227	1,842	
Oklahoma	1	960		1,360	31,790		7,659	98	985		41,402	9,133	
South Carolina	1		2,000	1,900	36,299	3,309	18,819	11,763	778		74,328	18,850	
Tennessee	1	2,500	2,400	1,638	17,600	900	13,548	4,000	2,306		45,033	7,096	
Texas	1	3,156	2,000	715	37,071	927	71,465	44,237	4,121		165,045	119,174	
Virginia	1	2,470	1,700	1,920	13,513	572	14,558	4,542	46,077		87,047	9,621	3,200
West Virginia	1		1,900		32,000	1,000	8,200		1,993		47,002		3,200
United States	15	11,104	23,040	12,575	262,985	15,884	187,661	85,967	61,984	1,696	682,900	166,791	

TABLE 36.—*City and county normal schools—Personnel and property, 1917-18.*

States	Number of reports	Personnel						Property				
		Number of teachers including the principal.		Number of different students attending.¹		Number of graduates from normal course.		Library.		Number of reports.	Value.	
		Men.	Women.	Men.	Women.	Men.	Women.	Number of reports.	Bound volumes.		Library, apparatus, machinery, furniture.	Ground and buildings.
1	2	3	4	5	6	7	8	9	10	11	12	13
United States	79	236	742	277	8,071	132	3,276	70	163,111	61	$226,171	$4,703,447
District of Columbia	2	4	27	8	206	4	105	2	13,979	2	69,000	502,000
Illinois	1	6	28	34	1,300	4	355	1	23,000	1		994,267
Indiana	2	18	38		158		65	2	5,062	2	11,500	45,000
Kentucky	1	6	30		113	0	46	1	3,100	1		181,669
Louisiana	1	3	16		132		47	1	2,997	1	7,500	40,000
Maine	1	1	9	18	17	9	9	1	1,129	1		
Maryland	2	6	28		280		136	1	1,500	1	2,500	50,000
Massachusetts	1	6	18	5	249	4	91	1	4,000	0		
Michigan	3	1	17	1	377		149	2	6,700	2	18,300	
Minnesota	1		2		14		14	1	500	1		245,000
Missouri	1	50	28	37	210		86	1	20,000	1	88,329	174,525
New Jersey	2	6	66		170		66	1	1,480	1	30,000	211,000
New York	9	32	142		1,907	17	869	0	23,063	7	639,512	1,195,773
Ohio	23	43	76	60	745	15	450	9	14,616	17	7,450	330,066
Pennsylvania	5	20	130	81	757	50	228	2	8,710	2	22,850	531,667
Wisconsin	24	31	63		1,422	29	569	25	33,275	21	57,730	305,500
Colored only.												
District of Columbia	1	4	9	8	108	4	52	1	4,270	1	29,000	180,000
Maryland	1	2	2	12	69	5	19	1	1,500	1	2,500	
United States	2	6	11	20	177	9	71	2	5,779	2	31,500	180,000

¹ There were an additional number of 1,031 nonresident students in extension courses.

TABLE 37.—*City and county normal schools—Receipts and expenditures, 1917-18.*

	Receipts.								Expenditures.										
States.	Student fees for educational services.		Public funds for—				All other sources.		Salaries of principals and directors.		Salaries of other instructors.		Other expenses of instruction and administration.		Operation and maintenance, sundry and fixed charges.		Total current expenses reported.	Outlays for sites, buildings, etc.	
			Increase of plant.		Current expenses.														
	Reports.	Amount.	Reports.	Amount.	Reports.	Amount.	Reports.	Amount.	Number of reports.	Amount.	Number of reports.	Amount.	Number of reports.	Amount.	Number of reports.	Amount.		Number of reports.	Amount.
1	2	3	4	5	6	7	8	9	10	11	12	13	14	15	16	17	18	19	20
United States	20	$6,010	9	$38,350	42	$269,825	16	$9,596	71	$154,120	55	$907,189	49	$132,310	41	$170,485	$1,364,104	11	$54,831
District of Columbia	0		0		0		0		2	5,000	2	44,250	2	7,945	2	13,931	71,126	2	2,748
Illinois	0		0		0		0		1	5,600	1	114,867	1	4,410	1	34,255	158,832	1	3,616
Indiana	0		0		0		0		2	4,000	2	19,197	1	200	0		23,497	0	
Kentucky	0		0		0		0		1	2,000	1	21,033	1	3,897	1	10,667	37,597	1	11,243
Louisiana	0		0		0		1	301	1	1,755	1	17,190	1	765	1	720	20,430	0	
Maine	0		0		0		0		1	1,400	0		0		0		1,400	0	
Maryland	0		0		0		0		2	5,400	2	14,060	2	1,550	1	3,200	24,200	0	
Massachusetts	0		1	3,000	0		0		0		0		0		0			0	
Michigan	0		0		3	33,270	1	446	2	4,700	3	34,188	3	2,652	1	1,250	42,790	0	
Minnesota	0		0		1	1,200	1	212	0		1	1,100	1	312	0		1,412	0	
Missouri	0		0		0		0		1	4,600	1	29,439	1	68,506	1	19,432	121,579	0	
New Jersey	0		0		1	40,282	0		2	8,900	2	54,572	1	635	1	3,920	68,027	0	
New York	0		0		11	2,000	1	1,500	9	28,900	9	311,907	5	24,133	2	18,795	413,735	0	
Ohio	2	1,220	5	250	0		0		3	30,640	4	68,114	3	723	6	11,259	110,736	3	150
Pennsylvania	0		0		0		0		3	7,575	2	70,654	3	7,249	1	20,147	105,625	0	
Wisconsin	18	4,790	3	38,350	25	170,833	12	7,137	21	43,750	24	76,828	23	9,331	24	32,909	162,818	4	37,074
Colord only.																			
District of Columbia	1	0	0		0		0		1	2,500	1	16,930	1	3,448	1	5,572	28,450	1	1,099
Maryland	1	0	1		1		1		1	2,400	1	2,850	1	1,000	0		6,250	0	
United States	2	0	1		1		1		2	4,900	2	19,780	2	4,448	1	5,572	31,700	1	1,099

TABLE 38.—*Private normal schools—Personnel, 1917–18.*

States.	Schools reporting.	Summer sessions reporting.	Instructors. Number of reports.	Total for year. Men.	Total for year. Women.	Summer session. Men.	Summer session. Women.	Half time or more in normal courses. Men.	Half time or more in normal courses. Women.	Students. Number of reports.	Total for year (resident). Men.	Total for year (resident). Women.	Summer session. Men.	Summer session. Women.	Normal courses (resident). Men.	Normal courses (resident). Women.	Extension and correspondence courses.	Graduates in 1918 (normal courses). Men.	Graduates in 1918 (normal courses). Women.
1	2	3	4	5	6	7	8	9	10	11	12	13	14	15	16	17	18	19	20
United States	57	17	55	367	571	111	129	106	157	55	2,827	6,742	343	1,471	1,533	4,462	461	142	1,839
Alabama	1	0	1	16	24			0	0	1	461	600			1	18	0		68
California	2	0	2	2	19				4	2	11	132				132			124
Connecticut	4	1	4	13	27			9	17	4		260		16	11	260		2	
District of Columbia	1	0	1		4					1		6				6			
Florida	1	0	1		4				4	1		8				8			5
Illinois	7	4	7	53	83	18	25	25	60	7	254	1,024	25	314	117	1,024		25	323
Indiana	4	3	4	57	55	37	51	8	9	4	655	1,501	128	465	123	866		29	135
Kentucky	1	0	1	3	8			2	6	1	8	8			0	18			2
Maryland	2	1	2	12	6	11		11	5	2	161	25			113	25		17	4
Massachusetts	7	1	6	27	94	1	16	5	16	6	1	894	96	10	9	828	127	17	297
Michigan	2	2	2	8	18	8		4	7	2	84	171			13	171			49
Minnesota	2	0	2	12	5				1	2		114				27		8	25
Missouri	1	0	1	2	9			1	1	1		45				45			18
Nebraska	1	0	1	7	14			2	2	1	40	49			2	4			2
New Jersey	1	1	1	11	10	11	10	11	10	1	52	146	10	161	52	146	198	15	14
North Carolina	1	0	1	11	18			4	1	1	118	207				10		0	3
Ohio	5	0	4	21	26				5	5	48	276				254		5	112
Oregon	1	1	1	3	22	2	6	5	2	1		85	3	102	14	16		0	8
Pennsylvania	4	1	4	9	18	3	5	0	14	3	13	190	0	0	13	180	100	0	44
South Dakota	1	0	1	7	5				0	1	20	137			14	128		0	19
Tennessee	1	0	1	8	10			1	2	1	116	144			15	44			18
Texas	2	0	2	1	13	14	14		6	2	629	44	78	351	14	44		2	30
Virginia	2	1	2	53	55	0	2		2	2	63	595	3	20	1	170	18	7	43
West Virginia	1	0	1	9	11			16		1	93	80			21	8			1
Wisconsin	2	1	2	23	7					2		44				36		5	5

Colored only.

Alabama	1	0	1	16	24			0	0	1	461	600			1	18	0	0	2
Kentucky	1	0	1	3	8			2	5	1	8	35			0	18			3
North Carolina	1	0	1	11	18				1	1	119	277				10		0	5
Pennsylvania	1	1	1	4	8	3	5		8	1	13	153	3	102	18	162	100	2	18
Tennessee	1	0	1	8	16			4	2	1	116	144			15	44			43
Virginia	1	1	1	53	54	14	14	1		1	629	593	78	351	14	167	0	7	1
West Virginia	1	0	1	9	11					1	63	89			1	8			
United States	7	2	7	104	139	17	19	7	16	7	1,408	1,830	81	453	44	427	100	11	72

¹ Several schools reporting total enrollment did not report these items.

¹ In extension courses, 263; in correspondence courses, 198.

TABLE 39.—*Private normal schools—Property and receipts, 1917-18.*

States	Property						Receipts										
	Bound volumes in library.		Library, apparatus, machinery, furniture.		Grounds and buildings, endowment.		Students' fees.				Public funds.		Private benefactions.				All other sources.	
							Tuition, etc.		Board, room, etc.				Increase of plant, endowment.		Current expenses.			
	Reports.	Number.	Reports.	Value.	Reports.	Value.	Reports.	Amount.	Reports.	Amount.	Reports.	Amount.	Reports.	Amount.	Reports.	Amount.	Reports.	Amount.
1	2	3	4	5	6	7	8	9	10	11	12	13	14	15	16	17	18	19
United States	45	153,872	35	$679,997	32	[1] $10,399,655	35	[3] $579,111	23	$407,220	6	$17,982	10	$292,950	12	$353,867	25	$826,522
Alabama	1	24,000	1	226,388	1	3,628,634	1	14,298	0		1	4,125	1	30,514	1	150,000	1	209,916
California	2	1,500	1	1,200	1	13,000	1	6,770	1	1,600	0		0		0		0	
Connecticut	1	1,205	1	26,241	2	109,700	3	26,580	1	48,639	1	500	0		0		1	3,500
District of Columbia	1	600	1	1,000	0		1	15,000	0		0		0		0		0	
Florida	1	40	0		0		0		0		0		0		0		0	
Illinois	7	9,107	4	32,732	2	450,500	6	108,696	6	124,153	0		2	3,000	1	3,000	5	13,732
Indiana	4	16,567	4	76,901	4	303,505	3	79,026	2	36,775	0		1	292	0		2	5,708
Kentucky	1	2,006	1	2,100	1	119,000	1	622	0		0		0		1	675	1	5,290
Maryland	2	1,850	1	5,000	1	205,000	1	3,000	0		0		0		0		1	22,261
Massachusetts	3	900	1	2,000	2	82,500	2	26,000	2	26,600	0		0		0		0	
Michigan	2	9,045	2	18,200	1	30,000	2	15,119	1	206	0		0		0		1	25
Minnesota	1	3,500	1	12,325	1	88,000	1	3,000	1	2,187	0		0		0		1	6,905
Missouri	1	400	1	800	0		1	4,500	0		0		0		0		0	10,549
Nebraska	1	2,000	1	16,285	1	83,800	0		1	2,391	0		0		0		0	
New Jersey	0		1	1,000	1	100,000	0		0		0		0		0		0	
North Carolina	1	6,100	1	15,525	1	179,064	1	11,327	1		0		1	9,031	1	6,532	1	28,184
Ohio	3	1,584	4	4,500	3	78,000	4	22,355	2	2,375	0		0		1	8,300	2	530
Oregon	1	3,256	1	20,000	1	78,000	0		0		0		0		0		0	
Pennsylvania	3	4,785	1	3,000	2	452,458	1	6,172	1	8,727	1	5,000	1	10,000	2	16,305	2	28
South Dakota	1	3,000	1	7,000	1	91,000	1	5,800	1	15,800	0		1	10,000	1	10,000	0	19,558

Tennessee	1	3,000	1	6,000	1	204,000	1	6,738	1		1		1	3,069	1	6,025	1	9,775
Texas	2	40,187	0		2	25,000	1	2,000	0		0	3,600	0		0		1	900
Virginia	1	7,000	2	174,000	0	3,638,703	1	106,553	1	3,240	1	206,351	1	146,064	1	164,918
West Virginia	1		1	7,500	0	284,801	1	10,427	1	2,487	0	1,193	0		1	11,178
Wisconsin	2	11,000	2	10,300	2	209,000	0		0		1	500	2	4,376	2	11,563
Colored only.																		
Alabama	1	24,000	1	236,388	1	3,528,634	1	14,298	1	4,125	1	30,514	1	150,000	1	209,916
Kentucky	1	2,008	1	2,100	1	119,000	1	622	0		0	9,081	1	675	1	5,290
North Carolina	1	6,100	0	16,525	1	179,064	1	11,327	0		1	10,000	1	6,532	1	28,184
Pennsylvania	1	3,210	1		0	262,488	0		1	5,000	1	3,069	1	11,675	1	10,789
Tennessee	1	3,000	1	6,000	1	204,000	1		0		1	205,351	1	6,625	1	9,775
Virginia	1	40,187	1	173,500	0	3,638,703	1	8,727	1	2,240	1		1		1	164,918
West Virginia	1	7,000	1	7,500	1	284,801	1	6,738	1	2,487	1	1,193	0	146,064	1	11,178
United States	7	85,503	6	441,013	7	8,200,650	4	134,492	4	13,852	6	259,168	6	324,461	7	440,000

1 Includes endowments amounting to $5,812,642. For amounts see Table 49.
2 Includes $43,510 for tuition, board, and room (items not separated).
3 Includes $3,660 for tuition, board, and room.
4 For board, room, and tuition.
5 Includes $15,503 for tuition, board, and room.

TABLE 40.—*Private normal schools—Expenditures, 1917–18.*

States	Salaries of principals and directors. Reports.	Amount.	Salaries of other instructors. Reports.	Amount.	Other expenses of instruction and administration. Reports.	Amount.	Operation and maintenance, sundry, and fixed charges. Reports.	Amount.	Total current expenses reported.	Outlays for sites, buildings, etc. Reports.	Amount.
1	2	3	4	5	6	7	8	9	10	11	12
United States	33	$61,506	42	$310,891	40	$161,129	40	$886,708	$1,420,234	12	$100,171
Alabama	1	5,180	1	60,506	1	96,058	1	235,614	397,360	1	77,006
California	1	2,500	2	4,658	2	250	2	3,268	10,686	1	700
Connecticut	2	3,965	3	13,947	3	6,286	2	42,876	67,004	1	4,097
District of Columbia	1	1,000	1	1,660	0		1	12,000	14,660	0	
Florida	1	1,120	1	1,520	1	225	0		2,865	0	
Illinois	5	11,600	7	55,536	7	30,145	7	90,072	187,333	3	12,517
Indiana	2	4,700	3	28,103	3	8,387	3	62,277	113,467	1	500
Kentucky	1	800	1	3,134	1	122	1	208	4,264	1	1,500
Maryland	0		1	3,700	2	613	1	20,167	21,480	0	
Massachusetts	0		2	12,900	2	3,500	2	10,546	26,996	1	200
Michigan	0		2	9,120	2	1,301	2	3,801	14,222	0	
Minnesota	1	1,960	1	7,172	1	468	1	2,628	11,868	0	
Missouri	1	1,900	1	1,800	1	100	1	900	4,500	0	
Nebraska	1	1,200	1	2,875	1	315	1	4,687	8,757	1	6,900
North Carolina	1	1,500	1	6,705	1	2,536	1	26,891	37,632	0	
Ohio	4	6,900	4	17,957	4	2,263	4	7,546	34,666	0	
Pennsylvania	3	6,453	3	19,348	3	4,486	3	15,692	45,951	1	199
South Dakota	1	1,534	1	12,589	1	196	1	6,716	21,315	0	
Tennessee	1	2,000	1	12,948	1	630	1	5,943	21,524	0	
Texas	2	2,294	2	3,000	1	140	0		5,364	0	
Virginia	1	1,200	0		0		1	315,006	317,108	0	
West Virginia	1	1,500	1	9,742	1	952	1	5,198	17,392	1	1,952
Wisconsin	2	2,000	2	15,299	1	2,204	2	13,718	33,781	0	

Colored only:												
Alabama	1	5,180	1	60,508	1	96,058	1	235,014	397,380	1	77,000	
Kentucky	1	800	1	3,134	1	122	1	208	4,264	1	1,500	
North Carolina	1	1,500	1	6,705	1	2,538	1	26,891	37,683	1	6,900	
Pennsylvania	1	3,000	1	6,022	1	2,590	1	11,283	22,905	1	199	
Tennessee	1	2,000	1	12,948	1	630	1	5,945	21,524	0		
Virginia	0		0		0		1	315,908	315,908	0		
West Virginia	1	1,500	1	9,742	1	962	1	5,198	17,392	1	1,952	
United States	6	13,980	6	99,069	6	102,888	7	601,058	816,965	5	88,157	

Location	Institution	Weeks in year, including summer session.	Weeks in summer session.	Length of teachers' training course, in years.	Entrance requirements to teachers' training course; completion of—	Graduates from the teachers' training course (1918). Men.	Graduates from the teachers' training course (1918). Women.	Model school, (A) maintained by this institution; (B) public school.	Practice school, (A) maintained by this institution; (B) public school.	Hours of practice required in teachers' training courses.	Enrollment in model and practice schools.
1	2	3	4	5	6	7	8	9	10	11	12
Alabama:											
Daphne	State Normal School	42	6	4	2 and 4 years of high school	3	9	A, B	B	27	100
Florence	do	48	12	4,2	2 years of high school	14	87	A	A, B	135	184
Jacksonville	do	48	12	4	2 years of high school	20	34	A, B	A	180	132
Livingston	do	48	12	4	do	4	75	A	A, A	120	100
Montgomery	State Colored Normal School	42	6	4	Eighth grade	9	20	A	A	72	296
Moundville	State Normal School	38	6								
Normal	Agricultural and Mechanical College for Negroes	38	6	4	3 years of high school	2	3	A, B	A, B		171
Troy	State Normal School	48	12	4	2 years of high school	10	52	A	A		113
Arizona:											
Flagstaff	Northern Arizona Normal School	46	8	6,2	Eighth grade, high school	0	65	A	A	190	216
Tempe	Tempe Normal School of Arizona	38			High school	4	74	A	A	190	231
Arkansas:											
Conway	Arkansas State Normal School	43	6	6,2	Eighth grade, high school	9	25	A	A	120	65
Pine Bluff	Branch Normal College (colored)	40	4	6,2	High school	3	4	B			
California:											
Arcata	Humboldt State Normal School	44	6	2	do	7	47	A	A	44	124
Chico	State Normal School	43	6	2	do	6	105	A	A	270	400
Fresno	do	38	6		do	4	131	A	A	240	380
Los Angeles	do	38			do					195	631
San Diego	do	36	12	4,3,2	do	0	95	A	A, B	300	463
San Francisco	do	36	6	2	do	6	316	A, B	A, B	305	884
San Jose	do	50	10	2	do	12	349	A, B	A, B	180	785
Santa Barbara	State Normal School of Manual Arts and Home Economics			2	2 years beyond high school	19	58				
Colorado:											
Gunnison	Colorado State Normal School	42	6	3,2	High school	1	34	B	B	90	1,262

Location	School				Entrance requirement						
Connecticut:											
Danbury	State Normal Training School	43	6	2			80	B	B	200	1,000
New Britain	do	38		3			90	B	B	180	1,000
New Haven	do			3	do		100	B	B		1,225
Willimantic	do	40	0	2	do	4	90	B	B	660	610
Georgia:											
Athens	State Normal School	36	4	4	Eighth grade	1	161	A	A	54	144
Milledgeville	Georgia Normal and Industrial College	36		4,2	High school and two-thirds high school		222	A	A	120	232
Valdosta	Southern Georgia State Normal College	40	4	2,1	4 and 3 years of high school		28	A	A, B	91	134
Idaho:											
Albion	State Normal School	45	9	2	High school	2	81	A, B	A, B	300	380
Lewiston	do	45	9	2	do		74	A	A	225	288
Illinois:											
Carbondale	Southern Illinois State Normal University	42	6	6,2	Eighth grade, high school	27	68	A	A	180	180
Charleston	Eastern Illinois State Normal School	42	6	6,2	do	7	54	A	A	110	245
De Kalb	Northern Illinois State Normal School	45	6	3,2	Eleventh grade, high school	12	140	B	B	280	676
Macomb	Western Illinois State Normal School	42	6	4,2	High school	16	60	A	A	240	180
Normal	Illinois State Normal University	48	12	4	do	19	164	A	A	130	1,201
Indiana:											
Terre Haute	Indiana State Normal School	48	12	4	do	35	109	A	A	120	576
Kansas:											
Emporia	State Normal School	44	8	4,2	do	70	211	A	A	108	288
Hays	Fort Hays Kansas Normal School	45	9		do	10	40	B	B	144	474
Pittsburg	State Manual Training Normal School	42	9	4,2,1	do	34	220	A	A	90-380	277
Kentucky:											
Bowling Green	Western Kentucky State Normal School	46	6	2	2 years of high school	11	51	A	A	100	275
Frankfort	State Normal and Industrial Institute for Colored Persons	46	6	4	do	6	33	A	A	100	d
Richmond	Eastern Kentucky State Normal School	46	6	2	High school	2	28	A	A	130	202
Louisiana:											
Natchitoches	Louisiana State Normal School	46	10	2	High school	28	231	A	A	130	499
Maine:											
Castine	Eastern State Normal School	38		2	do	1	35	A, B	A, B	60	110
Farmington	Farmington State Normal School	38		2	do	1	106	A, B	A, B	180	150
Gorham	Western State Normal School	37		2	do	6	108	A, B	A, B	140	445
Machias	Washington State Normal School	38		2	do	3	15	A	A, B	380	150
Presque Isle	Aroostook State Normal School	44	6		do	0	36	A, B	A, B	20	400
Maryland:											
Bowie	Maryland State Normal and Industrial School (colored)	42	6	3	Eighth grade	1	11	A	A	68	85
Frostburg	do	26		2	do	2	37	A	A	100	120
Towson	Maryland State Normal School	42	6	2	High school	1	88	A	A	180	140
Massachusetts:											
Boston	Massachusetts Normal Art School	36	0	4	do	1	24	B	B	780	484
Bridgewater	State Normal School	39		3,2	do	8	160	A	A	470	780
Fitchburg	do	48	8	4,2	do	16	135	B	B	120	390
Framingham	do	38		3,2	do		143	A, B	A, B	90	96
Hyannis	do	43	5	2	do	4	22	B	B		

Location	Institution	Weeks in year including summer session.	Weeks in summer session.	Length of teachers' training course, in years.	Entrance requirements to teachers' training course; completion of—	Graduates from the teachers' training course (1918).		Model school, (A) maintained by this institution; (B) public school.	Practice school, (A) maintained by this institution; (B) public school.	Hours of practice required in teachers' training course.	Enrollment in model and practice schools.
						Men.	Women.				
1	2	8	4	5	6	7	8	9	10	11	12
Massachusetts—Con't.											
Lowell	State Normal School	38	0	3, 2	High school		90	B	B	440	1,003
North Adams	do	38			do	0	69			724	1,600
Salem	do	36		4, 3, 2	do	3	98	B	B	600	590
Westfield	do	39		2, 1	do	0	87	A, B	A, B	390	500
Worcester	do	38		3, 2	d.		91	A, B	A, B	600	460
Michigan:											
Kalamazoo	Western Normal School	42	6	2	do	37	371	A	A	192-298	278
Marquette	Northern State Normal School	42	6	4, 2	do	18	212	A, B	A, B	120	261
Mount Pleasant	Central State Normal School	42	6	4, 2	do	17	178	A	A	120	250
Ypsilanti	Michigan State Normal College	40	6	4, 2, 1	do	72	789	A, B	A, B	50	532
Minnesota:											
Duluth	State Normal School	42	6	5, 2	Eighth grade, high school	1	85	A, B	A, B	120	201
Mankato	do	42	6	2	High school	7	174	A	A	180	437
Moorhead	do	42	6	5, 2	Eighth grade, high school	17	100	A, B	A, B	180	318
St. Cloud	do	42	6	5, 2	Eighth grade, high school	17	144	A, B	A, B	120	1,188
Winona	do	42	6	2	High school	6	165	A, B	A, B	38	392
Mississippi:											
Hattiesburg	Mississippi Normal College	48	6	5	Grammar school	6	25	A, B	A		17
Missouri:											
Cape Girardeau	State Normal School	48	10	4, 3, 2	High school	24	130	A	A	80	200
Jefferson City	Lincoln Institu (colored)	40		4	do	11	26	A, B	A, B	140	50
Kirksville	State Normal School	44	11	4	do	157	314	A	A	110	300
Maryville	do	48	12	4, 2	do	4	69	A	A		100
Springfield	do	46	10	4, 2	do	32	104	A	A	120	270
Warrensburg	do	46	10	4	do	64	199	A, B	A, B		300
Montana:											
Dillon	Montana State Normal College	48	12	3, 2	do	2	57	A, B	A, B	175	500

Location and name of school	Weeks in year		Entrance requirement (years)	Entrance requirement	Instructors	Students	Grade	Grade		By school authorities
Nebraska:										
Chadron, State Normal School	44	8	2	do	2	23	A	A	90	140
Kearney, do	44	8	2	do	10	64	A	A	27	150
Peru, do	44	8	6,2	do	13	128	A	A	64	152
Wayne, do	44	8		Eighth grade, high school	12	63	A	A	90	150
New Hampshire:										
Keene, do	42	6	2	High school		71	B, B	B, B	450	1,200[3]
Plymouth, do	26		2	do		51			495	255
New Jersey:										
Montclair, New Jersey State Normal School	40	0	2	do	8	250	B, B	B, B	400	600
Newark, do	40	6	2	do	21	431	A, B	A, B	400	
Trenton, do	40		2	do	8	392	A, B	A, B	450	260
New Mexico:										
East Las Vegas, New Mexico Normal University	44	8	4, 3, 2	do		28	A	A	10	
Silver City, New Mexico Normal School	44	8		do		28	A	A	240	160
New York:										
Brockport, State Normal and Training School	40	0	2, 1	do	3	69	A	A, B	600	253
Buffalo, State Normal School	44	6	2	d	19	210	B	A	400	473
Cortland, State Normal and Training School	40		2	d	4	146	A	A	300	380
Fredonia, do	39	6	2	d	5	95	A	A	600	312
Geneseo, Geneseo State Normal School	46		2	do	0	208	A, B	A, B	200	290
New Paltz, State Normal School	38		2, 1	d	1	126	A	A	500	700
Oneonta, do	42	6	2	do	3	263		A	570	468
Oswego, do	39		2	d	17	133		A	600	250
Plattsburgh, do	38		2	do	2	80				350
Potsdam, State Normal and Training School	39	0		d		101				
North Carolina:										
Cullowhee, Cullowhee Normal and Industrial School	38	6	4	Seventh grade	5	8	B, B	B, B	320	165
Elizabeth City, State Colored Normal School	36	4	4	Grammar grade					450	110
Fayetteville, do	36		4	Fifth grade			A, B	A, B	128	83
East Carolina Teachers' Training School	44	8	2	High school			B	B	132	158
State Normal and Industrial College	26	8	2	14 units high school			A	A		
Winston-Salem, Slater Industrial and State Normal School (colored)		4			5				32	291
North Dakota:										
Ellendale, State Normal and Industrial School	42	6	4, 3, 2	Eighth grade, high school	6	25	A, B	A, B	60	252
Mayville, State Normal School	42	6	4, 1	do	2	62	B	B	120	0
Minot, do	42	6	5, 1	do	3	59	A	A	180	283
Valley City, do	42		2, 1	High school	8	148			180	281
Ohio:										
Bowling Green, State Normal College	48	12	4, 2	do	2	65	A, B	A, B	180	225
do	48	12	4, 2	do	16	194	B	A	190	336
Oklahoma:										
Ada, East Central State Normal School	46	10	2	Eighth grade, high school	7	38	A	A	120	120
Alva, Northwestern State Normal School	46	10		High school	15	69	A	A	180	150
Southeastern State Normal School	46	10	6, 2	do	10	80	A	A	300	120
Edmond, Central State Normal School	46	10		do	24	160	A	A	180	199
Langston, Colored Agricultural and Normal University	46	10	2	Eighth grade, high school	8	39	A	A		30
Tahlequah, Northeastern State Normal School	46	10	2	do	5	15	A	A	180	120
Weatherford, Southwestern State Normal School	46	10	6, 2	Eighth grade, high school	7	34	A	A	180	119

[superscript header] Schools maintained in cooperation

[1] Public this.
[2] Side observation.
[3] Of these, 1,000 are in public schools.
[4] Joint session at Keene, N. H.

TABLE 41.—State normal schools—Items of general information, 1917-18—Continued.

Location	Institution	Weeks in year, including summer session	Weeks in summer session	Length of teachers' training course, in years	Entrance requirements to teachers' training course; completion of—	Graduates from the teachers' training course (1918). Men	Women	Model school, (A) maintained by this institution; (B) public school	Practice school, (A) maintained by this institution; (B) public school	Hours of practice required in teachers' training courses	Enrollment in model and practice schools
		3	4	5	6	7	8	9	10	11	12
Oregon:											
Monmouth	State Normal School	46	6	2	High school	6	185	A,B	A,B	180	12
Pennsylvania:											
Bloomsburg	do	40	6	4	3 years of high school	27	125	A	A	200	117
California	Southwestern State Normal School	40		4	do	12	128	A	A	80	180
Clarion	State Normal School	41		4	do	9	48	A	A	120	100
East Stroudsburg	do	40		4,2	Eighth grade, high school	23	114	A,B	B	180	140
Edinboro	do	40			2 year of high school	17	82	B	B	180	186
Indiana	Keystone State Normal School	40			do	12	289	A	A	200	286
Kutztown	Central State Normal School	40		4	do	47	105	A	A	180	142
Lock Haven	State Normal School	46		4	Eighth grade, high school	11	74	A,B	A,B	180	180
Mansfield	do	46		4,2	2 years of high school	45	146	A,B	A	180	247
Millersville	Cumberland Valley State Normal School	46		4,2	Eighth grade, high school	30	97	A	A	200	314
Shippensburg	State Normal School	46			Eighth grade	32	94		B	200	256
Slippery Rock	do	46		5,2	Eighth grade, high school	9	82	B	B	200	1 210
West Chester		46				38	322			163	1 389
Rhode Island:											
Providence	Rhode Island State Normal School	43	4	2½	High school		114	A,B	A,B	180	2 2,780
South Carolina:											
Orangeburg	Colored Normal, Industrial, Agricultural, and Mechanical College of South Carolina	38	4	4	Eighth grade	29	48	A	A	120	45
Rock Hill	Winthrop Normal and Industrial College	42	6	4,2	3 years of high school		176	A	A	80	401
South Dakota:											
Aberdeen	Northern Normal and Industrial School	48	12	4,2	Eighth grade, high school	9	95	B	B	250	360
Madison	State Normal School	48	12	2	Eighth grade	0	17	A	A	140	197
Spearfish	do	44	6	6,4,2	do		25	A	A	270	1 152
Springfield	do	48	12	6,4,2		6	54	B	B	108	
Tennessee:											
Johnson City	East Tennessee State Normal School	43	6	3,2	1 year of high school; high school.	18	94	A	A	120	295
Memphis	West Tennessee State Normal School										

Location	Institution				Basis of admission						
Murfreesboro	Middle Tennessee State Normal School	42	6	4	2 years of high school.	0	16	A	A	360	106
Nashville	State Agricultural and Industrial Normal School for Negroes.										
Texas:											
Canyon	West Texas State Normal College	48	12	4,2	14½ and 7 units.	5	47	A	A	180	225
Commerce	East Texas Normal College	43	10	4,2	14½ and 7 units.	29	4	A	A	72	160
Denton	North Texas State Normal College	46	10	4,2	do.	23	101	A	A	80	149
Huntsville	Sam Houston State Normal Institute	47	11	4,2	do.	47	72	A	A	60	142
Prairie View	Prairie View State Normal and Industrial College (colored).	45	9	4,2	1 year of high school.		110			12	30
San Marcos	Southwest Texas State Normal School	47	11	4,2	14½ and 7 units.		11	B	B	120	[1] 125
Vermont:											
Castleton	State Normal School	40	4	2	High School.		24	B	B	126	161
Johnson	do.	40	4	2	do.		22	A	A	173	
Virginia:											
East Radford	State Normal School for Women	48	12	3,2	do.		50	B	B	840	350
Farmville	do.	43	6	4,2	do.		168	A	A	270	217
Fredericksburg	State Normal and Industrial School for Women.	48	12	2,1	do.	0	43	B	B	270	900
Harrisonburg	do.	48	12	4	High school.	0	71	B	B	680	900
Petersburg	Virginia Normal and Industrial Institute (colored).	41	6	2	2 years and 4 years of high school.	1	11	A	A	193	233
Washington:											
Bellingham	State Normal School	45	9	3,2,1	High School.	29	391	A,B	A,B	150	532
Cheney	do.	47	11	3,2,1	do.	6	229	A,B	A,B	190	285
Ellensburg	do.	48	12		do.		109	A,B	A,B	90	250
West Virginia:											
Athens	Concord State Normal School	42	6	2,1	High school, 3 years of high school.	4	120	B	B	90	[2] 2,500
Fairmont	State Normal School	44	8	6	Eighth grade.	13	14	A	A	90	64
Glenville	do.	38	8	2	High school.		19	A	A	90	145
Huntington	Marshall College, State Normal School.	44	6	2,1	High school, 1 year of high school.	8	34	B	B	90	
Institute	West Virginia Collegiate Institute (colored).					5	34	B	B	135	[1] 203
Shepherdstown	Shepherds College, State Normal School.	43	6	2,1	High school.	5	28	B	B	80	158
West Liberty	State Normal School	43	6	2,1	do.		61	B	B	180	210
Wisconsin:											
Eau Claire	do.	43	6	2	do.	8	133	A,B	A,B	135	200
La Crosse	do.	41	6	2	do.	9	91	A,B	A,B	21	431
Menomonie	Stout Institute	43	6	4,2	do.	28	21	A,B	A,B	315–390	450
Milwaukee	State Normal School	43	6	3,2	do.	31	134	A,B	A,B	270	169
Oshkosh	do.	43	6	3,2,1	do.	19	76	A,B	A,B	180	185
Platteville	do.	43	6	3,4,1	do.	40	102	A,B	A,B		393
River Falls	do.	43	6		do.	22	183	A,B	A,B	135	280
Stevens Point	do.	43	6	3,2,1	do.	4	155	A	A	125	205
Superior	do.				do.	16	119	A,B	A,B		
Whitewater	do.	42	6	3,2,1	do.			A	A	100	

[1] Public schools.

[2] Of these 2,400 are in public schools.

[3] 14½ high-school units admit to the 4-year college course, 7 units admit to the 2-year normal course.

Table 42.—*State normal schools—instructors and students, 1917–18.*

Location of institution [1]	Instructors, including principal.				Instructors engaged half time or more.			Resident students.								Attendance weeks of resident students.	
	Whole year.		Summer.		Resident normal courses.		Exten-sion and corre-spond-ence courses.	In all courses.				In normal courses.		In other courses.	Non-resi-dent stu-dents in exten-sion and corre-spond-ence courses.	Teachers' training courses.	Other courses.
	Men.	Women.	Men.	Women.	Men.	Women.		Whole year.		Summer.		Men.	Women.				
								Men.	Women.	Men.	Women.						
1	2	3	4	5	6	7	8	9	10	11	12	13	14	15	16	17	18
Alabama:																	
Daphne	3	4	3			11	0	93	120	45	258	93	547	0	7	14,069	
Florence	11	11	11	10	10	11	0	17	547	3	10	16	35	11	0	[1]1,640	
Jacksonville	6	6	6	10	3	0	0	30	45			30	402		43	12,000	[1]396
Livingston	7	12	6	8	5	7		141	402	7	128	71	293	199	0	7,668	0
Montgomery	13	26	6	7	5	9			422								[1]3,184
Moundville																	
Normal	15	10	11	8	6	2	4	30	74	2	26	18	83	33	8	[1]1,376	[1]1,056
Troy	7	8	7	8	5	4	1		431				37	444			
Arizona:																	
Flagstaff	14	13	12	13	13	12	0	96	425	15	214	55	328	138	30	[1]11,565	[1]3,389
Tempe	16	19	12		18	19	0	120	330			9	169	272	0	[1]6,688	[1]10,184
Arkansas:																	
Conway	11	10	10	10	11	10	0	86	433	15	235	86	433		0	8,162	0
Pine Bluff	14	7	7		3	2	1	140	263	1	49	8	16	379		914	13,542
California:																	
Arcata	7	7	6	5	7	7	1	9	112	1	46	9	112		25	[1]3,614	
Chico	12	14	5	11	8	14		22	244	30	32	22	244		51	[1]3,580	
Fresno	20	22	5	6	10	20	0	15	316	9	100	15	316			7,200	
Los Angeles	20	19	8		20	70		57	1,246			57	1,246		611	39,116	
San Diego	6	24		17	6	19	0	5	453	5	394	5	453			10,944	
San Francisco	14	50	7		14	34	0	5	674			40	674	0	0		
San Jose	2	11	2	11	6	50	0	40	884	6	156	49	884		0	[1]10,104	
Santa Barbara					6	5		49	309			49	309				
Colorado:																	
Gunnison	14	23	14	28	14	28	0	86	462	25	325	25	306	127	135	[1]6,312	[1]4,582
Connecticut:																	
Danbury	22	42	16	6	6	36	0	103	486	108	346	103	486		79	[1]8,238	
New Britain	5	8			2	2			187				187				
New Haven	4	35							179				179				
Willimantic	5	22			4	9	0	4	100			4	100		0	4,021	

Institution																	
Georgia:																	
Athens	9	9	30				4	30				8						$1,512
Milledgeville	8	49																$5,040
Valdosta	4	15																1,760
Idaho:																		
Albion	8	14	4	8	6	14	77	8		51	186	61	8	380	59	31	10	
Lewiston	10	26	8	8	14	14	8	8			272	8		449		10		1,881
Illinois:																		
Carbondale	23	23	22	23	22	22	23	616		53	361	561	883	883	95	31	24,766	
Charleston	21	21	37	21	21	24	21	145		38	630	145	906	906		10	10,763	
De Kalb	13	13	17	13	11	17	36	36		17	522	38	538	538			16,548	
Macomb	23	23	60	23	16	43	174	174		64	566	78	671	671			10,008	
Normal	49	49	48	45	48	177	177		106	1,615	177	2,623	2,623	302	662	33,421		$7,055
Indiana:																		
Terre Haute	33	32	10	33	10	683	683		342	1,085	683	1,367	1,367			43,728		
Kansas:																		
Emporia	43	43	43	43	49	420	420		247	1,713	318	1,962	2,420	560	17	37,170		$11,302
Hays	16	16	40	43	10	215	215		60	240		672			125			
Pittsburg	40	40	40	41	41	483	483		204	1,060	306	1,611	1,611	531	112	16,978		10,314
Kentucky:																		
Bowling Green	16	10	29	10	20	264	264		14	49	264	977	977	0	0			$5,720
Frankfort	13	13	12	12	8	108	108		22	327	71	307	307	160		9,450		9,618
Richmond	12	12	14	12	71	71			472	472							
Louisiana:																		
Natchitoches	28	31	15	22	27	281	281		165	771	202	1,088	1,088	300	4	24,906		$9,908
Maine:																		
Castine	5	5	4	4	4	3	3				3	72	72			2,460		
Farmington	9	9	10	9	9	5	5				5	222	222			2,475		
Gorham	4	4	11	0	6	6					6	189	189			6,912		
Machias	2	2	13	13	10	10		1	46	10	43	43			1,887		
Presque Isle	1	1	1	2	2			3	342	2	128	128			2,309		
Maryland:																		
Bowie	4	3	2	4	3	6	6				6	79	79					
Frostburg	3	3	14	8	4	4				4	80	80	46				
Towson	8	14	14	8	8	8	5	5			5	415	460			7,770		$1,020
Massachusetts:																		
Boston	17	17	10	17	10	51	51		41	49	81	234	234		0	10,280		0
Bridgewater	9	28	27	7	28	28	18	18		18	423	423		0	16,796		
Fitchburg	12	22	12	22	29	76	76	13	174	76	307	307		0	11,854		0
Framingham	7	29	7	14	30	30		30	335	335		0	12,730		
Hyannis	11	14	11	40	214	214			12,735		
Lowell	5	40	5	98	120	120			7,914		
North Adams	4	11	4	24	21	21	321	321	114	4,313		
Salem	11	5	11	5	21	21	167	167		0	12,313		
Westfield	4	4	3	4	104	104		0	6,091		
Worcester	6	13	8	8			194	194		6,560		
Michigan:																		
Kalamazoo	40	58	48	45	34	293	293	283	832	64	1,423	1,303	150	647	26,894		$6,300
Marquette	13	13	28	20	13	69	69	43	491	43	576	560	41	14	18,276		
Mount Pleasant	15	15	25	25	15	248	248	248	604	225	621	621	235	14,168		
Ypsilanti	53	54	60	254	254	254	1,455	161	2,589	2,589	337	53,443		

1 For names of institutions, see Table 41.   2 Enrollment weeks.   3 Estimated.

TABLE 42.—*State normal schools—instructors and students, 1917-18—Continued.*

Location of institution	Instructors, including principal. Whole year.		Summer.		Instructors engaged half time or more. Resident normal courses.		Extension and correspondence courses	Resident students. In all courses. Whole year.		Summer.		In normal courses.		In other courses	Nonresident students in extension and correspondence courses	Teachers' training courses.	Attendance weeks of resident students. Other courses.
	Men.	Women.	Men.	Women.	Men.	Women.		Men.	Women.	Men.	Women.	Men.	Women.				
1	2	3	4	5	6	7	8	9	10	11	12	13	14	15	16	17	18
Minnesota:																	
Duluth	7	13	7	9	7	15		10	332	10	180	10	332			6,980	
Mankato	14	35	9	14	14	34		58	728	10	243	38	728		94	15,599	
Moorhead	17	27	15	12	17	27		64	812	21	507	64	812		0	18,579	
St. Cloud	15	33	12	17	16	33		64	821	29	547	29	821		0	18,585	
Winona	11	32	11	10	11	33		28	698	8	334	28	698		0	15,385	0
Mississippi:																	
Hattiesburg	18	11	18	11				92	745	176	607	92	745		91	14,700	
Missouri:																	
Cape Girardeau	32	32	33	19	33	31	0	383	881			383	881	72		30,367	12,336
Jefferson City	14	41	31	7	0	0	0	40	30	130	897	11	30	83	290		3,344
Kirksville	27	37	35	33	36	41		310	1,300	36	494	217	910	483	37	18,810	13,885
Maryville	26	45	16	35	11	8		101	716	250	850	52	800	265		111,04	4,085
Springfield	40	30	40	30				330	1,040	229		290	850	340	460	22,530	6,945
Warrensburg								316	1,472		1,104	224	1,182	274		36,248	
Montana:																	
Dillon	12	14	8	12	8	12		22	513	14	228	12	451	72	20	17,104	11,498
Nebraska:																	
Chadron	37	41	13	13	32	38		56	449	55	200	12	295	198		4,111	3,570
Kearney	18	33	18	33	18	35		191	1,134	48	780	90	729	507		12,644	4,351
Peru	19	39	19	35	19	33		107	786	47	843	31	211	723			
Wayne	18	32	15	13	15			135	610	25	400	135	610		40	116,990	
New Hampshire:																	
Keene	8	47	6	10	6	13	0	0	180			0	180	0	0	6,570	0
Plymouth	4	10			4	10	0	8	94			8	94	0	0	13,334	
New Jersey:																	
Montclair	4	21	6		4	21	0	15	592			13	592		0	21,100	
Newark	6	50			6	50		15	810			15	810		0	35,760	
Trenton	9	34							612				612				

New Mexico:
East Las Vegas
Silver City
New York:
Brockport
Buffalo
Cortland
Fredonia
Geneseo
New Paltz
Oneonta
Oswego
Plattsburg
Potsdam
North Carolina:
Cullowhee
Elizabeth City
Fayetteville
Greenville
Greensboro
Winston-Salem
North Dakota:
Dickinson
Mayville
Minot
Valley City
Ohio:
Bowling Green
Kent
Oklahoma:
Ada
Alva
Durant
Edmond
Langston
Tahlequah
Weatherford
Oregon:
Monmouth
Pennsylvania:
Bloomsburg
California
Clarion
East Stroudsburg
Edinboro
Indiana
Kutztown
Lock Haven
Mansfield
Millersville

1 Enrollment weeks.   2 Estimated.   3 Includes summer session of 1918.

Location of institution	Instructors, including principal							Resident students.							Non-resident students in extension and correspondence courses.	Attendance weeks of resident students.	
	Whole year.		Summer.		Resident normal courses.		Extension and correspondence courses.	In all courses.				In normal courses.		In other courses.		Teachers' training courses.	Other courses.
	Men.	Women.	Men.	Women.	Men.	Women.		Whole year.		Summer.		Men.	Women.				
								Men.	Women.	Men.	Women.						
	2	3	4	5	6	7	8	9	10	11	12	13	14	15	16	17	18
Pennsylvania—Contd.																	
Shippensburg	11	17	3	4				148	399	18	40	148	399	0	5	17,854	
Slippery Rock	10	15		2			0	88	344			88	344		0	15,243	
West Chester	19	18	7	12	11	14	1	146	743		90	116	743			[1] 32,890	
Rhode Island:																	
Providence	11	61	9	12	11	14	9	10	471	10	190	10	471		183	11,090	
South Carolina:																	
Orangeburg	40	19	7	8	16	12	1	284	489	8	13	144	310	319		[1] 11,186	[1] 10,848
Rockhill[2]	19	66	17	25	11	24	7	46	2,098	46	1,040	46	1,971	127	42	[1] 38,268	[1] 14,548
South Dakota:																	
Aberdeen	24	52	15	11	23	19		233	1,005	47	474	196	975	67	401	24,545	1,418
Madison	9	22	8	7				70	320	6	116	58	411		100		
Spearfish	12	28	8	19				165	471	4	211	54	215	107			
Springfield	12	16	7	5	12	28		63	237	8	83			31			
Tennessee:																	
Johnson City	13	15	13	15	13	15	3	140	692	100	400	140	692			[1] 11,175	[1] 3,301
Memphis														310		6,691	595
Murfreesboro																	
Nashville	17	26	9	23	11	14		130	252			15	57			[1] 14,625	[1] 14,451
Texas:																	
Canyon	22	18	22	18	22	18		215	116	75	125	215	116	231	0	[1] 16,632	2,376
Commerce	20	12	18	10	18	12	0	191	417	30	127	114	263	0	0	3,873	
Denton	31	27	34	27	33	27	0	424	2,102	212	1,488	424	2,102	27		27,359	
Huntsville	33	27	28	26	21	11	0	301	1,012	191	604	290	996			28,344	
Prairie View	24	11	24	11	4	10		300	932			300	932			24,253	
San Marcos	22	20	15	10				195	720	83	584	195	720				
Vermont:																	
Castleton	2	14	2	7	2	12	0	247	247		247	247	247	0	0	[1] 2,616	
Johnson	4	17	3	17	4	17		147	147		127	147	147		27	1,558	

Virginia:																	
East Radford	15	13	21	13	21	10	18			8		625	8	537	3	500	130		¹ 5,568
Farmville	8	27	11	3	18	7	36			0		922	0	300		647	275		6,974
Fredericksburg	9	34	7	6	12	9	18			20		460	20	185	12	245	217	0	5,071
Harrisonburg	16	14	34	14	20	13	33			118		1,316	118	1,063	13	1,007	317		4,140
Petersburg	22	10	45	10	22	3	17					750		258		406	449		15,715
Washington:																		
Bellingham	23	27	40	22	34	22	38			50		832	50	596		920	12	266	³ 450
Cheney	27	13	24	27	24	27	24			148	3	871	148			871	0	332	
Ellensburg	14		23	13	23	21	33			14		497	14			421	90	112	243
West Virginia:																		
Athens	13		10	4	9	8	9			0		310	0	104	3	200	162	56	² 2,232
Fairmont	8	6	7	6						0		172						8	9,000
Glenville	16	10	21		6		5			20		311	20		25		372	0	8,820
Huntington	5	2	10	2	4	3	5			118		182	118	139	13		215	51	700
Institute	4	2	9	2	4	4	8					156			10		69		2,530
Shepherdstown												108					126		
West Liberty																			
Wisconsin:																		
Eau Claire	33	6	15	9	8	27	77			28		372	7	174	23	355	22	0	1,132
La Crosse	13	10	27	11	8	18	18			165		626	25	190	135	585	71	135	1,800
Menomonie	13	13	18	23	11	20	55			174		308	133	157	174	308	356	11	
Milwaukee	30	19	53	16	70	33				284		1,519	33	572	108	1,339	69	37	9,534
Oshkosh	22	11	36	13		13				139		582	45	304	199	583		0	1,962
Platteville	22	16	20	9	4	19	18			100		225	13	139	100	370	295		3,146
River Falls	31	13	31	9	10	11	31			258		561	43	232	157	719	167		7,404
Stevens Point	26	9	12		9	16	11			112		719	24	291	112	452	118		0
Superior	17	9	19		9	13	19			57		580	3	296	18	295			3,672
Whitewater							9			121	0	455	18	170	63				3,827

TABLE 43.—*State normal schools—Property and income, 1917–18.*

Location of institution.[1]	Property.				Receipts.						
	Bound volumes in library.	Value of library, apparatus, machinery, furniture.	Value of grounds and buildings.	Endowment funds.	Student fees.		From productive funds.	Public funds for—		All other sources.	Total available for use.
					Tuition, etc.	Board, room, etc.		Increase of plant.	Current expenses.		
1	2	3	4	5	6	7	8	9	10	11	12
Alabama:											
Daphne	2,500	$3,500	$29,000	0	$600			$3,000	$5,000		$8,600
Florence	6,000	35,666	211,000	0	12,285	$22,273		0	20,000	$4,480	59,038
Jacksonville	2,500	18,000	125,000	0	7,480	10,667	0	0	20,000	1,088	39,235
Livingston	3,000	15,000	210,000	0	9,448	24,179	0		20,000	0	53,627
Montgomery	750	1,000	65,000	0	2,902				16,000	4,965	28,917
Mooreville											
Normal											
Troy	7,500	31,000	172,300	0	11,486	840 18,215	0 $397		4,000 20,000	24,022 098	29,538 61,041
Arizona:											
Flagstaff[3]	6,460	100,000	500,000		4,000	35,000		100,000	83,000		222,000
Tempe	11,200	115,865	423,825		2,458	44,814	2,491	52,500	110,000	4,750	216,978
Arkansas:											
Conway	4,407	35,506	201,007	0	5,081	19,006	900	31,996	47,430	0	113,612
Pine Bluff	2,150	1,537	88,500	0	786	246		0	12,000	13,586	27,357
California:											
Arcata	1,378	10,225	484,775		0	0	0	245,000	76,360	3,500	326,369
Chico	22,150	50,000	292,000					16,000	63,165	3,124	82,065
Fresno	8,000	38,417	417,000		923			19,000	77,475	1,085	99,031
Los Angeles	27,445	84,417	691,076						200,500	707	202,198
San Diego	18,307	45,197	310,100						85,841	0	85,845
San Francisco	22,246	75,814	240,000		0 1,716	0	0	750,000 3,846	85,150 60,500	2,659	845,500 66,002
San Jose	19,986	41,500	527,033 158,700		4,888	0	0	27,000	43,150	0	74,998
Colorado:											
Gunnison	6,000	8,500	60,000	0	6,500			19,655	65,184	11,000	102,239
Connecticut:											
Danbury	8,370	25,000	130,000		19,342	?			39,824		49,166
New Britain	11,000				20,615			21,201	42,274		84,089
New Haven	15,000	10,000	190,000		19,166				25,292		44,458
Willimantic	13,981	10,000	225,000		19,746	2,005		1,760	38,375	4,505	61,676
Georgia:											
Athens	10,091	20,000	475,000	$1,000	6,970	50,000			57,500		113,970
Milledgeville	8,500	100,000	440,000		6,440			53,000	67,500		76,540
Valdosta	3,500	12,000	140,700		3,788	18,992			20,000	8,961	116,064

Idaho: Albion	4,914	35,772	177,289	7,058	3,025	21,439		35,400	84,600	285	144,749
Lewiston	1,542	37,582	180,967		0	18,488		40,000	94,865	5,812	159,195
Illinois: Carbondale	20,162	38,102	552,840		6,650	15,310		25,150	129,100		177,150
Charleston	23,500	100,266	402,351		6,964	26,220		6,000	116,183		138,340
De Kalb	23,500	69,689	714,726		2,460	28,650		21,050	124,615	0	175,705
Macomb	17,764	148,311	645,205		7,346	4,666		70,970	117,885		185,875
Normal	34,000	168,317	762,500	166,226	18,703	3,297	6,644	58,653	174,765	30,425	391,644
Indiana: Terre Haute	76,699	315,000	1,000,000	0	7,000	0	0	98,347	227,499	9,000	339,816
Kansas: Emporia	43,831	68,500	820,000	255,357	34,331		12,384	50,000	109,000		248,715
Hays	20,000	25,000	300,000		8,000			47,500	72,500	11,500	139,500
Pittsburg	10,000	10,000	561,000		28,343			101,880	123,343		252,708
Kentucky: Bowling Green	9,673	30,000	365,000	0	4,686	1,929		0	75,000	9,134	90,000
Frankfort	3,701	9,372	124,000	0	295	11,456			21,000	14,102	46,946
Richmond		54,106	371,940		2,444	30,317			75,000	12,373	131,134
Louisiana: Natchitoches	9,916	158,720	341,600		12,610	103,687	6,273		68,750	2,293	158,003
Maine: Castine	3,000	10,000	108,000	0					25,000	0	25,000
Farmington	4,000	10,000	143,000	0					21,000	0	21,000
Gorham	1,000	25,000	220,000	0		6,000	0		11,000		15,000
Machias		3,500	79,200		0	0	0	0	11,036	500	22,036
Presque Isle	1,500	9,500	93,000		0						
Maryland: Bowie	250	2,500	32,000	1,500	360			10,000	10,000	449	10,449
Frostburg	1,300	25,000	64,000	0	948		0		10,000	1,377	11,377
Towson	4,300		805,000	0	60				60,000	689	94,337
Massachusetts: Boston	1,547		225,000		130	44,367		160,000	97,854	778	232,328
Bridgewater	12,000	25,000	875,500	0	650	24,715			132,996	0	132,996
Fitchburg	7,000		476,943	0	862	41,611			131,827	1,156	174,644
Framingham	5,654	20,250	376,073			12,696		0	30,270	291	41,284
Hyannis	2,700	32,300	134,093	0	650	19			60,142	2	66,813
Lowell	2,000		1,263,752		882	18,978			44,368		63,090
North Adams	6,900	20,000	305,317	0	276				72,965	204	172,905
Salem		40,000	566,000	0	200	15,947			60,096	282	77,148
Westfield	14,500		140,000			3,680			64,990		55,877
Michigan: Kalamazoo	17,000	118,251	467,100		18,373			170,000	170,000	921	169,294
Marquette	24,000	66,595	230,040		7,883			84,000	84,000	7,585	91,882
Mount Pleasant	20,700		492,819		4,699				102,333		107,175
Ypsilanti	45,300	188,852	804,588		32,222		143	116,522	235,000	98	339,335
							5,493				

1 For names of institutions, see Table 41.
2 This is less than the reported expenditures.
3 Data are approximates.
4 This is half of the amount for the biennium 1916-18.
5 Includes all student fees.
6 Not included in total of receipts for the institution.
7 Includes library apparatus, furniture, etc.
8 Appropriation covers period from Dec. 1, 1917, to Dec. 1, 1918.

Location of institution.	Property.				Receipts.							
	Bound volumes in library.	Value of library, apparatus, machinery, furniture.	Value of grounds and buildings.	Endowment funds.	Student fees.		From productive funds.	Public funds for—		All other sources.	Total available for use.
					Tuition, etc.	Board, room, etc.		Increase of plant.	Current expenses.		
1	2	3	4	5	6	7	8	9	10	11	12
Minnesota:											
Duluth	90,000	$40,000	$385,000		$5,665	$18,708	$950		$53,750		$154,700
Mankato	13,720	78,165	447,865		4,044	35,309	1,533		85,699		11,575
Moorhead	12,200	14,287	424,000		6,452			$19,230	102,655	$7,323	149,331
St. Cloud	15,212	59,631	375,000		5,000	18,600	1,720	5,000	87,225	8,089	122,716
Winona	13,000	25,000	430,000	$30,000			1,200		80,000		109,900
Mississippi:											
Hattiesburg	6,050	32,208	424,948		3,736			6,500	48,000	229	58,465
Missouri:											
Cape Girardeau	10,813	61,848	750,000	1,000	25,199	30,101	55	0	87,714	8,966	152,085
Jefferson City	3,914	4,638	205,000		22,000				33,682	6,983	40,665
Kirksville	30,000	65,000	290,000		12,573				91,000		113,000
Maryville	16,000	92,000	408,000	0	15,064				74,554	3,457	90,584
Springfield		70,000	432,000		36,580			18,144	81,039		96,108
Warrensburg	34,524								112,515		167,239
Montana:											
Dillon	10,220	18,000	269,000		3,835	30,248		52,500	75,000		161,583
Nebraska:											
Chadron	5,153	7,000	312,000		17,450	117,818			92,500	11,499	116,426
Kearney	15,000	30,000	467,000		3,110	1,672		7,645	90,000	7,400	114,956
Peru	27,418	130,000	475,000		3,500	1,656		11,500	100,000		108,000
Wayne	7,000	50,000			3,000	5,000					
New Hampshire:											
Keene	2,500	5,000	165,000	0	33,369	128,614	0	0	34,500	5,380	73,229
Plymouth	6,500	9,000	206,000	0	0			0	32,000	857	32,867
New Jersey:											
Montclair	8,997	58,976	398,080			24,250			97,825		122,075
Newark	10,748	70,000	650,000						129,150		129,170
Trenton	6,000	88,248	784,000	4,500		51,534	170	8,000	135,944	20	190,638
New Mexico:											
East Las Vegas	7,000	20,730	104,819		5,916	10,469	6,415	15,812	49,443	10,472	94,811
Silver City	8,000	26,000	176,000		6,050	115,549		17,000	46,500	29,638	104,588

Institution											
New York:											
Brockport	14,480	25,000	275,000		0		6,056				54,902
Buffalo	7,000	84,467	428,600			1,140	6,087				77,070
Cortland	14,433	308,000	272,000			733	6,669			1,620	86,667
Fredonia	5,000	10,000	325,000		0		51,299		61,140		52,340
Geneseo	11,864	55,528	200,000				111,323		52,000		29,742
New Paltz	9,000	21,833	320,000	250,000			4,381		74,186	1,200	78,000
Oneonta	7,000	51,833	320,000						64,936		74,186
Oswego	25,000	25,050	405,000		0				46,625		74,781
Plattsburg	10,000	25,050	175,000						57,856	28,000	46,625
Potsdam		58,900	641,000			11,910				9,845	419,569
North Carolina:											
Cullowhee	300	5,000	110,000						11,200		19,207
Elizabeth City	834	5,150	43,000		1,951		6,066		9,009		19,252
Fayetteville	450	2,100	42,914		1,482		6,087	256	9,900		12,946
Greenville	1,871	45,903	288,914		720		6,669	0	60,000		139,217
Greensboro	15,000		700,000		6,148		51,299		125,000		351,717
Winston-Salem	1,000	8,700	61,645		38,155		4,381		7,540		14,480
North Dakota:											
Ellendale	3,900	49,224	145,448	375,482	5,042		10,541	21,326	28,757	0	65,720
Mayville	6,940	51,296	226,975		2,663		15,906	2,009	63,980		123,739
Minot	6,960	2,750	225,999		8,255		17,508	361	58,870	6,336	91,330
Valley City	14,302	69,319	416,850		19,165		34,347	24,366	87,722		165,622
Ohio:											
Bowling Green	15,000	88,657	573,763		789		21,873		116,388	123,285	263,826
Kent	16,000	88,000	742,500				34,688		134,690	55,855	225,238
Oklahoma:											
Ada	4,797	22,729	119,782		0	0		0	49,498	2,100	51,598
Alva	7,000	24,997	180,000		0				82,100	3,100	55,200
Durant	4,000		128,675		3,683				62,454	20,893	76,930
Edmond	11,873	43,200	216,041						82,000	8,000	90,000
Langston	300	6,000	176,000				13,961		50,537		69,681
Tahlequah	4,000	30,126	122,300						42,000		62,000
Weatherford	8,000	25,000	185,000		4,010				66,817		70,827
Oregon:											
Monmouth	6,320	20,000	215,000		6,264			0	35,151	25,000	82,691
Pennsylvania:											
Bloomsburg	7,811	30,520	418,198		30,719		67,479		16,000	0	115,889
California	8,150	35,620	373,950		27,377		26,185		75,123		94,851
Clarion	4,000	43,000	310,000		14,236		18,364		16,000		57,315
East Stroudsburg	3,275	49,025	190,281		16,806	0	60,073		22,000		98,878
Edinboro	8,843	45,241	231,625		3,576		25,719		31,476	59,320	125,643
Indiana	8,038	110,000	655,000		47,952		166,696		16,000		248,648
Kutztown	6,040	79,429	701,875	0	84,612				16,000		120,191
Lock Haven	6,623	39,550	310,300		16,939			6,887	20,407		77,151
Mansfield	18,115	185,050	750,000		37,458		31,893		16,000		118,903
Millersville	7,243	70,200	681,846	0	24,732		62,486		16,000		100,102
Shippensburg	6,103	37,050	293,500		23,969		46,528		19,217		88,158
Slippery Rock	20,000	31,082	322,411		5,830		43,620		9,038		118,610
West Chester		70,000	850,000		48,000		41,842		33,095		193,000
							126,000		19,000		

1 Not included in total receipts for the institution.
2 This is less than the reported expenditures.
3 Includes equipment.
4 Of this amount, $39,354 was for payment of debt.

150407°—20——7

TABLE 43.—State normal schools—Property and income, 1917-18—Continued.

Location of institution.	Property.				Receipts.							
	Bound volumes in library.	Value of library, apparatus, machinery, furniture.	Value of grounds and buildings.	Endowment funds.	Student fees.		From productive funds.	Public funds for—		All other sources.	Total available for use.
					Tuition, etc.	Board, room, etc.		Increase of plant.	Current expenses.		
1	2	3	4	5	6	7	8	9	10	11	19
Rhode Island:											
Providence	23,600	$150,000	$650,000	0	$9,000				$74,000		$83,000
South Carolina:											
Orangeburg	550	25,000	307,000		2,432	$6,000	0	$44,500	20,000		0
Rockhill	20,649	141,709	945,822	0	46,790	134,330		3,414	114,076	$67,818	140,780
South Dakota:											
Aberdeen	8,480	32,307	490,900		20,069	3,358	$5,290	163,026	90,813		308,610
Madison	5,000	10,000	200,000		18,060		7,500		59,960		288,565
Spearfish	10,500	37,845	350,000		6,718	3,355		75,800	70,089		75,500
Springfield	3,000	28,500	121,500	$5,214	4,327	1,568	8,282	10,000	30,500		155,962
Tennessee:											
Johnson City	3,000	15,000	285,000	$1,000,000	4,496	21,371	2,047		83,319		64,673
Memphis											81,233
Murfreesboro											
Nashville	1,452	16,755	146,734		2,785	19,245			26,669	12,000	60,687
Texas:											
Canyon	13,000	100,000	340,000		11,767			89,171	72,275		125,507
Commerce	8,340	6,666	201,435		3,484			14,900	11,000	2,394	169,884
Denton	11,000	64,384	339,678		26,620			90,000	140,985	40,000	267,605
Huntsville	15,000	74,000	334,000		9,540			80,000	108,550		198,060
Prairie View	500	25,000	343,960		8,778	108,598	0	65,150	74,147		234,519
San Marcos	22,483	50,000	191,000	0	8,778	0	12,648	116,000	100,000	12,500	234,775
Vermont:											
Castleton	3,500	10,000	28,000		663	10,933	0		15,000		25,963
Johnson	7,028	12,712	16,000			2,677	39		25,100	2,180	30,566
Virginia:											
East Radford	4,000	47,000	263,000		3,530	23,912			88,000		78,652
Farmville	8,328	41,000	408,000		9,188	93,831			78,467	7,100	203,661
Fredericksburg	4,000	30,000	325,000	2,845	4,370	40,531	428	5,000	43,888	22,714	97,191
Harrisonburg	5,860	30,000	262,000	0	6,985	52,285	0	5,000	30,360	3,629	107,608
Petersburg	1,500	36,483	222,379		6,676	42,637		2,000		17,571	66,134
Washington:											
Bellingham	20,000	80,000	310,000		20,023	15,090		20,000	125,000	450	180,713
Cheney	16,000	35,000	492,000			15,200	800	10,900	126,000	0	159,290
Ellensburg	12,000	60,445	366,260	0	3,749	25,346		14,415	59,646		183,100

West Virginia:											
Athens	8,000	26,000	635,000	0	1,000	4,700		10,000	38,176		83,870
Fairmont	4,500	8,000	135,000	0					24,975		24,975
Glenville	7,285	68,888	280,000	0	11,081	16,606			72,500		100,086
Huntington	900	6,000	280,000	0	2,070	15,591			51,860	16,880	96,391
Institute	5,347	17,000	125,000	0	2,086	3,980			30,000		*36,065
Shepherdstown	5,000	6,000	92,000	0	1,317				13,780	412	16,100
West Liberty											
Wisconsin:											
Eau Claire	4,279	50,000	240,000	0	2,889			25,491	55,566	0	81,067
La Crosse	25,000	48,837	363,133	0	8,720			26,378	94,584		120,962
Menominie	9,973	151,579	598,770	0	34,948	21,725	37,734	9,700	138,785	0	148,485
Milwaukee	57,412	105,469	770,000	0	23,080			16,682	161,710		178,292
Oshkosh	18,608	100,000	825,000	0	10,458	4,697		189,422	126,168		315,560
Platteville	12,363	71,000	232,000	0	5,612			410,984	78,125		184,109
River Falls	26,350	59,603	240,475	0	5,600			13,300	95,948		109,248
Stevens Point	13,803	64,425	323,697	0	8,130			29,856	97,227		127,063
Superior	8,800	300,000	479,000	0	7,685	17,064		69,000	81,000	76	150,000
Whitewater	14,701	60,000	247,000	0	6,104	15,500	0	48,100	82,068	0	130,168

1 Includes all student fees, as board and room.
2 Land.
3 This is less than the reported expenditures.
4 Not included in total.

TABLE 44.—*State normal schools—Expenditures, 1917-18.*

Location of institution.[1]	Administration. Business.	Educational. Salary of principal.	Educational. Other expenses.	Instruction. Deans and teachers.	Instruction. Textbooks, supplies, etc.	Operation of school plant.	Maintenance.	Auxiliary agencies and sundry activities.	Fixed charges (rent, insurance, etc.)	Total current expenses.	Outlays (capital acquisition and construction).	Payment of indebtedness.
	2	3	4	5	6	7	8	9	10	11	12	18
Alabama:												
Daphne												
Florence	$22,516	$3,000	$1,720	$19,516	$4,062	$11,940	$18,188	$634		$82,176		0
Jacksonville	0	3,100	400	12,749	750	4,576	930	1,310	$918	25,433	0	$1,000
Livingston		3,100	1,000	12,989		6,276		1,500	1,200	34,459	1,660	
Montgomery	(*)	2,000	400	13,340	400	1,576	1,000	1,500	985	19,825	3,161	
Moundville												
Normal												
Troy	1,768	1,800	1,366	11,690	1,443	10,726	2,470	1,468		25,631		3,185
		3,100	1,200	18,370		14,301				44,129		
Arizona:												
Flagstaff[2]	7,000	5,500	2,500	58,600	15,000	22,800	8,800	3,000	2,274	123,900	73,600	
Tempe	1,208	4,400	3,345	66,936	9,179	20,653	7,844	50,683		156,402	56,112	
Arkansas:												
Conway	458	3,000	2,867	34,190	0	14,118	17,686	1,381	8,800	76,899	69,545	
Pine Bluff	700	2,040	650	12,646	5,704	3,643	610	680	400	98,922	914	
California:												
Arcata		4,000	965	13,598	9,000	2,422	2,000	3,003	0	96,876	7,000	0
Chico		2,598	1,330	38,897	1,286	8,980	2,200	2,700		60,106	15,000	
Fresno	3,870	4,500	1,800	52,785		7,411	2,884	2,500		73,543	16,486	
Los Angeles	1,779	6,000	3,772	149,683	827	20,090	8,425	7,000		191,780		
San Diego	1,802	4,000	600	52,535	2,831	8,159	13,622	3,994		85,416		
San Francisco	1,300	4,000	900	53,060	4,077	8,648	10,321	2,639		84,176		
San Jose		42,411	8,140	87,788	5,404	15,908	2,975	6,506		130,940	0	
Santa Barbara			3,009	27,656		5,818	1,307	1,611		46,816	20,000	
Colorado:												
Gunnison	8,964	4,060	2,415	43,665	2,800	6,087	5,500	7,210	400	81,081	1,500	1,016
Connecticut:												
Danbury	1,013	3,500	900	34,265	3,268	8,461	1,041	1,698		49,196		
New Britain	1,141	3,500	700	41,187	2,535	8,285	4,389	1,131		62,838	21,261	
New Haven	731	3,500	400	34,077	927	8,145	875	1,108		44,438		
Willimantic	719	3,500	700	29,668	2,602	7,632	2,874	2,644		50,126	1,750	
Georgia:												
Athens		3,960	1,700	54,199	1,896	12,641	8,148	3,565		79,908	90,093	
Milledgeville	620	2,500	1,360	21,664		13,205	4,606	1,177		46,968	89,489	
Valdosta												

Institution[1]	1	2	3	4	5	6	7	8	9	10	11	12
Idaho:												
Albion	2,017	3,575	275	29,878	2,594	16,731	5,880	2,212	278	63,240		33,400
Lewiston		8,500	4,388	55,280		15,827	20,216	5,049	700	104,927		
Illinois:												
Carbondale		6,000	3,400	66,406	11,361	21,660	8,200	7,700		123,226	6,000	
Charleston		6,000	1,235	69,000	2,160	42,660	2,105	5,466		130,676	730	
De Kalb		6,000	1,700	85,650	2,162	40,884	12,064	4,131	660	151,721	1,345	
Macomb		6,000	5,200	65,171	3,080	27,280	1,288	4,441		111,465	60,114	
Normal	2,602		2,710	128,117	13,690	39,043	4,570	8,617	185	190,212	56,608	
Indiana:												
Terre Haute	1,535	7,000	5,300	135,000	3,155	81,991	6,375	12,704	714	288,564	73,046	
Kansas:												
Emporia	1,321	5,000	15,562	146,705	8,000	21,187	2,260	14,300		207,075	50,000	
Hays		5,000	2,600	69,500	10,000	42,150		3,750		135,150	4,350	
Pittsburg		5,500	6,170	101,628	3,840	13,354	3,500	3,993		137,855		5,000
Kentucky:												
Bowling Green	3,200	4,200	4,325	52,261	2,665	8,990	9,826	950		85,009		
Frankfort	1,962	2,400	1,500	19,814	1,333	12,465	5,942	900		44,406		
Richmond		3,600	1,724	34,384		16,499	492			59,541		
Louisiana:												
Natchitoches	1,800	4,000	3,115	56,163	4,419	32,104	36,290	68,640	1,701	198,202	-1,545	
Maine:												
Castine	54	2,400	400	12,526	150	2,300	500	25		18,275	250	0
Farmington	142	2,600	515	13,400	385	3,180	425		0	20,480		
Gorham	1,366	2,600	500	14,000	500	6,000	500	400		24,100		
Machias	0	2,150	200	8,300	150	3,310	500	50		14,410		0
Presque Isle		2,200	120	11,616	600	6,950				22,036		0
Maryland:												
Bowie[5]		1,400		2,062	67	2,830	215	420		7,068		
Frostburg[4]		2,000	28	5,578	70	1,918	95	955		10,798		
Towson[5]		4,000	1,970	28,124	3,050	18,730	4,562	3,101	7	59,942		
Massachusetts:												
Boston		8,500	3,502	36,347	3,991	76,894	20,125			143,359	149,000	
Bridgewater		4,000	3,140	42,635	7,256	24,120	7,170	1,231		89,851		
Fitchburg[4]		4,500	3,349	45,313	3,306	114,396	12,973	1,837	0	174,844		
Framingham		3,250	1,600	15,075	1,275	10,317	2,655			34,179		
Hyannis		3,063	1,242	42,695	3,880	11,960	1,161			64,881		
Lowell[4]		3,250	3,325	20,833	2,583	28,081	3,891			61,983		
North Adams		3,500	1,800	44,684	5,625	16,497	4,249			76,355		
Salem		3,250	2,481	19,008	2,546	15,064	5,415	880	0	47,764		
Westfield		3,208	1,041	23,503	2,280	11,258	1,723			45,597		
Worcester	2,297							287				
Michigan:												
Kalamazoo	5,459	5,000	6,554	109,187		39,997	5,214	10,215	1,120	179,746	3,435	
Marquette	546	4,000	2,580	55,730		10,641	1,304	8,276		91,852		
Mount Pleasant	3,332	4,250	2,500	204,140	2,806	18,243	3,826	1,902	2,198	240,391	1,368	
Ypsilanti	6,441	5,500	12,361	153,688	21,943	54,325	4,052	12,240	2,309	272,759	116,522	

1 For names of institutions see Table 41.
2 Included in educational administration.
3 Data are approximate.
4 Annual salary is $4,000.
5 For year ending July 31, 1918.
6 December, 1916, to December, 1917.
7 Annual salary of $3,250.

TAABLE 44.—*State normal schools—Expenditures, 1917-18*—Continued.

Location of institution.	Administration.	Instruction.				Operation of school plant.	Maintenance.	Auxiliary agencies and sundry activities.	Fixed charges (rent, insurance, etc.)	Total current expenses.	Outlays (capital acquisition and construction).	Payment of indebtedness.
	Business.	Educational.		Deans and teachers.	Textbooks, supplies, etc.							
		Salary of principal.	Other expenses.									
1	2	3	4	5	6	7	8	9	10	11	12	13
Minnesota:												
Duluth	$1,950	$5,000	$2,650	$30,450	$860	$8,600	$8,800	$750		$52,100		
Mankato		5,000	3,631	53,035	4,205	17,533	5,064	3,049		93,467		
Moorhead		5,000	7,830	54,501	3,889	29,763	10,689	4,404		116,056	35,784	
St. Cloud	3,000	5,000	7,067	55,817	3,472	19,575	21,220	2,066		114,537		
Winona		5,000	4,900	54,000	5,500	24,400	9,000	3,300		109,900		
Mississippi:												
Hattiesburg	2,865	3,500	2,371	29,237	973	6,013	182	3,324		48,465	10,000	
Missouri:												
Cape Girardeau	1,257	3,900	10,278	61,862	4,069	26,126	22,728	8,237	$751	139,200	0	$4,315
Jefferson City	1,093			20,561		13,900	2,797			88,440		
Kirksville		5,000	3,000	68,348	2,000	16,632	2,000	12,585	1,900	110,700	3,000	
Maryville	337	4,000	2,900	44,440	2,000	14,148	9,640	3,338	3,300	84,610		
Springfield		4,000	1,980	71,098		12,500				96,226	6,000	
Warrensburg	1,500	4,000	780	79,568	6,000	6,860		9,962		102,285		773
Montana:												
Dillon		4,000	4,068	46,039	493	16,055	1,601	2,945	225	75,916	54,000	
Nebraska:												
Chadron		8,000	180	38,668	680	9,646	1,000	930		54,074	212,000	
Kearney		3,000	7,160	57,959	5,182	20,900	10,457	5,107		109,774	118,823	
Peru		3,000	4,900	65,800	5,800	19,820	6,800	7,910		114,080		
Wayne			4,480	56,500	8,000	20,400	6,000	4,100		97,480		
New Hampshire:												
Keene	62	3,500	948	41,683	5,496	18,751	930	400	966	71,568	0	
Plymouth		3,500	1,008	14,865	1,435	9,632	1,960	560		52,367		
New Jersey:												
Montclair	2,956	6,000	1,700	38,026	15,585	35,980	10,786	2,678		113,618		
Newark	5,699	6,500	3,347	75,601	8,677	11,801	7,265	6,458	1,634	128,867		
Trenton	1,524	4,400	2,580	57,108	13,273	85,108	43,585	8,697		161,440	2,944	
New Mexico:												
East Las Vegas	387	4,347	2,629	31,434	24,868	5,448	2,018	3,616	156	71,282		
Silver City		3,600	3,450	29,092	4,645	2,700	45,533			92,036	19	

New York:												
Brockport	200	3,800	900	27,375	2,940	8,928	7,622	1,150		51,770		
Buffalo		3,000	2,200	46,390	2,460	11,704	1,622	876	388	68,006		
Cortland		3,000		35,900	4,974	9,331	1,474			68,467		
Fredonia	250	3,300	1,000	34,300	1,500	8,284	2,297	3,800		61,816	8,760	
Geneseo	4,700	4,250		42,650	12,661	6,845	10,186	1,100		87,077		
New Paltz	400	3,800	2,000	32,000	1,800	9,646	2,100	2,566	26	60,520		
Onta.		3,800		51,750	3,519	9,327	2,124	2,500		74,786		
Oswego	1,200	3,800	2,100	41,558	3,400	14,357	9,937	1,900		74,783		
Plattsburg		3,800		31,350	1,450	475				74,626		
Potsdam	400	3,500	900	37,731		8,437	4,061	659	244	233,066		
North Carolina:												
Elon		2,000	330	9,398	597	3,816	945	346		15,444	925	
Elizabeth City	171	1,200	485	6,716	337	1,904	5,276	228	50	14,153	0	0
Fayetteville		1,200	288	3,869		1,908	8,121	4,640		12,576	18,592	0
Green'lle	3,141	3,600	1,684	28,743	1,681	61,340	18,721	35,492	326	113,338	56,071	
Negro	2,472	3,600	3,110	101,792	12,572	135,378	4,018	343		313,167	917	
Winston-Salem		1,000	414	4,094	246	3,232		151		13,498		
North Dakota:												
Ellendale	0	3,250	1,167	22,069	957	14,656	2,201	2,790	1,560	48,650	10,466	2,100
Mayville		4,000	1,373	27,410	483	19,247	6,379	1,737	1,206	61,334	60,000	
Minot	2,800	1,754	1,807	24,576	1,250	23,250	13,669	5,302	43	77,366	14,584	
Valley City	4,655	5,000	6,282	72,803	5,576	25,528	3,892		2,034	131,071		
Ohio:												
Bowling Green		4,300	870	52,071	2,835	1,059	812	6,856		90,326	57,000	
Kent	3,522	4,500	4,675	63,750	3,700	32,316	4,100	6,775		119,816	5,500	
Okla.:												
Ada		3,000	1,825	39,270	1,038	3,598	2,712	150		51,593	19,855	
Alva		3,000	1,846	31,428	1,668	4,284	710	3,069		4,966	8,000	
Durant		3,000	1,832	32,047	1,010	4,443	670	4,069		47,061	9,133	
E'mond		3,000	2,700	41,700		6,600	1,883	4,600		63,688		
Lawston	960			26,972		5,659	98	984		41,402		
Tahlequah		3,000	2,100	26,567		5,718	3,403	807		42,000	10,131	
Weatherford		2,950	1,558	31,557		6,771	1,961	4,976		49,673		
Oregon:												
Monmouth		3,600	1,400	30,644	14,292		1,000	3,500		54,436	28,255	
Pennsylvania:												
Bloomsburg	4,010	4,500		34,823	1,396	31,646	39,828	3,972	8,059	128,232	3,789	63,000
California	2,439	4,300	1,792	21,391	285	23,004	1,711	2,310	2,868	59,100	19,769	39,354
Clarion	2,300	2,500	900	15,199	3,800	25,409	1,165	3,054	1,136	55,453	173	1,688
East Stroudsburg	770	2,750	1,576	20,775	3,432	261	42,006	3,470		99,539		
Edinboro	1,416	3,350	790	16,978	3,672	16,742	1,284	17,703	789	62,724	59,186	3,296
Indiana	1,828	5,000	2,783	56,362	6,011	72,908	12,738	65,516	4,214	226,407	5,200	14,474
Kutztown	2,113	3,700		28,090	3,792	29,743	40,201	2,655	847	110,741	4,211	13,552
Lock Haven	2,741	3,000	1,980	18,182	3,883	20,772	22,396	3,382	484	76,519		10,000
Mansfield	1,016	3,000	1,260	19,044	3,804	31,436	43,036	7,768	6,406	115,770		
Millersville	1,200	4,000	480	24,436	3,505	36,766	4,723	4,962	494	82,693	3,217	30,000
Shippensburg		4,500	1,598	17,990	2,754	23,642	10,147	3,203	2,621	64,180	1,248	992
Slippery Rock	3,780	5,000	720	28,986	1,127	16,455	61,656	3,454	855	122,777		
West Chester			1,500	40,886	9,433	51,707	5,103	2,050	1,099	115,659	661	

1 From normal school fund.   2 Not ...ding dormitory expenses.   3 House rent in addition.   4 Includes salaries, fees, wages.   5 Paid by the State.

Table 44.—*State normal schools—Expenditures, 1917–18*—Continued.

Location of institution.	Administration.	Educational.		Instruction.		Operation of school plant.	Maintenance.	Auxiliary agencies and sundry activities.	Fixed charges (rent, insurance, etc.).	Total current expenses.	Outlays capital acquisition and construction).	Payment of indebtedness.
	Business.	Salary of principal.	Other expenses.	Deans and teachers.	Textbooks, supplies, etc.							
1	2	3	4	5	6	7	8	9	10	11	12	13
Rhode Island:												
Providence [1]		$4,000	$2,500	$47,500	$7,000	$17,000	$3,300	$1,700		$83,000		
South Carolina:												
Orangeburg	$21,598	2,000	1,360	86,299	3,309	18,819	11,763	778		74,328	$18,880	
Rockhill		5,000	4,838	71,340	8,836	40,128	26,457	67,640	$7,843	262,600	23,472	$2,023
South Dakota:												
Aberdeen	4,429	4,000	5,978	58,381	5,290	27,500	9,090	3,290		117,917	97,367	
Madison		3,000	1,100	34,000	5,060	25,626	4,700	1,698		75,100		
Spearfish		3,000	1,680	41,635	3,169	19,819	19,531	2,975		92,100		
Springfield	2,199	3,000	1,346	17,889	444	16,660	1,302	344		43,984	8,375	
Tennessee:												
Johnson City												
Memphis												
Murfreesboro												
Nashville [1]	2,500	2,400	1,900	17,600	900	13,648	4,000	9,806		45,068	7,066	
Texas:												
Canyon	6,000	2,000	1,000	59,943	3,643	6,500	27,314			102,787	47,225	
Commerce		3,000	6,711	43,083	7,475	2,000	600	1,200	1,560	66,087	106,360	
Denton	2,000	3,600	1,000	117,000	4,900	7,000	3,400	5,300		141,925	93,000	
Huntsville	1,700	2,000	1,638	60,060	1,927	9,146	8,700	4,121		98,395	119,174	
Prairie View	3,156	3,600	4,083	37,071	7,150	71,495	44,237	6,831	8,840	155,645	60,990	0
San Marcos [1]				64,551		20,780	5,040			115,945		
Vermont:												
Castleton		2,000	225	7,187	727	4,759	1,784	525	915	18,222		
Johnson		2,100	540	15,300	1,000	3,606	2,102	3,729		28,437		
Virginia:												
East Radford	2,453	3,000	1,581	16,661	597	15,013	18,686	4,997	559	63,440	16,300	1,301
Farmville	1,200	4,300	1,275	48,348	176	37,230	11,683	7,886	1,091	113,489		
Fredericksburg	1,782	8,000	1,000	29,882	1,171	20,704	7,470	6,080	676	99,716		
Harrisonburg	2,897	3,000	1,046	25,658	6,843	47,999	4,827	4,949	962	97,691	1,935	3,655
Petersburg	2,470	1,700	715	13,613	6,572	14,658	4,542	48,977	(*)	87,047	9,621	3,200

Washington:													
Bellingham	8,294	4,800	3,988	71,839	5,492	18,670	9,618	13,150	782	131,428	87,000	
Cheney		5,000	2,800	54,000		28,800	2,580	9,830		103,010	9,500	
Ellensburg	8,783	4,500	6,003	55,232	8,976	17,394	1,684			96,442	14,415	
West Virginia:													
Athens												0
Fairmont		3,000	680	27,000	1,600	6,560	1,600	8,550	20	43,570	10,000	
Glenville		2,500	240	15,000	500	2,800	500	1,850		28,380	0	
Huntington		3,600	2,380	39,050		7,987	10,000	1,200		64,197		
Institute		1,900	1,920	32,000	1,000	8,200		1,982		47,002		
Shepherdstown		2,500	14,760	17,460	1,016	5,990	500	807		43,053		
West Liberty		2,400	90	8,950	1,080	1,285	300	675		14,780		
Wisconsin:												0
Eau Claire		3,500	3,240	34,620	8,020	7,580	800	4,346	780	87,566	23,255	
La Crosse		4,250	2,618	63,402	8,072	10,098	8,145	6,280	702	93,555	1,628	
Menomonie	8,396	6,000	0	48,621	5,334	86,044	3,231	4,641	0	122,317	10,330	
Milwaukee		5,000	7,631	108,950	4,978	19,884	3,897	8,385	1,128	159,263	131,453	
Oshkosh		4,250	5,280	67,250	5,121	13,616	1,729	8,999		107,235	90,000	
Platteville		3,750	1,770	44,538	2,700	12,559	9,675	4,947	780	78,217	2,000	
River Falls	9,100	3,760	3,976	61,670	4,075	10,746	7,900	4,875	1,100	107,190	27,616	
Stevens Point		4,000	3,838	59,419	3,980	16,062	6,481	4,468	1,182	98,409		
Superior		4,250	3,620	56,925	8,695	14,650	408	5,140		98,688		
Whitewater		4,000	3,572	51,243	9,008	11,306	2,202	4,151	1,068	79,452	4,434	

¹ Estimated.   ² Includes insurance.   ³ Included under sundry activities.

TABLE 45.—City and county normal schools—General information and personnel, 1917-18.

Location	Institution	Number of weeks of sessions in year	Length of normal courses in years	Entrance requirements for normal courses; completion of—	Hours of practice required	Number of teachers, including principal — Men	Number of teachers, including principal — Women	Different students attending — Men	Different students attending — Women	Number of graduates from normal course (1918) — Men	Number of graduates from normal course (1918) — Women	Number of attendance weeks
Washington, D.C.	James Ormond Wilson Normal School	36	2	High school	90	4	18		197	0	54	23,582
Do.	Myrtilla Minor Normal	36	2	do	600	18	9	8	108	4	52	23,798
Chicago, Ill.	Chicago Normal College	45	2	do	50	3	25	34	1,300	4	355	31,290
Fort Wayne, Ind.	Fort Wayne Normal College	40	2	do	240	3	13		27		16	21,000
Indianapolis, Ind.	Normal Training School	38	2	do	950	3	23	0	126	0	49	3,698
Louisville, Ky.	Louisville Normal School	40	2	do	560	1	30		113	0	46	4,160
New Orleans, La.	New Orleans Normal School	36	2	do	60		16		132		47	2,376
Lexington, Mo.	Normal Training School	37	2	do	462		9		17		9	629
Baltimore, Md.	Colored Training School	36	2	do	450	2	9	12	69	5	19	651
Do.	Teachers' Training School	40	2	do	500	4	26	6	211	4	117	16,942
Boston, Mass.	Boston Normal School	40	3	do	500	6	18	5	269	4	91	10,940
Detroit, Mich.	Detroit City Normal School	40	3	do	120	1	13	1	352		126	12,639
Lockington, Mich.	Mason County Normal School	38	1	Eleven grades	95		2		12		12	450
Manistee, Mich.	Manistee County Normal School	40	1	3 years of high school	25		2	0	13	0	11	520
Albert Lea, Minn.	Albert Lea High School	36	1	do	90	0			14		14	504
St. Louis, Mo.	Harris Teachers' College	45	2	High school	500	59	28		210		80	8,400
Jersey City, N.J.	Teachers' Training School	40	2	do	220	4	40	0	93	0	30	3,630
Albany, N.Y.	City Normal School	40	2	do	700	2	26		77		36	2,580
Brooklyn, N.Y.	Albany Teachers' Training School	38	2		580	1	2		12		12	
Jamaica, N.Y.	Brooklyn Training School for Teachers	40	2	High school	400	13	39	20	832	8	413	34,080
New York, N.Y.	Jamaica Training School for Teachers	40	2	do	515	4	9	14	197	6	112	3,922
Rochester, N.Y.	New York Training School for Teachers	40	2	do	500	7	29	3	572	3	208	17,900
Schenectady, N.Y.	Rochester City Normal School	36	2	do	560	1	26		150		47	4,398
Syracuse, N.Y.	Schenectady Teachers' Training School	40	2	do		1	25		32		8	1,098
Watertown, N.Y.	Syracuse Training School for Teachers	40	2	do	120	1	3		69	0	26	2,000
Yonkers, N.Y.	Watertown Training School	38	2	do	950	3	3		13		13	434
Akron, Ohio	Yonkers Training School for Teachers	38	1	do	470	1	6		40		20	
Anna, Ohio	Perkins Normal School	38	1	do	350	3	4	2	22	0	13	836
Ansonia, Ohio	Shelby County Normal School	38	1	do	54	1	2	2	21			828
Berlin Heights, Ohio	Darke County Normal School	38	1	do	38	1	1		16	2	10	648
Canal Winchester, Ohio	Erie County Normal School		1	1 year of high school	87	3	3		13		13	432
—	Franklin County Normal School		1	High school	54	1	1	1	19	2	14	684
Chardon, Ohio	Geauga County Normal School	38	1	do	35	2	3		12		12	432
Cleveland, Ohio	Cleveland Normal School	44	2	do	300	8	11		274		164	

Location	School	(a)	(b)	Grade requirement	(c)	(d)	(e)	(f)	(g)	(h)	(i)	(j)	Enrollment
Columbus, Ohio	Columbus Normal school	40	3	do.	25	3	14	2		100	0	55	[1]414
Continental, Ohio	Putnam County Normal School	36	1	do.	64	2	1		2	10	2	9	[1]2,300
Dayton, Ohio	Dayton Normal School	40	2	do.	425	1	9			63		28	972
Dresden, Ohio	Dresden County Normal School	38	1	do.	64		1	1		15	1	12	323
Lancaster, Ohio	Fairfield County Normal School	36	1		64		1	6		11	0	5	365
Medina, Ohio	Medina County Normal School	36	1	High school	120	2	1			9	0	9	
Minerva, Ohio	Stark County Normal School	36	1	do.	64	2	2			17		10	[1]468
Monroeville, Ohio	Huron County Normal School	36	1	High school	64	1	3			15	0	15	
New Lexington, Ohio	Perry County Normal School	36	1	do.	64	1	1	8		13	3	13	450
Oak Harbor, Ohio	Ottawa County Normal School	36	1		54	8	3	2		9	1	9	
Plain City, Ohio	Madison County Normal School	36	1	High school	54	3	3	2		21	0	8	450
St. Clairsville, Ohio	Belmont County Normal School	36	1	do.	54	4	3	2		13	8	12	900
Scio, Ohio	Harrison County Normal School	36	1	do.	54	1	3	1		12	2	10	820
West Alexandria, Ohio	Preble County Normal School	36	1	do.	54	2	3			14	2	22	
West Liberty, Ohio	Logan County Normal School	38	1	High school	54	4	6			23	1	11	570
Wheelersburg, Ohio	Scioto County Normal School	38	2	do.	300		1			15		10	
Erie, Pa.	Erie Normal School	38	2	do.	500	4	13			15		10	[3]4,880
Harrisburg, Pa.	Teachers' Training School	40	2	do.	170		137	7		122	50	70	19,240
Pittsburgh, Pa.	Pittsburgh Training School for Teachers	40		do.	500	8		69		605		138	[2]2,760
Philadelphia, Pa.	Philadelphia Normal School for Girls	40	1	High school	65	1	2	8		35	6	16	[3]1,720
Do.	Philadelphia School of Pedagogy	40	1	do.	40	2	2	0		85	0	20	[3]1,440
Algoma, Wis.	Door-Kewaunee County Training School	42	1	Ninth grade	30	1	2	1		65	0	28	[3]1,929
Alma, Wis.	Buffalo County Training School	44	1	Tenth grade	38	1	5	3		78	1	41	[3]2,068
Antigo, Wis.	Langlade County Training School	40	1	do.	80	2	2	6		100	2	28	3,720
Berlin, Wis.	Green Lake County Training School	40	1	Tenth grade	50	1	2	4		50		23	1,930
Columbus, Wis.	Columbia County Normal School	46	1	High school	33	2	3	0		80		15	
Eau Claire, Wis.	Eau Claire County Training School	40	1	do.	20	1	4	0		85	0	18	1,400
Gays Mills, Wis.	Crawford County Training School	38	1	do.	25	1	2	13		35	0	45	
Grand Rapids, Wis.	Wood County Training School	46	1	do.	25	2	2	18		90	9	38	
Janesville, Wis.	Rock County Training School	40	1	do.	20	1	5	0		61		24	
Ladysmith, Wis.	Rusk County Training School	40	1	Eighth grade	20	1	3	1		71	0	27	[3]3,320
Manitowoc, Wis.	Manitowoc County Training School	42	1	Tenth grade	36	1	4	0		63	1	30	
Marinette, Wis.	Stephenson Training School	40	1	High school	67	1	2	4		33	4	22	1,277
Medford, Wis.	Taylor County Training School	40	1	do.	40	2	2			49		28	
Menomonie, Wis.	Dunn County Training School	40	1	do.	100	1	2	4		29	4	21	640
Merrill, Wis.	Lincoln County Training School	40	3	Eighth grade	100	1	8	1		58	1	13	2,022
New London, Wis.	Waupaca County Training School	40	1	High school	25	2	3	0		44	0	38	1,565
Phillips, Wis.	Price County Training School	40	1	do.	25	1	2	1		56	0	15	1,980
Reedsburg, Wis.	Sauk County Training School	40	1	do.	50	1	2	2		57	1	39	2,227
Rhinelander, Wis.	Oneida County Training School	40	1	Tenth grade		1	2	3		90	1	33	[3]3,920
Rice Lake, Wis.	Barron County Training School	40	1	do.		1	2	8		38		14	
St. Croix Falls, Wis.	Polk County Training School	40	1	High school				2					
South Kaukauna, Wis.	Outagamie County Training School	40	1	do.		2	8						
Viroqua, Wis.	Vernon County Training School	40	1	do.		1	3						
Wausau, Wis.	Marathon County Training School	40	1	do.			2						
Wautoma, Wis.	Waushara County Training School	40	1	Tenth grade			2						

1 Average enrollment.
2 Enrollment weeks.
3 Additional students in extension courses, 735.
4 Additional students in extension courses, 191.
5 Additional students in extension courses, 105.
6 Not including summer school.
7 Average for both semesters.

TABLE 46.—*City and county normal schools—Property, receipts, and expenditures, 1917–18.*

Location.	Institution.	Property. Bound volumes in library.	Value of library, apparatus, machinery, furniture.	Value of grounds and buildings.	Receipts. Student fees for educational services.	Public funds. Increase of plant.	Public funds. Current expenses.	All other sources.	Expenditures. Salary of principal or director.	Total salaries of other instructors.	Other expenses of instruction and administration.	Operation and maintenance of plant, sundry and fixed charges.	Outlays for sites, buildings, etc.
		3	4	5	6	7	8	9	10	11	12	13	14
Washington, D. C.	James Ormond Wilson Normal School	9,700	$40,000	$316,000	0				$2,500	$27,320	$4,497	$8,359	$1,649
Do.	Myrtilla Minor Normal	4,275	29,000	196,000					2,500	16,980	3,448	5,572	1,099
Chicago, Ill.	Chicago Normal College	23,000		994,257					5,500	114,667	4,410	34,255	3,616
Fort Wayne, Ind.	Fort Wayne Normal School	3,862	9,000	45,000					2,100	10,500			
Indianapolis, Ind.	Normal Training School	1,200	8,000		0				2,000				
Louisville, Ky.	Louisville Normal School	3,100	7,500	181,660					2,000	8,397	200	10,667	11,243
New Orleans, La.	New Orleans Normal School	3,997	40,000	40,000	0				1,755	21,083	3,897	720	
Lewiston, Me.	Normal Training School (city)	1,150		50,000				$301	1,400	17,190	765		
Baltimore, Md.	Colored Training School		3,500						2,400		1,000	3,200	
Do.	Teachers' Training School							0	3,000	2,350	550		0
Boston, Mass.	Boston Normal School	4,000	18,000	245,000		0	0		3,500	11,200	2,400	1,250	
Detroit, Mich.	Detroit City Normal School	6,500	300					446	1,200	31,500	192		0
Ludington, Mich.	Mason County Normal School	500	1,500	174,525			1,646	212		1,900	60		
Manistee, Mich.	Manistee County Normal School	20,000	58,329			$1,000	1,024			788	312		
Albert Lea, Minn.	Albert Lea High School						1,200			1,100			
St. Louis, Mo.	Harris Teachers' College	1,450	30,000	211,100	0				4,000	29,439	68,506	19,452	0
Jersey City, N. J.	Teachers' Training School	500		45,370					6,900	22,500		0	
Paterson, N. J.	City Normal School	6,915	584,312	250,000	0		40,292		3,000	32,072	635	3,920	0
Albany, N. Y.	Albany Teachers' Training School	3,163	20,000		0				5,000	3,000	100	0	
Brooklyn, N. Y.	Brooklyn Training School for Teachers	7,950	8,000					1,500	5,000	130,140	2,350	10,726	0
Jamaica, N. Y.	Jamaica Training School for Teachers	1,840							5,000	72,250	1,150		
New York, N. Y.	New York City Training School for Teachers	1,133		106,000					5,000	90,150	19,020		
Rochester, N. Y.	Rochester City Normal School	420	25,000						2,300	14,177	1,513	8,069	
Schenectady, N. Y.	Schenectady Teachers' Training School	242	2,700	67,000	0				2,700	26,000			
Syracuse, N. Y.	Syracuse Training School for Teachers	990	1,000				2,000		2,500	3,000			
Watertown, N. Y.	Watertown Training School								1,900	1,600			
Yonkers, N. Y.	Yonkers Training School for Teachers	1,200	3,500	96,000	$100				940	6,000	300	5,900	
Akron, Ohio	Perkins Normal School	325	3,500						950				
Anna, Ohio	Shelby County Normal School	240											
Ansonia, Ohio	Darke County Normal School												

Berlin Heights, Ohio	Erie County Normal School
Canal Winchester, Ohio	Franklin County Normal School
Chardon, Ohio	Geauga County Normal School
Cleveland, Ohio	Cleveland Normal School
Columbus, Ohio	Columbus Normal School
Continental, Ohio	Putnam County Normal School
Dayton, Ohio	Dayton Normal School
Dresden, Ohio	Dresden County Normal School
Lancaster, Ohio	Fairfield County Normal School
Medina, Ohio	Medina County Normal School
Minerva, Ohio	Stark County Normal School
Monroeville, Ohio	Huron County Normal School
New Lexington, Ohio	Perry County Normal School
Oak Harbor, Ohio	Ottawa County Normal School
Plain City, Ohio	Madison County Normal School
St. Clairsville, Ohio	St. Clairsville County Normal School
Scio, Ohio	Harrison County Normal School
West Alexandria, Ohio	Preble County Normal School
West Liberty, Ohio	Logan County Normal School
Wheelersburg, Ohio	Scioto County Normal School
Erie, Pa.	Erie Normal School
Harrisburg, Pa.	Teachers' Training School
Pittsburgh, Pa.	Pittsburgh Training School for Teachers
Philadelphia, Pa.	Philadelphia Normal School for Girls
Do.	Philadelphia School of Pedagogy
Algoma, Wis.	Door-Kewaunee County Training School
Alma, Wis.	Buffalo County Training School
Antigo, Wis.	Langlade County Training School
Berlin, Wis.	Green Lake County Training School
Columbus, Wis.	Columbia County Normal School
Gays Mills, Wis.	Crawford County Training School
Eau Claire, Wis.	Eau Claire County Training School
Grand Rapids, Wis.	Wood County Training School
Janesville, Wis.	Rock County Training School
Ladysmith, Wis.	Rusk County Training School
Manitowoc, Wis.	Manitowoc County Training School
Marinette, Wis.	Stephenson Training School
Medford, Wis.	Taylor County Training School
Menomonie, Wis.	Dunn County Training School
New London, Wis.	Lincoln County Training School
Phillips, Wis.	Waupaca County Training School
Reedsburg, Wis.	Price County Training School
Rhinelander, Wis.	Sauk County Training School
Rice Lake, Wis.	Oneida County Training School
St. Croix Falls, Wis.	Barron County Training School
South Kaukauna, Wis.	Polk County Training School
Viroqua, Wis.	Outagamie County Training School
Wausau, Wis.	Vernon County Training School
Wautoma, Wis.	Marathon County Training School
	Waushara County Training School

TABLE 47.—*Private normal schools—Items of general information, 1917–18.*

Location.	Institution.	Weeks in year, including summer session.	Weeks in summer session, 1917.	Years in teachers' courses.	Entrance requirements to teachers' training courses; completion of—	Graduates from teachers' training course (1918). Men.	Women.	Total number of hours of practice required in teachers' courses.	Enrollment in model and practice schools maintained by the institution.
1	2	3	4	5	6	7	8	9	10
Tuskegee, Ala.	Tuskegee Normal and Industrial Institute [1]	36		3	(?)				(?)
Berkeley, Calif.	Miss Barnard's Kindergarten Normal School	36		2	High school	0	31	468	40
Pasadena, Calif.	Broadoaks Kindergarten Normal School	36		2	do		37	108	13
Bridgeport, Conn.	Connecticut Froebel Kindergarten and Primary Training School	36		2	do		22	960	
Hartford, Conn.	Fannie A. Smith Kindergarten Training School	34		2	do		14	630	25
	Culver-Smith Kindergarten Training School	36	5	2	do		9	180	50
New Haven, Conn.	New Haven Normal School of Gymnastics	39		2	do	2	79	145	(?)
Washington, D.C.	Columbia Kindergarten Training School	32		2	do			80	
Miami, Fla.	Miami Kindergarten Normal School	32	6	2	High school	1	5	960	40
Chicago, Ill.	American College of Physical Education	42		2,3	do		26	108	
Do.	Chicago Kindergarten Institute	36		2	do	0	36	360	40
Do.	Chicago Normal School of Physical Education	42	6	2	do		68		
Do.	National Kindergarten and Elementary College	42	6	2	do		108	756	35
Do.	Pestalozzi-Froebel Kindergarten Training School	42	6	1,2	do		61	540	28
Chicago, Ill.	Technical Normal School of Chicago	40		2,4	do	0	22	48	109
Oak Park, Ill.	Concordia College	40		2	do	25		100	
Angola, Ind.	Tri-State College	48	12	2	do	12	30	180	146
Danville, Ind.	Central Normal College	48	12		do				
Indianapolis, Ind.	Normal College of the North American Gymnastic Union.	40	4	2	High school	17	28	144	
Do.	Teachers' College of Indianapolis.	39		4	do		72	420	200
Lexington, Ky.	Chandler Normal School.	34		4	Eighth grade.		2	660	88
Ammendale, Md.	Ammendale Normal Institute.	42	4	5	High school.	17		72	
Baltimore, Md.	Affordby Kindergarten-Primary Normal School.	36		2	High school.		4	300	35
Boston, Mass.	Perry Kindergarten Normal School.	34		3	do	1	21	210	
Do.	Posse Normal School of Gymnastics.	35		3	do	16	29		
Do.	Boyd Training School.	34		2	do		93	360	
Cambridge, Mass.	Wheelock Training School.	30		2	do		48	90	
Do.	Lesley Normal School.	30		3	do		100	40	
Springfield, Mass.	Sargent Normal School of Physical Education.	30		2	do		6	75	
Battle Creek, Mich.	Springfield Normal Kindergarten Training School. Normal School of Physical Education	42	6	2½	do		37	120	

Location	Name of school	(1)	(2)	(3)	Admission requirement	(4)	(5)	(6)	(7)
Grand Rapids, Mich.	Grand Rapids Kindergarten Training School	41	6	2	do.	4	12	700	*15
Madison, Minn.	Lutheran Normal School	38		1	do.	4	19	93	20
New Ulm, Minn.	Dr. Martin Luther College	40		2	Eleventh grade.		6	540	(2)
Kansas City, Mo.	Froebel Kindergarten Training School	38		2	Eighth grade.		18	80	
Santee, Nebr.	Santee Normal Training School (Indian)	35		2	Eighth grade.		2	100	22
Newark, N. J.	Newark Normal School for Physical Education and Hygiene.	36	6	2	High school.	15	14		
Raleigh, N. C.	St. Augustine's School[1]	33		2	2 years of high school.	0	8	350	100
Cincinnati, Ohio	Cincinnati Kindergarten Training School	32		3	do.		28	1,126	*120
Cleveland, Ohio	Cleveland Kindergarten Training School	38	6	3	High school.	0	24	380	(2)
Oberlin, Ohio	Oberlin Kindergarten Training School	38	4	3	do.	5	41	1,140	114
Toledo, Ohio	Law Froebel Kindergarten Training School	40		3	do.	0	17	30	*385
Woodville, Ohio	Woodville Lutheran Normal School	40		3	do.	5	4		150
Mount Angel, Oreg	Mount Angel Normal School	39		3	2 years of high school.	2	8	100	35
Cheyney, Pa.	Cheyney Training School for Teachers[1]	36		3	do.	7	5	200	250
Harrisburg, Pa.	Froebel Kindergarten Training School	36		4	2 years of high school.	0	6		*25
North Philadelphia, Pa.	Gratz College (Hebrew Normal)	34		2	2 years of high school.	2	33	265	47
Philadelphia, Pa.	Miss Hart's Training School for Kindergartners	36		4,6	High grade.		19	90	38
Sioux Falls, S. Dak.	Lutheran Normal School	32		4	Eighth grade.		18	128	*70
Morristown, Tenn	Morristown Normal and Industrial College[1]	36	0	2	High school.	0	23	1,080	(2)
Dallas, Tex.	Dallas Kindergarten Training School	32	0	2	do.	0	7	64	
Fort Worth, Tex.	Fort Worth Kindergarten and Teachers' Training School				do.				
Hampton, Va.	Hampton Normal and Agricultural Institute[1]	38	4	4	Eighth grade.	7	43	440	473
Norfolk, Va.	Norfolk Kindergarten Training School	34		2	High school.	0	0	510	42
Harpers Ferry, W. Va.	Storer College[1]	36		2	do.	2	1	90	(2)
Milwaukee, Wis.	National Teachers' Seminary	43		2	do.	3	5	80	205
St. Francis, Wis.	Catholic Normal School	40	5	4	Eighth grade.			120	8

[1] For colored people.
[2] Members of the senior class take this course.
[3] Public schools are used.
[4] Public schools also used.
[5] Parochial schools used.

TABLE 48.—*Private normal schools—Instructors and students, 1917–18.*

Institution.	Instructors, including principal.				Instructors engaged half time or more.			Resident students.								Non-resident students in extension and correspondence courses.	Attendance weeks of resident students.	
	Total for year.		Summer.		Resident teachers' training courses.		Extension and correspondence courses.	All courses.				Teachers' training, total for year.		Other courses, total for year.			Teachers' training courses.	Other courses.
	Men.	Women.	Men.	Women.	Men.	Women.		Total for year.		Summer.								
								Men.	Women.	Men.	Women.	Men.	Women.					
1	2	3	4	5	6	7	8	9	10	11	12	13	14	15	16	17	18
Tuskegee Normal and Industrial Institute, Ala.	[a]16	[a]24			0	0	0	461	600			1	18	1,042	0			18
Miss Harvard's Kindergarten Normal School, Calif.	1	12			1	4												
Broadoaks Kindergarten Normal School, Calif.	1	7						0	65			0	65		0		[a]2,340	
									67				67				[a]2,412	
Connecticut Froebel Kindergarten and Primary Training School, Conn.	1	5	13	1		3			33				33				455	
Fannie A. Smith Kindergarten Training School, Conn.		7				6			30				30				[a]1,020	
Culver-Smith Kindergarten Training School,		7	5						22		16		22				792	
New Haven Normal School of Gymnastics, Conn.	3	8		9	9	8		11	175				175				[a]5,900	
									6				6				[a]192	
									8				8				217	
Columbia Kindergarten Training School, D.C.	9	4				4			166	25	52	49	166				5,112	
Miami Kindergarten Normal School, Fla.		4			10	5		49	90				90		0	0	[a]2,880	0
American College of Physical Education, Ill.	13	6	18	6	5	11												
Chicago Kindergarten Institute, Ill.	11	19	12	8														
Chicago Normal School of Physical Education, Ill.	9	14		15	9	14		0	248	0	82	0	248	0			[a]6,186	
National Kindergarten and Elementary College, Ill.	3	26			1	15			322		116		322				7,875	
Pestalozzi-Froebel Kindergarten Training School, Ill.		10							188		63		188				5,055	
Technical Normal School of Chicago, Ill.		8				5			20				20					
Concordia College, Ill.	5	6		6	6	5		205	462	113	429	68	390	137			[a]2,720	[a]5,480
Central Normal College, Ind.	10			8	2	1		405	513			94		397			8,493	11,413
Normal College of the North American Gymnastic Union, Ind.	25	6	7		2			44	93	15	35	29	57				3,096	204

Teachers' College of Indianapolis, Ind.
Chandler Normal School, Ky.
Annasdale Normal Institute, Md.
Afflerdby Kindergarten-Primary Normal School, Md.
Perry Kindergarten Normal School, Mass.
Posse Normal School of Gymnastics, Mass.
Sloyd Training School, Mass.
Wheelock Training School, Mass.
Lesley Normal School, Mass.
Sargent Normal School of Physical Education, Mass.
Springfield Normal Kindergarten Training School, Mass.
Normal School of Physical Education, Mich.
Grand Rapids Kindergarten Training School, Mich.
Lutheran Normal School, Minn.
Dr. Martin Luther College, Minn.
Froebel Kindergarten Training School, Mo.
Santee Normal Training School, Nebr.
Newark Normal School for Physical Education and Hygiene, N. J.
St. Augustine's School, N. C.
Cincinnati Kindergarten Training School, Ohio.
Cleveland Kindergarten Training School, Ohio.
Oberlin Kindergarten Training School, Ohio.
Law Froebel Kindergarten Training School, Ohio.
Woodville Lutheran Normal School, Ohio.
Mount Angel Normal School, Oreg.
Cheyney Training School for Teachers, Pa.
Froebel Kindergarten Training School, Pa.
Gratz College (Hebrew Normal), Pa.
Miss Hart's Training School for Kindergartners, Pa.
Lutheran Normal School, S. Dak.
Morristown Normal and Industrial College, Tenn.
Dallas Kindergarten Training School, Tex.
Fort Worth Kindergarten and Teachers' Training School, Tex.
Hampton Normal and Agricultural Institute, Va.
Norfolk Kindergarten Training School, Va.
Storer College, W. Va.
National Teachers' Seminary, Wis.
Catholic Normal School, Wis.

1 For colored persons.
2 Includes only instructors in academic subjects.
3 Enrollment weeks.
4 Year October, 1917–August, 1918.
5 1918–19.
6 Not included in summary and total tables.

150407°—20——8

Table 49.—*Private normal schools—property, receipts, and expenditures, 1917–18.*

Institutions.	Bound volumes in the library.	Value of library, apparatus, machinery, furniture.	Value of grounds and buildings.	Student fees. Tuition, etc.	Board, rooms, etc.	Public funds.	Private benefactions. Increase of plant, endowment.	Current expenses.	All other sources.	Salary of principal.	Total salaries of other instructors.	Other expenses.	Other current expenses.	Outlays and payment of debt.
	2	3	4	5	6	7	8	9	10	11	12	13	14	15
Tuskegee Normal and Industrial Institute, Ala	24,000	$286,348	$3,528,634	$11,298		$1,125	$30,511	$150,000	$209,916	$5,180	$90,508	$90,058	$225,611	$77,006
Miss Barnard's Kindergarten Normal School, Calif	1,000	1,200				0	0	0	0	2,500	1,300	50	2,173	700
Broadoaks Kindergarten, Normal, Calif	560		13,000	6,770	$1,000						3,358	200	1,115	
Connecticut Froebel Kindergarten and Primary Training School, Conn			5,700	6,680	(3)							186		
Fannie A. Smith Kindergarten Training School, Conn				3,200		500			3,500	1,895	1,350	500	2,008	
Culver-Smith Kindergarten Training School, Conn	1,205	26,211	101,000	27,000	48,639					2,000	2,547	5,600		
New Haven Normal School of Gymnastics, Conn	600	1,000		15,000	(3)					2,000	10,050		40,898	4,097
Columbia Kindergarten Training School, D. C.	40		500	21,287	12,686		500		317	1,000	1,690	225	12,000	
Miami Kindergarten Normal School, Fla	300			8,954	11,595					1,120	1,520	900		
American College of Physical Education, Ill	50			30,370	21,448					3,500	8,250	4,857	6,261	
Chicago Kindergarten Institute, Ill	1,000	17,732		27,186	33,924				7,825	2,400	4,509	9,676	1,620	
Chicago Normal School of Physical Education, Ill	582	1,500	450,000	15,187	7,500						7,000	9,591	24,784	
National Kindergarten and Elementary College, Ill	125			3,500	45,000			3,000	2,500	1,800	10,857	3,921	32,301	0
Pestalozzi-Froebel Kindergarten Training School, Ill	6,050										7,540	850	7,576	
Technical Normal School of Chicago, Ill	5,483	12,000	118,000	38,426			2,500		1,500	1,500	3,500	350	6,145	9,417
Concordia College, Ill	2,500	26,000	90,000								13,840	2,500	11,385	2,500
Tri-State College, Ind		10,000									15,000		21,936	600
Central Normal College, Ind														
Normal College of the North American Gymnastic Union, Ind														
Teachers' College of Indianapolis, Ind	1,511	10,901	5,505	10,665	10,529		292		7,599	3,500	6,348	2,896	7,755	500
Chandler Normal School, Ky	7,013	30,000	90,000	29,935	26,246				109	1,290	16,755	2,991	32,596	1,500
American Normal Institute, Md	2,005	10,000	119,000	622					5,290	800	3,134	122	208	
Afforby Kindergarten-Primary Normal School, Md	1,500	5,000	205,000	3,000					22,261		700	213	19,517	
Perry Kindergarten Normal School, Mass	350							675				400	630	
Posse Normal School of Gymnastics, Mass														

School													
Sloyd Training School, Mass.	100	2,000	72,500	20,000	21,500	0	0	0	0	0	10,000	2,500	6,896
Wheelock's Training School, Mass.	200		10,000	8,000	4,800						2,000	1,000	3,700
Lesley Normal School, Mass.													
Sargent Normal School of Physical Education, Mass.	500	15,000	30,000	13,500	208			25	1,600	8,237	1,000	3,180	
Springfield Normal Kindergarten Training School, Mass.	7,785	3,200	[6] 88,000	1,619				6,905		883	301	621	
Normal School of Physical Education, Mich.	1,260	12,325		3,900	2,187					7,172	108	2,628	
Grand Rapids Kindergarten Training School, Mich.	3,500										315		
Lutheran Normal School, Minn.	400	800	[9] 83,800	4,500	2,391			10,549	1,700	1,800	100	900	
Dr. Martin Luther College, Minn.	2,000	16,245							1,200	2,575	315	4,667	
Froebel Kindergarten Training School, Mo.	1,000	1,000	100,000		(11)		9,031		1,500	6,705	2,636	26,991	
Santee Normal Training School, Nebr.	6,100	15,525	[10] 179,054	11,327			6,532	28,184					
Newark Normal School for Physical Education and Hygiene, N. J.	351	1,100	12,000	7,000	1,055			80	1,500	2,893	719	1,738	6,900
St. Augustine's School, N. C.	600	1,000	10,000	9,675	0		0	0	1,100	5,064	779	2,397	
Cincinnati Kindergarten Training School, Ohio	600	400	[13] 51,000	3,720	1,320		8,300	150	2,500	2,500	600	900	
Cleveland Kindergarten Training School, Ohio	3,256	2,000	76,000	1,960					1,800	7,500	165	2,510	
Oberlin Kindergarten Training School, Ohio	3,210	30,000	[14] 252,458										
Faw Froebel Kindergarten Training School, Ohio													
Woodville Lutheran Normal School, Ohio													
Mount Angel Normal School, Oreg.													199
Central Training School for Teachers, Pa.	1,300		[4] 290,000		8,727	5,000	10,000	11,575	10,739	3,000	6,022	2,590	11,293
Froebel Kindergarten Training School, Pa.													
Gratz College (Hebrew Normal), Pa.	275	3,000	91,000	6,172	15,800			3,730	8,819	963	7,046	100	2,237
Miss Hart's Training School for Kindergartners, Pa.	3,000	7,000	[14] 201,000	5,800	6,786	3,600	3,069	10,000		1,500	6,280	1,758	1,862
Lutheran Normal School, S. Dak.	3,000	6,000	25,000	2,230	2,000			6,625	9,775	1,824	12,589	185	6,716
Morristown Normal and Industrial College, Tenn.	200			700						1,224	12,948	630	5,946
Fallis Kindergarten Training School, Tex.											2,290		
Fort Worth Kindergarten and Teachers' Training School, Tex.													
Hampton Normal and Agricultural Institute, Va. [1]	40,187	173,500	[15] 3,768,703	960	108,552	2,240	255,351	149,054	164,918	1,000	720	140	315,908
Nordica Kindergarten Training School, Va.		500						900					
Storer College, W. Va.	7,000	7,500	[16] 283,501	463	10,427	2,487	1,193	2,063	11,178	1,200	9,712	932	5,198
National Teachers' Seminary, Wis.	9,000	8,500	[14] 175,000	15,503	(17)		500	2,313	10,951	1,500	13,209	2,201	3,178
Catholic Normal School, Wis.	2,000	1,800	181,000						642	800	2,050		10,540

[1] For colored people.
[2] Includes endowment funds of $2,259,073.
[3] Included under tuition, etc.
[4] Endowment.
[5] Includes endowment of $10,000.
[6] Includes endowment of $80,000.
[7] And board.
[8] Includes an endowment of $5,000.
[9] Includes an endowment of $2,000.
[10] Includes an endowment of $38,160.
[11] Included under tuition.
[12] Includes an endowment of $8,000.
[13] Includes an endowment of $112,900.
[14] Includes an endowment of $9,000.
[15] Includes an endowment of $2,513,703.
[16] Includes an endowment of $84,501.
[17] Includes board and room rent.

DEPARTMENT OF THE INTERIOR
BUREAU OF EDUCATION

BULLETIN, 1919, No. 82

MOTION PICTURES AND MOTION-PICTURE EQUIPMENT

A HANDBOOK OF GENERAL INFORMATION

By

F. W. REYNOLDS and CARL ANDERSON

WASHINGTON
GOVERNMENT PRINTING OFFICE
1920

LETTER OF TRANSMITTAL.

DEPARTMENT OF THE INTERIOR,
BUREAU OF EDUCATION,
Washington, October 21, 1919.

SIR: Motion-picture films have come to be recognized quite generally as a valuable and practical means of instruction in schools, colleges, and universities, and for clubs and societies organized for educational purposes. The number of persons making such use of them is now very large and is constantly becoming larger. To all these a handbook of general information on motion-picture equipment, installation, handling, and repair, prepared with special reference to their needs, will be very helpful. For this reason I recommend the publication of this manuscript, prepared under the direction of Mr. F. W. Reynolds, of the extension division of the University of Utah, and for some time connected with the educational extension division of this bureau.

Respectfully submitted.

P. P. CLAXTON,
Commissioner.

The SECRETARY OF THE INTERIOR.

3

EXPLANATORY NOTE.

No fact of the motion-picture world is more striking to-day than that of the interest in motion pictures for purposes of education. If the day of the motion picture in education has arrived—as would thus seem to be the case—and if the brains and money behind the production and distribution of motion-picture films for use in education should make the already existing source of supply of educational motion pictures not merely greater in volume but richer in content and variety and more easy of access—as would seem to be the very reasonable hope—then the problem of giving the day significance will promptly be with the users—the schools and the other organizations of whatever sort having immediate responsibility in education.

A part of the problem will, from the nature of motion pictures, be mechanical—relative to equipment and its installation and use and to the handling of motion-picture films.

It is with the hope of assisting users of motion pictures in the mechanical part of the problem that this pamphlet has been prepared.

In the course of the pamphlet is the interesting observation of the editor that high-school students who have learned to operate a motion-picture projection machine often give better exhibitions than professional theater operators. At any rate, the mechanical difficulties in the way of the use of motion pictures in schools are so easily overcome that they can in no way be urged as an objection to the use of motion pictures as an aid in education. The time is near when no school will be complete without its motion-picture projection machine, and no instructor well prepared or student mechanically inclined well taught without facility in its use.

F. W. R.

MOTION PICTURES AND MOTION-PICTURE EQUIPMENT.

Purpose of pamphlet.—There is no difference in the general principles involved between a picture-slide projector and a picture-film projector, and the slide lantern is rather well and widely understood. What difference there is between the two is in the mechanism for passing the pictures in succession through the cone of projecting light. The mechanism for moving the picture film past the projection aperture is not as intricate as at first glance one might be led to suppose.

It is to enable the educator to have at least a general knowledge of the mechanical elements involved in this new device for teaching, and to answer the more pertinent questions incident to the purchase, installation, and use of motion-picture machines that this pamphlet has been prepared. For assistance in its compilation indebtedness is acknowledged to the United States Bureau of Standards, the Eastman Kodak Co., and the Society of Motion Picture Engineers, or their publications.

Standard film only.—First of all the bureau deems it wise to caution schools and other users of film that the film furnished by the section of visual instruction is "standard film,"[1] that is, film of world-wide standard dimensions. It can not be used in any of the odd-sized machines on the market. This standard film is obtainable all over the world, and there are millions of feet available, in hundreds of thousands of subjects. This standard film is 1⅜ inches wide, with pictures thereon 16 to the foot and four perforations on each side of each picture on the film. Each single picture, or "frame," is ¾ inch by 1 inch, the latter dimension being the width of the pictures, i. e., across the film. The screen picture (motion picture) is, therefore, always three-fourths as high as it is wide. Because of this fact the size of motion pictures is almost invariably described by the width.

Portable v. nonportable projectors.—In the selection of a projection machine the first consideration is the resultant picture. It should be well lighted and of sufficient size for the audience. For an audience of 50 to 100 a well-made portable machine and a 5-foot screen are usually acceptable. For larger audiences it is obvious that a larger screen is required and in ratio a larger amount of light. For audiences of 500 to 1,000, a 10-foot screen is about right. A screen of

---

[1] For definition of the technical terms here used, see motion-picture nomenclature near close of this publication.

this size will require an arc light, though a special filament lamp may be used. Filament lamps used for projecting motion pictures are specially made for the purpose as to size and shape, but are in principle the ordinary electric bulb, which is in daily use in the home. The amount of light required is also measured by the kind of screen that is used. This subject of screen is treated in another paragraph.

Second-hand machines.—It is not generally wise to purchase a second-hand motion-picture machine of any kind. It is advisable by all means to put in a new equipment that will not be likely in a short time to disappoint.

Slide projection.—The older types of motion-picture machines are still made to project both lantern slides and motion pictures, though recently designed machines are made to project only motion pictures. One reason for this is that lantern slides are almost sure to be cracked or broken by the great heat incident to the strong light necessary to project motion pictures. The area of a lantern slide is about eight times the area of a motion picture " frame," and requires, therefore, much less light for the same screen brilliancy. Certainly a much more compact, lighter, and simpler apparatus can be built when the picture projector and the slide lantern are built each for its own purpose.

Luminant.—There are two acceptable sources of light for motion-picture projection, i. e., the electric arc for long throw and large screens and the electric incandescent lamp for shorter throws and smaller screens. Acetylene or other gas lights are not suitable. For large pictures and long throw (distance from machine to screen) the arc lamp only can be successfully used.

Incandescent lamps which are made specially for the projection of motion pictures give excellent results. They are of tubular bulb and filament construction which projects excellent, well-lighted pictures up to 12 feet in width and 75 feet throw. They are lighted by turning a switch and thereafter require no further attention.

Electric current.—For the operation of a motion-picture projector electric current is necessary, but as there is no standard in electric-current characteristics the projector manufacturer must know what current is available in the place where the projector is to be used. The usual voltage is 110. It may be that your electric-light company will advise you that your current is 220. They may prefer to sell you current on this basis, but it is also probable that inside of the building the 220 volts is distributed on a three-wire system. If so, this makes 110 volts available for your use.

This voltage may be either direct current (D. C.) or alternating current (A. C.). If your current is direct current, the projector manufacturer will need to know the voltage. If alternating current, advise him of the voltage, phase, and cycle.

When making inquiry about a projector, give above details about your electric current and ask the advice of the manufacturer as to the type of electric lamp and use of rheostat or transformer.

For motion pictures in the country a gasoline motor and electric generator are required. These outfits are built as a unit, are self-starting, use kerosene as engine fuel, and can be carried about with a projection machine, on a small automobile or on a trailer. Such an outfit and a good screen will produce good motion pictures.

Screen illumination and picture size.—The illumination of the screen depends upon the size of the screen and the "throw." The brilliancy of different size screens with a given light is in direct ratio to their areas; while the light required for a given area of illumination must be increased about 50 per cent of the increased "throw."

The size of any picture is increased with increased throw, although the same size picture can be obtained at different throws by changing the projecting lens.

Screens.—Motion pictures should be projected on the front of a screen; that is, on the side next to the audience. Projection through the screen from the back involves a loss of light of 50 per cent or more, in addition to which it strains the eyes.

Projection of pictures in the daytime can not, of course, equal pictures projected at night, unless the room can be made equally dark. Many assembly rooms in schools are equipped for daytime projection by fastening permanently around the inside of the window frame a strip of wood painted black and projecting from the window frame, and parallel with the sash, about 3 inches. When the window shade is pulled down between the window and this strip, the strip prevents light leaking into the room around the edges.

Even a small amount of daylight weakens the picture and strains the eye. Test out these conditions before you start projecting. A simple test is to darken the room, wait until the eyes have become adjusted to the conditions, and if you can then discern objects so that you can move freely about, there is still too much daylight entering the room.

Metallic-coated screens.—Wherever screen installation can be made permanent—that is to say, where the screen can be installed and stretched in a frame from which it does not have to be removed from time to time—a metallic-coated or highly reflective screen is by all means advisable. The screen and frame can be moved wherever space permits. There are a number of these screens on the market, and any reputable motion-picture equipment concern can be depended upon for information and advice in purchasing.

Plain white canvas-coated screens.—Where the screen can not be permanently installed as described (above), but must be rolled on a roller or folded, a plain white canvas screen coated with kalsomine, or any of the standard white coating formulas on the market, is advisable. Any motion-picture supply house will furnish either the coating material or the formula for same.

Film hazard.—Film is not dangerous in the way gasoline is, for it is not volatile. Nevertheless, smoking near film is criminal carelessness. Film in projectors catches fire if not moving, or not moving with sufficient speed, because of the great heat of the beam of electric light. We know that " light is heat," and in this case a great deal of light is concentrated on a small space. Most projectors have an automatic shutter that drops between the light and the film when the film stops moving, but even in this case if the light is left turned on for more than a few seconds it may make the fire shutter so hot that it, in turn, may ignite the film. The obvious rule is, when the film is not moving turn off the light.

Ninety-nine per cent of the standard motion-picture film manufactured to date is of the inflammable kind. Gasoline also is inflammable, but because it is efficient we use it in automobiles. When ignited, film burns with such speed that a small extinguisher or small stream of water usually fails to put it out. Smothering the flame with sand is successful. Because of the rapidity with which it burns and the heat thus generated, motion-picture film is dangerous when ignited. When we consider the millions of reels which are handled weekly by the express company, Post Office Department, and numerous theaters and compare it with the number of fires, we find that the percentage is very small, and that of all the film fires of known cause 50 per cent of them are due to smoking in or about the projection booth. This shows that the manufacture of projection machines has reached that point of perfection where the protection of the film against being set on fire by the heat of the lantern is almost automatic. The observance of the two following paragraphs will prevent possibility of a serious film fire:

1. Never remove film from the metal container in a room containing combustible materials or an open flame, fireplace, cigar, cigarette, etc. Never lay film or film container on or near a radiator or other heat-producing object.

2. Keep all film, excepting the one reel in use, in metal containers at all times.

Circular 75, United States Bureau of Standards, says:

Motion-picture films have the same general composition as the materials mentioned above, celluloid and similar materials, and municipalities have drawn up elaborate specifications to regulate their use so as to minimize the fire hazard. It is not to be understood that, with reasonable care, celluloid and similar materials constitute an unusual source of danger. They are not to be condemned by the public any more than would be petroleum or any other hazardous material, but it is desirable that their highly inflammable nature be known, that they may be handled with care when used about the house or person.

NATIONAL FIRE PROTECTION ASSOCIATION.

(Quarterly Bulletin, January, 1918, vol. 11, No. 3, p. 292.)

Motion pictures, fire record, common causes.

Classification.	Number. of fires.	Per cent of common causes.
Heating	2	4.8
Lighting	12	28.5
Boiler (or fuel)	1	2.4
Smoking	22	52.4
Lighting	1	2.4
Rubbish (or sweepings)	1	2.4
Miscellaneous	3	7.1
Total	42	-----

The fact that over one-half the fires due to common causes were the result of careless smoking speaks for itself.

Film should be handled with care. If, however, it is accidentally broken, no particular harm is done, for it may be spliced and be again ready for use. Lantern slides, however, can not be repaired if broken or cracked. The most frequent damage to slides comes from cracking by reason of the great heat of the arc lamp light cone of the motion-picture projector having a lantern slide attachment. It is practically impossible for a lecturer to describe a slide picture before the slide cracks, if projected by a motion picture machine (with lantern slide attachment). This is one of the reasons for recommending a separate lantern for slides, though compactness, simplicity, and lightness are often considerations of importance.

Storage.—No more than 10 reels should be kept in a room unless the room is fireproof throughout.

Wherever film is stored, it should be kept in metal containers or metal cabinets, and the room should have a permanent opening to the outside air. The door to this room should open outward and be equipped with a spring check. No artificial light should be used in the room except incandescent light, and the electric light should be protected with a wire guard. Patching and inspecting of film should be done in a room of this description.

Film splicing solution.—The solution used is collodion. If very viscous, an equal amount of acetone may be added. Where this is not convenient, add one-fourth alcohol and one-fourth ether to one-half collodion.

Dense film and poor slides.—The lack of expert knowledge is often the cause of disappointment in picture exhibitions. It should not be forgotten that films of different quality, ranging from the most beautiful photographically that are seen in the finest picture theaters where only the best are acceptable, to the poorest quality, dense, or thin, or frayed, or out of focus, or all of these in one ribbon, are sometimes given the educator because he is believed to be uninformed on the subject. A motion-picture film, like a stereopticon slide, should have clear high lights and soft shadows, with the half tones of infinite gradation, and of course should have the most minute details clearly defined. This will be readily understood when it is remembered that these miniature pictures, three-fourths by 1 inch, are often magnified to cover a 12 by 16 foot screen. Likewise, to get such a surface fully covered, a light cone of great intensities must pass through this small aperture on its way to the screen. It should also be remembered that tinted film cuts the light down, and unless tinted properly, may result in a loss of light equaling 79 per cent red tint, 62 per cent in orange, and 50 per cent tinted in blue. The selection of the tinting medium has an important bearing on the matter. for of two tinting mediums of the same color, one may be much more opaque than another. All that is here written applies to lantern slides. although obviously in lesser degree. If the screen pictures from tinted films seem underlighted, the probabilities are that the film is at fault and not the machine.

Shipping.—The United States Interstate Commerce Commission prescribes the way in which motion-picture films shall be shipped.

July 15, 1918. Revised regulations.

Par. 43. (*a*) Motion-picture films must be packet in spark-proof metal boxes or cans complying with Specification No. 321. Not more than eight reels (approximately 1,000 feet each) may be packed in one such outside container.

(*b*) Motion-picture films may also be packed in outside wooden boxes complying with Specification No. 19, provided each reel is placed in a tightly closed inside metal container. The gross weight of such a package must not exceed 200 pounds.

(*f*) Shipments of motion-picture film with advertising matter attached to the outside container must not be offered for shipment. Shippers desiring to include advertising matter with their shipments of motion-picture film must place the same inside the outside box containing the film.

Par. 1864. (*a*) Unless exempted on account of quantity or method of packing (see columns 3 and 5, list, par. 1807), all packages containing dangerous articles named in the list, paragraph 1807, and similar articles defined by paragraphs 1802 and 1806, inclusive, must be conspicuously labeled by the shipper. Labels should be applied when practicable to that part of the package bearing the consignee's name and address.

Par. 1865. Labels must be of diamond shape, with each side 4 inches long. The color is red for inflammable liquids and compressed inflammable gases. yellow for inflammable solids and oxidizing materials, green for noninflammable compressed gases, and white for corrosive liquids. Labels must conform to standards as to size, printing, and color, and samples will be furnished. on request, by the chief inspector of the Bureau of Explosives, 30 Vesey Street. New York City.

From the above it will be seen that motion-picture film to be shipped from point to point should be in a metal box, but when intended for only one shipment, such as from laboratory to buyer, it can be shipped in a wooden box, providing each reel is inclosed in a metal container. The shipping case must bear the yellow label previously described.

SHIPPING CONTAINER SPECIFICATION No. 19. (See par. 1822 (a).)

Boxes for inflammable solids or oxidizing materials and for mixed shipments of any dangerous articles which may be packed in the same outside container without violation of I. C. C. Regulations (except as provided in Specifications Nos. 2, 6, 17, and 18).

Effective October 1, 1914.

1. Boxes purchased hereafter for the shipment of inflammable solids or oxidizing materials, and for mixed shipments of any dangerous articles which may be packed in the same outside container without violation of I. C. C. Regulations (except as provided in Specifications Nos. 2, 6, 17, and 18), must comply with these specifications.

BOXES.

2. Boxes must be made of good sound white pine, or any wood of equal or superior strength, dry and well seasoned, and with no loose knots or knots liable to get loose in any part.

3. When the ends are single cleated, the cleats must run across the grain of the wood in the ends. The sides or tops and bottoms must extend out over the cleats, and the nailing must be staggered, at least 40 per cent of the nails being driven into the ends and at least 40 per cent into the cleats.

4. When the ends are double cleated, the sides, top, and bottom must extend out over the cleats and the nailing must be staggered, at least 40 per cent of the nails being driven into the ends and at least 40 per cent into the cleats.

5. Nailed boxes not cleated must have ends of one-piece material or must be tongued and grooved and glued; provided, that other joints may be used which after investigation made by the Bureau of Explosives are shown to possess strength equal to the tongued and grooved and glued joint.

6. All nails driven through sides, tops, or bottoms into ends or cleats or to fasten cleats to ends must be at not greater than $2\frac{1}{4}$-inch centers.

7. All nails driven through tops or bottoms into sides must be at not greater than 8-inch centers.

8. Gauge of nails used shall be not less than the following sizes, depending upon the thickness of lumber into which they are to be driven:

Twopenny into $\frac{7}{16}$-inch lumber.

Threepenny into $\frac{5}{8}$-inch lumber.

Fourpenny into $\frac{7}{16}$ to $\frac{1}{2}$ inch lumber.

Fivepenny into $\frac{9}{16}$ to $\frac{5}{8}$ inch lumber.

Sixpenny into $1\frac{1}{8}$ to $1\frac{3}{8}$ inch lumber.

Sevenpenny into $\frac{7}{8}$-inch or thicker lumber.

For example, nails driven through a $\frac{1}{2}$-inch side into a $\frac{3}{4}$-inch end must be sixpenny. Screws of equal efficiency may be used in place of nails.

MARKING OF BOXES.

9. Each box must be plainly marked with the words "COMPLIES WITH I. C. C. SPEC'N NO. 19," or, if desired, this marking may be indicated by a symbol consisting of a rectangle as follows:

I. C. C.—19.

The letters and figures in this symbol must be at least one-half inch high.

This symbol shall be understood to certify that the package complies with all the requirements of this specification.

When offered for shipment the package must also bear such other description as may be required by the I. C. C. Regulations for the particular article contained therein.

10. The thickness of lumber in the finished box must not be less than the following, except that a variation of 1/16 inch may be allowed for material 5/16 inch or less in thickness and a variation of 1/32 inch be allowed for material over 5/16 inch in thickness:

Box and contents not over 25 pounds gross weight.

	Ends.	Sides.	Top and bottom.	Cleats.
	Inch.	*Inch.*	*Inch.*	*Inch.*
For nailed boxes not cleated	3/8	1/4	1/4	....
For lock or dovetail corner boxes	3/8	3/8	3/8	....
For cleated boxes	3/8	3/8	3/8	3/8 by 1 3/8

15. (b).

Box and contents over 25 pounds but not over 75 pounds gross weight.

	Ends.	Sides.	Top and bottom.	Cleats.
	Inch.	*Inch.*	*Inch.*	*Inch.*
For nailed boxes not cleated	11/16	1/2	1/2	....
For lock or dovetail corner boxes	9/16	3/8	3/8	....
For cleated boxes	9/16	3/8	3/8	7/16 by 1 3/8

10. (a).

Box and contents not over 25 pounds gross weight.

	Ends.	Sides.	Top and bottom.	Cleats.
	Inch.	*Inch.*	*Inch.*	*Inch.*
Lock or dovetail corner boxes	3/8	5/16	5/16	....
Single-cleated boxes	3/8	5/16	5/16	3/8 by 1 3/8
Double-cleated boxes	5/16	5/16	5/16	3/8 by 1 3/8
Nailed boxes not cleated	1/2	5/16	5/16	....

10. (b).

Box and contents over 25 pounds but not over 75 pounds gross weight.

	Ends.	Sides.	Top and bottom.	Cleats.
	Inch.	*Inch.*	*Inch.*	*Inch.*
Lock or dovetail corner boxes	1/2	3/8	3/8	....
Single-cleated boxes	1/2	3/8	3/8	1/2 by 1 3/8
Double-cleated boxes	7/16	3/8	3/8	7/16 by 1 3/8
Nailed boxes not cleated	5/8	3/8	3/8	....

10. (c).

Box and contents over 75 pounds but not over 125 pounds gross weight.

	Ends.	Sides.	Top and bottom.	Cleats.
	Inch.	*Inch.*	*Inch.*	*Inch.*
Lock or dovetail corner boxes	5/8	3/8	3/8	....
Single-cleated boxes	5/8	3/8	3/8	5/8 by 1 3/4
Double-cleated boxes	1/2	3/8	3/8	1/2 by 1 3/8
Nailed boxes not cleated	7/8	1/2	1/2	....

SHIPPING CONTAINER SPECIFICATION NO. 32. (See par. 43 (a).)

Metal cases or cans for outside containers for inflammable motion-picture films.

Effective September 30, 1918.

1. Cans or cases must be made of sheet iron not less than 0.02 inch thick. These cans or cases must be lined throughout with hard fiber board at least one-eighth inch thick, or with some other equivalent insulating material approved for this purpose by the Bureau of Explosives.

2. Covers, if hinged, must be permanently attached to metal cases or cans by not less than two hinges which must be securely riveted, or they must be slip covers, closely fitting. The covers must be lined with insulating material of the same character and thickness as required for the body of the container.

3. Hinged covers must fit tightly against the shoulder of the body, and lap over or inside the body not less than seven-eighths inch on all sides. A strong metal hasp must fit over staple or eyebolt, and must be provided with a permanently attached catch to engage in staple or eyebolt.

4. Telescopic slip covers must fit tightly against the shoulder of the body and lap down over or inside the body not less than 3 inches (except that for a one-reel box the lap may be 2 inches). Telescope or slip covers must be secured to cans or cases by a strong, positive, mechanical device, made of metal. This device must be approved by the Bureau of Explosives both as to design and construction.

5. Each outside metal case or can must be plainly and permanently marked "Complies with I. C. C. Specification No. 32," or if desired, this marking may be indicated by a symbol consisting of a rectangle as follows:

I. C. C.-32.

The letters and figures in this symbol must be at least one-half inch high. The symbol shall be understood to certify that the package complies with all the requirements of this specification.

Projecting machines.—Which machine to install must be governed by the nature of your conditions and work.

If the machine is to be installed permanently in your school building, you are advised by all means to provide a standard professional machine, such as the Graphoscope, Motiograph, Powers, Simplex, etc. Your film projection will then not suffer in comparison with that of the theater. Prices for professional machines range from $225 to $500, according to equipment selected and the educational discounts offered by the manufacturers of these machines.

If you have occasion to move the machine from building to building, or if it is for use in the country, one of the so-called " portable " machines (employing standard width films, however) will be needed. The use of portable machines is inadvisable, except in sparsely settled communities. A motion-picture projector is a fine piece of machinery; constantly moving it from place to place is injurious in the same manner that it is to constantly move any piece of laboratory apparatus of fine adjustment.

A motion picture may cost $50,000 to make and if poorly projected because the machine is not in condition, or badly operated, or insufficient light, most of its value may be destroyed. Operating a motion-picture projector requires instruction, experience, and a knowledge of the " why."

In all permanent installations the use of motor-driven projectors is preferable to those operated by a hand crank. A motor-driven projector insures a steadier picture. Most beginners project at too low a speed. Speed up the action of your machine until you are approaching the point where the movements of the people or objects are unnatural. A speed slightly slower than this will be found the most efficient.

It is difficult to learn the operation of a motion-picture projector from a book of instructions. You might learn to operate a motor car in the same manner. From the standard of economic and satisfactory results, it is best to secure some instruction and information from an experienced operator. This is usually possible by inquiring at any place where motion pictures are shown. The following are a list of the items we advise learning from an experienced operator:

1. How to set up a projector properly, eliminating vibration of the picture.

2. How to operate the machine, including tension on the take-up, focusing, adjusting light so as to eliminate shadows on the screen, etc.

3. How to " thread " film through the mechanism.

4. How to rewind film, which side out and which end up.

5. How to patch a break in the film.

6. What labels, in addition to the address, are required by law on packages containing film.

Experience shows that young men and women in the schools who have learned to operate projectors are often able to give a better exhibition than the professional theater operators.

Installing a motion-picture projector.—The following are the rules to be observed:

1. Secure from the proper State authorities, city or county officials, and board of fire underwriters a copy of the existing rules and regula-

tions governing the installation and use of motion-picture apparatus and films. This will be a guide as to the handling and storage of film, insurance regulations, etc.

2. Decide upon a room or hall that is to be used.

3. Locate the place where the projector will stand and where the screen will hang.

4. Measure the distance between these two points.

5. Consult the company that manufactures your electric current and ascertain the voltage they can supply.

6. Secure from the company that insures the building a permit for the installation of a motion-picture projector.

7. Purchase projection outfit, metal cabinet with spring-hinged doors for holding reels, screen, booth, if required, pair of rewinders, patching block, bottle of cement, shipping labels, caution labels, special cement for fastening labels to metal shipping cases (glue or paste will not hold).

8. Engage competent electrician to install proper size cable for the electric current required. Also install on the ceiling of the booth one ordinary 16-candle power electric lamp, with pull chain switch.

9. Place inside of booth near door one pail of sand, one pail of water, and one small hand fire extinguisher. Also place sand, pail of water, and extinguisher near booth outside of door. Do not fill pail so full of sand that it can not be easily lifted and thrown out. This is best determined by a test.

Motion-picture standards.—The following have been adopted as standards by the Society of Motion Picture Engineers, and are promulgated to encourage uniformity and standard practice throughout the industry as a whole.

It is suggested that when making or contracting for the manufacture of motion-picture negatives you incorporate in your order the provisions of paragraphs B an C, and when ordering or manufacturing lantern slides, paragraphs D, E, and F.

A. *Film speed.*—A film movement of 60 feet per minute through motion-picture mechanisms shall be considered as standard speed.

B. *Frame line.*—The dividing line between pictures on motion-picture film shall lie exactly midway between the marginal perforations.

C. *Film perforation.*—The dimensions and location of film perforations shall be in accord with the illustrating diagram herewith.

D. *Lantern slide mat opening.*—A standard opening in mats of lantern slides for use in conjunction with motion pictures shall be 3 inches wide by $2\frac{1}{4}$ inches high.

E. *Lantern strip.*—A red binding strip to be used on the lower edge of the lantern slide, to indicate bottom of picture.

F. Thumb mark.—The thumb-mark spot on a lantern slide shall be located in the lower left-hand corner next the reader when the slide is held so as to be read against a light.

Projection lens mounting.—Picture-projecting lenses shall be so mounted that the light from the film picture aperture shall have an uninterrupted full path to the rear component of the lens.

Projecting lens height.—The standard height from the floor to the center of the projecting lens of a motion-picture machine shall be 48 inches.

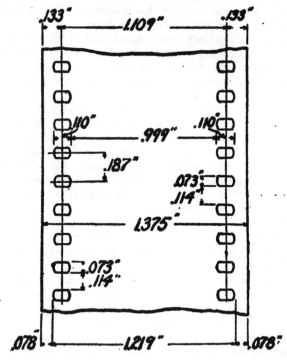

Projecting lens opening.—Shall have the equivalent focal length marked thereon in inches and quarters and halves of an inch, in decimals, with a plus (+) or minus (−) tolerance not to exceed 1 per cent of the designated equivalent focal length also marked by the proper sign following the figure.

Picture aperture.—The standard film picture aperture in a projecting machine shall be 0.906 inch wide and 0.6795 inch high, namely, $\frac{29}{32}$ inch and $\frac{87}{128}$ inch.

Reel.—The approved standard reel shall be 11 inches in diameter; 1½ inches inside width; with $\frac{5}{16}$-inch center hole, with a keyway

$\frac{1}{8}$ by $\frac{1}{8}$ inch extending all the way through; a 5-inch hub; and a permissible flange wabble of not more than $\frac{1}{16}$ inch.

Standard picture film.—Shall be $1\frac{3}{8}$ inches wide and carry a picture for each four perforations, the vertical position of the picture being longitudinal of the film.

Projection angle.—The maximum angle in picture projection shall not exceed 12° from a perpendicular to the screen surface (21.25 feet in 100 feet).

Projection lenses.—The focal length of motion-picture projection lenses shall increase in $\frac{1}{4}$-inch steps to 8 inches and from 8 to 9 in $\frac{1}{2}$-inch steps.

Standard reel or film.—Shall have black film leaders, with tinted (red, green, or blue) trailers; should have marking thereon embossed rather than punched in the film; and each reel of a multiple reel story should end with a title and the next reel begin with the same title.

Take-up pull.—The take-up pull on film shall not exceed 15 ounces at the periphery of a 10-inch reel or 16 ounces on a standard (11-inch) reel.

MOTION PICTURE NOMENCLATURE.

cine.—A prefix used in description of the motion-picture art or apparatus,

change-over.—The stopping of one projecting machine and the simultaneous starting of a second machine in order to maintain an uninterrupted picture on the screen when showing a multiple-reel story.

condensers.—In an optical projection mechanism, the lens combination which gathers the diverging rays of the luminant and converges them into the objective.

    collector lens.—The lens next the source of light.

    converging lens.—The lens which converges the light on the picture aperture.

    middle lens.—Of a three-lens combination, the lens lying between the collector lens and the converging lens.

dissolve.—The gradual transition of one scene into another.

double printing.—The exposure of a sensitive film under two negatives prior to development.

douser.—The manually operated door in the projecting machine which intercepts the light before it reaches the fire shutter.

fade-in.—The gradual formation of the picture from darkness to full-screen brilliancy.

fade-out.—The gradual disappearance of the screen picture into blackness (the reverse of fade-in).

footage.—Film length, measured in feet.

frame (noun).—A single picture of the series of a motion-picture film.

frame (verb).—The adjustment of the relative position between the aperture and the pictures on the film to bring them into register with each other.

frame line.—The dividing line between two pictures on a motion-picture film which forms the top and bottom, respectively, of adjacent pictures.

intermittent sprocket.—The sprocket (in motion-picture apparatus) which engages the film to give it intermittent movement at the light aperture.

lantern picture.—A still picture projected on a screen by means of an optical lantern.

lantern slide.—The transparent picture from which a lantern picture is projected.

leaders.—That piece of blank film attached to the beginning of the picture series.

magazine valve.—The film opening in the magazine of a motion-picture projector.

motion picture.—The synthesis of a series of related picture elements, usually of an object in motion.

motion-picture film.—The ribbon upon which the series of pictures are recorded.

motion-picture projector.—An optical lantern equipped with mechanisms for suitably moving motion-picture film across the projected light.

negative.—The developed film after being exposed in a camera.

objective.—The image-forming member of the optical system in picture apparatus.

positive.—The developed film after being printed through a negative; it may be one reel or more than one.

print.—Same as " positive."

projecting lens.—The lens (in an optical machine) which images the picture on the screen.

reel.—The flanged spool upon which film is wound for use in projecting machines.

reel.—An arbitrary unit of measure for film—approximately 1,000 feet of length.

rewind.—The process of reversing the winding of a film, usually so that the end to be first projected shall lie on the outside of the roll.

rewinder.—The mechanism by which rewinding is accomplished.

safety shutter (also known as the fire shutter).—The automatically operated door (in a projecting machine) which intercepts the light when the machine runs below normal speed.

screen.—The surface upon which a picture is optically projected.

shutter.—The obscuring device, usually a segmental revolving disc, employed to intercept the light during the movement of the film in motion-picture apparatus.

shutter.—Working blade (also known as the cutting blade or obscuring blade); that segment which intercepts the light during the movement of the film at the picture aperture.

shutter.—Intercepting blade (also known as the flicker blade); that segment which intercepts the light one or more times during the rest or projection period of the film.

sprocket.—The revolvable toothed member (in motion-picture mechanisms) which engages the perforations in the film.

still.—A picture printed from a single negative.

take-up (verb).—The process of winding the film (in a motion-picture machine) after it passes the picture aperture.

take-up (noun).—The mechanism which receives and winds the film (in a motion-picture machine) after it passes the picture aperture.

throw.—The distance to the screen from the objective lantern of a motion-picture projecting machine.

vision.—A new subject introduced into the main picture, by the gradual fading-in the fading-out of the new subject; as, for example, to visualize a thought.

DEPARTMENT OF THE INTERIOR
BUREAU OF EDUCATION

BULLETIN, 1919, No. 83

MONTHLY RECORD
OF CURRENT EDUCATIONAL
PUBLICATIONS

f

DECEMBER, 1919

WASHINGTON
GOVERNMENT PRINTING OFFICE
1919

MONTHLY RECORD OF CURRENT EDUCATIONAL PUBLICATIONS.

Compiled by the Library Division, Bureau of Education.

NOTE.

The record comprises a general survey in bibliographic form of current educational literature, domestic and foreign, received during the monthly period preceding the date of publication of each issue.

This office can not supply the publications listed in this bulletin, other than those expressly designated as publications of the Bureau of Education. Books, pamphlets, and periodicals here mentioned may ordinarily be obtained from their respective publishers, either directly or through a dealer, or, in the case of an association publication, from the secretary of the issuing organization. Many of them are available for consultation in various public and institutional libraries.

Publications intended for inclusion in this record should be sent to the library of the Bureau of Education, Washington, D. C.

PROCEEDINGS OF ASSOCIATIONS.

1881. **Pennsylvaria. University.** Schoolmen's week proceedings, April 10–12, 1919. Philadelphia, Pa., Pub. by the University, 1919. 447 p. by the 8°. (University of Pennsylvania bulletin, vol. 20, no. 1, October 1, 1919)

Commented upon in the Pennsylvania gazette, 18 : 121, October 31, 1919.

Contains: 1. W. H. Kilpatrick: The demands of present American life upon American education, p. 23–27. 2. A. E. McKinley: Educational reorganization during and after the war, p. 27–34. 3. H S. Magill: The organization of the teaching profession for more effective service, p. 35–39. 4. A code of ethics for the teaching profession, p. 42–46. 5. G. W. Flounders: Educational measurements in the building and maintenance of the course of study, p. 49–52. 6. E. S. Ling: The use of graphs in supervision, p. 52–55. 7. W. S. Monroe: The next step in the use of educational measurements, p. 64–72. 8. Harlan Updegraff and L. A. King: Second annual report of the Bureau of educational measure-

3

ments, p. 78–113. 9. W. S. Monroe: Reasoning tests in arithmetic, p. 113–19. 10. Harold Barnes: Reorganization of classes based on the Monroe silent reading tests, p. 119–23. 11. H. C. Morrison: Distribution of school funds in New Hampshire, p. 129–34. 12. Harlan Updegraff: Application of state funds to the aid of local schools, p. 134–66; Discussion, p. 166–70. 13. J. M. Gambrill: Americanization of the immigrant child—some underlying principles, p. 170–73. 14. I. B. Bush: Americanization work in the public schools of Erie, p. 174–77. 15. C. F. Weller: Community service for Chester and vicinity, p. 178–83. 16. S. E. Weber: Americanization work in the public schools of Scranton, p. 184–88. 17. G. H. Betts: Rural school consolidation and transportation, p. 192–97. 18. J. G. Becht: A study of school consolidation and transportation in Pennsylvania, p. 197–99. 19. T. A. Bock: Consolidation and transportation in Pennsylvania, p. 200–207. 20. G. H. Betts: The county institute, p. 208–12. 21. Carmon Ross: The status of teachers' institutes in Pennsylvania, p. 212–21. 22. Gertrude A. Golden: The Courtis arithmetic tests in a Philadelphia public school, p. 265–71. 23. A. L. Gehman: Emphasizing individual instruction, p. 271–76. 24. W. S. Monroe: The improvement of instruction through the use of educational tests, p. 277–86. 25. Mabel Skinner: An ideal course in civics for the high school, p. 287–97. 26. T. H. Briggs: The high school curriculum, p. 301–307. 27. W. R. Douthett: A study of occupations as a definite course in the high school, p. 312–22. 28. Anna B. Pratt: The educational counselor in the public schools, p. 322–27. 29. Muriel W. Brown: Educational guidance and the trade school, p. 327–36. 30. J. Y. Pennypacker: The relation of the college course to the high school student, p. 344–52. 31. C. E. Bennett: Theory and practice in the reading of classical verse, p. 364–77. 32. D. M. Robinson: Archaeology in the schools, p. 377–85. 33. J. A. Pratt: The vestibule school and its contribution to industrial education, p. 388–92. 34. Home economics and its function in the school [by] Ada G. Fish, p. 394–96; [by] B. Lillian Daix, p. 396–98; [by] Ruth F. Elliott, p. 399–401; [by] Mary K. Richards, p. 401–403; Discussion, p. 403–405. 35. W. H. Kilpatrick: Secondary mathematics from the point of view of general educational theory, p. 405–12; Discussion, p. 412–14. 36. C. H. Handschin: Tests and measurements in modern language work, p. 420–25. 37. F. P. Graves: The evolution of our universities, p. 441–47.

See also items 1896, 1968, 2006, 2043, 2056, 2057, 2075, and 2101.

EDUCATIONAL HISTORY AND BIOGRAPHY.

1882. **Haight, Elizabeth Hazelton.** The life and letters of James Monroe Taylor, the biography of an educator. New York, E. P. Dutton & company [1919] 891 p. front., plates, ports. 8°.

Dr. Taylor was for many years president of Vassar college, Poughkeepsie, N. Y.

1883. **Knight, Edgar W.** Reconstruction and education in South Carolina. South Atlantic quarterly, 18: 350–64, October 1919.

To be concluded.
A history of measures relating to public schools undertaken by the State government of South Carolina during the reconstruction period following the Civil War.

1884. **Musselman, H. T.** The story of a great public school system. Texas school journal, 37: 11–16, November 1919. illus.

The history and growth of the Houston (Texas) public school system.

1885. **Northrop, Cyrus.** "Reminiscences." Minnesota alumni weekly, 19: 13–27, October 27; 13–32, November 24, 1919.

Begins a series of President Northrop's reminiscences.

1886. **Tucker, William Jewett.** My generation; an autobiographical interpretation. Boston and New York, Houghton Mifflin company, 1919. xv, 464 p. plates. 8°.

By the president emeritus of Dartmouth college.

CURRENT EDUCATIONAL CONDITIONS.

GENERAL AND UNITED STATES.

1887. **Babbitt, Irving.** Rousseau and romanticism. Boston, New York, Houghton Mifflin company, 1919. xxiii, 426 p. 8°.

> This book is an indictment of present-day civilization and a defense of classicism. The author ascribes the origin of the faults of the modern system to Rousseau with his theory of a return to nature.

1888. **Brooks, Eugene C.** North Carolina's new educational system. South Atlantic quarterly, 18 : 279–88, October 1919.

> Sketches recent educational legislation in North Carolina, and says the people of every section of the State are responding readily to the call to make it possible to wipe out illiteracy and train the next generation in the ways of better citizenship.

1889. **Call, Arthur Deerin.** The war has not destroyed, I. Our hope in public education. Advocate of peace, 31 : 282–86, September–October 1919.

> Says, in conclusion, that the war has not destroyed our faith in the public schools. In the years to come we shall have to look more and more to the public schools for that stream of influences which shall overthrow devastating class antagonisms, socialize mankind above benumbing need, and put us all in the way of those permanent satisfactions which widen the meanings of life.

1890. **Cates, E. E.** Are our schools producing results?. Education, 40 : 154–58, November 1919.

> Discusses the lack of immediate and willing obedience to constituted authority on the part of the average American boy.

1891. **National education association.** Commission on the emergency in education. A national program for education. School and society, 10 : 525–27, November 1, 1919.

> A statement of policies adopted September 13, 1919.

1892. **Parkinson, Dera D.** A school program for South Carolina. Columbia, S. C., Pub. by the University, 1919. 23 p. 8°. (Bulletin of the University of South Carolina, no. 80, May 1919)

> A thesis submitted to the Department of education of the University of South Carolina in partial fulfilment of the requirements of the degree of Master of arts. A concise, clear-cut and comprehensive survey of the elementary and secondary schools of South Carolina.

1893. **Spaulding, F. E.** A national educational program suggested by experiences of war and prospective demands of peace. National education association bulletin, 8 : 5–11, November 1919.

> Says "There are three minimum, definite, comprehensive objectives, that American public education should at once set for itself. They are : first, essential elementary knowledge, training, and discipline ; second, occupational efficiency ; third, civic responsibility." Gives the necessary features of a program for the realization of these objectives.

1894. **Valentine, Roy Herbert.** A partial survey of the schools of Vermilion county, Indiana . . . June 1919. Newport, Ind., Hoosier state print, 1919. 82 p. 8°.

1895. **Watson, Foster.** National education and internationalism. Living age, 303 : 362–66, November 8, 1919.

> Reprinted from the Anglo-French review.
> Says that while the value of national education is irresistible, yet unmitigated self-centredness is as unwholesome in the nation as it is in the individual.

1896. **British association for the advancement of science.** Education at the British association. Journal of education (London) 51 : 671–73, October 1919.

> A résumé of the proceedings of the educational science section of the British association at the Bournemouth meeting, September 9–13, 1919.

1897. **Carpenter, Mary F.** School management in India and some of its problems. School and home education, 39 : 52–56, November 1919. illus.

1898. **Dewey, John.** Transforming the mind of China. Asia, 19 : 1103–08, November 1919. illus.

> China is learning that her readjustment to the impact of the western peoples can be effected only by a readjustment of her own age-long customs, that she must change her historic mind and not merely a few of her practices. This process of transformation of the Chinese mind seems to the outsider to progress slowly, but it should be allowed to develop in its own way.

1899. **Edmunds, Charles K.** Modern education in China. Journal of international relations, 10 : 174–97, October 1919.

> Continued from the preceding number of the Journal.
> Describes the various types of modern education in China.

1900. **Halévy, Élie.** La nouvelle loi scolaire anglaise. Revue de Paris, 26 : 596–621, October 1, 1919.

> A French account of the new English education act.

1901. **Hallays, André.** L'université de Strasbourg; sa renaissance et son avenir. Revue des deux mondes, 53 : 241–69, September 15. 1919.

> A survey of the past history, present condition, and future prospects of the University of Strasburg.

1902. **Martin, Percy A.** Four years of socialistic government in Yucatan. Journal of international relations, 10 : 209–22, October 1919.

> Incidentally discusses educational conditions in Yucatan.

1903. **Odum, Edward W.** German education and the great war. Bulletin of the Board of education of the Methodist Episcopal Church, South, 9 : 99–113, November 1919.

> Part of the opening address at the first official meeting of the Education association of the Methodist Episcopal Church, South, Memphis, Tenn., March 4–6, 1919.
> Also separately reprinted.

1904. **Reynolds, H. C.** Turning a leaf of the book of knowledge; how a literate China has been ordered by proclamation. Asia, 19 : 1143–47, November 1919. illus.

> The interesting story of the new simplified national phonetic writing for the Chinese language, officially adopted by a government decree in November, 1918. This new alphabet is making very successful progress.

1905. **Vasconcellos, A. Faria de.** A new school in Belgium; with an introduction by Adolphe Ferrière. Translated from the French by Eden and Cedar Paul. London, G. G. Harrap & co. ltd., 1919. 237 p. 12°.

> In this book, M. Faria de Vasconcellos describes the methods of instruction followed in the New school at Bierges-les-Wawre, Belgium, of which he is headmaster.

1906. **Vincent, George E.** Chinese progress in medicine, schools, and politics. American review of reviews, 60 : 515–18, November 1919.

> Shows how modern educational ideas are meeting a cordial reception in China.

1907. **Wells, H. G.** The undying fire, a contemporary novel. New York, The Macmillan company, 1919. 229 p. 12°.

> This work is a modern version of the book of Job, and presents a plea for the humanizing and socializing of education. Job Huss, the master of a modern school, overwhelmed by great misfortune, but inspired by the "undying fire," wrestles triumphantly with his tormentors and his comforters, in a discussion including everything from education to religion, agnosticism and the war.

EDUCATIONAL THEORY AND PRACTICE.

1908. **Baker, Elizabeth S.** The contribution of the teacher to the development of democracy. Kindergarten and first grade, 4: 343–45, November 1919.

> From the standpoint of an elementary teacher.
> Address given before the National education association, Milwaukee, July 1919.

1909. **O'Shea, M. V.** The medieval mind in education. School and society, 10: 561–68, November 15, 1919.

> Discusses the article by Mr. Ward on "Educational bolshevism," which appeared in the Outlook for September 24, 1919, in which the writer condemns our present educational system.

1910. **Preston, F. S.** Fundamental principles of education: the literary aspect. Journal of education and School world (London), 51: 728–30, November 1, 1919.

> A paper read before the educational science section of the British association, September 12, 1919. Advocates an acquaintance with the literature and history of other countries.

1911. **Sharp, Dallas Lore.** Patrons of democracy. Atlantic monthly, 124: 649–60, November 1919.

> This article calls the knowledge and practice of democracy the true end of American education. Neither life nor the getting of a living, but living together, this must be the single public end of a common public education hereafter. The writer urges that all American children be educated together in common schools through the high-school grade. After this preparation, specific vocational or technical training or a college course may be entered.

EDUCATIONAL PSYCHOLOGY; CHILD STUDY.

1912. **Franz, Shepherd Ivory.** Handbook of mental examination methods. 2d ed., rev. and enl. New York, The Macmillan company, 1919. 193 p. illus. 8°.

1913. **Garth, Thomas Russell.** Work curves. Journal of educational psychology, 10: 277–83, May–June 1919.

> "Examination of the work curves of over 700 third-fourth and seventh-eighth grade children yields no evidence to confirm Meumann's theory of distinct types of workers, but the tendency is to approximate the normal distribution curve."

1914. **Geneslay, F.** Physiologie de l'adolescence. Mercure de France, 135: 437–65, October 1, 1919.

> CONTENTS.—I. Durée de l'adolescence.—II. Croissance physique; Forme extérieure.—III. Développement des organes.—IV. L'instinct sexuel.—V. Déviation et exagération de l'instinct sexuel.—VI. Hallucinations et névroses.—VII. Hygiène et éducation physique.

1915. **Noe, J. T. C.** On study. Kentucky high school quarterly, 5: 66–73, October 1919.

> The writer says that the mastery of any subject is accomplished by sustained effort. Verbal learning is not real study—thinking alone educates and without thinking there is no mastery.

1916. **Ramsey, Carol.** The common school and the common child. American schoolmaster, 12 : 343–53, October 1919.

> Sets forth some of the facts and problems connected with the education of the individual child.

1917. **Toops, Herbert A. and Pintner, Rudolf.** Mentality and school progress. Journal of educational psychology, 10 : 253–62, May–June 1919.

EDUCATIONAL TESTS AND MEASUREMENTS.

1918. **Arthur, Grace.** An application of intelligence tests to the problem of school retardation. School and society, 10 : 614–20, November 22, 1919.

> A study made in the public schools of St. Paul, Minn. The results indicate that a child, with rare exceptions, can be made to work up to but not beyond the school grade corresponding to his mental age.

1919. **Chapman, J. Crosby.** The learning curve in typewriting. Journal of applied psychology, 3 : 252–68, September 1919.

> The method of this research was to test, each week in the school year, the speed of a mixed class, ages 16–18, in typewriting. The material used consisted of extracts from Addison's " Essays."

1920. **Christensen, Ione.** A mental survey of a training school. Utah educational review, 13 : 68–72, October 1919.

> Abstract of a small portion of a thesis prepared by Miss Christensen in partial fulfilment of the requirements for the master's degree in the University of Utah. It is a survey of the mental ages of the pupils of the University training school.

1921. **Doll, E. A.** " Scattering " in the Binet-Simon tests. Training school bulletin, 16 : 96–103, October 1919.

1922. **Evans, J. E. and Knoche, Florence E.** The effects of special drill in arithmetic as measured by the Woody and the Courtis arithmetic tests. Journal of educational psychology, 10 : 263–76, May–June 1919.

> "A carefully controlled experiment with the Studebaker economy practice exercises. The class with the special drill made five times as much improvement as the class with regular school work."

1923. **Foote, John M. and Henson, C. C.** A study of arithmetic in Rapides parish. Baton Rouge, La., Ramires-Jones printing company, 1919. 35 p. fold. table. 8°. (Louisiana. State department of education. Bulletin no. 11, September 1, 1919.)

> List of selected references, p. 35.

1924. **Gunther, Charles.** My experience with the Hillegas scale. English journal, 8 : 535–42, November 1919.

> The writer finds that with the Hillegas scale or some similar scale an experienced English teacher may arrive at the quality and progress of the theme work of students with reasonable accuracy, that it will be possible to maintain more even standards for promotion which will be reasonably free from temporary moods or caprices, and that the ratings given by a group of experienced teachers to a set of pupils' papers will be more uniform than those given when 'the per cent scale is used.

1925. **Hill, David Spence.** Standardized illustrative sentences for the Springfield spelling list. Journal of educational psychology, 10 : 285–90, May–June 1919.

> " The importance of using standardized materials in educational measurements is being increasingly recognized. This article presents standardized sentences for the 70 words of the Springfield (Ill.) spelling list, to 17,642 white and 3,677 colored children."

1926. **Lowell, Frances.** A group intelligence scale for primary grades. Journal of applied psychology, 3: 215–47, September 1919.

> This group scale offers a means for measuring the intelligence of large groups of children accurately enough to sort out all children of questionable normality. It also forms a basis for school promotions and demotions.

1927. **Pintner, Rudolf.** A non-language group intelligence test. Journal of applied psychology, 3: 199–214, September 1919.

> Tests that can be given to illiterates, foreigners, and deaf persons. Does not demand a knowledge of English in order to understand the directions for doing the tests.

1928. **Pittsburgh. Board of public education.** . . . Writing test, June 4, 1918. [Pittsburgh, 1919] 31 p. tables, diagrs. 8°. (Research and measurement bulletin no. 3)

1929. **Wood, E. R.** Investigation in arithmetic. Kentucky high school quarterly, 5: 1–49, October 1919.

> To be continued in the issue for January 1920.
> "The purpose of this study is to present a brief summary and evaluation of the various experimental studies that have been made in the field of arithmetic, and to emphasize the psychological and hygienic side, so that the way may be cleared for those who desire to devote time to this rich field of experimentation."

SPECIAL METHODS OF INSTRUCTION.

1930. **Charters, Jessie A.** The problem method of teaching ideals. English journal, 8: 461–73, October 1919.

> Says that the problem must grow out of some interest which the children already have. Emphasizes dramatization; many subjects, such as civics, history, and literature, lend themselves to dramatization.

1931. **Minor, Ruby.** Project-teaching in grade six. Elementary school journal, 20: 137–45, October 1919.

1932. **Sullivan, M. E.** Method in the teaching of reading. Ohio teacher, 40: 103–105, October 1919.

> Discusses some of the methods of teaching reading in the past and the failure of these methods to produce readers.

SPECIAL SUBJECTS OF CURRICULUM.

ENGLISH AND COMPOSITION.

1933. **Barnes, Walter.** Culture and efficiency; their relation to the English subjects. Education, 40: 135–47, 217–29, November, December 1919.

> An effort to determine whether the English subjects are essentially cultural or practical. Defines "culture" and "efficiency." Says they are not identical, not even similar. "Culture can not be practical; efficiency, though it assume the clothing and the manners of culture, remains efficiency." Life demands both. To make education complete the school should make contributions to both culture and efficiency. The English subjects should be cultural and practical, the one branch (literature) cultural, the other branch (grammar and composition) practical.

1934. **Barton, H. J.** The language tower. Illinois association of teachers of English bulletin, 12: 1–18, October 1, 1919.

> The value of Latin in the study of English.

1935. **Fretts, A. Alta.** Some proofs of the value of Latin for mastering a practical English vocabulary. Classical weekly, 13: 34–35, November 10, 1919.

> This paper was read at the thirteenth meeting of the Classical association of the Atlantic states, at Haverford College, April 5, 1919.

10 CURRENT EDUCATIONAL PUBLICATIONS.

1936. **Hawk, Hazel S.** Composition in high school. Inter-mountain educator, 15 : 56–61, October 1919.

1937. **Johnson, H. C.** The English language—its new importance and universality. Journal of the New York state teachers' association, 6 : 224–27, October 1919.

The teaching of the English language and the place of foreign languages in our schools, both elementary and secondary.

1938. **National council of teachers of English.** Committee on economy of time in English. Report of the subcommittee on composition and rhetoric. English journal, 8 : 554–68, November 1919.

A tentative report submitted for suggestions and constructive criticism.

1939. **Quiller-Couch, Sir Arthur.** The teaching of English. Journal of education and School world (London) 51 : 737–40, November 1, 1919.

Emphasizes the teaching of English. As regards the classics the author advocates the study of Greek as superior to Latin. It is the key to a more fascinating literature; and our scientific nomenclature is largely derived from it.

1940. **Sandwick, Richard L.** Teaching some American ideals through English composition. Journal of the New York state teachers' association, 6 : 209–17, October 1919.

1941. **Ward, C. H.** The next C. G. N. report. English journal, 8 : 519–26, November 1919.

Points out the ways in which the old report of the Committee on grammatical nomenclature proves wrong for classroom practice, and gives evidence of the radical changes that will be necessary when some new committee undertakes revision.

MODERN LANGUAGES.

1942. **Allen, Elizabeth S.** Learning Chinese for better business. Language schools are doing a great service to international trade. Trans-Pacific (Tokyo, Japan) 1 : 35–38, November 1919.

Describes particularly the work of the North China union language school at Peking, in which over 75 per cent of the teachers are Chinese and which trains both for the Christian missions and for business.

1943. **Wilkins, Lawrence A.** The war and world languages. Educational review, 58 : 289–302, November 1919.

Says that the German language is under "an eclipse that will continue; English is in the ascendancy, and French increasing. Spanish is rapidly being reinstated as one of the world languages." Advocates better teaching of French and Spanish.

ANCIENT LANGUAGES.

1944. **Burr, A. W.** Increasing the study of Latin. Classical journal, 15 : 116–19, November 1919.

1945. **Irland, Fred.** High school English. Classical weekly, 13 : 36–39, November 10, 1919.

Read before the thirteenth annual meeting of the Classical association of the Atlantic states, at Haverford college, April 5, 1919.
Shows the value of the classics as an aid in the study of English.

SOCIAL SUBJECTS.

1946. **Barnes, Harry E.** Psychology and history: some reasons for predicting their more active cooperation in the future. American journal of psychology, 30 : 337–76, October 1919.

Discusses the psychological interpretation of history. Predicts that a century hence a knowledge of that branch of psychology which Freud and his followers have elaborated will be regarded as "a tool of the historian which is as indispensable to his success as Giry's manual on diplomacy is to the present-day student of historical documents."

1947. **Hill, Howard C.** The social sciences in the University high school. School review, 27: 680–94, November 1919.

Gives an outline of a course used in the University high school (University of Chicago), entitled "General organization of survey of civilization," and "General organization of modern history (1763–1919)."

1948. **Morse, Anson Daniel.** Civilization and the world war; edited by members of his family. Boston, New York [etc.] Ginn and company [1919] xiv, 222 p. front. (port.) 12°.

Author was formerly professor of history in Amherst college. This book presents Prof. Morse's conception of civilization, of Germany, of the relation between the two, and of the means—a league of nations—for insuring the upward movement of humanity from the danger of a renewal of the world war.

GEOGRAPHY.

1949. **Cobb, Collier.** The teaching of geography in the high school. High school journal, 2: 203–10, November 1919.

Deals particularly with physical geography.

1950. **Cooper, Clyde E.** Status of geography in normal schools of the far west. Journal of geography, 18: 300–5, November 1919.

Presents an ideal plan for normal geography work, and invites correspondence to determine whether a survey of geography in the schools of the central and eastern parts of the country is warranted.

1951. **Parker, Edith P.** The partition of Africa—a seventh grade geography unit. Elementary school journal, 20: 188–202, November 1919.

A study of the story of Africa from 1884 to 1915 consumed the geography periods, in the School of education, University of Chicago, for five days. Current newspapers and magazines, maps, and other material were drawn on by the children.

SCIENCE.

1952. **Alden, George Ira.** The study of electricity by the deductive method. Worcester, Mass., Commonwealth press, 1919. x, 110 p. illus. 12°.

1953. **Downing, Elliot R.** The scientific method and the problems of science teaching. School and society, 10: 568–74, November 15, 1919.

Contains a list of tests in science which are already in existence.

1954. **Gray, A.** Scientific education and the teaching of physics. Science, n. s. 50: 377–83, October 24, 1919.

Concluding part of presidential address before the Mathematical and physical science section at the Bournemouth meeting of the British association for the advancement of science. Emphasizes scientific education rather than classical.

1955. **Kirkwood, J. E.** The case of general science. Education, 40: 159–70, November 1919.

Says that the course in general science in the high school is open to many objections. The place for the work that it contemplates is not in the high school, but in the seventh and eighth grades.

1956. **Tilden, William A.** Progress in science teaching. Nature, 104: 253–55, November 6, 1919.

A review of science teaching in Great Britain and Ireland.

MATHEMATICS.

1957. **Breckenridge, William E.** Applied mathematics in high schools. Some lessons from the war. Mathematics teacher, 12: 17–22, September 1919.

1958. Gray, John G. Number by development; a method of number instruction. Vol. II: Intermediate grades. Vol. III: Grammar grades. Philadelphia and London, J. B. Lippincott company [1919] 2 v. 12°.

Vol. I of this series, previously published, deals with Introductory number.

1959. Schlauch, William S. An experiment in motivation. Mathematics teacher, 12: 1–9, September 1919.

. The application of mathematics to problems in which the students are vitally interested. Experiments tried in the High school of commerce, New York city.

1960. Taylor, Joseph S. Subtraction by the addition process. Elementary school journal, 20: 203–7, November 1919.

Criticises the Austrian method, which has been tried in the public schools of New York city. The writer says that in one supervisory district the Austrian method of subtraction is not functioning.

1961. Wilson, Guy Mitchell. A survey of the social and business usage of arithmetic. New York city, Teachers college, Columbia university, 1919. 62 p. 8°. (Teachers college, Columbia university, Contributions to education, no. 100)

This study undertakes to determine the arithmetic actually used by adults in their social and business relations. The data were collected from the parents of sixth, seventh, and eighth grade pupils in towns and cities of the Middle West. The pupils of the chosen grades made daily reports of the problems actually solved by their parents during a period of two weeks. The results of the study indicate that many of the traditional processes of arithmetic should be entirely omitted from schoolroom practice, as being useless in later life of the pupils.

MUSIC.

1962. Gantvoort, A. J. Music for citizenship. American school, 5: 303–304, October 1919.

Read before the Music department of the National education association, Milwaukee, July 2, 1919.
Music as a promoter of good citizenship.

1963. Tiersot, Julien. L'art musical et l'enseignement public. Revue pédagogique, 75: 166–81, September 1919.

ELOCUTION.

1964. Gaylord, J. S. Speech improvement. Quarterly journal of speech education, 5: 358–67, October 1919.

Discusses the improvement of American speech. .

1965. West, Robert. Methods used in computing contest scores. Quarterly journal of speech education, 5: 319–33, October 1919.

Methods of computing the scores in oratorical contests.

THRIFT.

1966. Boyce, Thomas W. Education in thrift. Wisconsin journal of education, 51: 243–44, November 1919.

1967. Zook, George F. Teaching thrift in the schools. School and society, 10: 581–84, November 15, 1919.

Advocates a definite course in thrift for the schools, which shall be largely a course in money economy.

KINDERGARTEN AND PRIMARY SCHOOL.

1968. International kindergarten union. Proceedings of the twenty-sixth annual meeting . . . Baltimore, Md., May 19–23, 1919. 228 p. 8°. (Miss May Murray, secretary, Springfield, Mass.)

Contains: 1. Louise C. Sutherland: Report of the graphic arts committee, p. 65–70. 2. H. Grace Parsons: Report of committee on minimum essentials of kindergarten and primary education, p. 71–75. 3. A. D. Yocum: The kindergarten as a factor in democracy, p. 127–48. 4. Is it advisable to change the name "kindergarten?" Affirmative [by] Alice Temple, p. 148–54; Negative [by] Catharine R. Watkins, p. 154–58. 5. Edna D. Baker: Practical methods of developing initiative in students in the training school, p. 159–63. 6. F. C. Butler: America's duty to the next generation, p. 168–74. 7. Agnes L. Rodgers: The scope and significance of measurement in early elementary education, p. 174–83. 8. J. B. Watson: The pre-kindergarten age—a laboratory study, p. 184–206. 9. H. W. Thurston: Minimum standards of child welfare, p. 206–15. 10. Bertha Barwis: Unifying work of the primary grades, p. 215–18.

1969. Brady, Belle. Group teaching in the first grade. Kindergarten and first grade, 4: 354–57, November 1919.

An attempt made, in the first grade of the Normal training school at Superior, Wis., to work out the problem of giving opportunity to each child to advance as rapidly as he is able.

1970. Hall, Viola. A first-grade experiment. Elementary school journal, 20: 217–25, November 1919.

An experiment to test initiative and originality in pupils.

RURAL EDUCATION.

1971. Campbell, Macy. A dying school system for children who are just beginning to live. Midland schools, 33: 339–42, June 1919.

Shows why the one-teacher rural school is dying.

1972. Harvey, Marie Turner. The contribution of rural schools to democracy. American school, 5:265–66. 281, September 1919.

Read at the general session, National education association, Milwaukee, July 3, 1919.

"The teacher of the Porter rural school in Missouri gives a digest of a 7 years' experimental study of typical rural education problems as they were worked out in her school."

1973. Smart, Thomas J. The problem of rural education. School and society, 10: 540–46, November 8, 1919.

Shows the chaos of terminology used in the field of rural education, discriminates between "agricultural" and "rural" education, suggests a definition for the latter term and gives the immediate step necessary for the realization of its program.

SECONDARY EDUCATION.

1974. Fitzgerald, W. J. The junior high school. Catholic educational review, 17: 466–79, October 1919.

Paper read at the meeting of the Catholic educational association, St. Louis, 1919.

Considers the alleged advantages of the junior high school, and the objections brought against it as an educational proposition.

1975. Fuess, Claude Moore, ed. Phillips academy, Andover, in the great war. New Haven, Yale university press, 1919. 398 p. front., ports. 8°.

1976. **A handbook of American private schools; an annual survey. Fifth edition.** 1919–20. Boston, Mass., Porter E. Sargent, 14 Beacon street, [1919.] 761 p. 12°.

CONTENTS.—Introductory : Preface to the fifth edition, Development of the private school, The mission of the private school, Choosing the school, Development of the summer camp, School lectures, Progress in the private schools. Educational reconstruction in America, Educational literature of the year 1918–1919 Select bibliography for the academic year 1918–19.—Critical description of schools and summer camps.—Comparative tables.—Educational directories.—School and camp maps.

1977. **Kandel, I. L.** The junior high school in European systems. Educational review, 58 : 303–27, November 1919.

Intermediate education in Germany, France, and England.

1978. **Knight, Edgar W.** The academy movement in the South. High school journal, 2 : 199–204, 235–40, November, December 1919.

To be concluded.

1979. **McLaughlin, Henry P.** Building on a fund of school habits. Educational review, 58 : 279–83, November 1919.

Discusses various phases of high school discipline.

1980. **Obrien, Francis P.** The high school failures; a study of the school records of pupils failing in academic or commercial high school subjects. New York city, Teachers college, Columbia university, 1919. vii, 97 p. 8°. (Teachers college, Columbia university, Contributions to education, no. 102.)

1981. **Tildsley, John L.** The reorganization of the high school for the service of democracy. American school, 5 : 270, September 1919.

Read at the general session, National education association, Milwaukee, July 3, 1919.

1982. **Whitney, Frank P.** Provision for accelerant and retarded children in junior high school. School review, 27 : 695–705, November 1919.

Grouping children of junior high-school age according to ability as indicated by the proficiency marks.

TEACHERS: TRAINING AND PROFESSIONAL STATUS.

1983. **Almack, John C.** Keeping up in teaching. American school board journal, 59 : 27–30, November 1919.

The problem of self-improvement of teachers and some of the agencies for the improvement of teachers in service.

1984. **Ballou, Frank W.** Study of salary schedule. Boston teachers news letter, 8 : 6–8, November 1919.

The salary schedules in other cities in relation to the salary schedules of the various ranks in the city of Boston.

1985. **Boas, F. S.** Teachers and research. Contemporary review, 116 : 426–31, October 1919.

A discussion on some of the practical methods of promoting modern language research among teachers. An address delivered before the Modern language research association, England.

1986. **Boynton, F. D.** The effects of tenure and compulsory salary increment laws. Journal of the New York state teachers' association, 6 : 249–55, November 13, 1919.

The dangers arising from the tenure and compulsory salary increment laws in New York and suggestions for overcoming any undesirable tendencies in these laws.

CURRENT EDUCATIONAL PUBLICATIONS. **15**

1987. **Bricker, Garland A.** Training teachers of agriculture. Educational review, 58: 328–39. November 1919.

Expresses the conviction that teachers of agriculture must be specially trained. Gives experience with teachers not specifically trained.

1988. Bulletin of the American association of university professors, vol. 5, no. 6, October 1919. 84 p. 8°. (Pensions and insurance.)

1989. **Chancellor, William Estabrook.** The health of the teacher. Chicago, Forbes & company, 1919. 307 p. 12°.

1990. **Coffman, L. D.** [Teachers' unions and collective bargaining] Minnesota alumni weekly, 19: 6–7, November 10, 1919.

A letter written in response to a telegram signed by a little group of Minnesota teachers.
Dean Coffman is in favor of an American federation of teachers but not an American federation affiliated with the American federation of labor.

1991. **Dewey, John.** Professional organization of teachers. Journal of education, 90: 428, October 30, 1919.

Address originally published in the American teacher, in favor of teachers' unions and their affiliation with the American federation of labor.

1992. **Hibben, John Grier.** Are cheap teachers going to be good for your children? American magazine, 88: 15–16, 80, 82, September 1919.

Full-page portrait of President Hibben, p. 17.
In this statement, made to a member of the staff of the magazine, President Hibben of Princeton gives some startling facts regarding teachers' salaries. The pay is so small that the best teachers are likely to quit and leave the children to inferior instructors.

1993. **Johnson, S. W.** Minimum wage law for teachers in Iowa. American school board journal, 59: 40, 101, 103–104, October 1919.

1994. **Mardis, S. K.** How to make teaching a profession in Ohio. Ohio educational monthly, 68: 434–41, November 1919.

Teachers' salaries, etc., in Ohio.

1995. **Myers, C. E.** Should teachers' organizations affiliate with the American federation of labor? School and society, 10: 594–97, November 22, 1919.

Thinks that if teachers seek protection under the arms of "labor" they will be losers in freedom of spirit and that freedom which carries over in teaching and makes for democracy in education.

1996. **National education association. Commission on the emergency in education.** Teachers' salaries and salary schedules in the United States, 1918–19. By E. S. Evenden. Washington, National education association, 1919. 169 p. 8°. (Commission series no. 6)

Bibliography, p. 167–69.

1997. **New York state teachers' association. Committee on teachers' pensions.** The proposed retirement plan for New York state teachers. Preliminary report. Journal of the New York state teachers' association, 6: 197–204, October 1919.

A. R. Brubacher, chairman.

1998. **Oberlin college, Oberlin, Ohio.** [Committee on salaries] Increased salaries urged for faculties. Advances of fifty per cent asked for college trustees. Oeblin alumni magazine, 16: 32–37, November 1919.

Charles G. Rogers, chairman.
Gives charts showing the diminishing value of the dollar, the increase in living costs, etc.

1999. Oliphant, J. Orin. The vanishing profession. Northwest journal of education, 31: 72–73, November 1919.

In speaking of the critical period through which the teaching profession is passing, the writer says that unless a great change takes place soon, the public will be faced with two alternatives on the part of the teaching profession—dissolution or union.

2000. Patterson, Herbert. Common sense and teachers' contracts. School and society, 10: 553–56, November 8, 1919.

Thinks that no contract should be made which does not allow a teacher the right to resign, but says that common courtesy demands a notice of thirty days be given when one is about to resign.

2001. Seerley, Homer H. The American teacher in politics. 8 p. 8°.

Given at the Iowa state teachers' association, Des Moines, Iowa, November 7, 1919.
Also in American school, 5 :329–31, November 1919.
The writer says that the era of the teacher's separation from politics and of his isolation from popular propaganda and public work on the problems of society has ended and a new era of increased responsibility for existing conditions and of increased power to remedy evils and redress grievances existing in society has begun.

2002. Sierra educational news, vol. 15, no. 8, October 1919. (Teacher-training number)

Contains: 1. W. C. Wood: Problems of teacher training in California, p. 503–506. 2. A. F. Lange: The course for training secondary school teachers, p. 507–10. 3. Frederic Burk: The training of teachers, p. 511–14.

2003. Snedden, David. The professional improvement of teachers and teaching through organization. School and society, 10: 531–39, November 8, 1919.

Notes of an address given before the State teachers' association of Connecticut, October 24, 1919.

2004. Thomas, Charles Swain. Improvement of English teachers in service. English journal, 8: 543–53, November 1919.

Contains a suggestive scheme for self-measurement in English teaching.

2005. Vallance, H. F. The successful teacher. Ohio educational monthly, 68: 427–33, November 1919.

Speaks especially of the personality of the teacher and the essential characteristics of a successful teacher.

HIGHER EDUCATION.

2006. American association of collegiate registrars. Proceedings of the ninth annual meeting . . . Chicago, Ill., April 24–26, 1919. 160 p. 8°. (Ezra L. Gillis, secretary, University of Kentucky, Lexington, Ky.)

Contains: 1. C. S. Marsh: The American army university overseas and an estimate of its work for college credit, p. 22–27. 2. C. H. Judd : Some possible contributions of registrars to the solution of educational problems, p. 28–37; Discussion, p. 37–40. 3. A. C. Hall: A more uniform entrance certificate, p. 41–43; Discussion, p. 43–45. 4. R. L. Kelly: Some suggestions of college presidents, p. 51–60; Discussion, p. 60–62. 5. C. E. Friley: Some war benefits for the registrar, p. 63–71; Discussion, p. 71–73. 6. C. M. McConn: A study of registration procedure, p. 85–91. 7. K. C. Babcock: The efficient registrar— From a dean's point of view, p. 93–106. 8. W. D. Hiestand: The semester vs. the quarter plan, p. 108–19; Discussion, p. 119–21. 9. R. R. Newby: Some sidelights on the S. A. T. C., p. 124–30; Discussion, p. 130–32. 10. W. V. Bingham : The use of the army intelligence examination in university administration, p. 133–41. 11. E. J. Grant: The new plan for admission at Columbia, p. 142–45.

2007. **Beirne, Frank F.** The inadequate Rhodes scholar: a defense. Atlantic monthly, 124: 665–69, November 1919.

A reply to Dr. G. R. Parkin's criticism of American candidates for Rhodes scholarships in the September Atlantic.

2008. **Jones, Adam L.** Psychological tests for college admission. Educational review, 58: 271–78, November 1919.

Presents a few illustrations from a set of psychological tests used in testing candidates for one of the units of the Students' army training corps. Shows their feasibility for college admission.

2009. **Kerns, Shirley K.** College entrance requirements. Harvard alumni bulletin, 22: 116–18, October 30, 1919.

Advocates a reduction in the quantity of the college entrance requirements by one-fourth so that boys of to-day may have more leisure for self-education and cultivation.

2010. **Morrison, H. C.** Present day needs in higher education. School review, 27: 653–70, November 1919.

Advocates a better understanding and knowledge of Anglo-Saxon democracy and particularly of its American developments.

2011. **Schurman, Jacob Gould.** Twenty-seventh annual report by President Schurman, 1918–1919. Ithaca, N. Y., Cornell university, 1919. 83, xcviii p. 8°. (Cornell university official publication, vol. x, no. 18, October 1, 1919.)

The president's report covers pages 5–42 of this publication. The remaining pages comprise the comptroller's report and reports of the deans of colleges, the registrar, the librarian, and other officers.

Contains valuable material regarding the salaries of professors and instructors in American universities in general and in Cornell university in particular. Emphasizes the movement to increase the Cornell endowment. Has interesting sections on the necessity of fostering research, and on " Liberal scholarship, the soul of the university."

2012. **Straus, Percy S.** Just what is a college education worth? Some experiences in hiring college men and in getting jobs for them. American magazine, 88: 82–83, 112, 115–19, December 1919.

Mr. Straus is vice-president of R. H. Macy & company, inc., and chairman of the committee on employment of the Harvard club, of New York city. He says that a college man who regards his superior education as a very effective tool, not as a magic charm, is wanted in business and can succeed.

2013. **University of the Philippines, Manila.** Ninth annual commencement . . . April 4, 1919. Manila, Bureau of printing, 1919. 39 p. 8°.

Contains: George A. Malcolm: Philippine ideals realized through university efficiency, p. 5–16.

SCIENTIFIC RESEARCH.

2014. **Bogue, Robert H.** A system of cooperation between the college and industry. Science, n. s. 50: 425–27, November 7, 1919.

Chemical research and industrial problems described.

2015. **Gregory, Richard.** The promotion of research. Nature, 104: 253–55, November 6, 1919.

National provisions for scientific research work in Great Britain and Ireland.

2016. **Hill, Alexander.** Aspects of science at universities. Nature, 104: 255–57, November 6, 1919.

A review of scientific teaching and research work in the universities of Great Britain and Ireland.

SCHOOL ADMINISTRATION.

2017. **Allen, D. A.** Free textbooks: an opposing view. American school board journal, 59 : 87, 89–90, November 1919.

> The writer gives his objections to free textbooks.

2018. **Burris, W. P.** The Smith-Towner education bill. School and society, 10: 493–98, October 25, 1919.

> Letter addressed to the Committee on education of the Sixty-sixth Congress. The writer is opposed to a secretary of education in the President's cabinet and suggests an amendment to the Smith-Towner bill that would provide for a Federal Board of education consisting of nine members appointed by the President.

2019. **Gause, Frank A.** The efficiency department in a school system. American school board journal, 59 : 33–40. October 1919.

> The efficiency department of the Bay City (Mich.) schools and its function of determining how well the teaching corps of a school system is doing its work.

2020. **Good, H. G.** Early educational legislation in Ohio. School and society, 10 : 597–604, November 22, 1919.

> The aim of this article is to suggest that the forces which formed the school system of Ohio were American, not European forces, and that, in the period treated, the connection between legislative developments in Ohio and in the older states of the Union was close and clearly demonstrable.

2021. **Griffin, Orwin Bradford.** The administrator and the teacher. A philosophy of loyalty. American school board journal, 59 : 41–43, October 1919.

> Cooperation between the school administrator and the teacher. Teachers' meetings, classroom visits, etc.

2022. **Haisley, Otto W.** Simplifying enrollment and attendance records. American school board journal, 59 : 40–41, November 1919.

2023. **Hollister, H. A.** Why and how should we federalize education? School and society, 10 : 591–94, November 22, 1919.

> The writer does not approve of the proposed federal department of education, but suggests a commission that would be representative of the states and would convene at least once a year in Washington to consider educational needs.

2024. **Morrison, J. Cayce.** Methods of improving classroom instruction used by helping teachers and supervising-principals of New Jersey. Elementary school journal, 20 : 208–16, November 1919.

> Study based on a questionnaire sent to all supervising-principals and helping teachers of the state, in May 1918.

2025. **Spencer, Roger A.** The work of the school principal in supervision. Elementary school journal, 20 : 176–87, November 1919.

> Says that the standard test is the best means of eliminating poor methods and poor work, when it can be employed. The principal by using these tests avoids basing his criticism on his personal, unsupported judgment.

SCHOOL MANAGEMENT.

2026. **Allen, I. M.** Pupil responsibility as a training in democracy. Chicago schools journal, 2 : 2–8, October 1919.

> Also in American school, 5 : 305, 307, October 1919.

2027. **Farnham, Clinton E.** Supervised study. Education, 40 : 171–76, November 1919.

> Says that teachers should feel that the full time of the supervised study period belongs to the pupils and not to themselves, if a prepared lesson is expected for the next day.

2028. Janitorial services in school buildings. Variations in work and difficulties in maintaining economical conditions. American school board journal, 59 : 43–45, October 1919.

2029. Rorem, S. O. A grading standard. School review, 27 : 671–79, November 1919.

2030. Seymour, Martin A. School morals. American school board journal, 59 : 30–31, November 1919.

Gives eight requisites toward arousing and holding a proper school spirit: Constructive criticism, Cooperation, Commendation, Unselfishness, Loyalty, Square dealings, Conscientious and earnest effort, High ideals.

2031. Shumaker, J. H. The inner life of schools: what is it? Pennsylvania school journal, 68 : 141–44, October 1919.

Suggests remedies that may be introduced to improve the imperfections that attach to the inner life of schools, the moral atmosphere, etc.

SCHOOL ARCHITECTURE.

2032. Betelle, James O. Checking schedule for projected school buildings, a guide for school boards and superintendents. Milwaukee, Wis., The Bruce publishing company [1919] 32 p. 4°.

2033. Strayer, George D.; Engelhardt, N. L. and Hart, F. W. General report on school buildings and grounds of Delaware, 1919. Wilmington, Del., Service citizens of Delaware, Public library building, 1919. 222 p. illus. fold. table. 8°. (Bulletin of the Service citizens of Delaware. vol. 1, no. 3, October 15, 1919.)

SCHOOL HYGIENE AND SANITATION.

2034. Bierman, Jessie M. Growth of medical inspection in the public schools of the United States. Inter-mountain educator, 15 : 63–68, October 1919.

2035. Cooper, Frank Irving. Hygienic problems in schoolhouse construction. American school board journal, 59 : 37–38, November 1919.

Read before the Department of hygiene, National education association, Milwaukee, Wis., July 1919. Recounts some of the author's findings in studying several hundred schoolhouses for the Committee on standardization of schoolhouse planning and construction.

2036. Fairchild, R. W. The opportunity of education in medical inspection. American school board journal, 59 : 37–38, October; 35–36, 105, November 1919.

Gives a brief history of the recent growth of medical inspection of school children, five fundamental reasons for inspection, requisites of a good system, etc.

2037. The Health bulletin, vol. 34, no. 11, November 1919. (Published by the North Carolina state board of health, Raleigh, N. C.)

Medical inspection of schools number.

2038. Kenney, John A. How Tuskegee institute is promoting better health conditions in the South. Modern medicine, 1 : 627–30, November 1919. illus.

2039. McCastline, William H. Columbia university health service. Modern medicine, 1 : 621–26, November 1919. Illus.

"The health scheme at Columbia contemplates giving the graduate a stamp of physical health and efficiency in keeping with the standards of education upheld by the University. No student is graduated without fulfilling the compulsory credits in physical education."

2040. **McChesney, Bertha E.** Duties of the school nurse. American school board journal, 59 : 39, November 1919.

2041. **McVicker, V. E.** A health campaign for Ohio. Ohio teacher, 40 : 98–100, October 1919.

> Gives the special provisions of the Hughes act of Ohio with respect to schools, showing the relation between the schools and the public health system.

2042. **Preston, Josephine Corliss.** Rural health. American school, 5 : 301–302, October 1919.

> Report read before the National council of education, National education association, Milwaukee, June 30, 1919.
> Gives the present status of rural health and sanitation as revealed in reports received from 387 counties representing 44 states.

PHYSICAL TRAINING.

2043. **American physical education association.** Papers read before the Y. M. C. A. section . . . Chicago, Ill., April 11, 1919. American physical education review, 24 : 373–93, October 1919.

> Contains: 1. J. H. Gray: Physical education in India, p. 373–79. 2. Percy Carpenter: Latest news from Y. M. C. A. physical work in France, p. 380–85. 3. F. J. Smith: The present status of physical work in Canada, p. 385–89. 4. Anna L. Brown: Community physical education for women, p. 389–93.

2044. **Brown, Floyd L.** Reconstruction in physical education. Mind and body, 26 : 249–55, November 1919.

> Presents, in closing, a definite program for physical training in schools.

2045. **Evans, W. A.** Health education in industry. Modern medicine, 1 : 570–74, November 1919.

> Read before the eighth annual safety congress of the National safety council, Cleveland, Ohio, October 1–4, 1919.

2046. **Rowe, F. A.** Talks on physical training. Moderator-topics, 40 : 164–65, 169, November 20, 1919.

> Suggests a series of tests of physical efficiency for grading pupils.

SOCIAL ASPECTS OF EDUCATION.

2047. **Chancellor, William Estabrook.** Educational sociology. New York, The Century co., 1919. 422 p. 12°.

> A general introductory survey of the ground of sociology with particular reference to education, which prepares youth for society. The special fields entered are social movements, social institutions, and social measurement.

2048. **Oakley, George W., jr.** The country boy and the boy scout movement. School education, 39 : 50–51, November 1919.

> How the boy scout movement meets the great need of the country boyhood of America.

2049. **Preston, Josephine Corliss.** The wider use of the school plant. Community centers. Standardization. Olympia, Wash., F. M. Lamborn, public printer, 1919. 80 p. 8°. (Washington, Department of education. Bulletin no. 34, 1919)

2050. **Wright, H. W.** The social significance of education. Philosophical review, 28 : 345–69, July 1919.

> Read as the presidential address before the Western philosophical association, April, 1919.

CHILD WELFARE.

2051. Baldwin, Bird T. Iowa's research and welfare station for normal children. Iowa alumnus, 17: 30–35, October 1919. illus.

The work of the Child welfare research station of the State university of Iowa and its contribution toward the upbuilding and advancement of the so-called normal children.

Also separately reprinted.

2052. McCormick, B. E. Extravagance of school children, revealed in a close hand investigation of the schools of LaCrosse. Wisconsin journal of education, 51: 241–42, November 1919.

The investigation showed that in one Wisconsin high school the pupils are spending more than $50,000 a year on candy and movies.

2053. Thurston, Henry W. Minimum standards of child welfare. Kindergarten and first grade, 4: 357–59, November 1919.

Extracts from an address before the International kindergarten union, Baltimore, Md.

2054. U. S. Children's bureau. Minimum standards for child welfare, adopted by the Washington and regional conferences on child welfare. 1919. Washington, Government printing office, 1919. 15 p. 8°. (Conference series no. 2. Bureau publication no. 62)

MORAL EDUCATION.

2055. Donor's library on character education; compiled as an assistance to the collaborators in the $20,000 interstate research on methods of character education in public schools, 1919. Published at the expense of the donor of the award—100 copies. Volume I. Washington, D. C., National institution for moral instruction [1919] xii, 654 p. 8°.

RELIGIOUS EDUCATION.

2056. Association of Biblical instructors in American colleges and secondary schools. [Addresses delivered at the eighth annual conference . . . New York city, December 1918] Christian education, 3: 1–32, October 1919.

Contains: 1. W. C. Wheeler: Religious difficulties of college students and how to meet them, p. 12–14. 2. W. H. Wood: Necessary readjustments in our college curriculum, p. 16–19. 3. G. A. Barton: How to make our teaching contribute to the permanent peace of the world, p. 19–21. 4. Laura H. Wild: The use of the Bible in teaching national ideals, p. 25–29.

2057. Catholic educational association. Report of the proceedings and addresses of the sixteenth annual meeting, St. Louis, Mo., June 23–26, 1919. Columbus, Ohio, Catholic educational association, 1919. 590 p. 8°. (Catholic educational association bulletin, vol. 16, no. 2, November 1919) (Rev. F. W. Howard, secretary, 1651 East Main St.. Columbus, Ohio.)

Contains: 1. Cardinal O'Connell: The reasonable limits of state activity, p. 62–76. 2. H. S. Spaulding: Readjustment of the time element in education, p. 77–89. 3. J. A. Ryan: Vocational education in a democratic society, p. 90–99. 4. W. J. Fitzgerald: Differentiation in the curriculum of the grammar grades: viewpoint of junior high school, p. 100–14. 5. Brother Bernardine: Differentiation of studies in the seventh and eighth grades: viewpoint of vocational preparation, p. 115–30. 6. F. P. Donnelly: The principles of standardization, p. 137–52. 7. C. B. Moulinier: Social life in colleges, p. 153–58. 8. A. J. Burrowes: Attitude of Catholics towards higher education, p. 159–74. 9. Paul Folk: The college library in relation to college work, p. 175–83. 10. W. J. McAuliffe: The problem of Americanization, p. 184–91. 11. James J. Daly: The function of the classics in education, p. 196–205. 12. Sister Mary Antonia: The certification of teachers in Iowa and Nebraska, p. 220–24. 13. Sister Thomas

Aquinas: Certification of teachers in the Catholic schools of Wisconsin, p. 225–32.
14. Sister Magdalen: The certification of teachers in Indiana and Illinois, p.
233–38. 15. Mary A. Molloy: The parish schools—a study in school organization
and teacher training, p. 239–45. 16. J. V. S. M'Clancy: Americanization and
Catholic elementary schools, p. 252–60. 17. J. A. Nepper: School legislation in
Nebraska, p. 268–77. 18. John O'Grady: Vocational advisement, p. 279–88;
Discussion, p. 288–90. 19. Lawrence Sixtus: True and false methods of teaching arithmetic, p. 308–16. 20. W. A. Kane: The relations of a superintendent
to his teachers, p. 321–28; Discussion, p. 328–30. 21. W. F. Lawlor: Are any
changes needed in our elementary schools to meet post-war conditions? p. 331–35.
22. Brother Gerald: Grade school libraries, p. 338–53. 23. G. N. Sauer: Supervision and inspection of schools, p. 354–60. 24. John Schuetz: Entrance requirements for the junior high school, p. 362–72. 25. The social aims of education,
p. 373–81. 26. Brother Bernardine: Teaching pupils to appreciate good
literature, p. 392–408. 27. T. W. Turner: Actual conditions of Catholic education among the colored layman, p. 431–40. 28. E. A. Pace: The spirit of the
teacher, p. 443–49. 29. P. L. Blakely: The trend of educational legislation, p.
450–75. 30. T. E. Shields: The need of the Catholic sisters' college and the
scope of its work, p. 476–85. 31. Anthony Volkert: Uniform and adequate
classical training in our seminaries, p. 547–62. 32. M. J. O'Conner: The classics
in the preparatory seminary, p. 563–72. 33. J. J Jepson: Classical education
in the preparatory seminary, p. 573–82.

2058 **Betts, George Herbert.** How to teach religion, principles and methods.
New York, Cincinnati, The Abingdon press [1919] 23 p. 12°. (The
Abingdon religious education texts—Teacher training series, N. E.
Richardson, ed.)

2059. **[Council of church boards of education]** A partial report of the commission on the definition of a unit of Bible study for secondary schools.
Christian education. 2: 3–14. July 1919.

MANUAL AND VOCATIONAL TRAINING.

2060. **Arpe, G. F.** National supremacy, industrial education and cooperation.
School and society, 10: 501–509, November 1, 1919.

A paper read before the Central Ohio schoolmasters' club.

2061. **Benson, O. E.** Meeting America's peculiar needs in education. Journal
of education, 90: 481–83, November 13, 1919.

The Smith-Lever act and the Smith-Hughes act, the special field of each and
the opportunity for cooperation and blending of the two lines of work.

2062. **Buteau, J. A.** Notre enseignement technique industriel. Quebec, Imprimerie le Soleil, 1919. 124 p. plates. 12°.

2063. **Caillard, C.** École et industrie. École du travail, 1: cxlv–cll, clxxii–
clxxvi, October, November 1919.

Deals with the subject of the manufacture of articles in French industrial
schools.

2064. **Foulkes, Thomas Robert** and **Diamond, Thomas.** Teaching home repairs in the school shop. Manual training magazine, 21: 79–83, November 1919. illus.

The writer thinks that public school manual training courses should include
a course in "home mechanics" or "household repairs," and everybody in school
should finish such a course before completing the eighth grade.

2065. **McKinney, James.** The getting together of education and industry.
Industrial-arts magazine, 8: 471–74, December 1919.

After tracing briefly the history of industry and education the writer discusses the industrial problem of the twentieth century, the cooperation of the
captains of industry and the workers, and says that it is through the new movement of vocational education that education and industry can meet on a common
ground.

2066. **Park, Joseph C.** Shop management or suggestions for the young shop instructor. Vocationist, 8 : 3–15, October 1919.

Methods of conducting industrial classes.

2067. **Payne, Arthur Frank.** Vocational education as a preventive of juvenile delinquency. School and society, 10 : 509–13, November 1, 1919.

2068. **Reynolds, J. H.** Fifty years of technical education. Nature, 104 : 257–59, November 6, 1919.

Progress of technical education in Great Britain and Ireland.

2069. **Roux, J.** L'enseignement professionnel en Alsace et Lorraine. École du travail, 1 : cxxxviii–cxl, cliii–clv, September, October 1919.

2070. **Voorhees, Charity M.** Educating toward democracy. Education, 40 : 181–88, November 1919.

Emphasizes schooling in the factory.

2071. **Wyer, James I.,** *jr.* Half-baked cult menace to schools. Overdose of vocational training condemned as a mere contributor to commercialism and not a preparation for the real duties of life. State service (Albany, N. Y.) 3 : 55–61, October 1919.

An address delivered at the commencement of the New York State college for teachers, Albany, June 16, 1919.

Also in School bulletin, 46 : 58–61. November 1919.

A vigorous protest against the supplanting of the old-fashioned classics in education by the modern vocational training.

VOCATIONAL GUIDANCE.

2072. **Axton, Edward H.** The juvenile unemployment agency. Contemporary review, 116 : 448–53, October 1919.

Contrasts old system of education in England with modern scheme. Discusses continuation schools, etc.

HOME ECONOMICS.

2073. **Bunch, Mamie.** A course for home demonstration agents; the Illinois plan. Journal of home economics, 11 : 430–35, October 1919.

Presented at the meeting of the Extension section, twelfth annual meeting of the American home economics association, Blue Ridge, N. C., June 1919.

2074. **Davis, Helen Lee.** How to make home economics work function. Journal of home economics, 11 : 423–29, October 1919.

Given at the Inland empire teachers association, Spokane, Wash., April 3, 1919, and at the Oregon home economics association meeting, Portland, Oregon, May 17, 1919.

PROFESSIONAL EDUCATION.

2075. **National league of nursing education.** Proceedings of the twenty-fourth annual convention . . . held at Cleveland, Ohio, May 7–11, 1918. Baltimore, Williams & Wilkins company, 1919. 352 p. 8°. (Laura R. Logan, secretary, University of Cincinnati, Cincinnati, Ohio.)

Contains: 1. J. E. Cutler: How the public and the nursing profession are combining to supply nursing needs during and after the war, p. 115–24. 2. M. Adelaide Nutting: How the nursing profession is trying to meet the problems arising out of the war, p. 125–32. 3. S. S. Goldwater: The nursing crisis: efforts to satisfy the nursing requirements of the war, p. 132–39. 4. Elizabeth Burgess: The readjustment of the curriculum to meet war needs and its effect upon the hospitals, p. 142–51; Discussion, p. 151–59. 5. Jane A. Delano: Red cross aid versus the short-term course, p. 159–71. 6. Annie W. Goodrich: The plan for the Army school of nursing, p. 171–76; Discussion, p. 176–92. 7. Julia C. Lathrop: Child welfare, p. 292–96.

2076. **Flodin, John.** Essentials of engineering education. Industrial management, 58: 312, October 1919.

2077. **Greene, Roger S.** The Rockefeller foundation in China. Asia, 19: 1117–24, November 1919. illus.

> An account of the foundation's operations for the development of scientific medicine in China, by the establishment of medical schools and otherwise. Describes the Peking union medical college, reorganized by the foundation in cooperation with the church missions.

2078. **Hollis, Ira N.** Engineering colleges and administration. Bulletin of the Society for the promotion of engineering education, 10: 33–68, October 1919.

> The president of Worcester polytechnic institute presents the different phases of college administration.

2079. **Holmes, Oliver W.** The new century and the new building of the medical school of Harvard University. Boston medical and surgical journal, 91: 523–34, October 30, 1919.

> Reprinted from the issue of the Journal for October 18, 1883.

2080. **Hyde, Sarah E.** Adapting the model curriculum to the small school. American journal of nursing, 20: 129–33, November 1919.

> Work in a nurse training school.

2081. **Potter, A. A.** War experiences in engineering education. American school, 5: 269–70, September 1919.

> Read before the Department of higher education, National education association, Milwaukee, July 1, 1919.
> Shows how the experiences gained by engineering colleges during the war may be applied to engineering education.

2082. **Roe, Joseph W.** College training for industrial engineers. Yale alumni weekly, 29: 128–30, October 31, 1919.

> From an address on October 29 before the Society of industrial engineers, Cleveland, Ohio.

2083. **Tracy, John C.** Engineering at Yale. Yale alumni weekly, 29: 151–55, November 7, 1919.

> The situation in this profession throughout the country and Yale's imperative need to build up a strong department in it.
> From a paper read before the Yale engineering association, October 31, 1919.

CIVIC EDUCATION.

2084. **Deshel, M. C.** Safeguarding life and property. Outlook, 123: 298–301, November 12, 1919.

> Second paper of a series of articles by teachers of the New York high schools on community civics—a practical educational course in citizenship.

2085. **Hill, Howard C.** Community civics. Journal of education, 90: 479–81, November 13, 1919.

> Contains a topical outline of a course in community civics which attempts to remedy some of the defects in the prevailing courses.

2086. **Meers, G. Eunice.** Specific aims in the literature course. English journal, 8: 488–95, October 1919.

> Emphasizes training in citizenship. Gives lists of books treating of the subject.

2087. **National Catholic war council. Committee on special war activities.** A program for citizenship. Washington, D. C., National Catholic war council, 1919. 14 p. 12°. (Reconstruction pamphlets, no. 5, July 1919.)

2088. **Wilson, Woodrow.** Why teachers should study the principles of our government. South Carolina education, 1 : 3, October 1919.

Reprinted from the High school quarterly, Athens, Ga.

The duty of teachers in respect to the teaching of citizenship and patriotism, as given by the President of the United States in an address.

AMERICANIZATION OF IMMIGRANTS.

2089. **Bogardus, Emory S.** Essentials of Americanization. Los Angeles, University of Southern California press, 1919. 303 p. 8°.

This volume is based on the author's experience in Chicago at Northwestern university settlement, and on subsequent immigration investigations; it is an expression of experiences gained from teaching foreign-born laborers; it is a result of teaching the subject of "Americanization and immigration" to university students during the past seven years.

2090. **Carney, Chester S.** National conference on Americanization in industries. Journal of applied psychology, 3 : 269–76, September 1919.

Meeting was held at Nantasket Beach, Mass., June 23–24, 1919.

2091. **Fitzpatrick, Mary.** The need of immigrant education. Journal of education, 90 : 400–402, October 23, 1919.

2092. **Talbot, Winthrop.** The one language industrial plant. Practical aim of Americanization. Industrial management, 58 : 313–20, October 1919. illus.

Presents some of the most practical aspects of introducing language instruction for foreigners in industrial plants.

EDUCATION OF SOLDIERS.

2093. **Cave, Elmer L.** Development and operation of the educational program in the A. E. F. News letter of the State department of education (Olympia, Wash.) 1 : 3–11, October 1919.

A sketch of the plan and the machinery of the educational program as planned by the Educational commission corps, some objections that hindered the program, and the achievements.

2094. **Ridgley, Douglas C.** With the American expeditionary forces. School and home education, 39 : 60–62, November 1919.

This third article in a series deals with the Army schools in France.

EDUCATION OF WOMEN.

2095. **McLean, Katherine Sisson.** The effect of the war upon the education of women. American school, 5 : 297–98, 306, October 1919.

Read before the Department of higher education, National education association, Milwaukee, July 1, 1919.

2096. **Thamin, Raymond.** L'éducation des filles après la guerre. Revue des deux mondes, 53 : 512–32, October 1, 1919.

CONTENTS.—I. La femme de demain et l'éducation d'aujourd'hui.
To be continued.

NEGRO EDUCATION.

2097. **Brawley, Benjamin.** A short history of the American Negro. Rev. ed. New York, The Macmillan company, 1919. xvii, 280 p. 12°.

The following chapters of this book deal with educational and cultural conditions of the Negro: IX. Missionary endeavor; XI. The Tuskegee idea; XV. Self help in Negro education; XVI. Social and economic progress; XVII. Literature and art.

2098. **Mitchell, Ida,** *and others.* A study of association in Negro children. Psychological review, 26: 354-59, September 1919.

> Study consists of 300 association test records, the subjects being Negro children of New York city schools, in age groups of 25 ranging from 14 to 15 years, and about equally divided as to sex. Says that Negro children, on the whole, show "further departure than white ones from the normal adult associational standard."

2099. **University commission on Southern race questions.** Four open letters from the University commission on race questions to the college men of the South. [Lexington, Va., 1919] 8 p. 8°.

> CONTENTS.—I. Lynching.—II. Education.—III. Migration.—IV. A new reconstruction.

EDUCATION OF DEAF.

2100. **De Land, Fred.** Working in behalf of deaf children. Volta review, 21: 701-2, November 1919.

> Fourth article of series. Notes concerning the formation, growth, development, and work of the American association to promote the teaching of speech to the deaf.

EXCEPTIONAL CHILDREN.

2101. **National association for the study and education of exceptional children.** Report of the annual business meeting. . . held April 30, 1919, New York city. Bulletin of the National association for the study and education of exceptional children (Plainfield, N. J.) 1: 1-31, October, 1919.

> Contains: 1. Mrs. W. S. Stoner: The needed education, p. 11-12. 2. G. D. Strayer: School administration and the exceptional child, p. 14-15. 3. R. S. Copeland: The undernourished and defective child, p. 15-18. 4. W. A. Waterman: The boy scout movement, p. 20-21. 5. Misha Applebaum: Humanitarianism in education, p. 21-23. 6. M. P. E. Groszmann: [The individual adjustment of the exceptional child], p. 23-26.

2102. **Anderson, V. V.** Mental defect in a southern state. Mental hygiene, 3: 527-65, October 1919.

> Report of the Georgia commission on feeblemindedness and the survey of the National committee for mental hygiene. Among other things discusses the relationship of feeblemindedness to the public schools.

2103. **Camp, Pauline B.** Speech correction in the Grand Rapids schools. Volta review, 21: 732-34, November 1919.

> Discussion, p. 734-36.

2104. **Gillingham, Anna.** The bright child and the school. Journal of educational psychology, 10: 237-52, May-June 1919.

> The author gives a detailed account of a group of exceptionally bright children and shows why mere mental precocity is not a sufficient criterion for rapid advancement.

2105. **Montague, Helen.** Psychopathic clinic of the children's court of the city of New York. Mental hygiene, 3: 650-69, October 1919.

> Includes some interesting school records.

2106. **Roper, R. E.** Special treatment for special children. Child (London) 10: 1-9, October 1919.

> Remedial treatment of children in English schools.

2107. **Stedman, Lulu M.** An experiment in educational democracy. Sierra educational news, 15: 515-18, October 1919.

> The opportunity room for gifted children organized in the Training department of the Los Angeles state normal school.

2108. **Swift, Walter B.** Can stuttering be outgrown? Quarterly journal of speech education, 5: 368–74, October 1919.

2109. **Wembridge, Harry.** An investigation of mental deficiency among the juvenile delinquents of New York city. Journal of delinquency, 4: 186–93, September 1919.

LIBRARIES AND READING.

2110. **American library association.** Preliminary report of committee on enlarged program for American library service. Library journal, 44: 645–63, October 1919.

> Also condensed in Public libraries, 24: 319–22, October 1919.
> The library war service having ended ,the American library association plans to expand its activities so as to render a national service to all classes of the community.

2111. **Hopkins, Florence M.** Library work in school courses. Public libraries, 24: 393–94, November 1919.

> An address before the Library section of the National education association at Milwaukee, July 3, 1919.

2112. **Willett, G. W.** The reading interests of high school pupils. English journal, 8: 474–87, October 1919.

> Study based on a census taken of the pupils of the Hibbing (Minn.) high school, obtained by means of a questionnaire of 23 questions issued on March 21, 1918. Presents some interesting tabular statistics.

2113. **Wilson, Martha.** School library management. New York, The H. W. Wilson company, 1919. 126 p. 12°.

> A revised edition of School library management, published by the Minnesota Department of education in 1917.
> The book offers practical suggestions as to the equipment, organization, and administration of school libraries, and provides a reference aid for simple library methods.

BUREAU OF EDUCATION: RECENT PUBLICATIONS.

2114. The administration of correspondence-study departments of universities and colleges; by Arthur J. Klein. Washington, 1919. 54 p. (Bulletin, 1919, no. 56)

2115. Bibliography of home economics; by Carrie Alberta Lyford. Washington, 1919. 103 p. (Bulletin, 1919, no. 46)

2116. Education in parts of the British Empire. Washington, 1919. 104 p. (Bulletin, 1919, no. 49)

> Advance sheets from the Biennial survey of education, 1916–1918.

2117. Educational directory, 1919–20. Part 4. Special schools. Washington, 1919. 5 p. (Bulletin, 1919, no. 71, Part 4)

2118. Educational work of the Young men's Christian associations, 1916–1918; by William Orr. Washington, 1919. 60 p. (Bulletin, 1919, no. 53)

2119. The Federal executive departments as sources of information for libraries; comp. by Edith Guerrier. September 1, 1919. Washington, 1919. 204 p. (Bulletin, 1919, no. 74)

2120. Statement of the Commissioner of education to the Secretary of the interior for the fiscal year ended June 30, 1919. Washington, 1919. 67 p.

DEPARTMENT OF THE INTERIOR
BUREAU OF EDUCATION

BULLETIN, 1919, No. 84

THE UNIVERSITY EXTENSION MOVEMENT

By

W. S. BITTNER

ASSOCIATE DIRECTOR, EXTENSION DIVISION
INDIANA UNIVERSITY

WASHINGTON
GOVERNMENT PRINTING OFFICE
1920

CONTENTS.

4 CONTENTS.

LETTER OF TRANSMITTAL.

DEPARTMENT OF THE INTERIOR,
BUREAU OF EDUCATION,
Washington, October 21, 1919.

SIR: For two decades university extension work in this country has been increasing in volume. The growing recognition of the value of its various forms is indicated by the fact that within the last five years the total amount of appropriations for the support of university extension work has more than doubled, and the number of students has increased more than threefold. The need for extension education on a very large scale now and for the next few years at least is indicated by the following facts:

(1) There are now in the United States approximately four and a half million discharged soldiers, one-half of whom were overseas and all of whom have had impressed upon them in many ways the importance of education. It is a matter of common knowledge that these men, nearly all of them young men, are eager to take advantage of all available information for instruction in things pertaining to their vocations, to citizenship, and to general culture. Few of them will or can go to college; practically none of them will enter the ordinary public high schools; they are too old for this. Some, but comparatively few, will find their way into special vocational schools and part-time classes in industrial plants. A great majority of them must depend upon such opportunities as can be provided by extension education.'

(2) The shortening of the hours of labor and recent increase in wages have given to millions of working men and women time and means for self-improvement far beyond anything which such men and women have ever known before in this or any other country. The closing of the barrooms throughout the United States has relieved large numbers of men of the temptation to spend their leisure time and money in various forms of dissipation connected with the barroom. Everywhere these working men and women are eager for instruction, both for improvement in their vocations and for better living and more intelligent citizenship. Not only do they take advantage of such opportunities as are offered them by the organized agencies of education, but in many places they undertake to provide opportunities for themselves in their own time and at their own expense. Few of these have had any schooling beyond the elementary grades.

5

(3) Among the foreign-born population in the United States there are many, both of those who have taken out their citizenship papers and of those who have not, who, though able to read and write in English and are otherwise fairly well educated, know nothing of our country, its history, its ideals, the form and spirit of its government, of the agricultural and industrial opportunities offered in various parts of the country. Much might be done for them through educational extension work.

(4) Within the last few years millions of women have been given the franchise and now have all the privileges and responsibilities of active citizenship. The adoption of the nineteenth amendment to the Constitution of the United States will add millions more. When these women become voters, they will, by their ballots or otherwise, determine wisely or unwisely the policies of municipality, State, and Nation. They are conscientious; they realize they need instruction as to the duties and responsibilities of active citizenship and help toward an understanding of the many complex and difficult problems which, by their ballots, they will help to solve. Through their clubs and various other organizations educational extension workers can do much for them which could be done very hardly, if at all, in any other way.

(5) There are in the United States approximately twelve and one-half million boys and girls between the ages of 16 and 21 who are coming to their majority at a time when in order to make a living and assume the responsibilities and duties of life and citizenship more knowledge and training are needed than ever before. Two and one-half millions of these attain their majority each year; less than one-eighth are high-school graduates; only a little more than one-fourth have any high-school education. That a large per cent of them would take advantage of any adequate opportunities offered them for further instruction, either in class or by correspondence, is definitely proven by the response they make to the advertisements of all kinds of correspondence schools conducted for profit and by the efforts they make to provide for themselves the means of instruction. Still more of them might be induced to do systematic reading under direction, or to attend instructive and educational lectures. Such opportunities for their instruction might easily be organized on a large scale as a part of education extension work.

I am sure most of the thoughtful men and women of the country will agree that the institutions of higher learning, supported by all the people, have an important obligation to these millions who can never profit directly by the instruction given within their college walls.

For the purpose of giving information on a subject of such vast importance to the cause of education and the general welfare of the country at this time, I recommend for publication as a bulletin of the Bureau of Education the manuscript transmitted herewith on the university extension movement in the United States. This manuscript has been prepared at my request by Dr. W. S. Bittner, formerly connected with the educational extension division of this bureau and now associate director of the extension division of the University of Indiana.

Respectfully submitted.

P. P. CLAXTON,
Commissioner.

The SECRETARY OF THE INTERIOR.

PREFACE.

The informational material upon which this bulletin is based was collected by the writer while associate director of the division of educational extension in the United States Bureau of Education. This material now forms part of the collections of the Bureau of Education.

Special acknowledgment is made to President E. A. Birge, of the University of Wisconsin, whose permission was given to print the major portion of his paper on Service to the Commonwealth Through University Extension.

Attention is called to the chapter in this bulletin on Engineering Extension, written by Dr. J. J. Schlicher, formerly director of investigation in the division of educational extension, and to the other chapters, acknowledged specifically in footnotes, which were in large part the result of his work. Other members of the staff of the division, J. J. Pettijohn, A. J. Klein, F. W. Reynolds, and especially Mary B. Orvis, gave generous assistance in the preparation of this bulletin.

W. S. B.

8

THE UNIVERSITY EXTENSION MOVEMENT.

Of the liberal movements dominating the thought of the world to-day, the greatest of all is the sweep of education. No phrase or dissertation can compass the entire scope or catch all the essential elements of the newer education that is shaping itself. But everywhere one direction is apparent: The trend of education is toward the people in mass and group without regard to condition, class, or circumstance; toward men, women, and children as human beings having without distinction full claim on equal opportunity to enjoy the benefits of art and science. Literature, history, philosophy, all of the subjects that were once studied by a privileged few, are now being sought by a rapidly increasing number who have but recently acquired some leisure. The people are calling for knowledge, for that education which opens the door to complete living.

Educational extension is one of the terms that has been applied to the movement. It has come into use in the United States to describe the numerous ventures designed to meet the demand for knowledge and training. This demand is not uniform nor simple. It does not come from a single-minded public, from the people of one class. In one sense it is not a demand at all, but rather a multitude of impulses suggesting or rather seeking a way. Mr. Parke R. Kolbe says:

> The educational system of the United States represents not a uniform plan, developing in accordance with predetermined laws, but rather the result of innumerable separate initiatives whose aims and methods have been dependent upon their attendant conditions of inception and growth.

He says that our educational system "looks like a coat of many colors when reviewed geographically."[1]

Educational extension includes many devices and instruments of instruction. There are innumerable agencies, apart from schools, designed to "educate the public," to "put something over," to tell the "truth in advertising," to sell the community a "welfare" idea, to instruct the workman in rules of safety, scientific system, and better methods of increasing production. In the crafts and trades men devise ways of inculcating in their fellows commonly accepted principles of association and mutual action; they teach each other new methods, new techniques, and new ways to secure for their group accrued benefits of the industry or business. They have their chapels, classes, lecturers, teachers, their schoolmasters, and younger schoolmates.

---

[1] From School and Society, May 31, 1919, "The Colleges in the War," by P. R. Kolbe.

The employers, managers of great industries, have also appropriated every essential device of school and university not only to teach their workmen but also to educate themselves. They have their educational directors, schools, conferences, their laboratories, their service of specialists, their expert studies, their clubs and fraternities. They have tremendously developed the art of advertising, which, in the long run and in the best sense, may prove to be the basis of the finest technique of educational extension.

"Education is a curiously pervasive commodity. Analysis always proves it to be a part of nearly every large undertaking. It bobs up in everybody's bailiwick," says S. P. Capen.[1] He describes how the Federal Government had developed educational extension, including the work of the Bureau of Education: "As time has gone on other Government departments have found that certain portions of their work were educational. By the spring of 1917 the Government's educational activities involved the annual expenditure of more than 30 million dollars. They were carried on in no less than 20 different bureaus, commissions, and departments." Both the magnitude and the dispersion of these activities will doubtless cause surprise to anyone who has not studied the question.

Definition of educational extension.—Educational extension is not readily susceptible of definition, although the thing itself is very real. It is closely connected with the growing complexity of intercommunication in civilized countries. With every increased facility of intercourse through speech, press, and picture, through travel, cable, telegraph, telephone, through personal contact, through the innumerable mechanical, physical, and spiritual inventions of civilization, comes the means of increasing the scope and thoroughness of educational extension.

Of course, that form of education which is associated with schools and colleges and the children and youth who attend them has not been superseded by this comprehensive though vague new kind of education, which transcends all schools and barriers of age. But the traditional idea is expanding and changing with the impetus of new movements. The importance of considering the nature of educational extension is that its complexity, diversity, and ubiquity point to inevitable changes in the theory and practice of educational institutions as such, not so much perhaps in the primary elements of the public school system, but certainly in secondary schools and in the institutions of higher learning.

Not so very many years ago the private university, the State university, and the college were largely teaching institutions in a definitely limited sense, and the function of research was only grad-

---

[1] School and Society, May 24, 1919, "The Colleges in a Nationalized Educational Scheme," by S. P. Capen.

ually added. Even now the actual distinction between university and college is not thoroughly understood or recognized—the distinction that makes a university preeminently a discoverer of scientific fact, a laboratory and training center for advanced students, and a distributor of knowledge rather than a teacher of the youth or a school for elementary students of the professions. This latter field of endeavor belongs increasingly to the school and college, while the true university becomes more and more the graduate center, the scientific laboratory, the curator of the arts, and the administrator of educational extension.

Accordingly, the growth of university extension is a logical development of the new demand for universal education. Freedom, self-determination, the new democracy, equal suffrage, open diplomacy, and all the fresh catch words of the war and after the war, and the liberal movements linked with them—all have educational implications presupposing the diffusion of knowledge among the people. Undoubtedly the university, especially the State-owned institution, will play a progressively important part in educational extension.

In the United States and England, university extension is a well-defined movement with elaborate institutional organization and fairly definite methods and objectives which have broadened and deepened during the past 10 years. Inevitably it has reflected the spirit of the decade and has consciously taken up the task of developing new methods of adult education.

In spite of the fact that the movement is identified with universities and colleges, academic institutions which formerly were remote from the people and high above any suggestion of commonness and popularity, it is nevertheless quite ordinary, humble, and matter of fact in its intention. The man in the street can understand that university extension is "an organized effort to give to the people not in college some of the advantages enjoyed by the one-half of 1 per cent who are able to attend campus classes. It reaches out to the clerk, the workingman, the teacher, and the public official, and says to each 'If you can not go to your university, your university will come to you.' Agricultural extension makes better farmers, and general extension makes better workers, better teachers, and better citizens." In addition, the average man readily understands that the State university belongs to the Commonwealth and owes service to every citizen. He grasps, quickly, too, the nature and value of its services in research, instruction, and information. If there are some who naively rate these services too low, and who place the university instructor on a par with the characters of a cartoon or the "professor of dancing," there are many more who have a deep appreciation of the value of all university services; there are many who quickly realize the significance of university extension and who are eagerly receptive of its benefits.

A broader view of extension.—So, too, for the scientist, the scholar, and the man of affairs, university extension has gradually come to mean something definite and fine. He sees in the colorless phrase a rich implication of truth seeking and truth dissemination, the application of universal science and art to universal living. He sees in the newer university a central plant with great resources of investigation and research, a central group of scientists and specialists in technology, put at the service of the State, working for the whole citizenship and for each citizen who desires.

Academic views.—Some there are, academicians within the universities themselves, who, taking too literally the popular interpretations of university extension, rate the movement at ignorant par and decry the opening of the college gates to the people anywhere. They fear the effect of extension activities, not of course on the people, for even the most exclusive professor of the humanities or abstract mathematics is usually a thorough democrat, but on the seclusion and dignity and strength of the university itself. They wonder how a research professor can at the same time read, study, search, attend committees, and give "popular" lectures. They believe in detachment, undisturbed seclusion, freedom from practical pressure, as a *sine qua non* to the cultivation of science and art. Their misgivings have justification, but only in so far as the conception of "university" is too limited and narrow.

"University."—The true university should have both open gates and cloistered libraries, both practical, itinerant messengers and theoretical, isolated servants. Ivied walls and dusty laboratories may be legitimately, and picturesquely, part of the same university building that houses the office of the correspondence study department. A short course for Boy Scout masters may be held on the same campus where a learned conference of sociologists is discussing the theory of mob psychology. At the same institution there may be, and in many cases there are, groups of administrators concerned with a dozen different problems of resident instruction or extension work, while hundreds of teachers meet routine classes or correct correspondence study papers and prepare for community meetings. One faculty member may be testifying before a public utility commission, another conducting a social survey of a distant city, another preparing simple written lessons on prenatal care for mothers, another giving vocational guidance to students, and still others may be buried in historical files or seeking for a Greek hiatus or for missing data on a geological epoch.

The university is coming more and more to live up to its name. The ideal university and the practical institution growing toward the ideal take a high ground and look over a wide field of human endeavor.

"The phenomenal growth of university extension in the United

States in the past 10 years may be looked upon as indicative of a new interpretation of the legitimate scope of university service," wrote Dean Louis E. Reber, of the University of Wisconsin, in 1916.

Nevertheless, it is still maintained in many of our learned institutions that higher education should be removed from any possible intimacy with the common things of life. These institutions repudiate the idea that organized extension of their services may become a worthy function among their acknowledged activities—worthy not only in enabling them to reach greater numbers than the few who may assemble within their gates, but essentially so in its influence upon their own life and growth. Though with these, as with the more liberal, pursuit of the truth is the fundamental and all-embracing object of existence, they apparently fail to realize that truth does not belong to the cloister more than to the shops and homes or to the streets and fields, but is inseparably of them all.

The return of power to the institution is not, however, the main justification of university extension. Such justification exists primarily in the fact that the university is the one great source and repository of the knowledge which the people—all, not merely a few, of the people—need in order to reach their highest level of achievement and well-being.

Is it not a very uncharacteristic view of the field of the university which seems to limit its functions to those of a sealed storehouse, with facilities for giving out its invaluable contents only to the few who may be able to learn the cabalistic passes that unlock its doors? More in keeping with the modern spirit is the new slogan of unlimited service, which lays upon the university a command to retrieve to the world its losses from undiscovered talent and undeveloped utilities and to give freely to humanity the pleasures and profits of which so many are deprived by ignorance of the work of the masters of art and learning, and of the laws of sane living. For such purposes as these the university, in the fullness of its possessions and powers, must inevitably be acknowledged to be, in the words of President Van Hise, "the best instrument." [1]

The principle of extension accepted.—In the four years since 1915, the adverse criticism on the part of members of university faculties has materially diminished, partly because of the new impulse toward adult education · received from the war, and partly through the momentum of growth; even in the period before the war it was confined to comparatively few men, usually in departments which had little occasion for actual participation in extension work. With only two or three exceptions the administrative heads of State universities now accept without question the central idea of university extension, the principle that the State-owned institution has definite duties to perform for the people of the State, duties which are in addition to the task of educating the resident students. All State universities do perform such duties even when they have not secured substantial funds to organize a distinct extension machinery. Most private universities and colleges recognize a similar obligation to put their resources at the service of the community. The men who determine the policies of the institutions are in the great majority committed to recognition of extension and are in most States actively promoting it.

1 Reber, L. E., "University Extension," Annals, American Academy of Political and Social Science, Philadelphia, Sept., 1916, Publication reprint No. 1061.

. Frequently the State legislatures, even where the institutions of higher learning are not presumably in favor with the politicians, have backed substantially with public funds their belief in university extension. But no doubt the best approval is that which comes from the growing numbers of professors and instructors who have found new inspiration in successful community service.

HISTORY OF UNIVERSITY EXTENSION.

The possibility of developing the university into something more than the traditional institution of higher learning was thought of many years ago. The beginnings of university extension date back as far as the middle of the nineteenth century. George Henderson, formerly secretary of the Philadelphia Society for the Extension of University Teaching, wrote in one of his reports of a still earlier time:

The idea of expanding the influence of the university so as to meet the needs of a rapidly growing and progressive people dates back several centuries. Dr. Roberts, secretary of the London Society for the Extension of University Teaching, tells us: "In a fourteenth-century college endowment deed at Cambridge it is recorded how the college was founded out of a desire to see the number of students increased, to the end that knowledge, a pearl of great price, when they have found it and made it their own by instruction and study in the aforesaid university, may not be hidden under a bushel, but be spread abroad beyond the university and thereby give light to them that walk in the dark by-ways of ignorance." [1]

Beginnings in the United States.—The movement first took form as a result of the pioneer work of Prof. Stuart, of Cambridge, from 1867 on, when several English universities took up his lecture method with growing success. This early "aristocratic form as yet unmodified" was brought to the United States in 1867, and in the years of 1888 to 1892 showed a rapid development.[2] From then on the movement declined until about 1906, when new methods were adopted and a slow but systematic growth set in. The organized extension services established in this period—the majority in State universities—held their "First National University Extension Conference" in 1915. At that time representatives of 28 leading colleges and universities of the country organized the present National University Extension Association. Included in the membership were three institutions—Columbia, Chicago, and Wisconsin—which had consistently developed their extension work from the time it was begun in 1889 and 1892. The association is composed of the general extension divisions (institutional memberships) and is not concerned with agricultural extension, which has developed independently.

---

[1] Report upon the university extension movement in England, by. George Henderson, secretary Philadelphia Society for the Extension of University Teaching, in Columbia Papers, "University Extension Pamphlets," New York State Library.

[2] For full treatment of the early period, see Reber, L. E., "University Extension in the United States," Bull. 1914, No. 19, U. S. Bu. of Educ.

Present status.—The movement in its newer phase had a sounder basis than the earlier phase which had adopted in a superficial fashion the methods of the English universities. Extension work in both countries is now on a stable footing, but the extent and possibilities of the movement in this country are as yet barely comprehended. The extension divisions of Wisconsin, Minnesota, California, Iowa, and Massachusetts are widely known. In these States and in New York, North Carolina, Michigan, Indiana, Texas, Oklahoma, Oregon, Utah, and Washington the divisions have attained a considerable development. These divisions are in most instances administered by State universities. In addition, numerous extension services are well developed in these States and in practically all of the others by private institutions and State agricultural colleges.

On the basis of incomplete figures collected by Dr. John J. Schlicher,[1] it is estimated that university extension is reaching about 120,000 students through classes in branch centers and through correspondence study, together with an estimated number of about 2,026,000 through semipopular lectures; 5,553,000 through motion pictures and stereopticon lantern slides; 936,000 through outlines, bibliographies, and pamphlets used in debates and public discussion; 308,000 through institutes and conferences; 1,265,000 through bulletins and circulars. The States are spending over $1,513,000 directly on extension work entirely apart from the money spent for agriculture, in addition to putting at the disposal of the divisions the resources of the whole university plant—such resources as the services of faculties, libraries, laboratories, and the university publications.

RELATION BETWEEN THE ENGLISH AND AMERICAN MOVEMENTS.

The most striking characteristic of the English extension movement is its vital relation to the labor movement. University extension in England is actively cooperating with the workingmen's societies. Indeed, the whole rejuvenated educational movement which secured the enactment of the liberal Fisher bill in the war year of 1918 owes much to labor. Says Mr. I. L. Kandel:

It is not too much to claim that the representatives of labor and the Workers' Educational Association have played the most important part in stimulating public opinion, which only three months before the outbreak of the war received with very little interest the announcement of the chancellor of the exchequer that plans were being prepared for "a comprehensive and progressive improvement of the educational system."

Mr. Kandel points out that the reform of education in the island is "fundamentally a movement of the people." [2]

---

[1] The Federal Division of Educational Extension, leaflet published by the National University Extension Association, June, 1919.

[2] Education in Great Britain and Ireland, by I. L. Kandel, Bul., 1919, No. 9, U. S. Bu. of Educ.

The readiness of the university authorities and of the labor leaders to work with each other, the give-and-take character of their relationship, and the rapidly growing interest on the part of the industrial classes in cultural education, are facts which no American educator can afford to ignore. In spite of the social, political, and educational differences between England and America, these facts have an immense significance in our movement for extending higher education to the masses. To the extension worker they give a glimpse of new realities—realities that make the American movement seem relatively undemocratic and condescending. Here the university gives all; the students give little except their fees. In England the tutorial classes are actually controlled by the students, though they are taught according to university standards and by university men.

University extension in England has not always been wholly democratic in spirit. As Herbert W. Horwill said, it regarded labor "as clay in the potter's hand."[1] But a new spirit has manifested itself, chiefly through the Workers' Educational Association, which, according to Henry Seidel Canby, is the "training school whence many of the most alert political and economic thinkers in England have sprung or been inspired."[2] The adult education promoted by this association, with the full approval and sanction of the universities, is "distinctly a meeting of minds, designed to train the less skilled but with advantages for both (student and teacher)."[2]

The Workers' Educational Association.—The Workers' Educational Association, which was founded in 1903, has secured labor representatives on the governing bodies and committees of 60 universities. Its aim is "to articulate the educational aspirations of labor."[3] It consists of a federation of about 2,700 working-class and educational bodies, banded together for the purpose of stimulating the demand for higher education among working people, to supply their needs in cooperation with universities and other educational authorities, and to act as a bureau of intelligence upon all matters which affect the education of working people.

Tutorial classes.—The best known part of its work is that of the University Tutorial Classes. The tutorial class "is really the nucleus of a university established in a place where no university exists." It consists of a group of not more than 30 students who agree to meet regularly once a week for 24 weeks under a university tutor, to follow the course of reading outlined by the tutor and to write fortnightly essays.

---

[1] The Nation, May 10, 1919.
[2] Education by Violence, Harpers, March, 1919.
[3] Pamphlet of the Workers' Educational Association, "Its Aims and Ideals," William Morris Press, Manchester.

Every university and university college in England has appointed a joint committee composed of university representatives and working-class representatives to manage these classes. The classes meet for two hours each week, one hour being given to lecture and one to give-and-take discussion. The students choose the subjects of study after consultation with the tutor.

In the earlier years of the movement the subjects studied consisted almost entirely of economic history and economics. But these subjects were interpreted in a very catholic sense and included the consideration of a good many matters which could not, perhaps, figure largely in a university course in economics. At the present time the scope of the classes is tending to widen, and though economic history and economics still probably predominate, there are classes in literature, political science, general modern history, biology, psychology, and philosophy.[1]

In the year 1913–14 there were 145 standard university tutorial classes, containing over 3,200 students, in addition to a large number of other classes. The average age of students is about 30. In 1915 the association had 173 branches, 2,409 affiliated societies, 11,083 members, and 9 associations in overseas dominions. Its strength was maintained during the war. In 1916–17 there were 10,750 members; in 1917–18 there were 14,697.[2]

The Oxford report on extension movement.—It is characteristic of the recent English movement that these tutorial classes are the outgrowth of recommendations made in the famous Oxford Report of of 1908 by a joint committee of university and working-class representatives of Oxford on the Relation of the University to the Higher Education of Workpeople. The committee, which in turn was the outgrowth of a conference of working-class and educational organizations, held at Oxford in 1907, consisted of seven representatives of Oxford and seven representatives of the Workers' Educational Association.

The Oxford extension movement had been successful in "stimulating an interest in higher education among a large number of persons, especially women, who are unable to study in universities."[3] It had, according to the report, accomplished, "valuable pioneer work" leading to the establishment of universities and colleges, but it had not "undertaken to supply the continuous tutorial teaching of a university standard" which workpeople desired. The committee held that this work must be supplemented and reorganized.

The Oxford extension movement consisted in extra-mural lectures organized by university authorities for students who were not members of a university. The work involved the giving of courses of lectures, paid for by local committees who selected subjects

[1] Workers' Educational Association, "Its Aims and Ideals"

[2] Fifteenth An. Rep., 1918, The Workers' Educational Association, 16 Harper Street, London.

[3] Oxford Report, pp. 33–37, "Oxford and Working Class Education," second edition, revised, Oxford, the Clarendon Press, 1909.

provided rooms, and secured the audience. "The courses run in units of 6, 12, or sometimes 24 lectures, delivered at weekly or fortnightly intervals." Students sometimes prepare papers, take examinations, and are given certificates.

Objections to Oxford system.—"So long as the system is compelled to be financially self-supporting, so long must the lecturer attract large audiences,"[1] the secretary of the university extension delegacy is quoted as saying. Consequently—

both the lectures and the subject to be studied must be chosen not solely or chiefly on account of their educative value, but with a view to the probability of their drawing such numbers that the lectures will "pay." If the numbers attending a course fall off, however educationally valuable it may be, it must give place to another which is more likely to draw a large audience; and as one consequence of this, there is sometimes evident a distressing desire on the part of local committees continually to attack new subjects, instead of mastering thoroughly the old one. From the information before us, we believe that this is not due to any ignorance on the part of the centers as to the importance of regular study on systematic lines; on the contrary, we think there is a growing demand for facilities for such study—but solely to the fact that their better judgment had to yield before such irresistible financial considerations.[2]

A second defect, as seen by the committee, is found in the fact that the teaching offered is not sufficiently systematic, and in particular that—

individual students rarely receive the personal guidance and supervision which is offered to an undergraduate in Oxford and which is all the more necessary among work people because in an industrial city the means of knowledge—libraries, bookshops, and the atmosphere of culture—are less easy of access than they are in a university town.[3]

These objections—and, in addition, the problem of reducing the cost of the system—were disposed of by the committee in its suggestion that, "as far as the working-class centers are concerned, they should be recognized as merely subsidiary to the tutorial classes."[3]

Tutorial classes require systematic study.—Both problems have been met by these tutorial classes. They are now financed cooperatively by the university, the labor organization, and the board of education. Tutorial classes not only offer the student, but require of him, a remarkable devotion to systematic and thorough study. Those who enroll pledge themselves to study for three years, not to miss a single attendance from other than unavoidable causes, and to write 12 essays in connection with each of the three sessions of 24 lessons each. According to Albert Mansbridge:[4]

---

[1] Oxford Report, pp. 33–37, "Oxford and Working Class Education," second edition, revised, Oxford, at the Clarendon Press, 1909.

[2] Ibid, p. 37.

[3] Ibids, pp. 37–39.

[4] An address to the congress of the universities of the Empire, July, 1912. Quoted in pamphlet of Workers' Educ. Assoc.

The students have kept their pledges wonderfully. The percentage of attendance is often over 90. It is sometimes just on 100 per cent, which figure it has fallen short of only because of illness and overtime. The average percentage works out at 75, and this during a period in which there have been two general elections and violent labor unrest.

Nearly 700 students had in 1912 completed the three years' courses.

Reports as to the quality of the work done in the extension classes reiterate a frequent commentary on American extension work: It is "in some respects better and in others not so good as the work done in residence." Unfavorable economic conditions in England, as in America, make it extremely difficult for students to do their best work. On the other hand, maturity, earnestness, and determination go a long way toward overcoming these obstacles. The opinion of observers and of tutors seems to be unanimous that both students and tutors benefit enormously from the informal, democratic discussion, from the give-and-take between men accustomed to academic theory and men accustomed to dealing with the practical problems of the working world. As Margaret McMillan wrote:

There is not only a great body of facts coming always nearer to their (the students') consciousness than to that of the "educated," but the actual experience of all the play and interplay of economic forces is lightening for them continually a region that is dark to the pedant.[1]

Says a leaflet published by the Workers' Educational Association:[1]

One important principle laid down by the joint committee is that the teachers should actually teach in the universities. This completes the scheme, because it insures that the lessons that the teachers learn shall not be lost, but shall pass into the ordinary teaching of the universities; and this workpeople consider to be most necessary. It insures, too, that the teacher shall be in touch with every new advance in the study of science.

Leaders of the English movement insisted from the start that the tutors come from the university for the same reason that American educators insist upon it; namely, that they shall not be divorced from the traditions of learning. In the opinion of the joint committee, "it is essential that the extramural students of Oxford should be given guidance as systematic as that given those resident at the university."[2] The committee recommends that tutors be required to lecture regularly at Oxford, as well as in centers organized by the university extension delegacy.

Whatever one's opinion may be as to the need for a movement in this country corresponding to the tutorial class movement in England, an investigation of the Oxford report, the publications of the Workers' Educational Association, and the comments of first-hand investiga-

1 Education versus Propaganda, published by the Workers' Educ. Assoc.
2 Oxford Report, p. 39.

tors like Henry Seidel Canby, lead one to the belief that the movement offers much in the way of support and suggestion.

First of all, it gives to extension workers reassurance—a new faith in the desire of adult human beings for higher education. Working men and women of all classes are actually banded together in England many thousand strong to secure educational opportunities. And many hundreds of them are living up to the difficult pledge of doing systematic work of a university grade for a long period.

Influence in America.—A study of the English movement also convinces one of the great obligation that rests upon American universities to make a greater effort toward democratizing their extension work. Extension divisions have in the main ignored the possible contribution of working people and of organized labor to both the spirit and the subject matter of higher education. Extension divisions have offered opportunities to working people according to academic lights. But they have not said to working people, as Oxford University said in 1907, come and *help* us to work out a program for extramural education. And they have not to any very great extent emphasized the reciprocal nature of extension class work, its enormous possibilities for vitalizing education, for relating the university teacher to practical life. To study the English movement is to be convinced that the democratization of higher education through the cooperation of working people has not only greatly increased the amount of service to those who need it most but has also increased the quality of service both to intra and extra mural students. Moreover, though it began with the study of subjects of especial interest to the working classes, it has brought about a more universal interest in cultural subjects.

"There was a time," says Mr. Canby, "when you could stir any Britisher to talk—M. P., soldier, country gentleman, superintendent—merely by the question, 'What is going to happen in English education.'"[1] While Mr. Canby was talking on the situation that existed during the discussion of the Fisher bill in 1917 and 1918, he describes an interest that was manifested in numerous educational and semieducational movements during the last century and a quarter in England on the part of the working classes.

One of the earliest evidences of that interest was the rise of the adult school movement which appeared toward the end of the eighteenth century. Its purpose was to organize nonsectarian religious instruction for men and women laborers. With the aid of the Society of Friends, it established branches in nearly every part of England. There were in existence in 1909 over 1,600 schools for adults, with a membership of about 100,000.

---

[1] Harpers, March, 1919.

Contemporaneously with the adult schools, the Mechanics' Institutes, which flourished after the industrial revolution, were developed in an attempt to meet the need for technical education.

Cooperative societies.—The cooperative societies, which in 1909 included in their membership nearly one-sixth of the whole adult population, have for more than half a century played an important rôle in education. The societies developed an elaborate educational organization and set aside funds to provide a considerable income for educational purposes. They did three kinds of educational work: (1) The maintenance of continuation classes for children and young persons; (2) the organizing of *lectures and classes for adults;* and (3) the payment of fees and the granting of scholarships.

The organization of evening schools under the education act of 1902 caused some of these schools to be handed over to public authorities. While the idea of making better cooperators has been back of this movement, the instruction has necessarily been along the lines of history, theory, and principles of the movement, with economics and industrial and constitutional history so far as they have a bearing on cooperation. The movement also placed emphasis upon the training of men and women to take part in industrial and social reforms and civic life generally. Under the leadership of such men as Robert Owen and Arnold Toynbee, the movement has been strengthened "in the high line it has taken," says the report.[1]

Workmen's Colleges.—Workingmen's Colleges were established in England before the middle of the nineteenth century. In 1842 a People's College was started at Sheffield. Similar colleges were established in other cities, the London Working Men's College having the greatest success. In 1909 there were 2,387 entries in the college classes, 37 per cent of the students being engaged in manual occupations.

Ruskin College was established in 1899 to give workingmen, and especially those likely to take a leading part in working-class movements, an education which might help them in acquiring the knowledge essential to intelligent citizenship. The attitude of the college is one of political and religious neutrality. "The teaching is carried on partly by the correspondence school, which is designed to help the home reading of those who can not come to Oxford, but the chief concern is naturally with those students who reside at the college itself." In 10 years 450 students went into residence, representing many trades.

To this well-established movement for higher education among the workingmen the war has given great impetus. During the war, and since the return of the soldiers after the signing of the armistice,

---

[1] Oxford report, p. 5.

the interest of labor and of Government authorities in adult education has persisted and increased.

Arthur Greenwood states that the British committee of the ministry of reconstruction on adult education, which reported in 1918—

found it impossible to consider adult education apart from those social and industrial conditions which determine to a large extent the educational opportunities, the interests, and the general outlook of men and women. The committee pleads that "adult education and, indeed, good citizenship depend in no small degree * * * upon a new orientation of our industrial outlook and activities."

Instead of neglect of the worker, and a tacit admission of his inferiority, there is a recognition of the rightful claims of the personality of the worker in industry and of the justice of his plea for "industrial democracy." [1]

British and American progress.—Commenting on the program of the British Labor Party and on the American labor programs, Robert W. Bruere says:

The relevance of these programs of political and industrial reconstruction is that they express the judgment of the most influential body of workers in England and America as to the practical means that must be adopted to make the realization of their program for the democratization of educational opportunity possible. The growing prestige of the fourth estate is the characteristic fact of our generation.

He discusses the claim that labor is too radical, and concludes:

Men who dream of the democratization of knowledge, of science and the liberal arts, as the chief end of civilized government will not ruthlessly destroy the recognized material foundations of civilized life. Rather they will seek to strengthen those foundations and broaden them. For it is their eager and instinctive hunger for the spiritual values of life that principally accounts for their growing insistence upon the democratic principle of industry, for the humanization of industrial processes, for the more equal distribution of the benefits that accrue from the national surplus. Their programs of political and social reconstruction are inspired by their realization that it is only when men are guaranteed equality of educational opportunity that any man can be certain of access to the spiritual banquet of life. * * *

The test of governmental capacity will increasingly be the ability of those in positions of authority to find ways and means for the democratization of educational opportunity. [2]

Interest in cultural education.—In the United States it has frequently been assumed that the workman's interest in education was largely utilitarian; indeed, it has been considered desirable that school, college, and university curricula should be "more practical"; that the teacher, the clerk, the business man would take extension courses only when they would prove of advantage in "getting on," of immediate pecuniary use, or at least capable of eventual translation into material success. An opposite conclusion may be the right one. It may be that the average man and woman in this country, even the so-called uneducated workingman, may be desirous of educational opportunity of quite another kind. In England such

[1] Development of British Industrial Thought, Atlantic Monthly, July, 1919.
[2] The New Nationalism and Education, p. 181, by Robert W. Bruere, Harper's, July, 1919.

seems to be the fact, for that is the observation of Mr. Fisher, father of the English education bill, who says:

I notice also that a new way of thinking about education has sprung up among more reflecting members of our industrial army. They do not want education in order that they may rise out of their own class, always a vulgar ambition; they want it because they know that, in the treasures of the mind, they can find an aid to good citizenship, a source of pure enjoyment, and a refuge from the necessary hardships of a life spent in the midst of clanging machinery in our hideous cities of toil.[1]

No doubt Americans owe their interest in cultural education to much the same causes as do the English, but certainly not to class contentedness. American workmen do have the "vulgar ambition" to rise, and they are recognizing the importance of both practical and cultural education as aids to their individual enterprise.

Mr. Fisher adds, with reference to the features of the English education act which fix certain attendance limits and educational standards:

We argue that the compulsion proposed in this bill will be no sterilizing restriction of wholesome liberty, but an essential condition in a larger and more enlightened freedom, which will tend to stimulate civic spirit, to promote general culture and technical knowledge, and to diffuse a steadier judgment and a better informed opinion through the whole body of the community.

Herbert W. Horwill states that there is unanimous testimony that the Workers' Educational Association presents a spectacle of intellectual energy and enthusiasm which finds no parallel among the leisure classes.[2] The association aims at the satisfaction of the intellectual, esthetic, and spiritual needs of the workman student and thus gives him a fuller life.

George Edwin MacLean wrote, in 1917, with reference to both the English and American attitude toward education:

To-day the demand of the workingman, which can but perpetuate university extension and which is full of hope for democracy, is for something more than "bread and butter" education. It is a call for a liberal or human education, which is not so much "a means of livelihood as a means of life."[3]

He appends to his discussion of the English movement some pertinent questions:

The American workingman has had faith in his schools and has trusted especially the colleges and universities. Has not the time come for the labor organizations to strengthen their membership, and particularly their leadership, by courses of study conducted in connection with these institutions with the impartial spirit of truth believed to be preserved in them? May not these organizations assure the perpetuation of the federation of labor and of higher learning in America?

[1] From quotation, p. 79, Bull. Bu. of Educ., 1919, No. 9, Education in Great Britain and Ireland, by I. L. Kandel.
[2] The Nation, May 10, 1919.
[3] Studies in Higher Education in England and Scotland, by George E. MacLean, U. S. Bu. of Educ., No. 16, 1917.

Nietzsche.—It would be instructive to compare with the liberal estimates of education now prevalent in Europe and America some of the pre-war opinions of continental statesmen and educators. It is perhaps unfair to quote from Nietzsche, but some of his startlingly wild and bizarre statements afford by contrast an illuminating opportunity for securing perspective in estimating the significance of present-day conceptions of education and democratic university extension. J. M. Kennedy, in the introduction to a translation of Nietzsche's "The Future of Our Educational Institutions," says:

Nietzsche's idea was "that a bread-winning education is necessary for the majority," but "true culture is only for a few select minds which it is necessary to bring together under the protecting roof of an institution that shall prepare them for culture, and for culture only."

Nietzsche says:

Why this education of the masses on such an extended scale? Because the true German spirit is hated, because the aristocratic nation of true culture is feared, because the people endeavor in this way to drive single great individuals into self-exile, so that the claims of the masses to education may be, so to speak, planted down and carefully tended, in order that the many may in this way endeavor to escape the rigid and strict discipline of the few great leaders, so that the masses may be persuaded that they can easily find the path for themselves—following the guiding star of the States.[1]

The philosopher writes:

I have long accustomed myself to look with caution upon those who are ardent in the cause of the so-called "education of the people" in the common meaning of the phrase. * * * They were born to serve and to obey; and every moment in which the limping or crawling or broken-winded thoughts are at work shows us clearly out of which clay nature molded them and what trade-mark she branded thereon.[2]

He talks about "a natural hierarchy in the realm of the intellect." His conclusion is:

The education of the masses can not therefore be our aim, but rather the education of a few selected men for great and lasting works.[3]

THE WAR AND EDUCATIONAL EXTENSION.

The war has profoundly affected liberal opinion in every country. People have come to think less provincially. Not only have Americans been introduced to the international point of view—an introduction that has not yet ripened into thorough familiarity—but more significantly, as far as education is concerned, they have acquired a deeper realization of national unity. Proposals for reorganization of our educational system are no longer mere suggestions; they bid fair to find increasingly substantial expression and to shape legislation for the purpose of vitalizing local administration and re-

[1] Friedrich Nietzsche, On the Future of Our Educational Institutions, translated, with introduction, by J. M. Kennedy. T. N. Foulis, Edinburgh, 1909
[2] Ibid., p. 74.
[3] Ibid., p. 75.

moving the inequalities of educational opportunity in the various sections of the country.

During the war the idea that the whole nation spiritually, physically, industrially was on the firing line, rather than the soldiers alone, was thoroughly driven home. It has not, however, been widely recognized that the means of enforcing this idea, that the propaganda to win the war, was actually a wholesale adoption of educational extension methods. All the instruments and devices laboriously created or appropriated by the university extension movement during the last decade were utilized to mobilize public opinion and to teach the soldiers, sailors, and industrial fighters, and to train them in the practical technique necessary to make their blows effective against the opposing forces.

War-time education.—The war emergency revealed the necessity for the education of the people of the United States in the purposes, causes, and results of various policies of the Federal Government and of our allies and enemies as well. Some of the Federal bodies created for war purposes, such as the War Industries Board, the War Trade Board, the Fuel Administration, the Food Administration, and the Committee on Public Information, undertook and carried on through their own organizations in the States, through cooperating State agencies which they found in existence, and through private organizations, energetic and more or less effective campaigns of education along the lines of political and economic theory and practice. The War and Navy Departments, the Emergency Fleet Corporation and other Federal agencies planned, created, and conducted special training schools along industrial and vocational lines. In the educational war work of all kinds the State educational systems and the institutions of higher learning, both technical and academic, contributed equipment, direction, and a large proportion of the experienced teaching personnel.

New educational projects.—Dr. A. J. Klein says:

During the war the permanent educational institutions merged their efforts with those of less experienced persons and organizations which entered the field temporarily and in many cases without distinct consciousness of the real educational value of the work to be done. The result has been a very greatly increased interest in and knowledge on the part of the public of educational extension needs in the United States. From the realization of these needs, some important projects and proposals for Federal aid and encouragement to various lines of educational work have come from permanent educational forces with technical experience and knowledge of educational administration and methods. But many of the projects proposed have come also from persons and organizations with little understanding of the practical questions involved and with still less experience in continuous educational work. Some of those educational projects have already been started by departments of the Federal Government, and estimates looking to the continuance of the new work have been embodied in their appropriation bills or in special laws.

Confusion.—In some lines work has been undertaken and is being carried on independently by several departments of the Government. This has brought confusion and uncertainty to the permanently established State educational agencies. As one State superintendent of education expressed it, "I should welcome any kind of assistance and aid, as would every school officer, providing we may know 'Who is Who,' and not be compelled to be looking now to this authority and now to that authority for advice and counsel." This confusion has arisen from the eagerness of Federal departments to serve the country, from the great demand and urgent necessity for educational work, and from failure to form the educational program in cooperation with and to meet the needs of those who are in the States now charged with the responsibility of educating the boys and girls and adults whom Federal educational enterprises wish to reach.

Many of those educational projects have for their purpose the instruction and assistance to better citizenship of persons, minors and adults, not regular attendants at the public schools or institutions of higher education. The war educational program was most concerned with this class of persons. In peace time the university extension divisions of the States had been formed for this very purpose and when the war came they had had years of experience, much material and many practical, well-developed methods to meet the new pressure.

Demand for a Federal program.—It was natural, therefore, that the State extension divisions should take a most prominent part in educational war work. A review of the extent to which their resources were thrown into the work and a list of the leaders whom they contributed would show how important the expert service of the university extension divisions in the States was in furthering the war program.

It is also natural that the university extension divisions of the States should be interested in the steps that are taken to make certain features of this war work permanent, and that they should insist on a Federal program for after-the-war educational activities among the persons whom it was their business to instruct during peace times.

The university extension divisions have the experience and knowledge needed to carry on such work, and, since they are permanently established in the State educational systems, the burden of carrying on the labor of the programs inaugurated by enthusiastic and well-meaning persons will ultimately fall upon the extension divisions in large part, or require the setting up of duplicate administrative machinery.

If it is impossible in the present situation for them to have a determining voice in choosing which of those educational burdens shall be prepared for their shoulders, the minimum of assistance and knowledge which they demand is that the Federal Government establish some agency for keeping them informed of educational extension activities in other States and of the resources, aids, and agencies in the Federal Government itself which are at their disposal.

Federal aid.—For agricultural extension Federal aid has been provided most liberally, but no provision has been made for other important fields of extension work. Training and instruction of adults and others in subjects of civic and cultural value, in their professions, trades, and vocations, must not be neglected if we are to maintain intelligent Americanism. Proficiency in their work, knowledge of the latest advances in their lines of endeavor, understanding of the constantly fresh National and State and community problems, training for good citizenship of town and city inhabitants are as essential to the preservation of the prosperity and well-being of the agricultural classes and of all other classes in the Nation as is the education of the farmer himself.

For vocational education Federal aid has been provided through the Board of Vocational Education, and the board desires to utilize the university extension agencies in the States in the promotion of certain phases of vocational training.[1]

---

[1] Excerpts from mimeograph bulletin, "Summary Statement of Educational Extension," by Dr. A. J. Klein.

When the universities turned their energies to the task of mobilizing public opinion in support of the Government, the personnel of the extension divisions was extensively drafted for war service in the States, at Washington, and abroad. Speakers' bureaus of several State councils of defense were directed by extension officers. Every State university furnished numerous speakers in support of the Liberty loans, the Red Cross, etc. Thousands of motion-picture films and lantern slides on the war were displayed in every part of the States through the universities. In several States the training of Red Cross home-service workers was administered by the extension divisions; special training courses were given men in camps, and a large number of other war-service activities were conducted.

The adaptability of the extension machinery to national needs was proved during the war. The State divisions gave emergency courses in military French, in camouflage, in typewriting, in automobile mechanics, in food conservation, in home nursing, in reconstruction problems, in war aims, and in many other subjects of immediate national importance. The extension division of the University of Wisconsin prepared courses in English for the men at the Great Lakes training station and provided an instructor to advise the teachers at the station. Similar instances of extension division war service could be multiplied indefinitely.

War interrupted extension work.—The war-service work of the extension divisions seriously interrupted the normal activities in the States. The regular instructional work was continued with difficulty, through temporary arrangements carried out by inexperienced substitutes and by the extraordinary efforts of the small local clerical staff directed by officers on leave of absence.

Indiana eliminated its established community welfare service, institutes, and conferences. The director and two bureau chiefs gave full time to war service. Wisconsin discontinued community institutes and other activities; the chief of a department gave full time to direction of a Red Cross division. Other university extension divisions diverted their organization to war service.

FEDERAL DIVISION OF EDUCATIONAL EXTENSION ESTABLISHED.

Feeling that the university extension divisions had proved their adaptability to war-time and reconstruction needs, the National University Extension Association asked President Wilson to come to the assistance of the divisions in the emergency. The President set aside $50,000 for university extension work in a division of educational extension to be administered through the Bureau of Education in the Department of the Interior. This was done for several purposes, all of pressing importance. The State divisions needed a central clearing house to assist them in meeting the problems of recon-

struction. They needed assistance in reorganizing the extension
work interrupted by the war. It was clear that a national division
could salvage some of the educational resources and materials produced during the war. Further, the adoption of educational extension methods by Federal bureaus, national associations, and other
organizations threatened to create confusion and waste in the States,
and the national division could assist in establishing workable
methods and real cooperation.

The Federal division of educational extension was established in
December, 1918.[1] The President provided the funds for its maintenance out of his emergency appropriation, with the understanding
that the division would make the salvaged materials available to the
States through the machinery of the extension divisions which were
already established. At the same time the division was to act as a
clearing house for all matters of importance to the State extension
divisions and to the public libraries, particularly upon information
of special value to educational institutions during the immediate
post-war period.

During the six months of its existence the division succeeded in
organizing this service and in distributing to the States some of the
many Federal documents, war education courses, and motion-picture
films available in the several departments. It gave aid to the State
universities by distributing data on the methods and activities of the
different divisions. It sent out announcements and publicity materials, statistical data, budgets for extension divisions, and digests
of educational bills. It made available selected "package libraries"
of materials for the promotion of open-minded, impartial study and
discussion of such questions as Government ownership and operation
of railroads, Government control of prices, and reconstruction
measures. It distributed special references and bibliographies, university extension publications, information concerning the resources
offered by Federal departments, and suggestions for cooperative
efforts in educational extension. It also promoted Americanization
by gathering the experience of people who have been working among
foreigners, and of educators, and by making that experience available in summaries to the universities and State departments of
education.

The division carried on the work through its staff of experienced
educators and research men familiar with the resources of departments at Washington, and with those of the many semipublic agencies
such as the Red Cross and the other educational organizations.
The four main avenues of service established corresponded to the
avenues that have already proved themselves in the States—exten-

---

[1] This chapter is copied, with a few minor changes, from *The Federal Division of Educational Extension*,
by Mary B. Orvis, leaflet published by the National University Extension Association, June, 1919.

sion teaching, visual instruction, community-center promotion, and public discussion and library service.

The director, in addition to the work of organizing the division, gave advisory assistance to university authorities in the States, particularly to those establishing or developing new extension services. The director was called to Florida at the request of the legislature to appear before a joint session to present the facts concerning university extension. An appropriation of $50,000 was granted. He also conferred with legislative and faculty committees in Tennessee, Alabama, Oklahoma, North Dakota, Montana, Iowa, Ohio, Missouri, and Minnesota. Eight other States asked for similar services.

The heads of each of the four sections of the division performed for their particular avenue of extension a service similar to that performed by the director for the whole division; they kept officials in the States informed as to the development of the work in each State, and offered to each the benefit of the knowledge that a central office alone can accumulate.

Promotion of extension teaching.—The 120,000 persons who are studying through the State extension divisions are reached by means of correspondence study and classes held by university instructors in "extension centers." The Massachusetts department of university extension had 400 students in a gas automobile course which it gave in Boston; the Wisconsin division had about 2,000 students in engineering courses in Milwaukee. Thousands of farm men and women and small-town residents are studying such subjects as English composition, literature, history, and hygiene by correspondence. This work was promoted and standardized by the Federal division.

One hundred and forty-one different courses prepared for war-time instruction purposes were obtained from Government bureaus and departments by the division and passed out for continued use. These courses include simple and technical, vocational, cultural, and scientific subjects, and vary in size from pamphlets of a few pages to large and elaborately illustrated books. Engineering schools have found such courses as those of orientation and gunnery of value in the teaching of map making and the principles of mechanics. Extension divisions which give courses in vocational subjects are using large numbers of the Telephone Electrician's Manual, the Auto Mechanics and Auto Drivers' Instruction Manual, and the Motor Transportation Handbook, called to their attention by this service and furnished by the Government departments responsible for their preparation.

The War Department cooperated with the division of educational extension by putting at its disposal the psychological tests and systems of classification of personnel developed during the war, with a view to modifying them for civilian uses and making them available to the university extension divisions.

Soldiers' education.—Arrangements were made with the Federal Board for Vocational Education whereby the Federal board will use to the fullest possible extent the resources of the extension divisions in the rehabilitation and reeducation of soldiers, sailors, and marines who are compensable; and the extension divisions will cooperate with the Federal board by assisting in the guidance of men who are not legally compensable, but who need or desire educational assistance.

The division arranged with the Institute of International Education and other agencies to assist the universities in making their correspondence courses available to foreign students and to American residents abroad. Preliminary arrangements were made for securing through the institute English extension workers for lecture tours in this country.

A conference between the Red Cross and extension directors was arranged to discuss the whole question of cooperation between the State branches of the Red Cross and the State extension divisions.

Health education.—A cooperative arrangement between the Red Cross, the American Health Association, and other bodies interested in health education was projected whereby popular correspondence courses on health topics may be prepared and offered by the extension divisions of the States, free of charge to all the inhabitants of the United States.

The assistance of the National Automobile Chamber of Commerce was secured in the collection and preparation of course material on road transportation and traffic, as distinct from road construction. Extension divisions and universities have expressed their desire for such material in order that they may train the highway traffic experts who will be needed in the wise development and maintenance of a unified highway, railroad, and waterways system for the United States.

These examples illustrate the possibilities of the Federal division as a clearing house and cooperative agency for adult education.

Visual instruction service.—Over 3,000 school buildings contain projection lanterns, according to a recent survey made by the division of educational extension. Many others will be equipped if school authorities can be assured of a supply of films. Each one of these schools is a potential theater for educational motion pictures lent by the United States Government and by many public and semi-public agencies. The division acted as a collecting and distributing center for such films. It completed arrangements with extension divisions equipped in the States for the distribution of films sent out from Washington. Many reels were sent out to State extension divisions ready to distribute them. In States where there existed no central agency for visual instruction, the division negotiated with other departments, such as the State department of public instruction, for its establishment. The division did not distribute pictures directly to the users, but it operated through State machinery.

About 4,300 reels of motion pictures and 25,000 stereopticon lantern slides were acquired by gift or by loan during the period from January to May, 1919. These pictures represent in many cases merely the first consignment of lots of material which are to come to the Bureau of Education from the different governmental departments. The War Department agreed to supply the division of educational extension with enough duplicate negatives and positive prints to make a series of 12 motion pictures on the subject of the achievements of the war. The topics constituting this series are as follows: Camouflage in modern war; the work of the American engineers; lumbering in France; military communication; sports and entertainments for the soldiers; the transportation of men and supplies; the care of the wounded; modern ordnance; chemical warfare; feeding the Army; the Air Service; keeping the Army well.

Practically all motion pictures released by the Committee on Public Information during the war were transferred to the division for nation-wide circulation through educational channels.

The National Automobile Chamber of Commerce agreed to cooperate with the division in the production and distribution of a series of pictures on good roads. Many industrial firms turned over films to the division, which put them into circulation through the State extension centers.

The following report from the director of the division of educational extension, sent to the directors of extension and to officers in charge of motion-picture distribution in the States, gives a summary of the status of the film service of the United States Bureau of Education:

STATEMENT OF FILMS RECEIVED AND DISTRIBUTED.

Motion-picture films gathered to date...........................(feet).. 6, 120, 000
Distributed to date...(feet).. 3, 950, 000
Centers having received films to date.................................... 35
New centers now ready... 3
Centers still needed in order to cover United States...................... 16

Additional film for which negotiations are under way or which have been actually promised will be received in considerable quantity before January 1, 1920.

PRESENT STATUS OF FEDERAL SERVICE

Though efforts for an appropriation with which to continue the division failed, arrangements have been made by which the service in visual instruction will have attention. Two of the officers of the section, Mr. F. W. Reynolds and Mr. W. H. Dudley, are retained on the staff of the Bureau of Education, and though not permanently at Washington, will exercise such responsibility for the work as they can. Mr. R. E.

Egner, film inspector and shipping and record clerk, is to remain in Washington in immediate charge of the activities under way and in contemplation.

CONDITIONS GOVERNING THE MATERIAL.

The motion pictures sent out are free and must be shown free. Other conditions are that they be kept as busy as their interest warrants, that they be kept in proper repair, and that a record of their use be kept in the files of the center and be sent regularly to the Washington office.

The pictures in the main are deposited indefinitely with the centers. In the case of some of them there may be a request for a return to the Washington office or for a transfer to some other State center, but the terms of any such request will take the point of view of the center having possession. No plan for a definite and vigorous use of the material will be upset.

SUGGESTIONS AS TO THE MATERIAL.

The material sent out can be regarded only as a basis of a service in visual instruction. It will not in and of itself constitute a service. But in this connection attention should be called to the value of the material. That dealing with the war will increase, not decrease, in interest as time passes. It has been the plan of the officers of the section to get even more of this war material out to the centers, enough to make a pictorial review of the war by topics. The hope now is that this plan may be realized. Toward the plan, the material already sent out is a beginning.

Centers are not at liberty to make any changes in the pictures belonging to the series "The Training of a Soldier." The war features and the war reviews may be changed, however, and it may be that some of the centers will wish to use this material for experimental work in the assembly of pictures of their own.

All in all, the material should have lasting and real value. It is in the hope that it will have this that it has been salvaged and distributed.

REQUEST FOR COOPERATION.

The various distributing centers will discover many interesting ways in which to use the materials. It is requested that they report such discoveries to the Washington office, which, serving as a clearing house, will undertake to send accounts of them to other centers. This is important. The cooperation of the centers in an effort to secure as complete usefulness of materials as possible is earnestly requested.

NEW MATERIALS.

The officers of the section and the Washington office are still at work to secure additional material for the various centers. In this work they have the hearty cooperation of the newly organized National University Extension Association (Inc.), which is maintaining an office in Washington.

Word as to new material and as to the conditions under which it may be obtained may be expected at any time from the officers of the section, from the Washington office, or from the secretary of the National University Extension Association (Inc.)

APPRECIATION.

The section has had the warmest support from the departments of the Government, from allied organizations, and from various commercial and industrial companies. It also wishes to extend thanks to the distributing centers from which it has also had hearty support.

The section itself will have reward for its effort if, as is more than likely, a Federal permanent service in visual instruction is finally established.

Community center service.—The Community Center, a local democratic organization for community advancement, is another means of education that has been developed through the extension division machinery of the States and through the State departments of education. It is the logical place for showing educational pictures to adult audiences. It brings people together for the common good. It strengthens the existing freedom and self-government of the citizens.

Relations with 42 States were established by the division of educational extension for the promotion of the community centers, and arrangements were made to cooperate with the authorities in the remaining States. This section of the division was in contact with over 1,000 different local communities where community center organizations were being started, and more than 100 centers were projected in the spring of 1919. Members of the division were constantly in the field holding conferences in regard to this work. Outlines and plans for community organization, together with suggested programs for meetings, were distributed to the communities.

Public discussion and library service.—In practically all of the States the colleges and universities are carrying on an information and library service which reaches hundreds of thousands of people, giving them facts and sources of information. Nineteen extension divisions answered nearly 60,000 requests for information last year. This service disseminates information secured from authoritative sources on such public matters as municipal development, child welfare, public health, civics, and on miscellaneous subjects of interest to individuals, such as personal hygiene. This service is practical and specific. It meets a widespread demand for information—the same demand that floods Washington with requests for information on every conceivable subject. The State service needs a central agency which can supply materials and coordinate resources. The Federal division rendered such a service.

The package library.—All of the State universities and many other institutions carry on some kind of public discussion work. Large numbers of people are served, many of them members of high-school and college debating societies, city councils, women's clubs, civics clubs, and miscellaneous organizations. The extension divisions prepare, with the assistance of university faculties, lists of important subjects, bibliographies, and study outlines, and lend them to inquirers. Accompanying this specially prepared material go package libraries, which consist of from 5 to 100 pieces of literature, generally gathered together from Federal, State, and local public agencies, as well as from private associations and from magazines and newspapers.

The division of educational extension acted as a clearing house upon methods of improving the machinery for this State service and as an agency for distributing informational publications to each

153448°—20——3

State. It sent out in six months 14,700 pieces of material on current topics for inclusion in package libraries. This material was sent to the State divisions and has been lent by them many times to clubs and individuals. Thirty-eight different publications on the League of Nations, pro and con, or about 6,200 pieces, were sent out in two months' time. Fifty different publications, or about 1,500 pieces, on labor and reconstruction were sent in the same time, as were 30 different publications, or about 1,200 pieces, on the Government and the railroads.

These materials were made up by the State bureaus into package libraries, which give information on both sides of controversial questions. They usually contain lists of Government publications, programs, and statements by the interests especially affected, as well as pamphlets and magazine articles. The bibliographies give additional information of special value to extension divisions.

Use of Federal publications.—A particular effort was made to bring to the notice of the extension division agents the United States Government publications. Special investigations, reports of commissions, monographs issued by the Government bureaus, important statements of plans or reports on the operation of governmental agencies, speeches in Congress, hearings before committees are the very substance on which the policies of the National Government are based. All these and many others can be obtained free from governmental departments; others can be secured from the Superintendent of Documents. Most of them are practically unknown, however, even to intelligent people who take serious interest in public affairs. The library of the Superintendent of Documents contains over 200,000 separate publications. To make the people somewhat familiar with this material and to give them a first-hand acquaintance with the work done by the National Government was one of the primary aims of the division of educational extension.

Reference of inquiries.—In order to avoid futile reference from one Federal bureau to another, the division made arrangements with the inquiry office of the Department of Labor to refer inquiries on current public questions and other matters not easily answered in Washington to the university extension divisions in the States from which the inquiries come. This arrangement was designed to serve the additional purpose of acquainting the public with the informational resources of their State institutions.

The division established a working library of university extension publications of every kind. This library affords ready reference to any phase of the work offered in the United States and in England.

The division also issued, among others, the following mimeograph bulletins:

Adult Education: A brief statement of suggestive matter to be found in the report of the adult education committee to the English Minister of Reconstruction.

A Survey of the Public Discussion Work of the States, with explanations of successful devices.

An Exhibit of United States Publications.

Budgets for Public Discussion Bureaus.

Package Library and Club Service: A summary of work done by extension divisions and public library commissions.

National Library Service.—A direct service for the 18,000 libraries in the United States was maintained in the division. The libraries need to know more about the printed informational material issued by the Government. National Library Service helped librarians not only to secure that material, but also to familiarize themselves and their patrons with it. One Government department alone distributed last year nearly one hundred million copies of publications on hundreds of subjects. Obviously, no librarian can keep up with this output; yet the public has a right to expect the librarian to hand out the right information at the right time. The librarians have requested and demanded for years such a clearing house as National Library Service rendered through its printed pamphlets. Bulletins were issued telling of the work done and the services offered to librarians by the following governmental departments: Agriculture, Commerce, Labor, Treasury, and Interior. Each bulletin contains the story of the department, followed by news notes of the various activities. These notes contain material of current interest to librarians and are selected, prepared, and submitted by the information services of the different Government departments. Another feature of the bulletins is an up-to-date selected list of current available printed matter, posters, slides, and reels of films.

Training Americanization workers.—A tremendous amount of patriotic enthusiasm engendered by the war turned naturally last fall to the problem of making better citizens of our foreign-born people. Letters of inquiry sent out to the university presidents of the country last December by the division of educational extension, however, revealed the fact that only a very few institutions were awake to their opportunities and obligations in a movement obviously educational. All were anxious to do their part when their attention was called to the practical work that could be done. The most obvious duty was that of training special teachers for the foreign born.

The division immediately gathered together what information it could about the methods in use and sent it out in mimeographed bulletins to the universities and State education departments. It

also assembled a large collection of programs and pamphlets issued
by State councils of defense, State Americanization bureaus, private
agencies, and universities and colleges. In most cases pamphlets
could be secured in sufficient quantity to distribute them to a mailing list of about 250 of the leading educators of the country.

Three hundred copies each of several valuable publications and
English courses were secured from the Massachusetts extension
department, which was a pioneer in this movement. The California
State commission on immigration and housing also sent the division
300 copies of its study of the methods of Americanization. The
extension division of Iowa contributed several hundred copies of a
suggestive pamphlet for work among young people in high school
and college. Reed College, Oregon, gave 300 copies of an excellently
illustrated statistical survey of American cities, showing illiteracy
and foreign-born populations, along with other significant facts.
These are but a few of the many organizations that have helped
each other through the division of educational extension.

About 11,000 pieces of Americanization literature, almost entirely
of concrete specific value in planning courses for teaching immigrants,
were sent out to educators in six months. The division also answered
daily specific requests for assistance in such matters as the conduct
of surveys of civic instruction in State high schools, the finding of
suitable university instructors to train teachers, and the finding of
suitable courses in universities for individuals desiring to attend
summer sessions.

In Massachusetts, Colorado, and Wisconsin the extension divisions
have charge of State programs of Americanization. In other States
the divisions are doing more and more of the work. Wherever
educational institutions are doing Americanization work, they can
profit by the clearing house service of some central agency.

At least 19 universities and colleges gave courses in Americanization work during the summer of 1919. The division of educational
extension received ample testimony to the fact that it appreciably
assisted in establishing this new type of instruction. The fact that
in the first six months of its existence it had the opportunity to perform this very special kind of service for the Nation indicates something of the possibilities of a Federal division in future emergencies.

NATIONAL ASSOCIATION INCORPORATED.

University presidents and the members of the National University
Extension Association were desirous of continuing the work started
by the temporary Federal division. Accordingly the Secretary of
the Interior included in his estimates for the department an item to
provide funds with which the Bureau of Education could develop a
permanent extension service. Congress, however, did not appro-

priate the funds. A number of bills have been introduced to secure the establishment of a Federal clearing house for university extension.

In the summer of 1919, the directors of State university divisions agreed that, pending congressional action, a substantial agency should be created to continue the Washington clearing-house work. They worked out a plan in detail and created the National University Extension Association (Incorporated), with an office in the capital. The association, incorporated under the laws of the District of Columbia, is supported by the State extension divisions and by fees from different classes of membership. Its work is projected along lines similar to those followed previously by the Federal division. It cooperates with the staff of the Bureau of Education, supplementing the work the latter is able to do through the Government departments.

The following is a condensed statement of the work the incorporated association is undertaking:

1. It will collect and distribute data and material on the methods and activities of educational extension work in the United States and abroad.

2. It will make available selected materials prepared by educational, governmental, and other organizations on questions of general interest, such as Government ownership, price control, reconstruction measures, etc.

3. It will supply announcements and published material, statistical data, and digests of educational matters of special interest to extension and public welfare workers.

4. It will answer inquiries from members with reference to governmental activities, legislation, and administrative policies, in so far as educational extension interests are concerned.

5. It will make official and semiofficial connective relationships for cooperative educational extension work between member institutions and branches of the Federal Government or other organizations.

6. It will serve as a center through which cooperative efforts of member institutions may function. For example, extension lecturers on special subjects desired by a number of member organizations may be engaged through this office in long-time blocks, thereby increasing the bargaining strength of the members and eliminating most of the risk charges, the excessive overheads and traveling expenses, and making the final terms for the community using the services of the lecturers relatively low. A small fee to care for the office expense of such work will be charged. A similar advantage and arrangement can be had for some of the visual instruction material.

7. It will publish the results of research work in subjects of general interest to extension workers.[1]

There are several different types of membership in the association, making it possible for individuals as well as institutions to obtain assistance from the central office. While the association is governed chiefly by the directors of extension in State universities, other extension directors are eligible and any institution may arrange for clearing-house service.

---

[1] Statement issued by Dr. A. J. Klein, executive secretary, National University Extension Association, Incorporated, Munsey Building, Washington, D. C.

ESSENTIAL ELEMENTS OF UNIVERSITY EXTENSION.

''The American university emerges from the war with a new sense of confidence and of social obligation," says George Edgar Vincent. Undoubtedly the interpretation of that obligation includes definite assumption of the necessity of developing university extension. The following statements of the essential elements of a university extension policy are quoted in this bulletin because they throw light on the motive and direction of the movement.

SERVICE TO THE COMMONWEALTH THROUGH UNIVERSITY EXTENSION.

By President E. A. Birge.[1]

President Van Hise began his administration with the formal announcement of "service to the Commonwealth" as its motto, and he carried out that idea in ways never before tried on such a scale. Thus he has profoundly affected the practice of universities and has even modified the conception of a State university. I refer to the development of those lines of activity which for want of a better name are inadequately grouped under the name of university extension.

I find no evidence that President Van Hise entered office with any definite conception of university extension as a means of public service, or indeed that he entered on the rehabilitation of that branch of university work with any design of making it one of the prime factors in State university life. University extension was no unknown thing in the University of Wisconsin when he came to the presidency. It was established in 1892 and was organized in the ordinary form, with lectures and accompanying instruction in classes. Interest in it had declined in Wisconsin as it had everywhere, and on his accession it had little life. It so continued during four years, but in 1907 he reorganized the department, bringing to the university Louis E. Reber, first as director of university extension, later advanced to the position of dean of the extension division. He secured from the legislature of 1907 an annual appropriation of $20,000 for the work. The next legislature granted $50,000, and the income of the division from appropriations and fees has risen rapidly, until it now exceeds $275,000 annually. Thus university extension rose almost at once to a leading place in the university, surpassed in size only by the largest colleges, those of letters and sciences and of agriculture. This sum, devoted specifically to extension, is in addition to some $150,000 annually expended by the college of agriculture along similar lines. Altogether, nearly one-fifth of the operating expenses of the university other than those associated with the physical plant goes in that direction.

Enlargement of university teaching.—Here, then, was introduced into the life of the university and of the State a new factor and a new influence—not new indeed in the sense that it was something unheard of or something untried, but new in the sense that a scheme which had been attempted with limited success as a secondary method of extending knowledge was elevated to a primary position and brought into the first rank of university influences. Two principles underlie university extension. One of these could have been operative at any time in the recent past; the other belongs to our own day in its might and force. The first looks at it as an

---

[1] Excerpts from address delivered by President E. A. Birge, of the University of Wisconsin, in memorial to his predecessor, President Van Hise. MSS., 1919.

enlargement of university teaching—of individual opportunity for study—as a means of affording the chance of higher education to those persons who can not attend a university. Hence the historical name "university extension," connoting the enlargement of the area of university classes. The other point of view, though in some ways akin to this, is fundamentally different.

Application of knowledge.—This view starts not from the university as a center for teaching, but regards it as a center of learning, as the place where knowledge is accumulated and advanced. Into the university pour the streams of knowledge from all parts of the world in ever-increasing volume and rapidity of flow. Here, too, new, though smaller, currents arise, the contributions of the university to the stream of knowledge. The university is equipped by its libraries and its laboratories, most of all by the men and women assembled in its faculties, to receive this increasing knowledge, to sift it and judge its worth, to modify it or to increase it, and to hand it on to the students in its classes. But the university as thus defined is not equipped on another side and for another duty which belongs rather to our own day than to the past. This mass of knowledge, accumulating with a rapidity whose acceleration is almost portentous, is not, like that which scholasticism gained in the Middle Ages, wholly or primarily a subject for the discussions of scholars. It is also the knowledge which the members of the community must apply to the conduct of practical affairs, if these are to be ordered wisely and successfully. This is not a matter of education proper, either higher or lower, not a matter of teaching principles which the student will later apply in practice. It involves the transmutation of learning into such form that it can be directly used in the ordering of affairs. It means the extension of learning, the transmutation of science into practice, the application of knowledge to concrete problems of everyday affairs.

To convey learning to the people.—In this sense university extension is a far wider and more fundamental thing than in its older significance of extension by lectures and correspondence study. The latter is a sort of academic work of benevolence, the offering of education to those whom age or ill fortune deprives of the chance to study in the regular way. It does not differ in principle from the immemorial mission of endowments founded to bring such persons to university halls. But the new university extension involves new functions for the university and functions in large measure untried. Its aim is not so much education as the amelioration of life by the direct application of knowledge. It has become the duty of the university to reinterpret knowledge for the ends of practice and to convey learning so reinterpreted to the people in such a way as to make it immediately effective in life.

This function universities have longest applied and best worked out in agriculture, though even here matters are far from settled. A main work of the agricultural experiment stations is to act as an intermediary between pure science and practical farming. Experience has shown that many and various methods are needed to get this transmuted science into practice. Farmers' institutes, demonstration farms, short courses for farmers, young and old, county agricultural representatives, organized societies—all these as well as agricultural education in its proper sense, are needed to put at work efficiently and promptly the knowledge acquired and shaped by university and station.

University extension and problems of society.—This is a special case of a major problem of modern life, of modern life rather than of modern education—that of the methods of securing the utilization in practice of vast stores of knowledge ever enlarging in content and changing in application. The problem is by no means confined to agriculture, though both State and social considerations give it a peculiar importance and difficulty in that field. It exists everywhere in the field of society; and Wisconsin through its university under the leadership of President Van Hise is perhaps the first State to give it a generous recognition and to provide large means for beginning its solution in practice.

The problem thus offered by university extension presented itself to Dr. Van Hise in several aspects. There was present the older feeling of the necessity of carrying university education to all who can profit by it, whether these can come to the university or not. There was even greater need to the university of an organization by which it might express the results of learning directly to the public. Above all, there was in his mind the democratic ideal of the State and of the State university—an ideal ever before him and always dominant.

Utilization of knowledge.—He saw a State dependent for its prosperity, for its success in competition with other States, on the full and prompt utilization of the knowledge which science is so rapidly accumulating. He saw a university founded and maintained by the State to be the possessor and augmenter of this knowledge. But he saw also that a connection was lacking between the people of the State and the university. Knowledge accumulated at the center, but there was no way of realizing it in action at the periphery. University extension was the means devised to close this gap, to complete the State educational system by providing a definite agency which is to send out knowledge, transmitted in a workable form from the university to the State.

The execution of such a program is no simple or easy task. Social life still depends in large measure on tradition and rule of thumb, although at innumerable single points it needs the guidance of science. It is not ready to intrust its interests as a whole to science; nor is science ready to accept that responsibility, if it were asked to do so.

Thus, much of the work is partial, much is tentative, much is experimental. Many things will be tried and abandoned after trial. Many more which seem small and unimportant at first will prove ultimately to be of great value. Many matters will be undertaken from the central university which later will be turned over to local organizations. Still more important, the work will necessarily be in a sense fragmentary and broken, and not a connected whole like the teaching of a college or a department, but consisting rather of detached tasks, each addressed to a specific need of society or community. Their connection will be that of need for guidance and the possibility of meeting this need rather than any close intellectual or logical bond.

Faith in democracy.—It demands great power of initiative, great courage, and great faith in democracy to attempt such a policy on the large scale. Minor failures are sure to occur; experiments will be wrongly tried; men will be appointed who prove unfitted for novel tasks; and all these things mean just criticism and often unfriendly criticism. But the dozen years that have passed since President Van Hise initiated the policy have justified it. University extension in this sense has become accepted as an inevitable responsibility by universities, especially by State universities. It has entered as a war measure into the activities of national life and will perpetuate itself there during peace. No one who can read the signs of the times can fail to see that Wisconsin, under the leadership of President Van Hise, broke the way into a new and great field of university work. The life and the work of universities, the country over, have been permanently changed and enlarged by his influence, and the change has only begun to manifest its effect.

Uniting State and university.—With this conception of the duty of the university to the Commonwealth, President Van Hise united an unshakable faith in the intelligent good will of the Commonwealth toward the university in these new enterprises. He was confident not only that the State would support the university in these new enterprises, but also that it would see how the assistance given to the public in concrete cases was made possible and effectual by the entire university life behind it. He believed, therefore, that in thus uniting State and university at new and numerous points of contact, he was strengthening the institution in its highest functions; he was confident that the people would in a new sense and to a higher degree than before appreciate the intellectual forces represented in the university and would sustain all the parts of its great and complex life.[1]

I have emphasized this salient point in the presidency of Dr. Van Hise because, more than any other one thing, it represents that which will be most conspicuous in his work for the university; that which will remain visible when the history of years of successful administration has lapsed into the indistinguishable memory of past things well done. But it would be wrong to leave the story with this presentation for it would convey the idea that President Van Hise was fundamentally an educational reformer, interested primarily in his reforms and neglecting in his own thought the older and larger matters which make up the mass of university life. Such a view would wrong the memory of the president, wrong him even as the university has been wronged by the impression that Wisconsin is essentially an extension institution. Extension constituted the *differentia* of his administration, not its characteristics, as seen by us who lived and worked with him.

University's duty to increase knowledge.—His conception of the university went back to the days when he studied under Prof. Irving and when he took part as a young man in the early development of the university spirit and organization during the administration of President Chamberlin. Central in that conception were the ideals of scholarship and research—of the university's duty to increase knowledge and its equal duty to make knowledge live in the lives of its students. His was a working conception of research. He had, as all men must have who advance science, the pioneer spirit, the love of the new world, of the unbroken trail; he was ready to sacrifice ease, to endure hardship, to bear long-continued labor, if only the frontiers of knowledge might be advanced by him. Research meant specific problems to be solved at any cost of toil, not a "keeping in touch" with the advance of his science. * * * When, therefore, President Van Hise urged on his faculty the fundamental duty of research as part of their academic life, he spoke with full knowledge of his demands. * * *

He had a long and arduous experience in teaching science to large classes, not merely as stimulating his students to become specialists but also as part of a general education, as influencing the life and thought of students who will never pursue the subject in a serious way after they leave his class. * * *

Thus the catholicity of his university temper gave him points of contact with the life and influence of all types of teachers in his faculty. They were engaged in no line of work which he had not shared, none in which he had not succeeded, none whose value he had not weighed as a part of the life of the university whose earlier growth he had aided and whose later development he was now guiding. It was no small thing that he saw all of these matters primarily in relation to the university. He called on each one of us not merely to do his part in maintaining the university, but to put his full strength into helping its progress. He had found it a man's work to take his place in that group of men to whom we of to-day owe the existence of the university. From those who joined its faculty in the more fortunate day of larger opportunity he had every right to ask devotion and work comparable to opportunity. * * *

Public service.—Through all the urgent duties of the presidency he devoted his hard won leisure to writing and to public service, instead of to well-earned rest. He took the active part in the urgent discussions of the day which his broad training as an economic geologist warranted. He worked out the principles underlying the conservation of natural resources and the control of industries based on them and expressed the results not only in numerous addresses but in books. Thus the knowledge and

---

[1] The State of Wisconsin passed by referendum and in special session in 1919 two remarkable educational measures which are designed to give special opportunity to soldiers and sailors and others who served in the war. They apply the principle of an "educational bonus" and provide generous means for realizing it. There are special provisions for extension students, including the giving of free correspondence study courses and the holding of short courses, special schools, part-time day and evening classes.

trainíng accumulated in years of research and teaching were made increasingly effective for public service and were vigorously used for the public benefit. * * * *Extension the outcome of public necessities.*—Dr. Van Hise was not only familiar with the traditions of the university; he had been himself a powerful influence in creating them. He represented in his own person our academic ideals from elementary teaching to most advanced research. He saw the wide extent and variety of university effort in its relation to the institution. He saw the institution not only in its relation to learning, but also in that broader aspect in which it not only represents the State, but is itself the State organized for the higher intellectual life. And to all these qualities he further added a capacity for public affairs and a knowledge of them which lifted him out of the merely academic level and enabled him to see both university and State from a common point of view. Thus, while he embodied the academic traditions of the university, he was not confined by them or limited to them. He was completely in touch with his faculty, stimulating and guiding academic life and practice at all points. He was also able to conceive and execute policies like that of university extension, which were the outcome of a knowledge of public necessities rather than of academic development alone. He advanced the university along each of these lines while keeping both himself and the institution in full sympathy with the other.

WAR EXTENSION SERVICE.

By President E. A. Alderman.[1]

The fundamental duties of every university are to teach, to investigate, to disseminate truth, and to afford technical guidance to the people. My own ambition for the University of Virginia is to speed the time when no cry of help in any social need shall come up from any community in the Commonwealth that will not be met by immediate response from the forces and agencies assembled here at the university. If this was a normal peace-time aspiration, it is even more a war-time ambition. If it was our duty to discharge these obligations in peace through ordinary channels, it is even more our duty now to bring to bear all of our resources upon the novel and complex problems that face our democracy.

The University of Virginia, as soon as war was declared, hastened to concentrate its energies in helpful work for the Nation. It placed military training in its curriculum; it classified its resources of men and equipment; it organized and offered war courses of instruction; it organized a great base hospital unit, now ready for embarkation; its faculty, undergraduates, and alumni gave themselves to the Nation's need so generously that 20 per cent of them are now to be found with the colors. This sort of helpfulness will continue to go on as the need arises; but the university realizes that there rests upon it, in addition to this, a clear educational duty, not only to teach those who come to its walls, but to instruct all citizens who need guidance as to the causes of war, the character of American ideals, the avenues for public usefulness, the true ways to win peace, the nature of the responsibility that rests upon all Americans in this solemn moment of our national history, and the character of the reconstructive work that awaits us all when a just peace shall be won. The university wishes to discharge those duties to the extent of its power, and, if possible, in cooperation with high schools, grammar schools, and other educational bodies in practical and definite ways. It wishes to draw nearer to the people by offering them practical but inspiring instructions in a sound idealism, in all useful administrative work, in the mobilization of latent resources, and in all the fields that tend to give to a patriotic American knowledge of his privileges and duties in this testing time in the experiences of the Republic.

Our Republic can no longer rely on an unlimited quantity of untouched wealth. but must depend upon skill and training for the proper development of its resources. The times call imperatively, therefore, for educated leadership, whose greatest need

---

[1] Quoted from University of Virginia Record, Extension Series, November, 1917.

will be knowledge and the discipline of exact training. The ultimate mission of the State university in America will be to supply this training, not only to the fortunate few who can repair to its walls, but to all the people who constitute the life of the State. Universities must, therefore, in a peculiar sense, draw nearer to the people, young and old, in helpfulness and service. This is an old philosophy, indeed, but informed now by a new and vigorous spirit which will be satisfied with nothing less than a complete and pervasive program. University extension is the name given to this great connecting link between every part of a university and the actual conditions of life in the State which the university exists to aid and strengthen. The fundamental ideal of university extension is the ideal of service to democracy as a whole rather than to individual advancement. The University of Virginia, founded by the greatest individualist and democrat of the age, would be strangely false to its origin and genius if it did not seek to illustrate this idea. It has, of course, for years sought to render such service in indirect fashion and with limited means. It is now undertaking to inaugurate the great system in a more direct fashion, with the hope that the encouragement it receives will enable it to overcome all obstacles and to realize the great democratic purpose of bringing the university to every fireside and home in the Commonwealth. This sort of university extension necessitates large means, but when its advantages to the elevation of standards and life in the Commonwealth are seen, a sagacious and generous people will not fail, I believe, to provide for the maintenance of so vital an enterprise.

President Lowell, of Harvard University, says:

A college, to be of any great value, must grow out of the community in which it lives, and must be in absolute touch with that community, doing all the good it can, and doing what the community needs. Any institution not in close touch with the community around it is bound to wither and die. The institutions about us to-day which are doing the most good in the way of helping their respective communities are the great State universities of the Middle West. We must learn to do those things which others are doing.

Dean Bailey, of Cornell College, says:

All persons in the Commonwealth are properly students of a State institution, but very few of them have yet registered, nor is it necessary that any great proportion of them should leave home in order to receive some benefits of the institution. It is the obligation of such an institution to serve all the people, and it is equally the obligation of the people to make the institution such that it can exercise its proper functions; and all this can be brought about without sacrificing any worthy standards of education.

INSTITUTIONS PURSUING THE SEVERAL ACTIVITIES.

The following is a series of elementary definitions of terms used to designate different kinds of university extension work. After each definition a partial list is given of the State university extension divisions which have developed the specific service in whole or in part.

Extension teaching service.—A phrase used to distinguish the more formal and standard kinds of instruction from the informal methods of university extension, such as investigations, institutes, conferences, and various kinds of welfare work.

This phrase, or a similar one, is utilized by Arkansas, Colorado, Indiana, Pittsburgh, North Dakota, Utah, and Washington, to distinguish certain kinds of work from the kinds classified under "Public welfare service."

Correspondence instruction.—Teaching by mail. University instructors prepare written courses with detailed analysis, questions, and references, and require the student to do certain amounts of work, submit written reports, and answer specific questions for each lesson. Usually a year is given the student for completion of a standard course. Practically every important subject offered on the university campus is given by some extension division in the country. Man.· elementary subjects are given.

Used by the following universities: Arizona, Arkansas, California, Colorado, Florida, Idaho, Indiana, Iowa, Kansas, Kentucky, Maryland, Massachusetts, Minnesota, Missouri, Montana, Nebraska, North Carolina, North Dakota, Oklahoma, Oregon, Pittsburgh, South Dakota, Texas, Utah, Washington, West Virginia, Wisconsin, and Wyoming.

Extension class instruction.—Instructors meet students in classes arranged in different towns and cities of the State. Ordinary college subjects are taught and also special subjects like business psychology or commercial English, and vocational, cultural, and professional subjects, by regular instructors who come from the university. Frequently special instructors are secured outside the university faculty, men with practical experience and affiliations.

The classes closely resemble in subject matter and methods of teaching the classes regularly held in college and university Frequently the period set aside for lecture by the professor is supplemented by extended practical discussions to meet the problems of the mature extension student.

Used by the following universities: Arkansas, California, Colorado, Columbia, Massachusetts, Michigan, Minnesota, Missouri, Montana, Nebraska, Oklahoma, Oregon, Pittsburgh, South Carolina, South Dakota, Texas, Utah, Washington, and West Virginia.

Class and club instruction.—Such work is a combination of class and correspondence study. Instructors supply a course of lessons and also meet the class or club occasionally to give them personal guidance and to get their point of view and group difficulties. Papers are submitted by mail for correction at the university. Examinations are sometimes given to students desiring a special certificate showing completion of the work. This work does not count as university "credit;" that is, it does not offer opportunity to secure a university degree.

Used by the following universities: California, Indiana, Kansas, Michigan, Mississippi, North Carolina, and Texas.

44

Advisory mail instruction.—The instructor applies general principles of a correspondence course to the practical problems of an individual. For instance, a course on health in the home is made the basis of personal advice to a mother who wants systematic instruction in the principles of rearing children, and the instructor makes suggestions in reference to definite problems the mother presents from her own experience.

Used by the Universities of Kansas and New York.

Club study.—Extension officers recommend club programs, supply references, suggest books and lecturers, and furnish guides and other assistance in the preparation of club papers. The work is usually done for women's clubs, but is offered also to community center associations and civic clubs.

Used by the following universities: Arkansas, California, Indiana, Kansas, Nevada, North Carolina, North Dakota, Oklahoma, and Texas.

Directed reading courses.—A surprisingly large number of mature persons, even those who have had college training, welcome assistance in choosing selected reading material—not only fiction, or general literature, but also scientific books, pamphlets, and periodicals. Several extension divisions issue selected book lists, outline studies with bibliographies, club study outlines, and other helps to systematic reading.

Used by the Universities of Arkansas, Kansas, Oklahoma, Oregon, and Texas.

The United States Bureau of Education conducts home reading courses and proposes to utilize the State extension divisions in making them more widely available.

Lectures.—The old method of haphazard speaking by university professors is gradually being supplemented by a system of selective supply through the extension division, which uses outside resources as well as the university faculty to meet the needs of different groups of people.

Lectures in series are being developed to offer system and detail in the consideration of the subjects or problems. Frequently such lecture series are practically of the same character as those of regular class instruction, except that the routine of enrollment, assignment, examination, and accrediting is dispensed with.

Used by the following universities: Alabama, Arizona, Arkansas, California, Florida, Georgia, Idaho, Illinois, Kansas, Kentucky, Michigan, Minnesota, Mississippi, Missouri, Montana, Nebraska, New Mexico, North Carolina, North Dakota, Oklahoma, Oregon, South Carolina, Tennessee, and Texas.

Demonstrations.—University extension has developed a remarkably varied adaptation of laboratory methods in presenting the results of study and investigation. This is possible partly because of the increasing adequacy of the laboratory equipment of the local high schools. Extension courses in home economics frequently give considerable attention to practical demonstrations of the processes discussed in class. Engineering subjects are thus presented, as well as physics, chemistry, and other sciences. The same methods are often used in lecture series, short courses, institutes, and conferences, adding definite concrete instruction to extension work that otherwise may be merely suggestive, entertaining, or of a mildly intellectual character.

Used by the following universities: Arkansas, California, Colorado, Illinois, Iowa, Indiana, Kansas, Oklahoma, and Wisconsin.

Special visual instruction.—Exhibits consisting of actual materials, such as collections of minerals, or the various parts of machines and the different kinds of raw or manufactured materials involved in some industrial process, are sent to schools where the teachers use them in classroom instruction. The exhibits are designed to fit into the regular course of study pursued by the pupils. Lantern slides, motion-picture films, stereoscopic views, prints, and pictures of many different kinds are utilized also as supplements to classroom study. They are also used extensively as regular school material.

Used by the following universities: California, Indiana, Michigan, Pittsburgh, Oregon, South Dakota, and Wisconsin.

Merchants' short courses.—The short course for the farmer is a well-known instructional method developed by the agricultural colleges. Less well known but even more effective are the intensive lectures and discussions arranged for certain groups of merchants in the towns and cities. Such practical subjects as advertising, window display, bookkeeping system, etc., are treated by specialists, who, in lecture and conference, apply the principles to the peculiar difficulties of the men who attend the course.

Teacher-training courses.—The extension work done for public-school teachers varies from State to State and in many local communities. Sometimes the subject like the junior high school is offered in an extended series of lectures and discussion at intervals of a week or two throughout a year or more; other subjects are offered daily in the evening or afternoon. Most frequently, however, teacher-training courses are given in classes that meet once a week. A large proportion of courses for teachers given in residence are also offered in extension classes.

Public service.—Various phrases, such as *public service, public welfare service, department of general information and welfare,* are used to designate comprehensively certain groups of activities which are not definitely standardized or formal, like correspondence study and class instruction. Surveys, investigations, conferences, exhibits, institutes, publications, and many other devices and activities of university extension can not be readily grouped together in a rigid classification, but they all have one element in common, that of service to the public, a service that is relatively free to any person in the groups directly aided.

Institutes and short courses.—Institutes are specially prepared programs on certain topics, devices to inform large groups of people concerning special problems. Short courses are similar to institutes but are usually intended for smaller groups.

A *community institute* usually involves:

(a) Conferences with commercial club members and city officials on the chief needs of the community.

(b) Survey by specialists; preliminary meetings with local committees.

(c) A program of several days' duration arranged to attract every age and occupational group possible.

(d) The community problems presented by local men and women and by the university specialists through lectures, exhibits, demonstrations, etc.

(e) The formulation of plans for meeting the problems and first steps to carry them out.

(f) Follow-up work from the university.

A trade institute is similar to ordinary conferences held by any association, except that much of the organization is done by the university.

Used by the following universities: Arkansas, Colorado, Florida, Georgia, Illinois, Indiana, Kansas, Kentucky, Minnesota, Nevada, New Mexico, North Carolina, Utah, West Virginia, and Wisconsin.

Conferences.—Frequently universities arrange programs of discussion on topics of interest to special professional groups or of importance to the general public. Such conferences differ from community institutes in that they deal usually with but one general problem and usually they are technical and intensive. However, the conference is sometimes designed to arouse popular interest in some specific problem, such as tax reform, revision of the State constitution, child welfare, and housing.

Used by the following universities: Colorado, Florida, Georgia, Indiana, Iowa, Kansas, Michigan, New Mexico, North Carolina, West Virginia, and Wisconsin.

General information service.—The extension staff utilizes the personal and library resources of the university to answer inquiries of all sorts, from specific requests for the facts concerning public utilities, the history of railroad legislation, or communicable disease, to general requests for material on the causes of the war, the problems of reconstruction, the theories of astronomy, or how to equip a home.

Used by the following universities: Arizona, Arkansas, Idaho, Iowa, Kansas, Kentucky, Michigan, Missouri, Montana, Nebraska, New Mexico, Oklahoma, and Utah.

Business service.—Various kinds of assistance are rendered business men besides the merchants' short courses, which offer instruction in merchandizing, retail selling, etc. Information on particular business problems is furnished through bulletins, package libraries, and printed circulars. Some extension divisions give direct aid in the organization and development of commercial clubs or chambers of commerce.

Used by the following universities: Arkansas, Colorado, Iowa, Oklahoma, Pittsburgh, Utah, Washington, and Wisconsin.

Municipal reference.—Bureaus of municipal reference serve especially officials of town and city. They also cooperate with voluntary associations like civic clubs and chambers of commerce in their work of community development. The bureaus furnish information on special municipal problems. They hold conferences and publish bulletins on municipal affairs.

Used by the following universities: California, Cincinnati, Indiana, Iowa, Kansas, Michigan, Minnesota, Oklahoma, Washington, and Wisconsin.

Library service.—Books, pamphlets, and other printed matter are lent to individuals and groups. Some divisions circulate traveling libraries and undertake other work usually done by State library commissions.

Used by the universities of California, Michigan, Nevada, and Wyoming.

Package library service.—Small packages of up-to-date printed matter on questions or topics of current public interest are mailed to borrowers in the State. Debatable questions are presented by well-balanced selection of authoritative materials.

Used by the following universities: Arkansas, Idaho, Indiana, Iowa, Kentucky, Missouri, Montana, North Dakota, Oklahoma, Oregon, South Carolina, South Dakota, Virginia, and Wisconsin.

Discussion and debate service.—Special debate bulletins are printed and widely distributed. Contests between groups are organized, subjects of discussion suggested, references provided, briefs outlined, printed matter supplied. Most extension divisions assist or direct State high-school discussion leagues. Speakers are furnished to civic clubs, forums, parent-teacher associations, merchants' conferences, city councils, city clubs.

Used by the following universities: Alabama, Arizona, California, Florida, Georgia, Idaho, Indiana, Iowa, Kentucky, Maryland, Michigan, Minnesota, Nebraska, Nevada, New Mexico, North Carolina, Oklahoma, Oregon, South Carolina, South Dakota, Tennessee, Virginia, and Wisconsin.

Visual instruction.—The use of motion pictures, lantern slides, maps, exhibits of all kinds for conveying information, for technical instruction, for recreation, entertainment, and esthetic enjoyment. These materials are lent to clubs and institutions and circulated in the State. The following are common types of exhibits: Welfare exhibits on community topics, health, play, recreation, sanitation, gardening, landscape architecture, child welfare, public-health nursing, road building; industrial exhibits, safety appliances, wood and forestry materials, minerals, textiles; art exhibits, framed drawings, etchings, oil paintings, prints, copies of masterpieces.

The motion-picture service has developed under considerable difficulties, chief of which was the lack of a central collecting and distributing center for the whole country. Few universities have the financial resources necessary to support an extensive service. This difficulty has been partially met through an arrangement whereby the United States Bureau of Education maintains a film-distribution service to continue the work started by the temporary visual instruction section of the Federal division of educational extension. In 1919 the division supplied 4,000,000 feet of films to 38 distributing centers, including 29 State university extension divisions.

Used by the following universities: Alabama, Arizona, Arkansas, California, Colorado, Georgia, Idaho, Indiana, Iowa, Kansas, Massachusetts, Michigan, Minnesota, Mississippi, Missouri, Nebraska, Nevada, New York, North Carolina, North Dakota, Oklahoma, Oregon, Pittsburgh, South Dakota, Tennessee, Texas, Utah, Virginia, West Virginia, and Wisconsin.

Lyceum service.—Lectures, concerts, and entertainments of various kinds are secured for local committees by the extension division, acting as a clearing house for "talent." Some divisions organize circuits of Chautauquas.

Used by the following universities: Arkansas, Indiana, Kansas, Minnesota, Missouri, Montana, North Dakota, Utah, and Wisconsin.

Community center.—Community centers, originally called social centers, are local autonomous organizations designed to increase the number and effectiveness of activities which bring the people of a district together. The general idea behind the community-center movement is that of securing more cooperation between neighbors in the solution of community problems.

Extension divisions assist the movement by holding conferences, and community institutes, conducting investigations and social surveys, furnishing programs, speakers, exhibits, and other aids to local organizations, especially in developing the wider use of the public schools. The Wisconsin division was the first to organize systematic service in this field.

Used by the following universities: Colorado, Indiana, Kansas, Minnesota, North Carolina, Oregon, Texas, and Wisconsin.

Community drama and music.—Extension divisions assist local organizations in the development of entertainments, dramatic productions, and group singing, because of their value in encouraging local talent and in improving the tone of community life.

Lists of plays are printed and distributed, as well as practical bulletins giving directions for staging plays and for producing pageants and entertainment programs. Several divisions furnish the services of directors of community singing for special occasions. Others lend phonograph records, descriptions of folk games and dances, and organize literary and musical contests.

Used by the following universities: Indiana, Iowa, North Carolina, North Dakota, Oregon, and Wisconsin.

Americanization work.—Cooperation with various agencies in their efforts to assist the foreign born and to promote general understanding of American ideals. Practically all of the work of extension divisions may be regarded as important in this connection. The training of teachers of the foreign born and the holding of conferences for community welfare are two distinct types of Americanization work undertaken by extension divisions.

Used by the following universities: California, Colorado, Indiana, Kentucky, Massachusetts, Minnesota, Pittsburgh, and Wisconsin.

The following is a condensed description of the work of the Massachusetts department of university extension in Americanization:

In July, 1918, the department gave a summer course in "Methods of teaching English to immigrants." The membership of this class consisted of 35 teachers.

Since that time more than 2,000 teachers have been trained to give instruction to non-English speaking men and women. For the further development of this work additional funds were needed. The legislature appropriated $10,000.

According to the new legislation, cities and towns in Massachusetts are to be remunerated by the State at the end of each school year for one-half of their expenditures for immigrant education, including salaries of teachers.

During the winter classes were conducted in many cities and towns, and in the summer the course in the "Methods of teaching English to immigrants" was repeated, with the addition of a course in "Organization and supervision of Americanization."

Fifty-four cities and towns in Massachusetts were represented, and there were enrolled in addition students from five other States. Last year there was a total enrollment of only 35; this summer the enrollment totaled 111 students.

In addition there were conducted in various cities and towns 28 classes, consisting of foremen, leaders, and others holding responsible positions in different industries.

Child welfare.—Like health propaganda, the promotion of child welfare is a widespread undertaking which involves the utilization of practically all university extension devices. The most distinctive activity is the children's health conference, which consists of lectures, conferences, exhibits, physical examination of children, and consultations with parents. The community is given assistance in providing for permanent improvements in local conditions affecting children.

In several cases the divisions cooperate with State boards, child-welfare committees, parent-teacher associations, and other organizations.

Used in the following universities: Colorado, Indiana, Iowa, Kansas, Oklahoma, Texas, and Wisconsin.

Employment service.—Several divisions undertake the work of finding positions for university students and graduates, especially the placing of teachers. Other divisions assist incidentally the university officers who have charge of appointments.

Used in the universities of Oregon, Pittsburgh, and Washington.

Publications.—The publications of extension divisions are of various kinds. Most often they consist of circulars and pamphlets. Several divisions publish a regular series of bulletins, including announcements, programs, and popular informational discussions or essays on welfare topics. Frequently the proceedings of conferences and reports of surveys and investigations are printed as bulletins.

The extension division of Utah publishes the *Utah Educational Review;* North Carolina issues the *University News Letter;* North Dakota has issued a *News Bulletin.* The *Extension Monitor,* of Oregon, is a well-established periodical. The Washington division printed for a period the *University Extension Journal* as well as a special monthly bulletin entitled *Better Business.*

Service to schools.—All divisions cooperate directly with the teachers and officials of the public schools. Special courses of instruction are provided more often for teachers than for any other professional group. Many kinds of special aids to class room instruction are offered, including visual instruction materials, such as exhibits, maps, lantern slides, and motion pictures, advisory service in problems of school administration, assistance in preparing programs for school meetings, demonstrations of methods of teaching, etc.

Several divisions assist teachers in educational measurements. Others direct reading circle work, train teachers for vocational instruction in cooperation with the Federal Board of Vocational Education, and supervise or direct the training of Americanization workers, Boy Scout masters, Camp Fire guardians, and playground workers. In many States the divisions furnish instructors for county and city teachers' institutes.

The following definitions differ somewhat from those usually given to extension activities. The four activities or methods defined constitute the "Instruments of extension teaching," according to Wm. H. Lighty. In this classification *Extension teaching* is synonymous with *University extension.*[1]

Correspondence-study teaching.—The avenue of first consideration in extension teaching is that which addresses itself to those who can and choose to take up systematic, consecutive studies in which there is a continuous teacher and learner rela-

---

[1] Report of Dean of Extension Division, Univ. of Wis., Madison, 1918. Wm. H. Lighty, acting dean.

153448°—20——4

tionship. All such work is classified as correspondence-study teaching, whether it is done wholly by mail, and, therefore, at long distances; whether it is done in local class and conference groups; or whether it is conducted through any combination of degrees of use of either method.

Lyceum teaching.—The second avenue of university extension is that of lyceum teaching—platform instruction and inspiration.

Forum teaching.—The third avenue is found in the forum method of teaching conducted through the department of debating and public discussion.

Bureau teaching.—The fourth avenue is through the bureau method of teaching, by which the widest and most far-reaching forms of social leadership and social service are possible. Its methods are the least set or fixed, and its possibilities cover the widest range of educational service, whether through suggestion, stimulation, propaganda, and direction for the advancement of individuals and communities, or in response to the requests for information and instruction on the part of those already conscious of their needs.

THE CONTENT OF EXTENSION.

Necessarily most discussions of university extension deal with methods, kinds of activities, modes of organization and work, instead of with subjects, topics, and the specific content of instruction and service. Some extension directors believe that this failure to emphasize content is a mistake that might be avoided; that university extension should concentrate its attention on specific interests rather than on methods of teaching and propaganda.

Accordingly, it is contended that the properly organized extension division should have departments similar to those of the university teaching departments of sociology, economics, hygiene, fine arts, and the others. Instead of bureaus of correspondence study and class study in a department of extension teaching, the division should have many bureaus to correspond with the subject taught. Instead of bureaus of general information, public discussion, lectures, and visual instruction in a department of public welfare, the division should have bureaus of health, child welfare, municipal sanitation, food conservation, good roads, community center development, school improvement, markets, consumers' cooperation, and bureaus to correspond to other concerns of prime interest and importance.

There is considerable attraction to this point of view. Extension directors recognize the power of concrete ideas like good health or good roads. The campaign method of doing educational work has its value, and some subjects, like health, readily lend themselves to propaganda methods.

The following two sections on health and engineering are intended to give in some detail a survey of two fields of work which emphasize subject matter rather than method. Similar descriptions could be written of community center service, child welfare work, Americanization, community music extension, and economic betterment.

EXTENSION IN HEALTH.

One of the first fields of propaganda and instruction through various devices of university extension was that of health. Ever since the beginning of university extension, lectures and popular talks on health topics were given in many States by university instructors. The lectures deal with a large number of subjects, such as the following: Municipal and domestic sanitation, community recreation, water supply, garbage disposal, mental hygiene, medical inspection, physical handicaps of children, child hygiene, care of the teeth, prenatal care, first aid.

51

Lantern-slide sets, illustrating much the same topics as are treated in the lectures, are lent to individuals and organizations. Some of the more common topics thus illustrated are: Fresh-air schools, care of babies, the house fly, school hygiene.

In addition to lectures and lantern slides on health subjects, extension divisions have developed the exhibit to instruct the public. They have also used motion-picture films, stereoscopic views, microscopic slides, and pictures of every kind, as well as the clinic, the conference, the institute, and other informative methods to acquaint the people with the facts and principles of hygiene, sanitation, and other health problems.

Accordingly, health work of the university extension is not a distinct field, for it merges into various fields of extension practice. It is not practicable to mark off definitely the scope of health extension. It is connected with many general community problems like those of milk supply, water supply, pure food, and with even more general problems like those of play and recreation, child welfare, and home economics. One principle, however, runs through all of the work—the principle that educational propaganda should aim at the preventative rather than the curative handling of disease. Not much attention has been given by the extension divisions to instruction in medicine and surgery and clinical practice, though some attempt has been made to give instruction in practical nursing and the application of physical culture to remedial defects.

COURSES IN HEALTH.

The following institutions give general courses of instruction in hygiene and related subjects: University of California, University of Chicago, Indiana University, University of Kansas, Connecticut Valley Colleges, Boston College, University of Missouri, University of Nebraska, University of North Carolina, Columbia University, Peabody College for Teachers, University of Utah, and the University of Wisconsin. In most of these institutions the work is administered by the extension divisions.

New York University offers a correspondence course in public health. The catalogue describes the course as follows:

This course requires one week's residence in New York, the balance of the work being taken by correspondence. A new course begins each year on October 1, but health officers may commence at any time and finish at any time. The minimum number of hours of home study is 300, and the subjects are those selected by the Public Health Council. The reading matter consists of about 3,000 printed pages. Those taking the course must designate at least one month in advance what days are to be spent in the city, so that suitable arrangements may be made for inspections and laboratory work. Those who are able to do so are invited to attend as much of the summer-residence course as possible without extra charge.

The subject matter to be covered may be conveniently grouped as follows: Communicable diseases, bacteriology, legal questions of sanitation and treatment of nuisances, infant and child hygiene, schools, milk, foods, water, sewerage and sewage disposal, housing and industrial hygiene, vital statistics, quarantine, tuberculosis.

The following is a partial list of courses given by different institutions. The courses are offered usually through class extension. Sometimes the classes are given instruction through a series of lectures by several different specialists rather than by a single instructor.

Boston University.—Personal and public hygiene.

University of California.—First aid, domestic hygiene, Red Cross courses, courses in dietetics, sanitation, eugenics, motherhood, and public health.

University of Chicago.—Public hygiene.

Columbia University.—Nursing, psychology for nurses and social workers, child hygiene, public health, school hygiene.

Connecticut Valley Colleges.—Physiology and hygiene.

Indiana University.—Hygiene with special reference to the school child, dietetics, public health.

University of Kansas.—Prenatal hygiene, infant hygiene, home nursing, hygiene and sanitation.

University of Missouri.—Preventive medicine.

University of Nebraska.—First aid, home nursing, surgical dressing, dietetics.

University of North Carolina.—School hygiene.

Peabody College for Teachers.—Health teaching, health inspection in schools, mental hygiene, health problems.

University of Utah.—Public health, preventive medicine, health work in schools.

University of Wisconsin.—Home nursing, the prospective mother, the child in health, the child in disease, infants' clothes, study of the human body, health officers' work.

SPECIAL COURSES AND OTHER HEALTH WORK.

The extension divisions have developed several types of health instruction in addition to formal courses given in class and by correspondence. These types include vocational courses, expert service in various lines, and special devices for propaganda. The following institutions have such types of service: University of Colorado, Columbia University, Indiana University, University of Iowa, University of Michigan, University of Minnesota, Akron University, and the Universities of Oklahoma, Texas, Utah, Virginia, Washington, and Wisconsin.

University of Colorado.—The extension division provides single lectures and lecture courses on health subjects.

Lantern slides on public health are loaned to individuals and organizations in the State.

The division offers a four years' course for physicians and health officials. The work is conducted by correspondence throughout most of the year, supplemented by six weeks of residence work, including laboratory instruction during the summer. Students receive a certificate of public health on completion of the course.

At the sociology conference held at the university part of the sessions are devoted to public health.

Courses in clinical methods are offered to practicing physicians, nurses, and laboratory assistants to physicians.

The bureau of community welfare gives health information and instruction through community institutes and exhibits. Child welfare institutes are conducted in different parts of the State.

Columbia University.—The university gives courses in optometry and oral hygiene. The extension division has charge of the premedical work of students in the Long Island College Hospital.

Indiana University.—The extension division does propaganda work in health through all of its activities: Lectures, exhibits, demonstrations, conferences, and community institutes. It lends a number of lantern-slide sets and motion pictures on health subjects.

The supervisor of play and recreation works directly with the school officials of the State. The proceedings of conferences on play and recreation are published in bulletins.

The division cooperates with the State board of health, the board of State charities, and the State child welfare committee and with other organizations in health education.

The division was the first to cooperate with the Federal Children's Bureau in the weighing and measuring of children of preschool age. The work usually goes by the name of Children's Health Conferences. It was originally done in connection with community institutes held in the smaller cities of the State. Through the State child welfare committee this work was expanded to include most of the features of the children's year program of the Federal bureau.

Surveys of health conditions in small towns are made by university specialists. Some practical investigations of specific health and welfare undertakings in different communities have been made. The division has published a bulletin describing methods of feeding school children.

University of Iowa.—The child welfare research station at the university was established to study methods of child conservation. It cooperates with the extension division in disseminating the results of its investigations. The division holds child welfare and general social welfare conferences and institutes, at which considerable attention is given to health.

The social surveys conducted by the division include investigations of local health conditions.

University of Michigan.—The extension division offers lectures on a large number of subjects. The public health service includes, besides lectures, dental clinics, laboratory and hospital service, and service of the Pasteur Institute.

University of Minnesota.—Short courses are conducted for dentists. Health lectures on 23 different subjects are offered to the public.

University of Oklahoma.—The extension division provides lectures on health. It lends lantern slides and other visual materials.

In connection with community institutes and conferences, the division gives instruction in hygiene, sanitation, and child welfare.

University of Texas.—The extension division offers lectures by members of the faculty. The division of school interests cooperates with the State public health association in conducting community programs which give considerable attention to health matters.

University of Utah.—The extension division conducts State-wide campaigns for the promotion of physical welfare. Short health institutes are held in various parts of the State. The division holds conferences and institutes for child welfare. Most of the work is under the direction of a department of public health and preventive medicine.

The department reports that health institutes were conducted in the spring of 1919 in over 60 different places in the State. The number of lectures given varied from 1 to 21 at the different institutes and a total of over 15,000 people were reached. The department has issued a valuable report on the medical inspection of 346 school children in the Riverside school district of Salt Lake City. A number of bulletins have been issued on health topics. The following is a statement of the policy and methods of the health service.[1]

POLICY.

To push the work of health education in every legitimate way.

To make health education as complete and as far-reaching as possible.

To be patient with the laity and not expect immediate results, but keep at it.

To assume an attitude toward the medical profession that will merit their respect, confidence, and cooperation.

To render a real service to the people of the State.

WORK.

To train, not to treat.

To point the way leading to perfect health.

To extend a helping hand to those in need of advice or health education.

To prevent the preventable both in disease and physical defects.

To create in the minds of all classes a desire for physical fitness.

To make each generation stronger and better than the preceding one.

BULLETINS.

Should be as nearly accurate as possible from literary, educational, and scientific standpoints.

Should meet the demands of Utah. They should be adapted to the laity in rural districts rather than the slums of large cities.

Should be comprehensive in presentation, simple in language, and useful in subject matter.

Should aim at building up the reputation of the university for usefulness, not the building up of a practice for the author.

Should be ethical and should be conspicuous for their lack of advertisement either of preparation, methods, or men.

Should be free from criticisms of the medical profession, the nurses, or of anybody. Should breathe a spirit of service and helpfulness, not condemnation.

University of Virginia.—The university offers lectures on health subjects. It also sends a special representative to different communities in the State who assists in conducting school hygiene campaigns. He inspects school conditions and advises with officials and patrons.

University of Washington.—The extension division conducts graduate medical and dental courses and clinics with the assistance of local specialists.

The division has cooperated with the War Camp Community Service in instruction in social hygiene, also with nurses associations, in teaching the principles of public health nursing.

University of Wisconsin.—Most of the health work of the extension division is done through the bureau of health instruction, which conducts a press service, furnishes exhibits, and supplies lectures on health. The division cooperates with the State board of health and the Anti-Tuberculosis Association as well as with other organizations.

---

[1] Quoted from mimeograph leaflet of the University of Utah, 1919.

The department of general information and welfare conducts community institutes, children's health conferences, and local surveys. During the war the department organized Red Cross home service institutes and chapter courses.

The division publishes attractive bulletins on health subjects. It circulates extensively lantern slide sets, motion pictures, and other visual instruction materials for health propaganda in the State.

SUBJECTS OF BULLETINS.

Many extension divisions publish special pamphlets or bulletins dealing with public health, sanitation, and related problems. The following is a short list of a number of bulletins published by different extension divisions:

Colorado University.—Protection against typhoid. Municipal water supplies of Colorado. Insanity, its nature and causes.

University of Iowa.—Child welfare surveys. Hygienic conditions in Iowa schools. Iowa handbook on child welfare.

Indiana University.—How to conduct children's health conferences. Feeding of children at school.

University of Kansas.—Constructive juvenile effort in Kansas.

University of Missouri.—The feeding of children. Feeding the baby. The house fly.

University of Oklahoma.—A healthier world. The conservation of life.

University of Texas.—Food for infants and growing children. Pure milk and how to get it. Cleanliness and health.

University of Utah.—Infant mortality.

University of Wisconsin.—Guarding the public health. Nursing as a vocation. Wisconsin baby week. Some aspects of feeblemindedness in Wisconsin Chart on communicable diseases.

EXTENSION WORK IN ENGINEERING.[1]

By J. J. SCHLICHER.

Nearly all the extension work done in engineering is offered by the general extension divisions of the various institutions. Only in a few cases are the courses in engineering directly under the management of the engineering departments, and this is usually true of institutions which do not have a fully developed and unified extension system. Where such a system is maintained, and especially in the systems of the State universities, the work in engineering receives the same benefit as other work in the way of lectures, institutes, bulletins, visual instruction, expert advice, etc

The great bulk of the instruction in engineering, as in other subjects, is given in detached courses. A list of institutions giving such instruction follows. Those marked with a star give a more extensive list of such courses than the others.

University of Arizona, Tucson.
University of Arkansas, Fayetteville.
*University of California, Berkeley.
University of Colorado, Boulder.
Georgia School of Technology, Atlanta.
University of Idaho, Moscow.
Bradley Polytechnic Institute, Peoria.
*University of Iowa, Iowa City.

*Iowa State College of Agriculture and Mechanic Arts, Ames.
*University of Kansas, Lawrence.
*Johns Hopkins University, Baltimore.
*Massachusetts Board of Education, Extension Department, Boston.
Lowell Institute, Boston.
*Franklin Union, Boston.

[1] This chapter is a copy of a mimeograph bulletin prepared by Dr. J. J. Schlicher for the Division of Educational Extension, U. S. Bureau of Education, May, 1919.

*Northeastern College—Y. M. C. A., Boston.
*University of Minnesota, Minneapolis.
University of Missouri, Columbia.
*Washington University, St. Louis.
University of Nebraska, Lincoln.
Rutgers College, New Brunswick.
University of New Mexico, Albuquerque.
*Polytechnic Institute of Brooklyn.
*Columbia University, New York.
Union College, Schenectady.
Syracuse University, Syracuse.
University of North Carolina, Chapel Hill.
University of North Dakota, Grand Forks.
*University of Akron, Akron, Ohio.

*University of Cincinnati.
University of Oklahoma, Norman.
Carnegie Institute of Technology, Pittsburgh.
Lehigh University, Bethlehem.
Lafayette College, Easton, Pa.
*Pennsylvania State College, State College, Pa.
University of Pittsburgh.
Rhode Island State College, Kingston. .
Brown University, Providence.
*University of Texas Austin.
*University of Utah, Salt Lake City.
University of Washington, Seattle.
*University of Wisconsin, Madison.
University of Wyoming, Laramie.

A great number of different courses are offered. Among them the following are offered by three or more institutions. Courses which are not strictly technical, like those in various branches of mathematics, chemistry, and physics, have been omitted, even when they were especially adapted to the needs of engineering students.

Automobiles.
Architectural drawing and design.
Applied mathematics and mechanics.
Bridge design and construction.
Descriptive geometry.
Engineering mechanics.
Engines.
Electrical machinery.
Gas engines.
Heating and ventilation.
Highway engineering and road building.
Lumber and its uses.
Mechanical drawing.
Machine drawing.
Machine design.
Materials of construction.
Power plant testing.

Plumbing.
Reinforced concrete construction and design.
Refrigeration.
Railroad curves and earthwork.
Shop practice.
Surveying.
Strength of materials.
Steam engines and engineering.
Shop mathematics.
Sheet metal work and drafting.
Shop drawing and designing.
Structural design and drafting.
Telegraphy.
Telephony.
Wireless telegraphy.
Wiring.

Courses given by two institutions.—Automobile electricity, building construction, builder's and carpenter's estimating, engineering materials, engineering mathematics, electrical transmission, electrical power distribution and illumination, electric traction and transmission, electric meters, electric lamps and illumination, foundation and masonry construction, gas producers, irrigation, metallurgy, mining and milling, power plant economics, railroad engineering, sanitary engineering, structural steel drafting and design, structural mechanics, steel building construction, sewage disposal, turbines, testing of materials, works management.

Courses given by one institution.—Automobile mechanics, automobile engineering, contracts and specifications, carpenter's and builder's drawing, coal mining, concrete tests, cable telegraphy, construction of electrical apparatus, central electrical stations, compressed air, cupola practice, drainage, electrical shop work, electrical practice, elements of structures, engine testing, electrical drafting, estimating for architects and builders, electric railways, distribution systems, electric measurements, electric engineering mathematics, electrical contracting, electrotechnology, electrical design, engine running, electrical measuring instruments, electrical equipment of power plants, furniture making, foundry metallurgy, field astronomy, firing, fuels, gas practice, gas engine theory and design, gas engine ignition, gas power, graphics, graphic statics, household electricity, hydraulic engineering, heating and lighting for janitors, instrumental drawing, loft practice, locomotive engineering, locomotive maintenance, locomotive operation, logging railroads, map drawing, mechanical drafting, marine engineering, mechanics of materials, power plant design, power plant calculations, power plant operation, practical physics, pattern making, pavements, practical mechanics, plotting and computing, railroad drawing, seamanship and ordnance, shop mechanics, stationary engines, shop calculations, shop sketching, test methods, wireless telephony, works engineering, water power engineering, water supply.

In addition to these courses, extension work in engineering exhibits several well-defined characteristics which deserve to be mentioned. Most of these are due to the peculiarly close connection between instructional and occupational work in this line.

Part-time courses.—Various ways are adopted of combining the two. A variation, usually an abbreviation, of the regular four-year course is sometimes given, usually in the evening, to those who are employed during the rest of the day. Lowell Institute (Boston), under the auspices of the Massachusetts Institute of Technology, conducts a free evening school for industrial foremen, comprising an electrical, a mechanical, and a building course. Northeastern College (Boston Y. M. C. A.) offers two four-year courses—a part-time day course and an evening course—in mechanical, civil, structural, electrical, and chemical engineering. The University of Minnesota extension division gives groups of courses in architecture and in civil, mechanical, and electrical engineering. The work is given in the evening and extends over two to three years. The University of Wisconsin extension division suggests various groupings of its engineering courses, the groups consisting of from 4 to 10 courses each. The combinations are determined by the special requirements of some occupation. Thus there is a machine-design group, a gas-engine group, a refrigeration group, etc.

Cooperation.—An extensive form of cooperation, not usually classed as extension work, is carried on in engineering by the municipal universities of Cincinnati and Akron, and the Georgia School of Technology. This is the well-known plan of dividing the students into two sections, which alternate, two weeks at work and two weeks in the class. The requirements for entrance and graduation are virtually the same as for students taking the regular four-year course. Naturally, more time is required to complete the course. In the University of Cincinnati five years are fixed as the length of the course on the cooperative plan, the work continuing through 11 months of the year. A similar arrangement exists at the Georgia School of Technology.

The two institutions in Ohio, being supported by the cities in which they are located, also perform an extensive service in giving expert advice and in cooperating along this line with the industries of the city and with the city government. A similar form of cooperation exists in the University of Pittsburgh and New York University. The extension evening classes of the Georgia School of Technology are supported by appropriations granted by the city council of Atlanta.

Mining courses.—Several institutions which have not hitherto gone extensively, if at all, into the field of extension work, maintain a special form of this work in connection with the mines of the State. This is true of the Universities of Arizona, Kentucky, Nevada, and West Virginia, and of Pennsylvania State College.

In Arizona this work is conducted by the State Bureau of Mines, which is under the direction of the board of regents of the university. In addition to its more technical work, the bureau makes a study, for example, of recreation, organizations, and living conditions at the mines, and maintains a free film service and an information service. Some members of its staff are constantly in the field.

In Kentucky, classes are formed at the mines by the department of mines and metallurgy of the university. Besides lectures to disseminate information on the mineral resources of the State, courses of study are mapped out for the classes, examinations are given, and a certificate is awarded for the satisfactory completion of the work.

The Tonapah (Nevada) School of Mines gives secondary instruction in mining and milling subjects for those who wish to advance themselves without giving up their regular vocations. Classes are taught morning and evening to accommodate those changing shifts.

The engineering extension department of Pennsylvania State College cooperates with shop officers, the Y. M. C. A., the railroads, chambers of commerce, trade-unions, etc., in organizing classes and supplying books and instructors in engineering for men engaged in work, especially those who have not had a high-school education. Each course consists of 20 weekly assignments. The chief aim is to present the fundamentals of engineering in each case. A number of such courses are offered in mechanical, electrical, civil, and industrial engineering.

In West Virginia, instruction in mining centers is carried on jointly by a university instructor and a local instructor, usually a superintendent or foreman at the mine. The instructor from the university visits each center once or twice a month, giving supplementary lectures and demonstrations, and showing slides and films. Safety, sanitation, domestic science, etc., are also emphasized.

Institutes.—Professional institutes and short courses and expert information are often given, even by institutions which have no extension organization. Thus the Georgia School of Technology gives a three days' course in highway engineering for practicing engineers, and sends special information on request. The department of ceramic engineering in the University of Illinois offers a two weeks' industrial course in the principles underlying the manufacture of clay products, in cooperation with the clay and allied industries. It consists of lectures, laboratory work, practice in firing kilns, and discussion. The University of Michigan offers the advantages of its municipal, sanitary, and highway laboratories to the people and municipalities for making tests of materials, water, etc. A week's course in highway engineering is also given, consisting of lectures by experts. The University of Nevada gives a four weeks' prospector's course in prospecting, assaying, hygiene, etc., and laboratory work. The University of West Virginia conducts a four-day conference on good roads at the university, followed by a three-day school for general instruction in various parts of the State.

Work along all these lines is, of course, done by other institutions also, which maintain a complete extension system, including class and lecture work, a general information service, institutes, and conferences, visual instruction, etc. This includes the State universities listed and the Iowa State College of Engineering and Mechanic Arts, which has also established an extension system on the same lines as the State universities.

THE EXTENT OF EXTENSION SERVICE.

The activities of general university extension are exceedingly varied, and, with the exception of correspondence study and class study, not very definitely standardized. Accordingly, it is very difficult to give exact figures on the extent of service and the number of people served through the various activities. Even in the case of extension centers and classes held in different cities of the State, enrollment figures are hard to classify. In some institutions students in extension classes are listed informally, and do not appear in the statistical tables of the university. This is especially true of lecture courses in subjects not given for credit. Fairly exact figures can be obtained for correspondence-study students, though even here the same difficulty appears as in the case of class extension. Frequently students take correspondence-study courses without any intention of securing credit, and their names may not be listed in the enrollment figures. In addition, correspondence students may register any time in the year, and frequently they obtain extension of time, so that at any one date it can not be stated with exactness how many bona fide students are taking work.

Perhaps the best way to indicate the number of correspondence students in a single institution is to give a summary statement of all those who have enrolled during a certain period. For example, the correspondence-study department of Chicago reported May 1, 1919, that it has reached nearly 21,000 persons during the past 27 years. It is offering 450 credit courses in 40 different subjects. "It has made higher education possible to tens of thousands through pioneer work in university extension."

The Massachusetts department of university extension reports that in the courses by correspondence and the courses taken in classes the potential active enrollment on March 1, 1919, was 13,827. The enrollment from the establishment of the department, in January, 1916, to March 1, 1918, totaled 22,115.

The table following is a compilation of some of the reports furnished, September, 1919, in response to a questionnaire concerning the estimated number of persons served by extension divisions. Other reports contained figures which did not lend themselves to classification. In most cases the figures given in the table are necessarily approximate. They do not give a complete estimate of all the services, because data are seldom available for all items covered by the column heads. They include only the work of the organized extension services and not that of the university as a whole.

60

Column 2 includes all credit and noncredit extension class instruction and correspondence study of all kinds.

Column 3 includes lectures, single and in series, concerts, chautauquas, etc.

Column 4 includes all slides, films, exhibits, expositions.

Column 5 includes all services to clubs, package-library service, debates, etc.

Column 6 includes institutes, conferences, short courses, consultations.

Column 7 gives number of requests for information answered (other than by package libraries), and includes municipal reference, special bibliographies, etc.

Estimated number of persons served by 17 institutions, in the activities named, 1918–19.

Extension division or service.	Extension classes and correspondence study.	Lectures, concerts, etc.	Visual instruction.	Discussion and club service.	Institutes and conferences.	General information.	Number of copies of bulletins distributed.
University of Arkansas	1,584	(1)	165,000	1,900	(1)	15,000	60,000
College of the City of New York	3,660	25,500	(1)	(1)	(1)	(1)	(1)
University of Denver	256	20,000	(1)	1,400	(1)	(1)	8,500
Indiana University	2,256	25,100	43,000	19,969	101,250	3,000	30,000
University of Iowa	150	8,000	18,000	1,000	2,500	1,500	50,000
Massachusetts commission	1,184	(1)	(1)	(1)	(1)	(1)	(1)
Massachusetts department of university extension	15,450	(1)	(1)	(1)	3,500	600	50,000
University of Michigan	400	90,000	50,000	35,000	(1)	5,000	8,000
University of Missouri	607	7,500	10,000	15,000	(1)	2,000	5,000
University of Montana	130	20,000	12,000	1,695	(1)	121	500
University of Oklahoma	3,111	119,200	360,000	168,000	460	1,800	251,400
University of Oregon	1,400	120,000	80,000	15,000	1,000	800	25,000
Pennsylvania State College	3,900	(1)	(1)	(1)	300	500	2,000
University of Pittsburgh	437	13,000	607,502	31,800	(1)	(1)	50,000
University of South Dakota	400	(1)	5,000	5,500	(1)	(1)	1,500
University of Texas	1,360	50,000	116,100	488,445	18,500	23,801	290,000
University of Virginia	(1)	30,000	15,000	40,000	20,000	2,500	35,000
Total	36,285	529,300	1,481,602	819,709	147,510	56,622	

1 Activity not undertaken, or no report.
2 Correspondence study not included.
3 Classes not included.
4 236 schools served.
5 Figures for 1917–18.
6 Includes only class instruction and not other extramural work.
7 Includes 16 institutions.
8 Includes 12 institutions.
9 Includes 13 institutions.
10 Includes 8 institutions.

The following tabulated statements of the work of several extension divisions indicate approximately the number of persons affected by the different services.

UNIVERSITY OF MINNESOTA, EXTENSION DIVISION, 1917–1919.

Number of semester registrations in evening extension classes................ 5,118
Number of registrations in short courses..................................... 505
New registrations in correspondence courses................................. 386
Towns having lyceum courses... 354
Entertainments given on these courses....................................... 1,684

Single date addresses of various kinds..................................... 92
Towns using lantern slides.. 94
Sets of lantern slides used by these towns................................ 622
Towns using drama service.. 360
Plays sent out to these towns... 3,105
Towns served by the Municipal Reference Bureau........................... 125
Inquiries answered by the Bureau... 500

UNIVERSITY OF NORTH CAROLINA, BUREAU OF EXTENSION, 1918.

University news letter carrying results of economic and social surveys,
  weekly issues.. 12,000
Debaters in the High School Debating Union, 150 schools, 600 debaters,
  audience... 75,000
War information leaflets, stimulating patriotism........................... 60,000
After-the-war information leaflets, concerning reconstruction......total issue.. 10,000
Good roads institute for commissioner, engineers, etc.............attendance.. 125
Federated Women's Club members enrolled in study courses................. 825
Books and pamphlets lent in package library service....................... 3,219
Lectures delivered on 185 occasions...................................... 50,000
Community centers organized.. 5
North Carolina yearbook containing State studies...............total issue.. 2,500
Municipal reference service, film service, community drama service,
  persons affected... 10,000

UNIVERSITY OF OKLAHOMA, EXTENSION DIVISION, MAY 1, 1919.

Correspondence study... 861
Extension classes:
  Extension classes.. 39
  Community classes held (27), enrollment.............................. 213
  Study clubs organized (8), enrollment................................ 213
    Total number of classes.. 465
Entertainment:
  Extension lectures... 1,446
  Extension concerts... 526
    Total attendance.. 197,200
Visual instruction:
  Visual instruction lectures and slides circulated...................... 34,300
Conferences.. 300
Discussion and club service:
  Traveling libraries circulated... 103
  Debating class... 203
  Extemporary speaking, number of schools............................... 322
  Package libraries, number distributed................................. 1,028
  Current topics study, students enrolled............................... 7,408

UNIVERSITY OF PITTSBURGH, UNIVERSITY EXTENSION DIVISION, 1917-18.

Extra mural instruction department:
  Centers for credit courses... 11
  Centers for lecture courses.. 12
  Courses given for credit... 19

  Students taking credit courses... 345
  Noncredit attendance at courses.. 1,732

    Total.. 2,077

Public service department:
Lecture bureau—

    Lectures.. 1,342

    Total audiences... 290,095

Package library bureau—

    Briefs and bibliographies prepared............................. 104

    Loan libraries.. 103

Visual bureau—

    Centers using films... 107

    Exhibits... 779

    Attendance... 503,269

    Centers using slides.. 79

    Exhibitions.. 632

    Attendance.. 184,241

Appointment bureau—

    Teacher's branch—

        Positions secured... 213

        Applicants placed... 198

        Amount of salaries.. $159,119

    Undergraduate branch, students placed............................ 1,208

Relations bureau—

    Interscholastic literary contest omitted.

    Conference with secondary school principals held.

    Ninth annual conference of college, normal and secondary schools
    held.

UNIVERSITY OF WYOMING, EXTENSION DIVISION, 1917-18.

The following is taken from the official report published in the catalogue of the University of Wyoming:

STUDENTS IN RESIDENCE.

In graduate standing...............	2	Winter course......................	3
Seniors............................	26	Radio-buzzer class.................	27
Juniors............................	26	Summer school of 1917.............	261
Sophomores.........................	54		
Freshmen...........................	77		633
Special............................	44	Less names counted more than	
Nurses training school.............	3	once......................	30
University high school.............	68		
Music (not taking other subjects)....	42		603

EXTENSION.

Correspondence study department..	239	Training for industrial teachers.....	11
Extension study (Cheyenne), physical training for women	42	Total......................	292

Attendance at extension lectures, teachers' institutes, farmers' institutes, short courses, etc., is not counted in registration statistics. Careful estimates indicate, that direct educational service of all kinds has been given in 1917-18 to about 26,000 persons.

64   THE UNIVERSITY EXTENSION MOVEMENT.

MASSACHUSETTS DEPARTMENT OF UNIVERSITY EXTENSION.

The following tables are taken from the third annual report of the department:

Summary of total enrollment of students throughout the Commonwealth according to type of instruction—correspondence, class, and group. The period covered, January 19, 1916, when first student was enrolled, to November 30, 1917:

	Men.	Women.	Total.
Total correspondence enrollment	2,865	1,009	3,874
Total class enrollment	1,662	1,482	3,144
Total group enrollment	73	14	87
Total enrollment	4,600	2,505	7,105

Number of students who have completed courses since establishment of the department:

	Men.	Women.	Total.
Completed with certificates:			
In correspondence courses	370	123	493
In classes	249	352	601
In groups	9	....	9
Subtotals	628	475	1,103
Completed without certificates:			
In correspondence courses	59	31	90
In classes	49	88	137
In groups	6	....	6
Subtotal	114	119	233
Grand total			1,336

MASSACHUSETTS COMMISSION ON EXTENSION COURSES.

REGISTRATION IN COURSES, 1917–18.

Botany	21	German	34
Economics	49	History	103
Education	81	International law	18
English	580	Music	77
Fine arts	30	Spanish	73
French	114	Zoology	17
Geography	108		
Geology	40	Total	1,345

Since the establishment of the commission in 1910 the number of courses given each year and the registrations have been as follows:

	Courses	Registration.		Courses.	Registration.
In 1910–11	16	863	In 1915–16	24	1,544
In 1911–12	17	1,150	In 1916–17	21	1,435
In 1912–13	21	1,060	In 1917–18	29	1,345
In 1913–14	19	1,127	In 1918–19	..	1,184
In 1914–15	24	1,309			

REED COLLEGE, EXTENSION DIVISION.

TOTAL ATTENDANCE.

In 1911–12	3,360	In 1915–16	17,158
In 1912–13	6,577	In 1916–17	48,060
In 1913–14	11,288	In 1917–18	27,412
In 1914–15	13,547		

In extension lectures 88 courses have been given. Extension courses are open to everybody in Portland. Nineteen courses were given in seven different places in 1917–18.

INDIANA UNIVERSITY, EXTENSION DIVISION.

Registrations, Bureau of correspondence study, 1912–1919................... 1,519
    Hours of credit earned by correspondence study, 1917–18............... 310
    Hours of credit earned by correspondence study, 1918–19............... 354
    Courses completed by students in English, French, journalism, political
    science, and 15 other departments or subjects...................... 811
Class instruction, 1918–19:
    Students in Indianapolis center, first semester.......................... 425
    Students in Indianapolis center, second semester...................... 370

    Total... 795

    Students in Fort Wayne center, first semester, 1917–18................. 179
    Students in Fort Wayne center, second semester...................... 246

    Total... 425

    Total, 1918–19, second semester.................................... 311
    Students in classes at New Castle and 11 other cities, 1918–19......... 273
Public welfare service, 1918–19:
    Children tested.. 100,000
    Attendance at Red Cross institutes and chapter courses................ 250
    Schools enrolled in discussion league................................ 175
    Approximate attendance at league contests........................... 18,00
    Approximate attendance at lectures arranged by speakers' bureau..... 25,000
    Lecture series and institutes, attendance............................. 1,100
    Welfare and art exhibits circulated (29), number of exhibitions........ 158
    Package libraries and club study outlines supplied.................... 1,969
    Number of lantern slides lent....................................... 19,057
    Approximate attendance.. 27,500
    Informational bulletins published (10), copies distributed.............. 30,000

UNIVERSITY OF WISCONSIN, EXTENSION DIVISION.

Correspondence enrollments, 1916–1918............................... 12,923
Package libraries lent, 1917–18...................................... 6,663
Requests for information answered by Municipal Reference Bureau, 1916–
1918... 1,494
Cities served by Municipal Reference Bureau.......................... 128
Registration in classes for postgraduate medical instruction, 1918.......... 247
Lectures by faculty members, 1917–18................................ 551

July 1, 1918, to May 1, 1919.

Correspondence and class instruction, total enrollment, May 1, 1919........ 43,413
Lectures, concerts, etc., 1917–18, attendance......................... 451,700
Visual instruction, estimated attendance............................. 1,932,000
Individuals served by package library service......................... 169,571
Attendance at readjustment institutes and conferences.................. 11,356
Number of requests for information answered by information department.. 2,115

153448°—20——5

Partly to give an example of extension publicity, charts showing the extent of several types of the Wisconsin service of 1914–1916 are presented in the following pages:

CHART 1.—Extension instructs wherever the mail goes.

There are 648 spots on this map. Each spot represents a Wisconsin community in which some service of the extension division was used in one or more ways during the biennium 1914–1916.

There are 1,251 post offices in Wisconsin; 51 per cent of these were reached by extension service in the biennium 1914–1916.

CHART 2.—Distribution of package library service for the biennium 1914-1916. The University of Wisconsin, University Extension Division, Department of Debating and Public Discussion.

Explanation.—"Each spot represents 1 to 50 packages lent. In 45 cities over 50 packages were lent."

Number of package libraries lent in biennium 1914–1916 11,136
Number of package libraries lent in biennium 1912–1914 6,570
Number of package libraries lent in past 7 years 24,112

Increase in the number of packages lent during the biennium over the preceding biennium was 4,566, or 68 per cent. Number of packages lent in the past biennium was 46 per cent of the total lent in seven years. Packages were sent out at an average rate of 18 a day during 1914–1916.

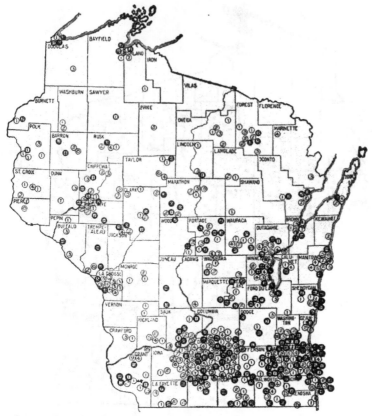

CHART 3.—Noncircuit or direct service in educational lantern slides and motion-picture films, 1915-1916. University of Wisconsin, The University Extension Division, Bureau of Visual Instruction.

Explanation.— White spots, slide service; *black spots,* film service. Spots represent schools and other organizations. Numbers indicate sets of slides or reels of film, July 1, 1915, to July 1, 1916. Represent service to 260 different places, 466 organizations; 89,625 slides, 1,499 reels of film shown. (These figures are gross—the totals of frequent relendings.)

WHAT THIS SERVICE WOULD HAVE COST IF RENTED.

Based on an average commercial charge of 5 cents each for slides, $1.50 a reel for films.
1914–1915:

43,876 slides at 5 cents each	$2,194
470 reels of film, at $1.50 each	705
1915–1916:	
89,625 slides at 5 cents each	4,481
1,499 reels of film, at $1 50	2,248
Total	9,628

CHART 4.—Routing circuit service in educational lantern slides and motion picture films. University of Wisconsin, The University Extension Division, Bureau of Visual Instruction.

Explanation.—Each spot represents one package weekly from November 1, 1915, to May 1, 1916. "Six circuits with 27 to 33 communities on each circuit."

Total number of slides in use, 13,808. Total number of slides shown on all, 400,820. Total number of reels of film in use, 120. Total number of reels of film shown on all, 3,617.

WHAT THIS SERVICE WOULD HAVE COST IF RENTED.

Based on an average commercial charge of 5 cents each for slides, $1.50 a reel for films.

1914–15:

7,200 slides used an average of 35 times each during season	$12,600
60 reels of film used an average of 35 times each during season	3,150

1915–16:

13,808 slides used an average of 29 times during season	20,021
120 reels of film used an average of 29 times during season	5,220
Total	40,991

DIRECTORY OF GENERAL EXTENSION SERVICES.[1]

The following list of institutions and extension activities is fairly complete and approximately accurate. The information was obtained from catalogues, announcements, and correspondence.

Since this bulletin is concerned chiefly with university extension, no attempt was made in compiling the directory to include all the agricultural colleges and the normal schools.

Institutions and extension activities.[2]

State, institution, place, officer in charge.	Activities.	Remarks.
Alabama: University of Alabama, University, J. S. Thomas, director extension division.	Extension lectures, debating and public discussion.	$10,000 appropriation for expansion, 1919.
Arizona: University of Arizona, Tucson, F. G. Lockwood, director extension division.	Lectures, correspondence study, general information service, field work by bureau of mines, debating and public discussion.	Organized 1912, reorganized 1919.
Arkansas: University of Arkansas, Fayetteville, B. C. Riley, director general extension division.	Correspondence study, club study, class study, lectures, concerts, visual instruction, package libraries, community institutes, general information, news service.	Organized 1914–15.
California: University of California, Berkeley, L. J. Richardson, director extension division.	Class instruction, lectures, public discussion and club service, municipal reference, general information, visual instruction.	Organized 1906, reorganized 1913.
California: Humboldt State Normal, Arcata, N. B. Van Matre, principal.	Correspondence instruction department, service of field supervision.	Organized 1917.
California: Junior College, Riverside, A. G. Paul, director of extension.	Extension classes, lectures.........	
Colorado: University of Colorado, Boulder, Loran D. Osborn, director extension division.	Correspondence instruction, class instruction, vocational instruction, lectures, visual instruction, community welfare, business and commercial development, library service, municipal reference publications.	Organized 1912; cooperates with two other State institutions.
Colorado: University of Denver, University Park, D. E. Phillips, director of extension college.	Extension classes and lectures for teachers, discussion, and club service.	Extension college, supported by tuition fees.
Colorado: Colorado State Teachers College, Greeley.	Correspondence study, group study courses, institutes, reading circles, surveys.	Cooperates with university and normal school.
Colorado: Colorado State Normal School, Gunnison, Grant Rutland, acting president.	Group study, correspondence study, reading circles, rural demonstration.	Cooperates with university and teachers' college.
Delaware: Delaware College, Newark, E. V. Vaughan, chairman committee on extension.	Extension lectures, movable house economics schools, service bureau, evening classes.	
District of Columbia: George Washington University, Washington, W. M. Collier, president.	Extension lectures, classes.........	Double sessions to accommodate Government employees.
District of Columbia: Howard University (colored), Washington, J. S. Durkee, president.	Correspondence study.............	
Florida: University of Florida, Gainesville, A. A. Murphree, president.	Conferences, lectures, correspondence study, employment bureau, debating, institutes.	$56,000 appropriated by legislature in 1919.
Florida: Florida State College for Women, Tallahassee, Edward Conradi, president.	Conferences, lectures, correspondence study, employment bureau, debating, institutes.	
Georgia: University of Georgia, Athens, D. C. Barrow, president.	Lectures, discussion service, institutes, conferences.	
Georgia: State Normal School, Athens.	Correspondence study.............	

[1] The directory is a revision of a mimeograph bulletin prepared by J. J. Schlicher.
[2] See succeeding pages for fuller tabulation of activities of State university extension services.

Institutions and extension activities—Continued.

State, institution, place, officer in charge.	Activities.	Remarks.
Idaho: University of Idaho, Moscow, E. H. Lindley, president.	Correspondence study, lectures, visual instruction, package libraries, public discussion, general information, welfare service.	Extension division organized 1914–15; at present the work has been partially discontinued because of insufficient funds.
Idaho: State Normal School, Albion, G. A. Axline, principal.	Correspondence study............	
Idaho: State Normal School, Lewiston, O. M. Elliot, principal.	Correspondence courses..........	
Illinois: University of Illinois, Urbana, E. J. James, president.	Advisory service in community problems, engineering short courses, movable schools, lectures.	
Illinois: Knox College, Galesburg, J. L. McConaughy, president.	Lectures; debate and discussion...	
Illinois: University of Chicago, Chicago, H. F. Mallory, secretary extension division; O. W. Caldwell, dean of University College.	Correspondence courses, extension classes; conferences; public lectures.	Organized 1892; offers 450 courses in 40 different subjects.
Illinois: Bradley Polytechnic Institute, Peoria, T. C. Burgess, president.	Extension classes................	
Illinois: Western Illinois State Normal School, Macomb.	Classes, institutes, teacher placement.	
Indiana: Indiana University, Bloomington, J. J. Pettijohn, director extension division.	Correspondence study, class instruction, extension lectures, conferences, public discussion, package libraries, general information, community institutes, visual instruction, surveys and investigations; welfare service; publications.	Center offices in Indianapolis, and Fort Wayne. Organized 1912; reorganized 1914.
Indiana: Butler College, Indianapolis, J. W. Putnam, director extension courses.	Classes......................	
Indiana: Goshen College, Goshen.	Correspondence courses.	
Iowa: University of Iowa, Iowa City, O. E. Klingman, director extension division.	Municipal service, business service, public discussion, educational service, visual instruction, child welfare work, public health service, patriotic league, correspondence study, conferences, publications.	Organized 1913.
Iowa: Iowa State College, Ames, R. A. Pearson, president.	Engineering extension, vocational courses, technical institutes, trade courses, bureau of technical service, correspondence study, extension classes, visual instruction.	Organized 1906, reorganized 1913. Ten-day courses held in six cities.
Iowa: Iowa State Teachers College, Cedar Falls, J. C. McGlade, director extension division.	Study centers, institutes, extension summer schools, lectures, concerts, lantern slides.	
Iowa: Des Moines College, Des Moines, J. A. Earl, president.	City extension classes, home study by correspondence.	
Iowa: Drake University, Des Moines, A. Holmes, president.	Home-study courses..............	
Kansas: University of Kansas, Lawrence, H. G. Ingham, director extension division.	Correspondence study, package libraries, club service, general information, lectures, concerts, municipal reference, child welfare work, visual instruction, short courses, institutes, conferences.	Organized 1909.
Kansas: State Normal School, Emporia, C. W. Salser, director extension division.	Appointments, educational measurements, correspondence study, lectures, visual instruction, service bureaus.	Organized 1914.
Kansas: State Agricultural College, Manhattan, W. M. Jardine, president.	Reading courses, vocational courses, home-study service.	Work done in addition to regular agricultural extension.
Kansas: Ottawa University, Ottawa, S. E. Price, president.	Assistance in debating and discussion.	
Kentucky: University of Kentucky, Lexington, Wellington Patrick, director extension division.	Correspondence study, short courses in engineering, lectures and institutes, public discussion, package libraries, club service, general information, welfare service, class instruction in mining.	Organized 1917–18.

Institutions and extension activities—Continued.

State, institution, place, officer in charge.	Activities.	Remarks
Kentucky: Berea College, Berea, M. E. Vaughn, superintendent extension department.	Lectures and demonstrations, traveling libraries, religious work.	
Louisiana: Tulane University, New Orleans, J. A. Lyon, chairman committee on extension.	Extension classes, work in agriculture and home economics.	
Louisiana: Louisiana State Normal School, Natchitoches, director extension department.	Employment, institutes, advice to teachers, extra-mural classes, correspondence study.	
Maine: University of Maine, Orono, K. J. Aley, president.	Correspondence study, assistance in debating.	
Maryland: Johns Hopkins University, Baltimore, E. S. Buchner, director of extension.	Extension classes in education; business economy and technical subjects given in evening classes; visual instruction.	Credit courses for teachers given first in 1909; special classes have been held since 1890.
Maryland: Maryland State College, College Park, Thomas B. Symonds, director general extension service.	Correspondence study, assistance in debating, package libraries, lectures.	Organized 1919.
Massachusetts: State board of education, Boston, J. A. Moyer, director department of university extension.	Extension classes, correspondence study, information service, surveys.	Established 1915–16.
Massachusetts: Commission on extension courses, Cambridge, J. A. Ropes, chairman of the commission.	Extension classes; courses carry credit toward the degree of associate in arts. The commission cooperates in the administration of the school of social work.	Established 1910; the commission represents 10 institutions.
Massachusetts: Harvard University, Cambridge, J. A. Ropes, dean of School of Arts and Sciences.	Conducts summer school of arts and sciences, shares in work of commission on extension courses, offers degree of associate in arts, gives extension courses in medicine.	Reorganized 1910, admission of special students is regarded as a branch of extension work.
Massachusetts: Lowell Institute, Cambridge, Prof. Charles F. Park.	Free evening lectures and extension classes.	
Massachusetts: Boston Museum of Fine Arts, Huger Elliot, supervisor of educational work, Boston.	Lectures on art	
Massachusetts: Franklin Union, Boston, Walter B. Russel, director.	Evening and Saturday extension classes in technical subjects.	
Massachusetts: Simmons College, Boston.	Extension classes.	
Massachusetts: Boston University, Boston, Prof. A. H. Rice, director.	Extension classes in college subjects.	
Massachusetts: School for Social Workers, Boston, Prof. J. R. Brackett, director.	Lectures on social and community subjects.	
Massachusetts: Lowell Textile School, Lowell.	Evening classes bearing directly upon their daily work for those employed in textile industries.	
Massachusetts: Massachusetts State Normal School, North Adams.	Correspondence study.	
Massachusetts: Connecticut Valley Colleges, Amherst, Charles W. Hobbs, executive secretary	Extension classes, mainly in collegiate subjects.	Amherst, International Y. M. C. A., Massachusetts Agricultural College, Holyoke College, Northfield Schools and Smith College, in cooperation with the Massachusetts Board of Education.
Massachusetts: Williams College, North Adams, I. Freeman Hall, superintendent.	Extension classes . . . . . , ...	
Michigan: University of Michigan, Ann Arbor, W. D. Henderson, director extension division.	Lectures and class instruction, visual instruction, public speaking and debating, library service, package libraries, conferences, school service, museum extension, municipal reference, advisory and other service in public health, engineering, etc.	Organized 1911.
Michigan: Michigan College of Mines, Houghton.	Extension lectures	
Michigan: State Normal College, Ypsilanti.	Lectures, classes, correspondence study.	
Minnesota: University of Minnesota, Minneapolis, R. R. Price, director, extension division.	Correspondence instruction, class instruction, short courses, municipal reference, lectures, lyceum, institutes, debating, community center and other welfare service.	Reorganized 1913.

Institutions and extension activities—Continued.

State, institution, place, officer in charge.	Activities.	Remarks.
Mississippi: University of Mississippi, University, J. N. Powers, chancellor.	Extension courses, lectures........	
Mississippi: Mississippi Agricultural and Mechanical College, Agricultural College, F. P. Gaines, director service bureau.	Correspondence study, general information, visual instruction, package libraries.	In addition to agricultural extension.
Missouri: University of Missouri, Columbia, C. H. Williams, director extension division.	Correspondence study, class instruction, lectures and lecture courses, lyceum service, public information service, package libraries, engineering extension.	Organized 1910, reorganized 1913. School of Social Work at St. Louis.
Missouri: State Normal School, Cape Girardeau, W. S. Dearmont, principal.	Correspondence courses, extension center, courses and public lectures, school service bureau.	
Missouri: Washington University, St. Louis, F. W. Shipley, director extension courses.	Courses in business, technical and other subjects, lectures.	
Montana: University of Montana, Missoula, E. O. Sisson, president.	Correspondence study, class instruction, lectures and lecture courses, lyceum service, public information service, package libraries, engineering extension.	Organized 1910, reorganized 1913.
Montana: Montana State School of Mines, Butte, C. H. Bowman, president.	Correspondence courses.........:..	
Nebraska: University of Nebraska, Lincoln, A. A. Reed, director extension division.	Correspondence study, class instruction, lectures, debating and public discussion, general information, welfare service, visual instruction, community drama service, professional service, Red Cross work.	Organized 1909.
Nevada: University of Nevada, Reno, W. E. Clark, president.	Library, club, and debate service, special mining school and classes; short courses.	
New Jersey: Rutgers College, New Brunswick, C. H. Elliot, director extension courses.	Lectures, extension classes, special courses for teachers, assistance in debating and public discussion.	Reorganized 1912.
New Mexico: University of New Mexico, Albuquerque, D. R. Boyd, president.	Correspondence study, lectures, extension teaching, debating and public discussion, general information, surveys and investigations, suggestive aid to communities, exhibits, conferences, institutes.	Reorganized 1919.
New Mexico: New Mexico Normal University, East Las Vegas, F. H. H. Roberts, principal.	Correspondence study.............	
New York: University of the State of New York, Albany, W. R. Watson, chief of division of educational extension; A W. Abrams, chief of division of visual instruction.	Lecture outlines, traveling libraries, reading circles, club study, lantern slides, pictures.	
New York: Columbia University, New York, J. C. Egbert, director extension teaching.	Extension classes in New York and elsewhere, lectures, institutes, home study.	Organized 1901, reorganized 1910; special courses offered by School of Practical Arts of Teachers College.
New York: Syracuse University, Syracuse, M. Elwood Smith, director extension courses.	Lectures, evening classes, extension work in forestry and landscape gardening, exhibits, demonstrations.	Department of Forest Extension organized in 1913.
New York: University of Rochester, Rochester, P. B. Gilbert, director extension courses.	Extension classes	
New York: State College for Teachers, Albany, R. H. Kirtland, chairman, committee on extension courses.	Extension classes, special courses for teachers.	
New York: Brooklyn Polytechnic Institute, Brooklyn; Charles A. Green, director extension courses.	Extension classes, afternoon and evening classes.	
New York: Adelphi College, Brooklyn, Mary Clarke, secretary extension courses.	Extension classes, evening classes..	Organized 1911.
New York: College of the City of New York, New York, director of extension courses.	Extension classes..................	Organized 1918.

Institutions and extension activities—Continued.

State, institution, place, officer in charge.	Activities.	Remarks.
New York: New York University, New York, James E. Lough, dean.	Extension classes, public-health correspondence study.	Extra-mural division opened 1908.
New York: Union College, Schenectady, Charles A. Richmond, president.	Extension classes.................	
North Carolina: University of North Carolina, Chapel Hill, L. R. Wilson, director extension division.	Correspondence study, lectures, debate and declamation, surveys, municipal reference, advisory school service, institutes, special bulletin series, visual instruction.	Organized 1911.
North Carolina: North Carolina Normal and Industrial College, Greensboro, Mary M. Petty, chairman extension work.	Lectures, club service, advisory service, commercial correspondence courses.	
North Dakota: University of North Dakota, Grand Forks, A. H. Yoder, director extension division.	Correspondence study, publicity and information, club service, package libraries, debate and declamation, lectures, lyceum service, visual instruction.	Organized 1901, committee on university extension.
Ohio: Miami University, Oxford, R. M. Hughes, president.	Extension classes, teachers' conferences, loan of slides, laboratory material.	
Ohio: Ohio University, Athens, William E. McVey, director extension work.	Extension classes, traveling libraries.	Organized 1910, work confined largely to southeastern Ohio.
Ohio: University of Akron, Akron, H. E. Simmons, director committee on extension.	Extension classes, cooperation with city authorities, lecture courses.	Cooperation in testing, home demonstration, playground work.
Ohio: Cleveland School of Education, Cleveland, Ambrose D. Suhrie, dean.	Extension classes.................	Cooperation with Western Reserve University and other local institutions.
Ohio: University of Cincinnati, Cincinnati, E. L. Talbert, director extension work.	Evening classes, cooperative courses in engineering, municipal reference service, home economics service.	
Ohio: State Normal College, Kent, J. E. McGilvery, principal.	Extension courses.................	Department of extension teaching.
Ohio: Toledo University, Toledo, A. M. Stowe, president.	Research, laboratory, and other service to the city.	Admits "extension students" for noncredit work.
Ohio: Denison University, Granville, C. W. Chamberlain, president.	Extension classes and lectures.....	
Ohio: Marietta College, Marietta, J. B. MacMillan, president.	Extension classes.................	
Oklahoma: University of Oklahoma, Norman, J. W. Scroggs, director extension division.	Correspondence study, lectures, public discussion and debate, general information, municipal reference, traveling libraries, public welfare service, visual instruction.	Organized 1905, reorganized 1913.
Oregon: University of Oregon, Eugene, John A. Almack, director extension division.	Correspondence study, class study, lectures, reading circles, visual instruction, community music, child welfare, public information, public discussion, other public service.	
Oregon: Reed College, Portland, W. T. Foster, president.	Extension lectures.................	
Pennsylvania: University of Pennsylvania, Philadelphia, E. F. Smith, provost.	Extension classes in finance and commerce, special courses for teachers.	Evening School of Accounts and Finance, T. J. Grayson, director.
Pennsylvania: University of Pittsburgh, Pittsburgh, J. H. Kelley, director extension division.	Correspondence study, class instruction, lectures, public discussion, debate, general information, package libraries, visual instruction, business development, community center, and other welfare work.	
Pennsylvania: Drexel Institute, Philadelphia, Hollis Godfrey, president.	Extension classes in domestic arts and science and physical training, cooperation with industries.	
Pennsylvania: Carnegie Institute of Technology, Pittsburgh, A. A. Hamerschlag, president.	Extension classes, night school and afternoon classes in business subjects, social work, etc.	
Pennsylvania: Lehigh University, Bethlehem, Percy Hughes, director extension courses.	Evening extension classes at Bethlehem and other towns.	

Institutions and extension activities—Continued.

State, institution. place, officer in charge	Activities	Remarks
Pennsylvania: Pennsylvania State College, State College, J. T. Marshman, director liberal arts extension; R. L. Sackett, director engineering.	Extension lectures, debating, correspondence, and evening courses, apprentice schools.	Organized 1906.
Rhode Island: Brown University, Providence, W. F. Jacobs, director university extension.	Lecture courses, extension classes.	Organized 1907.
Rhode Island: Rhode Island State College, Kingston, H. Edwards, president.	Home study courses.	Organized 1904.
South Carolina: University of South Carolina, Columbia, J. O. Van Meter, director extension department.	Correspondence study, class work, debating, package libraries, rural sociology, lectures, general welfare, assistance in teachers' meetings, etc., comparative engineering courses.	
South Carolina: Winthrop College, Rock Hill, David B. Johnson, president.	Lectures, demonstrations, community entertainment.	
South Dakota: University of South Dakota, Vermilion, J. C Tjaden, acting director.	Extension classes, correspondence work, visual instruction, debating, package libraries, lectures.	Reorganized 1918-19.
Tennessee: University of Tennessee, Knoxville, Charles E. Ferris, dean in charge extension division.	Lectures, debating, visual instruction.	
Tennessee: Peabody College for Teachers, Nashville, R. W. Salvidge, in charge of extension.	Correspondence courses, lectures.	
Texas: University of Texas, Austin, E. D. Shurter, director extension division.	Correspondence study, group study courses, class instruction, package libraries, lectures, short courses, general information, visual instruction, debating, school service, welfare service.	
Texas: Howard Payne College, Brownwood, J. A. Tolman, president.	Correspondence courses.	
Texas: Baylor University, Waco, Lula Place, chairman extension committee.	....do....	
Texas: Southwestern University, Georgetown, C. M. Bishop, president.	Correspondence study.	
Texas: Westminster College, Tehuacana, J. C. Williams, president.	....do....	
Utah: University of Utah, Salt Lake City, F. W. Reynolds, director extension division.	Correspondence study, extension classes, lectures and entertainments, general information, debating and discussion, visual instruction, institutes, health work and other welfare service.	Organized 1913-14.
Virginia: University of Virginia, Charlottesville, C. G Maphis, director of extension work.	Lectures, debating, package libraries, bulletins, appointments, high school quarterly, visual instruction.	
Vermont: University of Vermont, Burlington, Guy P. Benton, president.	Courses for teachers, school conferences, lectures, special extension classes on demand.	
West Virginia: University of West Virginia, Morgantown, L. B. Hill, director extension division.	Correspondence study, extension credit courses in various centers of the State; school of good roads, conferences, visual instruction.	Reorganized 1918.
Washington: University of Washington, Seattle, Edwin A. Start, director extension division.	Correspondence study, class instruction, lectures, general information, debate and discussion, package libraries, conferences, surveys, medical clinics and welfare work.	Organized 1912.
Washington: Washington State College, Pullman, F. F. Nalder, director general extension.	Debating and public discussion, home economics extension.	General extension division organized 1919.
Washington: State Normal School, Bellingham, G. W. Nash, principal.	Lectures, correspondence study, extension classes, advisory work.	

Institution and extension activities—Continued.

State, institution, place, officer in charge.	Activities.	Remarks
Wisconsin: University of Wisconsin, Madison, W. H. Lighty, acting dean extension division.	Correspondence study, class instruction, lyceum service, debating and discussion, package libraries, visual instruction, community institutes, health instruction, and other welfare work.	Organized 1892, reorganized 1906.
Wisconsin: Beloit College, Beloit, Dean G. L. Collie, chairman committee on extension.	Extension classes..................	
Wisconsin: Marquette University, Milwaukee, C. K. Atkinson, dean.	.....do............................	
Wyoming: University of Wyoming, Laramie, H. C. Dale, director of correspondence study.	Correspondence courses, lectures, extension classes, traveling libraries, general information.	Reorganized 1913; non-resident instruction.

NOTES ON STATE UNIVERSITY DIVISIONS.[1]

The following statement, with notes, is intended to give a brief survey of both the organization and the types of activities of each of the extension divisions in State universities.

The classification into departments and bureaus and the grouping of activities correspond in most cases to announcements and catalogues published by each institution. In some cases the list of activities does not correspond with the actual plan as followed in 1918–19, because several divisions have recently reorganized, and also because war-time service and later readjustments changed to some degree the normal process of extension work.

In order to avoid excessive repetition it was found necessary to condense greatly the descriptions of the divisions' services and to omit many minor items.

Statements are given for 28 State universities. Several others which have extension organization are not included, either because their activities are comparatively limited, as in the case of South Carolina, or because they are not yet definitely projected and developed, as in the case of the newly organized division at the University of West Virginia.

In order to afford opportunity for comparison with State university systems, descriptions are included of Columbia University, the Massachusetts systems of extension, the University of Chicago, and the Mississippi service bureau.

UNIVERSITY OF ARIZONA, UNIVERSITY EXTENSION DEPARTMENT.

Correspondence instruction.—The subjects taught include agriculture, architecture, astronomy, botany, education, history, philosophy, Spanish, etc. Two types of courses are offered—formal and informal, credit and noncredit courses.

Extension lectures.—These are usually given without cost to the community, though sometimes the expenses of the speaker are met by the local committee.

Public discussion.—The department offers service to schools, clubs, and other organizations interested in debate and public discussion. Considerable material is available and may be secured on request.

General information service.—Inquiries on public questions are answered by the department.

NOTES.

The work is being reorganized (1919) and will be considerably expanded. As in the case of several institutions, the University of Arizona conducts some extension work through other departments than that of extension. The bureau of mines does field work, conducts safety campaigns, offers first-aid and mine-rescue courses, circulates motion-picture films, and gives an information service on mining problems.

---

[1] These notes are based on tables prepared by J. J. Schlicher and incorporated in a mimeograph bulletin, "General Extension Work Done by Universities and Colleges in the United States," issued by the division of educational extension, May, 1919. Supplementary matter has been added to the tables, and a considerable number of changes have been made.

78 THE UNIVERSITY EXTENSION MOVEMENT.

UNIVERSITY OF ARKANSAS, EXTENSION DIVISION.

EXTENSION TEACHING SERVICE.

Correspondence study.—Some courses available are for university credit; others, such as directed reading courses covering practically the same ground, are not given for credit.

Club study.—Opportunity for study and reading is offered, particularly to teachers and club women. Upon request, a course of reading is outlined and a textbook selected; also several reference books are indicated, together with a full list of references and suggested topics for papers and reports. Courses in education, literature, social science, hygiene, economics, political science, and agriculture are offered.

Class study.—This department is supervised by members of the faculty. Classes usually meet at night.

Extension lectures and lyceum courses.—These are suited for programs of women's clubs, business men's leagues, institutes, conventions, commencement exercises and holiday programs.

The extension division acts as a clearing house for concert companies, assisting communities to secure lyceum courses.

PUBLIC WELFARE SERVICE.

Lantern slides and films.—Sets of slides, many of them accompanied by lecture outlines, are furnished free except for transportation charges. A partial list is in the catalogue. Films and phonograph records are also furnished.

Package libraries.—Packages of material for papers and debates on agricultural and present-day questions. State high school debating league. Plays and recitation materials.

Community institutes.—Two and three day programs, consisting of lectures, demonstrations, exhibits, conferences, and entertainment, are held in towns and cities. The institutes are designed to reach the various urban groups and deal with community problems. The general extension division, in conjunction with the agriculture extension, holds "Farmers' Chautauquas," lasting from one to three days.

General information.—Information on science, engineering, education, literature, or art is furnished free to individuals, clubs, civic societies, and public boards.

The general extension division works in close cooperation with the agricultural extension division. A well-developed press and publicity service is maintained.

UNIVERSITY OF CALIFORNIA, EXTENSION DIVISION.

Class instruction.—For cities and towns, courses are offered when a sufficient number of students can be secured for the same subjects. A list of these courses is given in special announcements. A special list is issued for southern California. Summer classes are given in San Francisco and Oakland.

Correspondence instruction.—Special business courses are offered. Among other courses given are music, sewing, millinery, education, and playground work, oral and dental hygiene, art appreciation, history, political science, journalism, foreign languages, technical subjects, secretarial training.

Bureau of lectures.—In series of 6 or 12 for clubs, organizations, or communities. Printed outlines accompany the lectures. Professional lecturers and musical companies are also furnished.

Bureau of public discussion.—The bureau promotes discussion of public questions and assists in organizing and conducting debating clubs and discussion centers.

The bureau publishes bulletins and cooperates with the State and county libraries in recommending material. It conducts the Interscholastic Public Speaking League of California.

Bureau of municipal reference.—The bureau acts as a clearing house for inquiries and information on municipal affairs, and maintains collections of books, public documents, etc., on problems of city government and administration. It is allied with the League of California Municipalities.

Bureau of general information.—The inquiries received, of whatever nature, are referred to various departments or individuals of the faculty.

Visual instruction.—The department collects and circulates large numbers of slides, films, and exhibits, and sends them in rotation to the public schools and to citizens.

NOTES.

Three main offices are maintained at Berkeley, San Francisco, and Los Angeles, besides centers at San Diego, Santa Barbara, Fresno, Sacramento, Red Bluff, and Eureka. Emphasis is placed on class, correspondence work and lectures.
During the war and in 1919, the division has been partially reorganized. The bureau of public discussion has been temporarily discontinued.

UNIVERSITY OF COLORADO, EXTENSION DIVISION.

DEPARTMENT OF INSTRUCTION.

Bureau of correspondence instruction.—Work is given in secondary subjects, vocational subjects, and subjects of university grade; credit is given for the last two.

Class instruction.—This is conducted under university instructors, local instructors or leaders from the classes. There is a list of courses given in the extension announcement.

Bureau of vocational instruction.—The bureau organizes classes among industrial groups, and combines certain welfare features with the instruction for coal miners, workers in sugar factories, etc.

DEPARTMENT OF PUBLIC SERVICE.

Lectures and visual instruction.—Lectures are given by university professors and others, both single lectures and courses. Stereoptican slides are sent out in circuits to the public schools for the purpose of supplementing by visual means the regular classroom instruction.

Business and commercial development.—Business surveys are made to determine business and trade activities and possibilities in Colorado communities. Business short courses are conducted for the purpose of giving business men new scientific knowledge of business and commerce. Cooperative work is undertaken with commercial clubs. Business correspondence study courses and classes are given for more formal instruction.

Information and library-extension service.—Books, magazines, and package libraries are sent out to high schools, clubs, and individuals for use in public discussions, debate, and for general information. General-information service is also afforded.

Bureau of municipal reference.—A municipal reference bureau is maintained for the purpose of furnishing information and suggestions to the municipal governments of the State.

Publications.—General university extension publications and pamphlets are written by members of the university faculty.

Community welfare activities and conferences.—Preliminary surveys are made of community needs, followed by an institute of three or four days' duration, participated in by university men, local speakers, and members of the State welfare commissions. In the follow-up work in these communities, the secretary of the welfare bureau acts as a general civic secretary.

UNIVERSITY OF FLORIDA, EXTENSION DIVISION.

The following is a copy of a portion of the bill introduced in the Florida Legislature appropriating money for university extension:[1]

"SECTION 1. The State board of control is hereby empowered and directed to extend the outside work of the educational institutions under its direction into all fields of human endeavor which, in its judgment, will best accomplish the objects herein expressed.

"SEC. 2. It shall be the duty of the board of control to gather information on all subjects useful to the people of Florida, and to carry it to them in ways that will help them most in the shortest time; to spread knowledge among them by taking it to them in an attractive way; to stimulate thought and encourage every movement among the people for their mutual improvement.

"SEC. 3. To carry out the provisions of this act, the board of control is hereby empowered to enlarge the work now done by the extension divisions of the University of Florida and the State College for Women, as it may from time to time deem advisable, and to employ all needful persons and appliances to carry on the work in the most efficient manner.

"SEC. 4. It shall be the duty of the board of control to seek out, among all the schools of Florida, every student who may by nature have a special aptitude and genius for some one branch of learning, and to encourage him in the prosecution of the study of that branch, to the end that he may become an expert and a leader in that subject."

UNIVERSITY OF IDAHO, EXTENSION DIVISION.

Correspondence study and forestry correspondence.—Courses for credit are given; courses to aid in preparation for teachers' certificates; classes for clubs and study groups. Correspondence courses in forestry are offered.

Lectures.—Lectures are conducted by members of the faculty.

Package libraries.—Package libraries are sent out by the general university library. The university catalogue of 1919 states that at present the work of university extension is devoted mainly to service in agriculture extension.

UNIVERSITY OF ILLINOIS, EXTENSION DIVISION.

"Extension work has not been organized as a separate administrative unit in the University of Illinois. Several departments, however, have initiated activities, both on the campus and in the State at large, which serve to make some facilities of the University available to groups of mature persons who are engaged in various industries and professions."[2]

The separate service "known as agricultural college extension offers courses in the principles and methods of extension work, conducts extension enterprises that do not deal with technical subjects, and cooperates with other departments in projecting their work in the State."

The department of ceramic engineering cooperates with the clay and allied industries by offering annually a two weeks' industrial course for those who have not the time or the preparation required for academic studies.

Correspondence work is done in home economics and club study. Requests for information on food, planning of the house, feeding of children, preparation of topics for club study are answered by the home economics department.

The department conducts movable schools, one or two weeks of instruction by one or more instructors.

---

[1] For the budget items see p. 104.

[2] Quoted from the catalogue of the University of Illinois, 1919.

Similar service is given to various organizations, academies, boys' and girls' clubs, chambers of commerce, civic leagues, library associations, woman's clubs.

THE UNIVERSITY OF CHICAGO.

Correspondence study department.—The department offers 450 courses for credit in 40 different subjects. During the past 27 years it has reached 21,000 persons. It has students in every State.

University college.—The university maintains separate offices and classrooms in the down-town section of Chicago. A large number of classes are conducted on business subjects and in the arts and sciences.

American institute of sacred literature.—The institute is a department of the university. As an organization it antedates the university by 10 years. It was incorporated in the university in 1905. It conducts all nonresident and biblical work. It offers the following: Outline Bible-study courses; the work of the ministers' guild; traveling libraries; survey courses for Sunday-school teachers; home-reading courses; advanced correspondence courses; publications.

INDIANA UNIVERSITY, EXTENSION DIVISION.

EXTENSION TEACHING SERVICE.

Bureau of correspondence study.—Courses are listed in extension announcement. Several hundred courses are open to any persons in the State. Academic requirements are exacted.

Class instruction.—Two centers are supported in Indiana, one at Indianapolis and one at Fort Wayne. Special announcements give the lists of courses offered. Credit and noncredit courses are given. Classes in special and practical subjects are offered. Classes are given on demand, in smaller cities of the State, under certain conditions.

Extension lectures.—Extension lectures are generally assigned to the members of the university faculty. Specialists from other States are also secured for short lecture tours.

PUBLIC WELFARE SERVICE.

Public conferences.—Public conferences are given on welfare and educational subjects. State conferences have been held on history teaching in secondary schools, educational measurements, taxation, and play and recreation. The proceedings are published in bulletins.

Bureau of public discussion.—The department offers service to debating societies, civic clubs, and literary clubs. Package libraries and bibliographies are furnished on present-day questions. It conducts a State High School Discussion League, cooperatively, on current subjects.

Package libraries.—Besides package libraries, outlines for reading clubs are supplied. Special service is given upon receipt of requests for information which can not be met by regular package library and bibliography service.

Bureau of visual instruction.—The bureau lends lantern slides and motion-picture films on academic and welfare subjects. It also lends exhibits of pictures, prints, photographs, and framed original paintings. Topical exhibits on the following subjects have been circulated: Health, visiting nurses, pure milk, housing, play and recreation, school surveys, parent-teacher activities, and child welfare. Programs and exhibits are offered on public welfare.

Surveys and investigations.—These are conducted to secure data necessary for intelligent community action, in cooperation with boards of education, chambers of commerce, civic societies, etc. In addition, investigations are made of special community problems, such as markets in small cities, and cooperative retail delivery

Community centers.—Assistance is given in organizing centers. General service supplements center programs with lectures, slides, etc.

Community institutes.—Programs of lectures, conferences, exhibits, demonstrations on community problems (generally a three days' program) are held in small cities, upon request. About 8 to 10 each year are held.

Publications.—Twelve bulletins are issued annually, on such subjects as training for citizenship, town beautification, etc. Also, there are printed a number of circulars on general welfare subjects and special subjects.

NOTE.

Several lines of special work, such as the promotion of community centers and parent-teacher associations, are supported. Child-welfare work is done in cooperation with the State boards and agencies like the Red Cross, the State child-welfare committee, and local clubs.   •

UNIVERSITY OF IOWA, EXTENSION DIVISION.

PUBLIC AFFAIRS.

Bureau of public administration.[1]—The bureau deals directly with problems of government and administration, especially with reference to (1) municipal administration, (2) township administration, (3) county administration, and (4) State administration of Iowa.

Bureau of municipal information.—The bureau is designed to be of service in handling all the phases of city, town, or village life in Iowa.

Bureau of social welfare.—The bureau cooperates with charity organizations, social centers, and all other agencies having for their aim the social betterment of communities. The bureau has made a number of surveys in the larger cities of Iowa, dealing with constructive charity. Survey service can be secured by commercial clubs, philanthropic agencies, or boards of supervisors.

Business administration.—Service through business institutes and by means of single lectures. Assistance is given in fields of business management, business organization, business surveys, salesmanship, and accounting service.

Debating and public speaking.—High schools are given direct aid by correspondence, personal interviews, and special bulletins.

Public health.—Work in public health is being carried on in cooperation with the American Red Cross. Classes in personal hygiene and home care of the sick are organized and taught in any locality upon request from any chapter.

Educational service.—This service has been chiefly concerned with the following types of work:

1. Fostering the use of educational tests and scales. Most of the standard tests and scales are kept in stock and sold at cost. Comparable results are available in many of these tests, and the bureau assists in the interpretation of results obtained and in planning remedial measures.

2. State-wide surveys have been made in the subjects of writing, arithmetic, and spelling.

3. On invitation of the superintendent and school board a survey of the school system of any district will be made and recommendations rendered. This service has been given to a number of communities during the past two years.

4. Cooperative studies. The bureau is a central agency for the coordination and direction of cooperative studies of educational problems lying in the general survey field. Correspondence is solicited from superintendents and principals concerning their special problems.

---

[1] The bureaus of public administration, municipal information, and social welfare deal more largely with the problems which have little or no connection with the public schools.

Lantern-slide service.—A large number of lantern slides especially made for Iowa schools have been prepared. These slides are divided into sets containing from 50 to 100 slides, each set being accompanied by a complete descriptive lecture.

Child welfare.—A child-welfare exhibit can be secured by any organization interested in this phase of social welfare.

Lectures.—These are provided for the community in accordance with special arrangements made by the extension division.

Package library service.—For high schools and similar institutions; for business men.

Correspondence study.—University credit is given under certain conditions.

Patriotic league.—This is distinct from the educational service. Bibliographies on the questions of the day, with suggestions as to how these can be handled in the various high-school activities. At present the league has an enrollment of approximately 22,000 high-school students.

NOTES.

Conferences are held on municipal affairs, school supervision, organization and administration, child welfare, and vocational education. There are conferences of Iowa newspaper men, commercial club secretaries, public health officials, and religious workers.

Special work in recreation is done, e. g., training camp for camp-fire girls and training camp for scoutmasters.

The extension division has conducted a number of short courses in retailing for the Iowa State Retail Association. Programs cover such topics as the following: Profitable business publicity, the community influences that shape business, etc.

UNIVERSITY OF KANSAS, EXTENSION DIVISION.

Department of correspondence study.—The department offers instruction in preparatory subjects and in vocational subjects, and also gives instruction of university grade.

Department of general information.—The department furnishes package libraries, prepares outlines of study for clubs, supplies material for debate, gives information on matters of general interest, recommends and furnishes plays and recitations, supplies lectures, commencement speakers, and concert companies.

Department of municipal reference.—Supplies information on municipal matters to officials and others.

Department of child welfare.—Assists schools, parents, and organizations in all matters pertaining to the welfare of the child.

NOTES.

The division also conducts merchants' short courses and five-day programs of classes and lectures on merchandising problems.

The division has developed a considerable visual instruction service, lending both slides and motion-picture films.

The division organizes regular extension classes in different cities in the State. These classes are conducted for university credit and for credit toward certificates of vocational training.

During the war the division conducted war conferences and community institutes and secured speakers on war topics.

UNIVERSITY OF KENTUCKY, DEPARTMENT OF UNIVERSITY EXTENSION.

Bureau of correspondence study.—Regular university studies may be taken for credit. Preparatory courses are also offered. The bureau furnishes study outlines and other assistance to clubs and individuals.

Bureau of lectures.—The university offers, through the bureau, lectures singly or in series; speakers for institutes; commencement addresses; lectures for special purposes, including Americanization.

Bureau of debating and public discussion.—The bureau supplies subjects for debates, with bibliographies, facts, and arguments on special subjects, guides, reports, and bulletins. The bureau fosters discussion by civic organizations, maintains package library service, and cooperates with the department of public speaking in holding State debating contests.

Bureau of general information and welfare.—The activities fall along the following lines:

1. Clearing house for inquiries.
2. Reports on special subjects.
3. Information on social conditions, municipal problems, etc.
4. Assistance in community dramatics.

The division of university extension was definitely organized in 1919. Previously extension work was conducted by a faculty committee.

MASSACHUSETTS BOARD OF EDUCATION, DEPARTMENT OF UNIVERSITY EXTENSION.

Correspondence instruction.—Academic courses are given as well as many special practical courses, such as retail salesmanship, household management, plan reading and estimating, safety engineering, civics for naturalization. Most courses contain 20 assignments or lessons. Shorter courses of 10 assignments have been successfully used.

Class instruction.—Subjects are taught by the usual class method in centers in different parts of Massachusetts. No tuition fees are charged.

Special information service.—In the department of university extension experts in a variety of subjects are employed as instructors. Thus there is available for students a wide range of expert information, in case an arrangement is provided to place it promptly and easily within reach of individuals. Such an arrangement has been provided, and there are indications that, as this service becomes generally known, it will be widely used.

Through its information service the department offers to answer or give expert opinion on any reasonable question that falls within its regular fields of study, namely, mechanics, mathematics, engineering, English, Spanish, French, civics, economics, history, business administration, household economics, education.

Publications.—The department publishes bulletins six times a year. They are of two kinds: Announcements of courses, and pamphlets to give permanent and readily usable form to educational material of special significance.

COMMISSION ON EXTENSION COURSES, CAMBRIDGE, MASSACHUSETTS.

The commission represents the following 10 educational institutions: Harvard University, Tufts College, Massachusetts Institute of Technology, Boston College, Boston University, Museum of Fine Arts, Wellesley College, Simmons College, Massachusetts Board of Education, school committee of the City of Boston. Courses of college credit are given by college professors. Students must meet college requirements.

Courses carry credit toward the degree of associate of arts at Harvard, Radcliffe, Tufts, and Wellesley. For this degree, 17 full courses are required of the student, which must include the equivalent of one full course from each of the following:

1. Language, literature, fine arts, or music.
2. Natural sciences.
3. History, or political and social sciences.
4. Philosophy, or mathematics.

UNIVERSITY OF MICHIGAN, EXTENSION DIVISION.

The extension division includes the following 13 bureaus:

University extension courses.—The extension division offers free extension lectures. The lectures are arranged in series, according to the credit plan. A list of these is given in the extension announcement. Extension courses are given for credit.

Visual instruction.—The bureau furnishes slides, charts, and films. A list of the slides available is published in the extension announcement.

Public speaking and debating.—The bureau conducts a high school debating league. Briefs and data are furnished.

Library extension service.—Package libraries are lent, together with bibliographies. Loans are made to other libraries; abstracts of articles are drawn up; advice and other service is given to individuals, to civic clubs, and other organizations.

Extension conferences.—Conferences on municipal, civic, and health problems are held for teachers, librarians, and others.

Public service, department of education.—The bureau makes inspection of schools, conducts school surveys, has a psychological testing service and a teachers' appointment service.

Museum extension service.—The bureau gives information, lends specimens, and publishes bulletins.

Municipal reference bureau.—Information is supplied on municipal problems and government administration. Documents and other material are lent.

Architecture and civic improvement.—Educational and advisory service. including lectures and class instruction.

Landscape design and civic improvement.—Lectures, counsel on city planning, and general advice.

Forestry extension service.—Lectures, advice, and testing of commercial woods.

Engineering extension service.—Courses in highway engineering, laboratory service, reports.

Public health service.—Service of the Pasteur Institute, and of a dental clinic; laboratory and hospital service; lectures.

NOTES.

"In connection with its extension service the University of Michigan seeks to operate, as far as possible, through the avenue of established university channels; it seeks to make use of such existing university facilities as are available. For example, its library extension service is carried on through the medium of the regularly organized library staff; questions relating to municipal affairs are referred to the municipal reference bureau; those touching on forestry to the forestry department; extension service affecting road improvement and sanitary engineering, to the municipal, highway and sanitary departments of the engineering college; matters relating to public health, to the medical schools, and so on. In other words, the policy of the University of Michigan is to render to the people of the State, through the medium of its extension division, the largest possible measure of public service commensurate with the equipment and facilities of an educational institution of university grade." [1]

---

[1] Bulletin of the University of Michigan, "Extension Service 1918-19."

UNIVERSITY OF MINNESOTA, EXTENSION DIVISION.

Correspondence instruction.—Courses are offered in collegiate, industrial, and business branches. Courses for credit.

Class instruction.—Classes are organized in larger cities. Courses are given for credit in science, literature, art, business, and engineering.

Short courses.—One and three-week courses in merchandising. A one-year course is given in business. Outlines of the courses are given in the extension announcement.

Municipal reference bureau.—Material is collected on city problems. The program of the League of Minnesota Municipalities is prepared by the bureau, whose secretary is editor of its official magazine, "Minnesota Municipalities." Conventions are held.

Lecture and lyceum service.—Single lectures are given, and also lectures in series. The department has charge of lyceum courses of popular lectures, concerts, and entertainments.

University weeks.—Six-day programs of educational lectures and entertainment by faculty members, students and professional musicians, designed to present the principal activities of university life.

Visual instruction.—The department sends out sets of slides, each with a syllabus or typewritten lecture. A list is given in the extension announcement.

Community drama service.—Plays suitable for amateur acting are selected and sent out. Advice is given as to costumes and scenery.

Community centers.—Service of an organizer for the promotion of wider use of schools and of greater town success. Advice, model constitutions, programs, etc.

Debating and general information bureau.—The bureau conducts a State high-school debating league and prepares bulletins and bibliographies.

UNIVERSITY OF MISSOURI, EXTENSION DIVISION.

Correspondence courses.—College and high-school courses. A list is published in the extension announcement. All college courses count toward graduation.

Lecture courses in extension centers.—Extension lectures are given on special subjects pursued at the centers. Lectures are given by an instructor, written papers are required, and a final examination is held. If the work is successfully done, credit is given.

Loan of books.—The university library lends books for study in the extension courses and also upon special application to high schools and individuals.

Package libraries and debating.—The university library and the Missouri State library commission send out packages of debating material free of charge, except for transportation. The material covers both sides of given questions and may be retained six weeks. The same material when not used in high schools is available for clubs and community centers.

Lantern slides.—The department furnishes to high schools sets of from 20 to 90 slides free except for transportation. A list is given in the extension announcement.

Art exhibit.—The department of art of the university sends out a special collection of exhibits to a number of the larger schools free except for transportation.

Bulletins of information.—Bulletins on subjects of general and special interest.

Municipal reference bureau.—The bureau furnishes information to cities and towns of Missouri on questions relating to civic affairs. Collections of bulletins and newspaper clippings on various topics, e. g., waterworks, sewers, lighting, paving.

School of social economy, St. Louis.—The school has been placed under the general direction of the division of university extension. It offers advantages for special training in sociology and social welfare work. Teaching and investigations are under the direct charge of Dr. George B. Mangold.

UNIVERSITY OF MONTANA, PUBLIC-SERVICE DIVISION.

Correspondence study department.—Courses are given through correspondence in the following departments of the college of arts and sciences: Art, business administration, English and literature, Greek, history, home economics, journalism, Latin, library science, mathematics, modern languages, psychology, zoology. Credit toward graduation is given by the university for correspondence work of collegiate rank, but the maximum credit toward a university degree which may be earned by correspondence study may not exceed one-half of the credits required for graduation.

Department of public lectures.—Lectures are given singly and in series. During the war a course of lectures on "Nations of the War" was given in some of the largest cities of the State. The extension division supplies lyceum courses and commencement speakers.

Extension courses in connection with the correspondence study department have been given in various cities of the State. The instructor lectures every two weeks to the class, which in the meantime prepares certain written work.

Bureau of public information.—The bureau was established for the purpose of furnishing information on all classes of subjects. Each letter of inquiry is answered carefully, and when full information is desired for debates, etc., package libraries are sent out by the university library.

At the College of Agriculture and Mechanic Arts, Bozeman, through the engineering extension service, courses are offered in shop calculation, drawing, design, electrical machinery, heat and steam, internal-combustion engines, etc.

UNIVERSITY OF NEBRASKA, EXTENSION DIVISION.

Correspondence study.—Credit and noncredit courses.

Instruction by lectures.—Nearly all the members of the faculty are available as lecturers.

Debating and public discussion.—The department maintains a loan library of books, periodicals, etc., relating to questions of the day. It issues bulletins on social topics and keeps in touch by correspondence or personal interview with civic leagues, town councils, library and school boards, business men's clubs, and high-school societies. It also conducts a high-school debating league.

General information and welfare.—The purpose of the department is to investigate problems—artistic, literary, historical, social, industrial, political, and educational—and also special problems in government and business, sanitation, lighting, banking. Information is given on request. It furnishes lantern slides and films to high schools and educational gatherings. Aid is given in dramatic art by sending out persons to drill individuals or groups, and by supplying appropriate selections.

Red Cross work.—Extension courses are offered in first aid, home nursing, surgical dressing, and dietetics. The university aids the department of civilian relief in instituting chapter courses.

NOTES.

Classes in commerce, engineering, history, and art are organized from time to time at Lincoln and Omaha. A bureau of professional service gives aid to school boards and others desiring to secure competent professional assistance by securing and transcribing information regarding vacancies and the qualifications of candidates.

UNIVERSITY OF NEVADA.

The university conducts three schools of mines, at Tonapah, Ely, and Goldfield. They give secondary training in mining and milling subjects. Classes are held in the morning and evening to accomodate shifts of workmen. The university offers a prospectors' short course of four weeks' duration, consisting of lectures and class work in assaying, mineralogy, geology, etc.

UNIVERSITY OF NEW MEXICO, EXTENSION DIVISION.

Correspondence study.—Correspondence study is under the direction of the university faculty.

Lectures.—Lectures are given in series, with syllabi, for study clubs, and single lectures for special groups and general audiences..

* *Extension teaching.*—In cooperation with educational institutions conducting continuation and evening schools.

Debating and public discussion.—Stimulated by State contests. Bulletins containing formulated questions with briefs and bibliographies, and library loan material.

General information.—On matters pertaining to education, State and local government, public health, civic improvement, and other subjects.

Surveys, research, and investigation.—These are made in fields and on subjects of community and State importance.

Suggestive aid.—Aid is given to county, town, and municipal boards, commissions, and councils, school boards, commercial clubs, civic and economic betterment associations.

Exhibits, conferences, and institutes.—These are held for public information upon vocational, educational, and social welfare matters.

The division was reorganized in 1919, and provision made for expansion of the work previously conducted.

COLUMBIA UNIVERSITY (NEW YORK), EXTENSION TEACHING DEPARTMENT.

The statutes of the university define extension teaching as instruction given by university officers and under the administrative supervision and control of the university, either away from the university buildings or at the university, for the benefit of students unable to attend the regular courses of instruction.

Students.—Courses in extension teaching are planned for two classes of students: (1) Men and women who can give only a portion of their time to study and who desire to pursue subjects included in a liberal education of the character and grade of a college or professional school, but without any reference to an academic degree; (2) those who look forward to qualifying themselves to obtain in the future academic recognition involving acceptance of the work which they may satisfactorily complete in extension teaching.

Courses of instruction.—Under the direction of the university council, courses are offered in extension teaching which count toward the degrees of master of arts and doctor of philosophy. Regular courses of instruction are offered in extension teaching which, in many instances, are coordinated so as to form at least the first years of collegiate and professional work, thus providing in the evening at Morningside Heights, and elsewhere, courses in subjects which are generally offered in the freshman, sophomore, and junior years of college, so that students may qualify themselves for admission with advanced standing to Columbia College and Barnard College or other institutions, as candidates for the degrees of bachelor of arts and bachelor of science.

There are also offered at Morningside Heights subjects which are required of students in the schools of mines, engineering, and chemistry. Evening courses are offered in architecture, leading to a certificate; also evening courses in business; and a series of courses intended to equip students for the position of private secretary.

A two-year course in practical optics is offered in cooperation with the department of physics for the special training of those who expect to become optometrists.

Teachers' college offers in cooperation with the department of extension teaching about 130 technical courses in the various fields of practical arts, i. e., household arts, fine arts, industrial arts, music, physical training and nursing, and health. In many of the courses the instruction is the same as that given in the regular classes of the school of practical arts. In other cases, special classes are organized to meet the needs of those desiring instruction in practical arts for use in the home.

A large number of other courses in varied subjects is given late in the afternoon and on Saturday, which repeat those in liberal studies offered in the colleges of the university. These are given in the same manner and often by the same instructors as the regular courses. In most instances university credit is granted.

Numerous courses are given at various *centers*. These are either regular courses of collegiate grade or short lecture courses without academic credit.

Lecture-study courses in certain subjects, forming 15 or 30 lectures alternating with quiz or conference hours, are given at Morningside Heights and at centers when requested.

Centers for the study of choral music are maintained at Morningside Heights and Brooklyn, and choral concerts are given during the year. The department of extension teaching also maintains the institute of arts and sciences.

Institute of arts and sciences.—The institute of arts and sciences is the nonacademic division of the department of extension teaching. The aim of the institute is to provide a popular late afternoon and evening program consisting of general lectures and events of a cultural nature.

The program is planned for busy men and women. The scope includes lectures, given singly or in series of six, on history, literature, art, music, household arts, science, and on current economic and social problems; it comprises also illustrated travel lectures, dramatic recitals, and vocal and instrumental as well as chamber music concerts.

The program is subscribed for as a whole. The annual dues are $10, payable in advance, with an enrollment fee of $5, payable only once, provided the enrollment does not lapse.

UNIVERSITY OF NORTH CAROLINA, EXTENSION DIVISION.

General information.—Literature is lent by the university. Study outlines on subjects of general interest.

Instruction by lectures.—Lectures for clubs, institutes, etc., on general or technical subjects. Popular lectures and lectures for special occasions.

Correspondence courses.—Credit toward graduation is given for some of the courses. Several are offered for the benefit of women's clubs.

Debate and declamation.—Bulletins are issued on a number of subjects for debate. Material is sent from the university library. The bureau conducts a high-school debating union.

County economic and social surveys.—Bulletins containing results are issued by the extension division.

Municipal reference aids.—The bureau studies municipal legislative problems and furnishes material bearing on them.

Educational assistance.—The school of education acts as a clearing house for teachers and principals.

Instruction in road engineering.—The university holds an annual road institute at the university campus, the institute consisting of a week's session of lectures, discussions, exhibits, and demonstrations. The bureau issues annual bulletins and circulars.

War information series.—A list of leaflets and publications is given in the university catalogue.

NOTES.

The university has conducted some extension work in medical instruction.

During 1918–19 the war information series of bulletins was supplemented by war information leaflets dealing with reconstruction problems.

The extension division has direct cooperation with the Federation of Women's Clubs, supplies club outlines, and gives other assistance.

The division conducts package library service on current public questions. It provides also a motion picture film service and aids to community drama.

UNIVERSITY OF NORTH DAKOTA, EXTENSION DIVISION.

I. BUREAU OF EDUCATIONAL COOPERATION.

Correspondence study.—Courses are given in college and vocational subjects under the direction of the university faculty. Credit toward graduation is allowed for one-fourth of the course. The catalogue contains a list of the courses offered.

Lectures.—Lectures are given in series, with syllabi, for study clubs; single lectures, for special groups and general audiences.

Concerts and recitals.—These are provided for music and culture clubs, and also for community lecture and entertainment courses.

Extension courses for club study.—The courses are organized for the purpose of encouraging cultural and vocational education.

Debating and public discussion.—The bureau promotes and directs interest in the study and discussion of public questions; selects questions for discussion and conducts the State high-school debating league and declamation contests. In addition it recommends literary material and bibliographies for assistance in the preparation of papers and speeches.

Visual instruction.—The bureau lends lantern slides and exhibits.

II. BUREAU OF PUBLIC INFORMATION.

General information.—General information is offered concerning municipal affairs and educational matters. Suggestive aid for individuals, school boards, commercial clubs, civic and economic betterment associations.

News service.—Service is given covering university activities and the general opportunities of education.

Conferences and community institutes.—These are held for public information upon vocational, educational, and social welfare matters.

Investigation and research.—Studies in economics; investigations of social and municipal conditions.

Library assistance.—Books, pamphlets, magazines, and clippings lent. The applicant provides postage.

The extension division was reorganized in 1919.

UNIVERSITY OF OKLAHOMA, EXTENSION DIVISION.

Department of public information and welfare.—The department furnishes information from the university's accumulation of material on all subjects pertaining to public welfare. The work of the department is extended through the following bureaus:

Municipal reference bureau.—The bureau gathers and distributes information concerning water, light, paving, drainage, sanitation, fire protection, parks, etc. Together with the bureau of information of the Oklahoma Municipal League it issues a quarterly bulletin, "Oklahoma Municipalities."

Commercial reference bureau.—The bureau gathers and disseminates information pertaining to business, commerce, manufacturing, markets, etc.

Bureau of social center development.—Aid is given in bringing about harmony and cooperation in communities, and also in rendering democracy more efficient.

Public discussion and club service.—The bureau promotes and assists debating through bulletins on important subjects. The bulletins give complete, impartial, and authoritative information on both sides of a question. More than 170,000 have been issued. Under current-events study, topics are selected for school classes, men's and women's clubs. Special bulletins are issued.

High-school debating.—Bulletins, with briefs, bibliographies, and other information, are furnished to high-school debating classes. The bureau conducts a State high-school debating league.

Traveling libraries.—Thirty-five rural and fifteen municipal traveling libraries in circulation.

OTHER DEPARTMENTS AND BUREAUS.

Correspondence study.—More than 700 courses are offered by the divison. These may be used extensively to complete the university course.

Extension classes.—These are intended particularly for teachers in various parts of the State. Syllabi and outlines are furnished.

Extension lectures.—Forty-five lecturers from the faculty are available, besides various musical organizations. Entertainments are provided for lyceum courses. The lectures and entertainments are given free, except for traveling expenses.

Community music bureau.—The department keeps musical instructors in the field who teach for two weeks at a place and endeavor to organize the musical resources. It has published a collection of about 60 songs, "Oklahoma Community Songs," about 6,000 copies.

Department of visual instruction.—The department offers, especially to rural communities, printed illustrated lectures on a variety of subjects. Motion pictures circulated.

Conferences.—Conferences have been held at the university on taxation, rural problems, and good roads.

Merchants' short courses have been held by the division; also State contests in music, ex tempore speaking, and declamation. The department of general information and welfare conducts community institutes and publishes informational bulletins on community welfare.

UNIVERSITY OF OREGON, EXTENSION DIVISION.

EXTENSION TEACHING.

Correspondence study.

Extension classes.—Intensive study classes are offered, extensive or general instruction classes (conducted largely by lectures), and also special classes.

Oregon Teachers' Reading Circle.—Certificates are offered upon completion of courses.

SOCIAL WELFARE.

Lectures.—Faculty members give a large number of lectures with no extra compensation.

Visual instruction.—Slides, films, exhibits, mineral sets, and microscopic slides. General university exhibits.

Community music and drama.—Direction and assistance is given in the presentation of high-school plays and in high-school music. A play-writing contest is conducted.

Public discussion and club service.—The bureau lends package libraries and conducts a high-school debating league. Women's clubs and other groups are supplied with study outlines, reference books, and personal instruction.

Red Cross service.—Lectures, exhibits, bulletins, institutes, service in civilian relief.

Child welfare.—The Oregon Child Welfare Commission, composed of five members of the university faculty, has arranged for a child welfare survey of the State. The commission has organized a psychopathic clinic which examines children free of charge and suggests lines of correctional treatment.

Public information.—The extension division is the distributing agency for such material as the university is able to gather and to put into usable form for the citizens of the State. Inquiries are answered by the division staff and university professors.

UNIVERSITY OF PITTSBURGH, DIVISION OF UNIVERSITY EXTENSION.

General education section.—Publications. Appointment bureau; the bureau conducts student employment, teacher appointment, and general alumni appointment. General information service. Educational meetings and conventions. Educational measurements.

Extra-mural instruction department.—Formal instruction. Class instruction is conducted by the regular university faculty. Courses for credit include a wide range of standardized university courses of the same grade as those offered on the campus.

Correspondence instruction. Formerly the extension division utilized those resources available from the University of Chicago. The division has assumed exclusive control and administration of this work and offers courses of its own.

Lectures.—The regular staff of the university is used by this bureau. Single lectures, with a wide range of subjects, are offered. No university credit is given.

Community center. The bureau does work in Americanization, conducts school and social surveys, investigations, research, and gives expert advice on community problems.

Public service department.—Informal instruction. Package Library Bureau. The bureau furnishes briefs, bibliographies, and club study programs. In addition to the stimulation of debates and literary activities in high schools, the bureau conducts a large debate and literary contest for high-school students on the university campus.

Visual Bureau. The bureau lends lantern slides owned by the university and educational motion picture films contributed by industrial concerns or furnished by the United States Bureau of Education.

School relations. The bureau has charge of high-school visitation, interscholastic contests, and student welfare.

Business and commercial development.—Business surveys; business short courses; cooperative work with commercial clubs.

UNIVERSITY OF SOUTH DAKOTA, EXTENSION DIVISION.

Correspondence courses.—The courses are based on textbooks, special reports, and special references furnished by the university library, and on special correspondence by the professor giving the course. A final written examination is given.

Extension classes.—The work is conducted by regular members of the faculty who meet extra-mural classes on Friday evenings and Saturdays in various parts of the State. Classes are held every four weeks and written work is done in the interim. Courses offered in education, sociology, economics, fine arts, and languages.

Department of visual instruction.—Slides, films, and charts are circulated in the State.

UNIVERSITY OF TEXAS, EXTENSION DIVISION.

EXTENSION TEACHING.

Correspondence instruction.—Courses are given for university credit, entrance credit, preparation for teachers' examination. Courses cover many subjects, including business and vocational work. Courses in law are given without credit.

Group study courses.—These are offered for women's clubs, teachers, business men, labor unions, mothers' clubs, literary societies, etc. Instruction is given through the medium of an outlined course, the instructor keeping in touch through correspondence and personal visits. A reference library is available. The courses are a combination of the correspondence and lecture plan.

Extension classes.—Classes not provided for in the regular university curriculum are conducted either by university instructors or other competent persons.

PUBLIC WELFARE SERVICE.

Bureau of home welfare.—Lecturers and demonstrators attend fairs and county educational meetings. "One-week schools" are held for women's organizations. Bulletins are published.

Division of information.—The division furnishes instruction and entertainment by exhibits, slides, films, music, etc. It also circulates package libraries and answers requests for information.

Public lectures and publicity.—Information is given on questions of the day, and on phases of literature, science, and art.

School interests.—A university interscholastic league has been organized. The bureau conducts contests in debate, declamation, spelling, vocational work, and athletics. It strives to promote the school as a community center, particularly in rural districts. It conducts county educational campaigns. The university provides two rural specialists for educational campaigns in rural districts.

UNIVERSITY OF UTAH, EXTENSION DIVISION.

Bureau of instruction.—Extension classes and correspondence study. Courses in business, trades, and industries, mining, and special courses for teachers and for mothers. Classes are formed upon the application of 10 people for the same work.

Bureau of public service.—Community and health institutes are conducted by the bureau. Child welfare work is supervised. Cooperative work is done with the State and National Government in baby-saving campaigns. The general work of the bureau covers water supply, sanitation, recreation, playgrounds, public improvements, lighting systems, street pavements, libraries, social conditions and needs, public accounts.

Visual instruction.—Slides and films circulated in the State.

General information service.—The bureau invites inquiries upon any subject about which it may be supposed to possess information. It disseminates information through bulletins and the press. It conducts a high school debating league.

Lectures and entertainments.—The bureau acts as an exchange for lecturers and artists. A list of the lectures available is published in the extension announcement.

Teachers' service.—With the cooperation of the State board of education and the Utah Educational Association, the extension division publishes "The Utah Educational Review."

Americanization and educational work.—Special lectures, institutes, training of teachers, vocational instruction.

UNIVERSITY OF VIRGINIA, EXTENSION DIVISION.

Instruction by lectures. Debate and public discussion. Package libraries. Virginia high school quarterly. Bureau of publication. Bureau of appointment. War extension service.

State Geological Survey and State Forestry department. These two departments devote practically all their time to extension work.

Moonlight schools, medical dispensaries, and rural life conferences are carried on by the Y. M. C. A. extension service. The conference is in connection with the summer school, and is held for one week. The proceedings are published and widely distributed.

UNIVERSITY OF WASHINGTON, EXTENSION DIVISION.

DEPARTMENT OF INSTRUCTION.

Correspondence study in academic and noncredit courses.

Extension classes are held in seven different cities. Evening classes are held at the university.

DEPARTMENT OF COMMUNITY SERVICE.

The bureau of lectures offers medical lectures and clinics. Lectures are offered in series, and in courses.

Bureau of debate and discussion.—The bureau circulates package libraries, bibliographies, etc. It also issues debating bulletins, containing outlines of subjects of debate.

Bureau of municipal and legislative research.—The bureau collects statutes, ordinances, charters, and other documents. The chief of the bureau is secretary and treasurer of the League of Washington Municipalities which issues a bulletin entitled "Washington Municipalities."

Bureau of civic development.—The bureau extends advice to centers and civic clubs, and gives general service to community centers.

State tax conference. Annual newspaper institutes. School surveys. Mineral collections. Educational surveys. General information. Publications. Journals, bulletins, circulars of information, etc.

NOTE.

Some extension work not administered by the extension division is as follows: Psychological clinics; laboratory examination of children. The college of mines issues bulletins, holds a three months' training session for miners, and does laboratory work.

UNIVERSITY OF WISCONSIN, EXTENSION DIVISION.

Department of correspondence study.—Instruction is given by correspondence and in class groups. A list of the courses offered is given in the extension announcement.

Department of instruction by lectures.—University, lectures are given singly and in series. In addition are offered concert recitals and reading programs. Institutes, conventions, commencements, etc., are provided for.

Department of debating and public discussion.—Bulletins, with facts, arguments, and selections of bibliographical character, are available on a number of questions. Package libraries, newspaper clippings, documents, publications. Study outlines and programs for clubs. Assistance in the writing of essays, themes, and orations.

Department of general information and welfare.—This department constitutes a clearing house through which inquiries on general matters are given attention. Various methods of disseminating information are utilized, including publication of nontechnical reports and the employment of experts for welfare work in local communities. Other activities supervised or conducted by this department are community institutes, social service institutes, special conferences, vocational institutes, exhibits, community center promotion, service to civic and commercial clubs.

Bureau of municipal reference.—The bureau collects and furnishes technical information on all subjects of organization and administration and other problems.

Municipal and sanitary engineering service.—Assistance is given communities in the solution of problems of municipal and sanitary engineering.

Bureau of community music and drama.—The bureau offers the service of a leader for the organization of community choruses, dramatic clubs, lectures, etc. It prepares school and community programs, organizes literary and musical contests, lends phonograph records, and gives other assistance.

Health instruction bureau.—The bureau conducts a news health service, cooperates with State boards in health propaganda, assists in training public health nurses, publishes nontechnical bulletins on health subjects.

Bureau of visual instruction.—The bureau makes studies of materials and methods of illustrative teaching. It collects, produces, and distributes lantern slides, motion pictures, and other materials for use by schools and organizations.

Slides and films are lent in circuits, especially among schools. In addition, service is given to schools and civic organizations not in circuits. During the year 1917–18 nearly 42,000 lantern slides on more than 250 subjects and 510,000 feet of motion-picture film on 175 subjects were available to borrowers. Seven circuits were established for 21 weeks in succession.

In 1918–19 the available stock of slides was greatly increased and the number of films made available for lending was nearly doubled. The bureau secured and put in circulation many slides and films on war emergency, patriotism, Red Cross, food conservation, and other timely subjects. The number of borrowers increased greatly over the period 1914–1916. In the biennium of 1916–1918 there was a growth of over 70 per cent in the number of slides sent out and nearly 250 per cent in the number of films lent.

Bureau of postgraduate medical instruction.—Six-day courses of instruction are given to physicians by lecture and clinic. Courses were held in nine different cities in 1918–19.

NOTES.

The division conducts a press service, which sends a weekly bulletin to 400 Wisconsin newspapers.

The university has established a chair of Americanization, and the extension division cooperates with the professor in charge of the work.

Much of the local work is administered through six districts with resident staff officers in the following cities: Milwaukee, Oshkosh, La Crosse, Superior, Wausau, and Eau Claire.

UNIVERSITY OF WYOMING, EXTENSION DIVISION.

Division of correspondence study.—Credit courses are given under limited conditions. Noncredit courses are also offered. Courses are given in accounting, agriculture, education, engineering, home economics, etc.

Traveling libraries.—Traveling libraries are lent to individuals and organizations. They consist of 20 or more books of fiction, history, science, travel, etc.

Lecture courses and university centers.—Lecture courses are arranged free except for expenses. Courses are offered in literature, education, political science, etc. Combinations of class, correspondence, and club study are held in different centers of the State. The centers are under the direction of local leaders, and the work is supervised by university professors.

General information.—Inquiries received through the mail on special and general subjects are answered through the division by specialists in the various university departments.

GENERAL EXTENSION IN AGRICULTURAL COLLEGES.

Several agricultural colleges are developing general extension service in addition to agricultural extension. This is the case in Mississippi, Maryland, and Maine, where general extension has not been established heretofore. In Washington the State college at Pullman has obtained legislative appropriation for general extension. Doubtless the agricultural college will divide the field of work with the University of Washington.

The Mississippi Agricultural and Mechanical College maintains, besides the cooperative extension division, a "service bureau," or "extramural division of the college work."

The service bureau is a branch of the Mississippi Agricultural and Mechanical College which seeks to expand into the broadest possible field the varied activities of the institution. To this end the bureau endeavors to act (1) as a clearing house to make available for the whole State the valuable information accumulated by the agencies of investigation and research which are parts of the college; (2) to extend through the department of correspondence study the exact knowledge imparted by the department of collegiate instruction; (3) to offer through the package libraries to schools, clubs, and other organizations, and interested individuals, the resources of compact and accurate libraries on a host of present-day topics of the moment; (4) to collect and to lend, through the department of visual instruction, both slides and films of an educational nature; (5) to supervise the agricultural work and the publicity department.[1]

The department of correspondence study offers courses in agricultural engineering, astronomy, chemistry, civics, dairy husbandry, education, English, home economics, poultry husbandry, public discourse, business law, etc.

The general information service disseminates information both through newspapers and by correspondence. "It invites requests for any kind of material which has relation to the economic, social, intellectual, or religious life of the people."

Visual instruction.—The department lends slide sets on subjects in agriculture, "industry, patriotism, and general culture," and reels of motion pictures on similar subjects.

The package library department lends packages on over 300 subjects "of interest to students of educational or civic topics."

---

[1] Excerpt from catalogue of Mississippi Agricultural and Mechanical College, 1918.

THE ORGANIZATION OF EXTENSION WORK.[1]

The following discussion is based upon replies to a questionnaire addressed to the directors of 29 leading extension divisions in the country. Replies were received from 24 institutions. They are the extension divisions of the State Universities of Arizona, Arkansas, California, Colorado, Indiana, Iowa, Kansas, Michigan, Minnesota, Missouri, North Carolina, Oklahoma, Oregon, South Dakota, Texas, Utah, Washington, and Wisconsin, the University of Pittsburgh, Columbia University, Ohio University, the State Teachers' Colleges of Colorado and Iowa, and the Massachusetts Board of Education.

The information contained in the replies shows a very considerable variety of organization and administrative procedure, certain leading tendencies, and many local peculiarities.

RELATION OF EXTENSION WORK TO THE UNIVERSITY.

The position most commonly occupied by the extension division is one coordinate with the schools or colleges of the university. This is true in Kansas, Missouri, Oregon, Indiana, Texas, Pittsburgh, Utah, and Wisconsin. The extension division of Wisconsin is ranked as a coordinate college, with a dean and faculty. In Minnesota it occupies a position between a department and a school, in Columbia and Colorado one similar to a school; in Michigan it is coordinate with the departments and schools. It is on the same level as a department in Arizona, Iowa Teachers' College, and Ohio University. It represents the extension activities of the various departments and schools in Washington, Iowa, and North Carolina. It cooperates with the departments in California.

The management of the extension division is usually independent of the faculty, though a partial exception is regularly made in the case of regulations pertaining to extension work done for credit. The management is subject to a committee of the faculty for the determination or recommendation of policies in Washington, Missouri, Colorado Teachers' College, California, and Arizona, and cooperates with an advisory committee in North Carolina. In Colorado it is independent, but subject to an advisory committee of the senate in such matters as credits, standards, and general interests.

The director of extension work, together with the associate directors and heads of bureaus, are generally ranked as members of the faculty, even when they do not teach in the university. In some cases they are also listed separately (Minnesota,

---

[1] This chapter is condensed from the mimeograph bulletin on the same subject, prepared by Dr. J. J. Schlicher, and issued by the Division of Educational Extension, March, 1919. A few minor changes have been made and additions incorporated. For further treatment of certain phases of organization, see "Class Extension Work in the Universities and Colleges of the U. S.," by A. J. Klein, Bul. 62, 1919, U. S. Bureau of Education.

Colorado, Oregon, California, Pittsburgh, Iowa, Oklahoma, Utah, Iowa Teachers' College, Colorado Teachers' College). In Indiana they are so listed when they do not do residence work. In Arkansas and Utah the director is ranked only as 'an administrative officer. The same is true of all the administrative officers of the extension division in North Carolina.

In Colorado the extension work of the western slope is carried on jointly by the State University, the State Teachers' College, and the State Normal School, under a supervisor appointed by an extension board. The supervisor is supported by the three institutions and has the rank of assistant professor on the faculty of each.

When the administrative officers of extension work and those giving their whole time to extension teaching are included as members of the faculty, the director is usually ranked as a professor, and the heads of bureaus as assistant professors, instructors, etc. In one case, where the extension work is subject to a committee of the faculty, the director is an associate professor. In two institutions, Wisconsin and Pittsburgh, the director ranks as dean. In one other there is some prospect of this rank for the director, and that of professor for the heads of bureaus. The rank of administrative officers seems to be determined by the salary paid them. Hence the advent of deans of extension work will be more than a change of titles for the director and his staff.

Appointment.—Appointment of the director and other administrative members of the extension staff is, as a rule, made in the usual way by the president of the university and the board of trustees or regents, other influences being unofficial and advisory. The following peculiarities and modifications are found. In California all appointments are recommended to the president by a committee of the university senate, called the University Extension Administrative Board. In Colorado the director is appointed by the president, and all other appointments are made on the director's recommendation. In Columbia the salaries of the assistants to the director are determined by him with the approval of the president. In Michigan the appointments are made by the board of regents. In Minnesota the director and assistant director are appointed by the president. In North Carolina the director is appointed by the president, and the assistants by the president and director. In Washington the heads of bureaus are appointed through joint recommendation. In Utah important appointments are submitted by the president to the dean's council. In Massachusetts the administrative officers of extension are appointed by the governor.

In the appointment of instructors for extension work there is some variety of practice. The departments of the university are usually consulted and usually must approve instructors and courses for which credit is to be given, but the selection of instructors and courses, as a rule, is made by the extension division. In individual instances they are nominated or recommended by the departments concerned, or all instructors to be appointed must be approved by them, or the departments select them with the approval of the director or upon suggestions by him as to the kind of instructor wanted. A distinction is sometimes made between instructors doing correspondence work and others, but the usual distinction depends on whether they are to offer credit courses, and on whether they are regular members of the faculty giving part time to the extension work or extension instructors giving all their time. Cases occur where the departments and faculty have no control over instructors whatever, even when credit is to be given for their work, but this is exceptional. Quite as exceptional are the cases where the departments have full control of the appointment of instructors. This situation is, however, scarcely a normal one, and seems to be found where extension work has in the past been done by individual members of the faculty, and a full-fledged extension division has not yet been formed.

Extension work done outside the division.—In 14 of the 24 institutions no extension work, outside of that in agriculture, is done except under the direction of the general extension division. In a few even agricultural work is under its management. In nine States more or less other extension work is done outside of it, as follows:

University of Arizona—Engineering and mining, the former being carried on by the college of engineering; the latter, under a separate State appropriation, by the State bureau of mines.

University of Colorado—Educational surveys.

University of California—Some lectures and institute work.

Colorado State Teachers' College—Department of psychology cooperates with juvenile court, department of sociology with the county court, department of education with the churches, etc.

Indiana University—Vocational teacher-training courses in the cities; some follow-up work for patients discharged from the hospital of the school of medicine.

University of Iowa—The clinical psychologist and State epidemiologist do extension work independently, the latter being employed jointly by the extension division and the State board of health.

University of Kansas—The school of education controls the work of its school-service bureau; members of the faculty visit teachers' institutes independently of the extension division.

University of Oklahoma—The school of education does its extension work independently. Two heads of departments act as secretaries, respectively, of the State Municipal League and the State Electric Light and Power Association.

University of Texas—The bureau of municipal research and the bureau of economic geology, which are units in operation, act independently of the extension division.

The arrangements just mentioned for extension activities outside of the extension division are by most directors considered satisfactory. There is very little evidence of friction, and the only serious objections made are on the ground of duplication of machinery and waste of effort. One director, whose division controls all the extension work of his institution, would encourage the departments to go ahead on their own initiative when there is no spirit of antagonism.

ADMINISTRATION.

In the subdivision of extension activities into what are usually called departments or bureaus there is the greatest diversity. Arizona has 2 such subdivisions, Arkansas 5, California 7, Colorado 9, Colorado State Teachers' College 5, Columbia 4, Indiana 8, Iowa 7, Iowa State Teachers' College 3, Kansas 4, Massachusetts Board of Education 3, Michigan 12, Minnesota 7, North Carolina 10, Oklahoma 5, Oregon 5, Pittsburgh 8, South Dakota 8, Texas 5, Utah 10, Washington 13, Wisconsin 4. Arkansas, Colorado, Indiana, Pittsburgh, and Utah group their activities under two main heads—instruction and public service. To these the name "bureau" is sometimes affixed also.

In a few cases the management of the different bureaus is practically independent, but as a rule the director exercises more or less complete supervision or control. New policies are determined in about half the divisions by consultation between the director and the individual head of the bureau concerned. The rest are about equally divided between those where a common consultation of all members of the staff is held and those where both individual and common consultation are found. When a distinction is made, general policies are determined by the latter, details by the former method. In California general policies are determined by the director and the administrative extension board of the university senate.

Local centers.—Local centers, with more or less definite administrative management of their own, are maintained by some of the extension divisions.

California has four local centers—at Los Angeles, Stockton, San Diego, and Fresno, with representatives of the extension division in charge.

The joint arrangement between the University of Colorado, Colorado State Teachers' College, and Colorado State Normal School has already been mentioned, by which through a committee representing the three schools the extension work of the western slope is put under the direction of a superintendent, who devotes his whole time to it. The committee, which consists of the director of extension at the university and the presidents of the other two institutions, selects the superintendent, outlines his duties, and has referred to it monthly reports of his work for its approval.

The director of extension at Columbia generally appoints some representative who acts as secretary for the local interests, merely looking after the registration and banking of the tuition fees under the direction of the bursar of the university.

In the two centers of the Indiana division the local officer in charge stands in the same relation to the director as the members of the main staff at the university. The chief duties of the local management are to arrange and conduct classes in the vicinity of the center.

In Kansas a local committee has charge, including the director, one member appointed by him, and others elected by the local center. It arranges and conducts the program of entertainment and education for one year and cooperates with the extension division in securing the greatest possible use of the services of the university for the community. The membership of the local center is composed of those who pay the membership fee, which entitles them to all programs for the year. They elect a president and act through committees for the various kinds of extension service to be obtained, lectures, musical recitals, social welfare, community surveys, etc. A local secretary, appointed by the director, conducts the correspondence, takes charge of slides and films, follows up the work of the committee and the program, and keeps things moving and active generally.

The Massachusetts division has one local center, at Springfield, whose manager is responsible to the agent in charge of class instruction, and attends to publicity and the organization of classes.

The North Carolina local centers are in charge of a separate member of the staff, who cooperates with a local committee.

The University of Oregon has a local center at Portland, with a director and secretary.

South Dakota is planning the appointment of paid local secretaries, who are to keep the class fully advised of matters concerning it, make local arrangements, and keep the extension idea prominently before the public.

The extension division of Wisconsin has six local districts, with headquarters at Milwaukee, Oshkosh, La Crosse, Superior, Wausau, and Eau Claire. Each has a district representative at its head, and one or more organizers, in addition to clerks and stenographers. Each has also one or more local instructors in engineering and in other lines much in demand. The chief of the bureau of health instruction has his headquarters at Milwaukee. The district representatives are chosen by the dean of extension, as are also the organizers, after consultation with the district representatives. The latter are responsible to the dean for the staff and work of their districts

Local instructors work under the direction of the home office at the university. The duties of the local staff are to survey the educational needs of committees and serve them through the various types of extension service. The district representatives are called into conference at the university once or twice a year, and at other times individually when necessary. They hold weekly conferences with their men for plans and reports on their work. Monthly reports are made by district representatives and instructors, and daily reports by the organizers.

INSTRUCTION, LECTURES.

The great bulk of extension instruction and lectures is given by regular members of the faculties. The following extension divisions report instructors[1] giving full time to extension work: Kansas 3, Minnesota 2, Oregon 6, California 4, Colorado 3, Columbia 195, Indiana 4, Massachusetts Board of Education 14, Pittsburgh 3, Iowa 7, Michigan 1, Colorado State Teachers' College 1, Iowa State Teachers' College 30 (summer), Ohio University 3, Utah 1, Wisconsin 60. Only a few institutions have lecturers devoting all their time to extension work. Indiana has 5, Oklahoma 1, Wisconsin 25. The members of the regular faculty devoting part time to extension instruction range from 2 to 107 (Columbia); of lecturers, from 2 to 115 (Michigan). The average number of part-time instructors per institution is 29, of part-time lecturers 24.

Instructors and lecturers are employed from outside the faculty and extension staff by nearly all the divisions. The following classes of such additional help are mentioned: Instructors at distant points, business and professional men, lawyers, doctors, lecturers in popular courses, travelers, instructors from the public schools, instructors for special work (vocational and commercial, e. g., wireless telegraphy), instructors for scout masters and camp-fire training camps, specialists in Americanization, community organization, municipal government and health subjects, superintendents of mines and factories, speakers at institutes and conferences.

Supervision.—The work of instruction thus done is sometimes closely supervised by the departments at the university under which it falls, through examination questions, outlines of the courses, and by other means. In Columbia each department has an extension committee for this purpose. In California, department secretaries cooperate with the assistant director in charge of instruction. Usually, however, the supervision is exercised through visits by the extension director or some member of the staff representing him. In two cases the school of education has a special part in this, and in one case the services of the State high-school inspector are thus employed.

Methods of determining the success of instruction or lecture work are various. In the order of frequency they are: Personal visits, usually by the director, confidential reports by reliable persons on the ground, conferences with superintendents, results as seen by subsequent requests for courses, careful analysis of the results of instruction by a tabulation of such items as attendance, reasons for absence, character of examination papers. The answers to questionnaires give evidence that it is a difficult problem, and usually several of the methods named are employed. It might be said that the tendency is toward accurate determination of results by such methods as the last one mentioned. At least, we find this method adopted by strong divisions whose finances permit them to do so.

---

[1] These figures do not include all administrators who have the rank of instructor but do no teaching.

Supervision of correspondence work by personal visits of instructors is found only in 6 out of 18 cases, and in several of these but little is done in this line, though it is considered desirable by several. Since correspondence work is usually conducted by regular members of the faculty, and is an individual matter so far as the student is concerned, correspondence and correction of his work is relied upon to check his work. The desirability of personal contact seems to be attested by the fact that several institutions which do a good deal of correspondence work make provision for it. The establishment of a number of local centers for extension work, with resident instructors, as we find in Wisconsin, makes this method of supervision relatively easy. As a new venture in this field should be mentioned the Helps for Community and Home Study Department just being established by Columbia.

Group study.—Group or class study, in which the instructor is not present at every meeting of the class, but periodically, is maintained by 9 out of 21 divisions replying. The success is reported as good by 4, as fair or as depending on circumstances, like local leadership, by 3, and as unsatisfactory by 2.

Help from outside the university and extension staff is secured when needed by most extension divisions. The institutions report the following purposes for which they secure such help: Instruction 11,[1] lectures 7, special and peculiar fields 3, institutes and conferences 6, correspondence work 2, grading correspondence papers 1, surveys and investigations 1, debating league 1, recreation camps 1, good roads and country life 1, community and child welfare 3, woman's clubs 1, expert informational work among teachers 1, promotion 2. Trained professional men and experts, the faculties of other colleges, former members of the university faculty, school superintendents and teachers, and National, State, and municipal officials are among the classes drawn upon for this purpose.

COOPERATION.

Fixed relations of cooperation are established by more than three-fourths of the extension divisions with a great variety of institutions, agencies, and organizations for business, charitable, general welfare, and general educational purposes. A large share of their effective work in these directions is done by extension divisions in this way, since it enables them to benefit by the accumulated experience, organization, and expert assistance of these bodies. Among them are the State and local chambers of commerce, rotary clubs, art clubs, the Federation of Women's Clubs, the Red Cross, hospitals, boards of education, the State board of health, the State Library Commission, colleges, universities and high schools, the States Relations Service, the State board for vocational education, various industrial organizations, the Anti-Tuberculosis Association, the State Conference of Charities and Corrections, the Young Men's Christian Association and Young Women's Christian Association, the churches, the American Institute of Banking, the State League of Municipalities, the granges, the railroads, advertising clubs, and local or State welfare and business organizations of various kinds.

These forms of cooperation are, with very few exceptions, reported as yielding good results, and even a qualified statement on this point is rare.

Cooperation with other extension divisions is carried on to a certain extent and in certain lines by 17 of the institutions. The remaining 7 either have not established cooperation with other extension divisions or did not answer the question. The close cooperation of the extension division of Arkansas with the States Relations Service deserves special mention. In the cooperation between the State institutions of Colorado expenses are shared and efforts pooled to provide the west slope with extension work. ·Slides, films, and to a limited extent lectures, are exchanged by Indiana, and there is reciprocation also in the exchange of mailing lists. The relations between the extension divisions of the State institutions of Iowa are deter-

---

[1] These figures should be larger, for most reports list only one or two purposes as examples.

mined by the extension council of the State board of education. In Kansas the State Agricultural College supplies the extension division of the university with demonstrators and lecturers in home economics for community institute programs, their local expenses being paid by the university extension division. The cooperation between Minnesota, North Dakota, and Wisconsin is in securing and routing lyceum talent. Oklahoma exchanged publications and package library material and has cooperation in correspondence study. The latter is found in a limited degree also in Oregon and in Colorado, which also exchange slides to a limited extent. Pittsburgh has used the correspondence-study division of the University of Chicago for its work in this line. It is a common practice to refer requests from outside the State to the extension division in the State where the correspondent resides.

BUDGET.

The appropriations for extension work are as a rule made either directly by the legislature or by the board of regents of the university, upon an estimate submitted by the director and approved by the president. The two methods of providing funds are about equally common. In one institution the president alone makes the assignment for the extension division.

Fees are charged by all of the 24 divisions reporting except two. They are regularly charged for correspondence work, and nearly always for class instruction also. In several cases a fee is charged only for credit courses. One division which has until now not charged fees for class instruction will do so hereafter. In the case of lectures the fee most commonly goes directly to the lecturer, together with the expenses of the trip. In isolated cases no charge is made for lectures, except the expenses of the lecturer. Fees are also charged in some cases for community institutes, short courses, service to women's clubs, current-topics study, first-aid instruction, industrial classes, and the use of slides and films.

The fees are sometimes paid into the extension fund; sometimes, and with about the same frequency, into the general university fund; or, in Massachusetts, into the State treasury. In the former case sometimes a fixed division is made between the divisions and the instructor, 50–50 in one, 20–80 in another, and 10–90 for the regular faculty and 30–70 for local instructors in a third. In the last-named case 20 per cent goes to the local administration for the expense of supervision. When the fees are paid into the university fund, this is in several instances done as a mere form, since they are reappropriated to the division or subject to its call for certain payments in instruction.

Methods of payment.—The payment to instructors is made according to several different methods. Sometimes regular members of the faculty receive no extra compensation for extension work; sometimes they are paid according to a scale, in which their regular salaries, the nature of the course or lecture and the attendance at the lecture or class, as well as the frequency of its meetings, may be factors. Local or outside instructors are sometimes paid according to the fees received from their work, even when regular instructors are not thus paid, but more commonly they are engaged for a specific purpose and paid a sum agreed upon. Two institutions pay the fees up to a certain amount, one of them with a certain guaranty in addition. Another makes the pay depend on fees received for class work within certain limits of attendance. Assistance for grading and correcting correspondence-study papers is, at least in some cases, paid by the lesson or assignment.

Other kinds of income received by the extension divisions are of such a varied character that they are difficult to estimate. Practically all the divisions receive considerable local help, which if counted as actual income would bulk large. Equally difficult is it to determine how much service the extension work receives from the faculty members and from the general administrative staff of the university. In some institutions, telephone, telegraph, and express charges are paid from the general university fund and not charged against the extension budget. Divisions in some instances receive special appropriations from the State board of education, some obtain gifts of the cost of printing special bulletins, others receive financial assistance from industrial or commercial corporations for conducting work for employees or the community.

Little effort is made to establish a fixed budget for the different bureaus of a division, the assignment of funds depending on the needs as they arise. In several very distinctly defined lines of work, like that of the institutes of arts and sciences at Columbia, and the summer extension work of the Iowa State Teachers' College, a fixed separation of funds is the established practice.

The traveling expenses of instructors and lecturers and other agents are paid by the extension division in 7 States, by the community in 7, by the State in 6, by the university in 4. Communities do not, however, always pay these expenses, even in the States referred to, since there is usually an alternative. In some cases the administrative expenses are excepted and paid by the extension division or the State. In two cases the expenses are met out of the fees.

In a similar manner, institutes or conferences are financed by the university in 5 cases, by the extension divisions in 4, by the State in 2, by cooperation of the community and the extension division in 3, by the community in 1, by one of the three methods in 3, by special appropriation in 2, by the State board of education in 1.

Slides, films, and package libraries are furnished free, except for cost of transportation, and in some cases for damage, in 9 States, in one of which it is provided that no admission fee be charged. In 2 additional States transportation one way only is charged.

THE FLORIDA BUDGET.

The following is a partially itemized budget for general extension as provided by act of the Florida legislature in 1919:

SECTION 5. The sum of $50,000, or so much thereof as may be necessary, is hereby appropriated out of the general revenue fund to carry out the work herein authorized, for a period of two years and one month from June 1, 1919, to June 30, 1921, and shall be expended as follows:

Salary of director...one year.. $3,000
Salary of field agent...do.... 3,000
Salary of office assistants, stenographers, filing clerks, and librarians...do.... 2,700

Extra pay for professors engaged in outside work, estimated for 352 days at
$5 per day...one year.... $1,760

Extra pay for 10 students assisting in work in office at $300 each.....do.... 3,000

Pay for lecturers and entertainers....................................do.... 500

Traveling expenses for field agent, estimated 150 days at $7 per day..do.... 1,050

Traveling expenses for professors and students engaged in outside work.do.... 1,290

Traveling expenses for lecturers and entertainers....................do.... 500

Contingencies, telegrams, researches, advertising, and extra salaries ...do.... 1,500

[Appropriations for items listed above may be transferred from one to another as need
may arise.]

Subscription for periodicals......................................one year.. 500

Printing...do.... 1,200

Stamps..do.... 1,500

Purchase of correspondence courses..................................do.... 1,000

Purchase of slides and films..do.... 2,000

Purchase of filing cases, writing machines, and other office furniture..do.... 500

Total... $25,000

For second year.. $25,000

For the two years.. $50,000

UNIVERSITY POLICY.

The following is a condensed statement of the place and function of an extension division in university policy. The propositions are taken from a preliminary draft of the by-laws proposed for a western university.

SECTION 1. *Fundamental considerations.* The university is under obligations to serve, within its means, all the people of the State.

The department of instruction is the unit of university activity, whether on or off the campus.

A school of the university is an administrative device by which certain major interests of the people may be more efficiently served. Departments that contribute to the activity of a school retain their integrity and independence as structural units of the university.

Only stringent necessity should make it necessary for the board of regents to establish more than one department covering the same field.

SEC. 2. *The field of the extension division.* The extension division is coordinate with the other divisions called schools. It is the administrative device by which the university serves the people of the State who can not come to the campus for instruction, or who, if they come to the campus, take only such work, especially provided, as their regular vocational duties permit them to take.

SEC. 3. *The extension division and the departments.* The departments of the university must do their teaching work beyond the campus through the extension division, and credit extension classes must be given with the general understanding of the departments concerned.

SEC. 4. *The extension division and schools.* In such of its teaching work as is designed to count toward a university degree the extension division represents the schools, and such work must be given with the understanding of the schools concerned.

SEC. 5. *Independent organization authorized.* The extension division may be authorized to undertake work independently of the departments or schools.

SEC. 6. *Classification of extension workers.* Members of the extension staff, who give instruction in a recognized field of knowledge should be classified also with the staff of the departments in question.

Clerks and administrative officers should be classified only with the extension staff.

SEC. 7. *Classification of extension students.* All students taking credit courses by extension should be classified as of the school in which their major work lies. They should, however, determine this classification themselves, on their application cards at the time of registration or on forms otherwise provided by the registrar. All extension students not so fixing their classification in schools and all other extension students shall be classified merely as extension students. This section does not in any way prohibit the extension division from maintaining and publishing lists of all students doing extension work.

LIST OF EXTENSION PUBLICATIONS.[1]

UNIVERSITY OF CALIFORNIA—EXTENSION DIVISION.

BULLETINS.

Volume 1. 1915–16.

No. 9. Part 1. Bureau of Correspondence Instruction. (General information.)

No. 11. Bureau of Class Instruction. (Announcement of courses, 1915–16.)

No. 14. Bureau of Public Discussion. (Constitution and rules and regulations of the Interscholastic Public Speaking League of California.)

No. 15. University extension service for teachers.

Volume 2. 1916–17.

No. 8. Correspondence courses in gasoline automobiles, advanced shop mathematics, etc.

No. 16. Compulsory health insurance.

No. 19. Military service.

No. 21. Single house legislature.

No. 23. Some suggestions regarding possibilities of service in view of the war.

Volume 3. 1917–18.

No. 1. Bureau of Class Instruction. (Announcements of courses 1917–18.)

No. 2. The newsprint situation.

No. 3. League to enforce peace.

No. 4. Schedule of classes (August).

No. 5. Preliminary announcement for Southern California.

No. 6. Preparing the way for peace. (Stereopticon lecture outline.)

No. 7. Steps toward democracy in Europe. (Syllabus of six illustrated lectures.)

No. 8. From north to south in Europe. (Syllabus of six illustrated lectures.)

No. 9. Episodes in American history and exploration. (Syllabus of six illustrated lectures.)

No. 10. Revelations of intrigue. (Stereopticon lecture outline.)

No. 11. Constitution, Public Speaking League.

No. 12. Correspondence course in music.

No. 13. Courses in philosophy, political science, economics, and history. (Correspondence.)

No. 14. Judging the debate.

No. 15. Astronomy, oral and dental hygiene, zoology. (Correspondence.)

No. 16. Stereopticon lecture outline.

No. 17. The single tax.

No. 18. Use and care of the gasoline automobile. (Correspondence.)

No. 19. Disaster and its reaction. (Stereopticon lecture outline.)

No. 20. Government monopoly of the manufacture of munitions of war.

No. 21. Correspondence courses in business subjects.

No. 22. Schedule of classes (January).

No. 23. Illustrated lectures on art.

No. 24. Constitution, rules and regulations, junior section, Interscholastic Public-Speaking League.

---

[1] This check list of university extension publications was originally prepared by Dr. Schlicher from records in the office of the division of educational extension. The list includes those bulletins and circulars sent to Washington and those tabulated in the publications of several divisions.

Volume 3. 1917-18—Continued.

Nos. 26, 30, 37, 38. Correspondence courses in journalism, business, technical subjects, and education.

No. 32. Illustrated war lectures.

No. 35. Extension courses offered in southern California.

No. 40. Schedule of classes.

Volume 4. 1918-19.

No. 1. Six-year presidential term.

No. 4. Correspondence courses in sewing, etc.

No. 5. Correspondence course in art appreciation.

In addition, numerous circulars dealing with instruction, exhibits, etc., are issued.

UNIVERSITY OF COLORADO—EXTENSION DIVISION.

(Extension bulletins are contained in the University of Colorado bulletin with separate numbering.)

BULLETINS.

No. 1. High school and college conference. (Abridged reports, 1896, 1898, 1903, 1909, 1910.)

No. 2. University extension division. (General statement, 1912.)

No. 3. Protection against typhoid, 1912.

No. 4. Municipal water supplies of Colorado. By C. C. Williams. 1912.

No. 5. Correspondence study centers. (Lectures and addresses. 1912.)

No. 6. List of serials in University of Colorado library, 1913.

No. 7. The practical value of birds. By Junius Enderson. 1913.

No. 8. A week of applied sociology—conference of social workers, 1913.

No. 9. Report of the week of applied sociology, 1913. (Program.)

No. 10. Correspondence study classes, lectures, etc.

No. 11. Graduate courses in medicine, 1913.

No. 12. Insanity, its nature, causes, and prevention. By Francis Ranely. 1913.

No. 13. Colorado Sociological Conference. (Social welfare, education. Program, 1914.)

No. 14. Sociological Conference, 1914. Report.

No. 15. Colorado high school and college courses, 1912, 1913, 1914. (Abridged reports.)

No. 16. Colorado Sociological Conference. (Program, 1915.)

No. 17. Community welfare conferences. (Suggested organization and programs.)

No. 18. University extension. (Announcement of courses, October, 1915.)

General Series.

No. 99. Colorado Sociological Conference and Colorado Municipal League. (Administrative efficiency in a democracy. Program, 1916.

No. 118. Extension courses in clinical laboratory methods, September 7, 1917.

No. 132. University extension courses. (General announcements, November, 1918.

Constitution of the Colorado high school debating league.

The war is over—let's go!

Business and industrial courses, September, 1915.

Telling stories to children.

Program suggestions for women's clubs. (Program, 1917.)

Social education and public health.

INDIANA UNIVERSITY—EXTENSION DIVISION.

BULLETINS.

Volume 1. 1915–16.
- No. 1. Correspondence study.
- No. 2. Municipal home rule. (High School Discussion League, October, 1915.)
- No. 3. Lantern slides, 1915.
- No. 4. The community schoolhouse.
- No. 5. First loan exhibit of pictures.
- No 6. Early Indiana history.
- No. 7. Indiana local history.
- No. 8. Westminster Abbey.
- No. 9. Reference aids for schools.
- No. 10. Community welfare programs.
- No. 11. Play and recreation.
- No. 12. Extension courses of instruction at Indianapolis, August, 1916.

Volume 2. 1916–17.
- No. 1. Play and recreation. (Four papers read at a conference, 1916.)
- No. 2. High School Discussion League. (Compulsory military service for the United States.)
- No. 3. Correspondence study. (Courses.)
- No. 4. Extension courses at Fort Wayne, January, 1918.
- No. 5. Community institutes.
- No. 6. Third Conference on Educational Measurements. (Report.)
- No. 7. Package libraries.
- No. 8. Class instruction.
- No. 9. Extension courses at Fort Wayne, September, 1918.
- No. 10. A new constitution for Indiana. (Club study outline.)
- No. 11. City markets. By Frank T. Stockton.
- No. 12. Extension courses of instruction at Fort Wayne.

Volume 3. 1917–18.
- No. 1. Cooperative retail delivery. By W. S. Bittner.
- No. 2. High School Discussion League. (War finance in the United States.)
- No. 3. Financing the war. By Ray S. Trent.
- No. 4. Extension courses of instruction at Fort Wayne.
- No. 5. Vocational recreation in Indiana, 1916.
- No. 6. Club study outline—subjects: America's war problems the background of the great war.
- No. 7. Women in industry. By Ray S. Trent.
- No. 9. Extension courses of instruction at Fort Wayne.
- No. 10. Extension courses of instruction at Indianapolis.
- No. 11. Public Markets. By Walton S. Bittner.
- No. 12. Correspondence study. (List of courses.)

Volume 4. 1918–19.
- No. 1. High School Discussion League. (Universal service for citizenship.)
- No. 2. Extension courses at Fort Wayne, October, 1918.
- No. 3. Extension courses at Indianapolis, November, 1918.
- No. 4. Fifth Conference on Educational Measurements, 1918.
- No. 5. Town and city beautification.
- No. 6. School and community service.
- No. 7. Visual instruction.
- No. 8. Feeding children at school.
- No. 9. Americanization.
- No. 10. Speakers' bureau.

Volume 11.

No. 10. A new constitution for Indiana. (Outline and students' speeches, January, 1914.)

No. 6. Debating and public discussion. (A manual for civic discussion clubs June, 1913.)

Volume 13.

No. 7. A manual of pageantry. By Robert Withington.

Volume 15.

No. 8. Extension division announcement, 1917–18.

Volume 16.

No. 6. Extension division announcement, 1918–19.

A new constitution for Indiana. (First annual contest, Indiana High School Discussion League, June, 1914.)

Topics of interest to women's clubs.

Baby-saving campaign and child-welfare institute. (Program.)

Programs of community institutes.

CIRCULARS OF INFORMATION.

Visual instruction. (Second loan exhibit of pictures.)
Visual instruction. (Third loan exhibit of pictures.)
Club study. (Departments and courses of study.)
Extension lectures. (A list of speakers and subjects.)
Public library lectures. (A list of speakers and subjects.)
Commencement lectures. (A list of speakers and subjects.)
Community institutes. (Explanation and suggested programs.)
Community institutes. (Methods of organization.)
The fourteen-minute speech.
Public discussion. (Package libraries.)
Public discussion. (Debates.)
State High School Discussion League.
Visual instruction. (Equipment.)
Visual instruction (Third loan exhibit of pictures.)
Visual instruction. (Motion pictures.)
Play and recreation.
Fourth exhibit of pictures.
Problems of the war.

UNIVERSITY OF IOWA—EXTENSION DIVISION.

BULLETINS.

No. 1. Street lighting. By Arthur H. Ford.

No. 2. Rate-making for public utilities. By Wm. C. Raymond.

No. 3. Engineering as a profession. By Wm. C. Raymond.

No. 4. Store lighting. By Arthur H. Ford.

No. 5. Economy of time in arithmetic. By Walter H. Jessup.

No. 6. Vocational guidance in high schools. By Ervin E. Lewis.

No. 7. Ninth annual announcement of the Iowa High School Debating League. By Glenn N. Merry.

No. 8. Waterworks statistics of 38 cities of Iowa, with the meter rates of 70 cities. By John H. Dunlap.

No. 9. Work, wages, and schooling of 800 Iowa boys in relation to the problem of vocational guidance. By Ervin E. Lewis.

No. 10. Principles of advertising. By Philip J. Sodergren.

No. 11. Hygienic conditions in Iowa schools. By Irving King.
No. 12. Tenth annual announcement of the Iowa High School Debating League. By Glenn N. Merry.
No. 13. Employers[1] welfare work in Iowa. By Paul S. Pierce.
No. 14. Iowa handbook on child welfare.
No. 15. Present attainment in handwriting of school children in Iowa. By Ernest J. Ashbaugh.
No. 16. Child welfare surveys and bibliography.
No. 17. Correspondence courses.
No. 18. High school plays. By Glenn N. Merry.
No. 19. Culture and women's clubs. By Thomas H. MacBride.
No. 21. Loan collections of lantern slides.
No. 22. Municipal accounting. By Russell A. Stevenson.
No. 23. Eleventh annual announcement of the Iowa High School Debating League. By Glenn N. Merry.
No. 24. Arithmetical skill of Iowa school children. By Ernest J. Ashbaugh.
No. 25. Standards of measuring junior high schools. By Ervin E. Lewis.
No. 26. The social survey. By Bessie A. McClenahan.
No. 27. The Iowa desk book of newspaper practices. By Conger Reynolds.
No. 28. Twelfth annual announcement of the Iowa High School Debating League. By Glenn N. Merry.
No. 29. German submarine warfare against the United States, 1915–1917. By Louis Pelzer.
No. 30. Newspaper English. By Sam B. Sloan.
No. 31. The Monroe Doctrine and the War. By Harry G. Plum.
No. 32. The conservation of sugar. By Ernest Horn and Maude M. McBroom.
No. 33. The fifth annual recreational camp for girls.
No. 34. Iowa Training Camp for Scoutmasters.
No. 35. Conference for Religious Workers.
No. 36. The overdraft evil as illustrated by conditions in Iowa banks. By Nathaniel R. Whitney.
No. 37. Survey of the high schools of Des Moines. By Ervin E. Lewis.
No. 38. Thirteenth annual announcement of the Iowa High School Debating League.
No. 39. Loan collections of lantern slides.
No. 40. Iowa Patriotic League. (Bibliography.)
No. 41. Survey of the school buildings of Muscatine. By Ernest J. Ashbaugh.
No. 42. Parent-teacher associations in Iowa.
No. 43. Iowa spelling scale. By Ernest J. Ashbaugh.
Programs of Retail Merchant's Conferences.

UNIVERSITY OF KANSAS—EXTENSION DIVISION.

BULLETINS.

Training for debating, with model briefs, 1910.
The recall of judges, with bibliography and references, 1913.
Constructive juvenile effort in Kansas.
Announcement of the Kansas High School Debating League, August, 1918, with bibliography and references on compulsory arbitration (also list of debates since 1910–11).
Announcement of extension lectures, lecture courses, and concerts, with general information, 1915.
Suggestions for forming child welfare organization.
Merchants week lectures, 1915. (Report.)
Bulletin of the Department of General Information.

Correspondence study courses, 1918.
The cigarette problem.

Department of general information.
Play service.
Visual instruction, 1918–19.
Commencement addresses, 1918.
Public speaking in high schools.
The cigarette problem.
How to enter the child welfare movement.
Juvenile thrift and industry.
Home and school gardening.
Child welfare in war time.
Women's clubs, debating outlines, package libraries, 1918–19.
Plays for schools, 1918.
Public speaking in the high school.
Service of the university extension division.   (Description of departments.)

MASSACHUSETTS BOARD OF EDUCATION—DEPARTMENT OF UNIVERSITY EXTENSION.

BULLETINS.

Volume 1. 1916.
    No. 1. Correspondence courses, 1916.
    No. 2. Correspondence and group-study courses, 1916.
    No. 3. News bulletin.
    No. 4. Courses for class instruction.
    No. 5. Courses for correspondence instruction.
    No. 6. Courses to be offered in cooperation with public libraries in Massachu-
        setts.
Volume 2. 1917.
    No. 1. Second annual report on university extension.
    No. 2. Educational extension opportunities in Massachusetts.
    No. 3. Bureau of Class Instruction and Bureau of Correspondence Instruction.
        (List of courses May, 1917.)
    No. 5. Food thrift.
    No. 6. Courses offered for correspondence instruction, November, 1917.
Volume 3. 1918.
    No. 3. Courses offered for correspondence instruction, May, 1918.
    No. 5. Courses offered for class instruction, 1918–19.
    No. 6. Courses offered for correspondence instruction, 1918–19.
University extension courses, 1918–19, offered by the Boston commission on exten-
  sion courses.
Public document No. 113. Third annual report of the board of education—depart-
  ment of university extension, January, 1918.

UNIVERSITY OF MISSOURI—EXTENSION DIVISION.

BULLETINS.

No. 2. School-improvement agencies, 1913.
No. 3. Consolidation of schools in Missouri, 1913.
No. 4. Correspondence courses in high-school subjects, 1913.
No. 6. Preservation of food in the home, 1914.
No. 7. Care of free textbooks, 1914.

No. 9. Abnormal and defective children, 1914.
No. 11. The house fly, 1914.
No. 12. Correspondence courses in high-school study, 1915.
No. 13. Announcements of the extension division, 1915–16.
No. 14. Technical manual arts for general educational purposes, 1916.
No. 15. Country roads, 1916. (2 parts.)
No. 16. Hand work in grades 1 to 6, 1916.
No. 19. Correspondence courses in high-school subjects, September, 1916.
No. 20. Announcement of the extension division, 1916–17.
No. 21. Manual for the mental and physical examination of children, 1916.
No. 22. Better highways, 1916.
No. 23. The feeding of children, 1917.
No. 24. Feeding the baby, 1917.
No. 25. Extension division—Announcement, 1917–18.
No. 26. Extension division—Announcement, 1919–20.
Constitution of the Missouri High-School Debating League.
Announcement of the extension division, 1912–13.

UNIVERSITY OF MINNESOTA—EXTENSION DIVISION

Americanization training course, 1918–19.
Community centers.
Effective debating.
Programs of merchants' short courses.
University extension lectures, 1918–19.
Correspondence courses, 1918–19.
Announcement of evening courses, 1918–19.
University extension—What and why?
Handbook of extension service.
Community service.
The key to opportunity.

UNIVERSITY OF MICHIGAN—EXTENSION DIVISION.

Library extension service, 1918–19.
Michigan High-School Debating League.
Extension credit courses, 1918–19.
Extension service, 1918–19.

UNIVERSITY OF NORTH DAKOTA—EXTENSION DIVISION

High-School Debating League.
High-school declamation contest, high-school universal contest, 1918–19.
Play festivals.
Extension division—Announcements.
University extension lectures.
Correspondence study.

UNIVERSITY OF NORTH CAROLINA—EXTENSION DIVISION.

BULLETINS.

Debate and declamation.
Compulsory military training.
Woman suffrage.
Addresses on education for use in declaiming, essay writing, and reading.

153448°—20——8

The initiative and referendum.
Public discussion and debate.
Ship subsidies.
The enlargement of the Navy.
Government ownership of railroads.
Compulsory arbitration of industrial disputes.
Announcement and regulations of the High School Debating Union of North Carolina.
    1918–19.
Selections for speaking in the public schools.

County economic and social surveys.

Cooperative institutions among the farmers of Catawba County.
Syllabus of home-county club studies.
Country life institutes.
The North Carolina Club Year-Book, 1915–16.
Sampson County: Economic and social.
The North Carolina Year-Book, 1916–17.
Local study clubs.
Correspondence courses, extension lectures.

Extension circulars.

Our country-church problem.
Our Carolina highlanders.
Wealth, welfare, and willingness in North Carolina.
County government and county affairs.
The country church.

Educational information and assistance.

A professional library for teachers in secondary schools.
The teaching of county geography.
Measurement of achievement in the fundamental elementary-school subjects.

War-information series.

War-information service.
The Lafayette Association.
A program for extension for a time of war.
Why we are at war with Germany.
Single lectures concerning the war.
Extension courses and lectures.
Will you keep the freedom our soldiers win?
National ideals in British and American literature.

Extension leaflets.

The American university and the new nationalism.
The community pageant.
Reconstruction and citizenship.
Studies in the social and industrial condition of women as affected by the war.

UNIVERSITY OF ARKANSAS—EXTENSION DIVISION.

Community programs.
A community forum.
Club programs.

UNIVERSITY OF OKLAHOMA—EXTENSION DIVISION.

DEBATE BULLETINS.

No. 12. A student's manual of debating and parliamentary practice.
No. 13. The initiative and referendum. (Out.)
No. 15. Unicameral legislatures. 72 pages.
No. 16. Guaranty of bank deposits. 80 pages. (Out.)
No. 17. Woman suffrage. 80 pages. (Out.)
No. 18. Consolidation of rural schools. 32 pages.
No. 20. The preferential.ballot. 56 pages.
No. 21. Government ownership of railways. 116 pages.
No. 22. The single tax. 162 pages.
No. 24. Workmen's compensation, 132 pages.
No. 26. Selling munitions of war. 64 pages.
No. 27. Municipal affairs.
No. 28. Continuing the Monroe doctrine. 148 pages.
No. 29. Proceedings Third Annual Convention—Oklahoma Municipal League.
No. 30. Teachers' pensions. 52 pages.
No. 33. Correspondence study, Sept., 1917.
No. 34. Compulsory arbitration of labor disputes.
No. 36. Current events study. 96 pages.
No. 37. Oklahoma municipalities.
No. 38. Current events study, 1917–18.
No. 39. Oklahoma municipalities.
No. 40. Woman suffrage No. 2. 80 pages.
No. 41. Studies on current topics. 80 pages. Part 1. The Great War.
No. 43. The city-manager plan. 77 pages.
No. 44. Social problem. 156 pages.
No. 45. Catalogue of material on war and the problems of peace, general subjects, debates.
No. 46. Problems of personal development.
The study of current topics.
List of illustrated lectures and stereopticon slides.
Debating contests.
Traveling libraries.
Department of community music.
Current events study.
Conference on taxation, 1914. (Program.)
Conference on rural economic problem, 1916. (Program.)
Visual instruction.
The Extension Division. (Departments and activities.)
Constitution of the Oklahoma High School Debating League.
Debating contests.

UNIVERSITY OF OREGON—EXTENSION DIVISION.

EXTENSION MONITOR.

Volume 5. 1916–17.
Volume 6. 1917–18.

LEAFLET SERIES.

Home study courses for teachers, 1918.
Lecture courses and study classes, 1918.
Summer classes for university credit (Portland center), 1918.
Emergency courses for men in war industries, 1918.
Putting the eyes to work, 1917.

Train for citizenship, 1918.
Institute lectures and subjects.
Oregon High School Debating League, 1917–18.
Correspondence study catalogue, October, 1918.

UNIVERSITY OF TEXAS—EXTENSION DIVISION.

(Extension bulletins are included in the University of Texas bulletin, but without separate numbering.)

BULLETINS.

No. 284. Intercollegiate debates on old-age insurance, banking and currency reform, 1913.

No. 30. A constitutional tax for the support of higher educational institutions in Texas, 1915.

No. 31. Woman suffrage.   (Bibliography and selected arguments, 1915.)

No. 35. School literary societies, 1915.

No. 70. Christmas entertainments, 1915.

No. 4. How to conduct a baby health conference, 1916.

No. 16. Schoolhouse meetings; school-closing exercises, 1916.

No. 17. The beautification of the home grounds, 1916.

No. 26. The furnishing and decoration of the home, 1916.

No. 39. The planning of simple homes, 1916.

No. 40. Study outlines of Elizabeth Harrison's "Child Nature," 1916.

No. 41. Military preparedness, 1916.

No. 42. What help the teacher can get from the University Extension Department, 1916.

No. 47. Single tax, 1916.

No. 48. Care and preservation of food in the home, 1916.

No. 56. Programs for schoolhouse meetings, 1916.

No. 57. The mourning dove, 1916.

No. 62. Universal military training, 1916.

No. 67. A study of rural schools in Travis County, 1916.

No. 72. A play for San Jacinto night, 1916.

No. 1708. What the Baby Health Conference teaches.

No. 1711. Pure milk and how to get it.

No. 1717. School savings banks.

No. 1730. Visual instruction through lantern slides and motion pictures.

No. 1739. How a superintendent may aid his teachers in self-improvement.

No. 1740. Announcement of correspondence courses.

No. 1748. The bobwhite.

No. 1756. Food conservation to help win the war.

No. 1765. Announcement of extension work for war service.

No. 1769. How to organize and conduct a school and community fair.

No. 1804. Food for infants and growing children.

No. 1805. Red Cross program for schools.

No. 1807. Announcement of group-study courses.

No. 1809. Lantern slides for war service.

No. 1830. Constitution and rules of the University Interscholastic League.

No. 1831. University aid for Community Councils of Defense.

No. 1832. War songs for community meetings.

No. 1833. The extension loan library and list of free bulletins.

No. 1834. Words for the spelling matches of the University Interscholastic League.

No. 1837. Patriotic programs for community meetings.

No. 1842. Play and athletics.

Valentine and Washington Birthday celebrations.

UNIVERSITY OF SOUTH DAKOTA—EXTENSION DIVISION.

Yearbook of the High School Debating League.
Extension center work.

UNIVERSITY OF UTAH—EXTENSION DIVISION.

Community thrift.
School and community survey and community welfare work.
Infant mortality.
Health lectures.
Correspondence study courses, 1918–19.
Circulars containing announcements.
The Utah Educational Review, published by the Extension Division, contains
frequent announcements and news of extension work.

UNIVERSITY OF VIRGINIA—EXTENSION DIVISION.

UNIVERSITY OF VIRGINIA RECORD: EXTENSION SERIES.

Volume 1. 1915–16.
    No. 1. High School Literary and Athletic League. (Literary societies in sec-
ondary schools: Part 1, Organization; Part 2, Parliamentary forms and rules;
Part 3, Questions for debate, arguments and references.) (Ten questions.)
    No. 2. University extension lectures.
    No. 3. The Virginia High School Literary and Athletic League. (Compulsory
education.)
    No. 4. Religious activities and advantages at the University of Virginia.
    No. 5. Program for the use of Sundayschools and churches and the observance
of country-church day.
    No. 6. Announcement of the Curry Memorial School of Education.
    No. 7. Program of the Ninth Annual Rural-Life Conference, 1916.
Volume 2. 1916–17.
    No. 1. Official syllabus of Bible study for high school pupils.
    No. 2. The Virginia High School and Athletic League. (Compulsory Military
training.)
    No. 3. Bibliography of educational surveys and tests.
    No. 4. Principles involved in teaching of hand writing.
    No. 5. Summer school of music.
    Nos. 6–7. The Jewish Chautauqua Society and the University of Virginia.
    Nos. 8–9. The relation of the colleges and universities of the South to the national
crisis.
    No. 10. Albermarle Highway Association.
Volume 3. 1917–18.
    No. 1. A study of school recesses.
    No. 2. Virginia High School Literary and Athletic League. (Debate—"A league
to enforce peace.")
    No. 3. War Extension Service.
Catalog of the Houston Art League collection of prints.
Volume 4. 1918–19.
    Nos. 1–5. Government ownership and operation of railroads. (Debating Bulletin.)

ALUMNI BULLETIN OF THE UNIVERSITY OF VIRGINIA. THIRD SERIES.

Volume 5. No. 4. Rural-life Conference, 1912.
Volume 7. No. 4. Rural-life Conference, 1914.
Virginia High School Bulletin often contains extension news and announcements.

UNIVERSITY OF SOUTH CAROLINA—EXTENSION DIVISION.

General extension bulletin.
South Carolina High School Debating League.
School surveys.
The school as a social center.
Cooperative courses in the school of engineering.

UNIVERSITY OF WASHINGTON—EXTENSION DIVISION.

Better Business. Monthly magazine. First number in March, 1916. $1.50 a year.
The University Extension Journal. Quarterly (1914).

BULLETINS.

No. 2. The social and civic center.
No. 3. State roads and permanent highways.
No. 4. The recall of judges.
No. 6. The single tax.
No. 7. The making of a newspaper.
No. 9. Immigration. (Debate outline.)
No. 10. The better newspaper.
No. 11. Supplementary lectures in journalism, 1913–14.
No. 12. Taxation in Washington.
No. 14. Government ownership of telegraph and telephone.
No. 15. Newspaper production.
No. 16. Supplementary lectures in journalism.
No. 17. Survey of the Port Townsend public schools.
No. 18. Ethical aspects of journalism.
No. 19. Supplementary lectures in journalism, 1915–16.
No. 20. Military training in the public schools.
No. 21. Ores, coals, and useful rocks of Washington.
No. 22. Some newspaper problems, 1917.
Circulars of Information.

UNIVERSITY OF WISCONSIN—EXTENSION DIVISION.

INFORMATION AND WELFARE BULLETINS

Chart on communicable diseases, 1917.
Commercial organizations and charitable control, 1915.
Community music and drama, 1918.
Eye in industrial accidents, September, 1916.
Food conservation through utilization of garbage waste, 1918.
General prospects, 1913.
Guarding the public health, 1913.
Industrial education and dependency, 1918.
Meadowgold (a play), 1914.
Municipal and sanitary engineering, 1914.
Nursing as a vocation for women, 1917.
Newspaper conference proceedings, 1913.
Organized poor relief work in Wisconsin, 1915.
Vocational conference papers, 1913.
Vocational education and guidance for disabled soldiers, 1917.
Wisconsin baby week, 1917.
Public recreation, 1915.
Some aspects of feeble-mindedness in Wisconsin.
Tuberculosis, 1909.

Milwaukee Bakers' Institute, 1910.
The manual arts as vocations, 1918.
Prenatal care.

COMMUNITY INSTITUTE BULLETINS.

De Pere Community Institute program, 1914, 1915.
Kaukauna Community Institute program, 1915.
Mayville Community Institute program, 1915.
Menomonee Falls Community Institute program, 1914.
Middletown Community Institute program, 1914.
Neillsville Community Institute program, 1914.
New London Community Institute program, 1914.
Stephens Point Institute, 1913.
Sauk City Community Institute; Results and opinions, 1913.
Organizations of community institutes, 1915.

MUNICIPAL REFERENCE BUREAU BULLETINS.

Assessed valuation and tax rates of Wisconsin cities, 1918.
Comparative salaries of city officials in Wisconsin.
Juvenile probation in Wisconsin, 1914.
Municipal coal yards, 1918.
Municipal special reports, 1918.
Uniform municipal accounts, 1915.
Voting machines in Wisconsin, 1915.
What is the municipal reference bureau? 1915.

SOCIAL CENTER BULLETINS.

Lessons learned in Rochester, 1911.
The rural awakening, 1912.
Schoolhouse as a local art gallery, 1912.
Social center in the southwest, 1912.
Social center movement, 1911.
The community center a means of common understanding, 1911.
Parent-teacher associations, 1918.

DEBATING AND PUBLIC DISCUSSIONS.

A league of nations. (Debating bulletin.)
How to judge a debate.
Municipal home rule.
Triangular Discussion League. (American Song Contest.)
The great war.
Initiative and referendum.
The recall.
School literary societies—training for citizenship.
Modern European history and the great war.
Debating manual.
Service and the State by the university extension division.
Biennial report of the dean of extension.

INDEX.

121

O

DEPARTMENT OF THE INTERIOR

BUREAU OF EDUCATION

BULLETIN, 1919, No. 85

DEVELOPMENT OF AGRICULTURAL INSTRUCTION IN SECONDARY SCHOOLS

By

H. P. BARROWS

Professor of Agricultural Education, Oregon
State Agricultural College

WASHINGTON
GOVERNMENT PRINTING OFFICE
1920

CONTENTS.

PREFATORY STATEMENT.

This bulletin represents a thesis presented by the late Harry Percy Barrows to the faculty of George Washington University in 1919 for the degree of doctor of philosophy. It furnishes an historic record that should be very helpful in the future development of instruction in agriculture in this country. Since secondary instruction in agriculture was developed first in the institutions that later became the colleges of agriculture, this paper covers in a masterly way the early development of collegiate agriculture.

Soon after the manuscript for this bulletin was presented for publication the author suffered a severe attack of influenza, which was followed by pneumonia and later resulted in his death at Berkeley, Calif., May 3, 1920. It should be understood, therefore, that the author was not permitted to examine the printer's proof nor to make such changes in the text as frequently suggest themselves upon reading the printed copy.

C. D. JARVIS,
Specialist in Agricultural Education,
U. S. Bureau of Education.

July 15, 1920.

4

DEVELOPMENT OF AGRICULTURAL INSTRUCTION IN SECONDARY SCHOOLS.

Chapter I.

HISTORY OF AGRICULTURE IN SECONDARY SCHOOLS.

EARLY DEVELOPMENT.

Lines not clearly drawn.—It is not easy to trace the development of agriculture in the secondary or high schools as such, because in the earlier days of our educational history distinctions were not made between elementary, secondary, and collegiate instruction as they are made now. The development of much of the agricultural instruction in the agricultural colleges should be classed as secondary agriculture when judged by present-day standards. In establishing the land-grant colleges there was not so much the intention to establish schools of college rank as to give some direct aid to the farmers. The discussions of the Morrill bill in Congress bring out the fact that many of those who voted for it did not realize that they were voting to establish colleges, just as some of the Members of Congress who voted for the Smith-Hughes Act thought they were voting to aid the elementary schools. A consideration of the early development of secondary agriculture must be of necessity a review of the general effort to improve agriculture by means of education.

Agricultural societies.[1]—Probably the first organized effort to improve agriculture was by means of agricultural societies and fairs. George Washington and Benjamin Franklin were members of the first society for the promotion of agriculture, which was organized in Philadelphia in 1775. About the same time a similar society was organized in South Carolina, which proposed, among other things, to establish the first experimental farm in the United States. In 1792 a small volume representing the transactions of the New York Society for the Promotion of Agriculture was published. This society, organized in 1791, was followed by a similar organization in Connecticut in 1794.

The establishment of fairs and exhibits was an outgrowth of the work of the agricultural societies and the desire of men going to ex-

---

[1] See Dabney, C. W., Agricultural education. *In* Monograph No. 12. Butler's Monographs in Education. New York, American Book Co., 1910. Pp. 5–8.

pense in importing improved types of farm animals from Europe, to exhibit their importations. The first fair was held in Massachusetts in 1804. In 1809 the Columbian Agricultural Society, composed mostly of farmers in Maryland and Virginia in the vicinity of the National Capital, was organized to further agriculture by means of fairs.

From the beginning the various State and local agricultural societies and fair associations have been strong factors in the direct improvement of agriculture and in securing additional means for improving the lot of the farmer. There have been, however, several movements of a national nature, which have had a wide-spreading influence. Most notable of these are the National Grange (Patrons of Husbandry), organized in 1867, and becoming a national society in 1873, and the Farmers' Alliance. While these organizations spread their influence chiefly in the North and West, their place was filled in the South by such organizations as the Brothers of Freedom and the Farmers' Educational and Cooperative Union.

Many of the societies have been instrumental in securing national and State aid for the promotion of agricultural instruction in the schools.

Development of the land-grant colleges.[1]—The first proposal to have the Federal Government aid in the training of farmers was made by Representative Justin S. Morrill, of Vermont, in 1857. Due to the able plea of Mr. Morrill in behalf of the farmer, and to his skill in parliamentary procedure, the bill passed the House by a narrow majority, but was held up in the Senate. The bill finally passed both House and Senate in 1859, only to be vetoed by President Buchanan. Soon after the Thirty-seventh Congress met, in December, 1861, the bill was again introduced and finally passed both Houses. On July 2, 1862, President Lincoln signed the bill which has been since known as the Morrill Act.

This act provided for Federal aid as a stimulus to State aid in establishing colleges of agriculture and mechanic arts. Inasmuch as the Federal aid given was in the form of grants of public land, the institutions established have become known as the land-grant colleges.

Agricultural colleges had already been established in the following States: New York, Pennsylvania, Michigan, Connecticut, and Maryland, before the land-grant act was passed. In other States, notably Kansas, Iowa, Wisconsin, Massachusetts, and New Hampshire, departments of agriculture were established in connection with existing institutions, which departments afterwards developed into colleges which secured the benefit of the land-grant act. Such institutions

---

[1] See Kandel, I. L., Federal Aid for Vocational Education. Carnegie Foundation for the Advancement of Teaching. Bulletin No. 10, 1917. Pp. 3–58.

as Harvard, Yale, and the Universities of Virginia and Georgia made some advancement in agriculture as a science before the Federal-aided agricultural colleges were established.

The act of 1862 was soon accepted by the legislatures of the States then loyal to the Federal Government, and, after the war, it was extended to and accepted by the States out of the Union during the war. Many of the colleges established were not colleges when judged by present-day standards for other lines. They were not strictly agricultural and mechanical colleges in that they did not confine their work to the training of farmers and mechanics. A perusal of the curricula of those colleges of earlier days shows that some of them did not approach very closely to practical agricultural training. Nevertheless, they performed a needed function in extending public education of a more or less special nature to a greater number of the common people, performing for a relatively small number the function performed now by rural high schools to great numbers of farm boys and girls. Yet a relatively large number did not receive training in agriculture and did not return to the farm, hence in a large measure these institutions failed in filling the mission for which they were established. The fact that they were appreciated, however, is shown by the increased appropriations made for these institutions. No sooner had the colleges become established than Senator Morrill and his colleges began a campaign for additional funds. Their efforts were unsuccessful, however, until 1890, when the so-called second Morrill Act was passed. This act provided for each college then established an additional sum of $15,000 for that year and an annual increase of that amount thereafter of $1,000 until the annual appropriation should reach $25,000 for each State. These funds were further supplemented in 1908 by what is known as the Nelson amendment, which provided for an additional sum of $15,000 to be given that year and additional sums of $5,000 for four succeeding years; united, the total appropriation from the Federal Government would be $50,000 each year.

The agricultural experiment stations.—At the time several of the first agricultural colleges were established provision was made for investigational work to go hand in hand with the instruction of students. The act providing for the establishment of the Maryland Agricultural College also provided that the college should establish a model farm upon which a series of experiments might be conducted. It may be remembered that the early settlers of this country spent a great deal of time and effort as individuals in attempting to secure crops suited to the New World. They were very willing to let the State do this work. A great deal of the foundation for real investigational work was done by Dr. Samuel W. Johnson, who was appointed professor of agricultural chemistry in Yale. Many of the early leaders in research in agricultural science were Dr. Johnson's students.

Although many of the States established experiment stations in connection with the agricultural colleges, the greatest impetus was given this movement by the passage of the Hatch Act in 1887. This act provided $15,000 each year of funds from the sale of public lands toward the establishment and support of an agricultural experiment station in each State.

The Hatch fund was supplemented further in 1906, by the passage of the Adams Act. This act appropriated an annual sum of $5,000, with an increase of $2,000 each year until the total sum per year should be $30,000 for each State. The individual States now appropriate more money each year than does the National Government for research work.

The United States Department of Agriculture.[1]—George Washington, as President, favored congressional aid for agriculture, and so recommended it, but Congress at that time did nothing by way of direct aid for the farmer. In 1836 the Patent Commissioner, Henry L. Ellsworth, received a considerable quantity of seeds and plants from representatives of the Government abroad and distributed them to progressive farmers in this country. Although this work was begun without authority or financial aid, it lead to an appropriation of $1,000, made for such purpose in 1839. The Patent Office soon began collecting and disseminating statistics and other information as well as seeds. The work grew in this office until, in 1862, the same year the agricultural colleges were established, a separate department was organized, with a commissioner of agriculture at its head. In 1889 this department was raised to the first rank in the executive branch of the Government, and was put under the direction of a Secretary of Agriculture, a Cabinet member.

The Department of Agriculture in its phenomenal growth has without doubt branched out into lines of work undreamed of by those who worked so hard for its establishment. Its work is chiefly along three lines, viz: Research, regulatory supervision, and direct instruction. From the beginning the department has done a great deal in the way of directing investigation as well as to direct the agricultural research carried on in the States with Federal funds. As Government control of agricultural production and marketing has increased, the police duties of the department have been added upon. Through direct contact of its corps of trained specialists and by extensive correspondence and publications, the department has

[1] See Greathouse, C. H., Historical Sketch of the United States Department of Agriculture. U. S. Department of Agriculture, Division of Publications. Bulletin 3, 2d Rev., 1907.

aided the agricultural colleges in the direct education of the people. It has done a great deal to aid the colleges and schools of lower grade in their problems of instruction as well as research.

Agricultural extension work.—Largely as a result of the work of the experiment stations and the Department of Agriculture, a beginning was made in this country toward developing agriculture as a science. A great mass of scientific material pertaining to agriculture has been accumulated, while the most valuable resources of the country were being wasted by poor methods of farming. The agricultural colleges reached a relatively small number of students, and a large percentage of them did not return to the farm. Early in the history of the colleges, however, an effort was made to take their information directly to the farmer. Farmers' institutes[1] developed along with agricultural societies and fairs. It became evident in time that a more comprehensive program and a better organized plan were essential in reaching the men and women on the farm. Once again Federal aid was sought and secured in what is known as the Smith-Lever Act. This act, passed in 1914, provides for Federal aid to State agricultural colleges for agricultural extension work in cooperation with the United States Department of Agriculture. The money was not to be spent upon resident instruction, but provided for various means of instruction away from the college. At the beginning $10,000 for each State was appropriated, a total of $480,000. This sum increases year by year until an annual appropriation of $4,100,000 is reached. This sum is divided among the States in the proportion that rural populations bear to the entire rural population of the country. The States must meet the Federal appropriation dollar for dollar.

Inasmuch as this extension work has reached a large number of people and has secured direct results, it has been on the whole very well received. In the extension service an organization has been effected under the direction of the Department of Agriculture through which additional funds may be spent effectively as a war measure in increasing efficiency in the production and consumption of food.

It has been the experience of many extension workers in agriculture and home economics that time and money were more effectively spent upon boys and girls than upon mature farmers and their wives. In many cases it was found to be easier to reach the fathers and mothers through the boys and girls; hence the boys' and girls' club movement and other forms of extension work among young people have been given an increasing amount of attention. There is a strong tendency at the present time to link such work as closely as possible with the public school system.

[1] See History and Status of Farmers' Institutes in the United States and Canada. U. S. Department of Agriculture. Office of Experiment Stations. Bulletin 79.

SECONDARY SCHOOLS OF AGRICULTURE.

Schools affiliated with agricultural colleges.—Attention has been called to the fact that lines have not been closely drawn between agriculture of a secondary grade and collegiate agriculture in the land-grant colleges. Some of the institutions, however, have seen fit to draw the line closely from the standpoint of administration and have organized secondary schools and colleges in the same institution. Minnesota established the first school of agriculture in 1888. This school was established on the campus of the college of agriculture, which is a part of the State university, at St. Anthony Park, between Minneapolis and St. Paul. Although the buildings, equipment, and faculty of the agricultural college are used in the instruction of the secondary students, the school is maintained as a separate institution. Almost from the beginning the school has been successful and popular. It has furnished the people of Minnesota the type of education they have demanded to the extent that until very recently it has overshadowed the college of agriculture in the same institution. Although Minnesota established a similar school at Crookston in 1908 and another one at Norris in 1910, there has been a demand for secondary agriculture in the high schools of Minnesota unequaled in any other State.

Following the lead of Minnesota, in 1896 Nebraska organized a similar school in connection with the college of agriculture of the State university at Lincoln. Over half of the States have since organized special schools in connection with the agricultural colleges. In some States these schools use the same equipment and teaching force as the college, following the example of the first school organized in Minnesota. In other States the schools have a separate organization in a different part of the State. Such is the case in California at the University Farm School at Davis. This school, however, serves the university proper, in giving the courses which demand farm practice to students of college grade in addition to giving courses of a secondary grade.

District and county agricultural schools.—The independent schools of agriculture established through State aid may be classed largely as county schools and district schools. The districts served, however, vary from the congressional district to an indeterminate district which means that the school may serve the State at large.

Alabama was the first State to establish a system of agricultural schools. In 1889 the State provided for a school in each of the nine congressional districts. At each school a branch experiment station was established under the direction of the State College of Agriculture. Although these schools have not given courses of a distinctly vocational nature, they have furnished some practical work along with an academic training to a great number of young people who otherwise would not have received instruction beyond the elementary school.

Following the lead of her sister State, Georgia established agricultural schools in each of her 11 congressional districts in 1906. These schools have had much the same service as those in Alabama. Wherever they have been in charge of agricultural men there has been a strong leaning toward agricultural education, but in a number of cases the term " agricultural school " has been a misnomer, as practical agriculture has been subordinated to academic work. This criticism applies even more strongly to the congressional district agricultural schools established in Virginia in 1908. In most cases these schools have been very weak agricultural departments added to ordinary high schools, which until very recently have made little attempt to adapt their curricula to the needs of the rural community.

In 1909 Arkansas established four agricultural schools, each to serve a district comprising approximately one-fourth of the State. These schools were established upon a bigger, broader basis than the schools which serve a smaller district in other Southern States. They have been from the beginning more nearly real agricultural schools than any of the special schools of agriculture in the South. They have become ambitious in the growth, however, and at times there appears a rivalry between these schools and the State college of agriculture. Oklahoma also established schools to serve a large district, but as these schools have not had the support given the Arkansas schools, they have not prospered so well.

Wisconsin led out in the county agricultural school idea in 1901, when funds were provided for county schools of agriculture and domestic economy at Wausau and Menomonie. Since then such schools have been established in many other counties. County agricultural schools have later been established in several States.

The following States have established schools to serve the State at large or an indeterminate district: California, New York, Nebraska, Vermont, Colorado, and Pennsylvania. In Nebraska the State agricultural school at Curtis has definite connection with the State university. The State agricultural school at Fort Lewis, Colo., is also a part of the State agricultural college. In California, while the university farm school at Davis is a definite part of the State university, the California Polytechnic School at San Luis Obispo is an independent State institution.

Public high schools.—Although it is a relatively simple matter to trace the development of agricultural schools as such, it is very difficult to secure definite and accurate information concerning agri-

culture as taught in the ordinary high schools. The instruction may
vary from the application of courses in botany or chemistry in the
direction of agriculture, or the use of an elementary textbook for a
portion of a year, to the full-fledged.department of agriculture giving
a four years' course, taking more than half of the entire time of the
student. In some cases these departments employ more than one
teacher, have better equipment and offer more complete courses than
so-called agricultural schools. One of the marked tendencies in
recent progress in agricultural education is the getting away from
the idea that a consideration of secondary agriculture is necessarily
a consideration of a special school of agriculture. Classifications of
institutions into agricultural courses may mean little as to the nature
and extent of the agriculture taught. Agriculture has not dominated
in the curriculum of the majority of secondary agricultural schools
established in the past. A mere statistical study may have some
value in showing progress made, but it will need a great deal of explanation based upon first-hand study to show the real nature of the
work given.

A few years ago there was a tendency to judge the progress in
agricultural education by the number of institutions offering courses
and the number of students taking the work. While much of the
superficial teaching which went under the name of agricultural instruction has been eliminated and real progress made in the character of the work given, the apparent decline in interest shown in the
following statistics is due largely to a more careful inquiry into
work reported as agriculture.

The following is from the report of the Commissioner of Education for the year ending June 30, 1913:[1]

According to the most reliable information obtainable there were about 2,300
high schools in the United States teaching agriculture in 1912–13. This indicates an increase of about 300 over the previous year. This number includes
47 State agricultural schools, 40 district agricultural schools, 67 county agricultural schools, 18 agricultural departments of high schools, and the remaining ordinary schools giving courses in agriculture.

The following tables were compiled from reports made to the Commissioner of Education showing the progress in the next two years:

Report for 1914.

Institutions.	Courses.	Schools reporting.	Number of students.		
			Boys.	Girls.	Total.
Public high schools........................	Agriculture.......	1,553	21,702	10,319	32,021
Private high schools........................	......do............	124	1,767	579	2,346
Total................................	....	1,677	23,469	10,898	34,367

[1] Chapter IX, Progress of Agricultural Education, pp. 213–214.

Report for 1915.

Institutions.	Courses.	Schools. reporting.	Number of students.		
			Boys.	Girls.	Total.
Public high schools............................	Agriculture........	4,665	51,677	39,031	90,708
Private high schools...........................	....do............	253	2,579	1,861	4,440
Total....................................		4,918	54,256	40,892	95,148

These statistics were compiled from general data sent by the schools to the Bureau of Education. In the spring of 1916 the bureau attempted to gather more complete and definite information concerning the teaching of agriculture in the public high schools and in special agricultural schools of secondary grade. The following is a brief summary of the schools reporting:[1]

Agriculture in secondary schools, 1915-16.

Number of public high schools reporting teaching agriculture......... 2,175
    Established before 1901.. 19
    Established from 1901 to 1905................................... 83
    Established from 1906 to 1910.................................. 413
    Established since 1910 1,710
Reporting teaching agriculture primarily:
    As informational subject...................................... 1,521
    As vocational subject... 566
Number of persons teaching agriculture:
    Male.. 2,007
    Female 247
    Number of these with any special training in agriculture, including those with full four-year agricultural college courses, short-term courses, normal school agricultural courses, summer courses, etc 1,021
Number of students of secondary grade studying agriculture:
    Boys 24,743
    Girls 16,312
Number of schools using school land for instructional purposes....... 392
Number teaching through home-project method..................... 837
Number in which instruction consists wholly of classroom work....... 416
Number in which instruction consists of classroom work, with laboratory exercises and observation on neighboring farms................ 1,064
Number of special secondary agricultural schools supported in whole or in part by the States... 68
    Total cost of maintenance..................................... $766,000
Total number of teachers:
    Male 276
    Female 140

[1] From Report of Commissioner of Education for the year ended June 30, 1916, pp. 237-38.

Total number of pupils:
  Elementary—
    Male _____ 615
    Female _____ 464
  Secondary—
    Male _____ 3,883
    Female _____ 2,406

This summary does not include special schools of agriculture maintained by the State colleges of agriculture on the college campus. Schools of this type are maintained by the State agricultural colleges of California, Colorado, Idaho, Kansas, Mississippi, Nebraska, Montana, North Carolina, North Dakota, and Washington (school of science). Agricultural courses of secondary grade are given to special students in 20 other State colleges of agriculture.

In a publication [1] which gives the final returns from this investigation, 2,981 public high schools are reported as giving instruction in agriculture in 1915–16. Of these, 2,250 schools gave information as to the character of the work given. Only 2,166 of this number, however, were really teaching agriculture in a serious way. To understand the nature of the agriculture taught in these schools, we may consider the following facts:

(1) Date of introduction: Less than 1 per cent of these schools taught agriculture before 1900, and less than 1½ per cent introduced the subject between 1900 and 1905. Over 97.6 per cent of the schools introduced the subject since 1905, and 78.5 per cent since 1910.

(2) Nature of instruction: The schools were asked to indicate whether they were teaching agriculture with a vocational aim as definite preparation for farming, as information about agriculture, or for general cultural purposes. As many of the schools reported that they were teaching agriculture for two or all three reasons, it is evident that they did not have a distinct purpose in their instruction. Although 25 per cent of the schools reported the chief aim as being vocational, the character of the work indicates that many of the teachers have little conception of the meaning of vocational training. The instruction in many cases was confined to classroom only, or supplemented with some laboratory work. Some teachers thought their textbook instruction was vocational, as their students lived on farms. The summary of replies shows that 20 per cent of the schools confined their instruction to classroom work; 50 per cent supplement the classroom instruction with laboratory exercises and observation trips to the farms; and only 30 per cent combine classroom instruction and laboratory work with practical

---

[1] Monahan, A. C., and Dye, C. H. Institutions in the United States giving Instruction in Agriculture, 1915–16. Bureau of Education. Bulletin, 1917, No. 34.

farm work. Three hundred and thirty-seven were using the home-project plan, although in only 261 schools was the home work given supervision by the instructor in agriculture. The schools reporting, however, did not include many of the State-aided schools which are using this plan. Eighteen per cent of the schools reported school land for agricultural purposes. Of these schools 134, or about one-third of the number, had less than two acres.

(3) Training of teachers: There is a close relation between the nature of the instruction and the training of the teachers. Only 15 per cent of the teachers in the 2,166 reporting were graduates of agricultural colleges. In addition to these, 21 per cent had some training in agriculture in colleges or normal schools. In some cases this work was taken only in summer school or as short winter courses.

Private high schools.—Since the time that secondary schools were first developed in this country many of these schools have been organized outside the city with private funds. At such of these schools as have owned farms upon which students have lived away from home there has been more or less direct relation between the instruction of the school and farm life. Definite instruction in agriculture was inaugurated in a few of these schools before it was attempted in the public high schools. In a few cases the agricultural instruction has been of a vocational character from the beginning, as the instruction has been based largely upon the work of the farm. In placing the agriculture of our public schools now upon a vocational basis we may learn much from these private schools which have been working for a number of years upon problems connected with the use of land in agricultural instruction. We have learned considerable from such schools as the National Farm School, at Doylestown, Pa., the Baron de Hirsch School, at Woodbine, N. J., and the Berry School, near Rome, Ga. Where these schools have had a real vocational aim they have had a decided advantage in making their work practical, as the students are living on the school farm throughout the year.

It is very difficult to secure accurate statistics concerning private schools and especially to grade the work done. Although a number of private colleges and State institutions other than the Federal-aided colleges are giving courses in agriculture, in few cases is the instruction given of more than secondary grade when judged by the standards of the land-grant colleges. As the equipment and instruction for college agriculture is so expensive, few colleges attempt to compete with the Federal-aided institutions in college courses. Only 18 of these colleges and 160 secondary schools reported the nature of the work to the Bureau of Education in

1916. These schools reported 3,393 students taking courses in agriculture. A number of schools having a relatively large number of students did not report the number of agricultural students.

Normal schools.—Normal-school training in agriculture is mostly associated with elementary agriculture, as in most cases it is training for elementary schools. Methods of teaching most subjects in normal schools are often superior to those used in the high schools. As the teaching of agriculture is not an exception to this rule, we may very well give some attention in pages to follow to normal-school instruction in this subject. At this time we shall consider briefly the development of normal-school instruction in agriculture in the United States.

Many of the States have made agriculture a required subject in rural schools without providing for special training of teachers in that line. As a result, agriculture as taught in many of the elementary schools was a very perfunctory perusal of a textbook which in most cases was adapted neither to the pupils nor the section in which they lived. To overcome this difficulty some States have required agriculture as a subject for examination for the teacher's certificate, others have made special effort to provide for the training of teachers, some have done both, as will be noted in the data following:

Legislative enactment has made the teaching of agriculture a requirement in all common schools, or at least in rural schools, in each of the following States: Alabama, Arkansas, Florida, Georgia, Indiana, Iowa, Louisiana, Mississippi, North Carolina, North Dakota, Ohio, Oklahoma, South Carolina, Texas, West Virginia, Wisconsin, and Wyoming. Agriculture is one of the subjects for examination for teachers' certificates in the following States: Alabama, Arkansas, California, Florida, Georgia, Idaho, Indiana, Iowa, Kansas, Louisiana, Michigan, North Dakota (alternative), Mississippi, Missouri, Nebraska, New Mexico, North Carolina, Ohio, Wisconsin, Oklahoma, South Carolina, Tennessee, Texas, Virginia (alternative), West Virginia and Wyoming. About half the States have had printed outlines of courses in elementary agriculture, prepared either by the State agricultural college or the State department of public instruction. Up to the present time approximately 75 texts in elementary agriculture have been prepared. But with all the aid given teachers in service, nothing has taken the place of specific training as a part of the teacher training course. The following will indicate that some States have sensed their duty in training teachers for rural schools: Maine, Oklahoma, and Tennessee require instruction in agriculture in all State normal schools. Instruction in agriculture is a requisite for State aid to normal training in the high schools of Iowa, Missouri, and Nebraska. Nebraska also requires her normal schools to establish a course for rural teachers, including agriculture, household economy, and rural sociology. Kansas provides State aid for agricultural instruction in high school normal training classes, while elementary agriculture is required in the course of study in the county normal classes in Michigan, Nebraska, and Oregon.

In most cases the instruction involves subject matter only, and for the most part there is but one course in agriculture, and that is of an elementary nature. Some schools have been more recently paying more attention to the pedagogy of the subject and have been developing courses involving subject matter of a more specialized character. In a recent study [1] made by the United States Bureau of Education about half of the 114 schools reporting required agriculture of all students, the amount of required work ranging from only 20 hours, in the case of the New Jersey State Normal School, at Newark, to 190 hours required in the State normal school at Spearfish, S. Dak. The first district State normal school, at Kirksville, Mo., offered 1,344 hours of agriculture. The author, having visited this school, can testify as to the high standard of the work offered.

As a rule the normal schools have confined their efforts to training teachers of elementary agriculture, but in a few cases the department of agriculture in connection with normal schools have become ambitious to compete with the agricultural colleges in training teachers for secondary schools. This has meant duplication of extensive farm and school equipment. In a few cases normal schools and agricultural colleges have cooperated in the training of secondary teachers, the normal schools or school of education given the professional training and the agricultural colleges the technical training.

Schools for Negroes and Indians.—It is difficult to classify schools for Negroes according to grade of work done. When measured by standards set for schools for white people, the colleges for Negroes give instruction in agriculture mostly of secondary grade. In 1915–16 there were 17 of these institutions with a total of 2,053 students taking regular four-year courses in agriculture. Ten of these institutions serve also as State normal schools. In addition to these schools, 67 other institutions for Negroes above elementary grade reported agriculture as a part of the curriculum and 43 reported courses in gardening. Much of the agriculture as well as gardening given in the secondary schools is of a decidedly elementary character. Although the classroom instruction of both colleges and secondary schools for Negroes may not measure up to standards for institutions for white people, in many cases the colored schools have led in the

---

[1] Institutions in the United States giving instruction in agriculture, 1915–16, U. S. Bureau of Education, Bulletin, 1917, No. 34, pp. 6–8.

amount and character of practical training given. This is especially true of such institutions as Hampton Normal and Industrial Institute at Hampton, Va., and Tuskegee Institute at Tuskegee, Ala. Although education has been unfortunately associated with the idea of emancipation from labor in the minds of many Negroes, in these institutions the industrial spirit predominates. Students who will not work are not allowed to remain at the school. Combining farming and industrial interests with the school, the students may work their way through school in a large measure, having work which fits well in the course of study pursued.

Established soon after the Civil War by Col. Armstrong, and since his death conducted until 1919 under the able leadership of the late Dr. H. B. Frissell, Hampton has been a wonderful factor in developing Negro leadership. It was in this institution that Booker T. Washington secured the inspiration and training which enabled him to develop at Tuskegee a larger one. In both institutions training for agriculture and the industries predominate. At Hampton the instructors are mostly white people, while at Tuskegee the teachers are of the colored race. At both institutions older students are used as assistants in the training of the younger ones. As an example of the practical and helpful character of the instruction given, the following account of a course in dairying at Hampton is given:

The well-equipped dairy is run as a commercial creamery making the butter used at the institution from milk obtained from two large dairy herds maintained by the school. There were 12 students in the class, each of whom was given two months' practical work in the creamery, one month as assistant and one month as foreman. As it took but two men to do the work, it was arranged for a new student to enter each month, so that the dairy was always in charge of a student with one month's experience. The student entering one month as assistant became foreman the next month when the man over him left. The plan worked well in developing initiative, resourcefulness, and self-confidence. The students interviewed felt competent to take charge of a small dairy when they left the school. The students in charge of the dairy at the time the school was visited in 1915 were both Indians.

There has been considerable development in vocational agriculture in some of the Indian schools maintained under direction of the Department of the Interior. Such schools as the United States Indian Industrial School at Carlisle, Pa., were given practical instruction in agriculture before public high schools were making very much progress in that direction. Recently the Bureau of Indian Affairs has been making an effort to reorganize and standardize the agricultural instruction given to Indian students.

Schools for delinquents.—Industrial education has been so closely associated with schools for delinquents in the past that even now when the term "industrial school" is used many people think of a reform school. All of these schools which have been located on farms have required farm work of the inmates. In line of progress in the education of delinquent youth, over half of the State reform schools have now provided for definite classroom instruction to accompany the farm work of the students. Such schools as the one located on Thompsons Island, in Massachusetts, have been pioneers in vocational agriculture and have pointed the way for public schools to follow.

Definite agricultural instruction is becoming a part of the educational work of a number of State prisons. In 1914 the author assisted in the introduction of agriculture into the California State prison at San Quentin. Before the year was over nearly 300 students were enrolled. Correspondence courses in agriculture prepared by the college of agriculture of the State university were made the basis for the instruction given. The men organized an agricultural club which met weekly for a general session, usually under the direction of a specialist from the university. The general session was made up of sections, each pursuing a special course. As some garden work was done at the prison and a herd of swine kept, some of the work was made practical. A number of agricultural books and large numbers of bulletins were added to the library, which was used extensively for reference purposes. Illustrative material, including colored charts, mounted pictures, and lantern slides, were prepared by the students, some of whom showed marked ability in this line of work. In some States the agricultural instruction is given as a regular phase of prison instruction, while in others it is conducted as a phase of extension work under the direction of the State college of agriculture.

Chapter II.

STATE AID FOR SECONDARY AGRICULTURE.

PROGRESS IN STATE AID.

Chronology of State aid for secondary instruction in agriculture and home economics.

[Compiled by Miss M. T. Spethmann, U. S. Department of Agriculture.]

Laws passed.	State.	System adopted.	Initial amount to each school for maintenance.
1889............	Alabama...............	Congressional district...................	$3,000
1901............	California.............	Indeterminate district..................	[1] 50,000
	Wisconsin.............	County..................................	4,000
1905............	Minnesota.............	Indeterminate district..................	4,000
1906............	Georgia...............	Congressional district..................	10,000
	New York.............	Indeterminate district..................	10,000
1907............	Michigan.............	County..................................	12,000
1908............	Oklahoma.............	Judicial district (supreme court).......	12,000
	Virginia..............	Congressional district..................	2,000
1909............	Texas................	High school............................	2,000
	Arkansas.............	District...............................	40,000
	Maine................	High school or academy.................	([2])
	Minnesota............	High school............................	2,500
1910............	Louisiana............	....do.................................	1,250
	Nebraska.............	Indeterminate district.................	40,000
	Maryland.............	High school............................	800
	Vermont..............	Indeterminate district.................	10,000
	Mississippi..........	County.................................	$1,500-3,000
	New York.............	High school............................	$900-2,000
1911............	Massachusetts........	Public high school.....................	([3])
		Independent agricultural schools.......	([4])
	Kansas...............	Normal training high school............	250
	North Carolina.......	County.................................	2,500
	North Dakota........	....do.................................	3,000
		High school............................	2,500
	Wisconsin............	....do.................................	$500-700
	Colorado.............	Indeterminate district.................	15,000
	Maine................	High school............................	500
	Utah.................	Rural high school must teach agriculture to secure general State aid.	....
1912............	Arizona..............	High school............................	2,500
	Louisiana............	County.................................	$1,000-1,500
1913............	Kansas...............	Normal training high schools...........	([5])
	Indiana..............	High school............................	([6])
	Iowa.................	Consolidated schools, teacher training.	750
	Nebraska.............	High school............................	1,250
	New Jersey...........	County.................................	10,000
	Pennsylvania.........	Indeterminate district.................	5,000
	Tennessee............	County.................................	1,500
	Vermont..............	High school............................	200
	Texas................	....do.................................	[1] 50,000
1915............	Virginia.............	Congressional district.................	[7] 25,000

[1] Total:
[2] Two-thirds cost of instruction; $500 maximum.
[3] Two-thirds salaries.
[4] One-half net maintenance.
[5] $250 (making total of $500).
[6] Two-thirds cost of vocational instruction.
[7] Total additional aid.

The foregoing table does not show the progress that has been made in matters of administration and in getting results in general. Due to the lack of any organized system of agriculture for secondary schools, much money has been spent by the States without getting results in better-trained farmers. It will be noted that for the first 10 years of this period of independent State aid that all of the money went to the support of some form of special agricultural school; in fact until very recent years many have discussed the problem of secondary agriculture as if it had to do only with these agricultural schools. Because some of the districts in which they were established had no rural high schools of a general character, and because a system of vocational training in agriculture had not been developed, these schools have not been agricultural schools in a strict sense. Their history has been in a sense similar to that of the land-grant colleges; without restrictions as to their field and without a guide to follow, they have adapted themselves to immediate service along lines already laid down. In more recent years many of the States have turned more toward aiding existing high schools in establishing departments of agriculture. Money appropriated for this purpose has not always been spent strictly for the purpose for which it was appropriated. The chief reason for this is that States have appropriated the money without establishing a standard and without providing a State organization and a means of supervision and inspection so that a standard could be maintained.

More recently some of the States, having profited by the experience of these other States, have provided for a more definite system of vocational agriculture with State aid. They have not only provided money for establishing schools and for paying a part of the salaries of teachers in agricultural departments, but they have also provided adequately for State supervision. The work has been developed toward a definite end, definite standards have been set, and means have been taken to see that they were reached. The experience of most of the States has justified the belief that State aid and supervision is needed mostly in the teaching of vocational agriculture. In putting the work upon a vocational basis, it meant teachers with better training, hence more equipment and more expensive and better supervision of both teachers and students, all of which mean a greater outlay in money than ordinary instruction. Placing agriculture upon a vocational basis should mean more immediate returns in the increased capacity of the student in production. Local communities have not felt able to bear the added burden of expense, hence the State has come to their aid. Before a national program for aiding scondary schools in vocational agriculture was outlined there was a definite system of vocational agriculture established in the following States: Massachusetts, New York, Pennsylvania, New Jersey, and Indiana. As the national law giving Federal aid to vocational agriculture and the policy of the Federal board in its administration have been determined to a great extent by the work in these States, we shall consider them more in detail.

MASSACHUSETTS.[1]

In 1911 the Commonwealth of Massachusetts passed an act governing the establishment and maintenance of State-aided education in vocational agriculture as a part of its State plan for vocational education. The act provided a State fund to reimburse local boards of control for two-thirds of the salaries of instructors in high-school departments of agriculture and one-half the net sum expended in the maintenance of county schools of agriculture.

The provision of the act made it possible for departments of agriculture to be established in existing high schools under the control of the regular school authorities.

To avail itself of the act the city council or town meeting must pass an ordinance authorizing the school committee to establish such a department. While such a department is a part of the regular high school, it must meet a standard set by the State board of education and submit to direct supervision of the agents of that board. An advisory committee of 5 to 15 members is expected to aid in direction of the work in the local community. The instructor employed for such a department is expected to have a well-rounded training in practical agriculture, that he may aid in community work among farmers and supervise farm work of the students. He must devote all of his time to agricultural work. As a rule the instruction and supervision are rather intensive, 1 teacher not having over 20 students. Should as many as 30 students enter the department two instructors would be employed. With two teachers there is opportunity for division of work which permits of some specialization. Fifty per cent of the student's time in such a department is to be spent in vocational agriculture, the other half of the time being devoted to regular high-school subjects.

To establish a county school of agriculture there must be in each case a special act of the State legislature providing for a board of trustees, bond issues to cover the first cost of the school plant, and a tax levy for yearly maintenance. The first cost is estimated at from $75,000 to $100,000, and $20,000 for the first year's maintenance. Such an act must be submitted to the county concerned for referendum vote in the November election. The controlling board of such schools consists of seven members—three county commissioners serving ex officio and four members appointed by the governor, all serv-

---

[1] See Massachusetts Board of Education. Bulletin 72. Information Relating to the Establishment of County Agricultural Schools and Agricultural Departments. Also yearly reports of State-aided vocational agricultural education.

ing without pay. The board employs a director of the school, who serves as its executive officer and who is responsible to the State board for the management of the school.

These county schools having 100 or more pupils and employing a number of instructors afford a degree of specialization not possible in the high school department. The entire curriculum of these schools is more dominately vocational. Eighty per cent of the time must be vocational agriculture, 50 per cent being productive farm work. Of the 20 per cent of the time devoted to general education one-half of that time, 10 per cent of the entire time, must be given to instruction in citizenship, personal hygiene, occupational diseases, and accidents. These schools, like the high school departments, do not provide dormitories, as they are supposed to take students living at home on farms. The county schools, however, are all located on farms which are used for instructional purposes.

The home-project plan.—In giving instruction in agriculture to students living upon farms, the home-project method has been worked out in Massachusetts. This method is essentially an effort to apply the part-time idea to the teaching of agriculture. An effort is made to organize and direct the home work of the student and to connect it with the instruction of the school in such a way that its educational value is increased. When such work is so organized and directed it is made a part of the instruction of the school and accredited as such. As the practical work of the students' project is made an approach to the study of the principles involved, the project plan is a working out of the problem method on a rather extensive scale. To have the highest educational value a project should have the following essentials: It must involve new experience and the working out of new problems, extending over a considerable period of time; it should have direct supervision by competent authority; the work should be carefully planned at the outset and accurate records and accounts kept of the finance and methods involved; this record is made on the basis of a written report of the work. Each student before entering the work in agriculture must have provisions for carrying on suitable projects to be directed by the instructor in agriculture. A written agreement between the student, his parents, and the teacher is required. The student is expected to have individual responsibility for his project and to participate in the profits and losses. There is a definite relation between each project and the instruction offered. A course in poultry husbandry is based upon a poultry project, while a course in vegetable gardening is based on a garden project. If a student can not secure a suitable project at home he may be allowed as a substitute for a project the privilege of working upon a suitable farm; providing such work may link up in a definite way with the instruction of the school and may be given some direction by the instructor. A student in dairy husbandry may have no opportunity for dairy practice at home but secure a position to work mornings and evenings on a dairy farm; such work is considered to be as valuable from an educational point of view in some cases as the care of one or more cows on the student's own account at home.

The instructors are employed for 12 months and spend their summers supervising the student projects, aiding the boys' and girls' club work, and rendering general community service along agricultural lines.

From the standpoint of school administration the home-project plan has the advantage of securing farm practice under normal conditions with a minimum of equipment at the school. If adequate supervision is given the home work one instructor can direct relatively few students, especially if they are scattered over a wide area. In such cases transportation of the instructor or supervisor becomes a big item of expense. When the Massachusetts plan was being developed for the first year or two the overhead expense seemed all out of proportion to the results obtained, but as the work has developed, not only the number of schools and departments have increased, but the number of pupils per instructor as well, so that the overhead cost per pupil has been lowered. The State board has insisted, very wisely, upon records from which it is able to show that the money spent by the State has yielded immediate returns in dollars and cents. The following table will show the development of the work in the increase of students and the money earned:

Earnings of vocational agricultural students.

Year.	Number of students.	Earnings.
1912	70	$11,100.17
1913	89	17,982.51
1914	235	42,060.73
1915	413	56,254.75
1916	497	84,173.43

NEW YORK.[1]

When New York, in 1913, amended its laws relating to industrial schools passed in 1910, it had the benefit of some of the work done in Massachusetts. The plan worked out for agricultural education is modeled in a large measure upon the Massachusetts plan. New York has a number of special schools of agriculture of secondary grade which are to be in a greater extent independent in their organization and administrations. These schools are not included in the

---

[1] See University of the State of New York. Bulletin No. 626, 1916. Schools of Agriculture, Mechanic Arts and Home Making.

schools of agriculture, mechanic arts, and home making. These schools are of two types: Intermediate schools which base four years of vocational work upon six years of elementary training, and high schools which base their four-year courses upon eight years of elementary work. In both cases, although known as schools of agriculture, mechanic arts, and home making, they are, in reality, vocational departments of ordinary high schools under the direction of the principal of the general school. The law provides that the commissioner of education shall apportion from the State school money to each of these schools a sum equal to two-thirds of the salary of the first teacher and one-third of the salary of each additional teacher, provided:

(1) That the time of such teachers is devoted exclusively to such school. (2) That the school has at least 15 pupils. (3) That the school maintains an organization and course of study and is conducted in a manner approved by the commissioner of education through the division of agriculture and industrial education. In a city the board of education may establish one of these schools, but in a common school district the question of establishing such a school must be determined by vote in the annual district meeting or a special meeting called for the purpose. If the school authorities are not capable of giving the teacher and students technical aid with agricultural problems, it is suggested that an advisory board shall be appointed.

At the time the system was studied in 1915 these boards did not appear to be especially active and as helpful as it was hoped for.

Although the New York plan is in many ways similar to that of Massachusetts, it is not quite so intensive and a great deal more is left to the local communities. In 1916, 64 schools had availed themselves of the provisions of the law. In some cases the classes were much larger than in Massachusetts. With more schools and a larger number of students there was less intensive supervision of both teachers and pupils. Regarding the courses of study, it will be seen from the following that while the State sets a standard it allows leeway for adaptation:

COURSES OF STUDY.

The classroom and laboratory instruction in these schools and departments is to be based upon practical experience gained on the farm, at home, or elsewhere. It is therefore impossible to prescribe courses of study or to prepare adequate outlines for particular subjects. This does not mean that the course of study is to be changed to suit the whims of pupils who do not know exactly what they want or need. A definite course of study should be formulated at the beginning and followed until there is urgent need for a change. A well-balanced general knowledge of the whole field of agricultural science and practice should be represented in the course.

The following courses are not prescribed, but it is expected that any school desiring to make any change will secure the approval of the commissioner of education before doing so. Other subjects may, after approval, be substituted for those indicated below. It is expected that the arrangement of subjects and the content of those subjects will be suited to the community in which the school is located.

A suggested course in agriculture for intermediate schools of agriculture.

FIRST YEAR.	Hours a week.
English	5
Arithmetic	5
American history	2
Mechanical drawing and shopwork	3
Commercial and industrial geography	5
General agriculture	3
	23
SECOND YEAR.	
English	5
Mathematics	5
American history	3
Mechanical drawing and shopwork	5
Plant husbandry (growing clubs in the line of home project with plants)	5
	23

THIRD YEAR.	Hours a week.
English	3
Mathematics, including bookkeeping	5
Biology	5
Soils and fertilizers	5
	18
FOURTH YEAR.	
English	3
Agricultural physics and agricultural chemistry	5
Animal husbandry and dairying	5
Special agriculture to suit local conditions: Fruit growing, Grape culture, Market gardening, Poultry, etc.	5
	18

A suggested course in agriculture for high schools of agriculture.

FIRST YEAR.	Hours a week.
English	4
Algebra	5
Biology	5
Farm mechanics 5 and Poultry husbandry 2½	7½
	21½
SECOND YEAR.	
English	3
Plane geometry	5
Soils and fertilizers 5 and Farm crops 5	10
	18

THIRD YEAR.	Hours a week.
English	3
History 3 Economics 2 or History 5	5
Animal husbandry, including dairying 5 Fruit growing 5	10
	18
FOURTH YEAR.	
English	3
American history with civics	5
Chemistry or physics	5
Farm management	5
	18

Methods of teaching.—The home-project plan, as operated in New York, is somewhat of a modification of the plan as developed in Massachusetts. In Massachusetts the study of agriculture grows out of the project. In one class students may have a number of different projects, hence the project study is to a great extent individual study. In New York the project grows to a greater extent out of the course. A project may be started in the spring and an increasing amount of time given this practical work until by the time the summer vacation begins instructor and students are putting in a large share of their time upon the home-project work. The commissioner of education is empowered to give each school district an additional fund of $200 to extend the employment of the agricultural instructor through the summer months. Most of the teachers are so employed. Their chief duty in summer is to supervise the home work of the students, but in addition to this they render a great deal of community service to the farmers and collect material for teaching purposes during the winter months.

PENNSYLVANIA.

In 1911 the school code of Pennsylvania made the teaching of agriculture obligatory in all township high schools. Although much of the instruction under this requirement was perfunctory, it developed a feeling that agricultural instruction could be made well worth while if established on a different basis. The vocational education act, passed in 1913, provided State aid for departments of agriculture in high schools and for special vocational schools with agriculture and home-making dominating in the curriculum. These departments and schools are under the direct supervision of the bureau of vocational education, which is a part of the State department of public instruction. In 1916–17 there were 17 vocational schools and 18 vocational departments in high schools. There is little difference in the courses of study and method of instruction in the two types of schools. Local districts are encouraged to establish a department in connection with an existing high school. If such a school does not exist in a community which wishes the vocational work, or the existing school can not meet the requirements, a vocational school may be established. Such a school is in reality a general high school adapted to the needs of rural life. Districts which can establish neither schools nor departments may send their pupils to other districts for vocational training at State expense for one-half the tuition. The State reimburses local districts with vocational schools and departments for two-thirds the salary of the vocational teachers.

In giving aid to local communities the State makes it clear that the money must be used specifically for vocational education. It recognizes the fact that agriculture has value in general education, but defines vocational agriculture as follows:[1]

Vocational agriculture has a specific purpose, that of preparation for useful and efficient service in occupation connected with the tillage of the soil, the care of domestic animals, forestry, and other wage-earning or productive work on the farm. Moreover, this training is given to the individual who has already indicated an occupational aim in life, which aim this particular form of training is designed to meet.

The State requires that all teachers of agriculture shall be employed for 12 months and that their entire time shall be spent in teaching and supervising agriculture. The following suggestions are given with regard to the selection of teachers:

Qualifications of teachers.[2]—Great care must be exercised in the selection of teachers who are qualified to take charge of vocational agriculture in the public schools. In all cases the success or failure of this type of training will depend very largely upon the selection of a teacher. Only such teachers as understand the purpose and aim of vocational training and are familiar with vocational methods will be successful in this work.

Such teacher should have an equivalent of a high-school education. He should be a graduate of an approved agricultural college, or, in lieu thereof, should have at least two years' training in a higher institution of learning, supplemented with at least four short terms or an equivalent in approved agricultural courses of study.

He must have had sufficient practical farm experience to make him familiar with farming methods. This should have been such as to put him in sympathy with rural life and to make him appreciate its problems.

A teacher having a general well-rounded knowledge of agriculture is better prepared to meet the problems arising in such a school or department as is here contemplated than one who is a specialist in a limited field.

It is highly desirable that the teacher of agriculture should have had some experience in teaching in the public schools previous to his entering upon this work.

Ability to make and use working drawings is a valuable qualification, as is also a knowledge of the use of tools and the use of the forge.

Course of study.—In addition to the regular course of study, outlined for students over 14 years of age who may spend the entire 12 months in school work and related home project, both vocational departments and school provide part-time and evening classes for those who are spending all or a large part of their working day in farm labor. An effort is made to link the study of agriculture in both part-time and evening classes as closely as possible with the work in which the student is engaged. In the regular day-school courses the students are expected to spend half their time upon agri-

[1] Commonwealth of Pennsylvania. Department of Public Instruction. Vocational Division. Bulletin 1, 1913. Vocational Education in Pennsylvania. P. 9.
[2] Ibid., Bulletin 2, 1913. Agricultural Schools and Departments. P. 9.

cultural and related practical work. All courses must be approved by the department of public instruction. Although it is expected that courses will be adapted to meet local needs, the schools which have been studied follow quite closely the following course suggested by the State department:

Outline of suggested course of study.

FIRST YEAR.

	Hours
English	4-5
History and civics or other academic subject	4-5
Drawing	1
Shop work	2
Soils	5
Poultry raising	3
Farm forestry	2
Agricultural projects.	

SECOND YEAR.

English	4-5
One academic subject	4-5
Drawing	1
Farm crops	5
Vegetable gardening	3
Ornamental gardening	2
Farm bookkeeping	1
Agricultural project.	

THIRD YEAR.

	Hours.
English	4-5
Physics or other academic subject	4-5
Drawing	2
Farm animals, including dairying	5
Fruit raising	5
Agricultural projects.	

FOURTH YEAR.

English	4-5
Chemistry or physics	4-5
Farm mechanics	4
Rural law	2
Fertilizers	2
Farm management	8
Agricultural project.	

The nature of the work in agriculture given will be indicated by the description of the courses in the catalogue of the Lake Township Vocational School.

AGRICULTURE.

Poultry.—The study of poultry as a farm enterprise, including a study of poultry-house construction, the more important breeds of poultry, incubation, brooding, methods of rearing chickens, and the general care and management of the farm flock.

Vegetable gardening.—The work in this course includes practice in the management of hotbeds and cold frames, seed sowing, transplanting, and raising of early vegetable plants. The more important vegetables are started in detail and the planning of home gardens considered.

Soils.—During the last half of the freshman year a study is made of the origin, formation, classification, and physical properties of various soils, together with the relation of these to soil moisture, heat, and methods of soil management.

General science.—This course introduces the pupils to the fundamental facts of the common sciences so as to give the pupils this general knowledge before science work can be studied in detail in the junior and senior years.

Fruit raising.—Under this head the planting, training, care, fertilization, spraying, harvesting, and marketing of both tree fruits and small fruits are thoroughly studied. Laboratory work includes practice in grafting, mixing of spray materials, and field trips during which pruning is taught by having the pupils prune trees under supervision.

Dairying.—A general survey of the dairy industry, including a study of the separation and handling of milk, cream ripening and churning, and use of the Babcock test.

Animal husbandry.—A study of the history and characteristics of the different breeds of horses, cattle, sheep, and swine. Practice in judging animals and a study of feeding practices.

Farm crops.—A course including the study of the history, production, improvement, cultivation, harvesting, and marketing of cereals, hay, forage, fiber, and root crops.

Forestry.—The relation of forestry to agriculture, identification of tree characteristics, and uses of the various kinds of wood.

Ornamental gardening.—A study of the ornamentation of home grounds, including methods of planting and the selection of planting materials.

Mechanical drawing.—The study of methods of laying out to scale, inking, and tracing; reading of working drawings, etc.

Shop work.—The use of woodworking tools is taught by having the pupils make useful articles for the home and farm.

Farm bookkeeping.—The study and practice of double-entry bookkeeping as applied to business transactions of the farmer.

Farm mechanics.—Rope splicing, knot tying, lacing belts, study of gas engines, and farm machinery.

Fertilizers.—A study of the different kinds of fertilizers, proper mixtures for various crops, time and rate of application.

Farm management.—Planning the work of the farm, study of crop rotations, layout of fields, and other problems, including the making of financial statements of farm operations.

Rural law.—An elementary consideration of the law in its relation to the farmer.

Project work.—Each pupil is required to work out some project such as raising of some crop, poultry, or live stock each summer on his home farm under the supervision of his instructor.

Methods of teaching.—The home-project plan is in vogue in all of the schools and departments of vocational agriculture in Pennsylvania. The teachers of agriculture are known as supervisors and employed for 12 months in the year with the understanding that one of the most important phases of their work will be the summer supervision of projects. The project is preceded by a study of the subject in the classroom. The schools are encouraged to have classroom shops and a greenhouse equipped to give practical instruction to the students while at school. They are not encouraged, however, to supply farms or any land at the school for instruction in agriculture, as it is considered that the project work upon the home farm offers training under conditions more nearly normal and that an ordinary rural community is rich in resources of educational value in training for farming and rural life. As in Massachusetts and New York, an advisory board may be appointed. It is significant to note that it is advised that farmers be appointed who will cooperate with the teacher by allowing their farms, herds, and flocks to be used for teaching purposes.

NEW JERSEY.[1]

It was in 1913 also that the State of New Jersey established a system of State-aided vocational schools and departments. In brief the plan established is for the State to give money for the equipment and maintenance of approved vocational schools on a dollar for a dollar basis in proportion to the amount spent by the local community out of funds raised by local taxation to the amount of $10,000 annually.

The following is summarized from the rules of the State board of education which govern the establishment of vocational schools and departments:

1. Advisory boards must be appointed by the local boards of control, subject to the approval of the commissioners of education. The advisory boards should be made up of persons who have had actual successful experience in the occupations for which the school prepares. The efficiency of vocational schools should be measured largely by the ability of their pupils to meet the demands of the trades, industries, and occupations for which these schools give preparation. Whether the schools give instruction in agriculture, home economics, or industrial subects, the vocational work must be such as to prepare the pupil for wage earning by participation in actual projects and processes of a very real character. This requires an intimate and practical knowledge of actual conditions and practices in the work as it is carried on outside the school. Only those experienced as employers or employees can furnish this information. The task of establishing and maintaining these schools, on a practical basis, is so important and so difficult that the instructors in the school, who must themselves have had such experience, need also the advice and assistance of those having the practical knowledge of the industry or occupation and the conditions peculiar to it in the locality. The advisory boards have no power except to give advice and assistance to the local school authorities in carrying on the work.

The advisory board of an agricultural school or department must be made up of at least three successful farmers in the area served by the school and should represent the various agricultural activities taught.

2. A separate vocational school must be in a separate building and have a separate organization of curricula, equipment, pupils, and teachers.

3. A vocational department of another school must have a separate organization of curricula, pupils, and teachers as far as the vocational work is concerned.

4. The State board of education will not approve State aid for more than $10,000 for any district unless the applications from all districts amount to less than $80,000.

5. To receive State aid in any given year, application must be made before January 1.

6. In an all-day vocational school (a) not less than one-half of the time must be given to shop or farm work; (b) the shop must be conducted on a productive or community basis; (c) instruction must tend to become individual; (d) the shop must be carried on like the real shop outside; (e) the product must be useful; (f) the school day must not be less than six or more than seven hours in length; and (g) the agricultural vocational school must have its courses arranged as a series of projects.

[1] See New Jersey Department of Public Instruction. Bulletin No. 1, 1913. State-aided Vocational Schools.

7. The part-time class must give instruction of direct value to the pupil for the work in which he is engaged.

8. To secure approval, the part-time or continuation work must (a) deal with a specific group of workers; (b) add to the technical knowledge and mechanical skill of the workers; (c) provide efficient instruction; and (d) provide adequate amount of time.

9. An evening industrial or agricultural or household arts school must give short unit courses.

10. All vocational schools must provide for (a) shop or farm or household experience; (b) instruction in related subjects; and (c) instruction in academic subjects.

11. Schools must be convenient of location and access.

12. Schools must have adequate general and mechanical equipment.

13. Tuition may be paid by a district sending pupils to vocational schools and be reimbursed to the amount of $25 per annum for each pupil.

14. Districts may transport pupils either within the district or to other districts and be reimbursed for 75 per cent of the amount expended.

Vocational agriculture in Atlantic County.—The provisions of the State vocational education act for agricultural education have been taken advantage of to the greatest extent in Atlantic County. In this county a rather complete county system has been worked, but under a board of five members. Agricultural schools have been established in four centers: Pleasantville, Cologne, Hammonton, and Minotola, each in charge of a teacher employed for the full year, and all under the supervision of a county director. In these schools the students are classified as follows:

1. *Full time.*—Men and boys above 15 years of age taking at least 3 hours per day, 5 days a week, during the winter.

2. *Part time.*—Students taking less than the time prescribed for full-time students, spending their time mostly on project study. Part-time classes are held mostly at night.

3. *School pupils.*—Students over 15 years of age enrolled in the public schools, above the seventh grade, taking not less than 3 hours per week. Work consists chiefly of elementary project study, which is taken in lieu of a like number of hours of regular school work.

4. *Lecture course.*—For men and women meeting once a week or oftener in the winter to discuss agricultural problems of community interest.

5. *Night classes.*—Composed of men who meet once a week or oftener studying project problems and subjects of interest upon their home farms.

6. *Short course.*—For those unable to attend a full-time course a detailed study of a specific subject is made for a period of 2, 4, or 6 weeks.

As the work was in operation in 1915 when the school at Hammonton was visited, the aims and methods appeared to be more narrowly vocational than the agricultural work conducted in other States.

More mature students were reached and less effort made to link the work closely with other school work. The community is a center of intensive agriculture, including production of small fruits and peaches. Such a community would furnish a wealth of resources for a general education in agriculture, as the student could gain experience in many lines. Instead of encouraging the direction of training and the use of material from this point of view, the students were encouraged to become proficient in a special line. Students were encouraged to stay with a project for several years if necessary to secure the maximum financial returns, although it might be to the neglect of opportunity for new experience in other lines.

The entire county system of agricultural schools was at the service of the farmers of the section to aid them in their problems. In this work it took the place of a county farm bureau. The director in fact did act through a cooperative arrangement as county agent. For the use of the farmers in making analysis of soils, fertilizers, and spraying material, a chemical laboratory is maintained at Pleasantville. The agricultural instructors also aided in the organizations of farmers for cooperative buying and selling. In 1916 the staff took over the entire direction of the boys' and girls' agricultural clubs.

INDIANA.

In Indiana the vocational agriculture of the secondary schools is linked closely with elementary agriculture in the common schools and with the boys' and girls' club work directed by the agricultural extension department of Purdue University. The same act providing for vocational education provides for employing county agents. At the same time the vocational education law was passed in 1913 the legislature made the teaching of elementary agriculture mandatory in the public schools of towns and townships. According to the law the county agent is expected to "aid the county superintendent of schools and the teachers in giving practical education in agriculture and domestic science." The vocational education law provided for establishing either schools or departments which may receive State aid. In 1916 thirteen communities had established departments of vocational agriculture. The departments served the needs of the rural communities so well that there was no demand for special agricultural schools. In addition to the vocational teachers who are employed for 12 months, a number of other teachers are given special training and employed during the summer months to supervise the home project work. Twenty-one such teachers were employed during the summer of 1915, supervising the work of 700 pupils. The greater part of this work is considered a definite part of the boys' and girls' club work organized as a phase of agricultural extension.

Vocational agriculture may be given in one of the three following classes: (1) All-day vocational schools; (2) part-time classes; (3) evening vocational classes. The all-day school may be organized either as a separate school or as a distinct department of another school. When organized as a department the organization must be distinct from the regular' school. The following from a bulletin [1] giving plans for organization shows the point of view with respect to such organization:

Whether vocational education is conducted in a separate building or under the same roof as general education is not necessarily of vital importance. It is, however, absolutely necessary, if State aid be given, that the vocational work be so carried on that it may realize its dominant aim of fitting for useful employment in the shop, in the home, or on the farm. If vocational agriculture is organized under the first plan, the local community will have established a presumption in favor of efficient work in the eye of the department.

The following from the same publication [2] gives an idea of the nature of the work in the all-day schools or departments:

All-day agricultural schools.—In the all-day agricultural school pupils must give most of their time to practical business-like work in agriculture and its related sciences. Practical problems must be worked out on a real farm under the direction of the teacher. Since most of these activities must take place during the summer months, it will be necessary for the vocational teachers in an agricultural school to be employed for the entire year, with a vacation in the winter. Their entire time during the summer should be taken up with superintending the practical work of the students, while in the winter months their time would be devoted to the home-project work and to teaching the theory and science underlying the art of farming.

Part-time classes give vocational instruction to students over 14 and under 25 years of age, who are regularly and lawfully employed in the field of work for which instruction is provided and where the instruction is complementary to the work in which the pupils are engaged during the time they are not attending school. The Indiana law provides that—

when the board of education or township trustee of any city, town, or township has established approved vocational schools for the instruction of youths over 14 years of age who are engaged in regular employment, in part-time classes, and has formally accepted the provisions of this section, such a board or trustee is authorized to require all youths between the ages of 14 and 16 years who are regularly employed to attend school not less than 5 hours per week between the hours of 8 a. m. and 5 p. m. during the school term.

Evening classes in vocational agriculture are established for students over 17 years of age who are employed in agriculture during

---

[1] Department of Public Instruction. Bulletin No. 6; 1914. Vocational Education in Indiana. P. 18.
[2] Ibid., p. 20.

the day. The instruction in an evening class in agriculture must deal with the subject matter of the day's employment, and must be so given as to increase the efficiency of the student in his work.

Local communities desiring to establish any or all of these forms of vocational agriculture in partnership with the State, which pays two-thirds the cost of such instruction, are subject to the following provisions: (1) Local school authorities must provide the necessary money for the purchase or rental of lands and buildings adapted to the needs of the vocational department or school to be established and pay the cost of all necessary equipment. (2) They must assume entire responsibility for the conduct of the work and must initiate its organization. (3) They must accept standards set by the State, submit to State supervision, and receive approval of the work done.

Standards for agricultural schools and departments.[1]—1. Evidence of proper interest on the part of the community must be furnished the State board of education. There must be an assurance of not less than 15 and not more than 25 students for each day, part-time, or evening class organized. The location of the school must meet the hearty approval of the people of the community as well as the State board.

2. An advisory committee, consisting of five members, shall be appointed to "counsel with and advise the board and other school officials responsible for the management and supervision of" the vocational agricultural school or department. It is recommended that one or two members of the committee be women who are familiar with farm home problems.

3. The teacher of agriculture must be a graduate of a standard high school and a standard agricultural college or prove an equivalent training in technical agriculture. He must devote all of his time during the 12 months to the vocational work.

4. Laboratory equipment must be approved by the State board. There should be apparatus sufficient for thorough work of secondary grade in soils, crops, animal husbandry, dairying, poultry, horticulture, carpentry, and blacksmithing, or for such of these lines of work as are to be taken up. A complete list of books must also be submitted for the approval of the board.

5. The course of study must be worked out in detail and submitted at least 30 days before the beginning of the school term for the approval of the board. The course may be for one, two, three, or four years. Where the school authorities decide upon a four-year course the following is recommended:

---

[1] See Department of Public Instruction. Bulletin No. 7, 1914. Regulations Governing Vocational Agricultural Schools and Departments in Indiana.

Course of study.

FIRST YEAR.

	Rec.	Lab.
English	4	
Horticulture	3	2
Soils and fertilizers	3	2
Mechanical drawing and woodworking		2
Mathematics	3	
Home-project work		

SECOND YEAR.

English	3	
Civics	3	
Mathematics	2	
Dairying	3	2
Farm crops (not limited to botany)	3	2
Mechanical drawing and woodworking		2
Home-project work		

THIRD YEAR.

English	3	
United States history	3	
Farm accounting	3	
Physics (not academic)	3	2
Animal husbandry	3	2
Carpentry		2
Home-project work		

FOURTH YEAR.

Farm management (including marketing)	5	
Poultry	2	2
General history (elective)		
Farm mechanics and engineering	2	1
Chemistry (not academic)	3	2
Forging and blacksmithing	1	2
Home-project work		

6. Home-project work must be an integral part of the course of study for each student. This work must be carefully inspected and supervised by the instructor. Each pupil must make a written report of each project based upon a careful record. The instructor must not only submit these reports to the State board upon completion of the project but must also submit within three weeks of the beginning of the school term an outline of the work to be done by each student. The following projects are suggested. Feeding swine, sheep, cattle, or poultry for market; feeding poultry for egg production; caring for a dairy cow and her products; caring for a team of horses, or a brood sow; selecting, testing, and grading seeds for farm crops; poultry hatching, etc.; corn growing, gardening, canning fruits and vegetables; marketing farm products; and small fruit growing.

Chapter III.

AGRICULTURE AS TAUGHT IN SOME SECONDARY SCHOOLS.

Representative schools chosen.—The author has had abundant opportunity to visit secondary schools for the purpose of studying their organization and methods of teaching agriculture. From a large number studied the following have been chosen not because they were the best schools visited but because they were fairly representative of the type indicated:

District schools of agriculture: Fifth District Agricultural and Mechanical School, Monroe, Ga.

County schools of agriculture: Agricultural High School, Sparks, Md.; Bristol County Agricultural School, Segreganset, Mass.

Public high schools: Hannibal High School, Hannibal, N. Y.; Concord High School, Concord, Mass.; Hopkins Academy, Hadley, Mass.

Normal schools: State Normal School, Platteville, Wis.

Private schools for whites: Berry School, Mount Berry, Ga.

Private schools for Negroes:: Manassas Industrial School for Colored Youth, Manassas, Va.

FIFTH DISTRICT AGRICULTURAL AND MECHANICAL SCHOOL, MONROE, GA.

The district agricultural schools of Georgia.[1]—In 1906 the General Assembly of Georgia passed an act providing for the establishment and maintenance of an industrial and agricultural school in each of the 11 congressional districts of the State. The schools were to be definitely affiliated with the University of Georgia as branches of the State College of Agriculture. The university became interested in their supervision. A keen interest was aroused in each district, and sharp competition developed among different localities for the location of the schools. Liberal bids of land and cash were made, the total of the accepted bids amounting to approximately $439,000 in cash and 3,214 acres of land. Electric lights, water, and sewage disposal were furnished free to each school for five years.

These schools were to be of secondary grade, intermediate between the rural elementary schools and the agricultural college. The law

---

[1] For a detailed description of these schools, see U. S. Bureau of Education, Bulletin, 1916, No. 44. The District Agricultural School of Georgia.

stipulates that the principal shall be an intelligent farmer and that he shall be aided by a faculty capable of giving practical instruction in agriculture and mechanic arts along with the elements of an English education. The district agricultural schools of Georgia represent the most extensive State-aided system of special agricultural schools in this country.

Buildings and equipment.—The citizens of Monroe bid $31,000 in cash and 250 acres of land. This bid was accepted and the fifth district school located at Walker Station in Walton County, about 3 miles north of Monroe on the Gainesville Midland Railroad. Although local trains stop at Walker, the school is located in open country, forming a small community by itself. The buildings consist of an academic building and a boys' dormitory, both modern brick buildings valued at $15,000 each. A frame cottage built for the principal's residence is used at the present time as a girl's dormitory. In addition to the farm buildings, there is a school shop, a smokehouse, a powerhouse, and a laundry, which, with its equipment, is valued at $2,000.

As the school farm is considered the agricultural laboratory, there is no special provision made for inside laboratory instruction. The chemical laboratory is used for those exercises given. The school shop is provided with benches and tools for woodworking and a forge and anvil for ironworking. A separator and other equipment for handling milk is a part of the kitchen equipment. Likewise a canning outfit is used in putting up fruits and vegetables for use in the school dining room. A relatively large room of the academic building is used both for the principal's office and as a library. The library, having very few bulletins and reference books on agriculture, is used but little for agricultural study.

The school farm.—The 250 acres which comprise the school farm are for the most part excellent agricultural land valued at $100 per acre. About 30 acres are used for the school buildings and campus. Permanent pasture comprises 50 acres and 45 acres in woodland, leaving 125 acres in cultivation. Fifteen acres of the cultivated land are used for cotton as a cash crop, and all the remainder used to supply food to the student boarding house, either directly or indirectly through feeding farm animals.

The farm buildings include separate barns for horses, cows, and calves; a machine shed, poultry and hog houses. A new concrete silo has been built preliminary to building a modern dairy barn. The farm animals include 2 Percheron brood mares with 2 colts, 3 mules, 1 Hereford and 1 Jersey bull, 13 dairy cows, 18 head young cattle, and 75 hogs. The value of the live stock owned would approximate $3,500. Farm machinery to the value of $1,500 is owned.

In addition to the tools and implements commonly found on southern farms, there is a small grain separator, a gasoline engine, an ensilage cutter, a hay press, manure spreader, corn shredder, and an electric motor. The gross income of the farm for 1915 was $6,600, leaving a net profit of $1,173.29.

Students.—On September 28, 1916, there were 120 students, 79 of whom were boys and 41 girls. All the students live at the school except 2, who live on near-by farms, and 12 who live in Monroe. The following students are taking courses in agriculture: First year, 36 (8 of these are girls); second year, 29; third year, 13. Although the school was then filled to its capacity for students, registration was not restricted to residents of the fifth district. Students are registered from other parts of Georgia and from three other States.

Course of study.—The course of study [1] adopted for the district agricultural schools of the State in 1915 is in operation as far as equipment and time will allow. The work in poultry husbandry, dairying, and farm management is not given at the present time, nor the agricultural laboratory work suggested for the first year. Students are expected to have completed the elementary school of seven grades before entrance. Boys must be 14 and girls 13 years of age.

Standard of credit.—Although the State standard for graduation is but 14 units, most of the students are taking more nearly 17 units of work. Five class periods of 40 minutes are equivalent to 1 unit. In laboratory work the periods are 80 minutes long. No credit is given for farm practice. The school year consists of 36 weeks.

Methods of teaching.—The classes in agriculture visited were under two different instructors. One of the instructors, an experienced teacher, had excellent interest, as he sought opportunity to connect the lesson of the textbook with the daily farm experience of the students. The other teacher, without previous teaching experience, was called upon to take hold of a class for which he had no preparation. The students dragged through a recitation period by taking turns in reading from the textbook. Although an effort is made to utilize the farm experience of the students in the classroom recitation, there is no definite connection between the course of study and the planning of the school farm and no definite relation between the daily classroom recitation in agriculture and the daily farm labor.

Use of the school farm.—Although there is a lack of definite relation between farm work and class work, the dominating aim of the school farm is to furnish practical instruction to the students. Each student is required to spend 36 hours per week in farm practice. The

---

[1] For a description of the course of study with class schedule, see Bureau of Education, Bulletin, 1916, No. 44, pp. 19–28.

work consists of the regular labor of the farm in season under the supervision of one of the instructors or the farm superintendent. In order to distribute the work and provide for supervision, the first and third year students have class work in the forenoon and field work in the afternoon, alternating with the second and fourth year students. All of the farm buildings have been constructed by the students. Most of the students do more than 36 hours of farm work a week. A daily record is kept of all work done and the amount beyond the required hours is credited upon their board account at 5 to 10 cents per hour, according to the nature of the work and the age of the student. Surplus work is given to those who are in most need of the money. Several students have been able to pay their way by working on the school farm. A number of students are retained for the summer work, receiving as wages $18 per month and their board. A few students have paid board and received pay by the hour for their services. The students who remain in the summer secure some practice not to be obtained by most of them who return home. For example, the school cans a good part of its supply of certain vegetables and fruits during the summer.

Although the aim of the school farm is primarily educational, it is depended upon largely to supply the dormitory and as a source of revenue, hence it can not plan its work in such a way and grow such crops as to secure the maximum educational value. The students may know the practice involved in cotton production, hence there may be little necessity from an educational point of view for growing cotton, but the school has soil well adapted to cotton and needs it as a cash crop.

A definite rotation is maintained. The farm has shown continual improvement since the school was established, hence serves well as a general demonstration of good farming methods. The following shows the acreage of crops for 1916: 15 acres cotton followed by rye; 15 acres wheat followed by peas; 40 acres corn (partly for silage) followed by winter oats; 35 acres oats followed by peas for hay; 5½ acres alfalfa; 50 acres pasture; and 8 acres orchard.

It is interesting to note that when the question came up as to using the farm more specifically for educational purposes, the principal thought it could be done better with a farm of only 15 acres.

Social administration.—As most of the students live at the school, the problem of directing their social life is presented. The girls and boys are kept separate for the most part, the girls living in a separate building under the direction of a matron, and the boys living in the main dormitory under the direction of the principal and the male instructors. All of the students take care of their own rooms. They also do most of the other janitorial services and the work of the school boarding house. For the latter services the girls are given school credit and pay for overtime as the boys are in the case of farm work. Board and laundry are furnished to the students at the rate of $10 per month. As no tuition is charged and but one or two small fees exacted, the cost is comparatively low.

As the school is located in the country, the students have little opportunity to spend money. Their entire time is under the direction of the principal. From 7.20 to 4.20 they are supposed to be engaged in the classrooms or engaged in work or study, except for a brief period for dinner. Although the girls are required to dress in a neat uniform, the boys most of the time appear in the classroom and at the table in the same clothes they wear at farm labor. The following is a schedule of the usual work day:

6 a. m..—Arise.
6.25 a. m.—Room and person in order for inspection.
6.30 a. m.—Breakfast.
7.50 a. m.—Chapel.
8.10 a. m. to 12.15 p. m.—School or farm work.
12.15 p. m.—Dinner.
1 to 4.20 p. m.—School or farm work.
4.20 to 6.15 p. m.—Recreation if desired.
7 p. m.—Inspection.
9.30 p. m.—Light bell.
9.45 p. m.—Retire.

Saturday afternoons are frequently taken for athletic sports. At the time of the visit there was a very lively football game in which a team selected from the first and fourth years contested with a team representing the second and third years. Although this was strictly a school affair, there was no lack of interest. In the evening the students assembled for a short program, followed by a social hour in which the boys and girls joined together in simple dances and harmless games. The principal directs these affairs upon the assumption that it is natural for boys and girls of high-school age to come together in a social way, and that there is little danger if there is proper supervision.

On Sundays, Bible classes and simple services of a nonsectarian character are held for all. The problem of finding profitable, harmless pastime for Sunday has not been completely solved, however.

Local extension work.—By an arrangement with the State agricultural college, one of the instructors in agriculture is to spend one-half of his time as a farm demonstrator for Walton County. The man appointed to the position had not gotten his extension work fully under way at the time of the visit. Since the school was first established there has been considerable extension work among the farmers. The principal of the school is a practical farmer who was reared in the country; hence he is well qualified to act as a farm advisor. The school has cooperated with the farmers in the purchase of live stock and has used its pure-bred live stock for community breeding. The school farm has been a source of improved seed as well as pure-bred stock for breeding purposes. The school has taken active part in the county fairs held at Monroe. During the summer farmers' institutes are held at the school, where both men and women meet with experts from the State agricultural college. At the one held during the last summer there was an attendance of 75. A short summer school was held also for teachers. During the last session there were 130 in attendance. Two teachers of agriculture gave practical courses to rural teachers, preparation for work in canning being a prominent feature. During the coming year this course is to be extended and all supervisors in the district are to take part as instructors. It is not expected that the school will be able to accommodate all who apply.

Each summer the principal undertakes to visit the homes of all students living in the district that he may become acquainted with the parents and the conditions surrounding the home life of the students.

BALTIMORE COUNTY AGRICULTURAL HIGH SCHOOL, SPARKS, MD.

Baltimore County, Md., has for years maintained an efficient school system, the county serving as a unit for administration. Inasmuch as the county has extensive agricultural interests, in 1908 a special agricultural school was established to serve the whole county. This school is located in the open country, not near any city or village, but adjacent to a small railroad station. The school was opened for the year 1908-9 with an enrollment in the high school department of 50 students. A granite building with five classrooms is used for grade students as well as secondary students. At the time the author first visited the school, in April, 1915, there were 99 elementary students and 77 in the high school. Two teachers took care of the grade students in two of the rooms, while five teachers were employed in secondary work.

Although this school was established as an agricultural school, its aim is apparently not to train farmers in any narrow vocational sense, but to give a broad training for rural life without attempting to meet college entrance requirements. The course of study which follows might be adapted to the needs of any rural community.

Course of study.

FIRST YEAR.	Units.	SECOND YEAR.	Units.
Agriculture	1.0	Agriculture	1.0
Arithmetic	1.0	Algebra	1.0
English	1.0	English	1.0
Botany	1.0	Zoology	1.0
Manual training or domestic science	.4	Manual training or domestic science	.4
History	.6	History	.6

THIRD YEAR.	Units.	FOURTH YEAR.	Units.
Agriculture or domestic science	1.0	Agriculture or domestic science	1.0
Plane geometry	1.0	Solid geometry and advanced algebra	1.0
English	1.0	English	1.0
Chemistry	1.0	Physics	1.0
Physiology	.4	German [1]	1.0
Manual training or domestic science	.6	Manual training or domestic science	.6

COURSES IN AGRICULTURE.

First year.—Soils. Text: " Soils," by Fletcher. Warren's " Elements of Agriculture," used as a reference. A special laboratory manual is used.

Second year.—Farm crops. (Vegetables to be a part of the course next year.) Texts: " Cereals in America," and " Forage and Fiber Crops," by Hunt.

Third year.—Animal husbandry and dairying. Texts: " Types and Breeds of Farm Animals," by Plumb; " Milk and Its Products," by Wing; " Dairy Laboratory Guide," by Ross.

Fourth year.—Farm management and horticulture. Texts: " Farm Management," by Warren; " Principles of Fruit Growing," by Bailey.

COURSES IN SCIENCE.

Botany.—Text: " Botany for Schools," by Bailey. Herbarium of 50 specimens required.

Zoology.—Text: Last half of course spent in economic entomology. Twenty-five specimens of economic species required as a collection.

Chemistry.—Text: Clark and Dennis.

Physiology.—Text: "The Human Mechanism," by Hough and Sedgewick.

Agricultural instruction.—The principal of the school also serves as instructor in agriculture and is assisted by another man. Both instructors are graduates of the New York State College of Agriculture, the assistant having just taken up the work in place of a man who had accepted a position in the United States Department of Agriculture. The principal proved to be an especially capable instructor and rural life leader, giving good evidence of earning the

---

[1] German is elective, all other subjects are required. Recitation periods are for the most part 50 minutes long. In all courses in agriculture and all science except physiology there is one double laboratory period per week. Occasionally field trips require a longer period, or a whole day.

relatively large salary he received. The assistant, on less than half the salary, did not give evidence of having special aptitude for teaching. He had not been away from college long enough to get away from college material and methods.

Correlations.—Inasmuch as the science is taught by the men teaching agriculture, there is an excellent opportunity for correlation. There is also an effort to correlate the science with home economics in the case of the girls. The students in mechanic arts work mostly upon farm equipment, although most of the laboratory cases and special equipment for teaching were made by the students. Considerable time was given one year to the making of models of barns and other buildings. The instructor did not think the work worth the time put upon it. He thought the time would have been better spent in making smaller buildings which would be of practical use upon the farm.

The teacher of English believes in basing her work upon the work of the farm and other interests of the students. Some of the papers required in the agricultural classes are corrected as to composition by the teacher of English. The students gain excellent practice in publishing a paper, "The Agriculturist of Baltimore County."

Practical work in agriculture.—Although there are 8 acres of land, it was not used to any great extent as a school farm when the school was visited in 1915. The elementary students used part of the farm as a school garden. A few fruit trees and a few small plats of grasses had been planted as a basis for some work in plant introduction and breeding. In 1917, when the school was visited again, the principal of the school was making a special effort to promote potato production in the community, and about half an acre of the school land was used for tests of varieties and methods of treatment.

The surrounding farms are used extensively for practical work. The classes in horticulture spray and prune the orchards on surrounding farms. Occasionally the class spends a day in Baltimore studying such problems as the marketing of dairy products or in visiting dealers in farm machinery and equipment. For practical work in dairying an arrangement was made with the local creamery to let students come in and secure practice in making butter and in handling milk and dairy products.

At the time the school was established, before the home-project plan was developed, each student was required to carry on an "experiment" at home. All of the students live at home on farms, school wagons and private conveyances bringing those who do not live within walking distance. The early idea of having these students working out experiments at home has developed into something approaching the home-project plan, although there is no definite attempt to connect the home work with the instruction of the school or to give it adequate supervision. Projects as given in 1915 covered crop production, crop improvement, management of live stock, and farm management problems. A project may run through several years. Corn and potato projects are connected with the club work.

In connection with the course in farm management each student has made a survey of the home farm showing the size and shape of fields, the crops planted, and the location and arrangement of buildings. From the data gathered papier maché models were made showing elevation and slope as well as the size and shape of the fields, worked out to a scale with fair accuracy.

Equipment.—The basement of the buildings is equipped with laboratories for the work in science, home economics, and agriculture. Most of the special equipment in the agricultural laboratory is for somewhat technical exercises in soils and for testing dairy products. There was some farm equipment on hand, but little of it in use. A kerosene engine was used to run a cream separator and a feed mill, but the engine did not work well. A gasoline gas plant supplies gas for cooking, lighting, and laboratory purposes. Practical woodworking is conducted in the basement of the school building. No special metal work is given, although an outside shop is equipped with forges and anvils and such tools as a farm shop should have. Practice is given in the repair of farm equipment.

There is the beginning of a very good museum containing exhibits of seeds and other farm materials for use in the classroom. A stereopticon is used as an essential feature in visual instruction.

A fairly good library of agricultural books gives evidence that it is used. The students have bound many bulletins themselves. The teachers have personal files of bulletins which are used by the students.

Community work.—Inasmuch as the school had become somewhat widely known for the local extension work carried on by a former principal,[1] it was rather to be expected that there would be a possibility of this work being carried on to a neglect of the regular school work. The principal is employed throughout the year and is expected to put in some of his time in extension work; he stated, however, that he considered his duty to his students first of all and that the work among patrons was but a secondary matter. Experi-

---

[1] See Crosby, D. J., and Crocheron, B. H. Community Work in the Rural High School. U. S. Department of Agriculture. Yearbook, 1910. Pp. 177-188.

ence had shown that it was very easy to develop distrust among the farmers and that they did not take kindly to any form of exploitation. It was not considered advisable to have the new instructor do any great amount of work among the farmers until he had been tried out and had developed local experience. The winter short courses for farmers and their wives and the work for rural teachers in the county, inaugurated under a former principal, had been discontinued.

BRISTOL COUNTY AGRICULTURAL SCHOOL, SEGREGANSET, MASS.

The citizens of Bristol County took advantage of the Massachusetts State law, passed in 1912, providing for the establishment of agricultural schools and departments under State aid. The school opened its doors for the year 1913–14 at Segreganset, a small village in the center of the county. The school has a delightful location on a farm of more than a hundred acres on the west bank of the Taunton River.

Purpose of the school.—The school disavows any intention of giving a general education or of fitting students for a higher institution. The prospectus of the school states "this is a school for the farmer's boy who intends to stay on the farm and for any other boy who wants to become an intelligent farmer." The school is more distinctly vocational in its aims and methods than any school of agriculture the author has visited. The law prescribed that students shall be between the ages of 14 and 25 years. No prerequisite schooling or entrance examination is required. Students must show evidence of sincerity of purpose and good moral character before they are admitted.

Course of study.

FIRST YEAR.

	Credits.		Credits.
Spelling	2	Kitchen gardening	1
English	2	Farm practice and shop work	2
Farm arithmetic	2	Project study	5
Agricultural botany	2	Project management and work	7
Woodlot management and ornamental planting	1		
Small fruits	1		25

SECOND YEAR.

	Credits.		Credits.
Spelling	2	Swine husbandry	1
English	2	General farm experience	2
Farm measurements and mechanics	2	Project study	5
Soils and soil fertility	2	Project management and work	7
Poultry husbandry	2		25

THIRD YEAR.

	Credits.		Credits.
English	2	Orcharding	2
Farm records and accounts	3	Project study	5
Insect study	2	Project management and work	7
Plant diseases	2		—
Market gardening	2		25

FOURTH YEAR.

	Credits.		Credits.
English	2	Animal husbandry	2
Farm management	3	Project study	5
Farm crops	2	Project management and work	7
Seminar (subjects elective)	2		—
Dairying	2		25

Equipment.—The main building of the school was built at a cost of $30,000, the second story not having been completed. The building has been equipped for teaching purposes at a cost of $15,000. Although in practically open country, it is supplied with both water and gas. The school farm comprises 110 acres of land which is much better than the average of the county. In fact, some people have criticized the school because it gives practice to students under much better conditions than those which obtain at home. ·The land is a sandy loam partly on the river bottom, suitable for working early and late with a variety of crops. A very good dairy barn with two large silos has been built to replace one burned in 1915. This barn and other equipment of the farm, Mr. Gilbert, the director, claims to be within the reach of most progressive ·farmers in the county. An excellent herd of Ayrshires is being built up in spite˙ of misfortune by way of fire and infectious disease. Both manure and machinery are protected by a long shed. The poultry plant consists of a long laying house, an incubator cellar, and a brooder house, in addition to a group of colony houses located on higher grounds which are used by students for individual projects. The farm is well equipped with modern implements and machinery.

Teaching staff.—The director is assisted by three men in addition to the county agent, who makes his headquarters at the school. All of the men have agricultural training. The director, G. H. Gilbert, although a practical farmer, conducted a commercial school, which may account for the emphasis given at the school on business training.

Practical work.—No outside labor is employed on the school farm. All of the work is done by students under the direction of the instructors. All students who enter without having had farm experience are required to spend two afternoons a week in " farm laboratory work." Before graduation, each student must have two seasons on some good farm. This work is reported to one of the instructors who is given charge of the supervision of the students' work. Work done on farms other than the home farm of the students is classed as a "substitute for a project." At the time the school was first visited, May, 1916, over half of the 50 boys were working on substitutes for projects away from the school. Twelve to 15 students were boarding at the school. In many ways the school presented the appearance of a well-managed farm. Students and instructors ate dinner together in their working clothes. There were individual projects and class projects being carried on in all the common branches of farming. Although the director aims to make the farm fully productive, as he believes it will then serve best for educational purposes, it is not managed as a commercial proposition. As a money-making venture, the farm would be devoted to one or two lines instead of being highly diversified. Although the chief aim is to give students practice in all phases of farming, the farm serves well for demonstration purposes to patrons as well as students. There are a number of highly specialized farms in the community to which the students are taken frequently. When an opportunity is presented to place a student upon one of these farms for the summer, it is taken even though the student is taken out of school before the end of the spring term. The character of the work done upon the school farm is good. During the spring of 1916 and the summer of 1917 when the school was revisited, crops and farm animals were in excellent condition. It is true, however, that certain items must be charged up now and then to educational experience given the students. For example, a number of rows of peach trees were nearly ruined in the school orchard when the spraying was left entirely in the hands of the students.

Methods of instruction.—As a rule the mornings are confined to the classroom, while the afternoons are spent on the farm and in the shop. Although some conventional class work is done, instruction in the school is largely individual.

In order to encourage habits of thrift each pupil is required to keep in permanent form an account of his personal receipts and expenditures from the day he enters the institution. In the same book he later opens a business account with his project. At any time he can determine his loss or gain.

The school has organized a savings bank along lines similar to the Massachusetts cooperative banks. This bank was established primarily to give business experience and to encourage the savings habit. The student's project, as a rule, will require a cash balance to draw upon until cash returns come in for produce sold. The bank also provides a loan fund available to worthy students in financing their projects.

The extent of the students' earnings is shown in the following table:

Year.	Number of boys.	Farm work.	Other work.	Total earnings.
1914	24	$1,516.72	$77.70	$1,621.42
1915	47	4,858.45	651.80	5,510.25
1916	50	4,991.99	301.00	5,292.09

Extension work.—The cooperative agricultural extension work of the county, sustained by Federal and State funds, is under the direction of the school. One member of the faculty is assigned to spend all of his time in this work as county agent. All of the instructors do more or less extension work in connection with the supervision of home projects. Considerable time is given to the supervision of the boys' and girls' agricultural clubs of the county and in helping the teachers in the elementary schools to connect the club work with the instruction in agriculture. Farmers have been assisted in the cooperative purchase of supplies. The following record for one year will indicate the scope of this work: Ten carloads of lime, three carloads of seed potatoes, one carload of dairy cows, and several carloads of grain. The school has cooperated with local communities in holding fairs, and a number of special exhibits and meetings have been held at the school, including a county dairy conference, a Grange field day, a poultry day, and the county apple, corn, and potato show.

AGRICULTURAL DEPARTMENT OF HANNIBAL (N. Y.) HIGH SCHOOL.

Hannibal is a small village in the western part of Oswego County, N. Y., near the shore of Lake Ontario. It is in the midst of a section devoted to diversified farming and fruit growing. The principal of the school, S. R. Lockwood, who is also a farmer in the community, started a course in 1908 which he termed "academic agriculture." Although this course was of a very general and elementary nature, an effort was made to adapt it to the needs of the community. In 1911 State aid was given the school and an effort made to put the agricultural work on a vocational basis, although both boys and girls were taking the work. A year later home economics was added to the curriculum, leaving only boys to the attention of one teacher, with no other subjects. In 1914 the home-project plan was introduced. The school was visited in May, 1915, for the purpose of investigating the application of this plan to New York conditions.

154070°—20——4

Home projects.—The following projects were being worked out by the 20 students who were taking the course in agriculture:

1. Fruit—One acre mixed orchard.
2. Poultry improvement of home flock, introducing Rhode Island Red blood.
3. Poultry—One pair turkeys.
4. Poultry—Set 50 Plymouth Rock eggs in incubator. Not successful, trying it the second time.
5. Fruit—Has set out one-fourth acre of berries.
6. Dairying—Keeping a record of 10 cows.
7. Poultry—Sixty-two Plymouth Rock and White Leghorn hens.
8. Fruit—Three acres of pears; one acre mixed orchard.
9. Fruit.—Twenty-four pear trees.
10. Fruit.—Managing 4 acres of pears, 95 apple trees.
11. Poultry.—Seventy-five to 100 Buff Orpingtons; built new house.
12. Poultry.—Hatched 332 White Leghorn chicks from 450 eggs; had 302 May 10.
13. Potatoes.—One-half acre Irish Cobblers.
14. Fruit.—One-fourth acre red raspberries, also one-fourth acre lettuce and celery.
15. Poultry.—Setting hens and raising chicks.
16. Poultry.—Setting hens to build up flock.
17. Poultry.—Setting hens to build up flock and caring for a flock of 200.
18. Poultry.—Caring for flock of 58 hens.
19. Poultry.—Caring for flock of 55 Rhode Island Reds and White Leghorns.
20. Onions.—One-fourth acre.

Visits were made to the home of boys having representative projects.

The boy having project No. 8 had the management of 1 acre of old orchard and 3 acres of young pear trees. The orchard had been sprayed and the young orchard cultivated, so that the trees were in good condition when judged by the standards of the district. The boy's mother spoke well of the work of the school.

In project No. 10 a boy had the management of a large part of his father's old orchard. At the time of the visit it looked as if there would not be much in the way of returns to give encouragement to the boy. The trees were old; they had been planted too close together and had suffered from insect injury in previous years. so that there were very poor prospects for a crop. At the time of our visit the boy's elder brothers were spraying the orchard.

The project listed last is one-fourth acre of onions grown by one of the younger students on rich bottom land. The crop had made no headway at the time of the visit, but the land had been put into excellent condition for the crop. If this project were successful it doubtlessly resulted in a larger area of onions planted on the farm.

A student living on a neighboring farm had an acre of onions the year before. By applying modern methods this student succeeded in securing 790 bushels which he sold at 50 cents per bushel. His entire cost of production, including rent of land, was $99.69, leaving him a profit of $295.31 in addition to cash for 369 hours of labor. To accomplish this required the working out of a difficult problem; hence the project had a high educational value. It was found difficult to get the fine onion seed to germinate, as the winds shifted the light soil. A system of overhead irrigation was worked out which was not only helpful on this land but which was suggestive also of treatment for similar soils in the community.

AGRICULTURAL DEPARTMENT OF HOPKINS ACADEMY, HADLEY, MASS.

History.—This school, known earlier as the Hopkins Grammar School, was established in 1664 with funds provided in the will of Gov. Edward Hopkins. Although the school is still known by the name given it in 1816, Hopkins Academy, it is one of the public high schools of the State, serving the village and town of Hadley. The agricultural instruction in this school is a national outgrowth of the attempt of a former principal, F. E. Heald, to adapt the course in general science to the interests of the students and the needs of the community. In 1912, a special teacher of agriculture was employed, the work given in the school qualifying at that time for State aid as an agricultural department in an existing high school.

The students.—There are two methods of admission: First, any pupil who has passed from the grades into the high school may elect to take the agricultural course; second, any person over 14 years of age who is to take up or has taken up farming may apply for admission to this department. His application will be given consideration in the light of preparation and attitude.

No girls have taken the course so far. Although there were never more than 10 students up to 1915, in that year the class reached a total of 24.

Course of study.—The number of students being relatively small, the classes in agriculture are combined and courses given in alternate years, as shown in the following table:

Beginning 1912, 1914, 1916, and other even years.

CLASSES I AND II.	CLASSES III AND IV.
Agricultural science and projects applied to Hadley.	Agricultural science and projects applied to Hadley.
Kitchen gardening: Vegetables and small fruit.	Farm animals: Types, breeding, management.
Ornamental planting: Shrubbery, flowering plants, lawns.	Farm buildings: Sanitation and conveniences, plans, construction, upkeep.
Farm shop work: Making and repairing for home and school use—hotbeds, cold frames, etc.	Farm crops for keeping the animals, rotations, balancing, cultivation, etc.
	Farm machinery and implements, their use and repair.

Beginning 1911, 1913, 1915, and other odd years.

CLASSES I AND II.	CLASSES III AND IV.
Agricultural science and projects applied to Hadley.	Agricultural science and projects applied to Hadley.
Small animals: Poultry, sheep, swine, bees—types, breeding, management, rations, etc.	Fruit growing: Orcharding and small fruits not before dealt with.
Buildings and equipment for small animals—plans, cost, etc.	Market gardening: Markets, soils seeds, fertilizers, tillage.
Home-grown crops for small animals—kinds, quantities, seeds, soils, fertilizing, tillage, harvesting, storage.	Buildings and appliances, plans, devices, implements and machines, cost, use, and upkeep.
Farm shop work and other construction.	Farm shop work and other construction.

Home-project work.—The school was visited by the author on May 18, 1916, for the special purpose of studying the home-project plan in operation. The principal of the school seemed very much interested in the work in agriculture and was so much in favor of the home-project method that he was conducting his own garden as a home project under the director of the teacher of agriculture, from whom he frequently sought advice. The 16 boys who were in the agricultural work at that time all lived comparatively near the school and all had their projects at home except one who had his onion project upon the school grounds. The projects for the summer of 1916 were as follows:

1. 15 fruit trees, one-fourth acre onions.
2. 10 fruit trees, one-tenth acre onions.
3. 25 fruit trees, one-tenth acre onions, 55 hens.
4. 15 fruit trees, one-tenth acre onions, 6 hens.
5. 1 acre corn, one-tenth acre onions, one-tenth acre berries.
6. 1 acre corn, one-tenth acre onions, 8 fruit trees.
7. 1 acre corn, 9 fowls, 39 fruit trees.
8. One-fourth acre potatoes, 60 currants, 24 fruit trees.
9. 1 acre corn, 60 currants, 22 fruit trees.
10. One-half acre corn, one-seventh acre berries, 25 fruit trees.
11. One-fourth acre potatoes, 33 fruit trees, 12 pullets.
12. One-fourth acre onions, one-half acre potatoes, 5 fruit trees.
13. One-twentieth acre kitchen garden, 6 hens, 50 ducks, 1 pig.
14. One-twentieth acre potatoes, 15 fruit trees (works also on poultry farm).
15. One-half acre mangles, 2 acres corn (continues dairy work of last year's project).
16. One-fifth acre kitchen garden, 7 hens, 32 chicks (takes care of 5 horses and 1 cow).

It is interesting to note that although the school owns a little agricultural land, it is turned over to one of the students for an individual project rather than used by the class as a whole. There are numbers of farms within a short distance, however, and an abundance of teaching material within reach of the school. A flock of fowls is kept at the school and an incubator and brooder were in operation, the students doing some of the work. Pure-bred fowls and eggs are furnished students at a nominal price after interest in better stock is aroused through their projects. Two of the students' poultry projects were visited. In both cases the students needed the stimulation of a visit from the instructor, as the poultry had been somewhat neglected in the pressure of spring work connected with the production of onions and tobacco.

Classroom instruction.—The work of the classroom consists of a good deal of individual project study and informal round table discussions, most of which are based upon a study growing out of the home projects. A combination laboratory and classroom lends itself very well to this form of instruction. Double periods are used at all times. The work for the day may be a combination period of supervised study and recitation, a field trip, or a class practicum. A small library of selected books and bulletins in good working order gave evidence of considerable use. A stereopticon with sets of slides, charts, and collections of seeds and other agricultural products were used as illustrative material. Appropriate pictures on the wall gave evidence of the purpose for which the room was used. Other material aided in giving the room an agricultural atmosphere.

Most of the students taking the agricultural course are sons of hardworking farmers. A number of them could not attend school were it not possible for them to engage in productive labor at the same time. All of the projects are put upon a productive basis and the students encouraged to do other farm work that will add to their incomes. Accurate records are kept of the work done and the cash received. The following table shows the results of the past four years:

Year.	Number of boys.	Farm work.	Other work.	Total earnings.
1913	9	$1,891.96	$301.50	$2,193.46
1914	8	1,070.95	168.28	1,239.23
1915	24	3,389.27	204.85	3,594.12
1916	21	4,687.48	146.00	4,833.48

During the year 1916 the students in this school received a total of $278.75 as prizes for project products exhibited and judging contests.

Local extension work.—The work of the agricultural instructor in supervising the home projects of the students brings him into direct contact with the farmers of the community and their problems. Advice is sought and given as a matter of course. Inasmuch as Hadley is within a few miles of Amherst, the seat of the State agricultural college, the instructor may easily secure aid in connection with problems beyond his power.   E. J. Burke, the present instructor, is especially well qualified for work among boys and girls. All of the boys and girls met seemed to greet him with a smile. He has been given charge of the club work conducted among the younger children and is assisting the teachers in the elementary schools to connect their classroom instruction more closely with the practical club work conducted at home. Special success has been attained in such cooperative effort with the rural teacher at Russellville.

As a means of teaching the students practical pruning and spraying, the orchards of the community are used. A farmer's orchard may be sprayed or pruned as a demonstration to him, at the same time affording practice to the students, but after the students have learned how to do the work they must receive pay for their work which is done outside of school hours. In one or two cases, orchards which are a menace to the community as sources of infection have been sprayed each year by the students.

DEPARTMENT OF AGRICULTURE, STATE NORMAL SCHOOL, PLATTEVILLE, WIS.

Since the department of agriculture was established in connection with the Platteville State Normal School, in the fall of 1914, it has had a steady growth, so that to-day it represents one of the strong normal-school departments of agriculture in the United States. As the school is serving in the general training of farmers in the community as well as in the training of teachers, its organization and methods should be suggestive to high schools as well as normal schools. The purpose of the instruction given may be gleaned from the following, printed under the title, "Our educational creed":

We believe that the purpose of the department of agriculture of the Platteville State Normal School is to train students to use the materials of a farm for their highest educational advantages, to equip students to unify the interests of the home and the school, and to promote all of the interests which make for the establishment of permanent agriculture in southern Wisconsin. In this way it fits students for identification with the moral and social forces of the country working for its betterment.

We further believe that culture will not suffer by evolving it through the material affairs of man, a study of the soil it may be. We also believe that the education that is most worth while teaches vocational efficiency, the power of problem solving, general intelligence, and the right moral attitude in relation to the useful activities of everyday life.

Finally, we believe that the purpose of the department is to prepare teachers who are intelligent as to the affairs of the farm, who see dignity in its manual labor; yea, see in it the finest and most effective opportunities for training in responsibility and in the reward of success that comes from faithful application and attention to duty.

Organization and equipment.—As the school aspires to train teachers for high schools as well as elementary teachers, it is developing a staff of instructors and rather extensive equipment. At the time the school was visited, in the summer of 1917, the department was under a director of agricultural education assisted by two instructors, one of whom had charge of the school farm. A new agricultural and manual arts building was nearing completion. This brick building, with two stories and a basement, should provide room for classes, laboratories, and shops for the vocational work for some years to come.

The school farm consists of 26 acres of limestone soil typical of the section of southwestern Wisconsin in which the school is located. The farm is divided into three tracts. The first tract of 15 acres is used for demonstrating systematic rotation of crops and other modern practices in crop production. No experimental work is attempted. The second tract of 8 acres is used in a rotation of forage crops for the maintenance of live stock at the school. A third tract of nearly 3 acres contains a cottage for the farm manager, poultry houses, a small orchard, a school garden of half an acre, 1 acre for truck crops. The school garden is used by the pupils of the training school maintained in connection with the normal school. The remainder of this plot is used as an out-of-door laboratory in connection with the instruction in agriculture. The farm also furnished material for inside laboratory work and classroom instruction. The farm has a good team of horses and farm implements and machinery suited to a small farm in Wisconsin.

A modern dairy barn is planned with the idea of maintaining one dairy cow for each acre of land. The product of these cows will be sold as market milk and cream in Platteville. The students will be expected to do all the work. As the school is located in a dairy section, dairy husbandry is emphasized. The idea of maintaining a dairy herd is to give practice in milk production under conditions approaching the ideal, yet within the reach of the farmer. Cows have not been purchased to represent the dairy breeds to be used in judging. Instead of spending money for that purpose, the school has purchased a truck fitted as a van to accommodate a class of about 20 students. In the community there are excellent dairy herds representing the four leading breeds, and pure-bred draft horses, sheep, and swine. If there is to be a lesson in breed types or practice judging, it is a relatively simple matter for the teacher to take the class out to a neighboring farm.

When the school was visited early in July the school garden and all the field plots were in excellent shape. The farm was then being used in connection with the summer school.

Courses of study.—The department of agriculture acts as a service department in giving one or more courses in elementary agriculture to each prospective teacher enrolled in the rural-school department.

In 1916–17, 50 young women received such instruction. The department also offers a general institute or short course of one week in December and a winter course of nine weeks for young men who can not attend the regular school session. A correspondence course in agriculture is also offered.

To students regularly enrolled for agriculture the department offers three courses. The nature of these courses will be seen from the following outlines taken from the department circular:

Two-year course for high-school graduates.

FIRST YEAR.

FIRST SEMESTER.	Hours.	SECOND SEMESTER.	Hours.
Animal husbandry	5	Physics	5
Weeds	2	Horticulture	3
Chemistry	5	Psychology	5
Insect pests	2	Plant physiology	2
Plant diseases	1	Blacksmithing and cement con-	
Farm carpentry	3	struction	3
	18		18

SECOND YEAR.

	Hours.		Hours.
Agricultural education	5	Agricultural bacteriology	2
English composition	5	Dairying	3
Farm mechanics	5	Farm arithmetic	5
Soils	5	Crops	5
Teaching	5	Teaching	5
	25	Physical training	2
			27

Three-year course for high-school graduates.

FIRST YEAR.

FIRST SEMESTER.	Hours.	SECOND SEMESTER.	Hours.
Animal husbandry	5	Physics	5
Chemistry	5	Psychology	5
Weeds	2	Plant physiology	2
Insect pests	2	Horticulture	3
Plant diseases	1	Blacksmithing and cement con-	
Farm carpentry	3	struction	3
	18		18

SECOND YEAR.

	Hours.		Hours.
Agricultural education	5	Physiography	5
English composition	5	Crops	5
Farm mechanics	5	Farm arithmetic	5
Soils	5	Advanced civics	5
Poultry	5	Physical training	2
	25		22

THIRD YEAR.

	Hours.		Hours.
Agricultural economics	5	Agricultural bacteriology	2
Algebra	5	Dairying	3
Teaching	5	Trigonometry and surveying	5
School administration	5	Teaching	5
	—	Elective	5
	20		—
			20

Five-year course for graduates of the eighth grade of the elementary schools.

FIRST YEAR.

FIRST SEMESTER.	Hours.	SECOND SEMESTER.	Hours.
Arithmetic	5	Algebra	5
Geography	5	American history	5
Reading	5	Grammar	5
Elementary agriculture	5	Vegetable gardening	5
	—		—
	20		20

SECOND YEAR.

	Hours		Hours
Algebra	5	Plane geometry	5
Civics	5	Music	5
Composition	5	Zoology	3
Physiology, hygiene, and farm		Bees and beekeeping	2
sanitation	5	Composition	5
	—		—
	20		20

THIRD YEAR.

	Hours		Hours
Elementary physics	5	Physiography	5
European history	5	European history	5
Solid geometry	5	Literature	5
Poultry	5	Farm practice	5
	—		—
	20		20

FOURTH YEAR.

	Hours		Hours
Animal husbandry	5	Physics	5
Chemistry	5	Psychology	5
Weeds	2	Plant physiology	2
Insect pests	2	Horticulture	3
Plant diseases	1	Blacksmithing	3
Farm carpentry	3	Cement construction	2
	—		—
	18		20

FIFTH YEAR.

	Hours		Hours
Agricultural education	5	Agricultural bacteriology	2
English composition	5	Dairying	3
Farm mechanics	5	Farm arithmetic	5
Soils	5	Crops	5
Teaching	5	Teaching	5
	—		—
	25		20

1. Elementary agriculture.

This course is an introduction to the later differentiated courses in agriculture. In an elementary way, students are given familiarity with farm animals, farm crops, soils, weeds, insects, dairying, etc. The school farm and garden furnish the out-of-door laboratory.

2. Vegetable gardening.

The main purpose of this course is to teach students to operate successfully their home gardens. Some of the topics presented in classroom instruction are the purposes and values of home gardens, the ordering of seed catalogues, the selection of vegetables and the best arrangement of them in the garden, the ordering and testing of seeds, the making of a planting calendar, the construction and operation of a hotbed, the cultivation and protection of garden truck against noxious insects and plant diseases, and the best methods of harvesting, marketing, and preservation of products from gardens. The practical work is done in the home gardens.

3. Physiology, hygiene, and farm sanitation.

In the production of healthy folks there are two considerations: The individuals themselves and their surroundings. The first part of the course deals with the development of sanitary and hygienic habits, and the second part with the proper construction and management of the farmhouse to insure proper heating, ventilation, lighting, cleanliness, sewage disposal, etc. Some time is given to the sanitary housing of farm animals.

4. Bees and beekeeping.

Wisconsin is one of the States in the front rank in the production of honey. In this course, which is a supplement to the course in zoology, students are taught the varieties of bees and the life history of each sex in a hive, the conditions that favor the production of a maximum amount of honey, the structure of a hive, the summer and winter care of bees, the control of insect and fungous enemies, and the marketing and uses of honey. The apiary on the school farm furnishes the concrete materials for the course.

5. Poultry.

This course deals with the description of breeds and varieties of poultry; the production and marketing of eggs; the fattening and marketing of poultry; fall, winter, and summer care; incubation and brooding. Actual practice in poultry management is given in the poultry ranges of the school farm.

6. Farm practice.

Students taking this course will assist in the regular farm operations under the direction of the farm manager, who will instruct the students as to the practical application of the scientific principles of agriculture. Some of the operations which will be taken up are: Care and feeding of horses, cattle, swine, and poultry; such field operations as plowing, harrowing, disking, drilling grain, planting potatoes and corn, and application of manure and other fertilizers; and miscellaneous operations as gardening, caring for small fruit, and orchard practice.

7. Animal husbandry.

The first part of this course treats of the types and breeds of horses, cattle, swine, sheep, and poultry. The origin, improvement, introduction to this country, and the characteristics of each breed are emphasized. A thorough study is made of the relation between the form or conformation of the animal and its purpose. After the development of these principles, standard score cards are used in judging stock in Platteville and vicinity. The second part of the course considers the compounds of animal nutrition; the digestion and assimilation of food; the excretion of wastes; the nutrient values of such feeds as ensilage, straws, roots, tubers, grains, and seeds; the proper care in preservation of farm feed; and the compounding of balanced rations for special results in particular types of animals. If students come from the farm, they will be encouraged to interest home folks in conducting feeding experiments. Feeding statistics will be collected from local experimenters, for study and interpretation.

8. Weeds.

· This course makes the student acquainted with the weeds of the farm and garden; the root, stem, fruit, and seed characteristics that facilitate their dissemination; the best method for eradicating each weed, such as cultivation, rotation, and spraying; and the different farm crops. Each student is required to make an herbarium of the weeds studied, and a collection of their seeds.

9. Insect pests.

This course involves a study of the external structure, classification, and local distribution of insects; a consideration of insects in their relation to farm products, more especially horticultural products; the life history and habits of injurious and beneficial species; collecting, identifying, and mounting some of the most common insect pests; general and special methods of control; and practice in the preparation and application of control measures.

10. Plant diseases.

The annual damage in this country in the destruction of crops by plant diseases is about $500,000,000. In this course the student is made acquainted with the bacteria and fungi that are responsible for the common diseases of farm crops, the use of resistant strains, and the composition and application of fungicides.

11. Plant physiology.

In this course the life processes of the plant, as far as possible, are interpreted in terms of physics and chemistry. The emphasis in the study of these life processes will be with the plants of the highest order, the seed plants. The development of the subject takes this order: The study of the plant cell; the intake of materials by the plant through the forces of imbibition and osmosis; the outgo of plants through transpiration, guttation, and secretion; the translocation of food materials; the study of food necessary for the nutrition of plants; the synthesis of carbohydrates, proteins, and fats; independent versus dependent plants; the digestion and assimilation of foods; and respiration and fermentation, the two great phases of destructive metabolism in the plant. The structure of the plant will be emphasized only as it is necessary to understand its physiology.

12. Horticulture.

This course is designed to give the pupil a knowledge of the planning, planting, and cultivation of the home vegetable garden; the care and management of small fruits and their adaptation to Wisconsin soils and climate; practice in the construction of hotbeds and cold frames; laboratory work in planting and cultivating the school garden; pruning and spraying of orchards in the community; and judging and scoring fruits and vegetables.

13. Agricultural education.

This course has for its object a consideration of the specific purpose of agricultural instruction in its relation to the general aims of education; a discussion of the organization of agricultural courses for high schools; the proper use of the school garden or the school farm; the unification of the interests of the school and the home through home project work, short courses in agriculture, social center work, farmers' institutes, and high-school fairs. This course also includes a study of the teaching process in relation to accepted sociological, biological, and psychological principles.

14. Soils.

This course offers instruction in the origin and composition of soils; methods of measurement of their varying physical conditions; the relation of texture of different types of soils and water content to the best time for cultivation; the history of the mineral nutrient theory; the source, loss, and ways of restoration of each of the 10 essential elements, with particular emphasis on the elements, nitrogen, phosphorus, potassium, and calcium; the use of fertilizers; and the work of bacteria in making available the food materials to the plant.

Experiments will be performed in the laboratory and on plats to determine the water-holding powers of different soils, the capillary movements of waters under different conditions, and the possibility and different methods of conserving soil moisture.

15. Agricultural bacteriology.

In this course the students are made acquainted with the principles that underlie the science of bacteriology. Drill in the technique of bacteriological study is given to determine the structure of certain representative bacteria of characteristic groups, and to note their effects on various culture media. After this preparation students make bacteriological examinations of water, soil, milk, and butter.

16. Dairying.

. Since the major interest of the people of this community is dairying, much is made of this industry. Sanitation in the production, transportation, and distribution of milk is emphasized. Excursions are taken to inspect the equipment and methods of dairy practice, butter making and cheese manufacture. Careful determinations are made of the amount of butter fat, casein, albumen, sugar, and ash in milk. Students from farms are encouraged to improve dairy herds by enlisting the cooperation of their home folks in keeping records of daily milk production, and by making regular laboratory tests of butter fat in the milk. As soon as the dairy laboratory in the new building is available students will receive training in the pasteurization of milk and cream and the making of butter and cheese.

17. Crops.

The study of crops includes a consideration of the origin, botanical characters, the leading types, and varieties of the leading crops of this region; the preparation of the soil, planting, methods of cultivation, systems of rotation, harvesting, food values for man or animals, and principles and methods of breeding. Corn and grains are judged by the methods recommended in Wisconsin. The plant and seed characters of the different crops are acquired through laboratory study. Variety tests and some of the best methods in crop production are demonstrated on the school farm. Excursions are taken to show the effects of soil, methods of cultivation, and rotation on the different crops.

Methods of instruction.—In connection with using the school truck an effort is made to utilize the resources of the community for teaching: Pruned 238 apple trees, 32 currant, 12 raspberry, and 21 goose-in dairy husbandry spent several days as an apprentice in the Platteville creamery as a part of his course. Some of the students gained such proficiency in this work that one of them was retained by the local creamery at a good salary for the summer, while others received good positions in near-by creameries, upon recommendation of the manager. The work in horticulture was made equally as practical. In the spring of 1916 the class accomplished the following: Pruned 238 apple trees, 32 currant, 12 raspberry, and 21 gooseberry bushes, and 19 shade trees; sprayed 150 trees; treated seed oats for smut; made the hotbeds and took charge of the vegetable garden on the school farm. The students have built the poultry house and a shed for the farm machinery. In making hotbeds and farm buildings the work is in cooperation with the department of manual training, the courses of which are taken by the students in agriculture. There is an organized effort made for cooperation and correlation of subjects in other lines, particularly with the science courses and in English.

Local extension work.—In addition to offering short courses and correspondence courses in agriculture; the department staff give lectures on agriculture and rural life before farmers' institutes; farmers' clubs and rural social centers. Students give assistance to the rural schools and to boys' and girls' clubs in such practical work as construction of hotbeds and aid teachers in giving special lessons. In addition to pruning and spraying of trees, they have tested seed and milk and have treated oats for smut and potatoes for scab. The instructors have also assisted in community fairs.

Results.—The results of the local extension work is that the school "takes well" with the farmers of the community, and the demand for help is beyond the power of the department to satisfy. Although the department had been in operation but three years, when visited in 1917, it had trained 41 young men as teachers of agriculture. The enrollment of the regular agricultural students had increased from 24 the first year to 39.

Much of the success of the department is due to its director, Fred. T. Ullrich, who although trained primarily as a teacher of science has adapted and applied his scientific training to educational and agricultural problems in southwestern Wisconsin.

THE BERRY SCHOOL, MOUNT BERRY, FLOYD COUNTY, GA.

The history of the Berry School, although one of the most interesting chapters in the development of the South, is too long a story to relate at this time. The scheme grew out of an effort on the part of Miss Martha Berry to broaden the lives of the people living near her in the mountain section of Georgia. A start was made with a Sunday school in a little log cabin. The school proper was opened in an unpretentious way in 1902. To-day the school owns over 5,000 acres of land, a score of buildings with equipment reaching into several hundred thousand dollars, and is taking care of several hundred

farm boys and girls. The school is still a private institution incorporated under the laws of Georgia. Although it has a considerable
endowment, it is dependent upon the bequests each year for its running expenses, the income from the fees and labor of the students
being inadequate. Although the Berry School for Girls is a separate institution from the Berry School, which is for boys only, the
two are on the same grounds and under the same management, hence
they will be considered together.

Purpose of school.—A visit to the school impresses one with the
air of industry and the lack of the aristocratic atmosphere which
prevails in many of the private schools of the South. The reason
for this is in the nature of the students selected and the dominating
purpose of the school, which is " to develop efficient Christian manhood by affording to worthy boys and young men of limited means
from rural districts the opportunity to earn an education combining
mental, moral, and industrial training." Candidates for admission
must "(1) live in the country; (2) have attained the age of 16
years; (3) be financially unable to attend school elsewhere; and (4)
furnish evidence of physical, mental, and moral soundness." All
students are required to do at least 16 hours of work a week. Students who do not take kindly to work are not allowed to remain at
the school. All of the work, including the erection of many of the
buildings, is done by the students. A needy student may remain at
the school working for pay during the summer, although students
are not encouraged to remain at the school over 20 months in any
one continuous period. The school affords a wonderful opportunity
to young men who are willing to work, an opportunity to secure
training toward efficiency in workmanship and at the same time to be
directed in physical, mental, and moral development which should
mean much to the northwestern section of Georgia. The history of
the graduates of the school will show that it has meant much not
only to Georgia but also to other sections of the South in sending
forth inspired leaders who know how to do things. It is interesting
to note the student body and the contrast between the incoming students and those about to graduate.

Work in agriculture.—Although the school gives general industrial training for rural life, it is more nearly an agricultural school
than many of the special schools of agriculture. It is the aim of
the director to make it more and more an agricultural school. In
1917, when the school was visited, agriculture was organized as a
division coordinate with mechanics, academic subjects, and administration.

Of the 5,000 acres of land owned by the school, about 60 are used
as a campus, 1,000 are under cultivation, 500 used as pasture, and
the remainder in woodland. All of the agricultural land is in charge

of the department of agriculture. The farm is equipped with modern buildings and machinery, including a hothouse and an up-to-date dairy. At the time the school was visited students were working on extensive poultry buildings. The live stock consisted of 100 head of dairy stock, including calves and heifers, 200 head of swine, 150 sheep, 14 mules, 6 horses, and a flock of poultry.

While the farm is operated as a money-making venture, educational values are not lost sight of. The use of student labor is not a serious problem, because two of the essential points in selecting students is that they shall want to work and need to work. Each student is required to work approximately 16 hours a week. Additional work with pay is given needy students. The pay depends upon the character of the work done. As the farming is done on an extensive scale, using modern machinery and methods, most of the farming operations afford new experience to the students, many of whom come from little " one-mule " farms in the mountains.

The following account of a day's work at the school will indicate something of the manner in which the school is conducted:

The active day at the Berry School begins early. At 4 o'clock the kitchen fireman arises and goes to build the fires in the ranges. A half hour later the cooks and the morning dairy squad go to their work. The latter milk the cows and bring the milk from the barn to the dairy house before breakfast, which comes at 6.30.

Meanwhile, the full-time farm boys, who are working one term in order to pay for their board and tuition the next term, have arisen, eaten breakfast, and gone to their work by 6 o'clock. The students arise at 6 o'clock and have breakfast at 6.30.

At 7 o'clock the real work of the school day begins, and lasts until 5 o'clock in the afternoon, with intermission for chapel and dinner. The school is divided into three groups as nearly equal in size as possible. Each day two of these groups attend classes, while the third works for eight hours. A few students, however, have assigned work at other times. From 4 until 5.30 o'clock in the afternoon is recreation period. This is the time for games, exercise in the gymnasium, reading, or other recreation for those not on duty.

Supper is served at 5.30, followed by evening prayers. At 6.30 on school days the evening study period begins, lasting until 9.05. During this time each student must be in his room and studying. A relaxation period is given from 9.05 to 9.30. At 9.30 silent time begins, and at 10 lights go out and everyone is in bed except the night watchman, who still h·s to make his rounds.

On Saturday there is a social hour instead of the study hour, and on Sunday church services and Sunday school instead of the regular routine.

In order to accommodate an additional number of boys who desire to work their way through school, a farm of 500 acres is being developed about 5 miles from the main school at the foot of Mount Lavender. Here about 25 boys, for the work done for four or five months, are given credit for board and tuition at the regular school. While doing this farm work for the purpose of getting a start toward their regular schooling they are given instruction five nights a week in agriculture, arithmetic, English, reading, and spelling.

Near the school a model farm is operated, under the direction of a former student, as a demonstration to the pupils and people in the community. Students also assist in the work of this farm.

As suggested, the girls live and have their schooling apart from the boys. Agriculture and other industrial work form a large part of the curriculum of the girls' school. When the school was visited the girls were taking entire charge of six dairy cows and making a part of their product into butter and cheese. The cows and the stable were in excellent condition, in better condition than the main dairy at the boys' school. The garden of 4 acres was also in better condition than the main truck gardens of the schools. The girls were proud of their showing on the farm, as they were of the excellent rugs and baskets they were making.

Although some agriculture is required in all of the courses for boys and girls, the following course is offered for students who desire agriculture in the four-year high school.

Freshman.	Hours.	*Sophomore.*	Hours.
*Agriculture	4	*Agriculture II	4
*Bible II	2	*Bible III	2
*English V	4	*English VI	4
Gymnasium	2	Gymnasium	2
*History II	4	*History III and civics II	4
*Mathematics V	4	Mathematics VI (fall term)	4
Mechanics III (fall term)	8	*Mechanics IV	8
Science III	5	Science IV (spring term)	4
Singing	2	Singing	2
Spelling	2	Spelling	2
		Writing	2

Junior.		*Senior.*	
*Agriculture III	4		
*Bible IV	2	*Agriculture IV	4
*English VII	4	*Bible V	2
Gymnasium	2	English VIII (spring term)	4
History IV	4	Economics	4
Mathematics VII	4	Mathematics VIII and IX	4
*Mechanics V	8	Music	2
Music	2	*Science VII	6
*Science VI	6	Spelling	2
Spelling	2	Writing	2
Writing	2		

* Subjects required.

154070°—20——5

HIGH SCHOOL COURSES IN AGRICULTURE.

Agriculture I (farm crops).—For freshmen in the high school. A general course in agriculture bearing on: The soil—general classification, elementary composition of plants and their sources of supply, sources of nitrogen, phosphoric acid and potash; relation of the soil to plants; plant analysis. Plants—general classification, duration of life, how they grow, feed and produce, sexuality, crosses and hybrids. General field crops—horticulture and gardening; forestry; applied botany. Text used: Southern Field Crops, by J. F. Duggar, and Southern Gardeners' Manual, by J. S. Newman.

Agriculture II (animal husbandry).—For sophomores in high school. This course is designed to take up in detail animal life on the farm and treats: The importance of the subject, breeds of horses, cattle, sheep, poultry, and swine. Animal type, judging, heredity, breeding, selection, pedigrees, feeding, care, equipment, meat on the farm, preserving eggs, bees and honey. Text used: Beginnings in Animal Husbandry, by C. S. Plumb.

Agriculture III (dairying).—For juniors in high school. A practical course in this important subject treating on: The origin of domesticated cattle, the dairy type and breeds, starting a dairy herd, selection of cows and bulls, calf raising, development of the dairy heifer, management of dairy cattle, feeding for milk production, stables for cows, handling of manure, common ailments of cattle, milk records, testing milk, butter making, and milk as a food. Text used: Dairy Cattle and Milk Production, by C. H. Eckles.

Agriculture IV (farm management).—For seniors in high school. The farm as a business enterprise and as an avocation, personal characteristics desirable in a farmer, profits to be expected from farming, cost of living on farms, some thoughts for the farm boys, types of farming, maintaining the fertility of the soil, capital, methods of renting land, farm labor, farm equipment, farm layout, rotation, marketing, farm records and accounts, some successful farms. Text used: Farm Management, by C. F. Warren.

Farm mechanics V (mechanics).—This course, for high-school pupils, consists of a detailed study of field machinery, farm power and transmission devices; the operation, care, and maintenance of such machinery being studied thoroughly. The following list will serve as an index to the work covered: Plows, stalk cutters, harrows, manure spreaders, fertilizer distributors, planters, mowing machines, rakes, binders, ensilage cutters, steam engines and boilers, gas engines and the farm tractors. Text: Farm Machines and Farm Motors, by Davidson and Chase.

In all of these courses a textbook sequence is not followed closely. An effort is made to use the farm and shops as a laboratory and to use a seasonal sequence in the classroom that the classroom lesson may be correlated with farm practice. An effort is made also to correlate agriculture with other subjects, as will be seen from the description of a course given to students before they enter the regular high-school courses:

Country Life.—For fourth year grammar school. The aim of this course is to take the everyday activities of the boys on the farm and make these the basis for arithmetic, science, and agriculture. For example: The institution sells a beef to a butcher in Rome. The arithmetic work for the day is based on the business operations involved in the sale of the beef and the buying of feed with part of the receipts. The beef is sold on foot at 7 cents per pound. There is first a discussion as to why it does not bring 7½ cents, which is the the top of the market for this day. The good points of beef are brought into consideration. Cotton-seed hulls, bran, and shorts have been purchased. The price of each is stated. It appears that the price of the cotton-seed hulls was much higher. The reasons are ascertained. The relative food value of the three feeds is discussed, as are the reasons for mixing them in the ration.

Very likely the second part of the lesson for the day is devoted to gathering the corn from a plot in which an ear-row test has been made by the boys during the summer. The corn is husked, sacked, and weighed and the result of the experiment determined.

Most of the boys in this class have studied very little arithmetic in the rural communities from which they come. The practical way in which arithmetic, agriculture, economics, and current events are blended enables the quick assimilation of what otherwise would be dry and indigestible material. No definite textbook is used during this year, but the students are encouraged to accumulate and read bulletins on the subjects discussed in class.

Weekly excursions to various farm activities through the first three years of grammar school are conducted by the instructor, which serve as a basis for the more advanced work in the fourth year.

THE MANASSAS INDUSTRIAL SCHOOL FOR THE TRAINING OF COLORED YOUTH, MANASSAS, VA.

This institution is typical of a relatively large number of smaller schools maintained by northern philanthropists for Negroes in the South. This school is located near the historic Bull Run battlefield, near Manassas, which is the seat of Eastern College and one of the district agricultural schools of Virginia. Although the school may be classed as a secondary school, elementary instruction is given. The following from the school circular suggests the primary purpose of the school:

The aim of the school is to train for useful lives those boys and girls who from necessity or desire must enter as early as may be into some self-supporting occupation. It aims to teach Negro youth the need and importance in a democratic society of all kinds of useful labor intelligently done and as far as possible to send them back to their homes efficient teachers and leaders in industry and civic welfare. Through work as well as through books it aims to teach the value and dignity of work. The students attend to the upkeep and care of the school's 200-acre farm, the farm implements, the stock, the dormitories and cottages, * * *. Particular stress is laid upon the study and practice of agriculture and upon the adequate training and preparation of teachers for the colored elementary rural schools. But whatever course, the aims is not alone to make young men and women craftsmen; the aim is to make craftsmen better men and women.

Courses of study.—Students must be 14 years of age upon entrance. It is considered essential for the student to have the equivalent of elementary school training before entering the industrial courses, hence students who have not had this preparation are required to take a preparatory course in the elementary subjects. Although there is fairly good equipment for woodworking and ironworking and other industrial training given in addition to blacksmithing and carpentry, this training does not enter into the agricultural course as will be seen from the following:

Outline of the agricultural course.

[Figures indicate the number of 45-minute periods a week.]

FIRST YEAR.

	Periods.
American history	3
Arithmetic	3
Botany	2
Chemistry (elementary)	2
Field practice	33
Language	5
Military drill and athletics	3
Reading	5
Supervised study	15

SECOND YEAR.

	Periods.
Agronomy	3
Botany	2
Chemistry of soils	·2
Dairy husbandry	2
Field practice	33
Grammar	5
Literature	5
Military drill and athletics	3
Poultry husbandry	2
Supervised study	14

THIRD YEAR.

	Periods.
Accounting	3
Algebra	5
Animal husbandry	4
Field practice	32
Grammar and composition	5
Military drill and athletics	3
Physics	3
Supervised study	14

FOURTH YEAR.

	Periods.
Commercial geography	2
Composition and rhetoric	5
Farm management—Land tenure	3
Field practice	30
Geometry	·3
Military drill and athletics	3
Rural economics—Sociology	3
Supervised study	22

Instruction in agriculture.—The agriculture of the classroom is supplementary to farm work. For much of the farm work wages are paid. Several acres of the farm are turned over to the students to use as individual garden projects. The school was visited two different years, each time the garden plots being in excellent condition and paying a profit to each student. To be sure, the plots were not all cared for equally well, and while the profit was small in some cases, all students were stimulated by the hope of a financial reward. It was interesting to note the difference in attitude toward farm work on the part of the colored students and the white students in the same town. The 200 acres at the colored school were kept in good condition and were a source of considerable revenue to the school, the work being done largely with student labor. At the district agricultural school the school owned five acres for instructional purposes. Although a part of the garden was planted by the students, the care of the school land was given over mostly to the janitor, who already had more than he could do well.

As most of the produce of the farm is used at the school, the students learn much in storing and preserving food for winter use. One year the following products were canned: Five hundred gallons of tomatoes, 120 gallons of peaches, 75 gallons of pears, 70 gallons of peas, 40 gallons of sauerkraut, 40 gallons of mixed pickles, 3 barrels of string beans in brine, and 12 barrels dried. In addition to the above the farm yielded 100 bushels of sweet potatoes, 435 bushels of potatoes, 100 barrels of corn, 230 bushels of turnips, 100 bushels of stock beets, 67 bushels of wheat, 30 bushels of carrots, 31 bushels of parsnips, 17 bushels of onions, 5,000 head of lettuce, and 7,000 head of cabbage, the latter stored for winter use. The last time the school was visited, in the fall of 1917, an agricultural exhibit representing mostly the products of the farm was symbolical of abundance and indicative of thrift as well as good husbandry. Due to war conditions, there had been a shortage of seed beans of garden varieties. The school had responded to the need and there were bushels of bright beans of many varieties, all well cleaned and in excellent shape. The school was then planning to extend the season of practical garden work by putting in extensive hotbeds and frames for forcing vegetables.

The corn produced is fed mostly to swine on the farm, the pork being consumed at the school. The students do the killing and curing of the pork. The live stock was not of the best breeding. It seems difficult to get Negroes to appreciate and properly care for well-bred animals. At Hampton, however, there are some of the best herds, cared for in as good shape as at any school visited.

The classroom instruction as observed was very good. The students, although not timid, were especially well behaved and responsive in the presence of strangers. The teachers paid special attention to visual instruction. The making of models, so often confined to our primary instruction, was used effectively with the older students. The use of pictures and charts on the walls seemed overdone to some extent.

Community work.—The school is made an educational and agricultural center for the surrounding section and to some extent for northern Virginia. Teachers' and farmers' institutes and other organizations bring together rural leaders in the community and give opportunity to leaders from the outside to reach them. Proximity to the National Capital gives opportunity for local people to hear men and women of national importance frequently. The school exhibit and agricultural fair mentioned was the occasion of many of the local farmers getting not only stimulation from their neighbors but also from men from Government departments who were interested in their work and social problems.

Chapter IV.

FEDERAL AID FOR VOCATIONAL AGRICULTURE.

HISTORY OF THE MOVEMENT.

The Dolliver, Davis, and Page bills.—The passage of the Morrill Act and subsequent acts giving Federal aid to the agricultural colleges has been made a precedent for repeated attempts to extend Federal aid for agricultural education. The first of these attempts to aid the secondary schools was in 1910, when Senator James P. Dolliver, of Iowa, introduced a bill providing Federal grants " to cooperate with the States in encouraging instruction in agriculture, the trades and industries, and home economics in secondary schools; in preparing teachers for those vocational schools in State normal schools." About this time there was a strong movement on foot to secure Federal aid for extension departments in all of the land-grant colleges. This movement was in accordance with recommendations made in 1909 by a committee of the Association of American Agricultural Colleges and Experiment Stations. The recommendations of these committees later, in 1910, were incorporated into the Dolliver bill, and furnished a starting point for the bill passed in 1914 as the Smith-Lever Act. Representative Charles R. Davis, of Minnesota, championed the Dolliver bill in the House of Representatives, hence the bill is sometimes referred to as the Davis bill. In 1911 Senator Carroll S. Page, of Vermont, advocated Federal aid for vocational education in secondary schools along lines similar to those of the Dolliver bill. The Page bill and other efforts to aid school instruction lost out for the time being because public interest and congressional favor were centered on Federal aid for agricultural extension work for the colleges. After such aid was secured, in the passage of the Smith-Lever Act, effort was again put forth to secure Federal subsidy for vocational education in the secondary schools.

Commission on national aid to vocational education.—In January, 1914, Congress passed an act authorizing the President to appoint a commission of nine members to " consider the subject of national aid for vocational education and report their findings and recommendations not later than June 1 next." This commission consisted of the following members: Senator Hoke Smith, of Georgia; Senator Carroll S. Page, of Vermont; Representative D. M. Hughes,

71

of Georgia; Representative S. D. Fess, of Ohio; John A. Lapp, of Indiana; Miss Florence M. Marshall, of New York City; Miss Agnes Nestor, of Chicago; Charles A. Prosser, of Minneapolis, Minn.; and Charles H. Winslow, of Washington, D. C.

As a result of the efforts of the commission [1] bills were introduced into the Senate by Senator Hoke Smith, of Georgia, and into the House by Representative Dudley M. Hughes, of the same State, which finally passed both houses as "An act to provide for the promotion of vocational education; to provide for cooperation with the States for the promotion of such education in agriculture and the trades and industries; to provide for cooperation with the States in the preparation of teachers of vocational subjects; and to appropriate money and regulate its expenditure." This act, known as the Smith-Hughes Act, became a law when President Wilson gave it his approval in February, 1917.

THE SMITH-HUGHES ACT.

Purpose of the act.—The act which went into effect July 1, 1917, is in reality an effort on the part of the Federal Government to stimulate the States to provide a system of secondary education in agriculture, the trades and industries, and home economics and to extend the benefits of these forms of vocational education to all those over 14 years of age. By extending financial aid to the States the Federal Government is not establishing a national system of education, but it does purchase the right to participate in the control of State systems in that it sets up standards which the States must meet.

Financial aid extended.—In order to stimulate the States to expend money especially for vocational education, the act makes available certain funds from which the States are reimbursed for money expended, providing they meet the requirements of the act and reach the standards set by the Federal board of control. The following table [2] shows the total amounts appropriated:

[1] Report of the Commission on National Aid to Vocational Education. House of Representatives. Document No. 1004, 1914.
[2] From Federal Board for Vocational Education. Bulletin, 1917, No. 1. P. 62. Statement of policies.

TABLE 1. —*Annual grants by the Federal Government for vocational education under the Smith-Hughes Act approved Feb. 23, 1917.*

Fiscal year ending June 30.	Total.	Agriculture: For salaries of teachers, supervisors, and directors. (Sec. 2.)			Trade, home economics and industry: For salaries of teachers. (Sec. 3.)[1]			Teacher training: For salaries and maintenance of teacher training. (Sec. 4.)			For Federal Board for Vocational Education. (Sec. 7.)
		Total.	Allotted on basis of rural population.	Additional to provide minimum allotments to States.	Total.	Allotted on basis of urban population.	Additional to provide minimum allotments to States.	Total.	Allotted on basis of total population.	Additional to provide minimum allotments to States.	
1917–18	$1,860,000	$548,000	$500,000	$48,000	$566,000	$500,000	$66,000	$546,000	$500,000	$46,000	$200,000
1918–19	2,512,000	784,000	750,000	34,000	796,000	750,000	46,000	732,000	700,000	32,000	200,000
1919–20	3,182,000	1,024,000	1,000,000	24,000	1,034,000	1,000,000	34,000	924,000	900,000	24,000	200,000
1920–21	3,836,000	1,268,000	1,250,000	18,000	1,278,000	1,250,000	28,000	1,090,000	1,000,000	90,000	200,000
1921–22	4,329,000	1,514,000	1,500,000	14,000	1,525,000	1,500,000	25,000	1,090,000	1,000,000	90,000	200,000
1922–23	4,827,000	1,761,000	1,750,000	11,000	1,772,000	1,750,000	22,000	1,090,000	1,000,000	90,000	200,000
1923–24	5,318,000	2,009,000	2,000,000	9,000	2,019,000	2,000,000	19,000	1,090,000	1,000,000	90,000	200,000
1924–25	6,380,000	2,534,000	2,500,000	24,000	2,556,000	2,500,000	56,000	1,090,000	1,000,000	90,000	200,000
1925–26	7,367,000	3,027,000	3,000,000	27,000	3,050,000	3,000,000	50,000	1,090,000	1,000,000	90,000	200,000
Annually thereafter	7,367,000	3,027,000	3,000,000	27,000	3,050,000	3,000,000	50,000	1,090,000	1,000,000	90,000	200,000

[1] Not over 20 per cent for salaries of teachers of home economics.

A study of this table will bring out the fact that in addition to the $200,000 appropriated annually for the use of the Federal board, there are three separate funds, viz: (1) For salaries of teachers, supervisors, and directors of agriculture; (2) for salaries of teachers of home economics and industry; and (3) for the salaries and maintenance of teacher training. These funds are extended to the States on a fifty-fifty basis, i. e., each dollar of Federal funds must be matched by a dollar from the State or local community.

If the States do no more than match the Federal funds, there will be available after 1926 an annual appropriation of $14,334,000, in addition to the $200,000 used by the Federal board. As a matter of fact many of the States are doing more than meeting the Federal appropriation. In other words, in these States the act is working as it was intended to do, in stimulating the States to liberality with regard to State aid for vocational education.

It will be noted also that the funds increase year by year until the maximum for salaries of teachers is reached in 1925–26. The maximum for teacher training is reached earlier, in 1920–21. The act provides also that unless the teacher training fund is used by June 30, 1920, the other funds will not be available. These provisions arise out of the urgent and immediate need for teachers with special training for these lines of vocational training.

The funds for teachers of agriculture are allotted to the States on the basis of the relation of the rural population of the State to the rural population of the United States, the funds for salaries of teachers of trades and industries and home economics on the basis of urban population, and the teacher training funds on the basis of total population. The population of some States is so small that the alloted portion of the total appropriation would not be worth considering, hence a special appropriation was made to bring the minimum appropriation for each of the three funds to $5,000 for each State. For example, the portion of the $500,000 alloted to Connecticut, in 1917–18, for salaries of teachers and supervisors of agriculture was $1,164.33 based on rural population. To bring this allotment to $5,000, it was necessary to appropriate $3,835.67 from the special fund appropriated to guarantee the minimum allotment.

Federal and State administration.—The act created a Federal Board for Vocational Education consisting of the Secretary of Agriculture, the Secretary of Commerce, the Secretary of Labor, the United States Commissioner of Education, and three citizen members appointed by the President. One of these citizen members represents manufacturing and commercial interests, and one a representative of labor. In addition to the administration of this act, the Federal board is expected to make investigations relative to the various aspects of vocational education involved in the act. Such investigations may be carried on in cooperation with the various Federal departments.

Any State to take advantage of the Federal funds available must accept the enactment and designate or create a State board to cooperate with the Federal board in the administration of the act within the State. Provisions are made for the Government to accept the act to designate or create temporary boards of control in States where the legislatures did not meet in 1917.

State standards.—The act does not go into detail with regard to a general standard for vocational education, but leaves that for the Federal and State boards to work out for each State. Each State is expected to prepare a plan to submit to the Federal board showing the kinds of schools, equipment, courses of study, methods of instruction, qualifications of teachers and supervisors, plans for training teachers, and plan for supervision.

Although it is expected that each State will work out a plan to meet its individual needs, the act places several safeguards upon the appropriations that they may be spent for only those phases of education for which they were intended. The standards set for vocational agriculture may be summarized briefly as follows: (1) Federal money appropriated for the teaching of vocational agriculture can not be spent in the teaching of other subjects necessary to build a well-rounded course of training. (2) The Federal appropriation for the salaries of teachers, supervisors, and directors of agriculture must be spent only on salaries, equipment, and maintenance. One-half of the salaries must be provided from State and local funds. In the case of training and local funds for teachers, however, Federal money may be spent for one-half of the maintenance of such training. (3) Vocational agriculture must be under State supervision and control. (4) It must be of less than college grade and be designed to meet the needs of persons over 14 years of age who have entered or who are preparing to enter upon the work of the farm or of the farm home. In order that the instruction may be practical the act stipulates that the schools shall provide for directed or supervised practice in agriculture, either on a farm provided for by the school or other farm, for at least six months per year. (5) Although the act leaves to the State boards the minimum qualifications of teachers to be approved by the Federal board, it stipulates that in the training of teachers and supervisors such training shall be given only to those persons who have had adequate vocational experience or contact in the line of work for which they are preparing themselves as teachers, supervisors, or directors, or who are acquiring such experience or contact as a part of their training.

The Federal Board for Vocational Education.—Soon after July 1, 1917, when the act went into effect, the President appointed the three citizen members of the Federal Board for Vocational Educational. The board was organized as follows: David F. Houston, Secretary of Agriculture, chairman; William C. Redfield, Secretary of Commerce; William B. Wilson, Secretary of Labor; P. P. Claxton, Commissioner of Education; James P. Munroe, of Massachusetts, representing manufactures and commerce; Charles A. Greathouse, of Indiana, representing agriculture; and Arthur E. Holder, of Iowa, representing labor.

The board elected Charles A. Prosser, then president of Dunwoody Institute, as director. Mr. Prosser selected the following as assistant directors to form the executive staff: Layton S. Hawkins, agricultural education; Lewis H. Carris, industrial education; F. G. Nichols, commercial education; Josephine T. Berry, home economics education; and Charles H. Winslow, research. The entire country was divided into five geographical regions, with an agent for each branch of vocational education in charge.

As the vocational education act is couched in terms rather general, it became necessary at the outset for the Federal board to secure legal interpretations and to issue statements of policy regarding the administration of the act. As a rule the board has been broad in its interpretation of the act, but it has at all times made it clear that Federal money could be used only for bona fide training for useful employment in the vocations for which the act provided. In the case of agriculture, for example, the board will not sanction the use of Smith-Hughes funds for the ordinary form of academic agriculture usually taught in the high school. The work of the school must be intimately related to the supervised practice given on the farm which the act requires.

Considerable time during the first year has been spent in going over the plans submitted by the various States. The board has not attempted to standardize the kind of instruction to be given in the Nation at large, but has left each State to work out a plan which would seem best fitted to its local needs.

The board has not done as much investigational work in the field of agricultural education as it would most likely have done in normal times. No sooner was the board organized than it was called upon to aid in the emergency training of war workers along certain technical lines. Recently (June 10, 1918) Congress passed the bill known as the Smith-Sears Act which delegates to the Federal board the duty of reeducating disabled soldiers in some useful employment. This work of vocational rehabilitation includes agricultural training. It promises to be a work of enormous magnitude and one which may affect materially future plans for vocational training. It seems reasonable that the machinery established for the training of the cripples of war will be continued in operation for the benefit of the cripples of industry, if not for general vocational training.

Although most of the publications of the board for the first year deal with emergency war training, a general bulletin was published giving a statement of policies and one dealing with the organization and administration of agricultural education. In May, 1918, the board began the publication of the Vocational Summary, a monthly paper dealing with its various lines of work.

Without doubt the war handicapped the establishment of schools and departments of vocational agriculture. Not only was it difficult to secure teachers with proper training, but many of the older students who would have desired vocational training under normal conditions, either joined the Army directly or entered the Students' Army Training Corps. The following table [1] shows the results obtained up to the present time:

TABLE 2.—*Statistics of Federal-aided agricultural schools for year ending June 30, 1918.*

AGRICULTURAL SCHOOLS AND DEPARTMENTS.

	United States total.	Region.				
		North Atlantic.	Southern.	East Central.	West Central.	Pacific.
Schools	1,741	794	285	423	45	39
Pupils	15,187	3,649	4,648	4,681	921	1,288
Teachers	895	305	240	220	62	68

TEACHER TRAINING DEPARTMENTS.

	United States total.	Region.				
		North Atlantic.	Southern.	East Central.	West Central.	Pacific.
Centers	40	8	9	11	7	5
Pupils	1,534	155	193	1,010	79	97
Teachers	116	18	24	30	19	25

[1] Adapted from the Second Annual Report of the Federal Board for Vocational Education, 1918.

Chapter V.

TRAINING TEACHERS OF AGRICULTURE.

DEVELOPMENT OF AGRICULTURAL TEACHING.

General versus special meaning.—The term agricultural education has, in times past, and in the minds of many people to-day, a very broad application. It has been linked closely with the general development of agriculture, including the work of agricultural societies, fairs, the entire field of the agricultural colleges, the experiment stations and departments of agriculture, and the work done through the rural press and agricultural publications. To-day the tendency is to consider agricultural education a phase of education linked with school instruction, and related training. In other words, the tendency is to limit the meaning with all the limitations of the term education applied in a technical sense, and to further restrict it to organized training in agriculture. In the future it ought not to be so difficult for a worker in agricultural education to establish himself as a specialist in education rather than an agriculturist.

Demand for trained teachers.—The greatest drawback to placing agricultural training upon a better basis and to extend its usefulness in all grades of schools has been the lack of teachers trained specifically to teach agriculture and related branches. Most of the failures have resulted from a lack of preparation on the part of teachers or the failure to secure proper supervision or direction of the work because no one could be obtained to take hold of this work in the right way. Too often school officials have yielded to a popular demand for agriculture in the schools only to fail because the teachers who attempted the work were not properly trained. In recent years many have felt that the greater part of the responsibility for success rested upon the teacher, and more attention has been given to securing teachers with special training. Educational authorities have begun to realize that the place to begin effective agricultural education is in institutions for training teachers. So far it has not been possible to get young people to train for work not in operation, hence it has been impossible to establish teacher-training departments before the work was established in the schools. The two lines are developing together, but until teacher-training departments turn out a finished product the schools are in a sense putting up with makeshifts.

Attempts to meet the demand.—Where special teachers have been employed attempts have been made, as a rule, to secure graduates of agricultural colleges. Although these men may have had practical as well as technical training in agriculture in the past, as a rule they have not had training as teachers. In very few cases have they had special training in teaching agriculture. For the most part they teach largely as they have been taught. The college training in agriculture may have been good or bad for college students, but neither the subject matter nor the method, at its best, was suited to students in secondary schools. In a large number of schools visited, the author has seen the same subject matter which the teacher had in his college course given out to high-school students in much the same way that the teacher received it in college. The lecture method has been abused to a great extent. While textbooks have been used more extensively in recent years, too often they have been books not organized as textbooks at all, or books not written for secondary schools.

General agriculture has been taught mostly by teachers who have had little or no training in agriculture; often by teachers of biology or other sciences. Where these teachers have had special aptitude and training as teachers some very good work has been done, but too often they have been like the teachers of agriculture without special training in pedagogy. Where they have applied the laboratory method it has been for the most part with the technical aims, methods, and materials of the college. However effective it might have been for training scientists, it has not gone far in the training of farmers nor in aiding boys and girls to adjust themselves to rural conditions.

As a reaction against the lack of practical training given by such teachers in general courses, there has arisen a demand for agriculture to be placed upon a basis strictly vocational. In securing teachers for vocational agriculture some of the States have demanded that applicants must be first of all practical farmers. In many cases they have taken men who have had little technical training in agriculture and no special training as teachers. They have appreciated the need of such training, however, and have in some cases made provisions for the teachers to make up their lack of training in both lines while in service.

Development of departments of agricultural education.—Departments of agricultural education in connection with our agricultural colleges and universities have been the product of a gradual growth. In fact, there has been, up to the present time, a great range of variation in their organization and the work they have been attempting to do. In some cases they have been an outgrowth of schools or departments of education, giving more attention to the rural schools and the problems of teaching agriculture and other subjects. In other cases schools and colleges of agriculture have gradually given more attention to the problems of the elementary and high schools and the preparation of teachers in such subjects as agriculture and nature-study. Most of the agriculture taught in the secondary as well as the elementary schools in the past has been of a general and elementary nature. Some of the States have required such agricultural instruction in rural schools, and some have required certain training in agriculture on the part of teachers. The colleges and normal schools, in the past, have established courses for teachers in summer sessions and correspondence courses to meet this demand. For the most part these courses have involved subject matter rather than method. Some institutions have followed up this work by furnishing materials and suggestions upon teaching to teachers in service. The New York State College of Agriculture at Cornell University has done a notable work along this line. For nearly 10 years it has been sending out its Rural School Leaflets, and in other ways aiding elementary teachers, before courses were developed for training teachers for the secondary schools. Until very recently, in the discussions of agricultural teacher-training little attempt has been made to distinguish between elementary and secondary work. Special college courses for training teachers of agriculture were simply suggested as possibilities.[1]

With regular four-year courses established through the stimulus of State aid, a demand arose for teachers especially trained for the secondary schools. Some of the Southern States, however, which were first to inaugurate secondary agricultural schools, have been the last to establish departments of agricultural education and to develop courses especially for teachers. Departments of agricultural education were established and the work first placed upon a professional basis in the following institutions: University of Minnesota, Michigan Agricultural College, Massachusetts Agricultural College, and the University of California.

Agricultural education upon a professional basis.—The training required for the successful teaching of agriculture in secondary schools is such that it may be considered professional. The training given especially to develop teaching ability should be considered a phase of professional education, whether imparted in a school or department of education or in a school or department of agriculture.

---

[1] See Crosby, D. J., Training Courses for Teachers of Agriculture. U. S. Department of Agriculture. Yearbook, 1907. Jackson, E. R., Agricultural Training Courses for Employed Teachers. U. S. Department of Agriculture. Bulletin, 1913, No. 7.

A WORK FOR COLLEGES.

As a rule teachers of agriculture are required to have college training for teaching agriculture in the secondary schools. Departments of agricultural education are confining their efforts more and more to training teachers of the secondary schools, leaving the training in agriculture for elementary schools largely to the normal schools and high-school teacher training classes. Departments of agricultural education are also offering courses for general leadership in rural life and are aiding in the training of the following groups: Superintendents and supervisors of rural schools, boys' and girls' club leaders, county agents and other extension workers, supervisors and directors of vocational agriculture, and secretaries for rural community centers. A beginning is being made also in the special training of college teachers of agriculture. Few agricultural colleges have reached the stage where they are ready to act upon the realization that college instructors need special training as teachers. Very recently, however, the committee on instruction in agriculture of the American Association of Agricultural Colleges and Experiment Stations [1] has strongly recommended the improvement of methods, ending its report with the recommendation "that immediate and serious attention be given for means of improving the quality of teaching in the college course in agriculture, and as one of the means to that end it would urge the development of strong departments of agricultural education."

Factors involved.—(a) Agricultural training. A teacher of agriculture should have a broad general training in agriculture involving (1) scientific or technical training based on the natural sciences and their direct application to agriculture; (2) practical training and farm experience. As a result of the criticism that the training of the agricultural colleges is not sufficiently practical, more attention has recently been given to the requirements in practical agriculture both as a prerequisite to college courses in agriculture and as a part of such courses.[2] (b) Professional training. Training in education should involve: (1) A general foundation in educational psychology, and the general principles and methods of education with particular application to the adolescent; (2) special training in teaching agriculture in the secondary school; (3) opportunity for practice teaching and practical experience in leading young people and working with farmers. (c) Correlated general training. Inasmuch as the teacher of agriculture is expected to be a leader in rural life, his

---

[1] See 20th report of this committee. In 31st Annual Report of the Association, 1917.
[2] See 16th and 17th reports of the committee on instruction in agriculture of the American Association of Agricultural Colleges and Experiment Stations in the 27th and 28th Reports of the Proceedings of the Association, 1913, 1914.

training should include: (1) Such subjects closely allied to agriculture as rural sociology and rural economics; (2) such practical training for expression as public speaking and agricultural journalism; and (3) such general training for citizenship, cultural, and avocational pursuits as time will permit.

Limitations of a four-year course.—It is obvious that if we demand scientific and practical training in both agriculture and education, in addition to a broad training for leadership, we can not accomplish this in a four-year college course. A great deal will depend upon the previous training of the student. Students entering the agricultural courses may be grouped into three classes as follows: (1) Those who have been reared on a farm and have had an agricultural course in a secondary school; (2) those who have been reared on a farm and who have not had an agricultural course in secondary schools; (3) those reared in the city who have had neither instruction nor practice in agriculture. Students from the first group should furnish by far the best material for teacher-training courses and may secure the requisite technical and professional training in a four-year college course. The training of the other groups should be supplemented with additional instruction and practical experience. As a matter of fact many students do not fit entirely into any of these groups and as yet little attempt is made to classify them according to their previous training and experience. The average agricultural college student needs the full four years for agricultural and general training, leaving his professional training to be secured in addition to that. At the present time school boards in most States consider themselves fortunate to get a college graduate who has had an agricultural course and an aptitude for teaching to take the secondary work in agriculture. Even in States which require training in education for certification, this requirement is often waived for the teacher of agriculture. Special certificates are given to those who have not been trained as teachers. As a rule, however, strong departments of agricultural education have been developed only in those States which require training in agricultural education of their teachers of agriculture.

The present shortage of teachers and the tendency to take teachers without special training has made it necessary for departments of agricultural education to turn their attention to training teachers in service. In many cases those now teaching agriculture and related sciences furnish good material for an early supply of trained teachers.

Training in service is given in a number of ways, chief among which are the following: Summer sessions and winter short courses, correspondence courses, conferences, institutes and extension courses, and itinerant teacher training. Some of these methods may naturally overlap and may be used purposely in combination. The placing of agriculture upon a vocational basis, through the stimulus of Federal aid, has called for many teachers not familiar with vocational methods. These men have been placed in service and organized methods used to improve their training as well as their teaching in connection with the supervision of their work. In some cases the itinerant teacher training is done directly by the State supervisor, in other cases by the department of agricultural education of the teacher training institution. In still other cases the training is given through cooperation of the supervisory forces and the teacher training institution.

LAND-GRANT COLLEGES AND THE PREPARATION OF TEACHERS OF AGRICULTURE.

Extent and nature of the work given.—A study of the teacher-training curricula of the State agricultural colleges[1] made by the Bureau of Education, in 1917, showed that while nearly all of the 48 institutions claimed to offer four-year curricula for training teachers of agriculture only 40 of them had work worthy of inclusion in such training. The Bureau of Education does not regard the work bona fide unless the curriculum includes at least a two-hour course in special methods of teaching agriculture and at least one three-hour course in either psychology or education.

The work given varies from a special four-year curriculum in agricultural education to a regular agricultural curriculum with courses in education taken as electives or an educational curriculum with courses in agriculture taken as electives. The requirements for graduation vary from a total of 120 semester hours to a total of 216 semester hours. The hours required in agriculture vary from none to 77 and in education from 10 to 26. Many of the curricula leave no time for electives, while Cornell University, which requires no courses in agriculture, leaves 45 per cent of the student's time free for elective subjects. The history of education occurs oftener in the educational courses than any other course. Only 29 institutions offered facilities for practice teaching, and many of these were make-shifts when judged by high standards. Only 34 institutions supplied information concerning the number of students registered in agricultural education. Of the total of 859 students, 18 were women. Of the 513 students reported as graduating with professional training in agricultural education, 299 were known to be engaged in teaching or supervising agriculture in the school.

Stimulus of Federal aid.—The Nelson amendment to the agricultural appropriation bill, which was passed in 1907, increased the

---

[1] Jarvis, C. D. Vocational Teachers for Secondary Schools. Bureau of Education. Bulletin, 1917, No. 38.

Federal appropriation for the land-grant colleges and provided that " said colleges may use a portion of this money for providing courses for the special preparation of instructors for teaching the elements of agriculture and the mechanic arts." Some of the institutions have used these funds in establishing departments of agricultural education, others have used them in a general way in their work of aiding teachers of elementary agriculture, while a large number have done nothing until very recently in the way of agricultural education. Many of the agricultural men have taken the attitude that if the prospective teacher knew his subject he could teach it and that no professional training is needed. In institutions having schools or departments of education, agricultural students who expected to teach have been encouraged or required to take general courses in education, especially in States where such training was required for certification. The student in such cases was expected to make his own application of education to agriculture.

Placing agriculture upon a vocational basis in the secondary schools is doing a great deal to strengthen the demand for special courses in agricultural education. The Smith-Hughes Act not only raises the standard for teachers so that special training is required but also provides funds for that training. By 1921 there will be $1,000,000 of Federal funds available for teacher training, 60 per cent of which may be used for training teachers of agriculture, this sum to be duplicated from State funds. Since the Federal act was passed most of the States have either organized separate departments of agricultural education or have extended those already organized. In nearly every case some kinds of courses in special methods of teaching agriculture have been established. There has been considerable difficulty in securing men capable of handling such courses. To do justice to the work given, those in charge should have not only technical and practical training in both agriculture and education but also have practical experience in farming and in the supervision and teaching of agriculture in secondary schools. Some of the men giving teacher training work are agricultural men who have worked into educational lines since graduation, while others are men of training and experience in general education who have taken up agriculture in recent years. As the line of work which they are directing is new, it is not to be expected that the older men have special training for it.

Typical departments of agricultural education.—Every department of agricultural education is organized along lines somewhat different and has different conditions to meet within the institution; most of them, however, may be grouped into one of the following classes: (1) Departments in universities. having schools or departments of education; (2) departments in independent agricultural colleges which do not train teachers for general subjects. The departments described at this time are fairly typical of these classes.

DIVISION OF AGRICULTURAL EDUCATION: UNIVERSITY OF CALIFORNIA.

Organization and scope.—Agricultural education in the University of California is organized as a division in the college of agriculture. Because of the fact that the university maintains a college of letters and science in which general subjects are taught, and a school of education which gives professional training, the division of agricultural education gives only special training in the teaching of agriculture and closely related general science, nature-study, and rural education. Inasmuch as the division also has charge of correspondence courses in agriculture with related extension courses, a comparatively large staff is maintained, although the teacher training has been conducted mostly by two men. Recently the university has entered into cooperation with the State Board for Vocational Education to train teachers at the University Farm School at Davis and at other points in the State and to conduct itinerant teacher training among teachers in service.

Facilities for teaching.—In times past the division gave more attention to training for elementary work with school gardens, nature study, and boys' and girls' club work. School gardens are still maintained in Berkeley at the university and used in elementary teacher training, especially during the summer session. Prospective teachers of agriculture in the secondary schools up to the present time have been taken to the university farm at Davis, where a six-weeks' course in farm practice has been given in various farm operations that all teachers may become familiar with ordinary farm practice. High schools in the State are selected for a five-weeks' course in practice teaching.

Courses of study.—Students who desire to secure a recommendation from the division as teachers of agriculture in high schools of the State are expected to take a four-year course in agriculture, with agricultural education as a major. The work of the first two years is the same as for other students in agriculture. Although the work of the junior and senior years is largely elective, the student is expected to have completed, in addition to three stipulated courses in agricultural education, at least one course in each of the following agricultural divisions: Agronomy, pomology, plant pathology, entomology, farm management, animal husbandry, dairy industry, poultry husbandry, and veterinary science.

In addition to opportunity for special studies and individual work in agricultural education, the following courses were given in 1917–18.

(a) Agencies for rural progress: Country life problems, agencies for rural progress, and the best means of utilizing these agencies for the improvement of rural communities. Lectures, assigned readings, and reports.

(b) Elements of agriculture, nature study, and school gardens: Aims, material, and methods used in agricultural instruction in the elementary and grade schools; teaching plans; educational value of the school garden; the home garden and the value of the school garden; the home garden and the value of home project work in agricultural education. Practical garden work on the campus.

(c) High school farms, gardens and community work: Lectures, reports, and conferences on the utilization of land in connection with agricultural teaching; means by which the facilities of a school can be brought into intimate and helpful relation with the agricultural interests and home life of the community supporting the school; practice in planning and executing school farm problems and demonstrations.

(d) General science and first-year agriculture: The aims and values of a general science course in the high school; comparative study of typical courses and exposition of the peculiar adaptations to the general science work of an elementary agricultural course in which plant study forms the basis of continuity; the equipment, nature, and amount of practical work needed in the course, including field trips and excursions. Outdoor and laboratory exercises are considered in detail.

(e) Agriculture in secondary schools: Agricultural teaching, including its history; the teaching methods to be employed, and the equipment needed. A general consideration of the educational aims and values of the work and the organization of the course is followed by a detailed study of materials and methods involved in the teaching of elementary agriculture, dairying, animal husbandry, horticulture, etc. Lectures, readings, and assigned practicums.

(f) Rural school administration: Readings and classroom discussions of the fundamentals of rural school organization, management, and improvement.

(g) The practice of teaching agriculture: A five-weeks' practice course in selected high schools of the State. Making of lesson plans, practice teaching reports and conferences with supervising teacher and instructor. Supervised practice teaching; the observation of methods; and management of class and laboratory instruction by the local teacher. By arrangement with the department of education properly prepared students may satisfy the requirements in practice teaching for the teachers' recommendation by taking this course instead of Education 201 (The practice of teaching).

As a rule several of the above courses are given in the summer session. No work was given for elementary teachers during the summer of 1918. Usually large classes of public-school teachers register for this work.

Students.—In 1916–17 there were 37 men and 5 women registered, with a major in agricultural education. In 1916 there were 20 graduates in agricultural education, 13 of whom secured positions to teach or supervise agriculture.

DEPARTMENT OF RURAL EDUCATION: CORNELL UNIVERSITY.

Organization and scope.—For a number of years the New York State College of Agriculture has been doing a great deal to aid teachers in service with their problems of elementary agriculture and nature study. This work is now continued by the department of rural education, organized in 1914, although the main function of this department is to train teachers of agriculture for the secondary schools. Although the university maintains a school of education, the department of rural education in the college of agriculture is mostly independent, giving its general methods courses within the department. In addition to a force of workers who take care of the extension work in the State, three men are employed for the training of teachers of agriculture in secondary schools, one for general methods and two for special methods in agricultural education.

Agricultural education is offered as an option to agricultural students in the junior and senior years. In common with other agricultural students, considerable latitude is allowed for election of subjects to students preparing to teach agriculture. For graduation there is required, however, approximately the following: Cultural subjects, 14 hours; science, 38 hours; psychology and education, 14 hours; elective, 54 hours; making a total of 120 hours. The electives are selected with the advice of the department.

Facilities for teaching.—For practice teaching, seniors are placed as apprentices to some of the best teachers in the high schools of the State for half a year. Near-by schools and departments are used for practice by the classes in agricultural education. For example, at a time when the author visited a vocational department at Interlaken a class in agricultural education from the college at Ithaca had just been there to study the planning and equipment of the building used for vocational agriculture. One of the students of the college came to the school regularly to give the high-school students instruction in forge work.

The department is well equipped for practice in collecting, making, and using teaching materials, especially along the lines of visual instruction.

Courses of study.—The following courses were offered in the third term, beginning June 3 and ending September 28, 1918:

(*a*) Principles of teaching and practice—topics considered: The application of principles of educational psychology and the philosophy of education to the problem of school practice; the nature of study and its principal factors; the teacher's relation to the learning process, motivation, psychological versus logical thinking, interest and attention, motor control; the problem and the project as basis for the organization of materials; the use of first-hand sensory materials; the selection and arrangement of subject matter; teaching methods, lecture, textbook, development, recitation; assignment of lessons, questioning, practice; and classroom management.

(*b*) Agriculture in the high school: A study of the purposes of vocational agriculture, organization and presentation of subject matter, textbooks, and home project and extension activities of the high school. A one-day excursion is a part of the course.

(*c*) Principles of method: A detailed study of the principles underlying method with special reference to the teaching of vocational agriculture and home economics. Topics considered: The aims of education; education as essentially a dynamic process, illustrated in growth changes, hereditary expression, habit formation, play and manual activities, and in the expenditure of energy; the laws of learning, particularly those related to the organization of ideas; the function and structure of subject matter; the principles underlying various school practices, for instance, the project; interest in relation to learning; the basis for the organization of knowledge; the tests of teaching methods; how we think.

(*d*) Administration and supervision of agricultural education: This course treats: Administrative phases of agricultural education of secondary and college grade; Federal acts relating to agricultural education; comparative study of types of schools of agriculture; State systems of supervision. Visits to schools in New York and adjacent States is a required part of the course.

During the summer school, which extended from July 8 to August 16, 1918, the following additional courses were offered:

(*a*) Agriculture in the high school: A course for consideration of curricula, courses of study, school plot, home project, extension work, and the preparation of material as they relate to secondary school conditions. The work will be planned for those who have had technical preparation in agriculture. Lectures may be taken without laboratory work by special permission.

(*b*) Organization of college departments of agricultural education: This course is designed for those preparing for teaching training work in college departments of agricultural education. It deals with the study of agricultural college and high school curricula in agriculture with respect to the technical preparation of teachers of secondary agriculture, and the professional needs of the high school teacher of agriculture, practice teaching, graduate needs to be met by such departments, and the content of special methods course in agricultural education.

(c) Administration and supervision of vocational agriculture: This course is designed especially to meet the needs of State directors of agricultural education. The Smith-Hughes Act is used as a basis for the work. Topics receiving consideration are: Types of schools, plans for supervision, preparation of teachers, supervision of home-project work, curricula, and courses of study. Visitation of schools is a required part of the course. In addition to the instruction by members of the department, lectures will be given by several State directors. L. S. Hawkins, assistant director of the Federal Board for Vocational Education, will give the lectures for one week.

(d) The social and vocational aspects of education: A course designed to give students certain fundamental points of view in the interpretation of educational problems. Emphasis will be placed upon the changing social and vocational demands made upon the school and the initiative the school should take to better social and vocational conditions. The purpose is to acquire a workable point of view for social progress and to study its applications with special reference to education in a democracy.

Emergency courses in agriculture.—Due to the lack of trained teachers to take hold of vocational departments of agriculture during the war period the New York State College of Agriculture, at the request of the State department of education, offered emergency courses for the preparation of these teachers for a period of nine weeks, beginning July 29, 1918. These courses under the direction of the department of rural education, covered the following subjects: Farm shop, soils and fertilizers, dairy industry, poultry husbandry, animal husbandry, general fruit growing, agriculture in the high schools, farm management, and farm crops. Each of these subjects was taken up from the point of view and with regard to the needs of teachers of agriculture in the high school.

From August 5 to August 10 a conference of all agricultural instructors in the New York schools of agriculture, mechanic arts, and home making was held at the college.

Students.—During the school year 1916–17, 43 men and 4 women were registered in the regular college course in agricultural education. In 1916, 82 of the agricultural students who graduated had taken special training courses; 35 of these students secured positions as teachers.

DEPARTMENT OF AGRICULTURAL EDUCATION: AGRICULTURAL AND MECHANICAL
COLLEGE OF TEXAS.

Organization and scope.—As all teacher training in the college
is under the direction of this department, it includes general training in education as well as special work in agricultural education.
The chief efforts of the department are centered upon training
teachers of vocational agriculture for the secondary schools of the
State and in aiding those teachers in service. The latter work consists chiefly of visiting the schools and furnishing direct aid thereby,
in conducting extension classes where teachers may be brought together for regular courses, and in furnishing illustrative material
in the way of charts, slides, and exhibits.

Teaching facilities.—The department occupies three rooms in a
new modern building. One room is a model laboratory in which are
exhibited and demonstrated desirable forms of equipment for teaching the various courses in the high school. Laboratory materials are
also on display with suggestions as to their preparation and use.
Another room is equipped as a laboratory for the preparation of
illustrative materials. Various charts and mimeographed materials
are prepared, lantern slides made and colored, and various photographs and other pictures prepared for use in visual instruction.
The department library contains the newest books and bulletins on
agriculture suited to secondary schools as well as works on education.

In addition to three regular members of the staff, a professor of agricultural education and two associate professors of agricultural
education, two student assistants are employed in the department.

Courses of study.—Two four-year college curricula are offered:
One leading to the degree B. S. in agricultural education, and the
other to a B. S. in agriculture. The two curricula are nearly alike in
the first two years and may differ but little in the two uppear years,
the difference depending upon the courses the student may elect. Six
hours of electives are left open in each semester of the junior and
senior year of the first named curriculum, while half of the optional
credits must be in either agriculture or agricultural education in the
agricultural curriculum.

The department offers the usual courses in the following subjects:
Educational psychology, methods and teaching, schools administration, high school problems, and vocational education. The special
courses in agricultural education are described in the catalogue as
follows:

Administration of high-school agriculture: This course is a study of the
specific problems that confront the teacher in carrying on the work of the
department of agriculture in the high school. Among the topics discussed are:

The selection of subject matter suited to local conditions; agriculture in the curriculum; laboratory, field, and home exercises; visual instruction; supervision of home projects; laboratory and library equipment; use and management of school farm, and community or extension work. The laboratory period will be used for the preparation of teaching material, and for working out individual assignments connected with the work. Text: Materials and Methods in High School Agriculture, by Hummel.

Rural education: The primary purpose of this course is to make a study of rural education in its broad sense, with a view of preparing teachers and extension workers for more efficient service in rural communities. Some of the topics discussed are: Changes in rural education and the rural home, together with the factors effecting such changes; the school as a community center; other agencies to be coordinated; community play and recreation, and the redirected rural school. Text: Rural Life and Education, by Cubberly.

Agricultural extension and demonstration: This course is intended to give a survey of the whole field of extension in agriculture and home economics and to give practice that will prepare for actual field work. Among the topics discussed are: Evolution of extension in agriculture and home economics, general organization for extension, methods of extension, farm demonstration work, junior agricultural clubs, extension by experts, extension by railroads and commercial companies, and the training of extension workers.

Teaching: The purpose of this course is to give opportunity for students to get actual experience in teaching secondary agriculture under supervision. Lesson plans must be submitted by the student and approved by the critic teacher in advance of the lesson. The teaching methods and results of the student will be discussed in special conferences. Provision will be made for classes on the campus and near-by high schools. Application for this course must be made at least three months in advance.

To other courses—agricultural instruction and agricultural extension and demonstration—are modifications of courses described in the latter course. The student is expected to do some extension work as a part of the course.

In addition to other work offered in the summer session, a rural life school is conducted for six weeks. Courses which do not involve college credit are given in agriculture, rural education, rural sociology, and rural economics. These courses include modified forms of regular college courses intended for the training of high-school teachers of agriculture. A rural life conference, including a rural pastor's conference and a rural school conference, is held for one week.

During the summer of 1918, from June 3 to July 13, special courses were offered for teachers of vocational agriculture. These courses, which were arranged in conference with those in charge of the Smith-Hughes work in the State, included: Administration of high school agriculture; elementary crop production; and market types of horses and swine.

Students.—In 1916–17 120 men enrolled for agricultural education. In 1916 there were 32 graduates, 10 of whom secured positions as teachers of agriculture.

Organization and scope.—The department of agricultural education is a part of the school of vocational education, which embraces also departments of education, psychology, home economics education, industrial education, and commercial education. The college is expected to confine its teacher training largely to preparing teachers of vocational subjects in the secondary schools. General training in education and psychology is given, however, as a basis for the training of teachers of special vocational subjects. The function of the department of agricultural education is "to train men and women as teachers of agriculture in the colleges and secondary schools; to train extension workers in agriculture; and to develop leadership in rural life and education."

Teaching facilities.—Although teachers of agriculture have had some special training for a number of years as a part of the work of the department of industrial education, the department of agricultural education has been but recently organized and is not fully equipped. The idea in equipment is not to have elaborate equipment but to train teachers with such equipment and facilities as will be within their reach in secondary schools. A combination laboratory and classroom is being equipped with such illustrative and reference material and laboratory apparatus as should be used in a department of vocational agriculture in a high school.

The department of agriculture in the local high school is in charge of an instructor in agricultural education of the college. This department is used for practice teaching with the instructor acting as critic teacher.

Courses of study.—Students preparing to teach agriculture in the secondary schools register in the school of agriculture, taking the prescribed work for all agricultural students in the first two years. In the last two years instead of specializing in some branch of agriculture the work is largely prescribed to round out a more general training in agriculture and related science and to include 15 hours of professional training. This latter training includes educational psychology, principles of education, vocational education, secondary education in agriculture, and practice teaching.

Facilities are afforded for special students in agricultural education to graduates of normal and agricultural courses. In addition to seminars for these students and practice teaching classes, the following courses are offered:

(a) Secondary education in agriculture: The principles of education as applied to the teaching of vocational agriculture in secondary schools. Aims, methods, and materials adapted to the practical training of students over 14 years of age are considered; including the organization of courses, the collection and use of illustrative and reference materials, and the various phases of classroom and laboratory instruction.

(*b*) Seminar agricultural education: A discussion of special problems in the teaching of agriculture and in the administration of agricultural education which will be brought out in an effort to keep in touch with the progress of this phase of education. The seminar includes also a critical review of the current literature of the subject.

(*c*) Educational resources of the rural community: The special aim of this course is to prepare teachers for broader social service. The rural school, the farmhouse, the country church, farmers' organizations, and other agencies for rural progress will be considered with a view of working toward a better correlation and a greater cooperation in effort for rural development. Special attention will be given the rural school as a community center.

(*d*) Extension methods in agriculture: The history, organization, and methods of county agricultural agent work; lectures, assigned readings and practice in news writing, outlining program of work, drawing projects, chart making, conducting meetings, etc.

(*e*) Agriculture and general science for teachers: The aims, materials, and methods in general agriculture and general science with organization of courses for secondary schools. Special attention to supervision of productive projects to meet emergency needs.

(*f*) Elementary education in agriculture: The aims, materials, and methods of prevocational and educational agriculture in the elementary schools, the relation to nature study and the boys' and girls' club work. Special attention given to school and home gardens and such projects as poultry and rabbits.

The last-named course is given in the summer session and to teachers and supervisors in the elementary schools at Portland. Courses for the training of vocational teachers are also offered at Portland. Secondary education in agriculture is given as an extension course in the itinerant training of teachers of agriculture in service by the head of the department who serves also as supervisor of agricultural education in the State.

Students.—In 1916–17, 14 men were registered in the department of industrial education. In 1916 there were 12 graduates, all of whom secured positions as teachers.

PRACTICAL PHASES OF TRAINING.

The demand to place agricultural instruction upon a more practical basis and the standardization of vocational agriculture through Federal and State control are calling for the more practical training of teachers. The practical training as now given may be classified as follows: (1) Practice in agriculture; (2) practice in teaching; and (3) practice in the preparation and use of teaching materials.

Practice in agriculture.—In most of the colleges the problem of making the agricultural training practical is considered a problem for the various agricultural departments. Departments of agricultural education take the men with the training as they have received it in the various phases of agriculture. In some cases, however, as this training is not sufficiently practical to enable the prospective teachers to direct vocational work, the departments of agricultural education have been obliged to secure new courses of a practical nature or to bring about a reorganization of courses as given. Although most of the States have required two years of farm experience for teachers of vocational agriculture, it is found necessary to supplement this and round it out in the training course to meet their needs as teachers. Some States are using teacher training funds to give practical shopwork to prospective teachers. Other States find it essential to have prospective teachers, directors, and supervisors of productive farm projects carry out such projects themselves in much the same manner as they will expect of their students. Conducting practical farm projects on the college farm has been a feature of several of the emergency teacher training courses. It is possible that it may become a permanent feature of regular courses for teachers of vocational agriculture. It seems reasonable that the prospective teacher should secure some of his practical training in agriculture in the light of a need which differs from the specialist or scientist or even from the student who returns to the farm.

Practice in teaching.—Securing suitable practice in teaching is admitted to be one of the most difficult and expensive of all forms of teacher training. It is presenting many new difficulties to departments that train teachers of vocational agriculture. Some of the agricultural colleges offer vocational courses of secondary grade and in some cases students in agricultural education secure practice in teaching the students in such courses. The chief objection to such practice is that it is secured under conditions widely variant from the ordinary secondary school. The students are older as a rule and the methods used in teaching them are too often the same methods used in teaching regular college students. As a rule the equipment is the same as used for college students. It is often difficult to secure cooperation wherein such practice may be supervised by those trained in education instead of by those trained in some special phase of agriculture. In some cases the students do not even get this kind of practice. If they secure any practice at all it is in the nature of moot classes of their fellow students.

Some of the colleges depend upon local high schools to secure practice for their students. Under some conditions this plan works well. Where one school is used for a large number of students, abnormal conditions arise and the plan does not work well.

One of the best plans yet observed is the placing of prospective teachers in agricultural departments of rural high school as apprentice teachers for a period of several months. As the local teacher acts as critic teacher, the plan is limited by the number of schools available in which teachers are in charge who are qualified to direct the work of a teacher in training. It is necessary to give the work careful general supervision, which means close cooperation between those in charge of teacher training and those in charge of the agricultural instruction in the schools. As the student may be called upon to give up all other tasks for a whole semester, the work must involve sufficient credit or monetary compensation to induce students to take it. In New York some compensation is given such teachers in training. It will be seen that the expense of such a plan puts limitations upon it. In the future, perhaps, it will be desirable to put limitations on teacher training and at the same time to make the work more thorough. This plan promises much for the future.

Practice in the preparation and use of teaching materials.—Many of the special courses in agricultural education call for laboratory work as well as practice teaching. It has been interesting to note that some of the older men in charge of the work who went into agricultural education from other lines of teaching have not known what to do with laboratory periods, while many of the men who have had actual contact with the problems of making the work practical in secondary schools have not had sufficient time for all of the practical training they desire to give their students. Although the extent and nature of the work done depends much upon the equipment and organization, as well as the aims of the various departments, most of the instruction will fit into the following groups:

I. Preparing illustrative and laboratory material.
    1. Use of a camera.
    2. Use of a stereopticon.
    3. Making lantern slides.
    4. Collecting and mounting pictures.
    5. Chart making.
    6. Collecting and mounting insects and other small animals.
    7. Collecting and mounting plants.
    8. Preparing exhibits and collecting laboratory materials.
II. Use of reference material.
    1. Making collections of bulletins, etc.
    2. Classifying and cataloging reference material.
    3. Making, mounting, and indexing clippings.

III. Organization of subject matter.
     1. Working out curricula and courses of study.
     2. Preparation of lesson outlines and study outlines for projects.
     3. Preparing forms for records.
     4. Planning practicums and field trips.
     5. Preparation of survey outlines.
IV. Planning and making equipment.
     1. Drawing plans of classroom, laboratory, shops, etc.
     2. Planning equipment for classroom and laboratory.
     3. Making simple equipment and teaching devices.
V. Conducting practical exercises as adapted to secondary students.

The nature and extent of the last-named group of activities depend chiefly upon opportunities afforded the students for suitable practical work in their agricultural courses and the opportunities for carrying out practicums and field trips in connection with practice teaching. In some cases, even where the students secure practice of a technical nature in connection with their agricultural courses, practicums are planned and conducted in the training class as they would be handled for secondary students. Such work includes: Judging farm animals, judging farm products, testing seed, testing soil for acidity, use of the Babcock test, testing and preserving eggs, and such practical and simple exercises as fit well into the work of a secondary school.

Agencies for the advancement of agricultural education.—Many of the larger educational and scientific institutions and societies have been concerned for a number of years with problems of agricultural education as they relate to the general problems of education and agriculture with which these bodies deal. Chief among the national bodies may be mentioned the National Education Association and the American Association of Agricultural Colleges and Experiment Stations. Scarcely a year passes in which these bodies do not consider some phase of agriculture in the secondary schools. Regional and State teachers' associations very often find time on their programs and place in their reports for consideration of problems dealing with teaching agriculture in the high schools. It has been only within the last four or five years, however, that the problems of agriculture in the secondary schools have been given special consideration. Such special attention has been given chiefly by the following agencies:

1. Division of agricultural instruction, United States Department of Agriculture: In 1903 the Office of Experiment Stations of the United States Department of Agriculture received an appropriation for farmers' institutes and agricultural instruction in the following terms:

To enable the Secretary of Agriculture to investigate and report upon the organization and progress of farmers' institutes and agricultural schools in the several States and Territories and upon similar organizations in foreign countries, with special suggestions of plans and methods for making such organizations more effective for the dissemination of the results of the work of the Department of Agriculture and the agricultural experiment stations, and of improved methods of agricultural practice, including the employment of labor in the city of Washington and elsewhere and all necessary expenses, $20,800.

For a number of years work of a general nature, much of it propaganda for the development of agricultural education and farmers' institutes, was carried on by specialists in those two lines. Although the work has continued ever since with the same appropriation and the same authorization, its nature has been changed as the work to do became more specific and specialized. In 1914 a man was employed to give his entire time to the work of the secondary schools. This work is mostly along two lines: (1) Investigating the methods of organization and teaching in the schools; (2) organizing the information secured in the Department of Agriculture and the experiment stations for teaching purposes. Methods gleaned from the study of schools are suggested in connection with the materials organized for teaching. This material is sent out in the form of bulletins and documents. For two years the Agricultural Education Monthly served as a medium for reaching teachers of agriculture. Sets of lantern slides are prepared and loaned to teachers with lecture syllabi.

2. United States Bureau of Education: The Federal Bureau of Education for several years has considered aid to teachers of agriculture as one of its functions, but owing to limited funds it has been necessary to restrict its efforts to a few lines. A specialist in agricultural education has been employed for the past three years. Much of his time has been devoted to investigations concerning higher education in agriculture and the coordination of the whole program of agricultural instruction. The bureau has cooperated with the Department of Agriculture and other agencies in making investigations and has published a number of bulletins reporting the results of investigations and the proceedings of educational societies dealing with agriculture in secondary schools.

3. Conferences on agricultural education: Under the auspices of the Department of Agriculture and the Bureau of Education a number of regional conferences have been held, in which specific problems relating to the teaching of agriculture in secondary schools were discussed. As those attending the conferences were mostly engaged in the colleges as professors of agricultural education, or in State departments of education as supervisors of agriculture, the problems discussed pertained chiefly to training teachers and to the organization and direction of courses of study in the secondary

154070°—20——7

schools. The reports of these conferences, though not published for general distribution, were made available to those immediately interested.

4. The American Association for the Advancement of Agricultural Teaching: This association was organized in 1909 for the purpose, as stated in its constitution, " to promote the teaching of agriculture and to devise ways and means of increasing the efficiency of such instruction in elementary and secondary schools and in colleges and universities." Up to the present time the association has given most of its time to problems relating to secondary agriculture. Some of the proceedings of its meetings and reports of its communities have been published by the Department of Agriculture and the Bureau of Education. The committee on the use of land by high schools teaching agriculture has done a good deal to develop a rational use of the school farm and to promote the home-project plan.

5. Federal Board for Vocational Education: In addition to the general administration of vocational agriculture, as subsidized with Federal funds, the Smith-Hughes Act charges the Federal Board for Vocational Education—

to make or cause to have made studies, investigations, and reports, with particular reference to their use in aiding the States in the establishment of vocational schools and classes and in giving instruction in agriculture, etc. * * *

When the board deems it advisable, such studies and investigations concerning agriculture for the purposes of agricultural education may be made in cooperation with or through the Department of Agriculture. Such studies, investigations, and reports concerning the administration of vocational schools, courses of study, and instruction in vocational subjects may be made in cooperation with or through the Bureau of Education.

Inasmuch as the work of the Federal board is directly connected with the schools and that it has both authorization and funds for aiding the teaching of agriculture and other vocational schools in a direct way, it looks as if the governmental aid for this phase of teaching would center largely around the work of that board. Plans for cooperation with both the Department of Agriculture and the Bureau of Education have been made. These departments will do investigational work connected with the teaching and administration of agriculture in the secondary schools under the direction of the Federal board.

6. General agencies: Of the general agencies interested in agricultural education the most important at present are the National Education Association and the National Society for Vocational Education. At the present time a committee on agricultural education is working in connection with the commission on the reorganization of secondary education of the National Education Association on a report which promises to be not a reorganization but a

primary organization of secondary agriculture, as this branch of secondary education has never been really organized. The National Society for the Promotion of Industrial Education gave some attention to agricultural education. Now that this society has broadened its field and changed its name to the National Society for Vocational Education, it promises to give a great deal more attention to the problems of vocational agriculture in secondary schools.

Chapter VI.

SUMMARY OF STUDY.

RELATION OF SECONDARY TO COLLEGIATE AGRICULTURE.

It is not easy to draw a distinct line between agriculture as taught in the elementary and secondary schools and the colleges. As the teaching of agriculture was developed in the college, it is reasonable to assume that, in its early development, it was of an elementary nature. It has only been in recent years that the land-grant colleges have raised their agricultural instruction to college grade; even now much of the instruction of the colleges for Negroes and some of the other institutions is of a secondary grade. Many of the secondary schools are doing work in agriculture to-day more advanced than most of the colleges were doing a few years ago. The nature of the subject will always present difficulties in drawing lines between agriculture suited for the elementary schools, the secondary schools, and the colleges. The present-day tendency appears to be to consider elementary instruction of a general prevocational nature the work of the elementary schools and the junior high schools, and the work of the agricultural colleges largely the training of scientists and specialists, leaving to secondary schools and departments a large share of the vocational training of farmers.

KIND OF SCHOOLS.

As the teaching of agriculture was extended beyond the colleges, it was assumed apparently that schools of agriculture should be established with land and equipment for practical instruction at the school. Many of the agricultural schools established have not been real agricultural schools. In some cases agricultural departments have been more successful in teaching agriculture than the so-called agricultural schools. The question has arisen as to whether agriculture should be taught in the ordinary high school or in special schools of agriculture. From the study the author has made it would seem that there is place for instruction in agriculture in every high school serving a farming community, if the school is prepared to give the proper training to future farmers. There is also a place for a limited number of agricultural schools of secondary grade. The majority of students should receive their agricultural training in

100

the public high school while living at home on the farm.. The students who are not served by local high schools and the more mature students who wish more intensive training in agriculture the agricultural schools will aid the colleges in training.

PROBLEMS OF VOCATIONAL AGRICULTURE.

The practical training of farmers as undertaken by the schools presents many new problems. While we may agree that vocational agriculture-means the training of farmers, we do not know what the schools may do, and just how they may do it, in giving that training. We may learn something from the experience of the agricultural colleges, but their work has been in most cases better adapted to the training of scientists than farmers. High-school instruction has suffered from the college instruction which has in too many cases been taken over without adaptation to secondary students. Some of the secondary schools have taken long steps in the direction of solving some of the problems presented. A survey of what these schools have accomplished should be helpful before new studies are attempted. The author has had opportunity to study a large number of schools teaching agriculture. The chief problems studies are summarized in the following paragraphs:

Use of land.—Placing agricultural instruction upon a vocational basis means making the work practical. Practice in agriculture involves the use of land. Whether the school should own a farm or not is still a question much discussed. Some of the schools visited have used their school farms effectively in giving practical training. Others have been more successful in connecting the training given at the school with practice secured at home through the home-project plan. Other schools have used both the school farm and the home-project plan. It would seem from the study made that there is a place for both, if properly planned, directed, and adapted to educational needs. As a rule the home-project plan works best in agricultural departments of high schools where the students are living at home upon farms near the school. School farms are most needed in connection with agricultural schools where the students are living at the school, away from home.

Utilizing community resources.—In vocational training in agriculture there is a tendency to get away from technical laboratory training and to make the shop and the farm the laboratory of the school. Some of the schools doing most effective work not only use the home farms and the school land for practical training, but also use neighboring farms in the community. In fact, they look upon the entire community as the laboratory of the school and use all its resources as far as possible for teaching purposes. This attitude is exemplified in the Wisconsin normal school described, which, instead of investing in live stock and equipment for their school farms, invested in auto trucks with which to take classes into the community for field instruction.

Methods of instruction.—Vocational training in agriculture is introducing new problems in teaching. Not that new principles are involved, but that new applications must be made. The lecture method and technical laboratory methods evolved in the college do not function any better in teaching secondary agriculture than they do in teaching other phases of science in the high school. Textbook methods and laboratory training considered successful in science teaching in the high school need considerable adaptation in their application to vocational training in agriculture. The most successful schools based their school instruction upon practical farm projects and constructive work in the field and shop. Teachers were supervisors and directors of training as well as instructors. Classroom instruction of a nature less formal than academic instruction in the high school seems to meet the needs of instruction related to practical work. Individual project study means supervised study. The teacher in the classroom continues as a director and leader as he is out of doors, for a part of the time directing individual study and planning of work and then acting as leader in a round-table discussion of problems and principles of general interest and application.

Organization of subject matter.—The curricula and courses of study in operation in the various schools and suggested in the State plans show that general standards are not established. As a rule, where States have attempted to standardize the work by prescribing curricula and definite courses of study, the work has not been entirely satisfactory. Various sections of most of the States differ so widely in their agricultural needs and educational resources that standardized courses are a handicap unless they offer considerable leeway in their choice of subject matter and its application. The most successful courses noted were those adapted best to the interests of particular classes of students and to the needs of the community in which they live. It should be possible to bring vocational agriculture to a high standard in regard to the quantity and character of the work done without specifying the subjects to be taught.

Equipment.—What has been stated in regard to standardization of courses applies in a large measure to equipment. The two go together to a great extent. Some States have made little attempt to standardize courses and methods of instruction, but have specified equipment in detail. In some cases it would seem that the courses of study and methods were made to fit the equipment, instead of the equipment selected as it was needed in teaching. As long as the idea prevailed that practical agriculture could be taught in the laboratory or that a school farm is essential to practical training, extensive and expensive equipment seemed inevitable in a plan for agricultural training. The home-project plan and a wider use of community resources have reduced the need for equipment greatly. As the work is made more practical there is a tendency to equip shops and workrooms rather than laboratories. Incubators, pruning tools, hotbed sash, and spraying outfits are apt to be considered more essential than microscopes, glassware, and soil tubes. In some of the schools doing excellent work little expensive equipment was found. The success of the work depended upon the ability and resourcefulness of the teacher, who, with his students, gathered about him inexpensive teaching material, and who used the home farms and the resources of the community to a great extent. A good teacher may overcome the handicap of poor equipment, while a poor teacher has difficulty in making good with the best equipment available.

SUBSIDIZING AGRICULTURAL EDUCATION.

Accomplishments of State aid.—Vocational training in agriculture means a form of training more expensive than instruction in academic subjects. Even where no farm is used by the school, and equipment is maintained at a minimum, the cost is high because a highly trained, high-priced man must be employed to supervise and direct the work of relatively few pupils. The home-project method may be inexpensive as far as equipment is concerned but expensive for instruction and supervision, as one man can supervise but a few pupils. Realizing the importance of agricultural training and considering its cost, the majority of the States had provided, in some way, to encourage and support the work with State subsidy. While much of the money was misspent, because rational plans were not made and adequate supervision and inspection provided, most of the agricultural instruction worthy of consideration as a special branch of education was developed up to 1917 under the stimulus of State aid. It is to the success of State-aided agricultural instruction that we must accredit Federal aid for that work.

State systems as models.—It was the States which provided distinctly for vocational agriculture and made provision for supervision that the work might be carried out upon a distinctly vocational basis that contributed most to a national plan for vocational agricultural education. In this study considerable attention has been given the work done in Massachusetts, New York, Pennsylvania, New Jersey, and Indiana, because it was upon the work accomplished in these States that the Federal act for vocational education was modeled to a great extent. The chief purpose of the Smith-Hughes Act was to stimulate other States to provide for vocational education, including agriculture, as the above-mentioned States had done. We may continue to study what has been done in these States with profit, because they have had severeal years' start in working out problems. The author has received many suggestions from visiting schools in New York and Massachusetts which have been helpful to other States. The home-project plan and practical use of school land have been worked out well in some of the schools and departments in those States. The problem before us now is to adapt methods worked out for conditions in those States to meet conditions as found in other sections.

The granting of Federal aid undoubtedly means a new epoch for agriculture in the secondary schools, not only because of the direct financial aid and the State aid which it stimulates but also for new policies established and new standards set. Although the matter of organization and administration is left largely with the States, there is little doubt but that the tendency is in the direction of national standards. While it is too early to determine the extent to which national standards are going to effect work already started under State aid, it has been considered worth while to make a study of the various State plans for purpose of comparison.

For the present, most of the effort of the State departments of education is centered upon vocational agriculture as established according to Federal standards. The question arises as to whether other forms of agricultural instruction in secondary and elementary agriculture are to be neglected. It is a question whether specialized vocational training in agriculture may be maintained in an extensive way without more attention to vitalizing the instruction in general agriculture. Linking instruction in general agriculture in the upper grades, the junior high school, and the lower grades of the high school with boys' and girls' club work and other home work should serve in an excellent way as prevocational training for agriculture.

Although the matter of dual control has been passed up to the States, there are few States in which the administration of vocational education is not linked closely with the administration of general education. Inasmuch as there should be close relation between the elementary or prevocational work and vocational training, the supervision of both lines should be under the same direction.

Teacher training.—As the success of the work in the secondary schools depends in such a large measure upon the training of the teachers, the Federal funds provide for this important work. Some progress had been made in developing departments of agricultural education before Federal aid was given through the Smith-Hughes Act. The Nelson amendment to the Morrill Act provided that some of the funds for the land-grant college could be used for training teachers of agriculture. The author had made some study of teacher training as conducted in these colleges, and found that courses in agricultural education varied from courses consisting chiefly of the subject matter of general agriculture to courses consisting chiefly of general methods in education.

We are now in the process of developing special methods and means of organization in agriculture. Along with this development, agricultural education is being developed as a special line in the teaching profession. A great deal, probably too much, is expected of teachers of secondary agriculture. They are expected to know both the art of farming and the science of agriculture along general lines, as well as the art of teaching and the science of education. Departments of agricultural education are finding that this broad training can not all be given in the college. To secure men who have good prospects of succeeding in departments of vocational agriculture from the start, they are reaching out for men who have had either experience in forming or practice in teaching or both, and then rounding out their training in the college.

BIBLIOGRAPHY ON AGRICULTURE IN SECONDARY SCHOOLS.

I. SCHOOLS OF AGRICULTURE.

ARKANSAS. *Department of Public Instruction.* The Minnesota agricultural high schools. *In its* Biennial report, 1907-8. pp. 140-173.

ASSOCIATION OF AMERICAN AGRICULTURAL COLLEGES AND EXPERIMENT STATIONS. *Committee on Instruction in Agriculture.* Relations of high school agriculture to agriculture as taught in the land-grant colleges. 19th Report, 1916.

CROSBY, D. J. Special agricultural high schools. *In* National Education Association. Journal of proceedings and addresses, 1909. pp. 974-976.

DAVIS, K. C. County schools of agriculture in Wisconsin. *In* U. S. Department of Agriculture. Office of Experiment Stations. Report, 1904. pp. 677-686.

JOHNSON, A. A. County schools of agriculture and domestic economy in Wisconsin. U. S. Department of Agriculture. Office of Experiment Stations. Bulletin 242, 1911.

LANE, C. H. Arkansas State agricultural schools. U. S. Department of Agriculture. Office of Experiment Stations. Bulletin No. 250, 1912.

—— *and* CROSBY, D. J. The district agricultural schools of Georgia. U. S. Bureau of Education. Bulletin, 1916, No. 44.

MATSCHECK, W. Report of a survey made for the Milwaukee Taxpayers' League. Madison, Wis., Efficiency Bureau, 1916. 78 pp.
    Deals with Milwaukee's County School of Agriculture and Domestic Economy.

MICHIGAN. *Department of Public Instruction.* County schools of agriculture. *In its* 21st Annual report, 1908. pp. 35-42.

NELSON, C. J. N. The best type of agricultural high school. *In* North Dakota Educational Association. Proceedings, vol. 28, 1914. pp. 81-84.

OWENS, C. J. Secondary agricultural education in Alabama. U. S. Department of Agriculture. Office of Experiment Stations. Bulletin 220, 1909.

PUGSLEY, C. W. Agricultural courses for secondary schools (Nebraska). Nebraska University Journal, vol. 8, No. 8. pp. 43-46.

REYNOLDS, J. H. Agricultural high schools. *In* Southern Educational Association. Journal of proceedings and addresses, 1908. pp. 515-525.

SMITH, W. H., *and others.* County agricultural high schools, with course of study. *In* Mississippi Department of Public Education. Bulletin 8, 1913. pp. 61-67.

SNEDDEN, DAVID. Practical program for agricultural schools. Journal of Education, 77: 733-734, 1913.

WAJTA, J. F. Menominee County Agricultural School and what it does. *In* Michigan Farmers' Institutes. Bulletin 20, 1914. pp. 821-828.

II. HIGH SCHOOLS.

BROWN, H. A. The New Hampshire type of reconstructed rural high school. Vocational Education, 3 : 327–337, 1914.

—— The readjustment of a rural high school to the needs of the community. U. S. Bureau of Education. Bulletin, 1912, No. 20.

CRANDALL, B. R. Agriculture in the Idaho Falls High School. American School Board Journal, 49 : 17–18, 1914.

LANE, C. H. Agricultural instruction in the high schools of six eastern States. U. S. Bureau of Education. Bulletin, 1913, No. 3.

MICHIGAN AGRICULTURAL COLLEGE. Department of Agricultural Education. Report of agriculture in the high schools of Michigan. Bulletin 18, August, 1917.
    Reports for previous years also published.

MONAHAN, A. C., and PHILLIPS, ADAMS. The Farragut School—a Tennessee country life school. U. S. Bureau of Education. Bulletin, 1913, No. 49.

III. NORMAL SCHOOLS.

ABBEY, M. J. Normal school instruction in agriculture. U. S. Department of Agriculture. Office of Experiment Station. Circular 90, 1909.

BALCOMB, E. E. Agriculture in normal schools : Course of instruction and financial support. In National Education Association. Journal of proceedings and addresses, 1907. pp. 752–758.

EVANS, CHARLES, and FRENCH, W. L. The work of the normal school in preparing teachers of agriculture. In National Education Association. Journal of proceedings and addresses, 1908, pp. 1194–1199.

JOHNSON, D. B. Agriculture in normal schools. Conference for education in the South. Proceedings, 1910. pp. 242–250.

KIRK, J. R. Agriculture and domestic science in normal schools with special reference to preparing teachers for community work. In National Education Association. Journal of proceedings and addresses, 1911. pp. 1152–1156.

STORM, A. V. The relation of the agricultural college to the State normal school. In National Education Association. Journal of proceedings and addresses, 1913. pp. 516–521.

IV. TEACHER TRAINING.

ASSOCIATION OF AMERICAN AGRICULTURAL COLLEGES AND EXPERIMENT STATIONS. Committee on Instruction in Agriculture. Work of agricultural colleges in training teachers of agriculture for secondary schools. U. S. Department of Agriculture. Office of Experiment Stations. Circular 118, 1913.

BAILEY, L. H. On the training of persons to teach agriculture in the public schools. U. S. Bureau of Education. Bulletin, 1913, No. 1.

BOOK, W. F. The training and certification of teachers for agricultural industries and household arts subjects in the public schools of Indiana. Indiana Department of Public Instruction. Educational publications. Bulletin 5, 1914.

CROSBY, D. J. Training courses for teachers of agriculture. In U. S. Department of Agriculture. Yearbook, 1907. pp. 207–220.

JACKSON, E. R. Agricultural training courses for employed teachers. U. S. Department of Agriculture. Bulletin 7, 1913.

JARVIS, C. D. Vocational teachers for secondary schools: What the land-grant colleges are doing to prepare them. U. S. Bureau of Education. Bulletin, 1917, No. 38.

NATIONAL EDUCATION ASSOCATION. Preparation of teachers for agricultural education. In its Journal of proceedings and addresses, 1908. pp. 294-312.

PEABODY COLLEGE. The Seaman A. Knapp School and Farm (for the Training of Teachers). Bulletin 2, vol. 1, 1913.

TEXAS AGRICULTURAL AND MECHANICAL COLLEGE. Department of Agricultural Education. Agricultural education at the Agricultural and Mechanical College of Texas. Bulletin No. 1, 1918.

The training of teachers for agricultural instruction. Canada Agricultural Gazette, 3: 916-924, 1916.

V. ORGANIZATION AND SUPERVISION.

FEDERAL BOARD FOR VOCATIONAL EDUCATION. Agricultural education: Some problems in State supervision. Bulletin 26, 1918.

—— Agricultural education organization and administration. Bulletin 13.

BUTTERFIELD, K. L. A State system of agricultural education. In Massachusetts Agricultural College. Bulletin 8, No. 2. pp. 29-47, 1916.

MASSACHUSETTS BOARD OF EDUCATION. State-aided vocational agricultural education in 1912. Bulletin 3, 1913.

—— State-aided vocational agricultural education in 1914. Bulletin 3, 1915.
—— State-aided vocational agricultural education in 1915. Bulletin 5, 1916.
—— Information relative to the establishment and administration of county agricultural schools and agricultural departments. Bulletin 23, 1916.

MICHIGAN AGRICULTURAL COLLEGE. Department of Agricultural Education. Reports on agriculture in the high schools of Michigan. Bulletin 8, 1912; bulletin 12, 1913; bulletin 13, 1914; bulletin 15, 1915; bulletin 16, 1916.

NEW YORK (State). Education Department. Agricultural education in secondary schools. Bulletin No. 624, 1916.

—— —— Schools of agriculture, mechanic arts, and home making. Bulletins, 1910; No. 548, 1913; No. 626, 1916.

—— —— Vocational schools. Bulletin No. 566, 1914.

STEWART, J. S. Annual report of the eleventh district agricultural school of Georgia. Georgia State College of Agriculture.

STIMSON, R. W. The Massachusetts home-product plan of vocational agricultural education. U. S. Bureau of Education. Bulletin, 1914, No. 8.

○

DEPARTMENT OF THE INTERIOR
BUREAU OF EDUCATION

BULLETIN, 1919, No. 86

ADMINISTRATION AND SUPERVISION OF VILLAGE SCHOOLS

By

W. S. DEFFENBAUGH
SPECIALIST IN VILLAGE AND CITY SCHOOL ADMINISTRATION

AND

J. C. MUERMAN
SPECIALIST IN RURAL EDUCATION

WASHINGTON
GOVERNMENT PRINTING OFFICE
1920

CONTENTS.

3

ILLUSTRATIONS.

4

LETTER OF TRANSMITTAL.

DEPARTMENT OF THE INTERIOR,
BUREAU OF EDUCATION,
Washington, September 25, 1919.

SIR: In the United States there are more than ten thousand villages and towns having a population less than 2,500. These are usually not included in our discussion of rural schools and rural school problems, nor in our plans for rural school improvement. Nor are they generally included in plans for the improvement of city schools. Yet these villages offer excellent opportunities for combining many of the best features of both country and city schools, without the handicap of obstructing elements in either. Indeed, it is not improbable that in the future both the schools of the large cities and the schools of the open country may turn to the village schools for lessons in effective organization on the one side, and freedom of initiative and individuality on the other. At any rate, there is much need for careful study of the actual and the possible opportunities for education in these thousands of villages, in which nearly ten million of the people of the United States live.

For the purpose of calling attention to this neglected part of our systems of education, I have within the past two years called and directed several conferences of persons engaged in or directly interested in the work of village schools, and have had the results of a study of this subject prepared in the form of a manuscript, which I am transmitting herewith and which I recommend for publication as a bulletin of the Bureau of Education. It is my purpose to have more detailed studies made of particular phases of village school work, and studies of the special needs and opportunities of the schools in agricultural villages, mining villages, and mill villages. The results of these studies will be submitted for publication as they are completed.

Respectfully submitted.

P. P. CLAXTON,
Commissioner.

The SECRETARY OF THE INTERIOR.

5

ADMINISTRATION AND SUPERVISION OF VILLAGE SCHOOLS.

INTRODUCTION.

The village in America.—In general, any compact community of less than 2,500 population is considered a village. No data are available showing how many villages there are in the United States. The census report for 1910 gives 11,784 municipal corporations of less than 2,500 population. To these must be added the many small places that have not been incorporated for municipal purposes. In New England only a few villages are incorporated, the town [1] government serving the needs of the village as well as of the rural sec· tions of the town.

In 1910 the population of incorporated places of less than 2,500 was 8.8 per cent of the total population of the United States. If the unincorporated villages and the immediate territory for which the villages serve as trading centers were added, the population living in villages and within their influence would amount to probably 30 per cent or more.

There are several types of villages—the industrial, the agricultural, and the suburban.

·The industrial village may be either a mining or a manufacturing village, or both. As a rule it has no intimate relation with the surrounding country. If it is a mining town there are usually from 100 to 2,500 inhabitants, most of whom are engaged in mining. The men who work in the mines live in small houses, usually erected and owned by the company and rented to the miner. At one side of the town may be found the houses of the mine officials and store managers. Practically the entire population of the typical coal mining village is made up of foreigners—Slavs, Italians, and Poles. It is not unusual to find 10 to 20 different nationalities represented in a mining town.

The manufacturing town is somewhat different. A better class of houses is found, and a general higher average of intelligence, from the fact that greater skill is needed in a manufacturing than in a mining community.

---

[1] The New England town corresponds to the township in some other States.

The suburban village is really a part of the near-by city and should be classed with it. In the suburban village there are churches and schools, but the business interests of most of the inhabitants are in the city.

The agricultural village serves a community much larger than the village itself. It is only a part of a larger rural community. The country village serves as a trading center for the farmers of the neighborhood. Every week a large per cent of the farmers visit the village to trade at the stores, to have farm implements repaired, to deposit their money in the bank, or to attend meetings of fraternal organizations. The farmer's wife, too, goes to the village upon various errands. The young people look to the village for entertainment and amusement, as baseball games, picture shows, etc.

- *Special types of villages.*—Besides these types of village, several special types may be mentioned. For example, there exists in Utah a type not found to any extent in other States. As the early settlers were of one faith, they usually followed the commands given them by their spiritual leaders. Among the first of these commands was: " Till the soil; learn the lesson of the land; do not search for gold or other precious metals or minerals."

The people were sent out in groups to form settlements, build churches and schools, and also stockades for defense against the Indians, who at that time were none too friendly. Farms were selected either by the church officials or by the settler himself, but the farmer lived in the village. The distance to the farm varied from an "easy walking distance" (about a mile and a half) to 5 or 10 miles. When new settlers arrived, they formed groups beyond the 10 or 15 mile limit, and thus each village became a self-supporting social center. Because of this natural isolation, they became more united internally by the social, religious, and economic situations, and to a less extent were influenced by external conditions. Thus, when the village was created, the opportunity for a central consolidated school was offered.

The farmer living in a village is in almost daily contact with his fellow farmers. He avoids the isolation and loneliness of the open country farmer, who may go a mile or much more to find his nearest neighbor.

These so-called village farmers take great interest in schools, and enjoy many of the comforts of a semiurban life. In general, their lives are more complete and satisfactory than those of isolated farmers.

Another type of village is found in the section where there are abandoned mines. This offers a peculiar situation for the schools that once prospered and flourished in the midst of good live mining centers. Because of the absolue failure of the mines to produce ore in abundance, or in paying quantities, fine old buildings once used as stores, dwellings, or schools are now partially boarded up or entirely abandoned. These tell their story of better days now long past. One of these abandoned villages has an excellent school building of eight rooms, once inadequate to accommodate the numerous children enrolled; now but one room is in use, and that is ample to accommodate the present attendance. It is doubtful if any great number of these towns will ever again become active, flourishing business centers. However, a few have turned their attention to manufacturing certain commodities, such as brick, tile, etc., which may, in time, bring back some of their former economic prosperity. Towns of this type are found in Nevada, Idaho, Washington, California, and Oregon in the West, and in some of the middle Western States, as Ohio, Indiana, and Illinois.

The shifting of the lumber industry caused a few abandoned villages, for in some places the timber, once so abundant, was finally cut, and the mills were moved to other parts, where timber could still be had. Fortunately, however, the " stump land," left after the trees are gone, can be tilled; and the erstwhile lumberjack may become an efficient farmer, provided he can solve the problem of a cheap and economical way of clearing the logged-off land. The central school will remain in the town or village.

Another type of village is that created by the recent war. In sites where munition factories were located " mushroom " towns filled with war workers sprang into existence almost overnight. Large school buildings, at an unusually large cost, have been built in these towns, many of which are now abandoned because it is no longer necessary to manufacture munitions of war.

The agricultural village is usually thought of when the term village is used, and this type is kept chiefly in mind in the preparation of this bulletin.

ADMINISTRATION.

DIFFERENT PLANS IN OPERATION.

As might be expected in a country where each State makes its own laws regarding the administration of its schools, there are many methods of administering the village schools.

In New England a town school committee administers the schools of the village or villages within the town, and there is no village school board. In some States, as Pennsylvania, schools in incorporated villages are administered by a village or borough school board, while the schools in unincorporated villages are administered

by the township school board. In States where the district system
prevails the village and possibly some territory surrounding the village comprise a school district, which is under the control of a local
board. In some States, as in Maryland and Alabama, where the
county is the unit of school administration, the county board of education has control of all the villages in the county, just as the town
school committee in Massachusetts has control of the schools in all
the villages within the town.

The town system of New England, or the county system, is without doubt the best plan, by reason of the fact that the town school
committee may district the town or the county board the county along
natural community lines. In districting for school purposes boun-
dary lines of the incorporated village should be disregarded, especially in the agricultural sections of the country where the village
is an integral part of the rural community and all the children of
the community should attend the same school. In other words, since
the village is the center of life for a considerable territory, it should
be the consolidation center.

THE VILLAGE AS A CONSOLIDATION CENTER.

One student of the village in its relation to the country, in commenting on the natural school district, says:[1]

In the realm of education the identification of the natural with the legal
community is being realized to a considerable extent by the union high-school
movement in its various forms. In many States the town has long had an
independent school district somewhat larger than its municipal limits. It was
patronized also by many country youth living beyond the district. These paid
tuition in lieu of taxes, and were admitted or not at the pleasure of the town
educational authorities. The next step was to authorize the township to pay
the tuition for its high-school pupils in the town school and to compel the
school to receive them if it had room. Here many States stuck; the more
progressive, however, have enacted union high-school laws. Thus, in Wisconsin, any contiguous area of 36 square miles defined by section lines may
organize itself for high-school support and maintenance. So far forth this
allows the town center to associate its dependent country with it in the secondary phase of education. But the trade area of a town of 3,000 population
in a northwestern State with average density of population may be 100 square
miles instead of 36. Minnesota therefore goes farther: Any county, upon
petition of 25 per cent of its residents, must appoint a county school survey
commission, which redistricts the county on the basis of actual communities.
Education is thus freed from arbitrary political units and allowed to organize
on a basis of geographical and social facts. The report of the commission, with
maps and diagrams, then comes before the voters in a special election. Under
this law Douglas County, for example, with 20 townships and 648 square miles
of area, reduced its 84 district schools to 24, following in the main natural
rather than township boundaries.

---

[1] The Little Town, p. 200, Harlan Paul Douglass.

Commenting on the Minnesota plan, Prof. Cubberley observes: " If established in a little village, itself the natural center of a rural community, such central schools can become the very center both of the village and of the community life." [1]

An idea of natural communities may be had from the following diagram: [2]

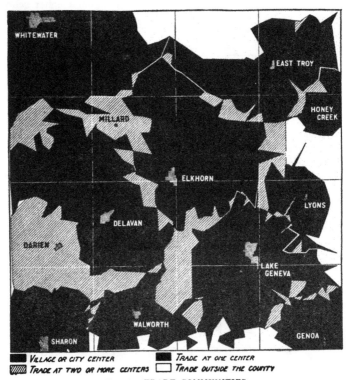

VILLAGE OR CITY CENTER   TRADE AT ONE CENTER

TRADE AT TWO OR MORE CENTERS   TRADE OUTSIDE THE COUNTY

FIG 1.—TRADE COMMUNITIES.

Twelve villages and small cities situated in the county serve as trade centers for the farm homes precisely as for the village and city homes, and all the homes trading at the same center form a trade community. Township lines 6 miles apart indicate the distance.

Why the village is not more often a consolidation point.—Even in many counties and townships where the school boards have authority to make school districts on community lines, with the village as part of the community, they have failed to do so. There are several reasons why a barrier has been set up between village and country schools. One, as already mentioned, is the fact that villages are per-

1 Cubberley. Rural Life and Education, p. 246f.
2 University of Wisconsin Bulletin No. 34.

mitted to have independent school systems, thus shutting off the children of the outlying districts. As a result there are often two or three one-room schools within a few miles of a village. In Pennsylvania, for instance, where the boundaries of the village school district are coterminous with the boundaries of the incorporation and the village school district is entirely independent of the township, only 4 per cent of the villages reporting have no one-teacher schools

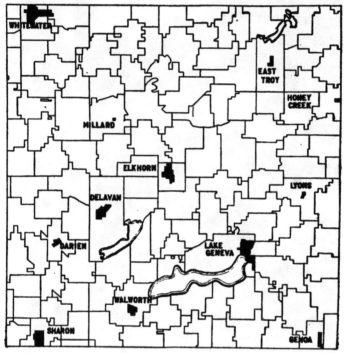

FIG. 2.—Shows the school districts in the county. If the school districts correspond to the natural districts, the number could be reduced to the number of village centers.

within a radius of 2½ miles; while 55 per cent have from 1 to 3 one-teacher schools, and 41 per cent have 4 or more one-teacher schools within that radius. The following table, compiled from replies by village school principals to a questionnaire shows the per cent of villages in several States having within a radius of 2½ miles of the village no one-teacher shool, one to three, and four or more such schools.

Per cent of villages having no 1-room schools, 1 to 3, and 4 or more within 2¼ miles.

States.	None.	1 to 3.	4 or more.	States.	None.	1 to 3.	4 or more.
	Per cent.	Per cent.	Per cent.		Per cent.	Per cent.	Per cent.
North Dakota..........	70	30	0	Indiana...................	35	55	10
Colorado.................	68	28	4	Iowa.....................	33	44	23
Florida...................	65	35	0	Maine....................	33	64	3
North Carolina...........	57	31	12	Wisconsin................	22	59	19
Idaho....................	50	50	0	New York................	15	52	33
New Jersey..............	47	47	6	Illinois...................	9	66	25
Oklahoma................	44	53	3	Pennsylvania.............	4	55	41
Maryland................	36	48	16				

The following map shows conditions in one township where the villages in the township have an independent school organization:

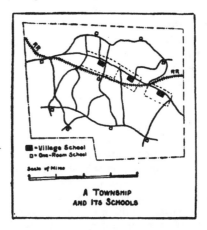

A TOWNSHIP
AND ITS SCHOOLS

It may be noted that there are 9 one-room schools within a few miles of one or another of the three villages. Two of the villages are contiguous. There is a high school in each of the three villages, one having a four-year course and the other two a two-year course. The school board in the township has to pay tuition to the village high school that the children living in the township attend. There are four school boards within the township lines. Other examples of like nature could be given.

Another reason why the village has not been more used as the consolidation center is that the country people hesitate to send their children to the village school for fear that they will be lured away from the farm, because the village schools do not teach subjects related to country life. It may be said that neither do the country schools, especially the one-room schools, teach subjects related to country life. The objection to the village as a consolidation point on the ground that the course of study is not suited to rural needs can be and should be overcome, not only for the sake of the country child but for the sake of the village child. If, however, the village schools are independent of the township or the country, the intro- -duction of such courses is not an easy matter, for the village school authorities too often look upon the city schools as models for the village to imitate.

Value of consolidated country and village schools.—It is evident that consolidation with the village would not make school conditions worse than they now are in many communities where there are 4 or 5, or even more, one-room schools within a few miles of the village. These one-room schools can not minister fully to the social and intellectual needs of the entire community, since a community as a rule is larger than the district served by the one-room school; neither do they tend to hold children on the farm; rather, they tend to drive them away. The course of study in the one-room country school can not be vitalized to any great extent, while the village school course can be.

If all the schools of a community are consolidated at the center of practical everyday life, the children of the entire community, village children as well as country children, may be brought to- gether. In consequence their vision would become broader. As it now is, with country children attending poor one-room schools and village children attending a better school, there is an enmity between them. The rural children frequently refer to the town children as " stuck-ups," and the village children speak of the country children as " Rubes." The village child would no longer be pitted against the country child if it were understood that each belongs to the same community and that both have the same interests.

Before there can be a reorganization and upbuilding of country life the villager and the countryman must cooperate. Neither can shut himself off from the other. The village must become a part of the community or it will become decadent, as have some villages that have tried to ape city ways instead of attempting to serve and work with the community upon which their prosperity depends. The lack of cooperation, however, can not be attributed entirely to the villager.

The farmer and the villager have in too many instances not thought together; each has been for himself. The signs of the times, however, point toward better cooperation. Rural life conferences in every State are bringing town and country in closer touch with those things common to the lives of both. One way to bring about co- operation is to think together. One school for the entire community will help bring about community thinking; that is, if there be de- veloped the type of school which meets the needs of the entire community, and if the school be made the center of all community activities of a recreational, social, and educational nature.

Instead of the weak one-room school and the village school, which are usually doing nothing more than attempting to teach the three R's, there should be a village community school with a course of study based upon rural life. If the country schools form a consolidation group by themselves and do not include the village, there will still be a line of demarcation between the village and the surrounding country, although they should be one.

Before it is possible for some States to have village community schools, the plan of having the village schools independent of the rest of the community must be abandoned and a town or county system substituted, thus making it possible for school boards to consolidate the schools of a community at or near its business center.

An illustration of a village as a consolidation point.—The consolidated school at Five Points, Chambers County, Ala., is an illustration of what a community school may do, not only for the village, but for the entire community as well. Before the establishment of the consolidated school at Five Points the village and the surrounding country were dead; there was but little interest in farming. There was no intellectual or social life. The entire community was becoming " deader " each year. Finally, through the influence of a few men and women, a consolidated school was organized at Five Points, a village of 300 population. What was a dead village with a few stores became alive.

Before consolidation, the most unattractive building at Five Points was the school building. It was weather-beaten and dingy, consisting of two classrooms—a large one with a stage, and a small one—and a dark and narrow hall. It was poorly equipped with uncomfortable homemade desks, and it had painted walls for blackboards. The absence of windowpanes reenforced the usual free ventilation of such an old building. It was uncomfortable, insanitary, and uninviting; yet the children, the most precious product of the village and its most valuable asset, were compelled to spend seven hours each day, five days a week, and seven months each year, in this makeshift of a school building. The children living in the country fared even worse, since they attended one or two teacher schools even poorer than the one at the village of Five Points.

Now the village children and country children living 6 or 7 miles from Five Points attend the same school, in a modern school building on 11 acres of land located about one-third of a mile from the center of the village.

There are four classrooms, four cloak rooms, a principal's office, and hallways on the first floor; and two classrooms and an auditorium seating several hundred people on the second floor. The basement is divided into two parts. One part is subdivided into three apartments—a furnace room, a manual training room, and sanitary toilets for boys. The other part contains a room for domestic science and sanitary toilets for girls. There is sufficient room left for a playroom for primary children, which is used on rainy days. Every modern convenience is enjoyed by the teachers and pupils of the school. Electric lights, steam heat, and sanitary toilets make the building modern and in sharp contrast to the old building and to the dilapidated houses formerly attended by the country children.

The 11-acre tract of ground upon which the school is located is sufficiently large for a lawn, a garden, a demonstration plat, a playground for the little children, and athletic grounds for the older ones. Playgrounds have already been laid off, and plans have been outlined for practical work in agriculture.

One of the State school officials says:

In the early spring of 1916 I visited the country schools, afterward consolidated with those at Five Points. The day was a fair one, and each teacher reported an attendance for that day to be about the average for the session. By school count there were 44 pupils in attendance at Five Points, 28 at one of the country schools, 26 at another, and 14 at another, making a total of 112 for all the schools in the consolidation. On the day of my visit one year later I found 190 pupils, or an increased attendance of 78. Four transportation wagons conveyed 90 children to school that day.

The term of schools under the old plan was seven months, and five teachers were doing the work in four different schools. Under the consolidated school plan the term is nine months, and the work is done by six teachers [the increased enrollment making more teachers necessary].

Before consolidation the high-school enrollment was 13; now it is 52. The increase in enrollment in the elementary grades has been 68 per cent, and in the high schools 300 per cent, while the expense of conducting the school has increased only 50 per cent.

The increased enrollment and better attendance are due to the fact that older pupils who had lost interest in school because of the inefficiency of the one-teacher schools have again enrolled. Under the old plan only a year or two of high-school work was offered. Now the course is four years.

The location of the consolidated school at Five Points has proved a blessing not only to the children, but to the adults. The whole community, country and town, has been organized into the Five Points Community Association, in which young and old alike are eligible to membership. This organization holds meetings biweekly at the school building. The people do not meet merely for the sake of holding a meeting, but to discuss community problems and current topics. The work of the community association is carried on by committees. A good idea of it may be had from the following outline:

1. *A committee on public schools.*—The duty of this committee is to improve and beautify school premises; to increase the supply of school apparatus; to build up a library; to provide playground equipment; to encourage school attendance; to provide instruction for the illiterate and others desiring a common-school education, but who are unable to attend the day school; and to encourage school visitation by patrons.

2. *A committee on health and community sanitation.*—It is the duty of this committee to obtain united effort of the community to maintain sanitary conditions; to combat epidemics; to exterminate germ-carrying insects; to provide for the distribution of health bulletins; and to invite speakers from time to time to discuss health problems before the association.

3. *A committee on literary, musical, and social culture.*—This committee provides occasional literary and musical entertainments and social gatherings; has charge of the magazine exchange; arranges educational games; organizes and conducts a story-tellers' league and a reading circle.

4. *A committee on agriculture and home economics.*—This important committee cooperates with the county demonstration agent and other agencies established for the upbuilding of agricultural interests; improves home-life facilities in the community; arranges for farmers' educational meetings from time to time; plans the organization of pig, poultry, and canning clubs; and introduces approved systems of cooperative industries.

5. *A committee on finances.*—This committee considers the needs of every department of work and proposes quarterly budgets for the intelligent guidance of the association in making appropriations. It devises ways and means of securing funds for the prosecution of the association's work.

The biweekly meetings are usually begun with a short business session, after which the association separates into departments, conferences, and study classes. There is a class in current events, another for story telling and child training, and a farmers' round table conference. The members of the association naturally group themselves in certain classes. However, they are at liberty to attend any group meeting which they may desire.

After the departmental meetings, the entire association assembles in the school auditorium for literary and musical entertainment and for general conference or a social hour. This part of the program is varied from time to time.

These meetings occupy about two and a half hours. The average attendance since the organization of the association has been about 200 persons.

154724°—20—Bull. 86——2

When there were several schools within a few miles of Five Points the community was divided. Now it works together, to the advantage of the village and of country people alike.

This one illustration shows how a decadent village community may be made alive by consolidating rural and village schools.

THE VILLAGE SCHOOL BOARD.

Size.—In villages having an independent school system the number of school board members varies, but not to the same extent as in city school systems. Three or five members usually constitute a village school board. The experience of city school. systems has demonstrated that the small board is preferable to the large one, and the tendency has been to reduce the sizes of city boards of education to not more than nine members. A village school system being simple, no one would advocate a board of more than five members. Many village schools are efficiently administered by a board of three members. In a small board responsibility can be definitely placed. The board can act as a committee of the whole and not through standing committees and discuss matters informally. The principal can sit at the table with the board and present and explain his plans to three or five members better than he can to a large board.

Term of office.—In many village school districts a majority of the school board is elected each year. In some districts all members of the board are elected at the same time every two or three years. A short term is not conducive to good schools; neither is complete renewal at the expiration of a term, no matter what its length. If the term is short, an entirely new board may be elected every few years, which tends to unsettle the policy of conducting the schools. When·a new man is elected to board membership it takes him some months to learn conditions and the best way of meeting them. If there is an entirely new board, which is possible with entire renewal at the end of a term, there is no one to guide the new members, except possibly the principal of schools. There may, however, be a new principal; in which case there will be no experienced leadership. If a board is composed almost entirely of new members, the principal who has worked to educate his board so that certain reforms may be brought about may find that he has to begin all over again.

Method of choosing.—Practically all village school boards are elected by popular vote. In a few instances the mayor appoints the board members. The prevailing opinion is that school boards should be elected. If the territory included in the village school district is larger than that of the village corporation, no other method should be considered. If the people vote directly for school-board members, the school question is brought directly to the attention of the public, while if the mayor or some of the village officials appoint the school board, the schools may be forgotten when the municipal officers are elected. If the mayor appoints the school board, it may listen to him in the management of the schools.

Board members should be elected at a special election held in the schoolhouse. By this method school-board members are more likely to be elected without regard to political parties. If elected at a regular election, partisan politics often enters into the choice of school boards. At a special election the voters exercise more care in voting for a candidate than at the regular election where village, county, and State officials are given more consideration than school officials.

Officers.—School boards usually organize with a president and a secretary from their own number. Where it is permissible for the board to elect a treasurer, he is generally chosen from their own number.

The only officer that should be chosen from the school-board membership is the president. If the county, township, or municipal treasurer is not custodian of the school funds, a trust company or a bank should be made the treasurer.

The village school principal may well be the clerk of the board. In large cities the secretary or clerk of the board is not a board member, but one skilled in accounts. He, with a clerical force, devotes all his time to the business affairs of the board. In the smaller cities school boards are beginning to make the superintendent's clerk the secretary of the board. In the village the principal can easily be the board's secretary. In the larger villages the stipend usually paid the clerk of the board should be used to employ, on part time, stenographic and clerical assistance for the principal. The clerk to the principal could keep the books of the board and assist in keeping other school records.

Function.—The function of the village school board is practically the same as that of the city school board. It represents the people in the management of their schools somewhat as a board of directors of a private corporation represents the stockholders.

In doing this the board legislates, decides upon policies of expansion, etc., and turns the technical execution of the work over to an expert manager or superintendent, who, in turn, names the other experts needed.

Since the dividends of a school system are not tangible, as are the dividends of a private corporation, school boards often do not use business methods in the administration of the schools. They go along in a hit-or-miss fashion, each member considering himself fully qualified to give advice as to the execution of the policies adopted by the board.

The first duty of a village school board is to employ a superintendent or principal of schools and hold him responsible for the management of the schools. If a superintendent or principal refuses to assume such responsibility, he should be requested to resign, so that some one with more courage may be employed.

In order that there may be a clear understanding regarding the duties of the principal and other employees of the school board, a few rules should be adopted and a general scheme of organization adhered to.

The following rules regarding the duties of the principal are suggested:

1. The principal of schools shall be the executive officer of the board of education and shall have oversight of the work of all other employees of the school board.

2. He shall recommend teachers and other employees. No teacher, supervisor, or janitor shall be elected by the board who is not recommended by the principal.

3. He shall have full responsibility for the promotion, assignment, and transfer of teachers.

4. He shall be held responsible for the general efficiency of the school system, for the development of the teaching force, and for the growth and welfare of the pupils.

5. He shall be responsible for all rules and regulations governing the admission, transfer, classification, and promotion of pupils.

6. He shall prepare, distribute, and collect all blanks and reports required by law and such other blanks and reports as he shall deem necessary for the intelligent and systematic conduct of the schools.

7. He shall select and recommend suitable textbooks (if the State or county adoption system does not prevail) and supplementary books. No book or apparatus shall be adopted by the board which is not recommended by the principal.

8. He shall prepare and recommend to the board for adoption the course of study for the elementary and the high school (provided there is not a mandatory State or county course of study).

9. He shall make monthly and annual reports to the board relative to conditions in the schools, and shall make recommendations for their increased efficiency.

10. He shall be responsible for the methods of instruction and management used by the teachers and shall have authority to hold such meetings of teachers as he deems necessary for their instruction and guidance.

11. He shall at least once each term report to the board upon the general condition of the teaching and supervisory forces, and especially with reference to those teachers or supervisors whose services are not proving satisfactory.

12. He shall first pass upon all complaints of parents and others who may appeal from his decision to the school board.

13. He shall have general oversight of the school property and report to the board what repairs are needed.

14. He shall have supervision of janitor work.

15. In order that the principal may comply with the foregoing rules, he should teach only part time in schools of fewer than 8 or 10 rooms, and in larger schools he should have practically all his time free for supervision.

Rules similar to the above help make clear the duties of the principal, but a principal who does nothing more than obey the rules laid down by a school board is a failure.

The proper relationship in a village school system may be illustrated as follows:

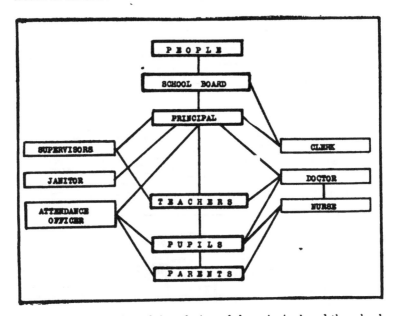

A further discussion of the relation of the principal and the school board in villages independent of the township may be found on page 24.

Business.—One of the weak points in the administration of many village schools is that business principles are often wholly ignored, school accounts are kept in a haphazard fashion, and public funds wastefully expended. No matter how small the school system, the clerk of the school board should keep a set of books showing amounts appropriated from different sources and to whom and for what purpose every dollar and cent has been paid. Public accounting requires as much care as private accounting.

Bookkeeping blanks based on the classification of expenditures following may be had from several publishing houses, or they may be printed by a local printer.

CLERK'S FINANCIAL RECORD.

EXPENSES INCURRED FOR FISCAL YEAR ENDING ...., 19....　I. GENERAL CONTROL.

Warrant.		To whom issued.	Amount.	Board of Education. Clerk's Office.	School election. School census.	Educational administration.	Other expenses.	Total.	Supervision.
No.	Date.								

II. INSTRUCTION.　　　　III. AUXILIARY AGENCIES.

Salaries of teachers.	Supplies used in instruction.	Text books.	Other expenditures of instruction.	Total.	Library.	Lectures and other auxiliary agencies.	Transportation.	Total.

IV. OPERATION OF PLANT.　　　V. MAINTENANCE OF PLANT.

Janitor wages and supplies.	Fuel.	Water, light, power.	Other expenses of operation.	Total.	Repair and upkeep of buildings and grounds.	Repair and upkeep of equipment.	Insurance.	Other expenses.	Total.

Grand total current disbursements.	VI.		VII. CAPITAL OUTLAY.				PAYMENTS OF INDEBTEDNESS.		
	Depreciation of plant (estimated).	Final grand total current disbursements.	Land.	New building.	Additional equipment, alterations, etc.	Total.	Short time notes.	Bonded principal.	Debt interest.
	Red ink	Red ink							

By distributing expenses under the different headings, as teachers' salaries, textbooks, etc., it is possible to ascertain the proportion of funds expended for these purposes. Data can also be compiled showing cost per pupil enrolled and in average daily attendance for instruction, operation of plant, etc. Just what proportion of funds should be expended for each item is not definitely known, but a fair estimate based upon practice in small cities would be as follows, and probably would not vary much from this for villages: Teaching and supervision, 70 to 75 per cent of the total current disbursements; supervision alone, 7 to 10 per cent; teaching alone, 60 to 68 per cent; janitors' salaries, 5 to 7 per cent; textbooks and supplies, 4 to 6 per cent; fuel, 5 to 7 per cent; repairs, 3 to 5 per cent.

Many school boards waste public funds by purchasing maps, charts, and apparatus that are not used or that have no educational value. Maps, charts, and apparatus are necessary, but it is unnecessary to pay exorbitant prices. No apparatus should be purchased without first being recommended by the principal of schools. If school boards would adhere to this practice, more money would be available for teachers' salaries, and apparatus suitable for school needs would be purchased.

THE VILLAGE SUPERVISING PRINCIPAL AND HIS WORK.

A supervising principal is one who does not teach or who teaches less than half time. Any principal who teaches most or all of the day should be classed as a teacher; probably head teacher or teaching principal would be the correct term.

No other school position carries with it a greater diversity of work than the supervising principalship of a village school. In a large or medium sized city school system the work of the superintendent is somewhat specialized, since he devotes most of his time to the larger problems of administration and organization. He supervises indirectly through his assistant superintendents, supervisors, and principals. In a small system of schools the principal must do a score or more of things. He must be an administrator, an organizer, and a supervisor. He must be an investigator, a school surveyor, a school-efficiency expert, a playground director, and a general utility man. He must write letters, usually without the aid of a stenographer; he must meet people with grievances and keep his temper; he must settle difficulties that arise between teacher and pupil, between pupil and pupil, and between teacher and parent; he must be the leader of educational thought in his community, educating school boards, teachers, and taxpayers as to the educational needs of the village. Thus one might continue to enumerate almost indefinitely the many things that require the direct attention of the supervising principal of a village school.

QUALIFICATIONS.

Since the duties of a village school principal are so multifarious, he should be a person of broad education. In general, he should be a college graduate who has had several courses in a school of education. School boards should not consider a young college graduate for a village school principalship who has not elected courses in education; yet comparatively few of the young men and women just out of college and applying for the principalship of village schools have made any extended study of school administration and supervision, especially of the administration and supervision of village schools.

The preparation necessary for the principalship of a village school should include a study of such school rather than a study of city schools. He should not only make a study of the village school but of the village community. Probably more young village school principals fail because they do not understand village habits and customs than 'for any other reason.

Since the scheme of organization of the village school is exceedingly simple, the principal deals directly with teachers and parents. He is also close to the pupils, knowing most of them by name and where they live in the village. Thus the administration of a village school system becomes largely a personal matter. The principal should for this reason know village life, its psychology and its sociology. He should know what forces are at work and how they can be manipulated and directed in the administration of the schools and in the socialization of the village community.

RELATION TO SCHOOL BOARD.

In villages having school boards of their own the school principal should stand in practically the same relation to the school board as does the superintendent of a city school system. He should nominate teachers; select textbooks if in a State where there is local adoption; prepare courses of study, if there is not a county or State course that he must follow; and even then he must elaborate and work out in detail such course. He must be free to assign teachers to the grades for which they are best suited. He should also prepare the annual budget for the consideration of the school board. These are some of the administrative duties of a village principal, and unless the school board requires them of him, it is wasting public funds by employing a principal. If, for instance, the teachers are not nominated by the principal but by the members of the school board, the teaching corps may not yield to supervision, owing allegiance to the school-board member who nominated them. If the school-board members are inclined to meddle in matters of school discipline and instruction, the teachers naturally look to them and ignore the principal.

The relation of a village school board to the principal of schools does not differ materially from the relation that a board of bank directors sustains to the cashier or the president of the bank, or that the board of directors of any private corporation sustains to the superintendent that it employs. The stockholders in a private corporation elect a board of directors to look after their interests in the conduct of the enterprise. These directors know but little about the technical details of the business they are empowered to administer. Few, if any, could do the work of one of the clerks or mechanics, much less supervise it: so they employ a superintendent to do this and hold him responsible for results. As another illustration, the relation of the board of directors of a hospital and the superintendent of the hospital may be mentioned. This board may be composed of laymen or of laymen and physiciahs, who appoint a superintendent of the hospital. None of the board members would think of interfering with the superintendent in his assignment of nurses, in administering medicine, and in other matters that are purely professional. If, in the opinion of the board, the superintendent is not skillful in his supervision, he is requested to resign and another is employed.

Some school board members are inclined to meddle in strictly professional matters, as school discipline, methods of instruction, promotion of pupils. Partly for this reason many village schools have remained on a low plane. If the directors of a business corporation attempt to dictate regarding matters upon which they are uninformed, or if the superintendent appointed by the board of directors of a private corporation is a figurehead, the corporation fails. The result is direct and the failure is known to all. If the principal of a village school is a figurehead only, the school fails; but the fact may not be known by the public, which often does not recognize what the duties of the school board and of the principal are and what a school should be. In brief, no board of directors, whether of a public or a private corporation, should attempt to do the work which it is paying an expert to do.

In county and township school systems, where the county or township school board administers the village schools, the principal should be subordinate to the county or township superintendent. He should have no direct relation to the school board, the board holding him responsible for results through the county or township superintendent. In other words, the village school principal in a county or township organization should have the same relation to the school board and the superintendent as the principal of a building or ward school in a city system has to the city school board and the city superintendent of schools.

SUPERVISION OF INSTRUCTION.

Notwithstanding the fact that there are a hundred and one matters that require the attention of a village school principal, he should give most of his attention to the supervision of instruction. Much of the poor teaching one finds in the village schools throughout the country is due largely to a lack of supervision or to the wrong kind. Of course, an exception must be made of those villages where politics, church membership, nepotism, and such things play a part in the selection of teachers, but in a village where the principal

selects his own teachers and exercises due care in their selection
something is wrong if many fail. There is a lack of supervision,
or poor methods are employed. If many pupils fail under the same
teacher year after year, the principal is not slow to declare that the
teaching is poor: It may be asserted with equal emphasis that if
many teachers fail year after year suspicion should point strongly
toward the principal. A village school principal is responsible for
the success or failure of the school system. Since success or failure
depends largely upon the kind of teaching, he must see to it that
teachers are employing good methods. This he can not do unless
he devotes much of his time to classroom visitation, to an analysis
of results, and to conference with teachers.

The methods of supervision employed by two village school principals illustrate the difference between good and poor methods.
Each of these villages employs about 20 teachers; the academic and
the professional preparation of the teachers in each village are practically the same. During the year the principal in one of these
villages visits each classroom about 15 times, averaging 15 minutes
each visit. Thus, approximately, 75 hours, or 12 school days out of
180, are devoted to visiting teachers for the purpose of supervising
instruction. In contrast the other principal visits each classroom
25 times a year, averaging an hour at each visit, a total of 83 school
days. In the former school the principal is not at all familiar with
the methods employed by the different teachers nor with the results
obtained; in the latter school the principal knows what each teacher
is doing and how she is doing it. In the one village the object of
the school is defeated to a large extent because the teaching is poor,
chiefly on account of a lack of supervision. The principal is tied to
his desk or is looking after details. In the other village the principal does not neglect necessary details, but he makes them subordinate to the larger matter of supervision of instruction, attending to
details before and after school hours and on Saturday mornings.

In many villages salaries are so low that well-qualified teachers
can not be obtained, the median salary for village school teachers
being between $500 and $600. Young inexperienced girls who have
had little or no academic or professional preparation must be employed. These must be trained in service. Even normal school and
college graduates, though they may have had the best instruction,
need to be broken into real school life situations. They need to be
shown how to apply their theories.

Before a principal can help his teachers he must diagnose classroom procedure and methods of instruction. He must observe the
teaching to see whether it conforms to certain standards. At the
outset a principal should inform the teachers of the standards by
which he is going to judge their instruction. He may, for example,
judge classroom instruction by the standards set up by Dr. Frank

McMurry, namely, (1) motive on the part of the pupils; (2) consideration of values by pupils; (3) attention to organization by pupils; (4) initiative by pupils. The principal may, when visiting a classroom, ask himself the following questions: Has the teacher reduced routine, as the passing of papers, leaving the room at recess periods, etc., to habit, so that there may be no waste of time? Is she supplementing and illustrating the text, or is she bound down to textbook questions and answers? Is she arousing interest in the class to such an extent that the pupils ask questions? Does she make careful and definite assignments of lessons?

A principal who desires a more detailed method of judging the efficiency of teachers may find the following efficiency record card, prepared by the department of education of the University of Chicago, helpful:

EFFICIENCY RECORD.

DETAILED RATINGS	V. P.	POOR.	MEDIUM.	GOOD.	EX.
I. Personal equipment— 1. General appearance					
2. Health					
3. Voice					
4. Intellectual capacity					
5. Initiative and self-reliance					
6. Adaptability and resourcefulness					
7. Accuracy					
8. Industry					
9. Enthusiasm and optimism					
10. Integrity and sincerity					
11. Self-control					
12. Promptness					
13. Tact					
14. Sense of justice					
II. Social and professional equipment— 15. Academic preparation					
16. Professional preparation					
17. Grasp of subject matter					
18. Understanding of children					
19. Interest in the life of the school					
20. Interest in the life of the community					
21. Ability to meet and interest patrons					
22. Interest in lives of pupils					
23. Cooperation and loyalty					
24. Professional interest and growth					
25. Daily preparation					
26. Use of English					
III. School management— 27. Care of light, heat, and ventilation					
28. Neatness of room					
29. Care of routine					
30. Discipline (governing skill)					
31. Definiteness and clearness of aim					
32. Skill in habit formation					
33. Skill in stimulating thought					
34. Skill in teaching how to study					
IV. Technique of teaching— 35. Skill in questioning					
36. Choice of subject matter					
37. Organization of subject matter					
38. Skill and care in assignment					
39. Skill in motivating work					
40. Attention to individual needs					
41. Attention and response of the class					
V. Results— 42. Growth of pupils in subject matter					
43. General development of pupils					
44. Stimulation of community					
45. Moral influence					
GENERAL RATING					

Recorded by................. .... Position............... ..... Date..................

EXPLANATION OF TERMS.

I. *Personal equipment* includes physical, mental, and moral qualities.

    1. *General appearance*—physique, carriage, dress, and personal neatness.

    3. *Voice*—pitch, quality, clearness of schoolroom voice.

    4. *Intellectual capacity*—native mental ability.

    5. *Initiative and self-reliance*—independence in originating and carrying out ideas.

    7. *Accuracy*—in statements, records, reports, and school work.

    10. *Integrity and sincerity*—soundness of moral principles and genuineness of character.

    13. *Tact*—adroitness, address, quick appreciation of the proper thing to do or say.

    14. *Sense of justice*—fair-mindedness, ability to give all a " square deal."

II. *Social and professional equipment* includes qualities making the teacher better able to deal with social situations and particularly the school situation.

    15. *Academic preparation*—school work other than professional. Adequacy for present work.

    16. *Professional preparation*—specific training for teaching. Adequacy for present work.

    17. *Grasp of subject matter*—command of the information to be taught or the skill to be developed.

    18. *Understanding of children*—insight into child nature; sympathetic, scientific, and practical.

    22. *Interest in lives of pupils*—desire to know and help pupils personally, outside of school subjects.

    23. *Cooperation and loyalty*—attitude toward colleagues and superior officers.

    24. *Professional interest and growth*—effort to keep up to date and improve.

    26. *Use of English*—vocabulary, grammar, ease of expression.

III. *School management* includes mechanical and routine factors.

    29. *Care of routine*—saving time and energy by reducing frequently recurring details to mechanical organization.

    30. *Discipline (governing skill)*—character of order maintained and skill shown in maintaining it.

IV. *Technique of teaching* includes skill in actual teaching and in the conduct of the recitation.

    31. *Definiteness and clearness of aim*—of each lesson and of the work as a whole.

    32. *Skill in habit formation*—skill in establishing specific, automatic responses quickly and permanently ; drill.

    33. *Skill in stimulating thought*—giving opportunity for and direction in reflective thinking.

    34. *Skill in teaching how to study*—establishing economical and efficient habits of study.

    35. *Skill in questioning*—character and distribution of questions ; replies elicited.

    36. *Choice of subject matter*—skill with which the teacher selects the material of instruction to suit the interests, abilities, and needs of the class.

    37. *Organization of subject matter*—the lesson plan and the system in which the subject matter is presented.

    39. *Skill in motivating work*—arousing interest and giving pupils proper incentives for work.

    40. *Attention to individual needs*—teacher's care for individual differences, peculiarities, and difficulties.

V. *Results* include evidence of the success of the above conditions and skill.

    41. *Attention and response of the class*—extent to which all of the class are interested in the essential part of the lesson and respond to the demands made on them.

    42. *Growth of pupils in subject matter*—shown by pupils' ability to do work of advanced class and to meet more successfully whatever tests are made of their school work.

    43. *General development of pupils*—increase in pupils' ability and power along lines other than those of subject matter.

    44. *Stimulation of community*—effect on life of the community, tending to improve or stimulate its various activities.

    45. *Moral influence*—extent to which the teacher raises the moral tone of the pupils or of the school.

Some such standards would make it clear to teachers what is expected of them. It has happened that teachers have failed of reelection and have not known why. If the principal would establish certain standards, it would be comparatively easy to point out wherein a teacher has failed. If there are no standards, the teacher can easily defend herself by saying, "I did not know that I was expected to do this."

Besides subjective standards there should be objective ones, a number of which have been prepared and are in common use. By using such tests a principal has a measure for comparing results within his school system and with other school systems in arithmetic, spelling, penmanship, and a few other subjects. If, for instance, the pupils of one teacher fall below the standard score in an arithmetic test and fail to make the progress that they should in a definite period, the principal is forced to the conclusion that something is wrong, that the course of study is not suited to the age and grade of the pupils or that the teaching is inferior. Such test will help the principal diagnose. In a recent school survey it was found that the score made in spelling was below standard in practically every grade. The cause of the poor showing was found to be in the method of selecting the words for study rather than in the methods of teaching, which were considered good. Unusual instead of common words were as a rule selected by the teachers, with the result that the children failed on a list of words in common use.

Results of standard tests.—Several principals and others who believe in much drill in arithmetic and other subjects say that standard tests have been eye openers, in that they have proved that drill in abstract work beyond a certain point is not only futile, but that it actually reduces accuracy, and that much drill in the tables and combinations, while it gives a higher speed, affects accuracy but slightly and is pretty sure to be fatal to a proper growth of reasoning. These tests have helped to show that good results in learning number combinations, acquiring skill in penmanship, and other mechanical subjects depend more upon the method of drill than upon the amount. Such tests should be used only as a means of diagnosing.

The value of such tests may be summarized as follows:

1. Pupils, teachers, and principals are enabled to see how far each pupil has progressed and where he is with regard to grade standard.

2. Individual differences of pupils in the same grade may be strikingly portrayed.

3. The particular weaknesses and strengths of individual pupils may be discovered.

4. A teacher learns where to economize in drill and the best methods to use in drill.

5. Principals and teachers may see how their schools compare with others.

Having made a study of classroom instruction by means of observation and by standard tests, the principal is then ready to prescribe. Supervision is more than inspection, more than diagnosis. A principal who gets no further than this may be likened to a physician who diagnoses a case and then fails to prescribe, which is as bad as prescribing without diagnosing. If teachers are using poor methods, if results fall below standard, a remedy must be prescribed. There must be constructive not destructive criticism; do, not don't. In fact often the least said about the faults of a teacher, the better. To mention a fault may make a teacher self-conscious and cause her to think first of how not to do, instead of how to do. That supervision is not effective " which observes only the faults, sets them down in a notebook, learns them by rote, and then casts them into the teacher's teeth." Pupils do not learn to spell by seeing words incorrectly spelled or by first thinking of an incorrect spelling. So it is with teachers in using methods of teaching. A fault is best eradicated by substitution, by substituting a good method for a poor one. To lead a teacher to do this is the difficult part, yet the absolutely necessary part in supervision.

Several methods by which a principal can help teachers may be suggested. The private conference to discuss the teacher's own particular problems is without doubt one of the best methods. If a supervisor has made careful note of her methods of instruction, he can without mere faultfinding lead her to do some thinking. Many of the foolish practices in teaching are due to the fact that the teacher does not have any guiding principles, or else does not apply them when face to face with a class of real boys and girls. If a principal will make use of the teacher's problems, he can help her grow. He might tell her what to do in a particular case, but to have her grow in power he should lead her to discover what to do, to discover guiding principles in teaching and classroom management.

Besides the private conference there should be the grade meeting, but in a small school system there are so few teachers teaching the same grade that such meetings would in many instances be nothing more than private conferences. Teachers of two or three grades should, however, be called together from time to time so that the third-grade teacher, say, would have an opportunity of becoming familiar with the aims of the first, second, and fourth grades, and so that the second-grade teacher might become acquainted with what the first and third grades are doing. Such meetings tend to make a teacher more than merely a teacher of a first or second grade. She realizes more clearly that her work is only a part of the general scheme and in order to teach intelligently she should know what the whole scheme is. Without such meetings a third-grade teacher, for example, is not likely to know what her children read in the first and second grades nor the amount or kind of number work done. If she has these facts, she can better observe the dictum: " Proceed from the known to the related unknown."

The teachers' meeting, where all the teachers assemble, has a place in every school system, and especially in the smaller systems, where there are no building or ward principals. At such meetings topics bearing upon general classroom management, general principles of teaching, and new movements in education should be discussed by the principal and teachers, by the principal from another village, by the county superintendent, or by a normal-school principal or teacher, or by a college professor of education. It is a good plan to have some teacher review a school-magazine article or a book on education. The general meeting can profitably be made a seminar, with the principal in charge.

Another type of meeting may be suggested—the nonprofessional—which adds variety and tends to have the teacher look away from his work to other interests. At such meetings topics of the day may be discussed. Some one—as the doctor, the lawyer, the banker, the merchant—may be invited to talk of his profession or business. A musical and literary program adds interest. There may be a social hour over the teacups. Teachers' meetings should not be confined wholly to " shop talk."

Too much emphasis can not be placed upon these types of conferences or teachers' meetings as a means of improving teaching practice, provided they have a high aim and emphasize principles rather than devices, though a discussion of devices has a place if the underlying principle is discovered.

A principal should give much time to preparing for a teachers' meeting. He should try to formulate the aims to be attained. If he does not make such preparation and comes to a meeting without having given it any thought, it will do harm rather than good. There will be no interest. Teachers' meetings can be made inspiring instead of stultifying, depending upon the amount of thought and planning expended upon them.

Another means of improving the quality of instruction is a carefully planned course of study. If there is no county or State course, the principal, with the assistance of his teachers, should work out a course. If there is a county or State course, it is usually very general and somewhat lacking in necessary detail. Such courses, however, usually afford a good basis upon which a principal may build. A course of study worked out in considerable detail is as necessary for the guidance of a teacher as a blue print is for a mechanic. If such course is provided, it will promote good teaching in many ways, among which may be mentioned the following: By giving as explicit direction as possible regarding the aim and purposes of teaching the several subjects; by organizing the subject matter around topics selected by specialists in the several subjects as of greatest importance, in order that teachers may not waste time in nonessentials, and in order that time may be saved by correlation whenever possible; by including suggestive lessons illustrating the fundamental principles in the methods suggested; by indicating materials available for supplementing and illustrating the text; by including suggestive outlines for teaching such subjects as geography and history.

In a small school system such course can be planned with the assistance of all the teachers. No better seminar topic could be suggested for a year's work in teachers' meetings than that of "working out a course of study," or syllabus. Nothing else would tend more to give the teachers a broader vision of their work. Much reading would be necessary. This would afford a motive for reading educational literature. The principal should, of course, direct the lines of study in preparing a course of study in which all the teachers take part, and at its completion his would be the last word. A caution is necessary. After a course of study has been prepared, it should not be considered final or good for all time. No sooner has a course of study been formulated than it must be revised. In other words, the course of study should be changing as our knowledge of the child becomes more nearly perfect and as the economic and social conditions of the community and of the country change.

Another means of improving instruction is for the principal to prepare a few questions for an occasional examination of the pupils. The term examination is no longer popular, from the fact that examinations have too often been the sole mode of judging whether a pupil should be promoted. The chief function of an examination question list is to help give direction to the teaching.

If the teacher makes the teaching of geography and history a mere mechanical process by asking the pupils to commit to memory numerous facts without bringing out their relation, a properly prepared set of questions will awaken the teacher to the fact that her pupils know nothing about the subject. As soon as a teacher discovers the type of question that the principal asks she will begin to use the same type in her teaching. Many teachers who are teaching unrelated facts are doing so because their principal asks for such in all the examination questions. If he would frame his questions so as to call for an organization of the facts or to call for some application it would not be long until the teachers would give up the habit of asking for detached facts. In this connection it must be empha-

A. A COUNTRY VILLAGE.

B. VILLAGE SCHOOL PLAYGROUND.

C. VILLAGE CONSOLIDATED SCHOOL.

A. THE VILLAGE SCHOOL ORCHESTRA.

B. HOME ECONOMICS CLASS.

SCHOOL BARN AT VILLAGE CONSOLIDATED SCHOOL.

HAULING COUNTRY CHILDREN TO THE TOWN SCHOOL.

sized that a principal should not give these examinations as tests for the promotion of pupils. They may in a general way be taken into consideration but not as counting entirely, or as a half or a fourth.

Still another method of improving teachers in service is for the principal and teachers to make a survey of the schools and of the community. One of the reasons many teachers fail is because they do not understand the community in which they are teaching. In another section suggestions are presented regarding the making of school and community surveys.

In general a principal may aid his teachers by holding private conferences with teachers by grade meetings, by general teachers' meetings, by working out a course of study with the assistance of the teachers, by giving an occasional test made up of questions that involve the use of the facts learned, and by making a survey of the schools and the community with the cooperation of the teacher. The principal can thus help his teachers if he does not rank her along with the factory girl who feeds pieces of metal into a machine and sees only one small part of the finished product. They should be considered just as capable of grasping general principles of teaching and of applying them to specific problems as the supervisor himself. When a principal views in this way his work of supervising teachers, he has made a good beginning.

INTERESTING THE COMMUNITY.

In reply to a letter addressed to principals of village schools asking for a list of problems they most often meet nearly every principal said that one of his great problems is, "How to interest the community in its schools." It is evident that, unless a community takes an interest in its schools, the stream of revenue does not flow freely, teachers are poorly paid, the teaching is of poor quality, discipline is difficult, attendance is poor, and so on.

In order to have a village interested in its schools the principal must be awake. He must take an active part in all community affairs and be a leader of educational thought.

One of the important functions of the village school principal is to be a leader in the improvement of educational conditions. In too many instances he is content to close the school building after the day's work and then to drift along with the sluggish current of village thought in educational and other subjects. Village community life is simple, but in most instances the members do not work together. An organizer and director of social and educational life is needed. The principal of the village school district, whether it embraces the village proper or the entire community, should be more than a pedagogue. He should be an educator in every sense of the term, a community leader, not a follower, a guide setting up ideals of accomplishment.

A word of caution is needed, however. Some village school principals in attempting to be leaders try to do everything themselves. A good leader has others do the work. If he does not, he will soon be broken down under a mass of detail. If, for instance, the principal wishes to have community meetings, it is not necessary that he be president of the community organization. The best plan is to have some member made president. The more persons that can be set to work, the better. Then, too, if the principal attempts to do everything himself, self-reliance on the part of the community is not developed. If the principal should leave the community, no leaders would have been developed. The work of the community leader is to develop leaders.

The business man is the first person that the village school principal should attempt to interest. There are very few business men who will not gladly support the schools if they are shown why more money should be expended. Many principals fail because they do not take the time or think it necessary to interest business men in the schools by means of school facts. One principal reports that he interested the business men in his village by asking them to make suggestions for the improvement of the schools. He invited them to send him a full statement on the following points:

In what respect do you find the pupils employed by you to be deficient? State fully and frankly the weaknesses of the public-school product. What suggestion can you give to help us in our work? According to the report of that principal, considerable interest was manifested by the business men, who are now speaking with approval of the work of the schools.

A village principal should be a member of the business man's club from the fact that he is in charge of the principal business in the village, the management of its schools. In a rural community the principal should affiliate himself with farmers' organizations and take part in farmers' institutes and other meetings of the farmers.

Another method of interesting a community in its schools is publicity. A principal who is managing a village system of schools need not fear to turn on the searchlight in regard to school expenditures. The sentiment is growing that the public should know how its money is expended and what the results are. There is no other way in a democracy.

Few village school principals publish school reports in pamphlet form for distribution among the taxpayers of the community. Such reports would be helpful. If, however, it is not possible to publish an annual report, the facts that would be embodied in such report should be published in the local and county newspapers. Even if a report is published. the newspaper should be used to give wider publicity to the facts in the report. Some of the facts that should be embodied in a village school report are listed on page 37.

A principal misses a great opportunity if he does not use the local and county newspapers to keep his schools before the public. Several principals have cooperated with editors of the local newspapers in an occasional educational issue. Many newspapers are glad to publish the names of the pupils who were not absent from school during the month. All school entertainments and community activities of the schools should be noted. The gist of papers presented at teachers' meetings should be published. If a school man from another village, the county superintendent, a college president, or a normal school principal visits the schools, the fact should be noted and if he addresses the teachers or pupils the important points should be given to the press. If any teachers are pursuing university extension courses or attending summer schools, the fact should be made known. This will show the public that the teachers are progressive. By publishing a list of teachers taking advanced work in academic or professional subjects and by commending them for this, some of those who have been inclined to stand still may feel that they, too, should become more progressive.

Some principals, however, object to using the newspapers on the ground that they are advertising themselves. A principal who was complaining about lack of interest among the parents of his town, when asked whether he reported the progress and needs of the schools through the local paper replied that he did not believe in advertising himself. He failed to grasp the idea that school news is not for the purpose of boosting a principal, but to keep the schools before the public and to call attention to their needs so that they may become more efficient.

In at least one school the principal addresses a monthly mimeographed letter to the parents. In these letters he discusses, among other things, the necessity of punctuality, regular attendance, and methods of preventing diseases among school children.

That the schools can work to advantage through women's civic improvement clubs and through parent-teacher associations has been thoroughly demonstrated. Such clubs are often instrumental in helping to broaden the scope of village school work, as in the introduction of courses in manual training and home economics.

Special visiting days for parents and school exhibits may be mentioned as other means of helping arouse interest in the schools.

THE SELF-SURVEY.

Previous mention has been made of the necessity of keeping the public informed regarding the condition and needs of the schools.

In order to present these facts the principal must make a thorough study of every phase of his schools and of the community. Many of the city and State school systems have been surveyed by persons employed especially for the purpose. Since few villages have funds available to pay for the services or even the expenses of a committee of experts, there have been few surveys of village schools. The fact that no funds are available for such work need not prevent a village school principal from making a survey of his school system. Every principal should himself conduct a continuous survey to discover the weakness and the strength of his school, and to invent means for strengthening the weak points and for enlarging the scope of the schools to meet community needs. Possibly principals in several villages could form a group, and by cooperating render one another much valuable assistance. If, for instance, 10 principals were to cooperate in making a study of classroom achievements, school attendance, retardation, unit costs, etc., norms could be established for these 10 villages. It would be an excellent plan for a group of principals to make a survey of these schools with the advice and cooperation of the school of education of the State university or of some other university. When the survey is completed, it would be possible for each principal to see how his school varies from the norm in unit costs, etc., and to discover ways of improving his school. The teachers in the village should be enlisted in a self-survey of the schools so that they may become better acquainted with conditions and not be mere teachers of a certain grade.

Several illustrations of self-surveys in small school systems may be given. The report of the principal of schools at Curwensville, Pa., shows what is possible for a principal in a small town to do to present to the public evidence of what the schools are doing and of their needs. The principal, in his report, explains as follows why he made a survey of his schools:

Due to the severe criticism thrust into the ears of school officials, both as to our own as well as to schools generally, we were very much interested to learn the true condition in Curwensville. We firmly believe in surveys, but in a small city school system it is almost beyond the financial grasp to hire an expert. So we determined to conduct an investigation and deal with problems as best we could.

Among the points investigated and reported upon were age distribution of pupils, promotion, medical inspection, achievements of pupils as determined by standard tests, junior and senior high schools, and costs.

An interesting example of an effort of a small public-school system to "survey" itself is found in "A Study: The Dansville (N. Y.) High School," by the supervising principal. This investigation consumed about 16 months of the principal's spare time and grew out of his feeling that the high school was not doing its proper work in comparison with the high schools in neighboring villages about the size of Dansville. When the work, which was aided to some extent by the teachers in the school, was completed it was presented to the board of education, by whose order it was published, so that it might be presented to the public.

The study led to 11 conclusions, which were offered not as "a program for immediate" action, but as "a sort of guide for the future." These conclusions pointed out the need of increasing the salary scale of teachers; a good library in or near the school building to supplement the work in the grades, and particularly that in the junior and senior high schools; the addition of a teacher trained in giving tests for mental deficiency; the addition of a department of agriculture and horticulture, and in home making; readjustment of the curriculum; the appointment of supervisors of play; more active concern about medical inspection; frequent parents' meetings; the organization of a group of mothers of children in the lower grades; a wider use of the school plant by broadening the work of the night school; and enlarging the district so as to increase the school revenue.

If every principal were to make a similar study of his school system it would be possible for him to formulate a plan for the development of his schools.

Outline for self-survey.—A principal undertaking to make a survey of his schools will find the following outline helpful. Part I suggests points to be studied in connection with the school itself and Part II the points to be studied regarding the community:

PART I. THE SCHOOLS.

I. *Efficiency of the Schools.*
  1. How the school holds pupils.
      a. Number of children 14 to 18 years of age in village and per cent in school.
      b. Number of children 6 to 14 years of age in village and per cent in school.
      c. Ratio of pupils above compulsory age limit to those below it. How this ratio has changed during the past five years.
      d. Number of pupils for each 100 beginners dropping out of school, at each age, at each grade; number of those leaving to enter school elsewhere; number for other causes.
      e. Per cent of those entering the first grade who complete the elementary-school course; the high-school course.

I. *Efficiency of the Schools*—Continued.
  1. How the school holds pupils—Continued.
    f. Per cent of those completing the elementary schools to enter high school.
    g. Per cent of those entering high school to complete the course.
    h. Per cent of high-school graduates who enter college; standing in college.
    i. Regularity of attendance. Average daily attendance based on number belonging; average daily attendance based on enrollment; average daily attendance based on school population.
    j. How school has improved during past five years in holding children in school.
  2. Progress of pupils through the school.
    a. Per cent of children of normal age for grade.
    b. Per cent of children over age for grade.
    c. Per cent of children under age for grade.
    d. Per cent who fail of promotion in first grade, second grade, etc.
    e. Per cent of failures in the different subjects.
    f. Number of years it takes each pupil to complete the course of study.
    g. Kind of work done by pupils repeating a grade in subjects in which they failed and in subjects passed.
    h. Causes of failures: Irregular attendance, frequent changes of schools, etc.
    i. How to lessen retardation.
    j. How much retardation has been reduced during past five years.
  3. How instruction in the schools reacts upon the home and lives of the pupils, especially instruction in music, art, literature, manual training, and domestic science.
  4. What those who have graduated from the high school within the past 5 or 10 years are doing; those who have graduated from the grammar school; those who left the grades without graduating; those who left high school without graduating.
  5. Ability of pupils in different subjects as determined by standard tests.
  6. Strong and weak points in teaching as determined by classroom visitation.
  7. How pupil's time is economized through course of study and through classroom methods.
  8. What the school is doing to direct pupils toward vocations. What more can it do?
  9. Provisions for exceptional children.
II. *Administration and Supervision.*
  1. Cost per pupil in elementary school and high school. Compare with cost in other villages.
  2. Cost per pupil recitation in high school, in the elementary school.
  3. Amount of real wealth in village for every dollar spent for school maintenance. Compare with other villages.
  4. Assessed valuation is what part of actual valuation? Compare with other villages.
  5. Present tax rate for schools.
  6. Bonded indebtedness for schools and for other purposes.
  7. Amount of local school tax paid by owners of real estate whose assessed valuation is $5,000 or more.
  8. Per cent of total school moneys received from State, county, and village.

II. *Administration and Supervision*—Continued.

9. Per cent of school moneys paid by business not owned principally by citizens—as railroads and industrial, mining, and commercial enterprises.
10. Possibility and feasibility of extending village school district so that small country schools may be consolidated with village schools.
11. Authority and duties of principal. List of things principal does in course of a week.

III. *Teachers.*

1. Academic preparation.
2. Professional preparation.
3. Number of years of experience within system; in other systems.
4. Ways in which teachers are improving themselves. What principal can do to help them improve.
5. Per cent of teachers leaving the school system each year and cause for leaving.
6. Salary schedule: How it tends to make teachers progressive. How salary schedules compare with those in other villages.

IV. *Buildings.*[1]

1. Heating and ventilation.
2. Lighting.
3. Seating.
4. Equipment.
5. How adapted to community use.
6. Janitorial service.

V. *Hygiene and Sanitation.*

1. Are hygienic and sanitary conditions standard?
2. The schools' responsibility for the health of children.
3. Medical inspection and school-nurse service.

PART II.—THE COMMUNITY.

I. *The People.*

1. Racial and national elements.
2. What the people do for a living. List of occupations and number engaged in each.
   a. Education and training required for occupations in the community.
   b. How much of this is provided by the school.
3. Social and recreational life.
   a. Of young children.
   b. Of high-school boys and girls.
   c. Of young men and women no longer in school.
   d. Of adults.
   e. Amount spent on amusements, moving-picture shows, etc. Compare with amount spent on schools.
   f. Provision for recreational activities through public library, lecture courses, clubs, Boy Scouts, Campfire Girls, community music, dramatics.

II. *Extent of Village Community.*

1. Population within village corporation.
2. Population outside corporate limits using village as trading center, church center, school center.

[1] This outline for a building survey is very general. The person making a study of the school building should provide himself with a Standard Building Score Card.

The principal who makes a study of some or all of the points suggested in the foregoing outline will have something concrete to present to his school board and to the public. If, for instance, the school is now holding pupils better than it has been, the fact should be shown. Unless the principal collects such data and tabulates them, he does not know whether the holding power of his school is improving.

Tables and graphs should be presented to help impress the facts upon the minds of the school board and of the public.

Tables for a school report or self-survey.—The. following illustrates the type of table that a principal may well include in his annual report.

A table and a graph showing the distribution of attendance is much better than a statement showing what per cent the attendance is of the enrollment. The table may be arranged as follows:

Distribution of attendance.

Period of attendance.	Boys.	Girls.	Total.	Per cent of whole number.
Attending less than 10 days.............				
10 to 19 days......				
20 to 29 days........				
30 to 39 days........				
(And so on for the remainder of the term.)				
Total (equal enrollment for term).........				

Comparison should be made with attendance of previous years.

In many schools few teachers know what per cent of the pupils fail by grades in the different subjects. A knowledge of these facts would assist in formulating a course of study. If, for instance, 20 per cent of the children in the second grade fail in arithmetic and 5 per cent in reading, it is evident that something is wrong. The promotion rate for the school should be known. If on an average 90 per cent of the pupils are promoted, only 478 out of 1,000 children entering the first grade would go through the eight grades without failing.

The table may be arranged as follows:

Per cent failures by studies and grades.

Pupils.	Reading.	Spelling.	Language.	Arithmetic.	History.	Geography.
FIFTH GRADE.[1]						
B {Boys.....						
Girls......						
Total.						
A {Boys.....						
Girls.....						
Total.....						
Per cent of failures on enrollment for term.........						

[1] The same form may be used for other grades.

A similar table should be prepared to show per cent of failures in the several high-school subjects.

Another table showing nonpromotion by grades and causes should be prepared thus:

Nonpromotion, by grades and causes.

Pupils.	Irregular attendance.	Physical defects.	Personal illness.	Mental incapacity.	Indifference.
.... GRADE.[1]					
B { Boys......					
Girls......					
Total......					
A { Boys......					
Girls......					
Total......					
Grand total { Boys......					
Girls......					
Total......					
Per cent of total......					

[1] Same form for each grade.

In compiling the age-grade data, children of the first grade 6 and 7 years of age are considered normal; all 8 years of age and over, over age. In the second grade, children under 7 years of age are considered under age; all 7 and 8 years of age, normal; and all 9 or more years of age, over age; and so on throughout the grades. A table should be prepared showing the per cent under age, normal, and over age; also a table showing the number and per cent of children over age in two and three or more years. These data should be compared with like data for several years previous to see to what extent retardation has been reduced.

The following are forms for tabulating other data regarding a village school system:

Enrollment, promotions, nonpromotion, by grades.

Pupils.	.... grade.[1]			Total, all grades.
	B.	A.	Total.	
Enrollment for term:				
In division for first time......				
Previously in division......				
Leaving school......				
Enrollment at date of this report......				
Per cent enrollment at date on enrollment for term......				
Promotions:				
Per cent on enrollment at date......				
Per cent on enrollment for term......				
Nonpromotions:				
From in division first time......				
From previously in division......				
Per cent nonpromotions on enrollment at date......				
Per cent nonpromotions on enrollment for term......				

[1] Similar columns to be inserted for all other grades.

Distribution of enrollment at date of this report, by ages and grades.[1]

Ages.	First.			Second.			Third.			Fourth.			Fifth.			Sixth.			Seventh.			Eighth.			Total.		
	Boys.	Girls.	Total.	Boys.	Girls.	Total.	Boys.	Girls.	Total.	Boys.	Girls.	Total.	Boys.	Girls.	Total.	Boys.	Girls.	Total.	Boys.	Girls.	Total.	Boys.	Girls.	Total.	Boys.	Girls.	Total.
6 years																											
7 years																											
8 years																											
9 years																											
10 years																											
11 years																											
12 years																											
13 years																											
14 years																											
15 years																											
16 years																											
17 years																											
18 years																											
19 years																											
20 years																											
Total by grades																											
Below normal age																											
Normal age																											
Above normal age																											

[1] Give age Sept. 1.

A permanent record card should be on file showing certain facts regarding each pupil. The following form is suggested:

ELEMENTARY SCHOOL RECORD SYSTEM—PROMOTION RECORD.	This card is to pass from teacher to teacher or from school to school as the pupil is promoted or transferred. It is to be filled out and sent to the principal's office when any change is made requiring a change in the office records. It is then to be sent to the teacher who has the pupil.	(a) School.	(b) Date of admission.	(c) Age Sept. 1.		(d) Grade.	(e) Room.	(f) Days present.	(g) Health.	(h) Conduct.	(i) Scholarship.
				Yrs.	Mos.						
				......	......						

(1) 1. Last name............	(2) First name and initial.......	ELEMENTARY SCHOOL RECORD SYSTEM—ADMISSION, DISCHARGE, AND PROMOTION CARD.
(3) Place of birth...........	(4) Date of birth.	(5) Vaccinated.
(6) Name of parent or guardian.	(7) Occupation of parent or guardian.	To be kept for every pupil and sent with the pupil when he is transferred to any school, either public or private, in the city or outside the city. Great care should be used to have the names complete and correct. Write all dates as follows: 1912-9-25.

(8) Residence. (Use one column at a time. Give new residence when pupil is transferred.)		(9) Date of discharge.	(10) Age.	
			Yrs.	Mos.

When a pupil is permanently discharged to work, to remain at home, or because of death, permanent illness, or commitment to an institution, this card is to be returned to the principal's office and a full statement of the cause of the pupil's discharge is to be made in the blank space remaining above.

Among the uses to which the card may be put are:
1. Amount of attendance of individual pupils for each year.
2. Classification of pupils by age and grade.
3. Number of times child has been retained in a grade.
4. Foreign birth as affecting progress.
5. Absence as affecting progress.

By referring to the permanent record cards of the children completing the eighth grade, a principal may ascertain how many years it has taken each pupil to complete the course. He may also discover how many children who entered the first grade eight years previous have remained in school. All these data help the principal analyze conditions. If few children complete the course in eight years, it is evidently too difficult or the teaching is not efficient. From the card record the following table may be prepared:

Graduates of elementary school, years in school.

	Boys.	Girls.	Total.
Taking 6 years			
Taking 6½ years			
Taking 7 years			
Taking 7½ years			
Taking 8 years			
Taking 8½ years			
Taking 9 years			
Taking 9½ years			
Taking 10 years			
Total			

The following table illustrates another use that can be made of the record card:

Effect of irregular attendance upon promotion.

Number of days present.	Number promoted more than twice.	Promoted twice.	Promoted once.	Not promoted at all.
180 days or more				
170 and less than 180				
160 and less than 170				
150 and less than 160				
140 and less than 150				
130 and less than 140				
And so on.				
Total				

Graphs for self-survey.—A few graphs are presented merely as suggestions. The reader is referred to the various school-survey reports of the United States Bureau of Education and of other agencies, to " School Statistics and Publicity " (Silver Burdett & Co.), and to " Standards for Local School Surveys " (D. C. Heath & Co.) for other suggestions.

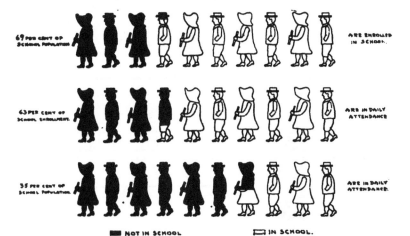

FIG. 5.—School population, enrollment, and attendance, 1918.

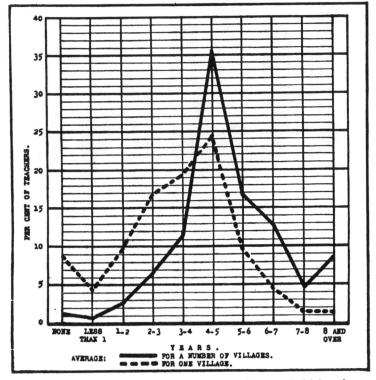

FIG. 6.—Number of years teachers have attended school beyond eighth grade.

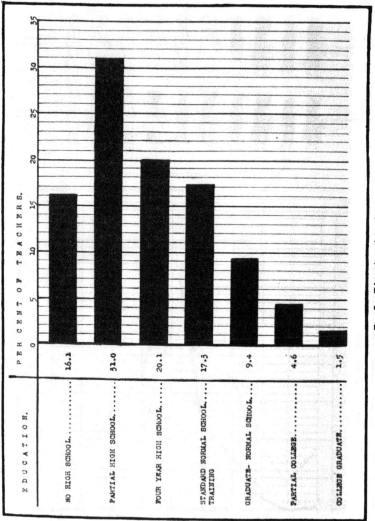

Fig. 7.—Education of teachers.

EDUCATION.	PER CENT OF TEACHERS.
NO HIGH SCHOOL............	16.1
PARTIAL HIGH SCHOOL........	31.0
FOUR YEAR HIGH SCHOOL......	20.1
STANDARD NORMAL SCHOOL TRAINING	17.3
GRADUATE—NORMAL SCHOOL....	9.4
PARTIAL COLLEGE............	4.6
COLLEGE GRADUATE..........	1.5

COURSE OF STUDY.

As it is.—Whether children take an interest in their own community depends partly upon what they study at school. But one finds the same facts taught and the same illustrations used in the agricultural town school that one finds in city schools. The elementary school course of study in village schools as carried out in practice is more bookish than that in the large city schools, where children are taught more about their environment. The village child is taught about city life through the several subjects of the elementary school course. Arithmetic, for instance, is not given a rural application, most of the problems solved being of the counting-house instead of the farm. The language lessons are based upon topics remote from the life and experience of the child instead of upon what is near, on the farm or in the village. Geography is begun, not at home, but at some distant point. Civics consists of an analysis of the national constitution instead of a first-hand study of the government of the village, the township, and the county. Nature study has a very subordinate place and is mostly bookish. Music, manual training, home economics, and physical training have found a place in comparatively few village schools.

The usual village high-school course is as formal or even more so than that of the elementary school. The subjects are English, Latin, algebra, geometry, ancient history, a science or two, usually with rather poor laboratory equipment, and possibly a modern foreign language. The subjects of agriculture and home economics are gradually working their way into the village school; but, strange to say, many farmers and housewives prefer that their children study Latin, mathematics, and other purely academic subjects instead of subjects vitally related to the community.

As it should be.—One of the fundamental principles in education is that instruction should begin with that which is familiar and simple and work out to that which is more remote and complex. To know things at home is to know the world. A farm-life course of study would prepare country children just as effectively to live anywhere as would a course made up of foreign language, mathematics, and other purely academic subjects. The village school should make use of home geography, of problems in arithmetic related to village life, of local history, of community civics; in fact, there is no subject in the elementary school course that can not be related to village life.

Agriculture may be taught in a practical way. Ground suitable for demonstration purposes may be had in or near almost every village. Boys living on farms may, by means of home projects, apply the principles of agriculture learned in the classroom and on the school demonstration plat. Science teaching may have rural application. Practical application of chemistry in an analysis of soils is possible. Botany may also be given a practical application in the study of the useful and useless plants of the region and of the best way of eradicating the noxious ones.

Then there is home gardening directed by the school. In many villages there are unsightly back yards and vacant lots that could be made attractive and productive if they were planted into gardens. It is true that many children living in villages cultivate gardens at home, but their efforts are undirected. If the work were supervised by the schools, many correlations of gardening with arithmetic, language, drawing, manual training, cooking, nature study, and other subjects would be possible.

The six-six plan.—The plan of organizing the course of study with six years in the elementary grades and six years in the high school can be easily applied to village schools. The high-school course of study should be divided into two parts of three years each, the first three years being generally known as the junior high school and the last three years as the senior high school. Not all villages should attempt to have both junior and senior high schools. In fact, some of the very small places should not attempt more than the six elementary grades, and three years of junior high school, especially if there is a senior high school not far away. Township and county boards of education that have jurisdiction over the village schools should seriously consider whether it is advisable to organize junior and senior high schools in every village in the township or in the county.

As it is, many villages are attempting to do 12 grades of work when there are only a few pupils in the tenth, eleventh, and twelfth grades. A few villages in each county should be selected for senior high schools. The density of population and other factors, of course, would determine the number of senior high schools.

What should be taught in the junior and senior high schools.— If villages were to adopt the six-six plan of organization, most of the subjects in the junior high school should be required. The subjects in this type of school might be the following: Three years of English; two of general mathematics; three years of history, including European beginnings and advanced American history; one year of community civics: one year of geography and elementary science; three years of physical education; one year of hygiene and sanitation; and three years each of music, art, current events, industrial arts, agriculture, and home economics. Not all of the required or of the elective subjects should be offered five times a week, once or twice a week being sufficient time for some.

The senior high-school course should continue the vocational and academic subjects begun in the junior high school with a higher degree of specialization in view. More electives can be offered. The number will depend upon the size of the school. The electives should not be so many that there are only three or four pupils in a class. If the school is small, some subjects can be offered in alternate years. A new and quite different course of study would be necessary in order that this plan may meet its full possibilities. The first six grades should be concerned chiefly with what are known as the fundamentals, or the tools. Topics for teaching purposes should be organized in relation to and from the point of view of the experience and environment of village and rural children. While the emphasis should be placed upon the "tools," the first six grades should not ignore the distinctly modern phases of education. Music, literature, and the fine arts should be taught largely for appreciation and not for technique. Nature study, elementary agriculture, school and home gardening, play, sanitation and hygiene, handwork of different kinds, dramatization and story telling should also have a place in the elementary school.

Extension of kindergarten work.[1]—According to recent statistics of the Bureau of Education, there were, approximately, 600 kindergartens, with 22,000 children enrolled during the school year 1917–18 in towns with under 2,500 population. While these figures are far below what they should be, they show that an increasing number of kindergartens are being opened in towns and villages. Fortunate are the little children who attend these kindergartens, for the town and village offer an ideal environment for kindergarten education. The modern tendency in kindergarten work is to have the children spend as much time as possible out of doors. Where weather and climate permit, there are out-of-door kindergartens, and even if a part of the activities take place within the kindergarten room, the children play their games out of doors. Under the trees are sand boxes, slides, and seesaws. In the city kindergarten too often there is no space available for this out-of-door play. Sometimes there is a roof garden, and weary little feet have to climb flights of stairs to reach the playground. Sometimes the city children are taken for one blissful day into the country, so that they may see pigs and cows and chickens, and experience all the other delights of the farm. But the village child has all this life at his very door, and nature unfolds her wonderful picture book from day to day. The child becomes acquainted with all the little creatures of wood and field. Pictures of birds and squirrels and butterflies are a poor substitute for the real thing. Window boxes and tin cans can never take the place of real gardens with enough space for each child to have his own plat.

[1] Prepared by Miss Julia Wade Abbot, Specialist in Kindergarten Education, U. S. Bureau of Education.

The country child not only has the opportunity to begin nature study by living with nature, but he is in daily contact with simple industrial processes in home and neighborhood. The country child is freed from the intricate organizations of city life; ambulances and police patrols, apartment life and department stores do not crowd upon his consciousness. He lives in a real home with a yard around it. He sees his mother cutting out clothes and making them for different members of the family. He sees her canning and preserving vegetables and fruits, and he is called upon to participate in the home activities which provide him with a wholesome round of duties. Farming country surrounds his village; he follows the work of the farmer through spring and summer and fall, and sees him gather the fruits of his labor. And there is need for a blacksmith's shop in the country, and the child "looks in at the open door," fascinated by the glare of the flaming iron and the primitive force of the hammer. In the village, the fire engine is still drawn by glorious, dashing creatures with long manes and tails, and faithful farm horses pull heavy loads of hay through the village street. The country child rides in the grocer's cart and is permitted to drive the horse; in exchange for which privilege he delivers the packages at every door. The village life provides a whole round of duties and pleasures suited to normal child life.

But the question may be asked, "If the town and village offer such opportunities for the right kind of development, why is it necessary to provide kindergartens for the children of these communities?" The answer to such a question is that education is always needed to show people how to appreciate and make use of the opportunities around them. Children in the country have all out of doors to play in, and yet such an authority as Dr. Thomas Wood declares that country children know little of how and what to play. The country has always been emphasized as the best place in which to bring up children, and yet statistics show that city children are more healthy than country children, because they have more intelligent care.

All children in city or country need the wise direction of their impulses and interests. While the city child needs to have what is wholesome and constructive selected from his too intricate environment, the country child needs to have his eyes opened to the wealth of material about him. And both city and country child need the stimulus of the social group, and the participation that results from working and playing with others.

Whether a small number of children in a community make necessary a kindergarten primary grade or whether a kindergarten is provided, this "beginning room" in the school of the small town should be a happy place where the youngest children enjoy the freedom and initiative characteristic of childhood. Only when children are encouraged to express themselves freely do we discover the needs and aptitudes of the individual child. In an article entitled " Mental Hygiene and the Public School," Dr. Arnold Gessell writes:

If there is, indeed, such a thing as human engineering, nothing could be more unscientific than the unceremonious, indiscriminating, wholesale method with which we admit children into our greatest social institution, the public school. We must supplement the matriculation examination with a period of observation which will not relax during the whole school career of the child, but which will be peculiarly intensive during the first year or first semester. The first year should be an induction year. The kindergarten and first grade then become a vestibule school where the child may be detained under a watchful semiprobationary régime which will discover and record his strength and his weakness.

The formal type of work so often prescribed for children who are beginning school is so machinelike in character that many discouraged ones fall by the way and have to repeat the first grade. The right beginning of school life in the kindergarten has a direct bearing upon the child's physical well-being, his mental alertness, and his social adjustment to the group, and should be a means of rendering more efficient any school system, whether in city, town, or rural community.

THE VILLAGE SCHOOL A COMMUNITY CENTER.

It is doubtful whether the social affairs in many villages to-day are on as high a plane and as educative and socializing as were the forms of social amusement once common, as debating societies, singing schools, spelling bees, etc. While it may not be desirable to conduct these old forms of amusements in the same manner as they once were, the fact remains that there must be a certain amount of social life in each community. At present the social life is usually confined to the one or more churches, to several lodges, to a moving-picture house showing films of doubtful value once or twice a week, or to traveling shows. Such forms of social life do not unite the people. There is no unifying element.

If the village school were organized to serve the entire community, it would have a tremendous influence in building up community social and intellectual life. It should be the educational center not only for children, but for young men and women and for older men and women. At the village community school farmers should meet to discuss farm problems and to hear lectures by the county demonstration agents and by professors of agriculture in the State college of agriculture. At such centers lectures on subjects of local, State, National, and international concern, entertainments, community singing, plays, moving pictures, and other activities should have a place. As it is, village school buildings are seldom open for public meetings. Now and then there is a school entertainment open to the public. Some villages maintain a lyceum course, but other activities are necessary if the school is to serve as a means of bringing the people together.

The village school must teach more than the three R's. It must broaden the lives of everyone in the community. One of the evils of village life is monotony and lack of fellowship. There is too much individualism and not enough cooperation, not enough thinking together. The village school serving as a center of community life for those who naturally congregate at the village for business purposes would tend to break up the isolation, lack of fellowship, and individualism. The school building, instead of the village store, should be the community center. In many villages there are few big topics of conversation. The village gossip and the store-box group are common characters. There is evidently need of some institution to create and conserve common interest. For this purpose there should be a common meeting place where there may be free and open discussion on the great topics of the day. Every village should discuss local improvements, cooperative methods of buying and selling, proposed State and National legislation. If an amendment to the State constitution is proposed, every person should know what the amendment is and what the effect of its adoption will be. No better place than the public-school building could be found to discuss such topics. In fact, the school building is the only logical place for such discussion, the one building in the village dedicated to democracy.

It is a good plan for the people of the community, country, and village to organize a community association. Officers should be elected and committees appointed. A good example of a community association is that at the village consolidated school at Five Points, Ala., described on page 15.

The following points regarding the organization of village communities for the discussion of public questions are suggestive:[1]

I. DIFFICULTIES TO OVERCOME.

1. Lack of social consciousness. Few people think in terms of the social unit. They are intolerant of an opinion differing from their own. Difference of opinion is taken as a personal matter or as dangerous.

2. Diffidence in the presence of an audience. Few can be prevailed upon to speak in public.

3. The inveterate talker who can not be suppressed, but talks every gathering to death.

---

[1] From paper read by U. J. Hoffman, at Conference on Village Schools, Chicago, Ill.

4. Lack of a leader and a greater lack of followers.

5. In an organization embracing the entire public there is not enough the sense of "ours" to give the necessary cohesion. It soon dies by indifference and falling away of members.

6. An organization just to talk in public dies, for soon all have said their say except the born bore.

II. SUGGESTIONS FOR OVERCOMING THE DIFFICULTIES.

1. Organize a community center to be made up of all the people of the community, and then let this be divided into clubs of about 15 members each. These clubs should consist of people who naturally affiliate and are or can be interested in the same subjects.

2. There should be. even in a small village, four clubs, two of men and two of women. There should then be a federation of these clubs to hold joint meetings once in two months. The clubs should meet every two weeks.

3. These should be study and working clubs; having something to learn and something to do. In Illinois a package of books on any subject may be obtained by paying transportation from the State library extension board.

4. The federation can arrange for the discussion of public questions by speakers of note or by themselves.

5. Little headway can be made in any special social undertaking without refreshments to arouse sociability. The clubs should meet at the homes of members and refreshments should be a feature at least once a month.

6. Much depends upon a capable leader for the federation and for the several clubs.

7. This work will not come by spontaneous generation. The Nation or the State must send out organizers and furnish suggestive plans, programs, courses of reading, etc.

While the foregoing plan may not be ideal, from the fact that it contemplates the breaking up of a community into clubs, it may be the only practical way to solve the problem of having public questions discussed in some communities. The ideal way is for the whole village community to organize, but difficult to put into practical operation, from the fact that there are social lines of cleavage in every village that must be broken down before all will come together as a community.

SUPERVISION OF SPECIAL SUBJECTS.

In most villages there is but little supervision of the teaching of music, art, and other so-called special subjects. In fact they are not included in many village-school courses of study.

How to provide supervision and expert teaching of these subjects is one of the problems of the village school. Several plans may be suggested.

If there are three or four villages within a few miles of one another, they might jointly employ the special supervisors needed. These could spend a day or two each week in each town, the amount of time given depending upon the number of teachers at each place. This plan has been found effective and economical.

If the village school is under the control of a county board of education, this board should employ supervisors of music and other subjects. Where this plan is in operation, the supervisors go over the county visiting all schools under the control of the county board. Some townships also have the same plan. If a township is too small to employ special supervisors, several could jointly employ the supervisors needed.

A plan successfully employed is that of departmentalizing the work of the elementary school so that the special subjects may be taught by special teachers. All the pupils report to one teacher for music, to another for art, and so on. Arithmetic, history, geography, and the other subjects not considered special are taught by the regular classroom teacher. The following program for a sixth grade illustrates how the plan may be worked out in practice:

PROGRAM OF GRADE 6.

MORNING.

First 90 minutes. 8.45 to 10.15 a. m.

6B. Regular classroom.
> 8.45– 8.55. Opening exercises—10 minutes.
> 8.55– 9.10. Spelling—15 minutes.
> 9.10– 9.45. Reading—35 minutes.
> 9.45–10.15. Geography—30 minutes.

6A. Special rooms.
> 8.45– 9.30. Home economics, manual training, Monday, Wednesday; physical training, Tuesday, Thursday, Friday.
> 9.30–10.15. Drawing, Tuesday, Thursday, and Friday; home economics and manual training, Monday and Wednesday; double periods for home economics and manual training.

Second 90 minutes. 10.15 to 11.45 a. m.

6A. Regular classrooms.
> 10.15–11.45. Spelling, arithmetic, geography, as for 6B.

6B. Special rooms.
> 11.00–11.45. Same as for 6A in first 90-minute period.

AFTERNOON.

First 80 minutes. 1.00 to 2.20.

6B. Regular rooms.
> 1.00–1.40. Arithmetic—40 minutes.
> 1.40–1.55. Writing—15 minutes.
> 1.55–2.20. History—25 minutes.

6A. Special rooms.
> 1.00–1.40. Composition.
> 1.40–2.00. Music.
> 2.00–2.20. Physiology and hygiene.

Second 80 minutes.

6A. Regular rooms.
    2.20–3.40. Reading, writing, and history, as for 6B in first period.
6B. Special rooms.
    2.15–3.40. Same as for 6A in first period.

A study of this program shows that while the B division of a grade is in the regular classroom during the first 90-minute period, the A division is having work with the special teachers. The program is reversed for the second 90-minute period. Similar programs can be worked out for each of the other grades.

No supervisors are needed if the teachers of the special subjects are skilled. If the county board does not provide supervisors, and if it is not possible for several villages to employ jointly the necessary supervision, the special subjects may be well taught by the departmental plan just outlined.

THE VILLAGE LIBRARY.

Comparatively few villages have libraries accessible to the general public. Mr. Harlan Douglass says:

The library itself as a public institution is not existent in most of the little towns. There are less than 2,000 in the entire United States, and four-fifths of their readers live in the North Atlantic and North Central States.

In many villages there are a few books in the school building for the use of the pupils, but as a rule these books are inferior, not adapted to the age of the pupils, and they are seldom used. In many village communities the churches formerly had Sunday school libraries, but this plan proved a failure in most instances from the fact that the books were poorly selected. The real depository of the village library is the public school. If the school is to serve the community, there should be a library room full of books not only for children but for adults. There should be children's stories, fiction, history, biography, books of travel, and books on farming and other vocations.

If there is a county library, the village library should be a branch of it. If there is no county library, the local school board or the county board should make appropriations each year for library maintenance.

In some village communities it is almost a hopeless task to introduce a library, because the people have not formed the reading habit. If the teachers interest the children in reading, it will be comparatively easy to have them cooperate in raising funds to purchase books. Many, in fact the majority. of village school libraries were started with funds raised by entertainments. This plan will no doubt have to be used for some time in many communities. If the school board does not make appropriations, there is no other way except by private donations. The plan of having books donated can not be recommended, since so few persons have books suitable for a school library. The books should be purchased by the principal and teachers, with the advice of some librarian familiar with the needs of a village community.

If the library is to be popular, books in which children and adults are interested must be provided. The first money raised for a library, especially if the amount is small, should be expended for books to read rather than for encyclopædias, compendiums, and books of useful facts. These are necessary, but as a rule they should not be purchased with the first library money. Reference books should be provided out of regular school funds, and most school boards can be induced to purchase such books, while it is rather difficult to persuade them to purchase story books and other reading material that appeal to children.

The village library should be open to adults of the community as many hours in the week as possible. The library room should be a reading room where there are current magazines. One of the teachers could act as librarian during the school year. The library should be open during the vacation period, but if it is not possible to have it open every day. one or two days a week could be designated as library day. If the principal of schools is employed for the entire year, as he should be, he could act as librarian several times a week. If the school board will not provide funds to keep the library open during vacation, it might be possible to have some of the citizens donate funds for this purpose.

Village school principals and teachers should, however, make it emphatic that the school library is an essential part of a school and should be supported by public funds.

THE SCHOOL TERM.

The usual school term in villages is eight or nine months. In several States the term provided by public funds is insufficient to keep the schools open more than six or seven months, but in many instances a tuition fee and donations are necessary to make it possible to continue the term several months longer. This is a deplorable condition. but true nevertheless.

The village school term should be at least 9 months—11 would be better—and should be the ideal toward which to work. In most villages there is nothing in particular for the children to do during the summer months. This is especially true in mining and manufacturing communities. In the farming sections the older boys and girls assist with farm and house work, but the younger children are idle. In such communities the school term could be extended for the primary grades at least. Gardening under the direction and supervision of the schools would be more practical. More play could be introduced. Field excursions would be feasible. School during the summer months would not necessarily mean that the children would have to sit at their desks six hours a day.

Where summer schools have been conducted the health of the children has not suffered. The schoolrooms are ventilated naturally. There is no artificially heated air. No arguments can be offered against a long term, except that the expense of maintaining a school term of 10 months will be greater than for a term of 8 months.

BUILDINGS AND GROUNDS.

There is no distinct type of village school architecture. It frequently happens that village school buildings in design do not compare favorably with some of those in the rural districts of the same county. A majority of the very old buildings are almost hidden by the numerous additions that have been from time to time built about them. Many of these old buildings should have been torn down or abandoned when the first additions were proposed. They now make uncomfortable quarters for the children and are poorly heated, ventilated, and lighted. They are inconvenient for the teacher in her classroom work and are also veritable fire traps that should be condemned by the State authorities.

The farmer who moves into the village from the farm usually objects to the high taxation necessary to maintain the village schools, and for that reason village schools in growing villages have been built to accommodate only the present enrollment, with no outlook for the increased enrollment in the years to come. In any growing village this is poor economy and means trouble for the future boards of education. Every bond issued for the purpose of building a new school building will invariably increase the taxation. Every effort should then be made to consolidate the districts near the village and extend the district lines that the village may become a center of a larger area with an increased valuation, which will materially reduce the taxation and at the same time provide better buildings for both country and village children. Every village should provide for the construction of a permanent school building, built of strong material, brick, stone, or concrete. This building should be built on the unit plan, and if sufficient ground can be obtained, it should be but one story in height.

Buildings for community use.—Any school building in the village should be built for the use of the entire community and should contain a large auditorium with a specially arranged booth, conforming to the State laws, for moving pictures, a good swimming pool, and a room for the community library. In this building, or in a building especially constructed for the purpose, provision should be made for teaching manual training, domestic science, and agriculture. Where the school building is situated on ground well drained and high, large and convenient basements are useful not only for community use but for playrooms for the pupils during rainy days. However, care must be exercised to keep this basement free from dampness and well ventilated.

School buildings should be attractive.—The style of architecture in the village schools and the driveways or other approaches to the school building should be attractive, at least equal in convenience and beauty to that of the best home in the village. Neat approaches add to the beauty as well as to the convenience of every school building. Town pride should assist in planning a building that would reflect the refined taste and good judgment of an intelligent people.

Ample halls and classrooms.—Narrow, dark, and poorly ventilated halls are not only a menace to health, but sources of great danger in cases of fire. Halls in modern school buildings should serve several definite purposes. They provide for the overflow of crowds when the auditorium is filled. They provide also a place for exercise on rainy days or during the period devoted to calisthenics.

Location of the village school.—In Spanish countries the schools are usually located in the center of the town, in what is called the town square or plaza. This plan has not been followed in laying out the towns in the United States; but, if possible, a central location should be secured, with ample grounds that may be used by the village for a park. If, however, sufficient space in a central place can not be secured, it is much better to have the pupils walk a longer distance if that is necessary in order to provide ample grounds for the building. The adults will not object to going this increased distance for community gatherings of various kinds.

Recreation and playgrounds.—Village boys and girls enjoy all forms of healthy recreation and play. They have a great advantage over children in the sparsely settled communities on account of the numbers and the opportunities for getting together for a good romp. In every village can be seen around the streets or in the principal street or the public square, if there be one, children meeting and enjoying themselves in some form of healthy exercise. They come in sufficient numbers to permit a team to play basket ball, volley ball, or baseball. Too often they encounter many difficulties from merchants who object to the children playing in front of their stores, and the town marshal has frequently to warn the boys that they must not play on certain busy streets. This is one of the results of a very ancient and mistaken idea that it is not necessary to provide playgrounds in a village.

When land was cheap and every opportunity was offered to secure a central location for parks or playgrounds it was thought very foolish to spend the public money to purchase such a site as would give the children of that generation and future generations an opportunity for good healthy exercise. Yet these parents frequently used to quote a familiar motto that "All work and no play makes Jack a dull boy." Records show that in our Western States ample sites have frequently been offered to the villages by patriotic citizens if the town council would enter into an obligation of caring for the land, improving it, and using it for a public park. Yet many of these village fathers positively refused to accept these generous offers, because they claimed it was a useless expenditure of the "hard-earned" money of the taxpayers.

To-day children can hardly bless the memory of these dear, departed village councilmen. The school ground, if centrally located, should be the recreation ground for the village. It should have a running track or place sufficiently large to make one. A county meet or township meet should be one of the annual events of the year. The New England States had their "training days"; the central Western States have had their "dicker days." The township fairs have been important features of recreation in these States. To-day more interest is taken in athletics in rural schools and village schools than ever before, and yet in less than 50 per cent of the village schools is sufficient ground provided for these meets and exercises. It is better to locate a school out on the edge of the village, with good, large, ample playground, than to have it centrally located with no opportunity whatever for recreation, and every village school ground should contain at least 5 acres of well-drained, well-graded land. This should be well provided with play apparatus for the pupils—preferably that made by the pupils in the manual-training department.

The following diagram illustrates what village school grounds should be like:

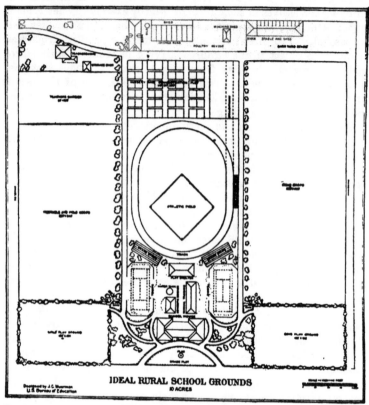

FIG. 8.—Ground plan of an ideal community school, prepared in miniature by the Bureau of Education for the Panama-Pacific Exposition. Provision is made for housing the teacher and in other ways making the school a real center for village community life.

The teacher's home.—Most villages contain a hotel or inn, but very seldom does a teacher care to board at such a place. Much has been said concerning lack of opportunity to find a good boarding place in the rural districts. This same difficulty is encountered by a majority of the teachers of the small villages. As the usual village school has from two to eight teachers, it is often desirable to provide a suitable building as a home for the teachers. While many State laws do not permit the building of a teacher's cottage, there is no objection to a building where domestic science can be taught. The teacher's home may be used for this purpose if built within a short distance from the school building. It becomes more difficult each year for a teacher to find a suitable boarding place in a good village home.

The village schools should, by all means, have at least one male teacher, and that teacher may be normally expected to be a married man. To provide for him a decent, respectable home would tend to retain his services much longer, and to increase his interest in the community. From reports received by the United States Bureau of Education from villages that provide a home for the teacher, a great majority state emphatically that its effect is beneficial upon the school, that they are able to retain good teachers longer, and that the teacher is a real, integral part of the community, and that his influence outside the school is as great as his influence in the school. If this teacher should be interested in agriculture, he may be employed for the full 12 months of the year to teach agriculture and direct home gardening during the summer months. It is highly desirable, however, that he remain in the district and live upon the school grounds. This offers protection to the school property that otherwise would be open to vandals during vacation periods. More than 300 teacher's homes are now provided in the villages.

HEALTH.

For generations the general health of the village has been the special province of that honored individual, the doctor. His word regarding individual health as well as the general sanitary condition of the village was considered law, and no one disputed it. His fees were nominal, if collected at all, and his advice was freely given upon every occasion. " The village preacher and the village doctor " have been considered the most important men in the village. The day of the village doctor, if not entirely past, is rapidly fading away. His influence is not as great as it was in the years that are gone. Village people, when there is continued illness, generally go to the city, where hospital treatment is offered. The village doctor now refers his serious cases to a specialist in the city. .

In a great many villages, very little, if any, provision is made for general sanitary conditions that directly affect the health of the inhabitants. Reports from every State note the frequent neglect of efficient sanitary inspection of the villages. What is everybody's business is nobody's business. No one has authority to order the drainage to be properly made in the smaller villages. Breeding places for flies and injurious insects are allowed to go unnoticed. The water in the wells is not examined, and the well owners themselves seem to think it unnecessary. It is not to be wondered that frequent epidemics of typhoid, malaria, and other diseases are reported. Officials of the board of health claim that the expense of putting some of the villages in good sanitary condition is too great a burden to be placed upon the taxpayers of the village. If this be true, a portion of this burden might well be borne by the State. Village councilmen should be compelled to enforce any health regulation given them by the State board of public health, and this board should provide adequate inspection for all villages.

The village school can do much to bring about better sanitary conditions. In some villages the principals and teachers have inaugurated "clean-up days" for the entire village, beginning with the school grounds. "Swat-the-fly" campaigns have done much to call the attention of village people to the fact that the housefly is a menace and that garbage and manure heaps in the back yards and alleys are breeding places for the fly.

Community civics should have a place in the program of studies in every village school. Included with this should be studies of community sanitation. Village life being simple, it lends itself especially to a study of such problems.

If there is a high school in the village, the classes in the sciences should make a study of the water supply, the milk, and other foods sold in the village.

In brief, there are many ways by which the principal and teachers in a village school may interest the community in health programs.

Leaflets of the United States Health Department and of the United States Bureau of Education could be distributed to the homes through the village school children. In fact, there are numberless ways by which the principal and teachers may help improve health conditions in the village. They should ask the State and National health departments for suggestions.

SUMMARY.

1. The village, especially in an agricultural region, should be part of the rural community. The village school should, therefore, be a community school serving the farm child as well as the village child.

2. The village school should not be independent of the township or county school system, but should be administered by a township or a county board of education.

3. The village school course of study should be based upon the life of the community. If the village is in a farming region, the course of study should be a country-life course. Music, art, physi-

cal training, home economics, and manual training should have a prominent place in the program of studies.

4. In the smaller villages only elementary and junior high-school work should be attempted. Pupils in these villages belonging to grades 10, 11, and 12 should attend a high school in some larger village or the township or county high school.

5. There should be a kindergarten in every village.

6. The school grounds should be large enough for a school garden, agricultural demonstration plats, play, shrubbery, and trees. Ten acres is not too much. The school grounds could well be the village park.

7. The school buildings should contain, in addition to regular classrooms, an auditorium, library room, laboratories, kitchen, shops, etc.

8. Every village school should contain a library. It should be a branch of the county library, if there be such.

O

DEPARTMENT OF THE INTERIOR
BUREAU OF EDUCATION

BULLETIN, 1919, No. 87

STATISTICS OF STATE UNIVERSITIES AND STATE COLLEGES

FOR THE YEAR ENDED JUNE 30

1919

WITH STATISTICAL SUMMARY OF HIGHER EDUCATION, PUBLIC
AND PRIVATE, FOR THE YEAR 1917-18

WASHINGTON
GOVERNMENT PRINTING OFFICE
1921

STATISTICS OF STATE UNIVERSITIES AND STATE COLLEGES.

For the Year Ended June 30, 1919.

This annual bulletin, formerly prepared and· published by the National Association of State Universities, has been published by the Bureau of Education for the past 11 years. The data given are taken from reports received from the offices of the presidents of the various institutions, and the figures printed are substantially as given in those reports.

Directory of State universities and State colleges.[1]

[Names in *italics* are institutions endowed by the Federal Government under the Morrill Acts.]

Location.	Name.	President.
Auburn, Ala.............	*Alabama Polytechnic Institute*..........	Spright Dowell, LL. D.
Montevallo, Ala.............	Alabama Technical Institute and College for Women..............	T. W. Palmer.
University, Ala........	University of Alabama..............	George H. Denny, LL. D.
Tucson, Ariz.............	*University of Arizona*..............	R. B. von Klein Smid, A. M.
Fayetteville, Ark...........	*University of Arkansas*.............	John C. Futrall, A. M.
Berkeley, Calif........	*University of California*..............	David P. Barrows, LL. D.
Boulder, Colo.............	University of Colorado.............	George Norlin, Ph. D.
Fort Collins, Colo.............	*Colorado Agricultural College*..........	Chas. A. Lory, LL. D.
Golden, Colo..............	Colorado School of Mines..........	Victor C. Alderson, Sc. D.
Greeley, Colo...........	Colorado State Teachers College.......	John G. Crabbe, Ph. D.
Storrs, Conn.............	*Connecticut Agricultural College*.......	Charles L. Beach, B. S.
Newark, Del........	*Delaware College*.................	Walter Hullihen, Ph. D.
Gainesville, Fla.........	*University of Florida*................	Albert A. Murphree, LL. D.
Tallahassee, Fla..........	Florida State College for Women.....	Edward Conradi, Ph. D.
Athens, Ga.................	University of Georgia................	David C. Barrow, LL. D., chancellor.
Atlanta, Ga.................	Georgia School of Technology.........	Kenneth G. Matheson, LL. D.
Dahlonega, Ga..	North Georgia Agricultural College....	Gustavus R. Glenn, LL. D.
Honolulu, Hawaii...........	*University of Hawaii*.................	Arthur L. Dean, Ph. D.
Moscow, Idaho.............	*University of Idaho*.................	Alfred H. Upham, Ph. D.
Pocatello, Idaho.	Idaho Technical Institute[2]...........	Charles R. Frazier, B. L.
Urbana, Ill.................	*University of Illinois*..............	David Kinley, LL. D.
Bloomington, Ind.............	Indiana University..................	William L. Bryan, LL. D.
La Fayette, Ind.............	*Purdue University*.................	Winthrop E. Stone, LL. D.
Ames, Iowa.................	*Iowa State College of Agriculture and Mechanic Arts*.	Raymond A. Pearson, LL. D.
Cedar Falls, Iowa.............	Iowa State Teachers College..........	Homer H. Seerley, LL. D.
Iowa City, Iowa.............	State University of Iowa.............	Walter A. Jessup, Ph. D.
Lawrence, Kans.............	University of Kansas..............	E. H. Lindley, Ph. D.
Manhattan, Kans.............	*Kansas State Agricultural College*.....	William M. Jardine, LL. D.
Lexington, Ky.............	University of Kentucky..............	Frank L. McVey, Ph. D.
Baton Rouge, La.·.............	*Louisiana State University and Agricultural and Mechanical College.*	Thomas D. Boyd, LL. D.
Orono, Me.................	*University of Maine*..............	Robert J. Aley, LL. D.
College Park, Md.............	*University of Maryland*..............	Alfred F. Woods, D. Agri.
Amherst, Mass..............	*Massachusetts Agricultural College*.....	Kenyon L. Butterfield, LL. D.
Cambridge, Mass..............	*Massachusetts Institute of Technology*...	Elihu Thomson, acting.
Ann Arbor, Mich..............	University of Michigan.............	Marion Le Roy Burton, LL. D.
East Lansing, Mich...........	*Michigan Agricultural College*........	Frank S. Kedzie, Sc. D.
Houghton, Mich..............	Michigan College of Mines.............	Fred W. McNair, Sc. D.
Minneapolis, Minn.............	*University of Minnesota*............	Lotus D. Coffman, Ph. D.
Agricultural College, Miss....·.	*Mississippi Agricultural and Mechanical College.*	W. H. Smith, B. S.
Columbus, Miss..............	Mississippi State College for Women.....	J. C. Fant, Ph. D.
University, Miss.............	University of Mississippi.............	Joseph N. Powers, chancellor.
Columbia, Mo.............	*University of Missouri*.............	Albert Ross Hill, LL. D.
Bozeman, Mont..............	*Montana College of Agriculture and Mechanic Arts.*	Alfred Atkinson.

[1] Corrected to Jan. 25, 1921, in so far as changes have been reported to this bureau.
[2] Junior college.

3

Directory of State universities and State colleges—Continued.

Location.	Name.	President.
Butte, Mont.	Montana State School of Mines.	Charles H. Clapp, Ph. D.
Missoula, Mont.	University of Montana.	Edward O. Sisson, LL. D.
Lincoln, Nebr.	University of Nebraska.	Samuel Avery, LL. D., chancellor.
Reno, Nev.	University of Nevada.	Walter E. Clark, Ph. D.
Durham, N. H.	New Hampshire College of Agriculture and Mechanic Arts.	Ralph D. Hetzel, LL. D.
New Brunswick, N. J.	Rutgers College.	Wm. H. S. Demarest, LL. D.
Albuquerque, N. Mex.	University of New Mexico.	David S. Hill, LL. D.
Socorro, N. Mex.	New Mexico School of Mines.	Fayette A. Jones, LL. D.
State College, N. Mex.	New Mexico College of Agriculture and Mechanic Arts.	R. W. Clothier, Ph. D.
Albany, N. Y.	New York State College for Teachers.	Abraham R. Brubacher, Ph. D.
Ithaca, N. Y.	Cornell University.	Albert W. Smith, acting.
Syracuse, N. Y.	New York State College of Forestry (at Syracuse University).	Franklin Moon, M. F.
Chapel Hill, N. C.	University of North Carolina.	Harry W. Chase, Ph. D.
West Raleigh, N. C.	North Carolina College of Agriculture and Engineering.	Wallace C. Riddick, C. E.
Agricultural College, N. Dak.	North Dakota Agricultural College.	Edwin F. Ladd, LL. D.
University, N. Dak.	University of North Dakota.	Thomas F. Kane, LL. D.
Athens, Ohio.	Ohio University.	Edwin W. Chubb, Litt. D., acting.
Columbus, Ohio.	Ohio State University.	Wm. O. Thompson, LL. D.
Oxford, Ohio.	Miami University.	Raymond M. Hughes, M. S.
Chickasha, Okla.	Oklahoma College for Women.	G. W. Austin, B. S.
Norman, Okla.	University of Oklahoma.	Stratton D. Brooks, Ph. D.
Stillwater, Okla.	Oklahoma Agricultural and Mechanical College.	James W. Cantwell, A. M.
Corvallis, Oreg.	Oregon State Agricultural College.	Wm. J. Kerr, Sc. D.
Eugene, Oreg.	University of Oregon.	Prince L. Campbell, A. B.
State College, Pa.	Pennsylvania State College.	
San Juan, P. R.	University of Porto Rico.	Paul G. Miller.
Kingston, R. I.	Rhode Island State College.	Howard Edwards, LL. D.
Charleston, S. C.	The Citadel, the Military College of South Carolina.	O. J. Bond, A. M., supt.
Clemson College, S. C.	Clemson Agricultural College.	Walter M. Riggs, E. M. E.
Columbia, S. C.	University of South Carolina.	Wm. S. Currell, Ph. D.
Brookings, S. Dak.	South Dakota State College of Agriculture and Mechanic Arts.	Ellwood C. Perisho, M. S.
Rapid City, S. Dak.	South Dakota State School of Mines.	Cleophas C. O'Harra, Ph. D.
Vermilion, S. Dak.	University of South Dakota.	Robert L. Slagle, Ph. D.
Knoxville, Tenn.	University of Tennessee.	Harcourt A. Morgan, B. S. A.
Austin, Tex.	University of Texas.	Robert E. Vinson, LL. D.
College Station, Tex.	Agricultural and Mechanical College of Texas.	Wm. B. Bizzell, D. C. L.
Denton, Tex.	College of Industrial Arts.	F. M. Bralley.
Logan, Utah.	Agricultural College of Utah.	Elmer G. Peterson, Ph. D.
Salt Lake City, Utah.	University of Utah.	John A. Widtsoe, LL. D.
Burlington, Vt.	University of Vermont and State Agricultural College.	Guy W. Bailey, A. B.
Blacksburg, Va.	Virginia Polytechnic Institute.	Julian A. Burruss, A. M.
Charlottesville, Va.	University of Virginia.	Edwin A. Alderman, LL. D.
Lexington, Va.	Virginia Military Institute.	Edward W. Nichols, supt.
Williamsburg, Va.	College of William and Mary.	J. A. C. Chandler, Ph. D.
Pullman, Wash.	State College of Washington.	Ernest O. Holland, Ph. D.
Seattle, Wash.	University of Washington.	Henry Suzzallo, Ph. D.
Morgantown, W. Va.	West Virginia University.	Frank B. Trotter, LL. D.
Madison, Wis.	University of Wisconsin.	Edward A. Birge, LL. D.
Laramie, Wyo.	University of Wyoming.	Aven Nelson, Ph. D.

TABLE 1.—*The teaching force in State universities and State colleges for the year 1918–19.*

Names of institutions.	Men.	Women.	Total.	President's salary.	Deans Max.	Deans Min.	Professors Max.	Professors Min.	Associate Max.	Associate Min.	Assistant Max.	Assistant Min.	Adjunct Max.	Adjunct Min.	Instructors Max.	Instructors Min.	Assistants Max.	Assistants Min.	Tutors Max.	Tutors Min.	House: President.	House: Professors.
1	2	3	4	5	6	7	8	9	10	11	12	13	14	15	16	17	18	19	20	21	22	23
Alabama Polytechnic Institute	69	0	69	$5,000	$3,000	$2,600	$3,000	$1,800	$1,800	$1,800	$1,800	$1,500			$1,500	$1,000	$700	$250				0
Alabama Technical Institute and College for Women	2	35	37	4,000	3,000		1,500	1,200	1,200	1,000	1,800	810			630	360	200	100			Yes	0
University of Alabama	83	5	88	7,500	3,900	3,000	3,000	2,500	2,500	2,400	2,200	1,800			1,800	1,200	1,000	200		$800	Yes	0
University of Arizona	45	12	57	7,500	4,500	3,000	2,800	1,600	2,300	1,950	2,000	1,700			1,600	1,400	1,200	1,200	$1,200	400	Yes	0
University of Arkansas	115	21	136	7,500	4,500	3,000	2,750	2,100			2,400	1,500			1,400	1,200			4,000		No.	2
University of California	795	80	875	12,000	6,000	3,500	8,000	3,000	4,000	2,400	2,800	1,700			2,300	800	2,000	250			Yes	0
University of Colorado	100	32	132	6,000	2,700	2,500	3,700	1,800			1,600	1,300			1,200	800	750	100			Yes	0
Colorado Agricultural College	50	32	80	6,000	2,600	2,000	3,000	1,800	2,500	1,600	1,800	1,300			1,500	800			2,000	300	Yes	0
Colorado School of Mines	32	2	81	6,000			3,500	1,700	2,000		1,800	1,300			1,800	1,000	1,200	780			Yes	0
Colorado State Teachers College	19	0	19	6,000	3,200	2,450	2,800	1,600			1,700	1,200			1,500	1,000	600	200			No.	0
Connecticut Agricultural College	39	42	81	4,200	3,500	3,200	2,800	2,250	2,300	2,000	2,200	1,300			1,800	800		200			No.	0
Delaware College	47	7	54	4,000	4,000	3,300	2,600	2,000			1,750	1,500			$1,800	800					No.	10
University of Florida	36	11	47	6,000	4,200	2,300	2,100	2,000	1,800	1,800	2,000	1,400			1,600	800					No.	0
Florida State College for Women	53	62	62	4,000	4,000		2,100	2,000	1,800	1,600	1,750				1,500	800			600	100	No.	2
University of Georgia	11	20	31	5,000			3,200	2,400			1,700	1,300			1,600	1,000					Yes	0
Georgia School of Technology	81	0	81	5,000	3,600	3,000	3,720	1,500			1,800	1,500	$1,500	$1,500	1,500	1,050	960				No.	0
North Georgia Agricultural College	13	7	20	12,000	2,250	2,000	3,000	1,200							1,650	1,000					No.	0
University of Hawaii	14	1	15	7,500	2,250	2,250	3,250	1,250	1,800	1,800	600	600			1,650	200	1,800	180		100	Yes	0
University of Idaho	60	14	74	7,500	5,000	3,500	5,000	2,600	2,250	2,100	1,900	1,300			1,300	700	800	50	900		No.	0
Idaho Technical Institute	11	5	16	7,000	4,500	2,000	3,600	1,600			2,300	1,500			1,200	1,200	1,200	600			Yes	0
University of Illinois	644	143	787	7,000	4,800	4,800	3,500	2,100	2,800	2,000	2,700	1,400			1,800	1,000	1,200	800	900	200	No.	2
Indiana University	175	31	206	7,000	2,500	2,500	2,100	1,400	3,000	1,000	1,900	1,200			1,400	900	900	405	120	60	Yes	0
Purdue University (Ind.)	165	20	185	10,000	2,500	3,500	3,200	1,200	2,400	3,250	3,250	1,000			1,400	2,000	2,000	400			Yes	0
Iowa State College of Agriculture and Mechanic Arts	223	95	318	6,000	4,500	3,500	3,600	2,000	2,500	2,000	2,000	1,500			1,400	400	900				No.	0
Iowa State Teachers College	35	43	78	6,000	4,800	2,000	3,000	2,100	2,800	2,400	2,700	1,400			1,800	1,000	1,200	600	900	200	Yes	0
State University of Iowa	174	44	218		6,000	2,500	3,500	1,400	3,000	1,000	1,900	1,200			1,400	900	900	800			Yes	0
University of Kansas	228	71	299	6,000	6,000	3,500	3,200	1,500	2,400	2,900	3,250	1,500			1,400	2,000	1,000	400			No.	0
Kansas State Agricultural College	130	50	180	6,000	6,000	3,500	3,200	1,500	3,000	1,400	2,200	1,350			2,200	1,100	1,800	900	2,200	900	No.	0
University of Kentucky	89	11	100	8,500	6,200	6,200	3,300	1,500	2,100	2,000	2,000	1,500			1,500	750			400	200	Yes	0

TABLE 1.—The teaching force in State universities and State colleges for the year 1918-19—Continued.

Names of institutions.	Professors and instructors — Men.	Women.	Total.	President's salary.	Deans. Maximum	Deans. Minimum	Professors. Maximum	Professors. Minimum	Associate professors. Maximum	Associate professors. Minimum	Assistant professors. Maximum	Assistant professors. Minimum	Adjunct professors. Maximum	Adjunct professors. Minimum	Instructors. Maximum	Instructors. Minimum	Assistants. Maximum	Assistants. Minimum	Tutors and others. Maximum	Tutors and others. Minimum	House in addition to salary for— President.	House in addition to salary for— Professors.
Louisiana State University and Agricultural and Mechanical College	106	10	116	$5,000	$4,000	$2,200	$2,500	$1,900			$1,500	$1,200	$1,800	$1,200	$1,350	$600	$300	$300	$2,400	$600	Yes	0
University of Maine	64	11	75	6,000	3,000	2,700	2,100	2,000	1,900	1,600	1,500	1,200			1,400	800					Yes	0
University of Maryland	38	1	39	10,000	3,500	2,700	3,250	2,000							1,500	1,200					No	0
Massachusetts Agricultural College	60	1	61	7,500	4,400	3,600	3,000	2,000	2,500	2,000	2,500	1,750			2,400	1,000					No	0
Massachusetts Institute of Technology	218	4	222																		Yes	
University of Michigan	433	5	438	10,000	7,900	3,200	5,000	2,000	3,000	1,800	2,400	1,600			2,100	900	900	300			No	4
Michigan Agricultural College	121	24	145	6,500	3,800	2,400	3,500	2,500	3,150	2,100	2,800	1,500			2,480	820	1,200	250			No	0
Michigan College of Mines	21		21	5,000			4,000	2,250	2,100		2,700	1,500			1,500	900	900				Yes	0
University of Minnesota	775	133	908	12,000	7,900	3,000	6,000	1,800	4,000	2,050	3,000	1,500			2,750	750	1,500	500	800		Yes	2
Mississippi Agricultural and Mechanical College	94	4	98	3,500	2,750	2,250	2,000	1,800	1,500	1,500	1,400	1,000			1,100	720				240	Yes	0
Mississippi Industrial Institute and College	6	70	76	3,500	3,500	2,000	2,200	1,600			1,200	900			720	480					Yes	1
University of Mississippi	31	1	32	5,500	5,000	2,000	2,000	2,000	2,000	1,200	1,200	1,200			1,200	1,000	300	150	100		Yes	0
University of Missouri	227	14	241	9,000	4,500	3,600	3,600	2,400	2,400	1,800	2,500	1,500			2,000	1,000	1,200	300	300	100	Yes	2
Montana College of Agriculture and Mechanic Arts	24	7	31	6,000	4,500	2,400	3,000	2,000			2,500	1,500			2,000	750	1,600	1,320			Yes	0
Montana State School of Mines	8		8	5,000			3,250	2,250			2,650	1,400			1,800	1,200					No	1
University of Montana	42	14	56	6,000	3,300	2,400	3,000	2,100	2,400		2,200	1,000			2,000	1,400	1,500	1,300			No	0
University of Nebraska	267	70	337	6,000	3,850	2,500	1,400	1,400		1,200	2,000	800			1,800	600	1,400	200			No	0
University of Nevada	38	10	48	7,500	3,600	3,000	3,000	2,000	2,750	2,200	2,600	1,800			1,800	1,320	1,100	800	500	300	Yes	0
New Hampshire College of Agriculture and Mechanic Arts	65	8	73	6,000	3,600	2,800	2,500	2,100	2,750	2,100	2,300	1,600			1,200	1,200	1,100	800		300	Yes	0
Rutgers College (N. J.)	90	8	98	6,000			3,600	2,500	2,500	2,000	2,400	1,800			1,800	1,200	1,000	500		500	Yes	0
University of New Mexico	23	7	30	4,800	2,300		2,300	1,500	1,500	900		900			400	500					No	0
New Mexico School of Mines	7		7	3,000			2,000	1,200							1,200	1,200					Yes	0
New Mexico College of Agriculture and Mechanic Arts	33	7	40	6,000	3,000		2,250	1,800			1,800	1,350			1,350		400	1,200			Yes	0
New York State College for Teachers	32	25	57	6,000	4,500	2,200	3,500	3,000		2,000	2,400	2,000			1,820	1,500	1,500	1,200	2,000	2,000	Yes	0
Cornell University (N. Y.)	708	74	782	10,000	5,250	4,500	4,500	2,500			2,000	1,000			1,300	800	500	400	88	88	Yes	0

Institution																				
New York State College of Forestry (at Syracuse University).	21	0	21	5,000		3,000		2,000		1,900	1,700			1,400	1,200		840			No...	0
University of North Carolina.	101	0	101	9,000	3,250	5,000	2,650	2,000	2,000	2,000	1,900	1,700	1,200	1,500	700	63		Yes.	0
North Carolina College of Agriculture and Engineering.	90	0	60	4,500	3,000	2,500	500	500	1,350	1,600	1,500	1,200	1,800	500	200	75		No...	0
North Dakota Agricultural College.	125	35	160	5,000	3,600	2,600	1,700	2,100	1,700	1,800	1,600	1,600	1,500	1,080	50		No...	0
University of North Dakota.	47	30	77	6,000	3,500	3,400	2,400	2,350	2,100	2,300	1,600	2,000	2,000	700	125		Yes.	0
Ohio University.	57	41	98	6,000	3,000	3,040	1,750	2,200	2,000	2,050	1,000	1,530	1,000	350		Yes.	0
Ohio State University.	531	128	659	10,000	3,200	3,500	2,500	2,500	1,750	1,900	1,200	1,700	1,000	900	150		Yes.	0
Miami University (Ohio).	53	17	70	6,000		4,500	2,000	2,000		1,900	1,800	1,200	900	150		Yes.	1
Oklahoma College for Women.	5	28	33	4,500	3,000	3,000	2,400	1,800	2,100	2,000		1,600	1,200	900	500		Yes.	0
University of Oklahoma.	171	32	203	7,500	2,500	3,000	2,400	2,500	2,100	2,400	1,700	1,600	1,100	1,200	900	840	Yes.	0
Oklahoma Agricultural and Mechanical College.	61	28	89	7,500	2,400	2,400	2,000	1,800	2,000	2,000	1,200	1,600	1,400	1,000	500	1,000	Yes.	0
Oregon State Agricultural College.	91	120	120	7,000	3,600	2,800	1,800	2,600	1,700	2,500	1,600	2,000	855	500	1,200		No...	1
University of Oregon.	107	39	146	5,000	3,000	2,500	1,600	2,000	1,600	2,400	1,400	1,600	200	200		Yes.	3
Pennsylvania State College.	183	17	200	9,000	6,000	1,800	2,000	2,500	2,450	1,800	1,400	1,600	1,000	1,200		Yes.	2
University of Porto Rico.	43	29	72		3,500	3,000	1,800	2,000	1,700	2,000	1,500	1,400	765	1,200			2
Rhode Island State College.	24	6	30	4,500	2,700	2,000	2,000	2,000	2,000	900	1,800	450		
The Citadel, the Military College of South Carolina.	16	0	16	4,000		2,500			1,500						
Clemson Agricultural College (S. C.).	68	0	68	5,360	4,500	2,950	2,200	2,020	1,500	2,000	1,400	1,400	1,200	900	1,200		No...	0
University of South Carolina.	35	3	38	4,200	2,400	2,400	2,600	1,800	1,800	1,400	1,700	1,400	375	500		Yes.	0
South Dakota State College of Agriculture and Mechanic Arts.	41	15	56	4,200	3,000	3,000	1,300	2,200	1,700	1,700	1,400	900		No...	2
South Dakota State School of Mines.	13	14	14	3,500		3,000		2,000	1,650	1,200		1,200		
University of Tennessee.	37	13	51	5,700	2,600	2,600	2,400	1,500	1,400	1,700	1,600	1,550	800	300		No...	0
University of Texas.	141	154	154	6,000	3,500	2,700	2,500	2,000	1,900	2,000	1,200	1,800	1,800	125		No...	0
Agricultural and Mechanical College of Texas.	168	47	215	7,000	3,600	3,250	3,500	2,500	2,000	2,250	1,800	1,800	450	100	450	No...	0
College of Industrial Arts (Tex.).	119	0	119	4,000			3,250	2,750				1,400	1,400	1,200	1,000		Yes.	2
Agricultural College of Utah.	5	72	77	5,500	3,500	2,500	2,500	2,100	1,650	1,700	1,250	1,700	1,200	800		No...	0
University of Utah.	55	13	68		3,000	3,000	3,000	2,200	2,100	2,200	1,700	1,600	1,200	300		Yes.	0
University of Vermont and State Agricultural College.	127	42	169	7,000	3,000	3,000	2,300	2,300	1,800	1,800	800	500		No...
Virginia Polytechnic Institute.	91	5	96	6,000	3,200	2,800	2,100	1,650	2,000	2,100	1,000	1,800	1,600	300		Yes.
University of Virginia.	55	0	55	8,000		3,600	2,600	2,100	2,000	2,100	180		Yes.
Virginia Military Institute.	83	0	83	4,950			2,100	2,300	2,400	2,300	1,800	800		Yes.
College of William and Mary (Va.).	35	0	35	3,100	3,400	2,300	2,300	2,100	2,400	2,500	2,000	2,100	1,200	800		Yes.	50
State College of Washington.	15	2	17	3,150	3,200	2,400	3,000	2,400	2,500	3,000	2,400	1,000	1,200	350		Yes.	250
University of Washington.	101	39	130	12,000	4,000	4,000	4,000	4,000	2,500	2,400	2,300	2,000	1,200	350		Yes.	50
West Virginia University.	151	11	190	3,000	3,300	2,400	4,000	2,000	2,400	2,400	2,000	1,800	750	350	50	Yes.	4
University of Wisconsin.	100	111	111	7,000	4,000	2,750	2,750	3,100	2,000	2,200	1,500	2,000	1,080	780	250	Yes.	0
University of Wyoming.	397	104	501	5,250	3,000	3,000	2,820	2,220	2,200	3,100	1,800	2,160	750	450	50	Yes.
	38	15	53	5,040	3,120	3,000	2,220	1,440	1,620						

Table 2.—Student enrollment in State universities and State colleges for the year 1918-19.

Names of institutions	Preparatory department[1] Men	Women	Collegiate department Men	Women	Graduate department Men	Women	Professional departments Men	Women	All other students[2] Men	Women	Total (excluding duplicates) Men	Women	Total	Enrolled in 1918 summer school Men	Women	Enrolled in other short courses Men	Women	Law	Medicine	Dentistry	Pharmacy	Students in military drill
	2	3	4	5	6	7	8	9	10	11	12	13	14	15	16	17	18	19	20	21	22	23
Alabama Polytechnic Institute			1,182	12	9	1	74	2		29	1,265	15	1,280	163	206						38	38
Alabama Technical Institute and College for Women		202	0	242	0	0	0	0	0	1	0	473	473	25	180							1,028
University of Alabama			698	261	3	0	117	0	13	31	828	262	1,088	251	474	136	66	59	64		4	
University of Arizona			377	201	18	12	11	1	24	56	419	296	706	0	31	0	10	11				602
University of Arkansas			686	243	4	1	531	50	37	70	727	296	1,023	82	252							138
University of California			3,270	2,983	333	479	118	22	169		3,568	3,494	7,422	835	4,197			106	238	172	66	206
University of Colorado			844	542	29	28	74	0			834	687	1,575	98	578			36	77		27	3,196
Colorado Agricultural College			598	274		1					384	384	1,196	23	40							632
Colorado School of Mines	241	90	274	1							274	1	275	28	0							986
Colorado State Teachers College			125	1,003	31	67			63	496	284	2,121	2,405	45	896			62				152
Connecticut Agricultural College	120	350	125	33					21	6	174	39	185	200	42		7		0	0	0	100
Delaware College	16		210	87	5		62				146	87	297	2	187	88						121
University of Florida			458	0	0		0			65	210	0	210	91	343							185
Florida State College for Women	0	64	0	438	0	4	0				525	571	525	4	419		5		0	0	0	153
University of Georgia[3]			1,251	34	9		68	0			0	34	1,286	100	0				0			
Georgia School of Technology	251	0	170	0	0	0	0	0	16	34	1,251	0	421						0	0	0	1,100
North Georgia Agricultural College			54	13	3	1	0	0	9	19	71	47	118									63
University of Hawaii	26	7	449	185	10	10	561				458	209	667	297		2			0	0	0	647
University of Idaho	90	87	18	20	3	1	31	44			105	107	212									
University of Illinois			4,650	1,639	261	102		7	17	6	5,372	1,785	7,157		451			80	281	168	111	3,072
Indiana University[3]			2,218	214	12	10	31				2,278	237	2,511			51	5				38	1,770
Purdue University (Ind.)	341	46	2,257	563	48	29	612		13	9	2,318	626	2,944	122	239			0	243			
Iowa State College of Agriculture and Mechanic Arts	95	1,959	146	1,218	12	64			3	241	256	3,262	3,518	147	2,452							4,332
Iowa State Teachers College			1,642	1,180	167	228	242	30	128	240	2,421	663	4,103	406	663			0				
State University of Iowa	29	52	2,133	1,331	78	171	612	40		841	2,610	1,834	4,444	245	517			65	243	274	50	707
University of Kansas	181	58	1,010	440	14	10	63	0	106		1,216	592	1,808	66	453	558	25	87	169		36	1,758
Kansas State Agricultural College																						968

Institution																			600
University of Kentucky	844		234	11	1	86	3	28	9	969	247	1,216	97	75	86	13	89		237
Louisiana State University and Agricultural and Mechanical College	738		412	14	4	32	1	7	10	789	427	1,216	141	294			33		400
University of Maine	529		183		1	9	1	12		529	183	712					10		227
University of Maryland	216		9	3	3			26	5	231	15	246	7	61	63				363
Massachusetts Agricultural College	332		22	9				6		356	28	384							
Massachusetts Institute of Technology	1,903		14		66	862	48		0	1,845	15	1,890	487	20			184	81	1,157
University of Michigan	6,345	11	1,423	36		41	0			7,320	1,537	8,857	779	522					5,500
Michigan Agricultural College	553		334	113				12	5	605	334	939	82	98	359	0	347	258	305
Michigan College of Mines	154		0		110	580	67	26	3	154	0	154							1,087
University of Minnesota	1,844	789	1,818	206						3,719	2,376	6,095	453	906		0	147	347	1,146
Mississippi Agricultural and Mechanical College	1,064	17	0	3	0		242		0	1,346	0	1,346	229	588	34			113	
Mississippi Industrial Institute and College			874		0	174	8		14			888				0	16		1,492
University of Mississippi	395		78	5	62	165	21			572	86	658	8		78	9	106	36	210
University of Missouri	2,115		1,100	65						2,345	1,246	3,591	214	567		13			59
Montana College of Agriculture and Mechanic Arts	196		132					30		196	132	327		190	97		20		100
Montana State College of Mines	91		1	1	10	25	19		135	91	1	92	31	262	471	3	98	22	
University of Montana	184		369	106	154	527	36			201	372	573	167	544	16	0		45	92
University of Nebraska	2,026	68	1,493	2						2,727	1,837	4,564	5	65				84	309
University of Nevada	122		141							134	144	298				12			361
New Hampshire College of Agriculture and Mechanic Arts	254		60	11				170	105	494	165	580	70	350	70				152
Rutgers College (N. J.)	424	92	52	3	0		1	1	0	528	62	590	79	96			348		283
University of New Mexico	180	7	97		0			7	19	197	116	313	4					55	1,550
New Mexico School of Mines	18	5	18		0			2				31							
New Mexico College of Agriculture and Mechanic Arts	279	2	25	1	8		8	98	40	307	82	389	15	0	58	22	228		92
New York State College for Teachers	65		550	217	69	416	55	21	39	177	782	959	54	494		0	52	0	811
Cornell University (N. Y.)	3,311		1,576							1,700	1,700	5,644	172	817					
New York State College of Forestry (at Syracuse University)	110	0	0		3		9			110	0	110		0	10				
University of North Carolina	878	154	22	26		133				1,123	35	1,158	97	515	0	0		35	
North Carolina College of Agriculture and Engineering	888		92	4	1			2	2	886	2	888		477	364		21		667
North Dakota Agricultural College	210		397	3	3	101	5	16	16	229	109	338	81	160	230	16			299
University of North Dakota	351		522	1						503	464	967	45					85	141
Ohio University	462		1,355	78	65	494	21			462	522	984	255	1,439	121			150	305
Ohio State University	3,142		472							3,714	1,438	5,152	425	485			34		981
Miami University (Ohio)	555		98	0	63	297	22	12	166	555	472	1,027	88	611		0		116	80
Oklahoma College for Women			929	42		1				0	336	336				0			1,575
University of Oklahoma	1,273	237								1,554	451	2,005	376	888	78		125		
Oklahoma Agricultural and Mechanical College	438	154	202	1	0	117	35	51	49	664	405	1,069	70	325	17	7		108	400
Oregon State Agricultural College	2,161	173	671	9	4			8	31	2,293	741	3,034	39	223	624	14		152	2,250

1 Including secondary schools.
2 Includes students in music, art, oratory, business, etc., unless they are enrolled in four-year courses leading to a collegiate degree.
3 No report.

TABLE 2.—*Student enrollment in State universities and State colleges for the year 1918-19*—Continued.

Names of institutions	Preparatory department Men	Preparatory department Women	Collegiate department Men	Collegiate department Women	Graduate department Men	Graduate department Women	Professional departments Men	Professional departments Women	All other students Men	All other students Women	Total (excluding duplicates) Men	Total (excluding duplicates) Women	Total (excluding duplicates) Total	Enrolled in 1918 summer school Men	Enrolled in 1918 summer school Women	Enrolled in other short courses Men	Enrolled in other short courses Women	Law	Medicine	Dentistry	Pharmacy	Students in military drill
1	2	3	4	5	6	7	8	9	10	11	12	13	14	15	16	17	18	19	20	21	22	23
University of Oregon			660	662	7	9	108	2	44	74	819	747	1,566	79	423			33	77			592
Pennsylvania State College			2,072	244	46	5			9	12	2,127	26±	2,388	584	59	74	5	33				1,112
University of Porto Rico	236	290	120	138			38	14	38	9	494	427	921	82	128						19	368
Rhode Island State College			206	47		2					206	49	255									130
The Citadel, the Military College of South Carolina			350								350	0	350	132	0							350
Clemson Agricultural College (S. C.)			788	0	10	6	40	1	38		825	0	825		0							825
University of South Carolina		38	470	38					8	25	470	70	540		230	49		41				107
South Dakota State College of Agriculture and Mechanic Arts	53	33	297	118	4		18	6	14	5	386	162	548	45							24	248
South Dakota State School of Mines	18		67	0							85	0	85	24	85	36	82	67	70			
University of South Dakota			207	272	2	1	139	7			455	304	760	161	661	5	0	45	71		6	92
University of Tennessee	29	9	377	193	37	43	172	45	7	24	535	728	725	371	968			388	211	59	39	199
University of Texas			1,717	999			591				2,141	1,081	3,222									1,050
Agricultural and Mechanical College of Texas	477	0	1,821	0			12	0		100	2,310	1,850	2,310	890	52	34	2		117			1,700
College of Industrial Arts (Texas)		300		1,450								337	1,950	600								
Agricultural College of Utah	139	78	215	159	8		158	6	5		354	437	791	31	201	156	28	47				261
University of Utah	60	48	1,209	466	20			0			1,406	481	1,889	106	558	10	0		90		39	1,100
University of Vermont and State Agricultural College			356	198	41	9	90		5	4	433	203	656	14	194				111			270
Virginia Polytechnic Institute			487	0	8						495	0	495	124	804			86				407
University of Virginia			964	0	20		207				1,191	1,632	1,673	34	16	133						673
Virginia Military Institute	161		673	25	12	67			76	46	673	1,025	2,002	390	1,404		28				328	268
College of William and Mary (Va.)		60	180	436	36	60	90	23	21	118	190	588	2,996	305	263	10	0	83	90		61	2,535
State College of Washington			784	1,522	14	10	104	10	201	14	1,070	379	2,379	305	1,404			21	111		8	464
University of Washington			1,231	374	155	128	61		10	62	1,274	2,700	6,265	657	1,446		5	77	37		29	703
West Virginia University		61	965	2,658	2	6					3,566	240	540	14	263				114			118
University of Wisconsin			2,699	111							300											
University of Wyoming	70		218																			

TABLE 3.—*Property and income of State universities*

	Names of institutions.	Property.				
		Bound volumes in libraries.	Value of library, scientific apparatus, machinery, and furniture.	Value of grounds (including farm).	Value of buildings.	Endowment funds.
	1	2	3	4	5	6
1	Alabama Polytechnic Institute	33,550	$240,753	$30,000	$785,500	$284,500
2	Alabama Technical Institute and College for Women	9,115	80,000	15,000	660,000	345,416
3	University of Alabama	27,000	180,000	350,000	950,000	950,000
4	University of Arizona	30,000	170,906	199,420	662,880	10,500
5	University of Arkansas	31,500	297,000	127,000	400,000	132,666
6	University of California	458,000	3,006,098		10,570,404	6,674,027
7	University of Colorado	114,931	400,000	200,000	1,000,000	80,000
8	Colorado Agricultural College	42,164	164,828	225,000	755,000	
9	Colorado School of Mines	15,500	283,488	83,914	455,009	
10	Colorado State Teachers College	52,000	131,868	170,000	525,980	
11	Connecticut Agricultural College	15,250	130,000	63,315	867,566	256,000
12	Delaware College	27,000	258,272	354,944	1,015,861	300,998
13	University of Florida	35,500	120,000	185,000	426,000	198,080
14	Florida State College for Women	11,000	80,000	85,000	515,000	
15	University of Georgia [3]					
16	Georgia School of Technology	15,000	280,000	150,000	600,000	155,000
17	North Georgia Agricultural College	4,000	6,000	20,000	85,000	
18	University of Hawaii	24,514	141,280	151,816	67,211	
19	University of Idaho	43,000	424,078	70,000	698,414	1,500,000
20	Idaho Technical Institute	7,500	24,660	54,500	240,252	
21	University of Illinois	440,325	2,505,089	1,071,080	4,116,952	649,012
22	Indiana University [3]					
23	Purdue University (Ind.)	51,795	584,000	225,000	1,611,500	444,500
24	Iowa State College of Agriculture and Mechanic Arts	70,885	1,207,080	261,841	2,857,532	689,779
25 / 26	Iowa State Teachers College	51,000	250,000	50,000	2,000,000	
	State University of Iowa	183,500	1,530,854	573,636	2,964,226	
	University of Kansas	125,212	450,874	125,000	1,500,000	151,000
	Kansas State Agricultural College	62,464	410,011	612,460	1,003,684	491,746
	University of Kentucky	36,201	261,170	252,487	755,635	184,075
	Louisiana State University and Agricultural and Mechanical College	49,329	246,095	259,992	588,544	318,713
	University of Maine	60,000	317,565	15,000	709,673	256,921
	University of Maryland	5,000	192,311	85,800	573,397	
	Massachusetts Agricultural College	58,563	669,833	114,693	1,000,321	361,000
	Massachusetts Institute of Technology	136,965	1,587,000	2,610,000	6,296,000	9,396,553
31	University of Michigan	413,666	2,489,639	891,203	4,694,818	1,393,304
34	Michigan Agricultural College	44,786	226,000	110,377	1,239,650	
37	Michigan College of Mines	28,515			786,745	
38	University of Minnesota	280,000	2,658,000	2,658,420	6,230,943	1,945,197
39	Mississippi Agricultural and Mechanical College [3]					
40	Mississippi Industrial Institute and College	15,000	75,000	225,000	562,500	
41	University of Mississippi [3]					
42	University of Missouri	223,770	1,348,321	804,141	1,988,855	1,577,021
43	Montana College of Agriculture and Mechanic Arts	17,860	254,330	96,000	453,000	812,558
44	Montana State School of Mines	9,000	51,000	32,000	120,000	
45	University of Montana	45,000	141,000	120,000	375,000	
46	University of Nebraska	140,640	784,146	1,505,219	2,535,288	878,058
47	University of Nevada	32,750	192,700	291,290	274,978	329,140
48	New Hampshire College of Agriculture and Mechanic Arts	40,000	140,000	50,000	800,000	950,000
49	Rutgers College (N. J.)	102,300	284,000	479,008	1,041,279	923,997
50	University of New Mexico	13,000	60,500	70,000	214,241	830
51	New Mexico School of Mines [3]					
52	New Mexico College of Agriculture and Mechanic Arts	18,323	220,425	75,810	221,306	
53	New York State College for Teachers	4,914	37,000	100,000	420,000	
54	Cornell University (N. Y.)	605,526	2,835,878	374,611	6,642,909	14,976,546
55	New York State College of Forestry (at Syracuse University) [3]					
56	University of North Carolina	88,316	363,051	125,500	866,414	241,030

[1] Includes appropriations for experiment stations, farmers' institutes, and extension work.
[2] Including students Army Corps and other war activities.
[3] No report.

and State colleges for the year 1918-19.

		Income.					Analysis of State appropriations.			
Student fees, excluding board and room rent.	From productive funds.	From the State.[1]	From United States Government.	Private benefactions.	From all other sources.	Total working income.	Mill tax rate.	Receipts from mill tax.	Appropriation for current expenses.[1]	For building and permanent improvements.
7	8	9	10	11	12	13	14	15	16	17
$18,334	$21,440	$148,917	$143,671	....	$21,262	$353,624	....	$17,611	$91,306	$40,000	1
13,785	20,849	36,000	....	....	16,606	87,240	....	....	36,000	....	2
63,500	59,337	87,500	88,918	....	....	299,255	....	....	87,500	....	3
8,437	10,205	338,391	96,004	$1,700	71,520	526,257	....	....	293,391	45,000	4
17,465	9,143	228,039	120,838	....	20,282	395,767	‡	189,109	38,930	....	5
353,989	279,645	1,980,422	128,631	270,794	¹1,229,000	4,242,481	....	....	1,879,411	101,011	6
98,910	4,000	564,734	....	....	43,056	710,700	½	350,000	74,734	140,000	7
16,926	17,798	341,891	106,774	....	91,033	574,422	¼	161,920	94,476	85,495	8
15,526	....	114,932	....	....	27,054	157,512	¼	114,932	....	....	9
37,940	....	256,546	....	....	2,191	296,677	¹⁄₁₆	184,546	....	72,000	10
34,761	25,295	149,233	79,890	....	126,511	415,690	....	....	149,233	....	11
21,819	28,820	62,010	85,200	60	76,455	274,364	....	....	62,010	....	12
5,473	20,054	229,575	82,298	3,750	7,387	348,537	....	....	170,713	58,862	13
17,000	2,064	115,036	....	....	....	135,100	....	....	115,036	....	14
											15
105,655	2,000	125,000	....	....	12,300	244,955	....	....	100,000	25,000	16
2,500	....	26,500	....	....	29,500	58,500	....	....	26,500	....	17
1,426	....	22,729	....	....	8,492	82,647	....	....	22,729	....	18
4,779	104,302	299,250	100,881	....	62,194	571,406	....	....	225,836	73,414	19
1,759	....	204,172	529	....	....	206,460	....	....	164,172	40,000	20
271,245	32,451	2,306,934	196,708	126,536	378,475	3,312,349	1	2,056,934	....	250,000	21
											22
80,413	31,447	581,168	156,259	....	432,406	1,281,693	⁷⁄₁₀	446,143	110,500	24,525	23
95,544	33,591	1,232,186	155,734	6,695	371,134	1,894,884	....	....	1,132,186	100,000	24
43,190	....	389,500	....	....	17,906	450,596	....	....	389,500	....	25
113,108	23,243	1,208,541	....	....	763,671	2,108,563	....	....	803,541	345,000	26
67,744	7,512	777,000	²366,905	....	97,334	1,316,495	....	....	664,500	112,500	27
55,581	20,743	700,123	140,944	....	551,311	1,468,702	....	....	650,123	50,000	28
17,272	9,452	397,251	²389,678	3,000	209,935	1,026,588	¹⁄₁₀	299,696	97,555	....	29
12,610	14,555	278,250	118,213	....	157,185	580,813	....	....	196,250	82,000	30
65,360	9,915	180,008	104,102	9,915	46,254	415,554	....	....	180,008	....	31
7,476	6,544	196,977	117,113	8,093	16,265	352,468	....	....	196,977	....	32
5,865	10,613	456,335	82,370	....	145,519	700,702	....	....	368,000	88,335	33
551,845	301,232	....	22,265	187,408	43,940	1,206,690	....	....	100,000	....	34
435,492	77,913	1,375,860	1,860	74,783	1,103,679	3,069,587	‡	1,050,000	110,860	215,000	35
31,383	70,712	585,783	153,113	1,047	457,124	1,299,162	¼	560,000	25,783	....	36
13,955	....	72,700	....	....	6,120	92,775	....	....	72,700	....	37
308,323	199,168	1,893,478	142,146	....	²919,446	3,462,361	⁷⁄₁₀	313,978	138,978	175,000	38
											39
29,798	9,449	75,000	....	....	....	114,247	....	....	75,000	....	40
											41
117,350	91,846	790,156	160,542	239,146	172,040	1,453,730	....	....	786,720	3,436	42
10,845	....	315,762	109,258	....	40,276	476,141	....	....	315,762	....	43
1,798	....	50,500	²1,180	....	6,076	59,554	....	....	38,500	12,000	44
13,303	....	290,000	....	....	12,424	315,727	....	....	220,000	70,000	45
92,646	51,518	1,431,272	127,506	....	249,093	1,952,035	1	528,191	425,938	477,143	46
2,484	13,392	255,090	92,915	....	24,369	388,230	½	133,097	21,993	100,000	47
31,473	39,866	59,467	97,467	101	117,318	345,692	....	....	59,467	....	48
35,153	45,467	226,040	116,807	65,322	....	488,789	....	....	226,040	....	49
3,236	37,585	105,480	....	....	60,149	206,450	....	....	105,480	....	50
											51
3,727	17,000	132,619	107,635	....	51,802	312,778	....	....	132,619	....	52
6,090	....	182,682	....	....	....	188,772	....	....	182,682	....	53
507,728	705,109	890,984	169,536	820,738	784,018	3,878,113	....	....	883,540	7,444	54
											55
63,274	13,258	213,756	....	6,892	71,534	368,714	....	....	194,167	119,590	56

TABLE 3.—*Property and income of State universities*

Names of institutions.	Bound volumes in libraries.	Value of library, scientific apparatus, machinery, and furniture.	Value of grounds (including farm).	Value of buildings.	Endowment funds.
1	2	3	4	5	6
57 North Carolina College of Agriculture and Engineering.	10,000	$369,698	$110,073	$664,768	
58 North Dakota Agricultural College	28,948	310,987	95,000	595,000	
59 University of North Dakota	76,420	341,154	115,510	638,410	$1,773,963
60 Ohio University	47,530	225,000	535,148	1,070,100	148,251
61 Ohio State University	196,295	1,783,468	2,050,033	3,173,986	1,045,331
62 Miami University (Ohio)	52,724	241,794	75,200	807,357	129,400
63 Oklahoma College for Women	6,000	8,000	30,000	300,000	
64 University of Oklahoma	31,700	291,410	116,389	1,150,586	3,670,000
65 Oklahoma Agricultural and Mechanical College.	10,000	55,000	60,000	1,056,752	
66 Oregon State Agriculture College	43,000	439,350	472,019	1,087,763	202,664
67 University of Oregon	87,500	251,016	319,000	546,871	55,000
68 Pennsylvania State College	71,271	780,701	152,180	1,810,587	676,372
69 University of Porto Rico	6,300	95,563	55,902	185,650	10,971
70 Rhode Island State College	22,700	146,712	14,900	325,000	
71 The Citadel, the Military College of South Carolina.	6,500	68,899	500,000	400,000	
72 Clemson Agricultural College (S. C.)	19,349	470,728	304,100	1,237,094	58,539
73 University of South Carolina	57,000	260,534	645,000	437,500	
74 South Dakota State College of Agriculture and Mechanic Arts.	24,152	99,000	125,000	595,000	451,059
75 South Dakota State School of Mines	7,200	60,000	17,000	96,000	
76 University of South Dakota	38,000	220,000	50,000	665,000	
77 University of Tennessee	45,243	291,337	856,850	514,701	425,000
78 University of Texas [1]					
79 Agricultural and Mechanical College of Texas.	20,000	692,116	158,063	1,929,708	209,000
80 College of Industrial Arts (Tex.)	12,000	200,414	95,500	790,673	
81 Agricultural College of Utah	32,900	212,043	29,500	888,900	
82 University of Utah	73,891	300,000	48,000	877,700	110,000
83 University of Vermont and State Agricultural College.	102,346	277,000	100,000	1,500,000	732,085
84 Virginia Polytechnic Institute	27,962	215,227	80,000	576,000	
85 University of Virginia	115,000	340,433	600,000	1,492,126	2,690,454
86 Virginia Military Institute	22,000	27,995	37,500	690,768	43,
87 College of William and Mary (Va.)	16,000	75,621	75,000	260,000	151,
88 State College of Washington	73,000	356,663	148,073	1,289,013	943,
89 University of Washington	93,687	.481,656	1,061,250	1,169,350	7,327,
90 West Virginia University	67,000		500,000	1,500,000	115,
91 University of Wisconsin	263,000	1,896,582	2,137,311	4,952,312	709,
92 University of Wyoming	43,768	310,000	110,000	520,000	547,

[1] No report.
[2] Including Students Army Training Corps, and other war activities.
[3] Includes receipts from mill tax.
[4] Fertilizer tax.

and State colleges for the year 1918–19—Continued.

			Income.				Analysis of State appropriations.			
Student fees, excluding board and room rent.	From productive funds.	From the State.	From United States Government.	Private benefactions.	From all other sources.	Total working income.	Mill tax rate.	Receipts from mill tax.	Appropriation for current expenses.	For building and permanent improvements.	
7	8	9	10	11	12	18	14	15	16	17	
$32,902	$7,500	$227,834	$153,834	....	$64,892	$486,962	....	....	$202,834	$25,000	57
8,034	78,105	234,387	111,865	$6,000	59,569	497,960			174,387	60,000	58
20,923	63,671	261,437	....		²112,613	458,643			186,294	75,143	59
23,932	12,032	252,490	....		24,959	313,413	⅛₁₀	....	²227,840	24,650	60
128,359	61,810	1,671,405	149,282	9,000	205,722	2,225,578	⁶₁₀		²1,671,405		61
32,001	17,642	220,530	....	277,008	13,384	560,565	₁₁₀		²196,580	23,950	62
....	50,000	105,000	1,648			156,648			5,000	100,000	63
32,452	102,456	910,185				1,045,093			353,456	546,729	64
5,990	....	568,124	141,895		34,091	750,100			368,124	200,000	65
40,177	11,388	600,626	105,562		48,862	806,615	₄/₁₀	$383,228	202,398	15,000	66
31,458	8,119	467,760	....			503,337	₇/₁₀	296,260	67,500	100,000	67
61,077	31,020	623,439	219,128		231,213	1,165,877			588,805	34,634	68
4,465	2,233	98,846	50,589		2,832	158,965			94,043	4,803	69
6,273	....	40,000	90,764		63,289	200,326			40,000		70
....		179,749	....		16,804	196,553			79,749	100,000	71
13,576	9,266	312,571	178,764		9,431	523,608	(⁴)	....	312,571		72
15,249	....	128,191	....		11,365	154,805			109,979	18,211	73
12,539	68,241	378,078	111,584	14,769	87,097	672,308			174,026	204,052	74
²60,028	4,784	62,875				127,687			62,875		75
14,014	16,046	157,500	....		3,741	191,301			157,500		76
46,348	24,210	244,068	152,204	4,130	41,474	512,434	½	241,068			77
....											78
36,541	10,450	937,944	218,381		756,138	1,959,454			702,816	235,128	79
33,280	....	195,923	6,840		22,493	258,536	(⁵)	147,033	191,723	4,200	80
6,559	....	343,113	98,529		60,757	508,958	(⁶)	366,973	23,000	173,080	81
....	9,005	553,374		20,203	274,727	857,310			14,700	171,700	82
74,809	42,264	67,150	97,958	20,809	165,020	467,710			67,150		83
28,310	....	237,275	140,785		308,712	715,082			237,275		84
99,649	101,962	150,000	....	187,894	99,061	638,566			150,000		85
43,111	6,058	160,600	¹25,642		15,235	250,646			60,600	100,000	86
3,566	8,777	52,000				64,343			52,000		87
24,794	74,684	440,458	112,829		261,799	914,564	(⁷)	318,187	122,271		88
147,398	61,609	698,268	6,582		22,330	936,187	(⁸)	625,013	14,611	58,644	89
36,475	11,318	490,510	122,251		81,168	741,722			426,510	64,000	90
368,488	44,331	1,915,927	147,962	117,028	617,984	3,921,458	½	1,382,349	439,452	94,126	91
7,721	25,065	154,664	94,372	617	23,912	306,351	½	105,309	12,000	37,355	92

ᵇ 28.34 per cent of 28 per cent of the State levy of 2 mills.
ᶜ 64.43 per cent of 28 per cent of the State levy of 2 mills.
⁷ A little less than one-third of 1 mill.
⁸ A little less than one-half of 1 mill.

The program of higher education requires buildings, equipment, and a superior teaching force. During the last few years the cost of buildings and equipment in colleges and universities has risen tremendously, just as it has in all parts of the business world. As yet the cost of salaries has not risen to the same extent as the cost of living, and unless the people wish to see their higher institutions staffed with men of inferior ability, it will be necessary to pay salaries sufficiently large to attract teachers of merit and ability.

Other conditions have added greatly to the cost of higher education, particularly the great increase in college enrollment in recent years. From 1890 to 1918 the increase in student attendance was 309 per cent at the public institutions and 113 per cent at the privately supported institutions. In three years, from 1917 to 1920, the increase of attendance was 31 per cent at publicly supported institutions and 20 per cent at privately supported institutions. This year it appears that the increase in attendance over last year is about 10 per cent. It goes without saying that these great increases in college attendance require corresponding increases in the funds devoted to higher education. It seems reasonable to suppose, therefore, that the great additions to the expense of building, equipment, and teachers' salaries, accompanied as they are by an unprecedented student enrollment, will require State legislatures to appropriate funds the amount of which was little dreamed of a few years ago.

Such a condition is not a matter for apprehension. When the State appropriates money to its departments of government, it is paying its current expenses. When the State appropriates money to education, it is making a wise investment which will yield manifold returns. Liberal support of higher education is good public economy and wise forethought for the future.

The people of this country are committed to free elementary and secondary education. They believe that higher education should be within reach of every young man and woman capable of profiting by it. How shall we pay for higher education? It does not seem desirable that the proportion of the income of State colleges and universities raised through the imposition of students' fees should be increased much, if any. Already the average proportion of the total income derived from this source is 22 per cent. The proportion of income received from the Federal Government has until the last few years steadily declined. State universities and colleges can not

16

expect to secure funds through private benefactions. This leaves only the States to support their higher institutions. Reassessments on property valuations, increased rates of taxation, and new forms of taxation in order to provide adequate support for higher education are possible solutions to which State legislatures will have to give their attention during the forthcoming session.

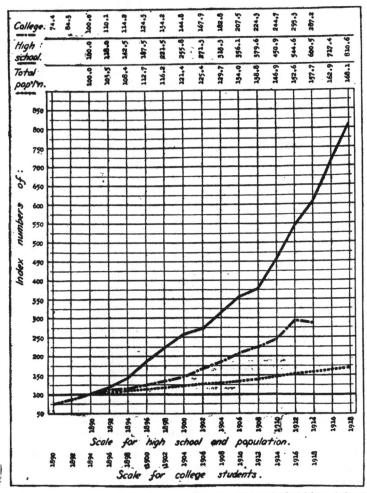

FIGURE 1.—Index numbers showing the comparative rates of increase in the total population, the total public high-school enrollment, and the total number of students in collegiate and resident graduate departments of colleges, universities, and technological schools from 1870–1918. The curve for college students has been shifted to the left to compensate for lag.

With the hope that the Bureau of Education may be of some
assistance in putting this matter clearly before the people of each
State, some comparative statistics have been included in this bulletin.
It was necessary to draw these figures from the reports for 1917–18
(later figures for the privately supported colleges are not yet available).
It is believed that the tables have been so simplified as to make them
more useful for the purposes of the campaign for increased financial
support now facing every State institution in the country.

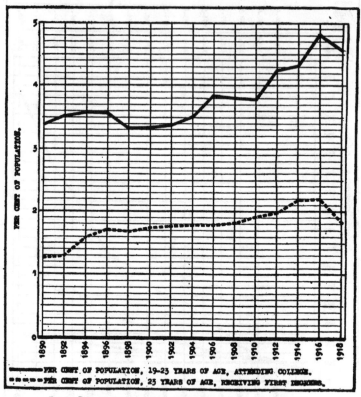

Fig. 2.—Per cent of population attending college and graduating, 1890–1918.

The accuracy of the tables showing the rank of various States in
a number of particulars is, of course, subject to a number of qualifications. Certain States have a larger proportion of adult population
than others; in some States there are located colleges and universities
which draw from the whole Nation; in some States an unusually
large proportion of students go to higher institutions located in other
States; some States are more wealthy than others; and still others

have a larger high-school population to draw from. These inequalities are bound to occur and should qualify all deductions which seem apparent at first examination. It is believed, however, that the several tables ranking the States in certain particulars are, notwithstanding these qualifications, of sufficient accuracy and worth to make them very useful in the promotion of State campaigns for the more adequate support of higher education.

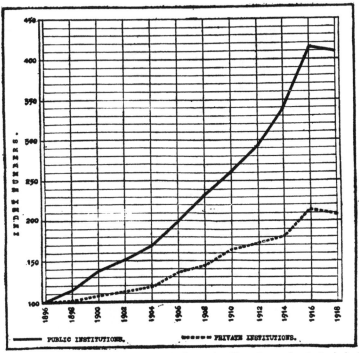

Fig. 3.—Index numbers of students in public and private universities, colleges, and professional schools, showing the rate of increase.

Because the statistical reports received by the Bureau of Education make no division of the income received for collegiate and subcollegiate instruction, respectively, it was found necessary to include the preparatory students attending colleges and universities with the regular college students in order to estimate the average income per student. "High-school attendance," therefore, includes only those students enrolled at public and private high schools. The total number of preparatory students at colleges and universities in 1917–18 was 44,660.

The item entitled "Teachers needed in secondary schools in September, 1920," is taken from a careful estimate made in each

State by the Bureau of Education in May, 1920. In order to see the force of this item the number of teachers needed in the secondary schools should be compared with the total number of college graduates for the year 1917–18. Since the total number of graduates in any one State did not in June, 1920, greatly exceed the number two years previous, it is apparent that each State can use a very large proportion of its college graduates as teachers in the secondary schools.

TABLE 4.—*College attendance compared with population, 1917–18.*

States.	Per cent of students in colleges and universities to total population.	States.	Per cent of students in colleges and universities to total population.	States.	Per cent of students in colleges and universities to total population.
District of Columbia.	1.66	South Dakota	0.37	Mississippi	0.20
Iowa	.72	Michigan	.36	Idaho	.19
Colorado	.65	Indiana	.34	Kentucky	.19
Massachusetts	.56	Virginia	.33	Rhode Island	.19
Nebraska	.55	Vermont	.32	Alabama	.18
Oregon	.54	Wisconsin	.31	Louisiana	.18
Kansas	.51	Montana	.29	Wyoming	.18
California	.50	North Dakota	.29	Arizona	.17
Illinois	.50	Washington	.29	Oklahoma	.17
Minnesota	.45	Maine	.28	Florida	.16
Ohio	.44	Nevada	.28	Delaware	.15
Utah	.44	Tennessee	.28	West Virginia	.12
New York	.42	South Carolina	.26	Arkansas	.11
Maryland	.41	Connecticut	.24	New Mexico	.11
New Hampshire	.40	Texas	.24	New Jersey	.10
Pennsylvania	.38	North Carolina	.23		
Missouri	.37	Georgia	.22	United States	.36

TABLE 5.—*Students in public and private universities, colleges, and professional schools, 1917–18.*

States.	Public institutions.			Private institutions.		
	Number.	Enrollment.	Per cent of total public and private.	Number.	Enrollment.	Per cent of total public and private.
Alabama	3	2,002	46.55	8	2,299	53.45
Arizona	1	475	100.00	0		
Arkansas	1	730	37.96	8	1,193	62.04
California	7	7,578	48.98	15	7,893	51.02
Colorado	4	4,547	68.15	5	2,125	31.85
Connecticut	1	186	5.94	6	2,945	94.06
Delaware	1	336	100.00	0		
District of Columbia	2	1,423	22.84	8	4,807	77.16
Florida	2	850	56.22	2	662	43.78
Georgia	3	1,978	30.20	15	4,572	69.80
Idaho	2	661	76.42	1	204	23.56
Illinois	2	5,195	16.39	45	26,497	83.61
Indiana	2	4,312	45.06	16	5,258	54.94
Iowa	3	7,635	47.43	20	8,464	52.57
Kansas	3	4,352	45.44	17	5,226	54.56
Kentucky	2	1,320	28.84	12	3,256	71.16
Louisiana	1	838	25.29	5	2,476	74.71
Maine	1	871	40.25	3	1,293	59.75
Maryland	1	206	3.66	16	5,428	96.34
Massachusetts	1	503	2.34	26	20.969	97.66
Michigan	5	8,339	73.24	11	3,047	26.76
Minnesota	3	6,061	57.59	15	4,479	42.41
Mississippi	3	2,305	58.34	7	1,646	41.66
Missouri	2	4,074	31.69	29	8,781	68.31
Montana	3	1,394	100.00	0		

TABLE 5.—*Students in public and private universities, colleges, and professional schools,* 1917-18—Continued.

States.	Public institutions.			Private institutions		
	Number.	Enrollment.	Per cent of total public and private.	Number.	Enrollment.	Per cent of total public and private.
Nebraska	1	4,028	56.43	8	3,110	43.57
Nevada	1	324	100.00	0		
New Hampshire	1	562	31.66	2	1,213	68.34
New Jersey	0			11	3,142	100.00
New Mexico	3	474	100.00	0		
New York	4	9,813	22.17	42	34,456	77.83
North Carolina	2	1,418	25.05	17	4,242	74.95
North Dakota	2	1,524	66.43	2	770	33.57
Ohio	6	10,601	45.47	38	12,711	54.53
Oklahoma	3	2,966	71.96	3	1,156	28.04
Oregon	2	3,184	65.85	10	1,651	34.15
Pennsylvania	1	2,192	6.64	48	30,835	93.36
Rhode Island	1	243	20.59	1	937	79.41
South Carolina	4	1,602	36.97	12	2,731	63.03
South Dakota	3	1,521	55.61	4	1,214	44.39
Tennessee	1	833	12.87	17	5,640	87.13
Texas	3	4,666	42.75	14	6,247	57.25
Utah	2	1,989	100.00	0		
Vermont	1	591	51.12	3	565	48.88
Virginia	5	2,319	31.40	23	5,066	68.60
Washington	2	4,240	86.74	2	648	13.26
West Virginia	1	986	56.93	3	746	43.07
Wisconsin	1	4,286	54.07	10	3,641	45.93
Wyoming	1	347	100.00	0		
United States	1 110	110,900	31.23	560	244,231	68.77

1 Does not include the U. S. Military or Naval Academy.

TABLE 6.—*Attendance at public universities, colleges, and professional schools compared to population, 1917-18.*

States.	Per cent attending colleges, etc.	States.	Per cent attending colleges, etc.	States.	Per cent attending colleges, etc.
Colorado	0.45	Arizona	0.17	Alabama	0.08
Utah	.44	Wisconsin	.17	Illinois	.08
Dist. Columbia	.38	Vermont	.16	Georgia	.07
Oregon	.36	Delaware	.15	West Virginia	.07
Iowa	.34	Indiana	.15	North Carolina	.06
Nebraska	.31	Idaho	.14	Kentucky	.05
Montana	.29	New Hampshire	.13	Arkansas	.04
Nevada	.28	Mississippi	.12	Louisiana	.04
Michigan	.27	Missouri	.12	Rhode Island	.04
Minnesota	.26	Oklahoma	.12	Tennessee	.04
Washington	.26	Maine	.11	Pennsylvania	.02
California	.24	New Mexico	.11	Connecticut	.01
Kansas	.23	Florida	.10	Maryland	.01
South Dakota	.21	South Carolina	.10	Massachusetts	.01
Ohio	.20	Texas	.10	New Jersey	.00
North Dakota	.19	Virginia	.10		
Wyoming	.18	New York	.09	United States	.12

TABLE 7.—*Percentage of students in universities, colleges, and professional schools compared to high-school attendance, 1917–18.*

States.	Per cent in colleges, etc.	States.	Per cent in colleges, etc.	States.	Per cent in colleges, etc.
Dist. Columbia	64.68	Nevada	21.18	Indiana	13.93
South Carolina	40.45	Missouri	21.13	Washington	13.06
Colorado	34.63	Ohio	21.09	New Mexico	13.19
Maryland	34.48	Alabama	20.65	Oklahoma	12.69
Tennessee	30.02	Kentucky	19.75	Rhode Island	12.47
Illinois	28.20	North Dakota	19.44	Montana	12.30
Iowa	27.26	Minnesota	18.95	Vermont	11.91
Mississippi	27.25	Louisiana	18.87	Connecticut	11.77
Oregon	25.76	Kansas	18.52	Delaware	11.56
North Carolina	24.71	California	17.41	Arizona	11.08
New York	24.46	Florida	16.91	Wyoming	10.70
Virginia	23.95	Michigan	16.67	Maine	10.51
Georgia	23.94	Texas	16.46	West Virginia	10.05
Massachusetts	23.76	New Hampshire	16.07	Idaho	7.88
Pennsylvania	23.57	Arkansas	15.38	New Jersey	5.66
Nebraska	23.54	Wisconsin	15.15		
South Dakota	21.52	Utah	14.78	United States	20.81

TABLE 8.—*Receipts per student from public sources for public universities, colleges, and professional schools, 1917–18.*

Maryland	$1,875	Wisconsin	$450	Utah	$289
Tennessee	1,495	Oklahoma	442	Maine	288
Connecticut	1,429	Texas	437	Washington	286
Massachusetts	1,016	New Hampshire	400	Vermont	283
Arizona	963	South Carolina	397	Ohio	274
Delaware	841	North Carolina	386	Georgia	266
New Mexico	742	Iowa	381	Michigan	248
Nevada	732	Pennsylvania	374	Virginia	225
Idaho	724	Kansas	366	Colorado	221
Wyoming	710	Minnesota	334	Missouri	215
West Virginia	628	Kentucky	329	Mississippi	208
South Dakota	612	Nebraska	324	Alabama	162
Rhode Island	537	Louisiana	323	New York	135
Montana	494	Indiana	322	Dist. Columbia	68
Florida	489	California	312	New Jersey	
Illinois	480	North Dakota	301		
Arkansas	466	Oregon	289	United States	384

TABLE 9.—*Receipts of universities, colleges, and professional schools from all public sources per capita of population, 1917–18.*

States.	Receipts per capita.	States.	Receipts per capita.	States.	Receipts per capita.
Nevada	$2.07	Washington	$0.73	Missouri	$0.25
Arizona	1.68	Michigan	.66	Mississippi	.24
Montana	1.42	Vermont	.59	Virginia	.23
Iowa	1.31	North Dakota	.58	North Carolina	.22
Delaware	1.30	Ohio	.55	Connecticut	.21
Wyoming	1.29	New Hampshire	.54	Massachusetts	.20
South Dakota	1.27	Tennessee	.54	Pennsylvania	.20
Utah	1.27	Indiana	.49	South Carolina	.20
Idaho	1.04	Florida	.44	Arkansas	.19
Oregon	1.04	Texas	.44	Georgia	.18
Nebraska	1.01	West Virginia	.43	Kentucky	.18
Colorado	.99	Illinois	.39	Alabama	.14
Minnesota	.87	South Carolina	.38	Louisiana	.14
Kansas	.85	Maine	.32	New York	.12
New Mexico	.81	Maryland	.28	New Jersey	.07
California	.76	Dist. Columbia	.27		
Wisconsin	.75			United States	.45

Table 10.—*Per cent of income of public and private universities, colleges, and professional schools derived from the various sources, 1917–18.*

States.	Public.				Private.			
	From productive funds	From United States Government, State, or city.	From private benefactions.	From student fees and other sources.	From productive funds.	From United States Government, State, or city.	From private benefactions.	From student fees and other sources.
1	2	3	4	5	6	7	8	9
United States	3.9	72.9	0.7	22.5	27.7	3.8	14.3	54.2
Alabama	19.8	60.9	0.8	18.5	4.6		8.2	87.2
Arizona	3.3	82.3		14.4				
Arkansas	1.7	92.0		6.3	9.7		5.6	84.7
California	6.2	65.2*	3.3	25.3	43.3		6.4	50.3
Colorado	2.1	79.7		18.2	30.2		3.7	66.1
Connecticut	1.5	57.3		41.2	37.4		45.2	17.4
Delaware	6.2	66.6	7.1	20.1				
District of Columbia	6.1	45.3	1.4	47.2	12.8		15.3	71.9
Florida	2.6	68.5	10.6	18.3	36.9		14.9	48.2
Georgia	3.8	74.4	0.3	21.5	13.2		43.7	43.1
Idaho	17.9	77.0		5.1	23.7		56.4	19.9
Illinois	1.0	81.1	1.2	16.7	37.8		13.0	49.2
Indiana	3.9	70.9		25.2	27.4		6.7	65.9
Iowa	1.5	72.8		25.7	20.4		14.6	65.0
Kansas	1.5	73.2		25.3	15.4		16.6	68.0
Kentucky	1.4	58.2	0.4	40.0	19.9		12.2	67.9
Louisiana	3.8	70.4		25.8	39.0		11.1	49.9
Maine	2.6	65.1		32.3	46.0		31.3	22.7
Maryland	0.2	98.3		1.5	5.3	8.1	15.3	71.3
Massachusetts	1.5	72.6		25.9	32.1	2.4	12.2	53.3
Michigan	4.1	57.6	3.6	34.7	24.2		27.6	48.2
Minnesota	2.0	69.2		28.8	14.2		20.7	65.1
Mississippi	6.4	46.5	0.3	46.8	7.0		6.3	86.7
Missouri	6.0	66.2		27.8	28.1		14.3	57.6
Montana	4.3	84.2		11.5				
Nebraska	3.3	75.0		21.7	34.6		19.6	45.8
Nevada	5.1	79.7		15.2				
New Hampshire	10.7	60.1		29.2	33.9	2.6	15.4	48.1
New Jersey					26.5	13.1	21.4	37.0
New Mexico	10.2	73.2		16.6				
New York		97.2		2.8	25.2	8.7	8.4	57.7
North Carolina	2.5	68.8	0.6	28.1	22.1		7.8	70.1
North Dakota	17.4	58.5		24.1	8.3		34.6	57.1
Ohio	4.6	76.0	0.7	19.3	29.7	0.4	22.8	47.1
Oklahoma	10.1	82.0		7.9	16.6		28.9	54.5
Oregon	2.0	84.1		13.9	29.2		13.2	57.6
Pennsylvania	2.8	77.0		20.2	23.9	11.3	7.9	56.9
Rhode Island	1.2	64.3		34.5				
South Carolina	2.1	68.7		29.2	10.7		12.5	76.8
South Dakota	5.4	83.9		10.7	30.0		21.8	48.2
Tennessee	1.9	91.6	0.3	6.2	25.1	1.5	16.4	57.0
Texas	7.2	62.6	0.2	30.0	35.2		8.7	56.1
Utah		82.3		17.7				
Vermont	9.2	42.7		48.1	22.0	22.2	1.4	54.4
Virginia	9.6	39.6	1.1	49.7	16.7		12.7	70.6
Washington	5.7	72.3		22.0	22.0		0.5	77.5
West Virginia	0.9	87.8		11.3	19.1		2.6	78.3
Wisconsin	1.3	66.2	0.8	31.7	20.1		11.7	62.2
Wyoming	6.9	74.9	0.3	17.9				

STATES.			STUDENTS IN HIGH SCHOOL TO EACH 100C IN TOTAL POPULATION.
UTAH	20.2	9.4	
CALIFORNIA	27.0	1.5	
KANSAS	26.5	1.0	
IOWA	24.9	1.7	
VERMONT	21.7	4.8	
MAINE	22.9	3.5	
DISTRICT OF COLUMBIA	16.5	7.2	
NEW HAMPSHIRE	18.7	6.0	
INDIANA	23.1	.9	
IDAHO	20.7	3.1	
MASSACHUSETTS	20.8	2.8	
MONTANA	21.5	1.8	
NEBRASKA	22.3	1.0	
MINNESOTA	20.5	2.3	
MICHIGAN	20.4	1.4	
WASHINGTON	20.7	.8	
OREGON	20.2	.9	
OHIO	20.0	1.0	
CONNECTICUT	17.4	3.3	
WISCONSIN	19.2	1.3	
COLORADO	18.2	.8	
NEW JERSEY	16.5	1.5	
ILLINOIS	16.6	1.2	
MISSOURI	16.4	1.2	
SOUTH DAKOTA	16.3	1.0	
WYOMING	15.8	1.3	
NEW YORK	15.3	1.7	
PENNSYLVANIA	14.4	1.5	
ARIZONA	13.9	1.9	
NORTH DAKOTA	14.7	.6	
RHODE ISLAND	13.0	1.8	
TEXAS	13.4	1.0	
VIRGINIA	11.9	1.9	
OKLAHOMA	13.3	.3	
DELAWARE	11.8	1.6	
NEVADA	13.3	.0	
WEST VIRGINIA	11.4	.6	
MARYLAND	9.8	5.0	
KENTUCKY	8.5	1.3	
FLORIDA	8.7	.8	
GEORGIA	8.1	1.2	
LOUISIANA	8.1	1.2	
TENNESSEE	7.2	2.1	
NORTH CAROLINA	7.2	2.0	
ALABAMA	7.7	1.0	
NEW MEXICO	7.7	.6	
MISSISSIPPI	6.3	1.0	
ARKANSAS	6.5	.4	
SOUTH CAROLINA	5.3	1.2	
UNITED STATES	15.6	1.5	

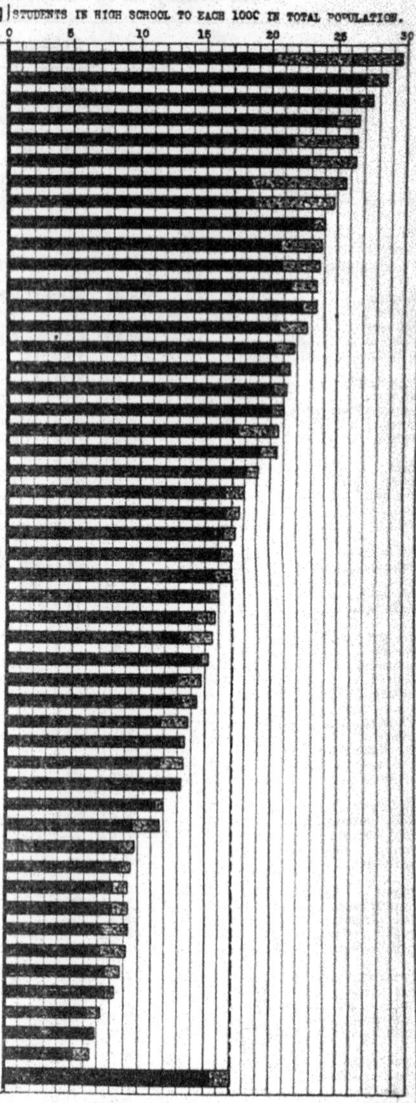

PUBLIC HIGH SCHOOLS.   PRIVATE HIGH SCHOOLS.

FIGURE 4.

TABLE 11.—*Universities, colleges, and professional schools—Students and graduates, 1917-18.*

	Institutions reporting.		Enrollment.									Students graduated.			Teachers needed in secondary schools in September, 1920.	High school attendance.	High school graduates.
			Public Institutions.			Private institutions.			Public and private.								
States.	Public.	Private.	Men.	Women.	Total.	Men.	Women.	Total.	Men.	Women.	Total.	Men.	Women.	Total.			
1	2	3	4	5	6	7	8	9	10	11	12	13	14	15	16	17	18
Alabama	3	8	1,357	645	2,002	1,842	757	2,299	2,899	1,402	4,301	177	82	259	221	20,836	2,038
Arizona	1	0	232	243	475	0	0	0	232	243	475	19	13	32	47	4,285	450
Arkansas	1	8	422	308	730	555	638	1,193	977	946	1,923	47	42	89	148	12,607	979
California	7	15	3,515	4,063	7,578	4,219	3,674	7,893	7,734	7,737	15,471	538	702	1,240	605	88,852	9,566
Colorado	4	5	1,727	2,820	4,547	1,135	990	2,125	2,862	3,810	6,672	186	295	480	124	19,269	2,344
Connecticut	1	6	161	25	186	2,561	384	2,945	2,722	409	3,131	788	2	790	120	26,601	3,940
Delaware	1	0	216	120	336				216	120	336	32	25	57	37	2,907	1,205
Dist. of Columbia	2	8	1,155	449	1,604	3,209	1,417	4,626	4,364	1,866	6,230	143	150	293	26	9,652	1,073
Florida	2	8	354	490	850	246	416	662	600	912	1,512	23	51	74	163	8,939	1,631
Georgia	3	15	1,947	31	1,978	2,029	2,643	4,572	3,976	2,674	6,560	184	160	385	330	27,365	2,128
Idaho	2	1	392	299	661	58	146	204	450	415	865	25	30	55	113	10,971	1,167
Illinois	2	45	3,090	1,496	5,195	14,021	12,476	26,497	17,720	13,972	31,692	841	1,026	1,867	996	112,993	14,609
Indiana	2	16	2,539	1,773	4,312	3,126	2,132	5,258	5,665	3,905	9,570	436	300	745	672	68,711	11,311
Iowa	2	20	2,962	3,083	7,635	2,552	4,912	8,464	7,504	8,596	16,099	491	607	1,098	1,214	59,062	7,835
Kansas	3	17	2,439	1,913	4,352	2,314	2,912	5,226	4,753	4,825	9,678	359	425	784	278	51,714	4,632
Kentucky	2	12	782	538	1,320	1,990	1,286	3,256	2,772	1,804	4,576	102	85	187	208	23,838	1,982
Louisiana	1	5	580	258	838	1,739	737	2,476	2,319	995	3,314	97	68	165	261	17,564	3,788
Maine	1	3	643	228	871	917	376	1,293	1,560	604	2,164	149	75	224	191	20,399	3,180
Maryland	1	10	201	5	206	3,517	1,911	5,428	3,718	1,916	5,634	185	159	344	83	16,336	3,116
Massachusetts	1	26	470	33	503	12,937	8,022	20,959	13,407	8,055	21,462	1,117	1,342	2,459	334	90,338	13,255
Michigan	5	11	6,099	2,240	8,339	1,934	1,113	3,047	8,033	3,353	11,386	667	430	1,097	378	68,285	8,373
Minnesota	3	15	3,731	2,350	6,081	2,811	1,668	4,479	6,542	4,018	10,560	320	434	754	910	53,447	7,441
Mississippi	3	7	1,300	1,005	2,305	324	1,322	1,646	1,624	2,327	3,951	115	198	313	178	14,499	1,556
Missouri	3	29	2,450	1,624	4,074	5,868	2,913	8,781	8,318	4,537	12,855	404	256	660	530	60,851	1,278
Montana	3	0	711	683	1,394				711	683	1,394	31	57	88	202	11,332	1,393
Nebraska	1	8	2,094	1,934	4,028	1,637	1,473	3,110	3,731	3,407	7,138	204	257	461	501	30,325	2,622
Nevada	1	0	154	170	324		0		154	170	324	6	15	21	11	1,530	2,182
New Hampshire	1	2	399	163	562	1,213		1,213	1,612	163	1,775	328	20	348	77	11,043	1,781

[1] Excluding United States Naval Academy.

TABLE 11.—*Universities, colleges, and professional schools—Students and graduates, 1917-18—Continued.*

States	Institutions reporting		Public institutions			Private institutions			Public and private			Students graduated			Teachers needed in secondary schools in September, 1920.	High school attendance.	High school graduates.
	Public.	Private.	Men.	Women.	Total.	Men.	Women.	Total.	Men.	Women.	Total.	Men.	Women.	Total.			
1	2	3	4	5	6	7	8	9	10	11	12	13	14	15	16	17	18
New Jersey	0	11				2,661	481	3,142	2,661	481	3,142	215	45	290	238	55,501	6,701
New Mexico	3	0	272	202	474				272	202	474	7	10	17	72	3,592	402
New York	1 4	42	5,062	4,751	9,813	23,712	10,744	34,456	28,774	15,495	44,299	1,796	1,872	3,668	1,220	180,925	18,096
North Carolina	2	17	1,394	24	1,418	2,026	2,216	4,242	3,420	2,240	5,660	212	88	400	396	22,903	1,197
North Dakota	2	2	836	688	1,524	250	520	770	1,086	1,208	2,294	62	101	163	270	12,108	953
Ohio	6	38	5,792	4,809	10,601	7,156	5,555	12,711	12,948	10,364	23,312	909	967	1,876	879	110,522	15,473
Oklahoma	3	3	1,687	1,279	2,966	530	626	1,156	2,217	1,905	4,122	107	134	241	406	32,474	3,034
Oregon	2	10	1,701	1,383	3,184	836	815	1,651	2,537	2,298	4,835	161	157	318	233	18,786	2,076
Pennsylvania	1	48	1,960	232	2,192	20,893	9,942	30,835	22,853	10,174	33,027	1,181	675	1,856	947	140,111	16,500
Rhode Island	1	1	194	49	243	688	249	937	882	298	1,180	93	57	150	12	9,466	162
South Carolina	4	12	1,538	64	1,602	1,042	1,689	2,731	2,580	1,753	4,330	317	159	476	120	10,713	543
South Dakota	3	4	851	670	1,521	351	863	1,214	1,202	1,533	2,735	47	76	123	297	12,707	1,399
Tennessee	1	17	579	254	833	2,650	2,990	5,640	3,229	3,244	6,473	127	145	272	225	21,561	2,014
Texas	3	14	2,445	2,221	4,666	2,751	3,496	6,247	5,196	5,717	10,913	219	364	583	886	66,980	6,457
Utah	2	0	1,143	846	1,989				1,143	846	1,989	72	78	150	92	13,456	1,206
Vermont	1	3	404	187	591	413	152	565	817	339	1,156	55	67	122	89	9,708	1,561
Virginia	5	23	2,316	3	2,319	2,040	3,026	5,066	4,356	3,029	7,385	305	171	476	176	30,840	2,470
Washington	2	3	2,050	2,190	4,240	497	151	648	2,547	2,341	4,888	138	299	437	402	35,794	4,631
West Virginia	1	3	653	333	986	347	399	746	1,000	732	1,732	92	42	134	172	17,226	2,131
Wisconsin	1	10	2,452	1,834	4,286	2,041	1,600	3,641	4,493	3,434	7,927	508	482	990	501	62,306	7,584
Wyoming	1	0	135	212	347				135	212	347	11	12	23	43	3,244	855

1 Excluding United States Military Academy.

Table 12.—*Universities, colleges, and professional schools—Financial summary, 1917-18.*

States	Appropriation from public sources for—		Income of public institutions.			Total income of private institutions, excluding additions to endowment.	Average income per student.			Productive funds.		
	Public institutions.	Private institutions.	For current expenses.	For increase of plant.	Total.		In public institutions.	In private institutions.	Total.	Public institutions.	Private institutions.	Total.
	2	3	4	5	6	7	8	9	10	11	12	13
Alabama	$324,206		$432,322	$100,000	$532,322	$902,282	$296	$269	$284	$1,334,190	$551,488	$1,885,678
Arizona	457,947		555,992	0	555,992		1,171	0	1,171	10,500	0	10,500
Arkansas	340,38		369,774	0	369,774	164,425	507	138	278	132,666	306,576	439,242
California	2,396,852		3,333,449	299,361	3,632,810	2,485,600	470	316	396	5,490,430	30,952,733	36,443,163
Colorado	1,006,591		1,110,150	152,000	1,262,150	2,345,413	278	163	241	282,783	2,144,897	2,427,680
Connecticut	265,783		371,353	92,057	463,410	3,598,874	2,491	1,222	1,297	255,000	25,962,180	26,218,180
Delaware	282,465		298,949	125,000	423,949		1,262	0	1,262	473,864	0	473,864
Dist. Columbia	101,000		225,236	0	225,236	870,962	157	181	176	310,386	1,156,472	1,466,857
Florida	415,291		491,501	114,594	606,095	150,604	713	227	500	579,168	214,271	214,271
Georgia	525,882		676,516	30,000	706,515	1,704,180	357	373	368		3,570,218	4,149,386
Idaho	478,447		525,229	96,000	621,229	24,623	940	122	747	1,500,000	116,706	1,616,706
Illinois	2,493,349		2,788,959	286,450	3,075,409	6,875,363	592	259	314	049,012	46,279,517	46,928,529
Indiana	1,390,212		1,775,266	186,108	1,961,274	671,489	455	166	296	1,318,400	5,153,195	6,471,595
Iowa	2,907,348		2,968,608	1,026,343	3,994,951	1,774,377	523	210	358	1,026,343	8,691,703	9,718,046
Kansas	1,592,947		1,963,506	192,500	3,176,006	1,888,589	500	164	317	491,746	2,925,224	3,416,970
Kentucky	433,698		745,428	0	745,428	988,190	565	303	379	187,185	4,752,118	4,939,303
Louisiana	270,461		383,923	0	383,923	567,443	458	233	287	318,713	6,480,156	6,798,869
Maine	250,904		385,156	0	385,156	357,373	442	276	343	252,050	3,935,852	4,187,909
Maryland	1,395,316	$80,775	265,039	174,000	439,039	988,696	2,131	184	255	115,000	7,550,557	7,665,557
Massachusetts	510,910	2 247,825	537,311	66,483	703,794	2 10,233,992	1,399	488	510	361,000	71,795,970	72,156,970
Michigan	2,071,786		3,397,922	200,000	3,597,922	501,194	431	164	360	1,327,412	2,402,089	3,729,501
Minnesota	2,032,317		2,813,219	125,250	2,938,469	1,269,955	334	284	389	1,785,570	3,612,045	5,397,615
Mississippi	480,272		906,495	34,000	1,032,495	215,094	448	130	316	700,000	579,000	1,270,000
Missouri	876,958		1,259,113	65,128	1,324,241	1,592,332	326	181	227	1,309,339	11,553,572	12,862,911
Montana	688,773		698,016	120,000	818,016		587	0	587	680,250	0	680,250
Nebraska	1,306,583		1,292,318	$4, 0	1,741,112	636,715	432	205	333	871,507	3,8, 50	4,673,657
Nevada	237,256		9,89	0	297,769		919	0	919	330,554	0	330,554

1 Excluding United States Naval Academy.
2 Including Massachusetts Institute of Technology, a private institution receiving land-grant funds.

TABLE 12.— Universities, colleges, and professional schools—Financial summary, 1917-18—Continued.

States.	Appropriation from public sources for—		Income of public institutions.				Total income of private institutions, excluding additions to endowment.	Average income per student.			Productive funds.		
	Public institutions.	Private institutions.	For current expenses.	For increase of plant.	Total.			In public institutions.	In private institutions.	Total.	Public institutions.	Private institutions.	Total.
1	2	3	4	5	6	7	8	9	10	11	12	18
New Hampshire	$224,650	$15,000	$333,823	$50,000	$373,823	$361,800	$665	$480	$538	$960,000	$3,438,961	$4,398,961
New Jersey	0	225,374	0	0	0	1,725,986	0	549	549	0	14,020,703	14,020,708
New Mexico	361,895	0	457,554	22,995	480,549	0	1,014	0	1,014	20,761	0	20,761
New York	1,330,873	1,201,058	1,358,452	41,185	1,399,637	13,812,077	143	401	344	0	77,384,699	77,384,699
North Carolina	547,226	0	731,324	63,812	795,136	839,802	561	197	289	216,548	2,943,544	3,160,092
North Dakota	458,734	0	784,316		784,316	51,661	515	67	364	2,051,180	339,457	2,390,617
Ohio	2,905,118	7,800	3,550,175	273,082	3,823,257	2,122,688	361	167	256	2,235,900	11,792,824	14,028,724
Oklahoma	1,311,190	0	1,073,388	526,000	1,598,388	105,339	539	91	413	3,670,000	417,947	4,087,947
Oregon	920,513	0	1,094,032	0	1,094,032	325,201	344	197	294	257,664	3,739,389	3,997,053
Pennsylvania	820,720	910,029	943,315	73,037	1,086,352	8,031,193	488	260	275	500,000	42,275,143	42,775,143
Rhode Island	130,682		205,097	0	203,097	538,973	536		338	370,989	1,221,754	1,592,843
South Carolina	635,515	0	879,885	45,520	925,405	232,137	678	197	491	390,941	1,245,149	1,636,060
South Dakota	931,556	0	683,008	426,861	1,110,409	0	730	191			0	
Tennessee	1,245,121	19,000	369,961	1,000,000	1,369,961	1,296,780	1,633	230	411	405,000	7,148,710	7,553,710
Texas	2,039,383	0	2,850,236	405,150	3,255,386	1,651,064	698	264	450	2,991,000	11,587,791	13,796,791
Utah	574,296	0	625,537	72,253	697,790	0	351	0	351	20,000	0	20,000
Vermont	167,343	48,800	391,529	0	391,529	219,906	662	389	529	1,053,525	1,032,668	2,095,193
Virginia	532,794	0	1,300,518	19,106	1,319,684	1,513,768	569	299	384	2,463,302	5,043,862	7,507,164
Washington	1,214,394	0	1,611,101	69,017	1,680,118	122,799	396	190	369	5,996,668	665,523	6,572,191
West Virginia	619,048	0	611,642	93,500	705,142	100,523	715	135	465	116,000	279,436	395,436
Wisconsin	1,928,080	0	2,762,466	150,570	2,913,035	779,899	680	214	466	704,399	6,124,840	6,829,299
Wyoming	246,218	0	297,304	31,483	328,787	0	948	0	948	239,339	0	239,339

3 Including Rutgers College, a private institution receiving land-grant funds.
4 Excluding United States Military Academy.
5 Including Cornell University, a private institution receiving land-grant funds.